The International Institute
for Strategic Studies

The Military Balance

2001·2002

OXFORD
UNIVERSITY PRESS

Published by **Oxford University Press** for
The International Institute for Strategic Studies
Arundel House, 13–15 Arundel Street,
London WC2R 3DX, UK

The Military Balance 2001·2002

Published by Oxford University Press for
**The International Institute
for Strategic Studies**
Arundel House, 13–15 Arundel Street,
London WC2R 3DX, UK
http://www.iiss.org

Director Dr John Chipman

Editor Col Christopher Langton

Defence Analysts
Ground Forces Phillip Mitchell
Aerospace Wg Cdr Andrew Brookes
Naval Forces Joanna Kidd
Defence Economist Mark Stoker
Armed Conflict Micaela Gustavsson

Editorial Susan Bevan
Assistant Editors Jill Dobson, James Hackett

Project Manager, Design and Production
Mark Taylor

Production Assistant Anna Clarke
Research Assistants Isabelle Williams, David
Ucko, Vitaly Gelfgat, Nikolai Rogosaroff
Cartographer Jillian Luff

This publication has been prepared by the
Director of the Institute and his staff, who
accept full responsibility for its contents.

First published October 2001

ISBN 0-19-850979-0
ISSN 0459-7222

The Military Balance (ISSN 0459-7222) is published
annually in October by Oxford University Press, Great
Clarendon Street, Oxford OX2 6DP, UK. The 2001 annual
subscription rate is: UK£78 (individual rate), UK£99
(institution rate); overseas US$129 (individual rate),
US$170 (institution rate).

Payment is required with all orders and subscriptions
are accepted and entered by the volume (one issue).
Please add sales tax to the prices quoted. Prices include
air-speeded delivery to Australia, Canada, India, Japan,
New Zealand and the USA. Delivery elsewhere is by
surface mail. Air-mail rates are available on request.
Payment may be made by cheque or Eurocheque
(payable to Oxford University Press), National Girobank
(account 500 1056), credit card (Mastercard, Visa,
American Express, Diners', JCB), direct debit (please
send for details) or UNESCO coupons. Bankers: Barclays
Bank plc, PO Box 333, Oxford, UK, code 20-65-18,
account 00715654. Claims for non-receipt must be made
within four months of dispatch/order (whichever is
later).

Please send subscription orders to the Journals
Subscription Department, Oxford University Press,
Great Clarendon Street, Oxford, OX2 6DP, UK *tel* +44
(0)1865 267907 *fax* +44 (0)1865 267485 *e-mail*
jnl.orders@oup.co.uk.

In North America, *The Military Balance* is distributed by
Mercury International, 365 Blair Road, Avenel, NJ 07001,
USA. Periodical postage paid at Rahway, NJ, and
additional entry points.

US POSTMASTER: Send address corrections to *The
Military Balance*, c/o Mercury International, 365 Blair
Road, Avenel, NJ 07001, USA.

Printed in Great Britain by Bell & Bain Ltd, Glasgow.

Contents

United States

NATO and Non-NATO Europe

Russia

Middle East and North Africa

Central and South Asia

East Asia and Australasia

Caribbean and Latin America

Sub-Saharan Africa

Analyses and Tables

The Military Balance is updated each year to provide an accurate assessment of the military forces and defence expenditures of 169 countries. The data in the current edition is according to IISS assessments as at 1 August 2001.

GENERAL ARRANGEMENT

Part I of *The Military Balance* comprises country entries grouped by region. Regional groupings are preceded by a short introduction describing the military issues facing the region, and significant changes in the defence economics, weapons and other military equipment holdings and acquisitions of the countries concerned. Inclusion of a country or state in *The Military Balance* does not imply legal recognition or indicate support for a particular government.

Part II contains analyses and tables. New elements in this edition include an analysis of developments in the European Rapid Reaction Force, while the subjects of tables this year include military airlift, military sealift and non-state armed groups.

The loose wall-map is updated from 2000 to show data on recent and current armed conflicts, including fatalities and costs.

USING THE MILITARY BALANCE

The country entries in *The Military Balance* are a quantitative assessment of the personnel strengths and equipment holdings of the world's armed forces. The strengths of forces and the numbers of weapons held are based on the most accurate data available, or, failing that, on the best estimate that can be made with reasonable confidence. The data presented each year reflect judgements based on information available to the IISS at the time the book is compiled. Where information differs from previous editions, this is mainly because of substantive changes in national forces, but it is sometimes because the IISS has reassessed the evidence supporting past entries. An attempt is made to distinguish between these reasons for change in the text that introduces each regional section, but care must be taken in constructing time-series comparisons from information given in successive editions.

In order to interpret the data in the country entries correctly, it is essential to read the explanatory notes beginning on page 5.

The large quantity of data in *The Military Balance* has been compressed into a portable volume by extensive employment of abbreviations. An essential tool is therefore the alphabetical index of abbreviations, which appears on the laminated card at the back of the book. For ease of reference, this may be detached and used as a bookmark.

ATTRIBUTION AND ACKNOWLEDGEMENTS

The International Institute for Strategic Studies owes no allegiance to any government, group of governments, or any political or other organisation. Its assessments are its own, based on the material available to it from a wide variety of sources. The cooperation of governments has been sought and, in many cases, received. However, some data in *The Military Balance* are estimates. Care is taken to ensure that these are as accurate and free from bias as possible. The Institute owes a considerable debt to a number of its own members, consultants and all those who helped compile and check material. The Director and staff of the Institute assume full responsibility for the data and judgements in this book. Comments and suggestions on the data presented are welcomed. Suggestions on the style and method of presentation are also much appreciated.

Readers may use data from *The Military Balance* without applying for permission from the Institute on condition that the IISS and *The Military Balance* are cited as the source in any published work. However, applications to reproduce portions of text, complete country entries or complete tables from *The Military Balance* must be referred to the publishers. Prior to publication, applications should be addressed to: Journals Rights and Permissions, Oxford University Press, Great Clarendon Street, Oxford OX2 6DP, UK, with a copy to the Editor of *The Military Balance*.

Explanatory Notes

ABBREVIATIONS AND DEFINITIONS

Abbreviations are used throughout to save space and avoid repetition. The abbreviations may have both singular or plural meanings; for example, 'elm' = 'element' or 'elements'. The qualification 'some' means *up to*, while 'about' means *the total could be higher than given*. In financial data, '$' refers to US dollars unless otherwise stated; billion (bn) signifies 1,000 million (m). Footnotes particular to a country entry or table are indicated by letters, while those that apply throughout the book are marked by symbols (* for training aircraft counted by the IISS as combat-capable, and † where serviceability of equipment is in doubt). A full list of abbreviations appears on the detachable laminated card at the back of the book.

COUNTRY ENTRIES

Information on each country is shown in a standard format, although the differing availability of information results in some variations. Each entry includes economic, demographic and military data. Military data include manpower, length of conscript service, outline organisation, number of formations and units and an inventory of the major equipment of each service. This is followed, where applicable, by a description of the deployment of each service. Details of national forces stationed abroad and of foreign-stationed forces are also given.

GENERAL MILITARY DATA

Manpower

The 'Active' total comprises all servicemen and women on full-time duty (including conscripts and long-term assignments from the Reserves). Under the heading 'Terms of Service', only the length of conscript service is shown; where service is voluntary there is no entry. 'Reserve' describes formations and units not fully manned or operational in peacetime, but which can be mobilised by recalling reservists in an emergency. Unless otherwise indicated, the 'Reserves' entry includes all reservists committed to rejoining the armed forces in an emergency, except when national reserve service obligations following conscription last almost a lifetime. *The Military Balance* bases its estimates of effective reservist strengths on the numbers available within five years of completing full-time service, unless there is good evidence that obligations are enforced for longer. Some countries have more than one category of 'Reserves', often kept at varying degrees of readiness. Where possible, these differences are denoted using the national descriptive title, but always under the heading of 'Reserves' to distinguish them from full-time active forces.

Other Forces

Many countries maintain paramilitary forces whose training, organisation, equipment and control suggest they may be used to support or replace regular military forces. These are listed, and their roles described, after the military forces of each country. Their manpower is not normally included in the Armed Forces totals at the start of each entry. Home Guard units are counted as paramilitary. Where paramilitary groups are not on full-time active duty, '(R)' is added after the title to indicate that they have reserve status. When internal opposition forces are armed and appear to pose a significant threat to a state's security, their details are listed separately after national paramilitary forces.

Equipment

Quantities are shown by function and type, and represent what are believed to be total holdings, including active and reserve operational and training units and 'in store' stocks. Inventory totals for missile systems – such as surface-to-surface missiles (SSM), surface-to-air missiles (SAM) and anti-tank guided weapons (ATGW) – relate to launchers and not to missiles.

Stocks of equipment held in reserve and not assigned to either active or reserve units are listed as 'in store'. However, aircraft in excess of unit establishment holdings, held to allow for repair and modification or immediate replacement, are not shown 'in store'. This accounts for apparent disparities between unit strengths and aircraft inventory strengths.

Operational Deployments

Where deployments are overseas, *The Military Balance* lists permanent bases and does not normally list short-term operational deployments, particularly where military operations are in progress. An exception is made in the case of peacekeeping operations. Recent developments are also described in the text for each regional section.

GROUND FORCES

The national designation is normally used for army formations. The term 'regiment' can be misleading. It can mean essentially a brigade of all arms; a grouping of battalions of a single arm; or (as in some instances in the UK) a battalion-sized unit. The sense intended is indicated in each case. Where there is no standard organisation, the intermediate levels of command are shown as headquarters (HQs), followed by the total numbers of units that could be allocated to them. Where a unit's title overstates its real capability, the title is given in inverted commas, with an estimate given in parentheses of the comparable unit size typical of countries with substantial armed forces. Guidelines for unit and formation strengths are: **Company** 100–200 • **Battalion** 500–800 • **Brigade (Regiment)** 3,000–5,000 • **Division** 15,000–20,000 • **Corps (Army)** 60,000–80,000.

Equipment

The Military Balance uses the following definitions of equipment:

Main Battle Tank (MBT) An armoured, tracked combat vehicle, weighing at least 16.5 metric tonnes unladen, that may be armed with a 360° traverse gun of at least 75mm calibre. Any new-wheeled combat vehicles that meet the latter two criteria will be considered MBTs.

Armoured Combat Vehicle (ACV) A self-propelled vehicle with armoured protection and cross-country capability. ACVs include:

Heavy Armoured Combat Vehicle (HACV) An armoured combat vehicle weighing more than six metric tonnes unladen, with an integral/organic direct-fire gun of at least 75mm (which does not fall within the definitions of APC, AIFV or MBT). *The Military Balance* does not list HACVs separately, but under their equipment type (light tank, reconnaissance or assault gun), and where appropriate annotates them as HACV.

Armoured Infantry Fighting Vehicle (AIFV) An armoured combat vehicle designed and equipped to transport an infantry squad, armed with an integral/organic cannon of at least 20mm calibre. Variants of AIFVs are also included and indicated as such.

Armoured Personnel Carrier (APC) A lightly armoured combat vehicle, designed and equipped to transport an infantry squad and armed with integral/organic weapons of less than 20mm calibre. Variants of APCs converted for other uses (such as weapons platforms, command posts and communications vehicles) are included and indicated as such.

Artillery A weapon with a calibre of 100mm and above, capable of engaging ground targets by delivering primarily indirect fire. The definition covers guns, howitzers, gun/howitzers, multiple-rocket launchers and mortars.

Military Formation Strengths

The manpower strength, equipment holdings and organisation of formations such as brigades and divisions differ widely from country to country. Where possible, the normal composition of formations is given in parentheses. It should be noted that where both divisions and brigades are listed, only separate brigades are counted and not those included in divisions.

NAVAL FORCES

Categorisation is based on operational role, weapon fit and displacement. Ship classes are identified by the name of the first ship of that class, except where a class is recognised by another name (such as *Udalay, Petya*). Where the class is based on a foreign design or has been acquired from another country, the original class name is added in parentheses. Each class is given an acronym. All such designators are included in the list of abbreviations.

The term 'ship' refers to vessels with over 1,000 tonnes full-load displacement that are more than 60 metres in overall length; vessels of lesser displacement, but of 16m or more overall length, are termed 'craft'. Vessels of less than 16m overall length are not included. The term 'commissioning' of a ship is used to mean the ship has completed fitting out and initial sea trials, and has a naval crew; operational training may not have been completed, but otherwise the ship is available for service. 'Decommissioning' means that a ship has been removed from operational duty and the bulk of its naval crew transferred. Removing equipment and stores and dismantling weapons, however, may not have started. Where known, ships in long-term refit are shown as such.

Definitions

To aid comparison between fleets, the following definitions, which do not necessarily conform to national definitions, are used:

Submarines All vessels equipped for military operations and designed to operate primarily below the surface. Those vessels with submarine-launched ballistic missiles are listed separately under 'Strategic Nuclear Forces'.

Principal Surface Combatant This term includes all surface ships with both 1,000 tonnes full-load displacement and a weapons system for other than self-protection. All such ships are assumed to have an anti-surface ship capability. They comprise: aircraft carriers (defined below); cruisers (over 8,000 tonnes) and destroyers (less than 8,000 tonnes), both of which normally have an anti-air role and may also have an anti-submarine capability; and frigates (less than 8,000 tonnes) which normally have an anti-submarine role. Only ships with a flight deck that extends beyond two-thirds of the vessel's length are classified as aircraft carriers. Ships with shorter flight decks are shown as helicopter carriers.

Patrol and Coastal Combatants These are ships and craft whose primary role is protecting a state's sea approaches and coastline. Included are corvettes (500–1,500 tonnes with an attack capability), missile craft (with permanently fitted missile-launcher ramps and control equipment) and torpedo craft (with anti-surface-ship torpedoes). Ships and craft that fall outside these definitions are classified as 'patrol' and divided into 'offshore' (over 500 tonnes), 'coastal' (75–500 tonnes), 'inshore' (less than 75 tonnes) and 'riverine'. The adjective 'fast' indicates that the ship's speed is greater than 30 knots.

Mine Warfare This term covers surface vessels configured primarily for mine laying or mine countermeasures (such as mine-hunters, minesweepers or dual-capable vessels). They are further classified into 'offshore', 'coastal', 'inshore' and 'riverine' with the same tonnage definitions as for 'patrol' vessels shown above.

Amphibious This term includes ships specifically procured and employed to disembark troops and their equipment onto unprepared beachheads by means such as landing craft or helicopters, or directly supporting amphibious operations. The term 'Landing Ship' (as opposed to 'Landing Craft') refers to vessels capable of an ocean passage that can deliver their troops and equipment in a fit state to fight. Vessels with an amphibious capability but not assigned to amphibious duties are not included. Amphibious craft are listed at the end of each entry.

Support and Miscellaneous This term covers auxiliary military ships. It covers four broad categories: 'underway support' (e.g. tankers and stores ships), 'maintenance and logistic' (e.g. sealift ships), 'special purposes' (e.g. intelligence collection ships) and 'survey and research' ships.

Merchant Fleet This category is included in a state's inventory when it can make a significant contribution to the state's military sealift capability.

Weapons Systems Weapons are listed in the following order: land-attack missiles, anti-surface-ship missiles, surface-to-air missiles, guns, torpedo tubes, other anti-submarine weapons, and helicopters. Missiles with a range of less than 5km, and guns with a calibre of less than 76mm, are not included. Exceptions may be made in the case of some minor combatants with a primary gun armament of a lesser calibre.

Aircraft All armed aircraft, including anti-submarine warfare and maritime-reconnaissance aircraft, are included as combat aircraft in naval inventories.

Organisations Naval groupings such as fleets and squadrons frequently change and are often temporary; organisations are shown only where it is meaningful.

AIR FORCES

The term 'combat aircraft' refers to aircraft normally equipped to deliver air-to-air or air-to-surface ordnance. The 'combat' totals include aircraft in operational conversion units whose main role is weapons training, and training aircraft of the same type as those in front-line squadrons that are assumed to be available for operations at short notice. Training aircraft considered to be combat-capable are marked with an asterisk (*). Armed maritime aircraft are included in combat aircraft totals. Operational groupings of air forces are shown where known. Squadron aircraft strengths vary with aircraft types and from country to country.

Definitions

Different countries often use the same basic aircraft in different roles; the key to determining these roles lies mainly in aircrew training. In *The Military Balance* the following definitions are used as a guide:

Fixed Wing Aircraft

Fighter This term is used to describe aircraft with the weapons, avionics and performance capacity for aerial combat. Multi-role aircraft are shown as fighter ground attack (FGA), fighter, reconnaissance and so on, according to the role in which they are deployed.

Bombers These aircraft are categorised according to their designed range and payload as follows:

Long-range Capable of delivering a weapons payload of more than 10,000kg over an unrefuelled radius of action of over 5,000km;

Medium-range Capable of delivering weapons of more than 10,000kg over an unrefuelled radius of action of between 1,000km and 5,000km;

Short-range Capable of delivering a weapons payload of more than 10,000kg over an unrefuelled radius of action of less than 1,000km.

A few bombers with the radius of action described above, but designed to deliver a payload of less than 10,000kg, and which do not fall into the category of FGA, are described as **light bombers**.

Helicopters

Armed Helicopters This term is used to cover helicopters equipped to deliver ordnance, including for anti-submarine warfare. They may be further defined as:

Attack Helicopters with an integrated fire control and aiming system, designed to deliver anti-armour, air-to-ground or air-to-air weapons;

Combat Support Helicopters equipped with area suppression or self-defence weapons, but without an integrated fire control and aiming system;

Assault Armed helicopters designed to deliver troops to the battlefield.

Transport Helicopters The term describes unarmed helicopters designed to transport personnel or cargo in support of military operations.

ARMS ORDERS AND DELIVERIES

Tables in the regional texts show arms orders and deliveries listed by country buyer for the past and current years, together with country supplier and delivery dates, if known. Every effort has been made to ensure accuracy, but some transactions may not be fulfilled or may differ from those reported.

DEFENCE ECONOMICS

Country entries in **Part I** show defence expenditure, selected economic performance indicators and demographic aggregates. **Part II**, *Analyses and Tables*, contains an international comparison of defence expenditure and military manpower, giving expenditure figures for the past two years against a bench-mark year in constant US dollars. The aim is to provide an accurate measure of military expenditure and of the allocation of economic resources to defence. All country entries are subject to revision each year, as new information, particularly that regarding defence expenditure, becomes available. The information is necessarily selective. A wider range of statistics is available to IISS members on request.

In **Part I**, individual country entries typically show economic performance over the past two years, and current-year demographic data. Where these data are unavailable, information from the last available year is provided. Defence expenditure is generally shown for the past two years where official outlays are available, or sufficient data for reliable estimates exist. Current-year defence budgets and, where available, defence budgets for the following year are also listed. Foreign Military Assistance (FMA) data cover outlays for the past year, and budgetary estimates for the current and subsequent years. Unless otherwise indicated, the US is the donor country. All financial data in the country entries are shown both in national currency and US dollars at current-year, not constant, prices. US dollar conversions are generally, but not invariably, calculated from the exchange rates listed in the entry. In a few cases, notably Russia and China, purchasing-power-parity (PPP) rates are used in preference to official or market-exchange rates.

Definitions of terms

To avoid errors in interpretation, an understanding of the definition of defence expenditure is important. Both the UN and NATO have developed standardised definitions, but in many cases countries prefer to use their own definitions (which are not in the public domain). For consistency, the IISS uses the NATO definition (which is also the most comprehensive) throughout.

In *The Military Balance,* military expenditure is defined as the cash outlays of central or federal government to meet the costs of national armed forces. The term 'armed forces' includes strategic, land, naval, air, command, administration and support forces. It also includes paramilitary forces such as the *gendarmerie*, customs service and border guard if these are trained in military tactics, equipped as a military force and operate under military authority in the event of war. Defence expenditures are reported in four categories: Operating Costs, Procurement and Construction, Research and Development (R&D) and Other Expenditure. Operating Costs include: salaries and pensions for military and civilian personnel; the cost of maintaining and training units, service organisations, headquarters and support elements; and the cost of servicing and repairing military equipment and infrastructure. Procurement and Construction expenditure covers national equipment and infrastructure spending, as well as common infrastructure programmes. It also includes financial contributions to multinational military organisations, host-nation support in cash and in kind, and payments made to other countries under bilateral agreements. FMA counts as expenditure by the donor, and not the recipient, government. R&D is defence expenditure up to the point at which new equipment can be put in service, regardless of whether new equipment is actually procured. The fact that the IISS definitions of military expenditure are generally more inclusive than those applied by national governments and the standardised UN format means that our calculated expenditure figures may be higher than national and UN equivalents.

The issue of transparency in reporting military expenditures is a fundamental one. Only a minority of the governments of UN member-states report defence expenditures to their electorates, the UN, the International Monetary Fund (IMF) and other multilateral organisations. In the case of governments with a proven record of transparency, official figures generally conform to a standardised definition of defence expenditure, and consistency problems are not usually a major issue. Where these conditions of transparency and consistency are met, the IISS cites official defence budgets and outlays as reported by national governments, NATO, the UN, the Organisation for Security and Cooperation in Europe (OSCE) and the IMF. On the other hand, some governments do not report defence expenditures until several years have elapsed, while others understate these expenditures in their reports. Where these reporting conditions exist, *The Military Balance* gives IISS estimates of military expenditures for the country concerned. Official defence budgets are also shown, in order to provide a measure of the discrepancy between official figures and what the IISS estimates real defence outlays to be. In these cases *The Military Balance* does not cite official defence expenditures (actual outlays), as these rarely differ significantly from official budgetary data. The IISS defence-expenditure estimates are based on information from several sources, and are marked 'ε'. The most frequent instances of budgetary manipulation or falsification typically involve equipment procurement, R&D, defence industrial investment, covert weapons programmes, pensions for retired military and civilian personnel, paramilitary forces, and non-budgetary sources of revenue for the military arising from ownership of industrial, property and land assets.

The principal sources for economic statistics cited in the country entries are the IMF, the Organisation for Economic Cooperation and Development (OECD), the World Bank and three regional banks (the Inter-American, Asian and African Development Banks). For some countries basic economic data are difficult to obtain. This is the case in a few former command economies in transition and countries currently or recently involved in armed conflict. The Gross Domestic Product (GDP) figures are nominal (current) values at market prices, but GDP per capita figures are nominal values at PPP prices. GDP growth is real not nominal growth, and inflation is the year-on-year change in consumer prices. Two different measures of debt are used to distinguish between OECD and non-OECD countries: for OECD countries, debt is gross public debt (or, more exactly, general government gross financial liabilities) expressed as a proportion of GDP. For all other countries, debt is gross foreign debt denominated in current US dollars. Dollar exchange rates relate to the last two years plus the current year. Values for the past two years are annual averages, while current values are the latest monthly value.

Calculating exchange rates

Typically, but not invariably, the exchange rates shown in the country entries are also used to calculate GDP and defence-expenditure dollar conversions. Where they are not used, it is because the use of exchange rate dollar conversions can misrepresent both GDP and defence expenditure. This may arise when: the official exchange rate is overvalued (as with some Latin American and African countries); relatively large currency fluctuations occur over the short-to-medium term; or when a substantial medium-to-long-term discrepancy between the exchange rate and the dollar PPP exists. Where exchange rate fluctuations are the problem, dollar values are converted using lagged exchange rates (generally by no more than six months). The GDP estimates of the Inter-American Development Bank, usually lower than those derived from official exchange rates, are used for Latin American countries. For former communist countries, PPP rather than market exchange rates are sometimes used for dollar conversions of both GDP and defence expenditures, and this is marked.

The arguments for using PPP are strongest for Russia and China. Both the UN and IMF have issued caveats concerning the reliability of official economic statistics on transitional economies, particularly those of Russia and some Eastern European and Central Asian countries. Non-reporting, lags in the publication of current statistics and frequent revisions of recent data (not always accompanied by timely revision of previously published figures in the same series) pose transparency and consistency problems. Another problem arises with certain transitional economies whose productive capabilities are similar to those of developed economies, but where cost and price structures are often much lower than world levels. PPP dollar values are used in preference to market exchange rates in cases where using such exchange rates may result in excessively low dollar-conversion values for GDP and defence expenditure.

Demographic data

Population aggregates are based on the most recent official census data or, in their absence, demographic statistics taken from *World Population Projections* published annually by the World Bank. Data on ethnic and religious minorities are also provided under country entries where a related security issue exists.

MILITARY DEVELOPMENTS

Ambitious plans are being drawn up for reforming the operational methods, structure and equipment of the US armed forces in line with the perceptions of how best to protect the US against current and future threats held by the new administration of President George W. Bush. The principal studies that may bring the changes about are the *Quadrennial Defense Review* (QDR), due to be presented by 30 September 2001, and the *Nuclear Posture Review* due to be completed in December 2001. It is not yet clear how far reaching the changes will be, as the outcome will be influenced by domestic political wrangling as well as by international reaction to the plans as they unfold. Domestic politics will probably be the most powerful brake on attempts to bring about radical change. In the meantime, no fundamental changes are slated for 2001 and 2002, as budgetary action is focused on armed forces pay, conditions of service, housing and base facilities, which, in effect, carry forward the previous administration's 'people first' policy towards the military. It is to improvements in these areas that the overwhelming majority of the largest increase in defence spending since 1985, some \$32.6bn, is being allocated in the 2002 defence budget. In the field of research and development, the biggest increase in funds is being applied to missile defence, for which \$8.3bn is sought in the revised budget request for fiscal year (FY) 2002 (a 60% increase over the initial request for 2002). This is the most contentious aspect of the administration's plans both domestically and internationally.

Breaking with the past

The broad aims of the Bush administration are clear, although the key decisions are yet to be taken and some important elements are yet to be clarified and agreed, both within the Department of Defense (DoD) and among the key departments dealing with security affairs. The new administration is intent on breaking from the past on nuclear deterrence, on reducing reliance on permanent overseas basing and on developing armed forces with powerful and rapid force-projection capabilities. A priority is protection for areas that the administration considers are now too vulnerable, including information systems and space-based assets for communications, navigation and surveillance. The administration believes the US has insufficient capability to defend against the weapons-of-mass-destruction (WMD) capabilities being developed by states such as Iraq, Iran and North Korea. This shortfall is in both defensive capabilities and in the means of attacking hidden WMD production facilities and delivery systems.

Where overseas basing is concerned, there appears to be a shift in focus away from Europe, where security threats that might call for large-scale combined-arms forces are thought to be less pressing, to Asia where such threats are perceived to be increasing, for example with the advancing military capabilities of Taiwan and China. This does not mean that the US is intent on a precipitous withdrawal from NATO-led operations in the Balkans. The administration, in particular Secretary of State Colin Powell, has been at pains to stress that as far as the current commitments in the Balkans are concerned 'in together, out together' still applies.

Achieving the capabilities to meet these threats requires changes affecting both personnel and weapons programmes. These changes are needed both to meet the military objectives with the right structure and equipment, and to make these objectives affordable, given the budget constraints that may arise from the administration's \$1.35 trillion tax-cutting plan and the general economic downturn. Major personnel cuts are being considered to help pay for the new technologies, power-projection capabilities, space defences, information-infrastructure defence and missile defences that are seen to be necessary. For example, a cut of nearly three army divisions (around 56,000 personnel) is being contemplated; the air force may lose 16 of its 61 fighter squadrons and the navy one or two of its 12 carrier groups. However these proposals are by no means certain to be presented to Congress after the QDR is completed at the end of October. Powerful opposition is already building up. For example, in August 2001, 80 congressmen from both sides of the house signed a petition to Secretary of Defense Donald Rumsfeld expressing strong opposition to cuts in army personnel. The administration's plans to save $3.5bn a year by closing bases (mostly in the US) will be another issue that will excite opposition in Congress. Any savings from this source would not be felt for four or five years in any case. The Joint Chiefs of Staff have conducted a study of the strategic guidelines set out by Rumsfeld which concludes that the armed forces need to be at least maintained at current strength to meet the administration's objectives and might even need to grow.

In the end, the budgetary constraint will probably be the biggest obstacle to radical change. Just to maintain the armed forces at the levels sought in the budget request for 2002, including replacement of worn-out equipment, could well require a further budget increase of as much as $30bn in 2003. To realise the administration's objectives, the intention is to drop the current armed forces objective of maintaining the ability to fight two major regional conflicts simultaneously. An alternative objective might be to have the ability to fight one major conflict while maintaining the capability to support other smaller operations that may already be in progress. It could be that this will become the strategy by default rather than design.

Strategic Weapons and Missile Defence

President Bush's 8 July 2001 meeting with Russian President Vladimir Putin in the margins of the G-8 meeting in Genoa began the process whereby Russia and the United States are seeking a new 'strategic framework', linking both strategic nuclear weapons and missile defence. While there are several apparent areas of agreement between Washington and Moscow, important issues of timing and substance present obstacles to an accord. On strategic weapons, both sides appear ready to accept substantial cuts in strategic nuclear forces to below Strategic Arms Reduction Treaty (START) II levels, perhaps to around 1,500 strategic nuclear warheads. Putin has already mentioned this figure, but the US administration is more cautious about committing to a precise number until its Nuclear Posture Review is complete. Moscow would prefer any new level agreed to be incorporated in a legally binding treaty, while Washington prefers a less formal approach of unilateral actions, political declarations and transparency measures. On missile defence, Moscow appears willing to modify the Anti-Ballistic Missile (ABM) Treaty, to relax constraints on testing and even allow for deployment of a limited missile defence system. The Bush administration in contrast, hopes to jettison the ABM Treaty entirely, to remove any constraints on US missile defence plans. This is likely to be the thorniest issue in the negotiations that got underway in August 2001. Washington's threat of unilateral withdrawal from the ABM Treaty has had a powerful effect on Russian willingness to modify the treaty's terms. However, Moscow will strongly resist complete abandonment of the treaty (encouraged by support from some US allies and China). Thus, the administration may be faced with a difficult choice between accepting amendments to the ABM Treaty allowing the US to proceed with a limited missile defence system within treaty constraints, and unilateral withdrawal from the treaty, which would remove constraints on missile defence but arouse strong international opposition. However, the strongest card in the US hand is Russia's need to make major reductions in strategic weapons for economic and technical reasons. Russia would have great difficulty in maintaining even START II levels of strategic nuclear warheads (3,000 to 3,500). Moscow therefore needs an arrangement that binds the US to reduce to levels that Russia can be confident of maintaining.

The dilemma for the Bush administration is made more difficult by timing constraints and domestic political considerations. The White House is pressing to resolve the issue with Russia, preferably by the end of this year and certainly well before the 2002 congressional elections, in which the Democrats stand a good chance of taking control of the House of Representatives and weakening the president's foreign-policy hand. For precisely the same reason, Moscow hopes to play for time and drag out the talks as long as possible (as they did successfully with the Clinton administration). Finally, and most importantly for the White House, the choice between accepting modifications to the ABM Treaty or walking away from it could have profound implications for the president's re-election chances in 2004. If the administration chooses to abandon the ABM Treaty rather than accept a compromise with Russia, this would help to mobilise Bush's conservative base and allow him to campaign on a strong defence theme. However, this would be at the cost of disenchanting Republican Party moderates and strengthening the Democratic accusation that the administration's 'unilateralist' foreign policy is isolating the United States. Accepting a limited deal with the Russians, on the other hand, would disappoint the president's strongest supporters, but deny a potentially critical campaign issue to the Democrats. In the end, this calculation of domestic political cost and benefit is likely to play a pivotal role in the decision on how to proceed with missile defence. The administration's difficulties would be greatly eased if a deal could be struck with Russia involving a new understanding on missile defences accompanied by major strategic-weapon reductions. This would defuse opposition both at home and abroad. Strategic nuclear warheads are currently around the 6,000 level. Reducing this number by thousands would be an important *acquis*, which could help strengthen the US' hand in international negotiations on multi-lateral WMD treaties, in particular, the Nuclear Non-Proliferation Treaty (NPT), and in developing policies for nuclear proliferation in South and East Asia and the Gulf. Current Russian and US holdings of strategic nuclear-delivery vehicles, governed by START I, are in Table 1.

Table 1 **Aggregate numbers of strategic nuclear delivery vehicles (START I)**[1]											
As declared on 31 Jan 2001	**US**		**Russia**		**Belarus**		**Kazakstan**		**Ukraine**		**Totals**	
ICBM	601	**687**[2]	750	**756**	0	**0**	0	**0**	16[3]	**27**[3]	1,367	**1,470**
SLBM	448	**464**	436	**504**	0	**0**	0	**0**	0	**0**	884	**968**
Bombers	295	**300**	80	**78**	0	**0**	0	**0**	6	**32**	381	**410**

Notes [1] These data are compiled from the annual declarations by the parties to the 1991 Strategic Arms Reduction Treaty (START) I and the 1992 Lisbon Protocols to that treaty

[2] The figures in bold (**123**) are the numbers declared on 1 January 2000

[3] There are no warheads with these missiles

Cooperative Threat Reduction (CTR) Programmes

During the 2000 presidential campaign, then candidate George W. Bush specifically endorsed CTR programmes with Russia, but his administration has been slow to develop its own approach to these issues. Due largely to budgetary pressures, the administration's request for CTR programmes in FY2002 is essentially unchanged on FY2001 for DoD and State Department programmes, with a reduction for Department of Energy (DoE) programmes (see Tables 2 and 3). After a comprehensive policy review lasting several months, the administration essentially endorsed the various State, DoD, and DoE programmes initiated by former presidents George Bush senior and Bill Clinton, with a few exceptions. In particular, the administration is considering several different options for the financially troubled plutonium-disposition programme for eliminating surplus Russian military plutonium. The administration is also considering options for restructuring the highly successful Highly Enriched Uranium (HEU) programme, in which Russian military HEU is blended down and exported to the US to fuel nuclear power stations. Whether the administration moves beyond the *status quo* and launches its own CTR initiatives depends on two factors. The first, although the administration denies any direct linkage, relates to strategic weapons. If the US and Russia reach agreement on a missile package, the administration is likely to seek substantially increased funds for CTR programmes, to, for example, help Russia accelerate destruction of strategic delivery systems and dispose of surplus fissile materials. Without a strategic agreement, especially if the US withdraws unilaterally from the ABM Treaty, funding and political support for CTR programmes in Washington and Moscow are likely to suffer. The second factor is that, like the Clinton administration, the Bush team has made clear that its support for CTR programmes is to some extent dependent on resolving concerns about Russian nuclear and missile leakage and conventional arms sales to Iran. To-date, however, the Bush administration has not developed a set of specific linkages to use as incentives and disincentives with the Russian government.

Table 2 Budget Authority for the Expanded Threat Reduction Initiative in the Former Soviet Union, FY1999–2002 US$m

	FY1999 Actual	FY2000 Actual	FY2001 Request	FY2002 Request
Department of Defense (DoD)	440	458	442	403
Department of Energy (DoE)	237	301	331	253
Department of State	41	251	141	140
Total	718	1,010	914	796

Table 3 Selected US Departments of Energy and Defense Programmes for nuclear non-proliferation and demilitarisation in the Former Soviet Union US$m

	Year started	Agency	Funding received to 1999	FY 2000 Actual	FY 2001 Est.	FY 2002 Req.
Export Control and Proliferation Prevention	1994	DoE	128	15	14	14
Cooperative Threat Reduction	1992	DoD	1,786	458	442	403
Materials Control, Protection and Accounting	1994	DoE	568	138	169	138
Arms Control		DoE	n.k.	109	148	101

DEFENCE SPENDING

With important studies yet to be completed, the only new data on US defence spending available by August 2001 is the amended budget request for FY2002, which is increased to $328.9bn inside the overall budget for National Defense. The proposed new figure is $18.4bn more than that originally outlined in Bush's budget submission to Congress in February 2001, *A Blueprint for New Beginnings*. The proposed FY2002 defence budget is $32.6bn higher than the $296.2bn enacted by Congress for FY2001, a rise of around 8% in real terms and the largest increase since 1985. The budget for FY2001 was itself boosted by the president's $6.4bn FY2001 supplemental appropriations request, primarily intended to address military quality of life and readiness.

The 2002 Defence Budget

The key purposes behind the increased budget request for FY2002 are stated as being to: improve morale; boost readiness; transform defence capabilities; and upgrade ageing facilities and equipment.

Morale The budget includes the largest increase in military pay and benefits in a generation, with a rise of at least 5% for every service member and up to 10% for enlisted grades and mid-level officers. Housing allowances are to be increased to improve the quality of housing and enable military personnel to afford private sector housing where this is appropriate. A big rise in the funding for military health care is included in the request, up from $12.1bn in FY2001 to $17.9bn in FY2002. Attempts to retain high quality personnel are being pursued through a stronger programme of selective enlistment bonuses, re-enlistment bonuses and other incentives.

Boosting Readiness The Operations and Maintenance budget is to climb from $108bn in FY2001 to $126bn in FY2002. The increased funding is to boost readiness by making more provision for flying hours, ship operations, training, weapon-system maintenance and repair, base operations, spare parts, force protection, utilities, and training range repair and support. The budget also makes a major investment in reducing the backlog of weapon-system maintenance, with the notable exception that there is no increase in the allocation for the army's 'Op Tempo'. This is the system for managing time away from home base, time between deployments, track mileage and the like. The funding request includes the items in Table 4.

Transformation of Defence Capabilities The budget emphasises the exploitation of 'leap-ahead' technologies, countering unconventional threats, improving research and testing infrastructure, and controlling the costs of weapons and intelligence systems. The budget request includes $61.6bn for procurement, to support the overhauling of systems that will remain essential until the next generation of capabilities is developed and fielded, and provide support for the long-term transformation envisaged. Funding increases to advance the plans for transformation build upon the $2.6bn Research Development Testing and Evaluation (RDT&E) initiative for 'leap-ahead' technologies already included in the original request for 2002 made in February 2001. The largest allocation by far for defence transformation is for missile defence with $8.3bn allocated to developing a full range of upper- and lower-tier systems. This represents a

Table 4 **Budget Request for Boosting Readiness**		
Selected Items US$bn	FY2001	FY2002
Aircraft operations/Flying hours	9.3	11.5
Army op tempo	2.7	2.7
Ship operations	2.8	2.9
Depot maintenance	8.5	9.3
Training	8.5	9.3
Facility/base support	17.9	20.7

$3bn increase over 2001. To help adjust the funding in support of the transformation, the administration has proposed cutting the B-1 bomber fleet from 91 aircraft to around 60, and retiring 50 MX *Peacekeeper* intercontinental ballistic missiles (ICBMs) from service. Other elements in the reshaping of US strategic and tactical nuclear forces include design studies to convert two *Trident* submarines to cruise-missile carrying submarines. Ahead of the finalisation of the strategy reviews, the budget request boosts funding for programmes that are considered urgent and critical such as close-in ship defence, E-2C *Hawkeye* radar modernisation, biological vaccines and miniature munitions. Two programmes under threat, but that are being kept going until the long-term plan is settled, are the F-22 *Raptor* fighter (13 on order for 2002) and the V-22 *Osprey* tilt-rotor aircraft for the Marine Corps (12 on order).

Upgrading Ageing Facilities While increased funds are requested for improvements in service housing and the renovation of barracks, schools, medical centres, and sports and recreation facilities for the military, the administration is planning a controversial move under the Efficient Facilities Initiative to achieve a 25% reduction in DoD bases in the US and elsewhere. This proposal, aimed at saving $3.5bn annually, is generating significant opposition in Congress as senators and representatives are under pressure to lobby for the retention of facilities within their states and districts.

Foreign Military Assistance

The FY2002 request for International Security Assistance (funded under the US Agency for International Development, now part of the State Department) is an estimated $6.2bn, compared to a revised $6.0bn in FY2001. Israel and Egypt head the military-equipment grant allocation. Israel will receive $2.04bn, enabling its government to meet cash flow requirements associated with the procurement of US systems, such as F-16I aircraft, the *Apache Longbow* attack helicopter and other advanced armaments. The economic-assistance allocation to Israel is cut by $720m. It is intended that Israel's Foreign Military Financing (FMF) will increase gradually by $60m a year to a level of $2.4bn by 2008, as economic support is phased out. Egypt will receive $655m in economic assistance and $1.3bn in FMF and Jordan will get $150m of economic support and $75m in FMF. Selected programmes from the International Affairs Budget are shown in Table 7.

Table 5 US National Defense Budget Function and other selected budgets, 1992, 1995–2002 US$bn

FY	National Defense Budget Function[1]		Department of Defense		Atomic Energy Defense Activities	Inter-national Security Assistance	Veterans Adminis-tration	Total Federal Government Expenditure	Total Federal Budget Surplus
	BA	Outlay	BA	Outlay	Outlay	Outlay	Outlay	Outlay	Outlay
1992	295.1	302.3	282.1	286.9	10.6	7.5	33.9	1,381	-290
1995	266.3	273.6	255.7	259.4	11.8	5.3	37.8	1,515	-164
1996	266.0	266.0	254.4	253.2	11.6	4.6	36.9	1,560	-107
1997	270.3	271.7	258.0	258.3	11.3	4.6	39.3	1,601	-21
1998	271.3	270.2	258.5	256.1	11.3	5.1	41.8	1,652	69
1999	292.1	275.5	278.4	261.4	12.4	5.5	43.2	1,702	124
2000	300.6	291.2	287.3	277.5	12.4	5.4	46.7	1,788	236
2001	310.5	n.k.	296.2	n.k.	13.5	6.0	50.7	1,856	280
2002[R]	343.3	n.k.	328.9	n.k.	13.3	6.2	51.7	1,960	231

Notes

FY = Fiscal Year (1 October–30 September)

[R] = Request

[1] The National Defense Budget Function subsumes funding for the DoD, the DoE Atomic Energy Defense Activities and some smaller support agencies (including Federal Emergency Management and Selective Service System). It does not include funding for International Security Assistance (under International Affairs), the Veterans Administration, the US Coast Guard (Department of Transport), nor for the National Aeronautics and Space Administration (NASA). Funding for civil projects administered by the DoD is excluded from the figures cited here.

[2] Early in each calendar year, the US government presents its defence budget to Congress for the next fiscal year which begins on 1 October. It also presents its Future Years' Defense Program (FYDP), which covers the next fiscal year plus the following five. Until approved by Congress, the Budget is called the Budget Request; after approval, it becomes Budget Authority.

[3] Definitions of US budget terms: **Authorisation** establishes or maintains a government programme or agency by defining its scope. Authorising legislation is normally a prerequisite for appropriations and may set specific limits on the amount that may be appropriated. An authorisation, however, does not make money available. **Budget Authority** is the legal authority for an agency to enter into obligations for the provision of goods or services. It may be available for one or more years. **Appropriation** is one form of Budget Authority provided by Congress for funding an agency, department or programme for a given length of time and for specific purposes. Funds will not necessarily all be spent in the year in which they are initially provided. **Obligation** is an order placed, contract awarded, service agreement undertaken or other commitment made by federal agencies during a given period which will require outlays during the same or some future period. **Outlays** are money spent by a federal agency from funds provided by Congress. Outlays in a given fiscal year are a result of obligations that in turn follow the provision of Budget Authority.

Table 6 National Defense Budget Authority, FY1999–2002 US$m

	1999	2000	2001 Estimate	2002 Request
Military personnel	70,649	73,800	75,400	82,300
Operations & maintenance	104,990	108,100	107,900	125,700
Procurement	50,920	55,000	62,100	61,600
RDT&E	38,290	38,700	40,800	47,400
Military construction	5,406	5,100	5,300	5,900
Family housing	3,591	3,500	3,600	4,100
Other incl net receipts	4,552	3,100	1,100	1,900
Total DoD	278,398	287,300	296,200	328,900
DoE (defence-related)	12,600	12,157	13,084	13,169
Other (defence-related)	1,149	1,202	1,250	1,262
Total national defence	292,147	300,659	310,534	343,331
Total (US$ 2000)	298,059	300,659	304,248	329,707
Real growth (%)		0.9	1.2	8.4

Table 7 US Agency for International Development: International Affairs Budget US$m

Selected Programmes	1999 Actual	2000 Actual	2001 Est.	2002 Req.
Assistance to the Newly Independent States of the FSU	847	835	808	808
Support for East European democracy including FY2000 supplement	550	1,158	674	610
Voluntary peacekeeping operations	n.k.	149	126	150
Contributions to UN and other peacekeeping operations	219	498	844	844
Economic support fund	2,593	2,792	2,314	2,289
International military education and training	50	50	57	65
Foreign military financing	3,400	4,788	3,568	3,674
Non-proliferation, anti-terrorism and related programmes	218	216	310	332
Wye Accord: Middle East Peace Process with FY2000 supplement	1,000	2,325	n.k.	n.k.
International narcotics and crime with FY2000 supplement (Plan Colombia)	517	1,321	324	217
International disaster assistance	388	227	299	200
Total	9,782	14,359	9,324	9,189

Funding for Contingency Operations

The allocations in Table 8 only partially cover the cost of contingency operations. Costs not covered are higher servicing and maintenance expenses arising from increased utilisation of equipment, and the cost of replacing equipment due to losses or major failures. The administration's budget request for FY2002 maintains the same level of allocation as its predecessor.

Table 8 US funding for contingency operations, FY2000–02 US$m

	2000	2001	2002
Kosovo	1,803	1,743	1,528
Bosnia	1,483	1,345	1,315
South-west Asia	1,139	1,277	n.k.
East Timor	56.8	n.k.	n.k.
Readiness/ Munitions & Other	n.k.	47.3	n.k.
Total	4,482	4,412	2,843

United States US

dollar US$		1999	2000	2001	2002
GDP	US$	9.2tr	9.9tr		
per capita	US$	33,100	34,300		
Growth	%	4.2	3.8		
Inflation	%	2.1	2.1		
Publ debt	%	59.3			
Def bdgt					
BA	US$	292.1bn	300.5bn	310.5bn	
Outlay	US$	275.5bn	291.2bn		
Request					
BA	US$	276.2bn	280.8bn	305.4bn	343.3bn
Outlay	US$	277.6bn	274.8bn	292.1bn	
Population				**281,404,000**	
Age		*13–17*	*18–22*	*23–32*	
Men		9,702,000	9,311,000	19,206,000	
Women		9,252,000	8,894,000	18,310,000	

Total Armed Forces

ACTIVE 1,367,700

(incl 199,850 women, excl Coast Guard)

RESERVES 1,200,600

(incl Stand-by Reserve)

READY RESERVE 1,175,000

Selected Reserve and Individual Ready Reserve to augment active units and provide reserve formations and units

NATIONAL GUARD 464,100

Army (ARNG) 357,200 **Air Force** (ANG) 106,900

RESERVE 710,900

Army 363,700 **Navy** 173,000 **Marines** 99,800 **Air Force** 74,400

STAND-BY RESERVE 25,600

Trained individuals for mob **Army** 700 **Navy** 7,200 **Marines** 900 **Air Force** 16,800

US Strategic Command (US STRATCOM)

HQ: Offutt AFB, NE (manpower incl in Navy and Air Force totals)

NAVY up to 432 SLBM in 18 SSBN

(Plus 16 *Poseidon* C-3 launchers in one op ex-SSBN redesignated SSN (32 msl), START accountable)

SSBN 18 *Ohio*

10 (SSBN-734) with up to 24 UGM-133A *Trident* D-5 (240 msl)

8 (SSBN-726) with up to 24 UGM-93A *Trident* C-4 (192 msl)

AIR FORCE

ICBM (Air Force Space Command (AFSPC)) 550

11 msl sqn

500 *Minuteman* III (LGM-30G)

50 *Peacekeeper* (MX; LGM-118A) in mod

AC (Air Combat Command (ACC)): 208 active hy bbr

15 bbr sqn (8 B-1, 5 B-52, 2 B-2A)

8 sqn (2 ANG) with 91 B-1B

5 sqn (1 AFR) with 93 B-52H (57 combat ready)

2 sqn with 20 B-2A

FLIGHT TEST CENTRE 5

1 B-52, 2 B-1, 1 B-2

Strategic Recce/Intelligence Collection (Satellites)

IMAGERY Improved *Crystal* (advanced **KH-11**) visible and infra-red imagery (perhaps 3 op, resolution 6in) *Lacrosse* (formerly *Indigo*) radar-imaging sat (resolution 1–2m)

ELECTRONIC OCEAN RECCE SATELLITE (EORSAT) to detect ships by infra-red and radar

NAVIGATIONAL SATELLITE TIMING AND RANGING (NAVSTAR) 24 sat, components of Global Positioning System (GPS); block 2R system with accuracy to 1m replacing expired sat

ELINT/SIGINT 2 *Orion* (formerly *Magnum*), 2 *Trumpet* (successor to *Jumpseat*), 3 name n.k., launched Aug 1994, May 1995, Apr 1996

NUCLEAR DETONATION DETECTION SYSTEM detects and evaluates nuclear detonations; sensors to be deployed in NAVSTAR sat

Strategic Defences

US Space Command (HQ: Peterson AFB, CO)

North American Aerospace Defense Command (NORAD), a combined US–Ca org (HQ: Peterson AFB, CO)

US Strategic Command (HQ: Offutt AFB, NE)

EARLY WARNING

DEFENSE SUPPORT PROGRAM (DSP) infra-red surv and warning system. Detects msl launches, nuclear detonations, ac in after burner, spacecraft and terrestrial infra-red events. Approved constellation: 3 op sat and 1 op on-orbit spare

BALLISTIC-MISSILE EARLY-WARNING SYSTEM (BMEWS) 3 stations: Clear (AK), Thule (Greenland), Fylingdales Moor (UK). Primary mission to track ICBM and SLBM; also used to track sat

SPACETRACK USAF radars at Incirlik (Tu), Eglin (FL), Cavalier AFS (ND), Clear, Thule, Fylingdales Moor (UK), Beale AFB (CA), Cape Cod (MA); optical tracking systems in Socorro (NM), Maui (HI), Diego Garcia (Indian Ocean)

USN SPACE SURVEILLANCE SYSTEM (NAVSPASUR) 3 transmitting, 6 receiving-site field stations in south-east US

PERIMETER ACQUISITION RADAR ATTACK

CHARACTERISATION SYSTEM (PARCS) 1 north-facing phased-array system at Cavalier AFS (ND); 2,800km range

PAVE PAWS phased-array radars in MA, GA; 5,500km range

MISCELLANEOUS DETECTION AND TRACKING RADARS US **Army** Kwajalein Atoll (Pacific) **USAF** Ascension Island (Atlantic), Antigua (Caribbean), Kaena Point (HI), MIT Lincoln Laboratory (MA)

GROUND-BASED ELECTRO-OPTICAL DEEP SPACE SURVEILLANCE SYSTEM (GEODSS) Socorro, Maui (HI), Diego Garcia

AIR DEFENCE

RADARS

OVER-THE-HORIZON-BACKSCATTER RADAR (OTH-B) 1 in ME (mothballed), 1 in Mountain Home AFB (mothballed); range 500nm (minimum) to 3,000nm

NORTH WARNING SYSTEM to replace DEW line 15 automated long-range (200nm) radar stations 40 short-range (110–150km) stations

DEW LINE system deactivated

Army 477,800

(incl 71,400 women)
3 Army HQ, 4 Corps HQ (1 AB)
2 armd div (3 bde HQ, 5 tk, 4 mech inf, 3 SP arty bn; 1 MLRS bn, 1 AD bn; 1 avn bde)
2 mech div (3 bde HQ, 5 tk, 4 mech inf, 3 SP arty bn; 1 MLRS bn, 1 ADA bn; 1 avn bde)
1 mech div (3 bde HQ, 4 tk, 5 mech inf, 3 SP arty bn; 1 MLRS bn, 1 ADA bn; 1 avn bde)
1 mech div (3 bde HQ, 4 tk, 2 mech inf, 2 air aslt inf, 3 SP arty bn; 1 AD bn; 1 avn bde)
2 lt inf div (3 bde HQ, 9 inf, 3 arty, 1 AD bn; 1 avn bde)
1 air aslt div (3 bde HQ, 9 air aslt, 3 arty bn; 2 avn bde (7 hel bn: 3 ATK, 2 aslt, 1 comd, 1 med tpt))
1 AB div (3 bde HQ, 9 AB, 3 arty, 1 AD, 1 air cav, 1 avn bde)
5 avn bde (1 army, 3 corps, 1 trg)
3 armd cav regt (1 hy, 1 lt, 1 trg (OPFOR))
6 arty bde (3 with 1 SP arty, 2 MLRS bn; 1 with 3 arty, 1 MLRS bn; 1 with 3 MLRS bn; 1 with 1 MLRS bn)
1 indep inf bn, 1 AB Task Force plus 1 inf bn (OPFOR)
10 *Patriot* SAM bn
2 *Avenger* SAM bn
2 Integrated Div HQ (peacetime trg with 6 enhanced ARNG bde - 3 per div)

READY RESERVE

ARMY NATIONAL GUARD (ARNG) 357,200 (incl 37,900 women): capable after mob of manning 8 div (1 armd, 3 mech, 3 med, 1 lt inf) • 18 indep bde, incl 15 enhanced (2 armd, 5 mech, 7 inf, 1 armd cav) • 17 fd arty bde HQ • 1 Scout gp • Indep bn: 1 inf, 36 arty, 19 avn, 11 AD (2 *Patriot*, 9 *Avenger*), 37 engr

ARMY RESERVE (AR) 363,700 (incl 45,100 women): 7 trg div, 5 exercise div, 13 AR/Regional Spt Comd, 4 hel bn (2 AH-64, 2 CH-47), 4 hel coy (CH-47), 2 ac bn (Of these, 205,000 Standing Reservists receive regular trg and have mob assignment; the remainder receive limited trg, but as former active-duty soldiers could be recalled in an emergency.)

EQUIPMENT

MBT some 7,620 M-1 *Abrams* incl M-1A1, M-1A2
RECCE 110 Tpz-1 *Fuchs*
AIFV 6,710 M-2/-3 *Bradley*
APC 15,400 M-113A2/A3 incl variants
TOTAL ARTY 5,836
    TOWED 1,547: **105mm**: 434 M-102, 416 M-119; **155mm**: 697 M-198
    SP **155mm**: 2,476 M-109A1/A2/A6
    MRL **227mm**: 881 MLRS (all ATACMS-capable)
    MOR **120mm**: 932 M-120/121; plus **81mm**: 624 M-252
ATGW 8,715 TOW (incl 1,379 HMMWV, 626 M-901, 6,710 M-2/M-3 *Bradley*), 19,000 *Dragon*, 950 *Javelin*
RL **84mm**: AT-4
SAM FIM-92A *Stinger*, 785 *Avenger* (veh-mounted *Stinger*), 99 *Linebacker* (4 *Stinger* plus 25mm gun), 483 *Patriot*
SURV Ground 122 AN/TPQ-36 (arty), 70 AN/TPQ-37 (arty), 66 AN/TRQ-32 (COMINT), 15 AN/TSQ-138 (COMINT), 24 AN/TSQ-138A **Airborne** 4 *Guardrail* (RC-12D/H/K, 3 RU-21H ac), 7 EO-5ARL (DHC-7)
AMPH 51 ships:
    6 *Frank Besson* LST: capacity 32 tk
    34 LCU-2000
    11 LCU-1600
    Plus craft: some 89 LCM-8
UAV 7 *Hunter* (5 in store)
AC some 271: 39 **C-12C/R**, 89 **C-12D/F/J**, 3 **C-20**, 43 **C-23A/B**, 11 **C-26**, 2 **C-31**, 2 **C-182**, 2 **O-2**, 1 **PA-31**, 23 **RC-12D/H/K**, 26 **RC-12P/Q/N**, 2 **T-34**, 22 **UC-35**, 4 **UV-18A**, 2 **UV-20A**
HEL some 4,715 (1,340 armed): 370 **AH-1S**, 740 **AH-64A/D**, 36 **AH-6/MH-6**, 735 **UH-1H/V**, 1,405 **UH-60AL/MH-60L/K**, 4 **UH-60Q**, 64 **EH-60A (ECM)**, 452 **CH/MH-47D/E**, 387 **OH-58A/C**, 385 **OH-58D** (incl 194 armed), 135 **TH-67** *Creek*, 2 **RAH-66**

Navy (USN) 366,100

(incl 52,050 women)
2 Fleets: Pacific, Atlantic
Surface combatants further divided into:
5 Fleets: **2nd** Atlantic, **3rd** Pacific, **5th** Indian Ocean, Persian Gulf, Red Sea, **6th** Mediterranean, **7th** W. Pacific; plus Military Sealift Command (MSC), Naval Special Warfare Command, Naval Reserve Force (NRF)

SUBMARINES 73

STRATEGIC SUBMARINES 18 (see p. 19)

TACTICAL SUBMARINES 55 (incl about 8 in refit)
  SSGN 33
    2 *Seawolf* (SSN-21) with up to 45 *Tomahawk* SLCM
      plus 8 × 660mm TT; about 50 tube-launched msl
      and Mk 48 HWT
    23 imp *Los Angeles* (SSN-751) with 12 *Tomahawk*
      SLCM (VLS), 4 × 533mm TT (Mk 48 HWT,
      Harpoon)
    8 mod *Los Angeles* (SSN-719) with 12 *Tomahawk* SLCM
      (VLS), 4 × 533mm TT (Mk 48 HWT, *Harpoon*)
  SSN 21
    20 *Los Angeles* (SSN-688) with 4 × 533mm TT (Mk 48
      HWT, *Harpoon*, *Tomahawk* SLCM)
    1 *Sturgeon* (SSN-637) with 4 × 533mm TT (Mk 48
      HWT, *Tomahawk* SLCM)
  OTHER ROLES 1 ex-SSBN (SSBN 642) (special ops,
    included in the START-accountable launcher figures)

PRINCIPAL SURFACE COMBATANTS 128
AIRCRAFT CARRIERS 12
  CVN 9
    8 *Nimitz* (CVN-68) (one in refit)
    1 *Enterprise* (CVN-65)
  CV 3
    2 *Kitty Hawk* (CV-63)
    1 *J. F. Kennedy* (CV-67) (in reserve)
  AIR WING 11 (10 active, 1 reserve); average Air
  Wing comprises 9 sqn
    3 with 12 F/A-18C, 1 with 14 F-14, 1 with 8 S-3B
    and 2 ES-3, 1 with 6 SH-60, 1 with 4 EA-6B,
    1 with 4 E-2C, 1 spt with C-2
CRUISERS 27
  CG 27 *Ticonderoga* (CG-47 *Aegis*)
    5 *Baseline* 1 (CG-47–51) with 2 × 2 SM-2 MR SAM/
      ASROC, 2 × 4 *Harpoon* SSM, 2 × 127mm guns,
      2 × 3 ASTT (Mk 46 LWT), 2 SH-2F or SH-60B
      hel
    22 *Baseline* 2/3 (CG-52) with 2 VLS Mk 41 (61 tubes
      each) for combination of SM-2 ER SAM, and
      Tomahawk; other wpns as *Baseline* 1
DESTROYERS 54
  DDG 54
    28 *Arleigh Burke* (DDG-51 *Aegis*) Flight I/II with 2
      VLS Mk 41 (32 tubes fwd, 64 tubes aft) for
      combination of *Tomahawk*, SM-2 ER SAM and
      ASROC 2 × 4 *Harpoon* SSM, 1 × 127mm gun, 2
      × 3 ASTT (Mk 46 LWT), 1 SH-60B hel
    4 *Arleigh Burke* (DDG-79 *Aegis*) Flight IIA, arma-
      ment as above
    22 *Spruance* (DD-963) with 2 VLS Mark 41 for
      combination of *Tomahawk* and ASROC *Harpoon*
      SSM, *Sea Sparrow* SAM, 2 × 127mm gun, 2 × 3
      ASTT, 2 SH-60B hel
FRIGATES 35
  FFG 35 *Oliver Hazard Perry* (FFG-7) (8 in reserve) all
    with *Harpoon* SSM, 1 SM-1 MR SAM, 2 × 3 ASTT
    (Mk 46), 1 × 76mm gun; plus either 2 × SH-60 or 1
    × SH-2F hel

PATROL AND COASTAL COMBATANTS 21
(mainly responsibility of Coast Guard)
  PATROL, COASTAL 13 *Cyclone* PFC with SEAL
    team
  PATROL, INSHORE 8<

MINE WARFARE 29
  MINELAYERS none dedicated, but mines can be
    laid from attack SS, ac and surface ships.
  MINE COUNTERMEASURES 29
    1 *Inchon* MCCS in reserve
    4 *Osprey* (MHC-51) MHC, 10 *Osprey* in reserve
    9 *Avenger* (MCM-1) MCO, 5 *Avenger* in reserve

AMPHIBIOUS 41
LCC 2 *Blue Ridge*, capacity 700 tps
LHD 7 *Wasp*, capacity 1,894 tps, 60 tk; with 5 AV-8B ac,
  42 CH-46E, 6 SH-60B hel; plus 3 LCAC
LHA 5 *Tarawa*, capacity 1,900 tps, 100 tk; with 6 AV-8B
  ac, 12 CH-46E, 9 CH-53; plus 4 LCU
LPD 11 *Austin*, capacity 900 tps, 4 tk, with 6 CH-46E hel
LSD 15
  8 *Whidbey Island* with 4 LCAC, capacity 500 tps, 40 tk
  4 *Harpers Ferry* with 2 LCAC, capacity 500 tps, 40 tk
  3 *Anchorage* with 3 LCAC, capacity 330 tps, 38 tk
LST 1 *Newport*, capacity 347 tps, 10 tk (in reserve)
CRAFT about 200
  72 LCAC, capacity 1 MBT; about 37 LCU-1610,
  capacity 1 MBT; 8 LCVP; 75 LCM; plus numerous
  LCU

COMBAT LOGISTICS FORCE 8
  4 *Supply* AOE
  4 *Sacramento* AOE

NAVAL RESERVE SURFACE FORCES 26 (counted in the
active totals)
  1 CV (*J. F. Kennedy*) fully op with assigned air wg, 8
  FFG, 5 MCM, 10 MHC, 1 MCCS (*Inchon*), 1 LST
  generally crewed by 70% active and 30% reserve,
  plus 22 MIUW units

NAVAL INACTIVE FLEET about 27
  3 CV, 2 BB, 8 LST, 5 LKA, 2 AO, 2 AF, 5 AG plus misc
  service craft

MILITARY SEALIFT COMMAND (MSC)
MSC operates about 110 ships around the world
carrying the designation 'USNS' (United States Naval
Ships). They are not commissioned ships and are
manned by civilians. Some also have small mil
departments assigned to carry out specialised mil
functions such as comm and supply ops. MSC ships
carry the prefix 'T' before their normal hull numbers.

Naval Fleet Auxiliary Force 33
5 AE • 6 AF • 2 AH • 13 AO • 7 AT/F

Special Mission Ships 26
2 AG • 1 AR/C • 5 AGOS (counter-drug ops) • 9
  AGOS • 8 AGHS • 1 AGM

Prepositioning Program/Maritime Prepositioning Program 32

1 ro-ro AK • 3 hy ro-ro AK • 1 flo-flo AK • 4 AK • 13 MPS AK • 4 LASH • 2 AOT • 2 AVB • 1 AG • 1 AO

Sealift Force 30

8 AKR • 17 ro-ro AKR • 5 AOT

ADDITIONAL MILITARY SEALIFT

Ready Reserve Force (RRF) 76

1 pass cargo, 2 mil auxiliaries, 9 tkrs, 64 dry cargo

National Defence Reserve Fleet (NDRF) 68 (plus RRF forces)

8 cargo, 13 mil auxiliaries, 22 tkrs, 25 dry cargo

Augment Forces

14 cargo handling bn (12 in reserve)

COMMERCIAL SEALIFT about 327

US-flag (152) and effective US-controlled (EUSC, 175) ships potentially available to augment mil sealift

NAVAL AVIATION 70,230

(incl 6,300 women)

incl 12 carriers, 11 air wg (10 active, 1 reserve) **Flying hours** F-14: 252; F-18: 252

Average air wg comprises 9 sqn

3 with 12 F/A-18C, 1 with 10 F-14, 1 with 8 S-3B, 1 with 6 SH-60, 1 with 4 EA-6B, 1 with 4 E-2C, 1 spt with C-2

ORGANISATION

AIRCRAFT

FTR 12 sqn

4 with F-14A, 5 with F-14B, 3 with F-14D

FGA/ATTACK 24 sqn

23 with F/A-18C, 1 with F/A-18A

ELINT 4 sqn

2 with EP-3, 2 with EA-6B

ECM 14 sqn with EA-6B

MR 12 land-based sqn with P-3CIII

ASW 10 sqn with S-3B

AEW 10 sqn with E-2C

COMD 1 sqn with E-6A (TACAMO)

OTHER 2 sqn with C-2A

TRG 16 sqn

2 *Aggressor* with F/A-18, 14 trg with T-2C, T-34C, T-44, T-45A

HELICOPTERS

ASW 20 sqn

10 with SH-60B (LAMPS Mk III)

10 with SH-60F/HH-60H

MCM 1 sqn with MH-53E

MISC 5 sqn

4 with CH-46, 1 with MH-53E

TRG 2 sqn with TH-57B/C

NAVAL AVIATION RESERVE (NR) 22,220

(incl 3,000 women)

AIRCRAFT

FTR ATTACK 3 sqn with F-18

AEW 1 sqn with E-2C

ECM 1 sqn with EA-6B

MPA 7 sqn with P-3C/EP-3J

FLEET LOG SPT 1 wg

6 sqn with C-9B/DC-9, 4 sqn with C-130T, 1 sqn with C-40A, 3 sqn with C-20

TRG 2 *Aggressor* sqn (1 with F/A-18, 1 with F-5E/F)

HELICOPTERS 1 wg

ASW 2 sqn: 1 with SH-60F/HH-60F, 1 with SH-60B

MSC 3 sqn: 2 with HH-60H, 1 with UH-3H

NAVAL AVIATION EQUIPMENT

(Naval Inventory incl Marine Corps ac and hel)

1,669 cbt ac plus 192 in store; 526 armed hel plus 28 in store

AIRCRAFT

192 **F-14** (72 **-A** (ftr, incl 14 NR) plus 26 in store, 75 **-B** (ftr), 45 **-D** (ftr) plus 1 in store) • 872 **F/A-18** (226 **-A** (FGA, incl 34 NR, 80 MC (47 MCR)), 33 **-B** (FGA, incl 2 NR, 4 MC), 405 **-C** (FGA, incl 79 MC), 142 **-D** (FGA, incl 85 MC), 32 **-E** (FGA), 34 **-F** (FGA) • 32 **F-5E/F** (trg, incl 22 NR and 2 MCR) • 27 **TA-4J** (trg) plus 10 in store • 119 **EA-6B** (incl 4 NR, 20 MC) plus 3 in store • 1 **A6-E** (FGA) plus 88 in store • 112 **AV-8B** (FGA, MC) plus 29 in store • 21 **TAV-8B** (trg, incl 14 MC) • 69 **E-2** (67 **-C** (AEW, incl 11 NR) plus 5 in store, 2 **TE-2C** (trg) • 260 **P-3** (1 **-B**, plus 26 in store, 226* **-C** (incl 70 NR) plus 13 in store, 12 **EP-3** (ELINT), 12 **NP-3D** (trials), 9 **U/VP-3A** (utl/VIP) • 113 **S-3** plus 1 in store (113 **-B**) • 101 **C-130** (20 **-T** (tpt NR), 77 **-KC-130F/R/T** (incl 77 MC (28 MCR)), 1 **-TC-130G/Q** (tpt/trg), 3 **-DC-130**) • 1 **CT-39G** • 38 **C-2A** (tpt) • 17 **C-9B** (tpt, 15 NR, 2 MC) • 9 **DC-9** (incl 9 NR) (tpt) • 7 **C-20** (2 **-D** (VIP/NR), 5 **-G** (tpt, 1 MCR)) • 63 **UC-12** (utl) (41 **-B** (incl 18 MC, 3 MCR), 12 **-F** (incl 6 MC), 10 **-M**) • 1 **NU-1B** (utl) • 2 **U-6A** (utl) • 99 **T-2C** (trg) • 1 **T-39D** (trg) • 17 **T-39N** (trg) • 55 **T-44** (trg) • 130 **T-45** (trg 74 **-A**, 56 **-C**) • 312 **T-34C** (incl 2 MC) • 11 **T-38A/B** (trg) • 21 **TC-12B** • 2 **TC-18F** (trg) • 17 **TA-4J** (trg) plus 10 in store

HELICOPTERS

102 **UH-1N** (utl, incl 98 MC (20 MCR)) • 25 **HH-1H** (utl, incl 7 MC) plus 9 in store • 154 **CH-53E** (tpt, incl 150 MC (16 MCR)) plus 11 in store • 44 **CH-53D** (tpt MC) plus 14 in store • 41 **MH-53E** (tpt, incl 12 NR, 5 MC) plus 3 in store • 234 **SH-60** (159 **-B**, 75 **-F**) • 40 **HH-60H** (cbt spt, incl 16 NR) plus 1 in store • 8 **VH-60** (ASW/SAR MC) • 50 **UH-3H** (ASW/SAR incl 10 NR) plus 2 in store • 18 **CH-46D** (tpt, trg) • 230 **CH-46E** (tpt, incl 230 MC (25 MCR)) • 48 **UH/HH-46D** (utl incl 9 MC) • 130 **TH-57** (45 **-B** (trg), 85 **-C** (trg)) plus 1 **-B** and 4 **-C** in store • 11 **VH-3A/D** (VIP, incl 11 MC) • 194 **AH-1W** (atk, incl 188 MC (37 MCR)) plus 2 in store • 44 **CH-53D** (tpt, MC) plus 14 in store

TILT ROTOR 21 V-22 (MC)

MISSILES

AAM AIM-120 AMRAAM, AIM-7 *Sparrow*, AIM-54A/C *Phoenix*, AIM-9 *Sidewinder*
ASM AGM-45 *Shrike*, AGM-88A HARM; AGM-84 *Harpoon*, AGM-119 *Penguin* Mk-3, AGM-114 *Hellfire*

Marine Corps (USMC) 171,300

(incl 10,100 women)

GROUND

ORGANISATION

3 div
  1 with 3 inf regt (9 bn), 1 tk, 2 lt armd recce (LAV-25), 1 aslt amph, 1 cbt engr bn, 1 arty regt (4 bn), 1 recce coy
  1 with 3 inf regt (9 bn), 1 tk, 1 lt armd recce (LAV-25), 1 aslt amph, 1 cbt engr bn, 1 arty regt (4 bn), 1 recce bn
  1 with 2 inf regt (6 bn), 1 cbt spt bn (1 AAV, 1 LAR coy), 1 arty regt (2 bn), 1 cbt engr bn, 1 recce coy
3 Force Service Spt Gp
Special Ops Forces incl 3 recce bn, 3 Force recce coy
1 bn Marine Corps Security Force (Atlantic and Pacific)
Marine Security Guard bn (1 HQ, 7 region coy)

RESERVES (MCR)

1 div (3 inf (9 bn), 1 arty regt (5 bn); 1 lt armd recce (LAV-25), 1 aslt amph, 1 recce, 1 cbt engr bn)
1 Force Service Spt Gp
Special Ops Forces incl 1 recce bn, 1 Force recce coy

EQUIPMENT

MBT 403 M-1A1 *Abrams*
LAV 400 LAV-25 (**25mm** gun) plus 334 variants incl 50 Mor, 95 ATGW (see below)
AAV 1,321 AAV-7A1 (all roles)
TOWED ARTY 105mm: 331 M-101A1; **155mm**: 596 M-198
MOR 81mm: 586 M-252 (incl 50 LAV-M)
ATGW 1,083 TOW, 1,121 *Dragon*, 95 LAV-TOW
RL 83mm: 1,650 SMAW; **84mm**: 1,300 AT-4
SURV 23 AN/TPQ-36 (arty)

AVIATION 36,310

(incl 2,030 women)
Flying hours 249 fixed wing (non-tpt), 365 fixed wing (tpt), 277 (hel)
3 active air wg and 1 MCR air wg
Flying hours cbt aircrew: 270
AIR WING no standard org, but a notional wg comprises
  AC 118 FW: 48 **F/A-18A/C/D**, 48 **AV-8B**, 10 **EA-6B**, 12 **KC-130**
  HEL 156: 10 **CH-53D**, 32 **CH-53E**, 36 **AH-1W**, 18 **UH-1N**, 60 **CH-46E**
  plus 1 MC C² gp, 1 wg spt gp

ORGANISATION

Aircraft

FTR/ATTACK 18 sqn with 208 F/A-18A/C/D (incl 4 MCR sqn)
FGA 7 sqn with 100 AV-8B
ECM 4 sqn with 20 EA-6B
TKR 5 sqn with 69 KC-130F/R/T (incl 2 MCR sqn)
TRG 4 sqn
  1 with 12 AV-8B, 14 TAV-8B; 1 with 40 F/A-18A/B/C/D, 2 T-34C; 1 with 2 F-5E (MCR); 1 with 8 KC-130F

Helicopters

ARMED 6 lt attack/utl with 159 AH-1W and 86 UH-1N (incl 2 MCR sqn)
TPT 15 med sqn with 210 CH-46E (incl 2 MCR sqn), 4 sqn with 38 CH-53D; 6 **hy** sqn with 135 CH-53E (incl 2 MCR sqn)
TRG 4 sqn
  1 with 29 AH-1W, 12 UH-1N, 4 HH-1N; 1 with 20 CH-46; 1 with 6 CH-53D; 1 with 15 CH-53E, 6 MH-53E
SAM 3+ bn
  2+ bn (5 bty), 1 MCR bn with *Stinger* and *Avenger*
UAV 2 sqn with *Pioneer*

Marine Corps Aviation Reserve 11,700

(640 women); 1 air wg

Aircraft

FTR/ATTACK 4 sqn with 47 F-18A
  1 *Aggressor* sqn with 2 F5-E/F
TKR 2 tkr/tpt sqn with 28 KC-130T

Helicopters

ARMED 2 attack/utl sqn with 37 AH-1W, 20 UH-1N
TPT 4 sqn: 2 med with 25 CH-46E, 2 **hy** with 16 CH-53E
SAM 1 bn (2 bty) with *Stinger* and *Avenger*

EQUIPMENT

(incl MCR): 396 cbt ac; 188 armed hel
Totals included in the Navy inventory

Aircraft

248 **F-18A/-B/-C/-D** (FGA incl 47 MCR) • 112 **AV-8B** • 14* **TAV-8B** (trg) • 20 **EA-6B** (ECM) • 2* **F-5E/F** (trg, MCR) • 77 **KC-130F/R/T** (tkr, incl 28 MCR) • 2 **C-9B** (tpt) • 1 **C-20G** (MCR) (tpt) • 1 **CT-39G** (MCR) • 21 **UC-12B/F** (utl, incl 3 MCR) • 2 **T-34C** (trg)

Helicopters

188 **AH-1W** (GA, incl 37 MCR) • 98 **UH-1N** (utl, incl 20 MCR) • 7 **HH-1H** (utl) • 230 **CH-46E** (tpt incl 25 MCR) • 9 **UH/HH-46D** (utl) • 150 **CH-53-E** (tpt, incl 16 MCR) • 5 **MH-53E**, 44 **CH-53D** (tpt) • 8 **VH-60** (VIP tpt) • 11 **VH-3A/D** (VIP tpt)
TILT ROTOR 21 MV-22B

Missiles

SAM 1,929 *Stinger*, 235 *Avenger*

AAM *Sparrow* AMRAAM, *Sidewinder*
ASM *Maverick, Hellfire,* TOW

Coast Guard (active duty) 36,260 military, 5,850 civilian

(incl 3,540 women)
By law a branch of the Armed Forces; in peacetime ops under, and is funded by, the Department of Transport

Bdgt Authority

Year	1995	1996	1997	1998	1999	2000	2001
US$bn	3.7	3.7	3.9	4.0	4.6	4.1 expected	4.6 request

PATROL VESSELS 130

OFFSHORE 41

12 *Hamilton* high-endurance with HH-60J LAMPS HU-65A *Dolphin* hel, all with 76mm gun
13 *Bear* med-endurance with HH-65A hel
16 *Reliance* med-endurance with 25mm gun, hel deck plus 16 sea-going buoy tenders

COASTAL 89

49 *Farallon*, 10 *Point Hope*, 30 *Baracuda*, plus 4 coastal buoy tenders

INLAND, tenders only

13 inland construction tenders, 5 small inland buoy tenders, 18 small river buoy tenders

SPT AND OTHER 24

4 icebreakers, 19 icebreaking tugs, 1 trg

AVIATION (1,050 incl 50 women)

AC 20 HU-25 (plus 21 supt or in store), 26 HC-130H (plus 4 spt), 2 RU-38A, 35 HH-60J (plus 7 spt), 80 HH-65A (plus 13 spt), 1 VC-4A, 1 C-20B

RESERVES 8,000 incl 1,080 women

Air Force (USAF) 352,500

(incl 66,300 women) **Flying hours** ftr 205, bbr 178, tkr 224, airlift 284
Air Combat Comd (ACC) 4 air force, 23 ac wg **Air Mobility Comd** (AMC) 2 air force, 13 ac wg
The USAF introduced its Aerospace Expeditionary Force (AEF) concept on 1 Oct 1999. Almost the entire USAF – active force, reserve force and ANG – is being divided into 10 AEFs. Each AEF will be on call for 90 days every 15 months, and at least 2 of the 10 AEFs will be on call at any one time. The intention is that each AEF, with 10,000–15,000 personnel will comprise approx 90 multi-role ftr and bbr ac, 31 intra-theatre refuelling ac and 13 ac for intelligence, surv, recce and EW missions. At present, only 3 AEFs have stand-off, precision-engagement capabilities.

TACTICAL 82 ftr sqn

incl active duty sqn ACC, USAFE and PACAF (sqn may be 18–24 ac)
14 with F-15, 6 with F-15E, 46 with F-16C/D, 14 with A-10/OA-10, 2 with F-117

SUPPORT

RECCE 3 sqn with U-2R and RC-135
AEW 1 Airborne Warning and Control wg, 6 sqn (incl 1 trg) with E-3
EW 2 sqn with EC-130
FAC 7 tac air control sqn, mixed A-10A/OA-10A
TRG 36 sqn
1 *Aggressor* with F-16
35 trg with **ac** F-15, F-16, A-10/OA-10, T-37, T-38, AT-38, T-1A, -3A, C-5, -130, -141 **hel** HH-60, U/TH-1
TPT 28 sqn
17 strategic: 5 with C-5 (1 trg), 9 with C-141 (2 trg), 3 with C-17
11 tac airlift with C-130
Units with C-135, VC-137, C-9, C-12, C-20, C-21
TKR 23 sqn
19 with KC-135 (1 trg), 4 with KC-10A
SAR 8 sqn (incl STRATCOM msl spt), HH-60, HC-130N/P
MEDICAL 3 medical evacuation sqn with C-9A
WEATHER RECCE WC-135
TRIALS weapons trg units with **ac** A-10, F-4, F-15, F-16, F-111, T-38, C-141 **hel** UH-1
UAV *Global Hawk*, 2 sqn with *Predators*

RESERVES

AIR NATIONAL GUARD (ANG) 106,900
(incl 17,000 women)
BBR 2 sqn with B-1B
FTR 4 AD sqn with F-15, F-16
FGA 40 sqn
6 with A-10/ OA-10
27 with F-16 (incl 1 AD, 2 trg)
7 with F-15A/B (incl 3 AD, 1 trg)
TPT 27 sqn
24 tac (1 trg) with C-130E/H
3 strategic: 1 with C-5, 2 with C-141B
TKR 23 sqn with KC-135E/R (11 with KC-135E, 12 with KC-135R)
SPECIAL OPS 1 sqn (AFSOC) with EC-130E
SAR 3 sqn with **ac** HC-130 **hel** HH-60
TRG 7 sqn
AIR FORCE RESERVE (AFR) 74,360
(incl 15,760 women), 35 wg
BBR 1 sqn with B-52H
FGA 7 sqn
4 with F-16C/D (incl 1 trg), 3 with A-10/OA-10 (incl 1 trg)
TPT 19 sqn
7 strategic: 2 with C-5A, 5 with C-141B
11 tac: 8 with C-130H, 2 C-130E
1 weather recce with WC-130H/J
TKR 7 sqn with KC-135E/R (5 KC-135R, 2 KC-135E)

Journals Marketing Department (MB01)
Oxford University Press, Inc.
2001 Evans Road
Cary
North Carolina 27513
USA

Journals Marketing Department (MB01)
Oxford University Press
Great Clarendon Street
Oxford OX2 6DP
UK

SAR 3 sqn (ACC) with **ac** HC-130N/P **hel** HH-60
ASSOCIATE 25 sqn (personnel only)
4 for C-5, 2 for C-141, 1 aero-medical for C-9, 5 C-17A, 4 for KC-10, 1 for KC-135, 1 for *Aggressor* (F-16), 1 for F-16 trg, 6 for T-37, T-38, T-1 trg

AIRCRAFT

LONG-RANGE STRIKE/ATTACK 208 cbt ac: 94 **B-52H** (93 in service, 1 test) • 93 **B-1B** (91 in service, 2 test) • 21 **B-2A** (20 in service, 1 test)

RECCE 32 **U-2S** (31 in service, 1 on lease) • 4 **TU-2 R/S** • 9 **E-8C** (JSTARS) (8 in service, 1 test), 2 **E-9A** • 3 **RC-135S** (*Cobra Balls*), 2 **RC-135U** (*Combat Sent*), 16 **RC-135V/W** (*Rivet Joint*) • 162 **RF-4C** in store

COMD 33 **E-3B/C** (32 in service, 1 test) • 4 **E-4B** • 3 **EC-135** (plus 29 in store)

TAC 3,939 cbt ac (incl ANG, AFR); no armed hel: F-4 261 **-D, -E, -G** models in store • 740 **F-15** (523 **-A/B/C/D** (ftr, incl 100 ANG, 12 test)), 217 **-E** (FGA, plus 1 F-15A/B/C/D/E in store) • 1,412 **F-16** (100 **-A** (incl 95 ANG), 42 **-B** (incl 27 ANG), 1,088 **-C** (incl 408 ANG, 65 AFR), 182 **-D** (incl 39 ANG, 5 AFR) plus 365 F-16A/B in store) • 3 **F-22A** (2 YF-22A in store) • (213 **F-111**/33 **EF-111A** in store) • 52 **F-117** (incl 6* (trg), plus 1 test) • 249 **A-10A** (incl 76 ANG, 44 AFR), plus 105 in store • 118* **OA-10A** (FAC incl 26 ANG, 8 AFR) • 5 **EC-18B/D** Advanced Range Instrumentation (2 in store, 3 test) • 21* **AC-130H/U** (special ops, USAF) • 30 **HC-130N/P** (incl 10 ANG plus 8 AFR) • 30 **EC-130E/H** (special ops incl 8 ANG SOF) • 66 **MC-130E/H/P** (special ops incl 45 SOF (4-Ps ANG)) • 14 **WC-130H/J** weather recce, (AFR) plus 6 in store • 4 **WC-135B/C/W** • 3 **OC-135** ('Open Skies' Treaty) (2 in service, 1 in store) • 1 **EC-137D**

TPT 126 **C-5** (74 **-A** (strategic tpt, incl 12 ANG, 32 AFR), 50 **-B**, 2 **-C**) • 23 **C-9A/C** • 30 **C-12C/-D/-F/-J** (liaison) • 67 **C-17A** • 1 **C-18B** in store • 12 **C-20** (2 **-A**, 5 **-B**, 3 **-C**, 2 **-H**) • 78 **C-21A** (2 ANG) • 4 **C-22A/B** (3 ANG, 11 in store) • 2 **VC-25A** • 11 **C-26B** (ANG) • 7 **C-27** in store • 4 **C-32A** • 2 **C-37A** • 3 **C-38A** (ANG) • 526 **C-130B/E/H/J** (incl 216 ANG, 107 AFR), plus 13 in store • 6 **C-135B/C/E** (1 ANG, 5 test) • 2 **C-137C** (1 in service, 1 test) (VIP tpt) • 130 **C-141B** (incl 17 ANG, 44 AFR) plus 49 in store

TKR 546 **KC-135A/D/E/R/T** (incl 223 ANG, 69 AFR) plus 55 in store • 59 **KC-10A** tkr/tpt

TRG 180 **T-1A** • 110 **T-3A** • 13 **T-6A** • 1 **TE-8A** • 2 **TC-18E** • 3 **UV-18B** • 417 **T-37B** • 408 **T-38A/C** (147 in store) • 93 **AT-38B** (3 in store) • 3 **T-41** • 11 **T-43A** • 6 **CT-43A** (5 in store) • 2 **TC-135S/W**

HELICOPTERS

38 **MH-53M/J** *Pave Low* (special ops) • 3 **MH-60G** • 11 **HH-1H** (11 in store) • 104 **HH-60G** (incl 18 ANG, 23 AFR) • 62 **UH-1N**, 6 **TH-53A**

UAV

High Level – **RQ-4A** *Global Hawk* prototype
Tactical – 8 **RQ-1A/B** *Predator*

MISSILES

AAM 9,200+ AIM-9P/L/M *Sidewinder*, 4,300+ AIM-7E/F/M *Sparrow*, 4,500+ AIM-120 A/B AMRAAM
ASM 27,000+ AGM-65A/B/D/G *Maverick*, 8,000+ AGM-88A/B HARM, 70+ AGM-84B *Harpoon*, 1,173 AGM-86B ALCM, 207 AGM-86C ALCM, 408 AGM-129A, 100+ AGM-130A, 110+ AGM-142A/B/C/D, AGM-154 *JSOW*

CIVIL RESERVE AIR FLEET (CRAF) 683

commercial ac (numbers fluctuate)
LONG-RANGE 501
passenger 271 (A-310, B-747, B -757, B-767, DC-10, L-1011, MD-11)
cargo 230 (B-747, DC-8, DC-10, L-1011, MD-11)
SHORT-RANGE 95
passenger 81 (A-300, B-727, B-737, MD-80/83)
cargo 14 (L-100, B-727, DC-9)
DOMESTIC AND AERO-MEDICAL 34 (B-767)

Special Operations Forces (SOF)

Units only listed

ARMY (15,300)

5 SF gp (each 3 bn) • 1 Ranger inf regt (3 bn) • 1 special ops avn regt (3 bn) • 1 Psychological Ops gp (5 bn) • 1 Civil Affairs bn (5 coy) • 1 sigs, 1 spt bn

RESERVES (2,800 ARNG, 7,800 AR)
2 ARNG SF gp (3 bn) • 12 AR Civil Affairs HQ (4 comd, 8 bde) • 2 AR Psychological Ops gp • 36 AR Civil Affairs 'bn' (coy)

NAVY (4,000)

1 Naval Special Warfare Comd • 1 Naval Special Warfare Centre • 3 Naval Special Warfare gp • 6 Naval Special Warfare units • 6 SEAL teams • 2 SEAL delivery veh teams • 2 Special Boat sqn • 6 DDS

RESERVES (1,400)
1 Naval Special Warfare Comd det • 6 Naval Special Warfare gp det • 3 Naval Special Warfare unit det • 5 SEAL team det • 2 Special Boat unit • 2 Special Boat sqn • 1 SEAL delivery veh det • 1 CINCSOC det

AIR FORCE (9,320)

1 air force HQ, 1 wg, 14 sqn
8 with AC-130H, 13 AC-130U, 21 MC-130H, 20 MC-130P, 33 MH-53J/M, 5 C-130E
AETC (Air Education and Trg Comd) 1 wg, 2 sqn: 3 MC-130H, 4 MC-130P, 5 MH-53J, 4 TH-53A

RESERVES (AFRC 1,260, ANG 1,040)
1 wg, 2 sqn: 14 MC-130E, 1 C-130E
ANG
1 wg, 1 sqn: 5 EC-130E, 3 EC-130J, 3 C-130

Deployment

Commanders' NATO appointments also shown (e.g., COMEUCOM is also SACEUR)

EUROPEAN COMMAND (EUCOM)

some 98,000. Plus 14,000 Mediterranean 6th Fleet: HQ
Stuttgart-Vaihingen (Commander is SACEUR)
ARMY (53,000) HQ US Army Europe (USAREUR),
Heidelberg
NAVY HQ US Navy Europe (USNAVEUR), London
(Commander is also CINCAFSOUTH)
AIR FORCE (35,500) HQ US Air Force Europe (USAFE),
Ramstein (Commander is COMAIRCENT)
USMC 950

GERMANY

ARMY 42,300
V Corps with 1 armd(-), 1 mech inf div(-), 1 arty, 1 AD
(1 *Patriot* (6 bty), 1 *Avenger* bn), 1 engr, 1 avn bde
Army Prepositioned Stocks (APS) for 2 armd/mech
bde, approx 57% stored in Ge
  EQPT (incl APS in Ge, Be, Lux and Nl)
  some 541 MBT, 760 AIFV, 852 APC, 508 arty/
  MRL/mor, 134 ATK hel
AIR FORCE 15,100, 60 cbt ac
1 air force HQ: USAFE
1 ftr wg: 3 sqn (2 with 42 F-16C/D, 1 with 12 A-10
  and 6 OA-10)
1 airlift wg: incl 16 C-130E and 9 C-9A, 13 C-21, 2C-
  20, 1CT-43
NAVY 300
USMC 380

BELGIUM

ARMY 795; approx 22% of POMCUS **NAVY** 100 **AIR
FORCE** 530

GREECE

NAVY 240; base facilities at Soudha Bay, Makri
AIR FORCE 240; air base gp. Facilities at Iraklion

ITALY

ARMY 2,200; HQ: Vicenza. 1 inf bn gp, 1 arty bty
  EQPT for Theater Reserve Unit/Army Readiness
  Package South (TRU/ARPS), incl 116 MBT, 127
  AIFV, 4 APC
NAVY 4,400; HQ: Gaeta; bases at Naples, La
  Maddalena, 1 MR sqn with 9 P-3C at Sigonella
AIR FORCE 4,140; 1 AF HQ (16th Air Force), 1 ftr
  wg, 2 sqn with 42 F-16C/D
  Deliberate Force Component 86 F-16C, 4 AC-130,
  8 EC-130, 26 F-15, 18 F-15C, 21 EA-6B, 10 KC-135,
  12 F-117, 7 UH-60, 22 A-10, 4 U-2, 3 P-3, 9 MH-53, 3
  MC-130, 4 MH-60
USMC 110

LUXEMBOURG

ARMY approx 21% of APS

MEDITERRANEAN

NAVY some 14,000 (incl 2,100 Marines). 6th Fleet
  (HQ: Gaeta, It): typically 3 SSN, 1 CVBG (1 CV, 6
  surface combatants, 1 fast spt ship), 2 LHD/LPD, 2
  AO, 1 AE, 1 AF, 1 AT/F. MPS-1 (4 ships with eqpt
  for 1 MEF (fwd)). Marine personnel: some 2,000.

MEU (SOC) embarked aboard Amph Ready
  Group ships

NETHERLANDS

ARMY 355; approx 7% of APS **AIR FORCE** 290
NAVY 10

NORWAY

ARMY 23: prepo incl 18 M-109, 18 M-198 arty, no
aviation assets **AIR FORCE** 50 **NAVY** 10

PORTUGAL

(for Azores, see Atlantic Command)
NAVY 50 **AIR FORCE** 940

SPAIN

NAVY 1,760; base at Rota **AIR FORCE** 360 **USMC** 70

TURKEY

NAVY 20, spt facilities at Izmir and Ankara
AIR FORCE 1,800; facilities at Incirlik. 1 wg (ac on
  det only), numbers vary (incl F-15E, F-16, EA-6B,
  KC-135, E-3B/C, C-12, HC-130, HH-60)
Installations for SIGINT, space tracking and seismic
  monitoring
USMC 220

UNITED KINGDOM

ARMY 390
NAVY 1,220; HQ: London, admin and spt facilities
1 SEAL det
AIR FORCE 9,550
1 air force HQ (3rd Air Force): 1 ftr wg, 72 cbt ac, 2
  sqn with 48 F-15E, 1 sqn with 24 F-15C/D
1 special ops gp, 1 air refuelling wg with 15 KC-135,
  1 recce sqn, 1 naval air flt
USMC 120

PACIFIC COMMAND (USPACOM)

HQ: Hawaii

ALASKA

ARMY 5,900; 1 lt inf bde
AIR FORCE 9,600; 1 air force HQ (11th Air Force): 1
  ftr wg with 2 sqn (1 with 18 F-16, 1 with 12 A-10, 6
  OA-10), 1 wg with 2 sqn with 42 F-15C/D, 1 sqn
  with 18 F-15E, 1 sqn with 10 C-130H, 2 E-3B, 3 C-
  12, 1 air tkr wg with 8 KC-135R

HAWAII

ARMY 15,500; HQ: US Army Pacific (USARPAC):
  1 lt inf div (2 lt inf bde)
AIR FORCE 4,580; HQ: Pacific Air Forces (PACAF):
  1 wg with 2 C-135B/C, 1 wg (ANG) with 15 F-
  15A/B, 4 C-130H and 8 KC-135R
NAVY 7,500; HQ: US Pacific Fleet
  Homeport for some 22 SSN, 3 CG, 4 DDG, 2 FFG, 4
  spt and misc ships
USMC 5,680; HQ: Marine Forces Pacific

SINGAPORE

NAVY 90; log facilities **AIR FORCE** 40 det spt sqn
USMC 160

JAPAN

ARMY 1,600; 1 corps HQ, base and spt units
AIR FORCE 13,480; 1 air force HQ (5th Air Force): 84 cbt ac
1 ftr wg, 2 sqn with 36 F-16, 1 wg, 2 sqn with 48 F-15C/D, 1 sqn with 15 KC-135, 1 SAR sqn with 8 HH-60, 1 sqn with 2 E-3 AWACS, 1 Airlift Wg with 16 C-130 E/H, 4 C-21, 3 C-9, 1 special ops gp with 4 MC-130P and 4 MC-130H
NAVY 5,200; bases: **Yokosuka** (HQ 7th Fleet) homeport for 1 CV, 9 surface combatants, 1 LCC **Sasebo** homeport for 4 amph ships, 1 MCM sqn
USMC 18,050; 1 MEF

SOUTH KOREA

ARMY 27,200; 1 Army HQ (UN comd), 1 inf div with 2 bde (2 mech inf, 2 air aslt, 2 tk bn), 2 SP arty, 2 MLRS, 1 AD bn, 1 avn, 1 engr bde, 1 air cav bde (2 ATK hel bn), 1 *Patriot* SAM bn (Army tps)
EQPT incl 116 MBT, 126 AIFV, 111 APC, 45 arty/MRL/mor
AIR FORCE 8,920; 1 air force HQ (7th Air Force): 2 ftr wg, 84 cbt ac; 3 sqn with 60 F-16, 1 sqn with 12 A-10, 12 OA-10, 1 special ops sqn, 5 MH-53J, 1 U-2
NAVY 300
USMC 100

GUAM

ARMY 40
AIR FORCE 1,600; 1 air force HQ (13th Air Force)
NAVY 1,850; MPS-3 (4 ships with eqpt for 1 MEB) Naval air station, comms and spt facilities

AUSTRALIA

AIR FORCE 70 **NAVY** some 40; comms facility at NW Cape, SEWS/SIGINT station at Pine Gap, and SEWS station at Nurrungar

DIEGO GARCIA

NAVY 650; MPS-2 (5 ships with eqpt for 1 MEB) Naval air station, spt facilities **AIR FORCE** 20

THAILAND

ARMY 40 **NAVY** 10 **AIR FORCE** 30 **USMC** 370

US WEST COAST

MARINES 1 MEF

AT SEA

PACIFIC FLEET 135,100 USN, 13,470 reserve, 11,000 civilians (HQ: Pearl Harbor (HI)) **Main base**: Pearl Harbor **Other bases**: Bangor, Everett, Bremerton (WA), San Diego (CA)
Submarines 8 SSBN, 27 SSN
Surface Combatants 6 CV/CVN, 13 CG, 25 DDG, 15 FFG
Amph 1 comd, 3 LHA, 3 LHD, 8 LSD, 1 LST, plus 1 AG, 59 MSC ships
Other 2 MCM, 8 auxiliary ships
Surface Forces divided between two fleets
3rd Fleet (HQ: San Diego) covers Eastern and Central Pacific, Aleutian Islands, Bering Sea;

typically 3 CVBG, 4 URG, amph gp
7th Fleet (HQ: Yokosuka) covers Western Pacific, J, Pi, ANZUS responsibilities, Indian Ocean; typically 1 CVBG (1 CV, 6-8 surface combatants), 2 LHD/LPD, 2 LSD/LST, 1 LCC, 4 AO, 3 MCM
Aircraft 363 tac, 203 hel, 77 P-3, 162 other

CENTRAL COMMAND (USCENTCOM)

commands all deployed forces in its region; HQ: MacDill AFB, FL
ARMY 2,100
AT SEA
5th Fleet HQ: Manama. Average US Naval Forces deployed in Indian Ocean, Persian Gulf, Red Sea; typically 1 SSN, 1 CVBG (1 CV, 6 surface combatants), 3 amph ships, 4 MCM

BAHRAIN

NAVY 680 **USMC** 45

KUWAIT

ARMY 2,600; 1 bde HQ; prepo eqpt for 1 armd bde (2 tk, 1 mech bn, 1 arty bn)
NAVY 10 **AIR FORCE** 2,000 (force structure varies)
USMC 80

OMAN

AIR FORCE 200 **NAVY** 60

QATAR

ARMY 37; prepo eqpt for 1 armd bde (forming)

SAUDI ARABIA

ARMY 790; 1 *Patriot* SAM, 1 sigs unit incl those on short-term (6 months) duty
AIR FORCE 4,050. Units on rotational detachment, **ac** numbers vary (incl F-15E, F-16, F-117, A-10, C-130, KC-135, U-2, E-3)
NAVY 20
USMC 250

UAE

AIR FORCE 390

TRAINING ADVISORS

NIGERIA 50 (to be 200)

SOUTHERN COMMAND (USSOUTHCOM)

HQ: Miami, FL
ARMY 2,100; HQ: US Army South, Fort Buchanan, PR: 1 inf, 1 avn bn
USMC 100
AIR FORCE 1,600; 1 wg (1 C-21, 9 C-27, 1 CT-43)

COLOMBIA

ARMY 160

HONDURAS

ARMY 850 **USMC** 70 **AIR FORCE** 200

JOINT FORCES COMMAND (USJFCOM)

HQ: Norfolk, VA (CINC has op control of all CONUS-based army and air forces)

US EAST COAST
USMC 19,140; 1 MEF

BERMUDA
NAVY 800

CUBA
NAVY 590 (Guantánamo) USMC 200 (Guantánamo)

ICELAND
NAVY 960; 1 MR sqn with 6 P-3, 1 UP-3
USMC 48
AIR FORCE 630; 6 F-15C/D, 1 KC-135, 1 HC-130, 4 HH-60G

PORTUGAL (AZORES)
NAVY 10; limited facilities at Lajes
AIR FORCE periodic SAR detachments to spt space shuttle ops

UNITED KINGDOM
NAVY 1,220; comms and intelligence facilities at Edzell, Thurso

AT SEA
ATLANTIC FLEET (HQ: Norfolk, VA) 108,000 USN, 17,000 civilians **Main base** Norfolk **Other main bases** Groton (CT), King's Bay (GA), Mayport (FL)
Submarines 10 SSBN, 28 SSN
Surface Combatants 6 CV/CVN, 14 CG, 21 DDG, 20 FFG
Amph 1 LCC, 2 LHA, 4 LPH, 6 LPD, 5 LSD, 6 LST, 1 LKA
Surface Forces divided into 2 fleets:
2nd Fleet (HQ: Norfolk) covers Atlantic; typically 4–5 CVBG, amph gp, 4 URG
6th Fleet (HQ: Gaeta, Italy) under op comd of EUCOM, typically 1 CG/BG, 3 DDG, 2 FFG, amph gp

Continental United States (CONUS)

major units/formations only listed

ARMY (USACOM) 345,300
provides general reserve of cbt-ready ground forces for other comd
Active 1 Army HQ, 3 Corps HQ (1 AB), 1 armd, 2 mech, 1 lt inf, 1 AB, 1 air aslt div; 6 arty bde; 2 armd cav regt, 6 AD bn (1 *Avenger*, 5 *Patriot*)
Reserve (ARNG): 3 armd, 2 mech, 2 med, 1 lt inf div;18 indep bde
NAVY 186,200
AIR FORCE 276,200
USMC 128,100

US STRATEGIC COMMAND (USSTRATCOM)
HQ: Offutt AFB, NE. See entry on p. 19

AIR COMBAT COMMAND (ACC)
HQ: Langley AFB, VA. Provides strategic AD units and cbt-ready Air Force units for rapid deployment

AIR FORCE SPACE COMMAND (AFSPC)
HQ: Peterson AFB, CO. Provides ballistic-msl warning, space control, worldwide sat ops, and maintains ICBM force

US SPECIAL OPERATIONS COMMAND (USSOCOM)
HQ: MacDill AFB, FL. Comd all active, reserve and National Guard special ops forces of all services based in CONUS. See p. 25

US TRANSPORTATION COMMAND (USTRANSCOM)
HQ: Scott AFB, IL. Provides all common-user airlift, sealift and land tpt to deploy and maintain US forces on a global basis

AIR MOBILITY COMMAND (AMC)
HQ: Scott AFB, IL. Provides strategic, tac and special op airlift, aero-medical evacuation, SAR and weather recce

Forces Abroad

UN AND PEACEKEEPING
BOSNIA (SFOR II): ε3,500; 1 div HQ, 1 inf bde plus spt tps **CROATIA** (SFOR): 130 **SFOR AIR ELEMENT** (OP JOINT GUARD) 3,200. Forces are deployed to **BiH, Cr, Hu, It, Fr, Ge** and **UK**. Ac include F/A-16, A-10, AC-130, MC-130, C-130, E-3, U-2, EC-130, RC-135, EA-6B, MH-53J and *Predator* UAV. **EAST TIMOR** (UNTAET): 3 obs **EGYPT** (MFO): 860; 1 inf, 1 spt bn **FYROM** (KFOR): 340 **GEORGIA** (UNOMIG): 2 obs **HUNGARY** (SFOR) 350; 230 Air Force *Predator* UAV **IRAQ/ KUWAIT** (UNIKOM): 19 obs **MIDDLE EAST** (UNTSO): 2 obs **WESTERN SAHARA** (MINURSO): 15 obs **SAUDI ARABIA** (*Southern Watch*) **Air Force** units on rotation, numbers vary (incl F-15, F-16, F-117, C-130, KC-135, E-3) **TURKEY** (*Northern Watch*) **Air Force** 1,400; 1 tac, 1 Air Base gp (ac on det only), numbers vary but include F-16, F-15, EA-6B, KC-135, E3B/C, C-12, HC-130 **YUGOSLAVIA** (KFOR): 5,400

Paramilitary

CIVIL AIR PATROL (CAP) 53,000
(incl 1,900 cadets); HQ, 8 geographical regions, 52 wg, 1,700 units, 535 CAP ac, plus 4,700 private ac

MILITARY DEVELOPMENTS

Regional trends

Amid reports of overstretched militaries in Western Europe, the main topic in 2001 has been the building of the European Rapid Reaction Force (ERRF). The December 2000 Nice summit failed to resolve the central question: the feasibility of having a 60,000-strong force ready for deployment by 2003. And there is less talk about 'rapid reaction' and more about 'planned options' for likely scenarios. Meanwhile, the Balkan crisis shows no sign of disappearing, with the crisis in Macedonia unresolved and NATO pledged to provide a brigade-size force to disarm rebels once there is a stable cease-fire agreement. NATO enlargement and its effect on NATO's relations with the Russian Federation will be a major issue as the selection of new member states approaches following the November 2002 NATO summit in Prague.

Terrorism continues to be a significant concern. In Spain, *Euskada ta Askatasuna* (ETA) has stepped up its bombing campaign, while in the UK, political debate over the future of Northern Ireland has been interspersed with terrorist attacks on mainland Britain by republican groups opposed to the Good Friday Agreement.

European Security and Defence Policy (ESDP)

Insufficient defence spending is the biggest obstacle to the creation of a European force by 2003 (see the essay on the European Rapid Reaction Force, or ERRF, on page 283). In particular, combat support capabilities – such as airlift and air-to-air refuelling – will have to be greatly enhanced if a credible force is to be fielded for peacekeeping operations either in Europe or beyond. Another problem is the operational overstretch of some European armed forces. For example, the UK has some 40% of its army deployed or preparing for operations. In this context, it is hard to see how any significant extra commitment can be taken on. Aside from these practical problems of capability, overstretch and finance, there are considerable political difficulties. Turkey, which is not an EU member, is reluctant to agree to a European force drawing on NATO assets, and France is against sharing key NATO capabilities. There is also the concern, voiced by Ireland after the December 2000 Nice conference, that in a pan-European force, national influence over decision-making on deployment of national forces may be diluted. Nevertheless, plans have gone ahead. The EU Military Staff (EUMS) became operational on 11 June 2001 and had its first meeting with the NATO Military Committee on 12 June.

NATO

The Balkans A positive sign in Balkans events was the agreement of 21 May 2001 between the Former Republic of Yugoslavia (FRY) authorities and the Liberation Army of Presevo, Medvedja and Bujanovac (UPCMB), and the subsequent handing-in of weapons by the UPCMB. Yugoslav forces were able to re-enter the de-militarised zone (DMZ) and 450 UPCMB members gave up their weapons. By 31 May 2001, the return of Yugoslav and Serb forces into one sector of the DMZ was complete. However, the activity of the National Liberation Army (NLA) in north-western Macedonia is presenting new challenges for NATO and European leaders. For some time, NATO has used Macedonia as a transit route for logistic support into Kosovo. NATO countries are obviously reluctant to get involved further, for fear of being drawn deeper into a potentially widening and lengthy conflict. Therefore, while NATO and EU leaders mediate in intense negotiations, NATO military planners are preparing for the deployment of a brigade-sized force of 3,000 to Macedonia if a stable cease-fire is attained. The UK-led force would only be deployed on condition that an effective agreement was in place between the warring parties and would have the specific task of collecting weapons handed in by ethnic Albanian rebels operating inside Macedonia. With 40,000 peacekeepers, mostly from NATO countries, already deployed in Kosovo, NATO may have difficulty finding extra troops to cope with anything more than the relatively limited task of overseeing the handing-in of weapons.

The diversity of national and foreign forces deployed in the Balkans (see Table 9) is an unusual and complex aspect of this peacekeeping operation.

Table 9 **Armed forces in the Balkans**				
	External Armed Forces		**State Armed Forces**	**Other Armed Gps**
	NATO	Non-NATO		
Bosnia-Herzegovina	ε19,000 (SFOR II)	ε1,650[1] (attached SFOR II)	24,400[3] 14,000[4]	Nil
Croatia	ε500 (SFOR)	Nil	ε58,300 plus 10,000 armed police	Nil
Macedonia	ε5,000 (from KFOR)	Nil	ε16,000 plus some 4,580 armed police	ε1,000–1,500[5]
FRY (except Kosovo)	Nil	Nil	ε105,500 plus 80,000 Ministry of Interior tps	Nil
Kosovo	ε32,920 (attached KFOR)	ε5,900[2] (attached KFOR)	Nil	ε1,000–1,500[6]

Notes
[1] Non-NATO contributions to SFOR II from Alb, A, Arg, Bg, Ea, SF, Irl, L, Mor, R, RF, Slvk, Slvn and Swe.
[2] Non-NATO contributions to KFOR from Arg, A, Az, Bg, SF, Ga, Irl, L, Mor, RF, Slvk, Slvn, Swe, CH, Ukr and the UAE.
[3] Forces of the Federation of Bosnia Herzegovina
[4] *Republika Srpska* Armed Forces
[5] National Liberation Army (NLA)
[6] Liberation Army of Presovo, Medvedja and Bujanovac (UCPMB)

NATO ENLARGEMENT

The question of NATO enlargement will become more prominent as the autumn 2002 Prague summit approaches. Altogether nine countries are applying for membership: Slovenia, Romania, Bulgaria, Slovakia, Estonia, Lithuania, Latvia, Albania and Macedonia. Croatia might also apply. It is very unlikely that all these candidates will be successful. On the other hand, in his speech at Warsaw University on 15 June 2001, President George W. Bush signalled a US willingness to consider a 'big bang' approach that would at least open serious talks about accession with all applicants. The most likely successes are Slovenia and Slovakia, followed by the Baltic states. The US favours the Baltic option, whereas some NATO European states, such as France, would like to see enlargement in south-eastern Europe, although the qualifications of the most strategically and economically significant NATO applicant in that region – Romania – have been slipping. There is also some support for accession by Bulgaria, Slovakia and Slovenia, but neither Albania nor Macedonia are likely to meet the criteria for membership in this round. The most contentious issue is the prospective membership of the Baltic States, which is strongly opposed by Russia. Moscow views the Baltic States as part of the Russian sphere of influence and a key strategic area. These countries are geographically, ethnically and historically close to Russia. The position of Kaliningrad, a Russian region separated from the Federation and flanked by potential NATO member Lithuania and current member Poland, is an added reason for Russian sensitivity about NATO membership for the Baltic states. Given this context, Russia's participation in the NATO *Baltops* naval exercise in July 2001 was an encouraging sign of willingness to cooperate militarily in the Baltic area.

Conventional Armed Forces in Europe (CFE)

Russian base closures in Georgia Following the 19 November 1999 Istanbul Declaration on the Adaptation of the Conventional Armed Forces in Europe (CFE) Treaty and the Bilateral Georgia–Russia Protocol on the closure of Russian bases in Georgia, Russian troops have withdrawn from the Vaziani airbase. The withdrawal was complete by the 1 July 2001 deadline and intense negotiations continue between the Georgians and the Russians over the closure of the other three bases – Gudauta, Akhalkalaki and Batumi. Gudauta, located in the separatist region of Abkhazia, was also to have been closed by 1 July 2001; however, the Russians, who maintain a peacekeeping force in this disputed region, claim that it is unsafe to close the base. The Abkhaz, who see the Russian presence as crucial to their future security and a deterrent to any Georgian military attempt to recapture Abkhazia, would resist such a move, possibly with violence. The Russian preference is for the base to be turned into a rehabilitation and logistic base for the peacekeeping force, thereby maintaining a foothold in the area. Georgia, which would not be able to verify any withdrawal of Russian troops from the disputed territory, has reached a compromise agreement with the Russians on the status of the base. Russian peacekeepers already deployed in Abkhazia will guard installations at the Gudauta base. They will be lightly armed, and the Georgian government is to approve a list of their weapons. All other military equipment is to be withdrawn from the territory.

Meanwhile, the phase-two closure programme for Akhalkalaki and Batumi is being held up, and there are difficulties in closing the Sagareju ammunition site. The Russians claim that it will take up to 15 years for them to pull out of Akhalkalaki, which is in the Samtskhe-Javakheti region, populated mostly by ethnic Armenians. The base is tied economically to the rouble, and is quite distinct from the rest of the country. The withdrawal of the Russian contingent – around 3,000 troops – would have a negative affect on the area's social and economic stability, since the base supports, directly and indirectly, a large proportion of the local population.

Moldova Under a commitment given in the Final Act of the Agreement on Adaptation of the CFE Treaty, signed by the CFE states on 19 November 1999 in Istanbul, Russia is complying with its CFE Treaty obligations to withdraw or destroy all its military equipment in the Moldovan region of Transdniestr by the end of 2001. Under the treaty, Russia must destroy or withdraw 108 main battle tanks, 214 armoured fighting vehicles, 7 combat helicopters and 125 artillery systems. On 1 July 2001, Russian military specialists began the destruction of 10 T-64 main battle tanks. Meanwhile, the Moldovan government has signed an agreement with NATO under which the alliance will assist Moldova in the destruction of mines and surplus munitions. This will be funded through NATO's Partnership for Peace Trust Fund.

Missile Defence and Europe US missile-defence plans have divided opinion in Europe. Some countries – notably the UK – have publicly supported President Bush's plans for missile defence; others, France in particular, have voiced strong opposition. Those opposed to the deployment of a missile-defence system claim that the end of the 1972 Anti-Ballistic Missile (ABM) Treaty would see the end of the existing arms-control regime, resulting in the proliferation of weapons of mass destruction.

Following meetings between presidents Bush and Vladimir Putin in Llubjana and Genoa, Russia has toned down its initial opposition to missile defence. This is despite the belief of influential figures in the Russian Ministry of Defence that the existing US plan for missile defence contains an anti-Russian element. However, the Russians acknowledge the validity of the concept of missile defence, having put forward their own ideas for such a system to defend Europe. The Russian proposal is for a flexible system of rapid response triggered by accurate threat analysis, rather than setting up a permanent structure. This proposal would require an upgraded S-300 air defence system and possibly an integrated multinational warning system. There is widespread scepticism about the feasibility of the Russian proposal. Critics claim that its purpose was solely to deflect Europeans from supporting the US missile-defence plans in Europe.

NON-NATO EUROPE

Sweden

As a result of taking a much broader definition of security, Sweden's armed forces are undergoing rapid reorganisation. The aim is to produce armed forces that can react rapidly and flexibly to a range of threats, both internal and external. Key aspects of the restructuring are new command-and-control systems; expansion of research and development; and reduction of military manpower.

Like the United States, Sweden hopes that by linking all elements of its armed forces into one-command-and-communications network, the forces' overall capabilities and flexibility will be greatly increased. To this end – and unlike the US – the Swedish Ministry of Defence is cooperating with commercial information-technology firms to create a command, control, communications, computer, intelligence, surveillance and reconnaissance (C4ISR) system, LedsysT, capable of meeting the challenges of various military operating environments and tasks. It is hoped that by using civilian technology, LedsysT will be easier to update than if military technology alone were used. Overall the unusually large part – some 50% – of the Swedish defence budget that is being spent on research and development is to ensure that the military platforms produced are capable of meeting new tasks such as rapid deployment, which are part of the new thinking.

The third aspect of Sweden's military restructuring is the rapid and sizeable reduction in defence personnel and platforms. In 2000, the Swedish Navy had 24 surface vessels; by 2005, it will have only 12. Submarines will be reduced from nine to five over the same period. The air force and army are being similarly reduced: in 2000, the air force had 13 fighter squadrons; by 2004, it will have only eight. The marked improvements in C4ISR systems and in platform capability are expected to result in greater capability for Sweden's armed forces, despite manpower reductions of nearly 50%.

Terrorism

Domestic terrorism in Western Europe has increased marginally since autumn 2000, with low-level attacks by Irish Republican Army (IRA) splinter groups in UK and more substantial operations by the Basque separatist group *Euskadi ta Askatasuna* (ETA) following the end of a 14-month cease-fire in 2000.

In Northern Ireland, the Provisional Irish Republican Army (IRA), the largest and most formidable anti-British republican group, has maintained a cease-fire. Since June 2000, it has allowed three limited weapons inspections of two arms dumps (representing a fraction of its estimated 100-tonne arsenal) in an effort to further the faltering peace process. During that period, however, four IRA members were prosecuted in Florida for gun running, and the IRA killed a member of a rival republican group in Belfast, executed several drug-dealers, smuggled weapons into Ireland and continued vigilantism in republican areas of Northern Ireland.

The dissident Real IRA and Continuity IRA appear to be converging organisationally and operationally, and are believed to be slowly increasing their ranks, which may now exceed 200. The Real IRA was added to the US State Department's list of proscribed terrorist organisations in May 2001. The two groups have purchased light and crew-served weapons as well as explosives from suppliers in Eastern Europe, and as a result of defections possess a small portion of the Provisional IRA's former stock. Three Real IRA members, suspected of attempting to buy arms, were arrested in Slovakia in July 2001. The group has mounted several attacks on the British mainland since September 2000, targeting the MI6 headquarters, a British Territorial Army barracks and BBC studios. There were no fatalities, but a young cadet was blinded. Both the Provisional IRA and the splinter groups have continued their illegal fundraising activities. They are unlikely to halt violence in the near future.

In July 2001, the Ulster Freedom Fighters (UFF), one of the two main loyalist paramilitary groups, withdrew its support for the Belfast Agreement. The UFF has maintained its seven-year cease-fire, but loyalists have increasingly feuded and engaged in violent political protest. The Progressive Unionist Party (PUP) – the political wing of the Ulster Volunteer Force, the other key loyalist paramilitary group – walked out of talks on disarmament. These developments reflect growing disenchantment with the peace process among loyalists, and make their return to violence more likely. All loyalist paramilitary groups appear to be engaged in criminal financial enterprises.

ETA has stepped up its terrorist campaign in Spain. In the period from the end of its cease-fire in November 2000 to mid-July 2001, the group killed 34 people. Although the Spanish security forces have had some anti-terrorist successes in the past year, ETA is well-supported by its illegal activities and appears to have sufficient supplies of explosives and small arms to continue its campaign at this level. Prospects for another cease-fire, though still low, may be better than they were a year ago. Voters manifested disapproval of ETA's emphatic return to violence, as *Euskal Herriatok*, ETA's political wing, lost seven of its 14 regional parliamentary seats in the May 2001 elections. On the other hand, Madrid has maintained an uncompromising stance on further autonomy, with strong public support. This resistance to ETA demands is likely to incite the group to continue rather than draw down its violent campaign.

In Turkey, the Kurdistan Workers' Party (PKK) continues relatively quiescent following its August 1999 cease-fire. Reportedly only 400–500 armed PKK guerrillas remain in scattered groups in south-eastern Turkey. In the period January–June 2001, there have been about 100 people killed, mostly PKK, in isolated clashes between security forces and militants. This is compared to 2,000 dead per year in 1997–99. PKK fundraising via narcotics sales and human trafficking appears to have fallen and the group now lacks the funds to mount an effective armed campaign. There is much PKK frustration at the government's failure to liberalise its policy on Kurdish cultural rights, which was supposed to occur after the cease-fire. Up to 5,000 PKK militants are in camps, mainly in northern Iraq, with a small number in northern Iran. In late 2000, both northern Iraqi Kurd groups, the Patriotic Union of Kurdistan (PUK) and the Kurdistan Democratic Party (KDP) aligned themselves against the PKK, but are as yet reluctant to act. The Turkish military, which maintains a small presence in northern Iraq, fears that the PKK will link up with non-Kurdish left-wing groups and launch a new campaign in Turkish urban areas. The military is believed to be contemplating an offensive in anticipation of this development, although the terrain and the PKK escape routes into Iran would make any military operation difficult. In any event, financial and political constraints on the group suggest that a surge in PKK terrorist violence in Turkey is highly unlikely in the short term.

Since the June 2000 assassination of British military attaché Brigadier Stephen Saunders in Athens by the terrorist group 17 November, the Greek government has taken stronger legal and administrative counter-terrorism measures. In the last twelve months, Greek anti-terrorist cooperation with other countries, in particular the US and UK, has improved. Given the staging of the 2004 Olympic Games in Athens, such developments are vital. More broadly, European efforts to thwart terrorists conducted or sponsored by the international terrorist, Osama bin Laden's *al-Qa'ida* group have borne results, with arrests of significant group members in the UK in December 2000; in Germany in February 2001; and in Italy in April 2001.

DEFENCE SPENDING

NATO Trends

In 2000, defence expenditure by European NATO countries continued the decline of recent years, falling by 6.7% in real terms from $177bn in 1999 to $165bn in 2000 (measured in constant 2000 US dollars). However, when measured in real local currency the defence spending of 7 out of the 15 EU nations rose. Spain, for example, increased its defence spending by 5.2%, and Greece by 4.8% when measured in local currency terms. Budgets set for 2001 suggest that the overall trend will continue, with a likely fall of around 5–8%.

The bigger picture, however, remains unchanged. European spending on research and development remains about a quarter of that spent by the United States and, with US R&D spending likely to increase over coming years, that gap will widen further. Likewise, the United States accounted for 62% of all NATO funds allocated to procurement in 2000. The overall defence spending increases proposed by the US administration for 2002 and beyond are unlikely to be matched by Europe.

Although **UK** spending on defence is budgeted to increase at around 1.5% a year, the National Audit Office reported that the 'smart procurement' process introduced in the 1998 Strategic Defence Review has yet to produce the intended efficiency gains. It noted that the UK's 25 major defence projects are running $2.7bn over budget and roughly four years late.

The first of four Boeing C-17 military cargo aircraft being leased by the Royal Air Force arrived in the UK in May 2001. The remaining three were due to be delivered by August 2001. The original contract, in the region of $750m, lasts for seven years, with the possibility of two further annual extensions. The aircraft were leased as an interim step pending the introduction of the A-400M.

In May 2001, **Greece** announced that it intends to extend its current five-year procurement plan worth Dr3.95tr ($10.1bn) until 2008. Although there will be no cuts, most new programmes will not be initiated until after 2005, including the procurement of the *Eurofighter*. Greece has

Table 10 **Defence R&D and procurement spending in NATO and non-NATO Western Europe, 1997–2001** constant 1999 US$m

	Defence Budget					Research and Development (R&D)					Equipment Procurement				
	1997	1998	1999	2000	2001	1997	1998	1999	2000	2001	1997	1998	1999	2000	2001
NATO															
Belgium	2,920	2,879	2,547	2,402	2,142	2	1	2	1	1	200	211	191	234	233
Denmark	2,836	2,760	2,552	2,283	2,260	5	5	5	1	1	353	365	335	333	224
France	34,031	31,942	29,497	26,538	24,257	3,975	3,385	3,025	3,053	3,145	6,726	5,847	5,902	5,317	5,450
Germany	28,444	27,052	25,423	22,871	20,154	1,547	1,467	1,313	1,299	1,286	3,075	3,594	3,865	3,413	3,389
Greece	3,750	4,037	3,426	3,195	3,217	19	24	22	24	26	1,193	1,339	1,324	1,351	1,378
Italy	18,973	18,201	16,239	15,704	14,861	781	555	310	218	291	2,185	2,491	1,982	2,276	2,291
Luxembourg	113	110	102	99	90	0	0	0	0	0	6	6	5	6	6
Netherlands	7,251	7,248	6,535	6,047	5,372	107	103	66	66	65	1,378	1,645	1,435	1,369	1,341
Norway	3,551	3,422	3,303	2,820	2,854	23	22	22	23	24	943	805	719	788	788
Portugal	1,767	1,617	1,332	1,267	1,268	4	4	4	4	4	366	379	416	371	366
Spain	6,179	6,123	7,358	6,857	6,621	252	206	177	175	174	1,053	813	774	1,065	1,062
Turkey	4,180	7,903	8,901	7,577	4,898	41	47	44	47	50	2,672	3,051	3,150	3,121	2,517
UK	35,603	38,090	35,945	33,890	32,608	3,632	3,938	4,067	4,026	3,986	8,808	9,732	8,596	8,537	8,597
Sub-total	149,599	151,384	143,453	131,808	116,026	10,387	9,757	9,058	9,052	9,105	28,957	30,276	28,695	28,182	28,454
Czech Republic	1,028	1,165	1,164	1,131	1,091	25	20	16	21	26	140	155	183	204	224
Hungary	692	673	745	776	773	2	12	12	12	12	135	186	186	235	255
Poland	3,119	3,429	3,219	3,104	3,557	57	96	80	83	88	494	526	486	697	713
Sub-total	4,840	5,267	5,128	5,010	5,422	84	129	108	116	126	769	867	855	1,135	1,192
Total	154,439	156,651	148,286	136,560	126,023	10,471	9,885	9,165	9,169	9,231	29,726	31,143	29,551	29,317	29,646
Canada	7,451	6,448	6,996	7,456	7,292	78	117	114	118	121	1,954	1,499	1,308	1,282	1,295
US (DoD)	281,243	276,618	278,398	281,601	284,448	37,873	37,824	38,290	37,932	39,340	44,662	45,657	50,920	53,909	59,878
US and Canada	288,694	283,066	299,143	294,922	300,595	37,951	37,941	38,404	38,050	39,461	46,616	47,157	52,228	55,191	61,173
Total NATO	443,133	439,717	433,680	425,618	417,763	48,422	47,826	47,570	47,218	48,698	76,342	78,300	81,779	84,508	90,819
Non-NATO															
Austria	1,858	1,835	1,664	1,497	1,513	10	10	10	10	10	322	416	300	312	323
Finalnd	1,908	1,929	1,695	1,583	1,351	9	10	14	8	8	697	901	615	624	618
Ireland	797	811	745	711	763	0	0	0	0	0	28	35	42	47	50
Sweden	5,197	4,885	4,525	4,405	3,997	165	167	98	104	103	1,739	1,972	2,294	2,179	2,114
Switzerland	3,878	3,700	3,169	2,893	2,602	80	72	64	64	63	1,714	1,580	1,368	1,300	1,261
Total	13,639	13,160	11,799	11,089	10,225	264	258	187	186	184	4,500	4,902	4,618	4,462	4,365

NATO and Non-NATO Europe

continued to affirm its intention to procure the *Eurofighter*, but the shift in timing will place the procurement after the country's next general election in 2004, which could bring a change in policy.

The **Polish** parliament approved a z105bn ($26.2bn) defence plan for the period 2001–06, stipulating that Warsaw will spend no less than 1.95% of its gross national product on defence in an effort to bring the Polish armed forces closer to NATO's military and interoperability standards. Further funds may also be allocated for the acquisition of 60 fighter aircraft.

France's move to all-professional armed forces is due to be completed by 2003. The defence budget has declined by around 15% since 1996. Most of the savings are from personnel reductions following the elimination of conscription. These freed-up funds have enabled a modest increase in procurement while keeping the operations and maintenance budget constant.

Italy boosted its defence budget in local currency terms from L32.8tr ($16bn) in 2000 to L34.2tr ($15.4bn) in 2001 to continue its major reorganisation and modernisation programme. Under current plans the army will be entirely professional by 2006. The first women entered service in 2000. The most significant funding increase was given to research and development, which rose to L673.6bn from L458.7bn. The air force chose the Lockheed Martin F-16 aircraft as its interim replacement for the ageing *Starfighters* and *Tornado* ADV currently leased from the UK. Italy will lease 34 fighter aircraft for 10 years, beginning mid-2003, until sufficient *Eurofighters* are fully operational. The Italian Navy ordered a 22,000-tonne aircraft carrier that will initially operate *Harrier* STOVL and EH-101 helicopters and will be commissioned in 2007.

Norway announced a radical armed forces restructuring plan in February 2001 calling for base closures and a large cut in personnel. In line with the European trend, the Norwegian Defence Ministry is shifting the role of its armed forces away from the defence of national territory to one of participating in out-of-area operations as part of an international coalition force. The defence budget is set to fall over the next four years. Cuts include reducing the army field force from six to three brigades, the disbandment of the fast-attack force equipped with 14 *Hauk* Fast Patrol craft and trimming the F-16 fighter fleet by ten to 48 operational aircraft.

The draft for the **German** defence budget for 2002 has been agreed as DM46.2bn, a reduction from the FY2001 budget of DM46.8bn; however, the Chancellor agreed on 29 May that a further DM500m would be released each year up to 2005–06. Taking this extra money into account, the overall reduction is only around DM300m. According to critics, the additional money represents only the finance necessary to cover the cost of reform, rather than an add-back for real defence needs. They question the German government's ability to reconcile the country's increasing security commitments to NATO and the EU with a shrinking defence budget. Germany's defence spending as a share of gross domestic product (GDP) is unlikely to rise to 2% and there is little public support for an increase.

Turkey

The dramatic devaluation of the Turkish lira in late 2000 cut the dollar value of the 2001 defence budget from around $7bn to $4.9bn. This was in line with demands made by the International Monetary Fund (IMF), which initiated a rescue package of $14bn as part of a major fiscal recovery programme. The procurement element of the budget was cut by $500m, placing many major programmes on hold or putting them under threat.

Major EU and NATO aircraft equipment programmes

A-400M To meet the requirement for airlift, EU countries plan to purchase up to 200 A-400M aircraft. No firm orders had been placed by 1 August 2001. Original letters of intent indicated a total order of 225, with a breakdown by country as follows: Belgium seven; France 50, Germany

73, Italy 16, Spain 27, Turkey 26, UK 25 and Luxembourg one. However, the order has already shrunk to 212 and may be further reduced as countries face economic recession. The earliest in-service date for the A-400M fleet is 2008. The acquisition of this aircraft will enable larger numbers of personnel with light and medium armour to be moved greater distances. Each aircraft is currently estimated to cost about $85m, although the final price will depend on how many are ordered.

Eurofighter Developed by Germany, Italy, Spain and the UK, the fifth-generation combat aircraft *Eurofighter* is expected to enter service in June 2002. The four consortium countries have so far ordered 620 aircraft between them, while Greece is committed to 60. A number of other countries have expressed an interest in purchasing the aircraft, including Australia, Chile, Brazil, South Korea, Saudi Arabia and Turkey. The cost of each aircraft ordered for the UK will be about £30m. Contracts for fighter's industrial support network are to be signed by the end of 2001.

Joint Strike Fighter (JSF) At present, flight-testing of the Boeing X-32 and Lockheed Martin X-35 JSF-concept demonstrator aircraft is continuing at pace, with the purpose of selecting the best design and starting the engineering and manufacturing development phase in October 2001. There will be three basic versions of the JSF: conventional, carrier-capable and short take-off/vertical landing capable (STOVL). The US Air Force plans to buy 1,763 aircraft to replace the F-16 and A-10. The US Navy will buy 480 to replace the F-14D and F/A-18C/D and the US Marine Corps is planning to purchase 609 to replace the AV-8B and F/A-18C/D. The UK is expected to order 150, to replace the *Harrier* GR7 and *Sea Harrier* FA2.

Non-NATO Europe

Defence spending in 2000 (measured in constant 2000 US dollars) by the non-NATO European countries was virtually unchanged as increases in spending by Romania and Yugoslavia were offset by decreases in Switzerland, Ukraine and Belarus.

In the Transcaucasus, **Georgia** cut its 2001 defence budget by 20% in dollar terms and took delivery of the first 11 of 120 T-55AM2 main battle tanks from the Czech Republic. The tanks were upgraded five years ago. It is the first time that Georgia has purchased significant quantities of weapons from another country since independence. In the **Ukraine,** the defence budget for 2001 rose in local currency terms by h750m to h3.1bn ($580m). The minimum needed to maintain the current armed forces is thought to be around h6bn ($1.1bn). The defence budget allocated just 14% to procurement, upgrades and weapons modernisation, detailing as priorities the procurement of 65 AN-70 aircraft and upgrades to the fleet of MiG29 and Su-25 attack aircraft. As in recent years, the gap between the official budget and the actual requirement was to be 'found through economies'.

Romania again significantly increased its defence budget in 2001, with a 30% rise to US$1bn, to finance the radical restructuring announced last year. The defence minister said that $200m would be spent on equipment purchases to help the effort to join NATO.

Austria made little change to its 2001 defence budget, but stated an intention to increase spending in 2002 to meet a goal of 1% of GDP. The army ordered nine S-70A *Black Hawk* transport helicopters, the first transatlantic defence order by Austria for twenty years.

Swedish defence spending was virtually unchanged as the new downsizing and reform process got underway. The old military structure is being streamlined and transformed into a more mobile and flexible force. An important aspect of reform is the merging of the chain of command into one operational and tactical command. The sweeping changes to force structure and the need for improved intelligence and command-and-control assets have led to around 50% of the defence budget being spent on procurement and research. Despite the projected fall in overall spending of almost 10% over the years to 2005, it is hoped that this level can be maintained.

Table 11 Arms orders and deliveries, NATO Europe and Canada, 1998–2001

Country supplier	Classification ⇩ / Designation	Quantity ⇩	Order date	Delivery date ⇩	Comment
Belgium US	FGA	**F-16**	110	1993	1998	Mid-life update. 88 AMRAAM on order
Aus	APC	**Pandur**	54	1997	1998	
Il	UAV	**Hunter**	18	1998	2000	
US	FGA	**F-16**	18	1999	2000	Upgrade; option on 18 exercised
Fr	trg	**Alpha Jet**		2000		Upgrade
Br	tpt	**ERJ-135/145**	4	2000	2001	
Canada US	hel	**B-412EP**	100	1992	1994	Deliveries to 1998 at 3 per month
dom	LAV	**LAV-25**	240	1996	1998	105 in 1997, 47 1998; deliveries continue
UK	ACV	**API-88/400**	2	1996	1998	Delivery May 1998
US	APC	**M-113**	400	1997	1998	Life extension update; deliveries continue
Ge	MBT	**Leopard** 1	114	1997	1999	*Leopard* C1A5 upgrade
dom	LAV	**LAV-25**	120	1998	2001	Follow-on order after initial 240
UK	SSK	**Upholder**	4	1998	2000	Deliveries to 2001
col	hel	**EH-101**	15	1998	2001	Ca designation AW520; deliveries to 2002
dom		**CP-140 Aurora**	16	2000	2001	Upgrade
US	FGA	**CF-18**	80	2000	2003	Upgrade to C/D status
dom	APC	**Bison**	199	2000	2002	Upgrade
dom	APC	**Grizzly**	246	2000	2002	
US	SAM	**Sea Sparrow**		2001	2003	To equip *Halifax*-class FFG
Czech Republic						
dom	MBT	**T-72**	140	1995	2000	Upgrade prog. Rescheduled in 1999
dom	trg	**L-39**	27	1997	1999	Originally for Nga; delivery to Cz airforce delayed
dom	FGA	**L-159**	72		2000	
col	UAV	**Sojka** 3	8	1998	2000	Upgraded *Sojka* III. Dev with Hu
RF	cbt hel	**Mi-24**	7	1999	1999	Arms for debt
Denmark Ge	MBT	**Leopard** 2A4	51	1998	2000	Ex-Ge army
Ca	tpt	**Challenger** 604	3	1998		
UK	hel	**Lynx**	8	1998	2000	Upgrade to *Super Lynx* standard
CH	APC	**Piranha** III	2	1998	1999	Option for 20 more; UN PKO use
Ge	APC	**M-113**	100	1999	2000	Upgrade. Deliveries until 2001
Fr	UAV	**Sperwer**	2	1999		
US	PGM	**JDAM**	400	2000	2000	Deliveries to 2004
US	tpt	**C-130J**	3	2000	2003	Option on 4th
dom	AG	**Stanflex** S3	2	2000	2006	
Swe	SSK	**Nacken**	1	2001	2001	
France col	hel	**Tiger**	215	1984	2003	With Ge; 1st batch of 60 ordered 1999
dom	FGA	**Rafale**	60	1984	1999	Deliveries of first 10 1999–02
dom	FGA	**Rafale**	234	1984	1999	ISD 2005
dom	MBT	**Leclerc**	406	1985	1992	311 delivered by 2000.
col	ASSM	**ANNG**		1985	2005	In dev with Ge
col	radar	**Cobra**	10	1986	2002	Counter-bty radar; dev with UK, Ge
dom	LSD	**Foudre**	2	1986	1990	2nd of class delivered 1998

Country supplier ⇩	Classification ⇩ / Designation	Quantity ⇩	Order date	Delivery date	Comment ⇩
dom	SSBN *Le Triomphant*	3	1986	1996	Deliveries to 2001; 4th order 2000 for 2007
dom	CVN *Charles de Gaulle*	1	1986	1999	Sea trials mid-1998
col	hel **NH-90**	160	1987	2003	With Ge, It, Nl; prod orders delayed.
col	ATGW *Trigat*		1988	2004	With UK, Ge
col	hel **AS-555**	44	1988	1990	Deliveries through 1990s
col	tpt **FLA**	52	1989	2005	Dev. Prog status uncertain
dom	FFG *Lafayette*	5	1990	1996	Deliveries to 2003
col	SAM **FSAF**		1990	2006	Future surface-to-air-family
col	hel **EC-120**		1990		In dev with PRC, Sgp
col	torp **MU-90**	150	1991	2000	With It and Ge. Deliveries 2000–02
dom	FGA *Mirage* 2000-D	86	1991	1994	45 delivered by Jan 1997
col	hel **AS-532**	4	1992	1996	Battlefield radar system *Horizon*
dom	FGA *Mirage* 2000-5F	37	1993	1998	*Mirage* 2000-C upgrade, deliveries to 2002
col	UAV *Eagle*				Dev with UK
col	sat *Helios* 1A	2	1994	1995	With Ge, It, Sp. *Helios* 1B for launch 1999
col	sat *Helios* 2	1	1994	2004	Dev with Ge
col	sat *Horus*		1994	2005	Fr has withdrawn funding
US	AEW **E2-D**	3	1994	1999	1st delivered Jan 1999
col	ALCM **SCALP**	600	1994	2000	2 orders for delivery over 11 years
col	hel **AS-532**	4	1995	1999	Combat SAR, requirement for 6
dom	SLBM **M-51**		1996	2008	To replace M-45; devpt continues
dom	APC **VBL**	120	1996	1998	20 delivered 1998
dom	SAM *Mistral*	1,130	1996	1997	To 2002
dom	recce *Falcon*-50	4	1997	1998	Deliveries to 2000
col	hel **BK-117**	32	1997	1999	
dom	msl *Eryx*	6,400	1997	1997	To 2002
dom	msl **LAW**	30,800	1997	1997	For delivery 1997–2002
col	ASM *Vesta*		1997	2005	In devpt
col	sat *Skynet* 5	4	1998	2005	Comms; devpt in 1998 with Ge, UK
dom	SSN **SSN**	6	1998	2010	Design studies approved Oct 1998
col	AAM *Mica*	225	1998	1999	Further 1,537 to be delivered from 2004
dom	APC **VBCI**	65	1998	2005	Up to 700 req
dom	AIFV **AMX-10**	300	1999	2001	Upgrade
Swe	APC **Bv 206S**	12	1999	1999	For units serving in Kosovo
col	FFG **mod** *Horizon*	2	1999	2005	Joint It/Fr project
dom	LSD **NTCD**	2	2000	2005	2 on order
dom	MHC *Eridan Class*	13	2000		Upgrade
dom	arty *Caesar*	5	2000	2002	
dom	MBT *Leclerc*	38	2000	2002	Upgrade to Mk 2 standard
dom	sat *Syracuse* 3	3	2000	2003	Comms
dom	LHD *Mistral*	2	2000	2005	
Swe	RL **AT-4CS**		2000		
Germany col	hel *Tiger*	212	1984	2003	With Fr. 1st order for 60 in 1999
col	FGA **EF-2000**	180	1985	2001	With UK, It, Sp; 44 ordered late 1998
dom	SPA **PzH 2000**	186	1986	1998	Req 594 units; 86 delivered by 2000
col	hel **NH-90**	134	1987	2003	With Fr, It, Nl; prod orders delayed
dom	MHC **Type 332**	12	1988	1992	Deliveries completed 1998

Country supplier ⇩	Classification ⇩ / Designation	Quantity ⇩	Order date	Delivery date ⇩	Comment
col	ATGW / *Trigat*		1988	2004	
col	tpt / **FLA**	75	1989	2008	Dev. Status uncertain
dom	SSK / **Type 212**	4	1994	2003	Deliveries to 2006
col	recce / *Fennek*	164	1994	2000	Joint dev with Nl. Prod in 2000
col	sat / *Helios* 1A	2	1994	1995	With Fr, It, Sp, *Helios* 1B for launch 1999
col	sat / *Helios* 2	1	1994	2001	Dev with Fr, It
col	tpt hel / **AS-532**	3	1994	1997	
col	sat / *Horus*	1	1994	2005	Dev with Fr
dom	FFG / **Type F 124**	3	1996	2002	Deliveries 2002–05.
dom	AOE / **Type 702**	2	1996	2000	1st delivered 2000
UK	hel / *Lynx*	7	1996	1999	
dom	AAA / *Gepard*	147	1996	1999	Upgrade. 1st of 147 delivered Jan 1999
col	sat / **Skynet** 5	4	1997	2005	With UK, Fr
col	AAM / IRIS-T		1997	2003	Dev with It, Swe, Gr, Ca, No
col	hel / **AS-365**	13	1997	1998	Delivery 1998–01
col	APC / **GTK**	200	1998	2004	NL and UK (MRAV)
dom	SAM / *Wiesel* 2	50	1998	1999	
US	SAM / *Patriot*	7	1998		Upgrade to PAC-3 configuration
US	SAM / *Patriot*	12	1998		*Roland/Patriot* cost total $2.1bn
US	SAM / *Roland*	21	1998		Air defence system
dom	APC / **TPz KRK**	50	1998	1999	
col	radar / **COBRA**	12	1998		
UK	hel / *Lynx*	17	1998	2000	Upgrade to *Super Lynx* standard
col	torp / **MU-90**	600	1998	2000	
col	ASM / *Taurus*		1998	2001	Dev with Swe (KEPD-350)
dom	FFG / **Type F 125**	8	1999	2010	Feasibility study stage
dom	AG / **Type 751**	1	1999	2002	Defence research and test ship
dom	AFV / **ATF-2K**	56	1999	2001	
dom	MBT / *Leopard* 2 A5	225	2000	2001	Upgrade to 2A6
dom	MRTT / **A310**	4	2001	2002	
dom	FSG / **Type 130K**	5	2001	2005	Deliveries to 2008
Greece US	FGA / **F-16**	80	1985	1988	Deliveries of 2nd batch of 40 1997–99
Ge	FFG / *Meko*	4	1988	1992	Deliveries to 1998; last 2 built in Gr
dom	AIFV / *Kentaurus*		1994	2000	In dev; trials in late 1998
US	hel / **CH-47D**	7	1995	2001	In addition to 9 in inventory
US	FGA / **F-4**	38	1996	1999	Upgrade in Ge; deliveries to 2000
US	AAM / **AIM-120B**	90	1997	1999	In addition to previous 150 AMRAAM
US	SP arty / **M-109A5**	12	1997	1999	135 delivered; option for further 12
Ge	MBT / *Leopard* 1A5	170	1997	1998	In addition to previous delivery of 75
US	SAM / **Stinger**	188	1998	2000	
US	trg / **T-6A**	45	1998	2000	Deliveries complete 2003
US	SAM / *Patriot* PAC-3	5	1998	2001	5 batteries, option for 1 more
Br	AEW / **RJ-145**	4	1998	2002	
Ge	SSK / **Type 214**	3	1998	2005	Deliveries to 2008
UK	MCMV / *Hunt*	2	1998	2000	1 in 2000. 1 in 2001
It	AK / **AK**	1	1999	2002	
Fr	hel / **AS-532**	4	1999	2002	Option on further 2
US	MRL / **MLRS**	18	1999	2002	
US	FGA / **F-16C/D**	50	1999	2002	Option on further 10

Country supplier ⇩	Classification ⇩ / Designation	Quantity ⇩	Order date	Delivery date	Comment ⇩
Fr	FGA	*Mirage* 2000-5	15	1999	2003	Option on 3 more
Fr	FGA	*Mirage* 2000	10	1999	2004	Upgrade 10 of existing 35
Fr	SAM	*Crotale* NG	11	1999	2001	9 for air force; 2 for navy
US	hel	S-70B	2	2000		Option on further 2
col	FGA	EF-2000	60	2000	2005	May increase to 90
dom	PFM	*Super Vita*	3	2000	2003	Option on further 4
dom	PCO		4	2000		
dom	AO		1	2000	2003	
RF	LCAC	*Zubr*	4	2000	2001	Final delivery 2001
US	AAM	AMRAAM	560	2000		
US	recce	C-12	2	2000		For photo-reconnaissance
Ge	SP arty	PzH2000	24	2000	2003	Deliveries to 2004
US	ACV	HMMWV	70	2000	2001	
Fr	ASSM	*Exocet* MM-40	27	2000	2001	Deliveries to 2004
Fr	AAM	*Mica*	200	2000		To equip *Mirage*
Fr	ALCM	SCALP	56	2000		To equip *Mirage*
US	hel	S-70B	8	2000		Upgrade including *Penguin* AAM
RF	SAM	SA-15	29	2000	2001	Aka Tor-M1; Additional 29.Original order for 21 units completed
Ge	SAM	*Stinger*	54	2000	2002	
Slvk	SPG	*Zuzana*	12	2000	2001	For Rapid Deployment Force
RF	ATGW	*Kornet*	278	2001		Two phase purchase
dom	PCO		2	2001		
Hungary Fr	SAM	*Mistral*	45	1996	1998	27 launchers, 110 msl delivered 1998
US	FGA	F-16	24	2001	2002	On lease
Italy dom	MBT	C1 *Ariete*	200	1982	1995	Deliveries to 2001
dom	AIFV	VCC-80	200	1982	2000	First ordered 1998; aka *Dardo*
col	FGA	EF-2000	121	1985	2002	With UK, Ge, Sp; 29 ordered
col	hel	NH 90	117	1987	2003	With Fr, Ge, Nl; prod order delayed
dom	APC	*Puma*	600	1988	2001	Deliveries to 2004
col	tpt	FLA	44	1989	2008	With Fr, Ge, Sp, Be, Por, Tu, UK
col	SAM	FSAF		1990	2006	Future surface-to-air-family
col	hel	EH-101	16	1993	1999	With UK. Navy require 38
dom	PCO	*Esploratore*	4	1993	1997	Deliveries to 2000
col	sat	*Helios* 1A	1	1994	1995	With Fr, Ge, Sp. *Helios* 1B for launch 1999
dom	CV	*Andrea Doria*	1	1996	2007	
US	tpt	C-130J	22	1997	2000	Options on further 2
Fr	tpt	*Falcon* 900EX	2	1997	1999	
Ge	SSK	*Type* 212	2	1997	2005	Licence-built in It; options for 2 more
dom	AGI	A-5353	2	1998	2000	2nd for delivery 2001
dom	hel	A-129I	15	1998	2001	New multi-role configuration
dom	PCO	*Aliscarfi*	4	1999	2001	1st batch of 4; 2nd expected after 2003
dom	LPD	*San Giorgio*	2	1999	2001	Upgrade to carry 4 hel
Ge	SPA	PzH 2000	70	1999	2004	Joint production
col	FFG	Modified *Horizon*	2	1999	2007	Joint It/Fr project
dom	AT	C-27J	12	1999	2001	
US	UAV	*Predator*	6	2000	2001	
US	AAM	*Stinger*	30	2000		For use on A-129
US	SAM	*Standard* SM-2	50	2000		

Country supplier ⇩	Classification ⇩ Designation	Quantity ⇩	Order date	Delivery date ⇩	Comment ⇩
dom	hel A-129	45	2000		Upgrade to A-129I standard
US	FGA F-16	34	2001	2003	7-year lease
US	tkr Boeing 767	4	2001		Option on further 2
NATO UK	trg *Hawk*	18	1997	1999	Option for 8 more
US	AWACS E3-A	18	1997	1999	NATO fleet upgrade
US	trg T-6A	24	1997	1999	Deliveries to 2000
US	ACCS	1	1999	2005	Air Comd and Control System
RSA	APC *Scout*	75	1999	2000	
Netherlands col	hel NH-90	20	1987	2003	With Fr, Ge, It
dom	LPD *Rotterdam*	2	1993	1998	Second due 2007
US	FGA F-16	136	1993	1997	Update programme continues to 2001
US	hel AH-64D	30	1995	1998	4 delivered 1998
US	hel CH-47C	7	1995	1999	
dom	FFG *De Zeven*	4	1995	2003	2 ordered 1995; 2 more ordered 1997
SF	APC XA-188	90	1996	1998	24 delivered 1998
US	MPA P-3C	7	1999	2001	Upgrade
col	APC PWV	200	2000	2006	Joint Programme
Ge	SPA PzH 2000	60	2000	2004	
Ge	MBT Leopard 2A5	180	2001		Upgrade to 2A6
Il	ATGW *Spike/Gil*	300	2001	2002	
Norway US	FGA F-16A/B	58	1993	1997	Mid-life update programme to 2001
US	AAM AMRAAM	500	1993	1995	84 delivered 1998; deliveries to 2000
dom	FAC *Skjold*	5	1996	1999	
US	MPA PC-3	4	1997	1999	Upgrade
Ge	AFV *Leopard* 1	73	1998	1999	Deliveries to 2000; for mineclearing
Sp	FFG *Nansen*	5	2000	2004	
Nl	MBT *Leopard* 2A4	52	2000		To be modernised
SF	APC XA-200	10	2000		
Poland dom	hel W-3	11	1994	1998	1 for Navy. First 4 delivered Jul 1998
dom	SAR PLZ M-28	3	1998	1999	
UK	SPA AS-90	80	1999	2001	Licence
Ge	FGA MiG-29	22	1999	2002	Upgrade
US	FFG *Perry*	2	1999	2000	2nd delivery 2003
Il	FGA Su-22	20	2000	2003	Upgrade
US	hel SH-2G	2	1999	2000	2 more due 2001
RF	hel Mi-24	40	2001	2003	To be completed by 2006
Portugal US	FGA F-16	20	2000	2003	Upgrade
col	hel EC-635	9	2000	2001	
Spain col	tpt FLA	36	1989	2008	With Fr, Ge, It, Be, Por, Tu, UK
dom	FFG F-100	4	1992	2002	Deliveries to 2006
col	FGA EF-2000	87	1994	2001	With Ge, It, UK; 20 ordered late 1998
col	sat *Helios* 1A	1	1994	1995	With Fr, Ge, It. *Helios* 1B 1999
Fr	hel AS-532	18	1995	1996	1st delivery 1996. Deliveries to 2003
US	tpt C-130	12	1995	1999	Upgrade programme
Aus	AIFV *Pizarro*	144	1996	1998	Licence. Requirement for 463
It	SAM *Spada* 2000	2	1996	1998	First of 2 batteries delivered
dom	arty SBT-1		1997	2000	Dev

Country supplier ⇩	Classification ⇩ Designation	Quantity ⇩	Order date	Delivery date	Comment ⇩
dom	MPA **P-3**	7	1997	2002	Upgrade
US	AAM **AIM-120B**	100	1998	1999	
Ge	MBT **Leopard 2**	235	1998	2002	Built in Sp. Includes 16 ARVs
It	AIFV **Centuaro**	22	1999	2000	aka VCR-105
US	ATGW **Javelin**	12	1999		
Fr	trg **EC120B**	12	2000	2000	Deliveries Jul 2000–Jul 2001
dom	AT **C295**	9	2000		To be delivered by 2004
col	hel **EC120B**	15	2000	2001	Training
No	SAM **NASAMS**	4	2000	2002	
US	hel **SH-60B**	6	2000	2004	Also upgrade of existing 6
Swe	APC **Bv-206S**	10	2000		Total requirement of 50
dom	MPA **P-3B Orion**	5	2001	2003	Upgrade
Turkey Ge	FFG **Meko-200**	8	1985	1987	7 by 1999; final delivery 2000, 4 built in Tu
Ge	SSK **Type 209**	8	1987	1994	Delivery of first 5 to 2003
US	APC **M-113**	1698	1988	1992	Final deliveries in 1999
Ge	PCM **P-330**	3	1993	1998	1st built Ge; 2nd and 3rd Tu; to 1999
US	tpt hel **CH-47**	4	1996	1999	
US	FFG **Perry**	6	1996	1998	Delivery of 5 1998–99. Last 2000
Il	FGA **F-4**	54	1996	1999	Upgrade; deliveries to 2002
US	MRL **ATACM**	72	1996	1998	36 msl delivered 1998
Fr	hel **AS-532**	30	1996	2000	To be completed by 2003
US	AAM **AIM-120B**	138	1997	2000	
US	ASW hel **SH-60B**	14	1997	2000	
dom	APC **RN-94**	5	1997		Dev
Il	AGM **Popeye 1**	50	1997	1999	For use with upgraded F-4 ac
Sp	MPA **CN-235**	9	1997	2000	
Fr	MHC **Circe**	5	1997	1998	Ex-Fr Navy. 3 in 1998, 2 in 1999
It	SAR hel **AB-412**	5	1998	2001	
Il	FGA **F-5**	48	1998	2001	IAI awarded contract to upgrade 48 Tu F-5
US	hel **CH-53E**	8	1998	2003	
US	SAM **Stinger**	208	1999	2001	
US	hel **S-70 Blackhawk**	50	1999	1999	Deliveries to 2001
dom	PCC	10	1999	2000	For coastguard
UK	SAM **Rapier Mk 2**	840	1999	2000	Licence; 80 a year for 10 years
US	FGA **F-16**	32	1999	2002	Licence; following orders of 240 in 2 batches
Ge	SSK **Type 214**	4	2000	2006	
Ge	MHC **Type 332**	6	2000		1st to be built in Ge, 5 in Tu. Last delivery 2004
US	hel **S-70B Seahawk**	8	2000		Heavy lift
US	radar **Sentinel**	7	2000		Including HAWK missiles
US	hel **AH-1Z King Cobra**	50	2000		
Fr	FFG **Type A69**	6	2000	2001	Second hand
US	APC **M-113**	551	2000	2001	Deliveries to 2004
US	AEW **Boeing 737**	6	2000		Option on 7th
RF	hel **Ka-62**	5	2001	2002	
United Kingdom dom	SSBN **Vanguard**	4	1982	1993	Deliveries to 1999

Country supplier ⇩	Classification Designation	Quantity ⇩	Order date	Delivery date	Comment ⇩
US	SLBM *Trident* D-5	48	1982	1994	Deliveries to 1999; original order 96
col	FGA EF-2000	232	1984	2002	1st batch of 55 ordered end 1998
dom	MHC *Sandown*	12	1985	1989	All delivered by 2001
dom	FGA *Sea Harrier*	35	1985	1994	Upgrade prog; deliveries to 1999
col	radar *Cobra*		1986	1999	Counter-bty radar in dev with Fr, Ge
col	hel EH-101	22	1987	2000	With It; for RAF; aka Merlin HM Mk 3
dom	SSN *Swiftsure*	5	1988	1999	Upgrade to carry TLAM
dom	SSN *Trafalger*	7	1988	2000	Upgrade to carry TLAM
dom	FGA *Sea Harrier*	18	1990	1995	Deliveries to 1999
dom	SSN *Astute*	3	1991	2005	Deliveries to 2008
dom	LPD *Albion*	2	1991	2003	Expected in 2003
dom	hel *Lynx*	50	1992	1995	Upgrade. Completion 1998–99
dom	MBT *Challenger 2*	386	1993	1998	78 delivered 1998
col	sat *Skynet 5*	4	1993	2005	With Fr and Ge
dom	LPH *Ocean*	1	1993	1998	Delivered 1998
col	SAM PAAMS		1994	2003	Dev with Fr, It. Part of FSAF prog
US	tpt C-130J	25	1994	1999	Option for 20 more
dom	FGA *Tornado GR4 ID*	142	1994	1998	Upgrade; deliveries to 2003
US	SLCM *Tomahawk*	65	1995	1998	Delivered. 20 fired in Kosovo conflict
dom	ASM *Brimstone*		1996	2001	1st 12 to be delivered 2001
col	ASM *Storm Shadow*	900	1996	2001	
dom	FGA *Tornado F-3*	100	1996	1998	Upgrade
dom	MPA *Nimrod MRA4*	21	1996	2005	To replace MRA2
US	hel WAH-64D	67	1996	2000	Deliveries to 2003
dom	AO *Wave Knight*	2	1997	2001	
dom	AK *Sea Chieftain*	1	1997	1998	18-month lease renewed 2001
col	AEW ASTOR	5	1997	2005	Delivery slipped from 2003
col	bbr FOAS		1997	2020	Future Offensive Air System, feasibility study with Fr
Ge	trg *Grob*-115D	85	1998	2000	
col	lt tk TRACER	200	1998	2007	With US; in feasibility phase
col	APC MRAV	200	1998	2006	Multi-Role Armoured Vehicle; with Nl, Ge
col	UAV *Sender*		1999		Devpt with US
US	SLCM *Tomahawk*	30	1999	2002	
dom	AGHS ECHO	2	2000	2002	Deliveries 2002 and 2003
dom	AT A400M	25	2000		UK to lease 4 C-17 in interim
dom	AAM *Meteor*		2000		To provide BVRAAM capability
US	tpt	4	2000	2001	To be leased
US	ASM *Maverick*		2000	2000	
dom	ALSL	4	2000	2003	Alternate landing ship logistics
dom	UAV *Watchkeeper*		2000	2006	Under dev
dom	SAM *Sea Wolf*	21	2000	2006	Mid-life upgrade programme
dom	TKR FSTA	30	2001	2004	
Swe	APC BvS 10	108	2001	2003	
dom	DDG *Type 45*	6	2001	2005	

Table 12 **Arms orders and deliveries, Non-NATO Europe, 1998–2001**

Country supplier	Classification ⇩ Designation	Quantity ⇩	Order date	Delivery date ⇩	Comment ⇩
Armenia PRC	AAA *Typhoon*	8	1998	1999	
Azerbaijan Kaz	FGA **MiG-25**	8	1996	1998	
Tu	PCC **AB-34**	1	2000	2000	
US	PCI	1	2001	2001	
Austria dom	APC *Pandur*	269	1997	1999	
Ge	ATGW *Jaguar*	90	1997	1998	
Nl	MBT *Leopard* 2A4	114	1997	1998	79 delivered in 1998
Swe	FGA **J-35**	5	1999	1999	
col	APC **ULAN**	112	1999	2002	Delivery to 2004. aka ASCOD
US	hel **S-70A**	9	2000	2001	Option for 3 more
Belarus RF	trg **MiG-29UB**	8	1999	1999	
Kaz	MBT **T-72**	53	2000	2000	
Bosnia-Herzegovina					
US	hel **UH-1**	15	1996	1998	Part of US-funded Equip and Train prog
UAE	arty **105mm**	36	1996	1998	
Et	arty **122mm**	12	1996	1998	
Et	arty **130mm**	12	1996	1998	
Et	AD **23mm**	18	1996	1998	
R	arty **122mm**	18	1996	1998	
R	arty **130mm**	8	1996	1998	
Bulgaria US	hel **B-206**	6	1998	1999	2 delivered
Croatia dom	MBT **M-84**		1992	1996	In production
dom	MBT *Degman*		1995	2001	
dom	MHC *Rhino*	1	1995	1999	
dom	PCI	1	1996	2001	
US	FGA **F-16**	18	1999	2001	Ex-US inventory
Il	FGA **MiG-21**	40	1999		Upgrade
Cyprus It	SAM *Aspide*	44	1996	1998	24 delivered
RF	SAM **S-300**	48	1997	1999	msl. Delivered to Gr, based in Crete
Gr	MBT **AMX-30**	37	1997	1997	Last 10 delivered 1998
Estonia SF	arty **105mm**	18	1996	1997	105mm. Deliveries 1997–98
SF	ML	2	1998	1999	Free transfer
Ge	MCMV *Lindau*	1	1999	1999	Free transfer
US	hel **R44**	4	2000	2000	
Da	FSG *Beskytteren*	1	2000	2000	Transfer
Finland dom	APC **XA-185**	450	1982	1983	XA180/185 series. Deliveries to 1999
US	FGA **F/A-18C/D**	64	1992	1995	Delivered by 2000. 57 made in SF
dom	ACV **RA-140**	10	1997	1998	Mine-clearing veh
SF	arty **K-98**	7	1998	2000	Additional 9 ordered 2001
dom	AIFV **CV 9030**	57	1998	2002	Up to 150 req
dom	APC **XA-200**	48	1999	1999	Deliveries to 2001
Il	UAV *Ranger*	3	1999	2001	9 ac and 6 ground stations

Country supplier ⇩	Classification ⇩	Designation	Quantity ⇩	Order date	Delivery date	Comment ⇩
US	ATGW	*Javelin*	242	2000		3,190 msl
Il	ATGW	*Spike*		2000		
dom	APC	XA-202	100	2000	2001	Option on further 70
Georgia Ge	MSC	*Lindau*	2	1997	1998	Free transfer; deliveries to 1999
UK	PFC		2	1998	1999	Free transfer
Ukr	PFM	*Konotop*	1	1999	1999	
Cz	MBT	T-55AM2	120	1998	2000	1st 11 Delivered 2000
US	hel	UH-1	10	1999	1999	
Ireland UK	PCO	*Roisin*	2	1997	1999	2nd delivered 2001
CH	APC	*Piranha* III	40	1999	2001	
Latvia Ge	MSC	*Lindau*	1	1999	1999	Free transfer
No	PCI	*Storm*	2	2001	2001	
Lithuania Ge	MSC	*Lindau*	1	1999	1999	Free transfer
Ge	APC	M-113	67	1999	2000	Free transfer
Ge	MCMV		1	2000	2000	Token price
Macedonia Kaz	APC	BTR-80	12	1997	1998	
Ge	APC	BTR-70	60	1998	1998	Free transfer
Bg	arty	152mm	10	1998	1998	Free transfer
Bg	arty	76mm	72	1998	1998	aka ZIS-3. Free transfer
Bg	MBT	T-55	150	1998	1999	36 type T-55AM2
Bg	arty	122mm	142	1998	1999	Free transfer
US	arty	105mm	18	1998	1999	Free transfer
Tu	FGA	F-5A/B	20	1998	1999	Free transfer
Ge	APC	*Hermelin*	105	2000	2000	
Ukr	hel	Mi-24	6	2001	2001	
Ukr	FGA	Su-25	4	2001	2001	
Ukr	hel	Mi-8MTV	8	2001	2001	
Romania dom	FGA	MiG-21	110	1994	1997	Upgrade programme with Il
US	tpt	C-130	5	1995	1998	
dom	hel	IAR-330L	26	1995	1998	Upgrade
Il	UAV	*Shadow*	6	1995	1998	
Ge	AAA	35mm	43	1997	1999	
R	trg	IAR-99	33	1998	2000	6 delivered 2000
Slovakia dom	MBT	M-2 *Moderna*		1995	2000	T-72 upgrade programme
Cz	APC	OT-64	100	1997	1998	Also 2 BVP-2 from UK for delivery to Indo
RF	trg	Yak-130	12	1997	1999	RF debt repayment. Delayed or cancelled
col	hel	EC-135	12	1997	1999	
col	hel	AS-532	5	1997	1999	
col	hel	AS-550	2	1997	1999	
dom	arty	*Zuzana* 2000	8	1997	1998	155mm. Deliveries 1998
Slovenia Il	mor	120mm	56	1996	1998	Mortar
Il	arty	M845	18	1996	1998	155mm 45 cal. towed arty

Country supplier ⇩	Classification ⇩	Designation	Quantity ⇩	Order date	Delivery date ⇩	Comment
dom	MBT	**M-55**	30	1998	1999	T-55 upgrade involving 105mm L-7 gun
Aus	APC	**Pandur**	70	1998	1999	
dom	MBT	**T-84**	40	1999	2002	Upgrade
Sweden dom	FGA	**JAS-39**	204	1981	1995	Deliveries to 2007. 18 delivered 1998
dom	AIFV	**CV-90**	600	1984	1993	To 2004. Extra 40 ordered 2001
dom	LCA		199	1988	1989	To 2001. 100 delivered by 1997
dom	PCI	**Tapper**	12	1992	1993	Deliveries to 1999. Coastal arty
US	AAM	**AMRAAM**	110	1994	1998	Option for a further 700
Ge	MBT	**Leopard 2**	120	1994	1998	New-build *Leopard* 2A5; to 2002
Ge	MBT	**Leopard 2**	160	1994	1997	Ex-Ge Army. Upgrade
dom	MCM	**YSB**	4	1994	1996	Deliveries to 1998
dom	FSG	**Visby**	6	1995	2001	Deliveries to 2006
CH	APC	**Pirahna**	13	1996	1998	Command variant. Deliveries continue.
col	AAM	**IRIS-T**		1997	2003	Dev with Ge
col	ASM	**KEPD 350**		1997	2003	Dev with Ge to 2002. Also KEPD 150
dom	LCA	**Transportbat**	14	1997	1999	
Fr	UAV	**Ugglan**	3	1997		
Fr	hel	**AS532**	12	1998	2001	Deliveries 2002
dom	SP arty	**Karelin**	50	1998		155mm. Dev
dom	PCI	**KBV 201**	2	1999	2002	
Ge	ARV	**Buffel**	10	1999	2002	
dom	FSG	**Visby**	2	1999	2008	
SF	APC	**XA-203**	104	2000	2001	
dom	APC	**Bv-206S**	15	2001		
It	hel	**A109**	20	2001	2002	
Switzerland US	AAM	**AIM-120**	100	1993	1998	
Il	UAV	**Ranger**	4	1995	1998	Licensed, 28 UAVs. Deliveries to 1999
Ca	APC	**Piranha** II	515	1996	1997	Deliveries to 2002
dom	AD	**Skyguard**	100	1997	1999	Upgrade
US	SP arty	**M-109**	456	1997	1998	Upgrade, deliveries to 2000
Fr	hel	**AS-532**	12	1997	2000	Deliveries to 2002
dom	APC	**Eagle** II	175	1997	1999	Final deliveries 2001
US	AD	**Florako**	1	1999	2007	Upgrade
Ca	APC	**Piranha** III	10	2000	2001	Up to 120 req
UK	AIFV	**CV-90**	186	2000	2002	Deliveries to run to 2005
Sp	tpt	**C295**	2	2000	2003	
dom	APC	**Eagle** III	120	2000	2003	
Ukraine dom	CG	**Ukraina**	1	1990	2000	
col	tpt	**AN-70**	5	1991	2003	Up to 65 req
RF	FGA	**Su-24**	4	1996	2000	Final 2 delivered 2000
dom	MBT	**T-84**	10	1999	2000	
RF	FGA	**MiG-29**			2001	Upgrade
RF	FGA	**Su-25**			2001	Upgrade

Belgium Be

franc fr		1999	2000	2001	2002
GDP	fr	9.4tr	9.8tr		
	US$	237bn	238bn		
per capita	US$	25,000	26,193		
Growth	%	1.8	3.1		
Inflation	%	1.1	2.5		
Publ debt	%	114.3	109.8		
Def exp	fr	136bn	140bn		
	US$	3.4bn	3.4bn		
Def bdgt	fr	100.8bn	99.4bn	102.6bn	
	US$	2.5bn	2.4bn	2.2bn	
US$1=fr		39.6	41.2	46	
Population				**10,179,000**	

Age	13–17	18–22	23–32
Men	306,000	310,000	685,000
Women	291,000	298,000	663,000

Total Armed Forces

ACTIVE 39,420

(incl 1,860 Medical Service; 3,230 women)

RESERVES 100,500

Army 71,500 **Navy** 3,300 **Air Force** 10,000 **Medical Service** 15,700

Army 26,400

(incl 1,500 women)

1 joint service territorial comd (incl 2 engr, 2 sigs bn)
1 op comd HQ
1 mech inf div with 3 mech inf bde (each 1 tk, 2 armd inf, 1 SP arty bn, 1 engr coy) (2 bde at 70%, 1 bde at 50% cbt str), 1 AD arty bn, 2 recce (incl 1 UAV), 1 MP coy; 1 recce bn (MNDC)
1 cbt spt div (5 mil schools forming, 1 arty, 1 engr bn – augment mech inf div, plus 1 inf, 1 tk bn for bde at 50% cbt str)
1 para-cdo bde (2 para, 1 cdo, 1 recce/SF bn, 1 arty, 1 AD bty, 1 engr coy)
1 lt avn gp (2 ATK, 1 obs bn)

RESERVES

Territorial Defence 11 lt inf bn (9 province, 1 gd, 1 reserve)

EQUIPMENT

MBT 132 *Leopard* 1A5
RECCE 119 *Scimitar*
AIFV 218 YPR-765 (plus 56 'look-a-likes')
APC 187 M-113 (plus 109 'look-a-likes'), 95 *Spartan* (plus 50 'look-a-likes'), 50 *Pandur* incl 'look-a-likes'
TOTAL ARTY 272
   TOWED 105mm: 14 LG Mk II
   SP 155mm: 108 M-109A2

MOR 107mm: 90 M-30; **120mm**: 60; plus **81mm**: 118
ATGW 420 *Milan* (incl 215 YPR-765, 2 M-113)
RL 66mm: LAW
AD GUNS 35mm: 51 *Gepard* SP
SAM 118 *Mistral*
AC 10 BN-2A *Islander*
HELICOPTERS 74
   ASLT 28 A-109BA
   OBS 18 A-109A
   SPT 28 SA-318 (5 in store)
UAV 3 *B-Hunter* systems (18 air vehs)

Navy 2,560

(incl 280 women)
BASES Ostend, Zeebrugge. Be and Nl navies under joint op comd based at Den Helder (Nl)
PRINCIPAL SURFACE COMBATANTS 3
FRIGATES 3
FFG 3 *Wielingen* with 4 MM-38 *Exocet* SSM, 8 *Sea Sparrow* SAM, 1 × 100mm gun, 2 × ASTT (Fr L5 HWT), 1 × 6 ASW rkt
MINE WARFARE 11
MINE COUNTERMEASURES 11
   4 *Van Haverbeke* MCMV (US *Aggressive* MSO) (incl 1 used for trials), 7 *Aster* (tripartite)
SUPPORT AND MISCELLANEOUS 11
   2 log spt/comd with hel deck, 1 PCR, 1 sail trg, 5 AT; 1 AGOR, 1 AG
NAVAL AVIATION
EQUIPMENT
   HELICOPTERS
   3 SA-316B *Alouette* III

Air Force 8,600

(incl 800 women)
Flying hours 165
FGA 3 sqn with 36 F-16 MLU
FGA/RECCE 1 sqn with 12 F-16A(R)/B
FTR 2 sqn with 24 F-16A/B ADI (12 MLU ADX by 2002)
OCU with 8 F-16B
TPT 2 sqn
   1 with 11 C-130H
   1 with 2 Airbus A310-200, 1 *Falcon* 900, 3 HS-748, 5 *Merlin* IIIA, 2 *Falcon* 20, 1 ERJ-135 (3 more ERJ-135/145 on order to replace HS-748, *Merlin* and *Falcon*)
TRG 3 sqn
   2 with *Alpha Jet* (1 flt with CM-170)
   1 with SF-260
SAR 1 sqn with *Sea King* Mk 48
EQUIPMENT
   90 cbt ac (plus 45 in store), no armed hel
   AC 129 **F-16** (72 **-A**, 18 **-B**, plus 39 in store (110 to receive mid-life update)) • 6 *Mirage* 5 (in store) •

11 **C-130** (tpt) • 2 **Airbus A310-200** (tpt) • 3 **HS-748** (tpt) • 2 *Falcon* **20** (VIP) • 1 *Falcon* **900B** • 5 **SW 111** *Merlin* (VIP, photo, cal) • 10 **CM-170** (trg, liaison) • 33 **SF-260** (trg) • 29 *Alpha Jet* (trg)
HEL 5 (SAR) *Sea King*
MISSILES
  AAM AIM-9 *Sidewinder*, AIM-120 AMRAAM
  ASM AGM-65G *Maverick*
  SAM 24 *Mistral*

Forces Abroad

GERMANY 2,000; 1 mech inf bde (1 inf, 1 arty bn, 1 recce coy)

UN AND PEACEKEEPING
BOSNIA/CROATIA (SFOR II): up to 450 (UNMOP): 1 obs **DROC** (MONUC): 1 obs **INDIA/PAKISTAN** (UNMOGIP): 2 obs **FYROM** (KFOR): 210 **ITALY** (SFOR Air): 4 F-16A **MIDDLE EAST** (UNTSO): 6 obs **WESTERN SAHARA** (MINURSO): 1 obs **YUGOSLAVIA** (KFOR): 800

Foreign Forces

NATO HQ NATO Brussels; HQ SHAPE Mons
WEU Military Planning Cell
US 1,425: **Army** 795 **Navy** 100 **Air Force** 530

Canada Ca

dollar C$		1999	2000	2001	2002
GDP	C$		949bn	1,038bn	
	US$		644bn	705bn	
per capita	US$		23,432	24,381	
Growth	%		3.7	4.0	
Inflation	%		1.7	2.7	
Publ debt	%		93	104.9	
Def exp	C$		12.4bn	12.0bn	
	US$		8.4bn	8.1bn	
Def bdgt	C$		10.3bn	10.8bn	11.4bn
	US$		7.0bn	7.3bn	7.7bn
US$1=C$			1.47	1.47	1.5
Population					31,750,000
Age		13–17	18–22		23–32
Men		1,008,000	983,000		2,022,000
Women		963,000	949,000		1,976,000

Ca Armed Forces are unified and org in functional comds. This entry is set out in traditional single-service manner.

Total Armed Forces

ACTIVE 56,800

(incl 6,100 women). Some 15,700 are not identified by service

RESERVES 35,400
Primary 20,700 **Army** (Militia) (incl comms) 14,000 **Navy** 4,000 **Air Force** 2,100 **Primary Reserve List** 600 *Supplementary* **Ready Reserve** 14,700

Army (Land Forces) 18,600

(incl 1,600 women)
1 Task Force HQ • 3 mech inf bde gp, each with 1 armd regt, 3 inf bn (1 lt), 1 arty, 1 engr regt, 1 AD bty • 1 indep AD regt • 1 indep engr spt regt

RESERVES
Militia 14,000; 18 armd, 51 inf, 19 arty, 12 engr, 20 log bn level units, 14 med coy
Canadian Rangers 3,250; 127 patrols
EQUIPMENT
  MBT 114 *Leopard* C-1/C-2
  RECCE 5 *Lynx* (in store), 195 *Cougar*, 203 *Coyote*
  LAV 150 *Kodiak* (LAV-III), 269 *Grizzly*, 199 *Bison*
  APC 1,214 M-113 A2 (341 to be upgraded, 82 in store), 61 M-577
  TOWED ARTY 213: **105mm**: 185 C1/C3 (M-101), 28 LG1 Mk II
  SP ARTY 155mm: 58 M-109A4 (plus 18 in store)
  MOR 81mm: 167
  ATGW 150 TOW (incl 72 TUA M-113 SP), 425 *Eryx*
  RL 66mm: M-72
  RCL 84mm: 1,040 *Carl Gustav*; **106mm**: 111
  AD GUNS 35mm: 34 GDF-005 with *Skyguard*; **40mm**: 57 L40/60 (in store)
  SAM 22 ADATS, 96 *Javelin*, *Starburst*

Navy (Maritime Command) 9,000

(incl 2,800 women)
BASES Ottawa (National), Halifax (Atlantic), Esquimalt (Pacific)
SUBMARINES 1
  1 *Victoria* SSK (UK *Upholder*)
PRINCIPAL SURFACE COMBATANTS 16
DESTROYERS 4
DDG 4 modified *Iroquois* with 1 Mk-41 VLS for 29 SM-2 MR SAM, 1 × 76mm gun, 6 ASTT, 2 CH-124 *Sea King* ASW hel (Mk 46 LWT)
FRIGATES 12
FFG 12 *Halifax* with 8 *Harpoon* SSM, 16 *Sea Sparrow* SAM, 2 × ASTT, 1 CH-124A *Sea King* hel (Mk 46 LWT)
PATROL AND COASTAL COMBATANTS 14
  12 *Kingston* MCDV, 2 *Fundy* PCC (trg)
SUPPORT AND MISCELLANEOUS 6
  2 *Protecteur* AO with 3 *Sea King* hel, 1 AOT; 1 diving spt; 2 AGOR

DEPLOYMENT

ATLANTIC Halifax (HQ): 1 SSK, 2 DDG, 7 FFG, 1 AO, 1 AK, 6 MCDV (Air Force Assets); 2 MR plus 1 MR (trg) sqn with CP-140 and 3 CP-140A, 1 general purpose and 1 (trg) hel sqn with 26 CH-125 hel

PACIFIC Esquimalt (HQ): 2 DDG, 5 FFG, 1 AO, 6 MCDV (Air Force Assets); 1 MR sqn with 4 CP-140 and 1 ASW hel sqn with 6 CH-124 hel

RESERVES

HQ Quebec
4,000 in 24 div; tasks: crew 10 of the 12 MCDV; harbour defence; naval control of shipping

Air Force (Air Command) 13,500

(incl 1,700 women)
Flying hours 210
1 Air Div with 13 wg responsible for operational readiness, combat air-spt, air tpt, SAR, MR and trg
EARLY WARNING Ca NORAD Regional HQ at North Bay: 47 North Warning radar sites: 11 long-range, 36 short-range; Regional Op Control Centre (ROCC) (2 Sector Op Control Centres (SOCC)): 4 Coastal Radars and 2 Transportable Radars. Ca Component – NATO Airborne Early Warning (NAEW)

EQUIPMENT

140 (incl 18 MR) cbt **ac**, no armed **hel**
AC 122 **CF-18** (83 -**A**, 39 -**B**) - 60 operational (5 sqns) and 62 fighter trg, testing and rotation • 4 sqns with 18 **CP-140** (MR) and 3 **CP-140A** (environmental patrol) • 4 sqns with 32 **CC-130E/H** (tpt) and 5 **KCC-130** (tkr) • 1 sqn with 5 **CC-150** (Airbus A-310) and 5 **Boeing CC-137** • 1 sqn with 6 **CC-144/144-U** (EW trg, coastal patrol, VIP/tpt) • 4 sqns with 4 **CC-138** (SAR/tpt), 7 **CC-115** (SAR/tpt), 27 **CT/CE-133** (EW trg/tpt)
HEL 12 **CH-113** (SAR/tpt) • 3 sqns of 29 **CH-124** (ASW, afloat) • 99 **CH-146** (tpt, SAR) • first of 15 **CH-149** delivered late 2001
TRG 2 Flying Schools **ac** 136 **CT-114** *Tutor*, 4 **CT-142 hel** 9 **CH-139** *Jet Ranger*
NATO FLIGHT TRAINING CANADA 12 T-6A/CT-156 (primary), (another 12 to be delivered by end 2000). First of 18 Hawk 115 (advanced wpns/tactics trg) delivered
AAM AIM-7M *Sparrow*, AIM-9L *Sidewinder*

Forces Abroad

UN AND PEACEKEEPING

BOSNIA (SFOR II): 1,200: 1 inf bn, 1 armd recce, 1 engr sqn **CROATIA** (UNMOP): 1 obs **CYPRUS** (UNFICYP): 2 **DROC** (MONUC): 6 incl 1 obs **EGYPT** (MFO): 28 **ETHIOPIA/ERITREA** (UNMEE): 6 obs **IRAQ/KUWAIT** (UNIKOM): 5 obs **MIDDLE EAST** (UNTSO): 10 obs **SIERRA LEONE** (UNAMSIL): 5 obs

SYRIA/ISRAEL (UNDOF): 191: log unit
YUGOSLAVIA (KFOR): 800

Paramilitary 9,350

Canadian Coast Guard has merged with **Department of Fisheries and Oceans**. Both are civilian-manned.
CANADIAN COAST GUARD (CCG) 4,700
some 101 vessels incl 29 navaids/tender, 11 survey/research, 5 icebreaker, 22 cutter, 4 PCO, 11 PCI, 12 fisheries research, 4 ACV, 3 trg; plus **hel** 1 S-61, 6 Bell-206L, 5 Bell-212, 16 BO-105
DEPARTMENT OF FISHERIES AND OCEANS (DFO) 4,650
some 90 vessels incl 35 AGOR/AGHS, 38 patrol, 17 icebreakers

Foreign Forces

UK 343: Army 200; Air Force 143

Czech Republic Cz

koruna Kc		1999	2000	2001	2002
GDP	Kc	1.8tr	2.0tr		
	US$	52bn	52bn		
per capita	US$	13,327	14,163		
Growth	%	-0.2	3.9		
Inflation	%	2.1	3.9		
Debt	US$	25.3bn	23.0bn		
Def exp	Kc	41.2bn	44bn		
	US$	1,155m	1,155m		
Def bdgt	Kc	41.5bn	44.0bn	44.7bn	
	US$	1,164m	1,154m	1,138m	
FMA (US)	US$	1.4m	1.6m	1.7m	
US$1=Kc		35.7	38.1	39.3	
Population				**10,218,000**	

Slovak 3% **Polish** 0.6% **German** 0.5%

Age	13–17	18–22	23–32
Men	333,000	408,000	811,000
Women	317,000	392,000	783,000

Total Armed Forces

ACTIVE 53,600
(incl 18,200 MoD, centrally controlled formations and HQ units; 25,000 conscripts)
Terms of service 12 months

Army 23,800

(incl 15,500 conscripts)
1 mech div HQ
1 rapid-reaction bde (2 mech, 1 AB, 1 recce, 1 arty, 1 engr bn)

2 mech bde (each with 3 mech, 1 recce, 1 arty, 1 AD, 1 engr bn)
1 SF 'bde' (bn)
1 arty, 1 SAM, 1 engr regt
9 trg and mob base (incl arty, AD, engr)

RESERVES

1 territorial def HQ: 2 trg and mob base, 1 engr regt, 8 territorial def comd

EQUIPMENT

MBT 652: 56 T-54, 55 T-55, 541 T-72M (140 to be upgraded)
RECCE some 182 BRDM, OT-65
AIFV 801: 612 BMP-1, 174 BMP-2, 15 BRM-1K
APC 403 OT-90, 7 OT-64 plus 565 AIFV and APC 'look-a-likes'
TOTAL ARTY 648 (120 in store)
  TOWED 122mm: 124 D-30
  SP 322: **122mm**: 49 2S1; **152mm**: 273 *Dana* (M-77)
  MRL 122mm: 109 RM-70
  MOR 93: **120mm**: 85 M-1982, 8 SPM-85
SSM FROG-7, SS-21
ATGW 721 AT-3 *Sagger* (incl 621 on BMP-1, 100 on BRDM-2), 21 AT-5 *Spandrel*
AD GUNS 30mm: M-53/-59
SAM SA-7, ε140 SA-9/-13
SURV GS-13 (veh), *Small Fred/Small Yawn* (veh, arty)

Air Force 11,600

(incl AD and 8,500 conscripts); 75 cbt ac, 34 attack hel
Organised into two main structures – Tactical Air Force and Air Defence
Flying hours 60
FGA/RECCE 2 sqn with 31 Su-22MK/UM3K, 7 L-159 (further deliveries in progress)
FTR 2 sqn with 37 MiG-21
IN STORE 5 MiG-23, 24 Su-25BK/UBK
TPT 2 sqn with 14 L-410, 8 An-24/26/30, 2 Tu-154, 2 Yak-40, 1 Challenger CL-600 **hel** 2 Mi-2, 4 Mi-8, 1 Mi-9, 10 Mi-17
HEL 3 sqn (aslt/tpt/attack) with 24 Mi-2, 9 Mi-8/20, 32 Mi-17, 34* Mi-24, 11 PZL W-3 (SAR)
TRG 1 regt with **ac** 24 L-29, 14 L-39C, 17 L-39ZO, 3 L-39MS, 8 Z-142C **hel** 8 Mi-2
AAM AA-2 *Atoll*, AA-7 *Apex*, AA-8 *Aphid*
SAM SA-2, SA-3, SA-6

Forces Abroad

UN AND PEACEKEEPING

BOSNIA (SFOR II): up to 490; 1 mech inf bn **CROATIA** (UNMOP): 1 obs (SFOR): 7 **DROC** (MONUC): 6 incl 5 obs **ETHIOPIA/ERITREA** (UNMEE): 2 obs **GEORGIA** (UNOMIG): 5 obs **SIERRA LEONE** (UNAMSIL): 5 obs **YUGOSLAVIA** (KFOR): 175

Paramilitary 5,600

BORDER GUARDS 4,000
(1,000 conscripts)
INTERNAL SECURITY FORCES 1,600
(1,500 conscripts)

Denmark Da

kroner kr		1999	2000	2001	2002
GDP	Kr	1,213bn	1,283bn		
	US$	166bn	162bn		
per capita	US$	24,800	25,900		
Growth	%	1.3	2.9		
Inflation	%	2.4	2.9		
Publ debt	%	55.4	48.3		
Def exp	Kr	19.5bn	19.4bn		
	US$	2.7bn	2.4bn		
Def bdgt	Kr	18.6bn	18.4bn	20bn	
	US$	2.6bn	2.4bn	2.4bn	
US$1=kr		7.3	7.9	8.5	
Population				5,308,000	
Age		13–17	18–22	23–32	
Men		141,000	148,000	375,000	
Women		136,000	144,000	363,000	

Total Armed Forces

ACTIVE 21,400

(about 5,600 conscripts; 685 women; excluding civilians)
Terms of service 4–12 months (up to 24 months in certain ranks)

RESERVES 64,900

Army 46,000 **Navy** 7,300 **Air Force** 11,600
Home Guard (*Hjemmevaernet*) (volunteers to age 50) about 59,300 incl **Army** 46,400 **Navy** 4,500 **Air Force** 5,500 **Service Corps** 2,900

Army 12,900

(incl 5,000 conscripts, 350 women)
1 op comd • 1 mech inf div with 3 mech inf bde (each 2 mech inf, 1 tk, 1 SP arty bn), 1 regt cbt gp (1 mech inf, 1 mot inf bn, 1 engr coy), 1 recce, 1 tk, 1 AD, 1 engr bn; div arty • 1 rapid reaction bde with 2 mech inf, 1 tk, 1 SP arty bn (20% active cbt str) • 1 recce, 1 tk, 1 AD, 1 engr bn, 1 MLRS coy • Army avn (1 attack hel coy, 1 recce hel det) • 1 SF unit

RESERVES

5 local def region (1–2 mot inf bn), 2 regt cbt gp (3 mot inf, 1 arty bn)

EQUIPMENT

MBT 238: 220 *Leopard* 1A5 (58 in store), 18 *Leopard* 2
RECCE 36 Mowag *Eagle*
APC 274 M-113 (plus 313 'look-a-likes' incl 55 SP mor), 22 *Piranha* III
TOTAL ARTY 475
 TOWED 105mm: 134 M-101; **155mm**: 97 M-114/39
 SP 155mm: 76 M-109
 MRL 227mm: 8 MLRS
 MOR 120mm: 160 Brandt; **81mm**: 338 (incl 53 SP)
ATGW 140 TOW (incl 56 SP)
RL 84mm: AT-4
RCL 1,151: **84mm**: 1,131 *Carl Gustav*; **106mm**: 20 M-40
SAM *Stinger*
SURV ARTHUR
ATTACK HEL 12 AS-550C2
SPT HEL 13 Hughes 500M/OH-6
UAV *Sperwer*

Navy 4,000

(incl 500 conscripts, 150 women)
BASES Korsøer, Frederikshavn, Vaerlose (naval aviation)
SUBMARINES 4
SSK 4
 2 *Tumleren* (mod No *Kobben*) with Swe Type 61 HWT
 1 *Narhvalen*, with Type 61 HWT
 1 *Nacken*
PRINCIPAL SURFACE COMBATANTS 3
CORVETTES 3
FSG 3 *Niels Juel* with 8 *Harpoon* SSM, 8 *Sea Sparrow* SAM, 1 × 76mm gun
PATROL AND COASTAL COMBATANTS 27
MISSILE CRAFT 5 *Flyvefisken* (Stanflex 300) PFM with 2 × 4 *Harpoon* SSM, 6 *Sea Sparrow* SAM, 1 × 76mm gun, 2 × 533mm TT
PATROL CRAFT 22
 OFFSHORE 4
 4 *Thetis* PCO with 1 × 76mm gun, 1 *Lynx* hel
 COASTAL 18
 6 *Flyvefisken* (Stanflex 300) PFC, 3 *Agdlek* PCC, 9 *Barsøe* PCC
MINE WARFARE 7
MINELAYERS 4
 2 *Falster* (400 mines), 2 *Lindormen* (50 mines)
(All units of *Flyvefisken* class can also lay up to 60 mines)
MINE COUNTERMEASURES 3
 3 *Flyvefisken* (SF300) MHC
SUPPORT AND MISCELLANEOUS 13
 1AE, 1 tpt; 4 icebreakers, 6 environmental protection, 1 Royal Yacht
NAVAL AVIATION
EQUIPMENT
 HELICOPTERS
 8 *Lynx* (up to 4 embarked)

COASTAL DEFENCE

1 coastal fortress; **150mm** guns, coastal radar
2 mobile coastal msl batteries: 2 × 8 Harpoon
RESERVES (Home Guard)
40 inshore patrol craft/boats

Air Force 4,500

(incl 100 conscripts, 185 women)
Flying hours 180
TACTICAL AIR COMD
FGA/FTR 3 sqn with 68 F-16A/B (60 operational, 8 attritional reserve)
TPT 1 sqn with 3 C-130H, 1 *Challenger*-604 (2 more on order for MR/VIP), 2 *Gulfstream* G-III
SAR 1 sqn with 8 S-61A hel
TRG 1 flying school with 28 SAAB T-17
CONTROL AND AIR DEFENCE GROUP
2 SAM bn: 6 bty with 36 I HAWK launchers plus STINGER
5 radar stations, one in the Faroe Islands
EQUIPMENT
 68 cbt ac, no armed hel
 AC 68 **F-16A/B** (FGA/ftr) • 3 **C-130H** (tpt) • 1 *Challenger*-604 (tpt) • 28 **SAAB T-17** • 2 *Gulfstream* G-III, 28 SAAB T-17
 HEL 8 **S-61** (SAR)
MISSILES
 ASM AGM-65 *Maverick*, GBU-12 and GBU-24 LGBs
 AAM AIM-9 *Sidewinder*, AIM-120A AMRAAM
 SAM HAWK, *Stinger*

Forces Abroad

UN AND PEACEKEEPING
BOSNIA (SFOR II):345; incl 1 tk sqn (10 *Leopard* MBT); aircrew with NATO E-3A ops; Air Force personnel in tac air-control parties (TACP). (UNMIBH): 1 obs
CROATIA (UNMOP): 1 obs **DROC** (MONUC): 2 obs
EAST TIMOR (UNTAET): 4 incl 2 obs **ETHIOPIA/ ERITREA** (UNMEE): 6 incl 4 obs **GEORGIA** (UNOMIG): 5 obs **INDIA/PAKISTAN** (UNMOGIP): 6 obs **IRAQ/KUWAIT** (UNIKOM): 5 obs **ITALY** (BAL-KAN AIR OPERATION): 6 F-16 **MIDDLE EAST** (UNTSO): 10 obs **SIERRA LEONE** (UNAMSIL): 2 obs **YUGOSLAVIA** (KFOR): 900: 1 inf bn gp incl 1 scout sqn, 1 inf coy

Foreign Forces

NATO HQ Joint Comd North-East

France Fr

franc fr		1999	2000	2001	2002
GDP	fr	8.8tr	9.2tr		
	US$	1.4tr	1.3tr		
per capita	US$	24,000	25,300		
Growth	%	2.9	3.2		
Inflation	%	0.6	1.7		
Publ debt	%	65.0	64.4		
Def exp	fr	239bn	243bn		
	US$	37.1bn	35.0bn		
Def bdgt	fr	190.0bn	187.9bn	189.0bn	
	US$	29.5bn	27.0bn	25.3bn	
US$1=fr		6.44	6.94	7.48	
Population					59,271,000
Age		13–17	18–22		23–32
Men		1,981,000	1,915,000		4,275,000
Women		1,892,000	1,834,000		4,090,000

Total Armed Forces

ACTIVE 273,740

(incl 19,150 conscripts, 18,760 women; incl 5,200 **Central Staff**, 8,600 (750 conscripts) *Service de santé*, 1,340 *Service des essences* not listed)
Terms of service 10 months (can be voluntarily extended to 12–24 months)

RESERVES 419,000

Army 242,500 **Navy** 97,000 **Air Force** 79,500
Potential 1,058,500 **Army** 782,000 **Navy** 97,000 **Air Force** 179,500

Strategic Nuclear Forces (8,400)

(**Navy** 4,700 **Air Force** 3,100 *Gendarmerie* 600)
NAVY 64 SLBM in 4 SSBN
  SSBN 4
  2 *L'Inflexible* each with 16 M-4/TN-70 or -71, SM-39 *Exocet* USGW and 4 × 533mm HWT
  2 *Le Triomphant* each with 16 M-45/TN-75 SLBM, SM-39 *Exocet* USGW and 4 × 533mm HWT
  AIRCRAFT
  28 *Super Etendard* strike; plus 16 in store
AIR FORCE
  3 sqn with 60 *Mirage* 2000 N(ASMP)
  TKR 1 sqn with 11 C-135FR, 3 KC-135
  RECCE 1 sqn with 5 *Mirage* IV P
  AIRBORNE RELAY 4 C-160H *Astarte*
  CBT TRG 6 *Mystere* 20, 6 *Jaguar* E

Army 150,000

(incl 17,100 conscripts, 9,150 women) regt normally bn size
1 Land Comd HQ

5 Regional, 4 Task Force HQ
2 armd bde (each 2 armd, 2 armd inf, 1 SP arty, 1 engr regt)
2 mech inf bde (each 1 armd, 1 armd inf, 1 APC inf, 1 SP arty, 1 engr regt)
2 lt armd bde (each 2 armd cav, 2 APC inf, 1 arty, 1 engr regt)
1 mtn inf bde with 1 armd cav, 3 APC inf, 1 arty, 1 engr bde)
1 AB bde with 1 armd cav, 4 para inf, 1 arty, 1 engr, 1 spt regt
1 air mobile bde with 3 cbt hel, 1 spt hel regt
1 arty bde with 2 MLRS, 3 *Roland* SAM, 1 *HAWK* SAM regt
1 arty, 1 engr, 1 sigs, 1 Int and EW bde
1 Fr/Ge bde (2,500): Fr units incl 1 armd cav, 1 APC inf regt

FOREIGN LEGION (8,000)

1 armd, 1 para, 6 inf, 2 engr regt (incl in units listed above)

MARINES (14,700)

(incl conscripts, mainly overseas enlisted)
11 regt in Fr (incl in units listed above), 10 regt overseas

SPECIAL OPERATIONS FORCES

1 para regt, 1 hel units, 3 trg centre

RESERVES

Territorial def forces: 75 coy (all arms), 14 coy (engr, spt)

EQUIPMENT
  MBT 809 (CFE: 1,151): 498 AMX-30B2, 311 *Leclerc*
  RECCE 337 AMX-10RC, 192 ERC-90F4 *Sagaie*, 1,019 VBL M-11
  AIFV 599 AMX-10P/PC
  APC 3,900 VAB (incl variants)
  TOTAL ARTY 794
    TOWED 155mm: 97 TR-F-1
    SP 155mm: 273 AU-F-1
    MRL 227mm: 61 MLRS
    MOR 120mm: 363 RT-F1
  ATGW 700 *Eryx*, 1,348 *Milan*, HOT (incl 135 VAB SP)
  RL 84mm: AT-4; **89mm**: 9,850; **112mm**: 9,690 APILAS
  AD GUNS 20mm: 328 53T2
  SAM 26 HAWK, 98 *Roland* I/II, 331 *Mistral*
  SURV RASIT-B/-E (veh, arty), RATAC (veh, arty)
  AC 2 Cessna *Caravan* II , 5 PC-6, 8 TBM-700
  HELICOPTERS 410
    ATTACK 262: 77 SA-341F, 155 SA-342M, 30 SA-342AATCP
    RECCE 4 AS-532 *Horizon*
    SPT 144: 24 AS-532, 120 SA-330
  UAV 6 CL-289 (AN/USD-502), 2 *Crecerelle*

Navy 45,600

(incl 1,700 Marines, 6,800 Naval Aviation, 3,310 women, 1,000 conscripts)

COMMANDS SSBN (ALFOST) HQ Brest **Atlantic** (CECLANT) HQ Brest **North Sea/Channel** (COMAR CHERBOURG) HQ Cherbourg **Mediterranean** (CECMED) HQ Toulon **Indian Ocean** (ALINDIEN) HQ afloat **Pacific Ocean** (ALPACI) HQ Papeete
ORGANIC COMMANDS ALFAN (Surface Ships) **ALFAN/Brest** (Surface Ships ASW) **ALFAN/Mines** (mine warfare) **ALAVIA** (naval aviation) **ALFUSCO** (Marines) **ALFOST** (SS)
BASES France Cherbourg, Brest (HQ), Lorient, Toulon (HQ) **Overseas** Papeete (HQ) (Tahiti), La Réunion, Nouméa (New Caledonia), Fort de France (Martinique), Cayenne (French Guiana)

SUBMARINES 10

STRATEGIC SUBMARINES 4 SSBN (see **Strategic Nuclear Forces**)
TACTICAL SUBMARINES 6
SSN 6 *Rubis* with F-17 HWT, L-5 LWT and SM-39 *Exocet* USGW

PRINCIPAL SURFACE COMBATANTS 35

AIRCRAFT CARRIERS
1 *Charles de Gaulle* CVN (40,600t), capacity 35–40 ac (typically 12 *Super Etendard*, 2 E-2C *Hawkeyes*, 5 hel; *Rafale M* ac to be carried 2002)
CRUISERS 1 *Jeanne d'Arc* CG (trg/ASW) with 6 MM-38 *Exocet* SSM, 4 × 100mm guns, capacity 8 SA-319B hel
DESTROYERS 3
DDG 3
2 *Cassard* with 8 MM-40 *Exocet* SSM, 1 × 2 SM-1MR SAM, 1 × 100mm gun, 2 × ASTT (Fr L5 HWT), 1 *Panther* hel
1 *Suffren* (Duquesne) with 4 MM-38 *Exocet* SSM, 1 × 2 *Masurca* SAM, 2 × 100mm gun, 4 × ASTT (Fr L5 HWT)
FRIGATES 30
FFG 30
6 *Floréal* with 2 MM-38 *Exocet* SSM, 1 × 100mm gun, 1 *Panther* hel
7 *Georges Leygues* with *Crotale* SAM, 1 × 100mm gun, 2 × ASTT (Fr L5 HWT), 2 *Lynx* hel (Mk 46 LWT); 5 with 8 MM-40 *Exocet* SSM, 2 with 4 MM-38 *Exocet* SSM
2 *Tourville* with 1 × 6 MM-38 *Exocet* SSM, *Crotale* SAM, 2 × 100mm gun, 2 × ASTT (Fr L5 HWT), 2 *Lynx* hel (Mk 46 LWT)
10 *D'Estienne d'Orves* with 1 × 100mm gun, 4 ASTT, 6 ASW mor; 4 with 2 MM-38 *Exocet* SSM, 6 with 4 MM-40 *Exocet* SSM
5 *La Fayette* with 8 MM-40 *Exocet* SSM, *Croatale* SAM, 1 × 100mm gun, 1 *Panther* hel

PATROL AND COASTAL COMBATANTS 39

PATROL, OFFSHORE 1 *Albatros* PCO (Public Service Force, based in Indian Ocean)
PATROL, COASTAL 23
10 *L'Audacieuse* PCC, 8 *Léopard* PCC (instruction), 3 *Flamant* PCC (Public Service Force), 1 *Sterne* PCC,

1 *Grebe* PCC (Public Service Force)
PATROL, INSHORE 15
2 *Athos* PCI<, 2 *Patra* PCI<, 6 *Stellis* PCI<, 5 PCI< (manned by *Gendarmerie Maritime*)

MINE WARFARE 21

COMMAND AND SUPPORT 1 *Loire* MCCS
MINELAYERS 0, but SS and *Thetis* (trials ship) have capability
MINE COUNTERMEASURES 20
13 *Eridan* (tripartite) MHC, 4 *Vulcain* MCM diver spt, 3 *Antares* (route survey/trg)

AMPHIBIOUS 9
2 *Foudre* LPD, capacity 470 tps, 30 tk, 4 *Cougar* hel, 2 *Edic* LCT or 10 LCM
2 *Ouragan* LPD: capacity 350 tps, 25 tk, 2 *Super Frelon* hel or 4 *Puma* hel
5 *Champlain* LSM: capacity 140 tps, tk
Plus craft: 5 LCT, 15 LCM

SUPPORT AND MISCELLANEOUS 30

UNDER WAY SUPPORT 4 *Durance* AO with 1 SA-319 hel
MAINTENANCE AND LOGISTIC 7
4 AOT, 1 *Jules Verne* AR with 2 SA-319 hel, 2 *Rhin* depot/spt, with hel
SPECIAL PURPOSES 14
8 trial ships, 2 *Glycine* trg, 4 AT/F (3 civil charter)
SURVEY/RESEARCH 5
4 AGHS, 1 AGOR

DEPLOYMENT

CECLANT (HQ, Brest): 4 SSBN, 1 CG, 10 DDG/FFG, 3 MCMV, 1 MCCS, 10 MHC, 1 diver spt, 3 AGS, 1 AGOR
COMAR CHERBOURG (HQ, Cherbourg): 1 clearance diving ship, 3 PCC
CECMED (HQ, Toulon): 6 SSN, 1 CV, 15 DDG/FFG, 4 LPD, 3 AO, 1 LSM, 2 diver spt, 3 MHC, 1 AR

NAVAL AVIATION (6,800 incl 480 women)

ORGANISATION
Flying hours *Super Etendard*: 180–220 (night qualified pilots)
AIRCRAFT
NUCLEAR STRIKE 2 flt with *Super Etendard*
STRIKE 1 flt with *Rafale M* (from 2002)
MR 1 flt with *Nord-262*
MP 2 sqn with *Atlantique*
AEW 1 flt with E-2C
TRG 3 units with *Nord-262 Rallye 880*, CAP 10
HELICOPTERS
ASW 2 sqn with *Lynx*
SAR/TRG 1 unit with AS-565MA*
EQUIPMENT
51 cbt ac (plus 28 in store); 29 armed hel (plus 18 in store)
AIRCRAFT
28 **Super Etendard** plus 16 in store • 16 **Atlantique*** 2 plus 12 in store • 11 **Nord 262** • 8

Fr

Xingu • 7 *Rallye* 880* • 8 **CAP-10** • 6 *Falcon* 10
MER • 2 *Falcon* 50 MER

HELICOPTERS
16 *Lynx* plus 16 in store • 13 **AS-565MA** plus 2 in
store

MISSILES
ASM *Exocet* AM-39
AAM *Mica*, AS 30 *Laser*

MARINES (1,700)

COMMANDO UNITS (400) 4 aslt gp
1 attack swimmer unit
FUSILIERS-MARIN (1,700) 14 naval-base protection gp
PUBLIC SERVICE FORCE naval personnel perform-
ing general coast guard, fishery protection, SAR, anti-
pollution and traffic surv duties: 1 *Albatross*, 1 *Sterne*, 1
Grebe, 3 *Flamant* PCC; **ac** 4 N-262 **hel** 4 SA-365 (ships
incl in naval patrol and coastal totals). Comd exercised
through *Maritime Préfectures* (Premar): *Manche*
(Cherbourg), *Atlantique* (Brest), *Méditerranée* (Toulon)

Air Force 63,000

(incl 6,300 women, 1,050 conscripts and strategic nuc
forces, excl 5,600 civilians)
Flying hours 180

AIR SIGNALS AND GROUND ENVIRONMENT COM-MAND

CONTROL automatic *STRIDA* II, 6 radar stations, 1
sqn with 4 E3F
SAM 11 sqn (1 trg) with *Crotale*, *Aspic*, SATCP and AA
gun bty (**20mm**)

AIR COMBAT COMMAND

FTR 6 sqn with *Mirage* 2000C/B/5F
FGA 6 sqn
3 with *Mirage* 2000D • 1 with *Jaguar* A • 2 with
Mirage F1-CT
RECCE 2 sqn with *Mirage* F1-CR
TRG 2 OCU sqn
1 with *Mirage* F1-C/B • 1 with *Mirage* 2000/BC
EW 1 sqn with C-160 ELINT/ESM

AIR MOBILITY COMMAND (CFAP)

TPT 14 sqn
1 hy with DC-8F, A310-300
6 tac with C-160/-160NG, C-130H
7 lt tpt/trg/SAR/misc with C-160, DHC-6, CN235,
Falcon 20, *Falcon* 50, *Falcon* 900, TBM-700, N-262,
AS-555
EW 1 sqn with DC-8 ELINT
HEL 5 sqn with AS-332, SA-330, AS-555, AS-355, SA-319
TRG 1 OCU with C-160, N-262, 1 OCU with SA-319,
AS-555, SA-330

AIR TRAINING COMMAND

TRG *Alpha Jet*, EMB-121, TB-30, EMB-312, CAP-10/-
20/-231, CR-100, N262

EQUIPMENT

473 cbt ac, no armed hel

AC 352 *Mirage* (10 **F-1B** (OCU), 23 **F-1C** (OCU plus 6
in Djibouti), 40 **F1-CR** (recce), 40 **F1-CT** (FGA), 5
MIVP (recce), 114 **-M-2000B/C/5F** (64 -C (ftr), 30 -
5F (upgraded C), 20 -B (OCU)), 60 **-M-2000N**
(strike, FGA), 60 **-M-2000D**) • 22 *Jaguar* (FGA)
(plus 98 in store) • 99* *Alpha Jet* (trg, plus 29 in
store) • 4 E-3F (AEW) • 2 **A 310-300** (tpt) • 2 **DC-
8F** (tpt) • 1 **DC-8E** • 14 **C-130** (5 **-H** (tpt), 9 **-H-30**
(tpt)) • 11 **C-135FR** (tkr) • 77 **C-160** (13 **-AG**, 60 -
NG (tpt/14 tkr) 4 **-H**) • 3 **KC-135** • 14 **CN-235M**
(tpt) • 19 **N-262** • 17 *Falcon* (7 **-20**), 4 **-50** (VIP), 2 -
900 (VIP)) • 17 **TBM-700** (tpt) • 6 **DHC-6** (tpt) • 32
EMB-121 (trg) • 92 **TB-30** (trg plus 50 in store) • 9
CAP-10/20/231 (trg) • 48 **EMB-312** (trg) • 2 **CR-100**
(trg)

HEL 3 **SA-319** (*Alouette* III) • 29 **SA-330** (26 tpt, SAR,
3 OCU) (*Puma*) • 7 **AS-332** (tpt/VIP) (*Super Puma*)
• 3 **AS-532** (tpt) (*Cougar*) • 4 **AS-355** (*Ecureuil*) • 43
AS-555 (34 tpt, 9 OCU) (*Fennec*)

UAV 4 *Hunter*

MISSILES

ASM ASMP, AS-30/-30L
AAM *Super* 530F/D, R-550 *Magic* 1/II, AIM-9
Sidewinder, *Mica*

Forces Abroad

GERMANY 2,700: incl elm Eurocorps
ANTILLES (HQ Fort de France): 3,800: 3 mne inf regt
(incl 2 SMA), 1 mne inf bn, 1 air tpt unit **ac** 2 C-160
hel 2 SA-330, 2 AS-555, 1 FFG (1 AS-365 hel), 2 PCI, 1
LSM, 1 spt *Gendarmerie* 860
FRENCH GUIANA (HQ Cayenne): 3,250: 2 mne inf
(incl 1 SMA), 1 Foreign Legion regt, 2 PCI 1 *Atlantic*
ac, 1 air tpt unit **hel** 2 SA-330, 3 AS-555 *Gendarmerie*
600
INDIAN OCEAN (Mayotte, La Réunion): 4,200: 2
Marine inf (incl 1 SMA) regt, 1 spt bn, 1 air tpt unit
ac 2 C-160 **hel** 2 AS 555, 1 LSM, 1 spt *Gendarmerie*
850 **Navy** Indian Ocean Squadron, Comd ALINDIEN
(HQ afloat): 1 FFG (2 AS-365 hel), 1 PCO, 2 PCI, 1
AOR (comd), reinforcement 2 FFG, 1 *Atlantic* ac
NEW CALEDONIA (HQ Nouméa): 3,100: 1 mne inf
regt; some 12 AML recce, 5 **120mm** mor; 1 air tpt
unit, det **ac** 3 CN-235 **hel** 2 AS-555, 5 SA-330 **Navy** 2
FFG (2 AS-365 hel), 2 PCI, 1 LSM, 1 AGS, 1 spt **ac** 2
Guardian MR *Gendarmerie* 1,050
POLYNESIA (HQ Papeete) 3,100 (incl *Centre
d'Expérimentation du Pacifique*): 1 mne inf regt, 1
Foreign Legion bn, 1 air tpt unit; 2 CN-235, 3 AS-332
Gendarmerie 600 **Navy** 1 FFG, 3 patrol combatants, 1
amph, 1 AGHS, 5 spt **ac** 3 *Guardian* MR
CHAD 900: 2 inf coy, 1 AML sqn (-) **ac** 1 C-160, 1 C-130,
3 *Mirage* F1-CT, 2 *Mirage* F1-CR **hel** 3 SA-330
CÔTE D'IVOIRE 680: 1 mne inf bn (18 AML-60/-90)
hel 1 AS-555

DJIBOUTI 3,200: 2 inf coy, 2 AMX sqn, 1 engr unit; 1 sqn with **ac** 6 *Mirage* F-1C (plus 4 in store), 1 C-160 **hel** 2 SA-330, 1 AS-555
GABON 750: 1 mne inf bn (4 AML-60) **ac** 2 C-160 **hel** 1 AS-555, 13 AS-532
SENEGAL 1,170: 1 mne inf bn (14 AML-60/-90) **ac** 1 *Atlantic* MR, 1 C-160 tpt **hel** 1 SA-319

UN AND PEACEKEEPING

BOSNIA (SFOR II): 2,200 **CROATIA: SFOR Air Component** 11 *Jaguar*, 10 Mirage 2000C/D, 1 E-3F, 1 KC-135, 1 N-262 **DROC** (MONUC): 6 incl 1 obs **EGYPT** (MFO): 17; 1 DHC-6 **ETHIOPIA/ERITREA** (UNMEE): 180 **GEORGIA** (UNOMIG): 3 obs **IRAQ/ KUWAIT** (UNIKOM): 11 obs **ITALY** (DELIBERATE FORGE): 6 *Mirage* 2000C/D, 3 *Jaguar* **LEBANON** (UNIFIL): 232: elm 1 log bn **MIDDLE EAST** (UNTSO): 3 obs **SAUDI ARABIA** (*Southern Watch*): 170; 5 *Mirage* 2000C, 3 F-1CR, 1 C-135 **SIERRA LEONE** (UNAMSIL): 1 obs **WESTERN SAHARA** (MINURSO): 25 obs (*Gendarmerie*) **YUGOSLAVIA** (KFOR): 5,100

Paramilitary about 100,700

GENDARMERIE about 100,700
(incl 6,277 women, 5,350 conscripts, 1,610 civilians) **Territorial** 62,930 **Mobile** 17,025 **Schools** 5,440 **Overseas** 3,430 **Maritime, Air** (personnel drawn from other dept.) 3,700 **Republican Guard, Air tpt, Arsenals** 4,530 **Administration** 3,650 **Reserves** 50,000
  EQPT 28 VBC-90 armd cars; 155 VBRG-170 APC; 781 **60mm, 81mm** mor; 5 PCIs (listed under Navy), plus 34 other patrol craft and 4 AT **hel** 12 SA-316/ 319, 30 AS-350 B/BA

Foreign Forces

GERMANY 300: elm EUROCORPS
SINGAPORE AIR FORCE 200; 18 TA-4SU *Skyhawks* (Cazaux AFB)

Germany Ge

deutschmark DM		1999	2000	2001	2002
GDP	DM	3.7tr	3.8tr		
	US$	1.9tr	1.8tr		
per capita	US$	23,500	24,500		
Growth	%	1.3	3.0		
Inflation	%	0.6	1.9		
Publ debt	%	63.5	61.3		
Def exp	DM	59.7bn	59.6bn		
	US$	31.1bn	28.8bn		
Def bdgt	DM	48.8bn	48.3bn	46.8bn	
	US$	25.4bn	23.3bn	21.0bn	
US$1=DM		1.92	2.07	2.23	

Population			82,442,000
Age	13–17	18–22	23–32
Men	2,394,000	2,232,000	5,168,000
Women	2,266,000	2,123,000	5,019,000

Total Armed Forces

ACTIVE some 308,400
(incl 118,400 conscripts, 6,200 women)
Terms of service 10 months; 12–23 months voluntary

RESERVES 363,500
(men to age 45, officers/NCO to 60) **Army** 294,800 **Navy** 9,500 **Air Force** 59,200

Army 211,800

(incl 94,300 conscripts, 4,100 women)
ARMY FORCES COMMAND
1 air-mobile force comd (div HQ) with 2 AB (1 Crisis Reaction Force (CRF)), 1 cdo SF bde •1 army avn bde with 5 regt •1 SIGINT/ELINT bde •1 spt bde
ARMY SUPPORT COMMAND
3 log, 1 medical bde
CORPS COMMANDS
I Ge/Nl Corps 2 MDC/armd div
II Corps 2 MDC/armd div; 1 MDC/mtn div
IV Corps 1 MDC/armd inf div; 1 armd inf div; 1 MDC
Corps Units 2 spt bde and Ge elm of Ge/Nl Corps, 1 air mech bde (CRF), 1 ATGW hel regt
Military District Commands (MDC)/Divisions
6 MDC/div; 1 div; 1 MDC comd and control 9 armd bde, 7 armd inf and the Ge elm of the Ge/Fr bde, 2 armd (not active), 2 armd inf (not active), 1 inf, 1 mtn bde
Bde differ in their basic org, peacetime str, eqpt and mob capability; 4 (2 armd, 1 inf and Ge/Fr bde) are allocated to the CRF, the remainder to the Main Defence Forces (MDF)
The MDC also comd and control 27 Military Region Commands (MRC). One armd div earmarked for Eurocorps, another for Allied Rapid Reaction Corps (ARRC) and one armd inf div for the Multi-National Corps North East; 7 recce bn, 7 arty regt, 7 engr bde and 7 AD regt available for cbt spt
EQUIPMENT
MBT 2,521: 751 *Leopard* 1A1/A3/A4/A5, 1,770 *Leopard* 2 (350 to be upgraded to A6)
RECCE 523: 409 SPz-2 *Luchs*, 114 TPz-1 *Fuchs* (NBC)
AIFV 2,110 *Marder* A2/A3, 133 *Wiesel* (with **20mm** gun)
APC 807 TPz-1 *Fuchs* (incl variants), 1,803 M-113 (incl 286 arty obs and other variants), 56 APCV-2
TOTAL ARTY 2,073
  TOWED 350: **105mm**: 17 Geb H, 138 M-101;

155mm: 195 FH-70
SP 155mm 605: 519 M-109A3G, 86 PzH 2000
MRL 229: **110mm**: 78 LARS; **227mm**: 151 MLRS
MOR 889: **120mm**: 394 Brandt, 495 Tampella
ATGW 1,973: 1,606 *Milan*, 157 RJPz-(HOT) *Jaguar* 1,
210 *Wiesel* (TOW)
AD GUNS 1,525: **20mm**: 1,145 Rh 202 towed; **35mm**:
380 *Gepard* SP (147 being upgraded)
SAM 143 *Roland* SP, *Stinger* (incl some *Ozelot* SP)
SURV 19 *Green Archer* (mor), 110 RASIT (veh, arty),
65 RATAC (veh, arty)
HELICOPTERS 568
ATTACK 204 PAH-1 (BO-105 with HOT)
SPT 364: 126 UH-1D, 107 CH-53G, 95 BO-105M, 35
Alouette II, 1 EC-135
UAV CL-289 (AN/USD-502)
MARINE (River Engineers) 13 LCM

Navy 26,050

(incl 4,200 Naval Aviation; 5,150 conscripts, 700 women)
FLEET COMMAND Type comds SS, FF, Patrol Boat,
MCMV, Naval Aviation **Spt comds** Naval Comms,
Electronics
BASES Glücksburg (Maritime HQ), Wilhelmshaven,
Kiel, Olpenitz, Eckernförde, Warnemünde
SUBMARINES 14
SSK 12 Type 206/206A SSC with *Seeaal* DM2 A3 HWT
SSC 2 Type 205
PRINCIPAL SURFACE COMBATANTS 14
DESTROYERS 2
DDG 2 *Lütjens* (mod US *Adams*) with 1 × 1 SM-1 MR
SAM/*Harpoon* SSM launcher, 2 × 127mm guns, 8
ASROC (Mk 46 LWT), 6 ASTT
FRIGATES 12
FFG 12
8 *Bremen* with 8 *Harpoon* SSM, 1 × 76mm gun, 2 × 2
ASTT, 2 *Lynx* hel
4 *Brandenburg* with 4 MM-38 *Exocet* SSM, 1 VLS Mk-
41 SAM, 1 × 76mm gun, 4 × 324mm TT, 2 *Lynx* hel
PATROL AND COASTAL COMBATANTS 28
MISSILE CRAFT 28
10 *Albatros* (Type 143) PFM with 4 *Exocet* SSM, and 2
533mm TT
10 *Gepard* (T-143A) PFM with 4 *Exocet* SSM
8 *Tiger* (Type 148) PFM with 4 *Exocet* SSM
MINE WARFARE 28
MINE COUNTERMEASURES 28
5 *Kulmback* (mod *Hameln*) MHC
12 *Frankenthal* (T-332) MHC
5 *Ensdorf* (mod *Hameln*) MSC
5 *Frauenlob* MSI
1 MCM/T-742A diver spt ship
AMPHIBIOUS craft only
5 LCU/LCM
SUPPORT AND MISCELLANEOUS 43

UNDER WAY SUPPORT 2 *Spessart* AO
MAINTENANCE AND LOGISTIC 16
1 *Berlin* spt
6 *Elbe* spt, 4 small (2,000t) AOT, 3 *Lüneburg* log spt, 2
AE
SPECIAL PURPOSE 21
3 AGI, 2 trials, 8 multi-purpose (T-748/745), 1 trg, 6
AT, 1 icebreaker (civil)
RESEARCH AND SURVEY 4
1 AGOR, 3 AGHS (civil-manned for Ministry of
Transport)

NAVAL AVIATION
ORGANISATION
Flying hours *Tornado*: 180
AIRCRAFT
FGA/RECCE 2 sqn with *Tornado*
MP 2 sqn with *Atlantic*, Do-228
TRG 1 sqn with *Tornado*, 1 sqn with *Atlantic*, Do-228
HELICOPTERS
ASW 1 sqn with *Lynx*
ASUW/SAR 1 sqn with *Sea King* Mk 41
1 SAR/ASUW/tpt wg with 1 sqn *Sea King* Mk 41
hel
TRG 1 sqn with *Lynx*
EQUIPMENT
67 cbt ac, 40 armed hel
AIRCRAFT
50 **Tornado** • 17 **Atlantic** (13 armed) • 4 **Do-228**
HELICOPTERS
15 **Sea Lynx** Mk 88 • 4 **Lynx** Mk 88A • 21 **Sea King**
Mk 41
MISSILES
ASM *Kormoran*, *Sea Skua*, HARM
AAM AIM-9 *Sidewinder*, *Roland*

Air Force 70,550

(incl 18,950 conscripts, 1,400 women)
Flying hours 150
AIR FORCE COMMAND
2 air comds (North and South), 4 air div
FGA 5 wg with 10 sqn *Tornado*; 1 wg operates ECR
Tornado in SEAD role
FTR 4 wg (with 7 sqn F-4F; 1 sqn MiG-29)
RECCE 1 wg with 2 sqn *Tornado*
SAM 6 mixed wg (each 1 gp *Patriot* (6 sqn) plus 1 gp
Hawk (4 sqn plus 2 reserve sqn)); 14 sqn *Roland*
RADAR 2 tac Air Control regts, 8 sites; 11 remote radar
posts
TRANSPORT COMMAND (GAFTC)
TPT 3 wg, 4 sqn with *Transall* C-160 (incl 1 OCU), 4 sqn
(incl 1 OCU) with Bell UH-1D, 1 special air mission
wg with Airbus A-310, CL-601, L-410S (VIP), 3 AS-
532U2 (VIP)
TRAINING
FGA OCU with 27 *Tornado*
FTR OCU with 23 F-4F

NATO joint jet pilot trg (Sheppard AFB, TX) with 35 T-37B, 40 T-38A; primary trg sqn with Beech *Bonanza* (Goodyear AFB, AZ), GAF Air Defence School (Fort Bliss TX)

EQUIPMENT

434 cbt ac (50 trg (overseas)); no attack hel

AC 131 **F-4** *Phantom* II (incl 7 in store), 8 **F-104**, 267 *Tornado* (189 FGA, 35* ECR, 41 Recce, 2 in store), 1 **MiG-21**, 3 **MiG-23** (2 in store) • 23 **MiG-29** (19 (ftr), 4* **-UB** (trg)) • 1 **Su-22** • 84 *Transall* **C-160** (tpt, trg) • 7 **A-310** (VIP, tpt) • 7 **CL-601** (VIP) • 4 **L-410-S** (VIP) • 35 **T-37B** • 40 **T-38A**

HEL 101 **UH-1D** (97 SAR, tpt, liaison; 4 VIP) • 3 **AS-532U2** (VIP)

MISSILES

ASM AGM-65 *Maverick,* AGM-88A HARM

AAM AIM-9 *Sidewinder,* AA-8 *Aphid,* AA-10 *Alamo,* AA-11 *Archer*

SAM *Hawk, Roland, Patriot*

Forces Abroad

FRANCE: ε300; elm Eurocorps
POLAND: ε70; elm Corps HQ (multinational)
3 MPA in ELMAS/Sardinia
US: **Army** trg area with 35 *Leopard* 2 MBT, 26 *Marder* AIFV, 12 M-109A3G **155mm** SP arty **Air Force** 812 flying trg at Goodyear, Sheppard, Holloman AFBs, NAS Pensacola, Fort Rucker with 35 T-37, 40 T-38, 23 F-4F; 27 *Tornado,* msl trg at Fort Bliss

UN AND PEACEKEEPING

BOSNIA (SFOR II): 1,900; 34 SPz-2 *Luchs* recce, 32 TPz-1 *Fuchs* APC, hel 4 CH-53, 4 UH-1D **EAST TIMOR** (UNTAET): 4 **GEORGIA** (UNOMIG): 11 obs **IRAQ/KUWAIT** (UNIKOM): 11 **ITALY** (SFOR II/KFOR): 200 Air Force, 3 Tornado recce **YUGOSLAVIA** (KFOR): 5,100; 63 *Leopard* 2 MBT, 31 *Marder* AIFV, 25 SPz-2 *Luchs* recce, 51 TPz-1 *Fuchs* APC, 6 *Wiesel* TOW ATGW; 3 CH-53, 8 UH-1D hel

Foreign Forces

NATO HQ Allied Rapid Reaction Corps (ARRC), HQ Allied Air Forces North (AIRNORTH), HQ Joint Command Centre (JCCENT), HQ Multi-National Division (Central) (MND(C)), Airborne Early Warning Force: 17 E-3A *Sentry,* 2 Boeing-707 (trg)
BELGIUM 2,000: 1 mech inf bde(-)
FRANCE 2,700: incl elm Eurocorps
NETHERLANDS 2,600: **Army** 2,300: 1 lt bde **Air Force** 300
UK 17,100: **Army** 17,100: 1 corps HQ (multinational), 1 armd div
US 58,080: **Army** 42,300: 1 army HQ, 1 corps HQ; 1 armd (-), 1 mech inf div (-) **Navy** 300 **USMC** 380 **Air Force** 15,100: HQ USAFE, (HQ 17th Air Force), 1 tac ftr wg with 4 sqn FGA/ftr, 1 cbt spt wg, 1 air-control wg, 1

tac airlift wg; 1 air base wg, 54 F-16C/D, 12 A-10, 6 OA-10, 16 C-130E, 9 C-9A, 9 C-21, 2 C-20, 1 CT-43

Greece Gr

drachma dr		**1999**	**2000**	**2001**	**2002**
GDP	dr	38.2tr	40.2tr		
	US$	107.4bn	113bn		
per capita	US$	13,700	14,624		
Growth	%	3.3	4		
Inflation	%	2.7	3.2		
Publ debt	%	104.4	103.8		
Def exp	dr	1.9tr	1.9tr		
	US$	5.3bn	5.6bn		
Def bdgt	dr	1,220bn	1,160bn	1,300bn	
	US$	3.4bn	3.3bn	3.3bn	
FMA (US)	US$	0.025m	0.035m	0.025m	
US$1=dr		319	356	388	
Population[a]			**10,683,000**	Muslim 1%	
Age		13–17	18–22	23–32	
Men		329,000	381,000	825,000	
Women		310,000	362,000	789,000	

[a] Excl ε350–400,000 Albanians working in Gr in 1999

Total Armed Forces

ACTIVE 159,170

(incl 98,321 conscripts, 5,520 women)
Terms of service **Army** up to 18 months **Navy** up to 21 months **Air Force** up to 21 months

RESERVES some 291,000

(to age 50) **Army** some 235,000 (Field Army 200,000, Territorial Army/National Guard 35,000) **Navy** about 24,000 **Air Force** about 32,000

Army 110,000

(incl 81,000 conscripts, 2,700 women)

FIELD ARMY

3 Mil Regions • 1 Army, 2 comd, 5 corps HQ (incl 1 RRF) • 5 div HQ (1 armd, 3 mech, 1 inf) • 5 inf div (3 inf, 1 arty regt, 1 armd bn) • 5 indep armd bde (each 2 armd, 1 mech inf, 1 SP arty bn) • 7 mech bde (2 mech, 1 armd, 1 SP arty bn) • 5 inf bde • 1 army avn bde with 5 avn bn (incl 1 ATK, 1 tpt hel) • 1 indep avn coy • Special Forces: 1 marine bde (3 bn), 1 special ops comd, 1 cdo bde • 4 recce bn • 5 fd arty bn • 10 AD arty bn • 2 SAM bn with I HAWK
Units are manned at 3 different levels
 Cat A 85% fully ready **Cat B** 60% ready in 24 hours
 Cat C 20% ready in 48 hours

RESERVES 34,000

National Guard internal security role
EQUIPMENT
MBT 1,733: 712 M-48 (13 A3, 699 A5), 669 M-60 (357 A1, 312 A3), 352 *Leopard* (105 -1GR, 170 -1V, 77 -1A5)
RECCE 130 M-8, 37 VBL, 8 HMMWV
AIFV 500 BMP-1
APC 308 *Leonidas* Mk1/Mk2, 1,669 M-113A1/A2
TOTAL ARTY 1,900
    TOWED 729: **105mm**: 18 M-56, 445 M-101; **155mm**: 266 M-114
    SP 413: **105mm**: 73 M-52A1; **155mm**: 141 M-109A1B/A2/A3GEA1/A5, 6 *Zuzana*, **175mm**: 12 M-107; **203mm**: 181 M-110A2
    MRL 122mm: 116 RM-70; **227mm**: 18 MLRS (incl ATACMS)
    MOR 107mm: 624 M-30 (incl 231 SP); plus **81mm**: 2,800
ATGW 290 *Milan* (incl 42 HMMWV), 336 TOW (incl 320 M-901), 262 AT-4 *Spigot*
RL 64mm: 18,520 RPG-18; **66mm**: 10,700 M-72
RCL 84mm: 2000 *Carl Gustav*; **90mm**: 1,314 EM-67; **106mm**: 1,291 M-40A1
AD GUNS 23mm: 506 ZU-23-2
SAM 1,000 *Stinger*, 42 I HAWK, 21 SA-15, 20 SA-8B, SA-10 (S-300) in Crete, originally intended for Cy
SURV 10 AN/TPQ-36 (arty, mor), 2 AN/TPQ-37(V)3
AC 43 U-17A
HELICOPTERS
    ATTACK 20 AH-64A
    SPT 9 CH-47D (1 in store), 76 UH-1H, 31 AB-205A, 14 AB-206

Navy 19,000

(incl 9,800 conscripts, 1,300 women)
BASES Salamis, Patras, Soudha Bay
SUBMARINES 8
SSK 8
    4 *Glavkos* (Ge T-209/1100) with 533mm TT, and *Harpoon* USGW (1 in refit)
    4 *Poseidon* (Ge T-209/1200) with 533mm TT and *Harpoon* USGW
PRINCIPAL SURFACE COMBATANTS 16
DESTROYERS 4
DDG 4 *Kimon* (US *Adams*) with 6 *Harpoon* SSM, 1 × 1 SM-1 SAM, 2 × 127mm gun, 2 × 3 ASTT, 1 × 8 *ASROC* SUGW
FRIGATES 12
FFG 12
    4 *Hydra* (Ge MEKO 200) with 8 *Harpoon* SSM, 1 × 127mm gun, 6 ASTT, 1 SH-60 hel
    2 *Elli* (Nl *Kortenaer* Batch 2) with 8 *Harpoon* SSM, *Sea Sparrow* SAM, 2 × 76mm gun, 4 ASTT, 2 AB-212 hel
    4 *Aegean* (Nl *Kortenaer* Batch 1) with 8 *Harpoon* SSM, *Sea Sparrow* SAM, 1 × 76mm gun, 4 ASTT, 2 AB-212 hel

    2 *Makedonia* (ex-US *Knox*) (US lease) with *Harpoon* SSM (from ASROC launcher), 1 × 127mm gun, 4 ASTT, 8 *ASROC* SUGW
PATROL AND COASTAL COMBATANTS 40
CORVETTES 5 *Niki* (ex-Ge *Thetis*) FS with 4 ASW RL, 4 × 533mm TT
MISSILE CRAFT 17
    11 *Laskos* (Fr *La Combattante* II, III, IIIB) PFM, all with 2 × 533mm TT; 8 with 4 MM-38 *Exocet* SSM, 5 with 6 *Penguin* SSM
    4 *Votis* (Fr *La Combattante* IIA) PFM 2 with 4 MM-38 *Exocet* SSM, 2 with *Harpoon* SSM
    2 *Stamou* with 4 SS-12 SSM
TORPEDO CRAFT 8
    4 *Hesperos* (Ge *Jaguar*) PFT with 4 533mm TT
    4 *Andromeda* (No *Nasty*) PFT with 4 533mm TT
PATROL CRAFT 10
    OFFSHORE 4
    2 *Armatolos* (Dk *Osprey*) PCO, 2 *Pirpolitis* PCO
    COASTAL/INSHORE 6
    2 *Tolmi* PCC, 4 PCI<
MINE WARFARE 14
MINELAYERS 2 *Aktion* (US LSM-1) (100–130 mines)
MINE COUNTERMEASURES 12
    2 MHC (UK *Hunt*)
    8 *Alkyon* (US MSC-294) MSC
    2 *Atalanti* (US *Adjutant*) MSC
AMPHIBIOUS 7
    5 *Chios* LST with hel deck: capacity 300 tps, 4 LCVP plus veh
    2 *Inouse* (US *County*) LST: capacity 400 tps, 18 tk
    Plus about 61 craft: 2 LCT, 6 LCU, 11 LCM, some 31 LCVP, 7 LCA, 4 *Zubr* ACV
SUPPORT AND MISCELLANEOUS 20
    2 AOT, 4 AOT (small), 1 *Axios* (ex-Ge *Lüneburg*) log spt, 1 AE, 3 AGHS, 1 trg, 2 personnel tpt, 6 AWT
NAVAL AVIATION (250)
EQUIPMENT
18 armed hel
    HELICOPTERS
    ASW 8 AB-212, 2 SA-319, 8 S-70B
    EW 2 AB-212
    MISSILES
    AAM *Penguin*

Air Force 30,170

(incl 7,521 conscripts, 1,520 women)
TACTICAL AIR FORCE
8 cbt wg, 1 tpt wg
FGA 11 sqn
    2 with A-7H, 2 with A-7E, 2 with F-16CG/DG, 2 with F-4E, 1 with F-5A/B, 2 with *Mirage* F-1CG
FTR 6 sqn
    2 with F-16 CG/DG, 2 with *Mirage* 2000 EG/BG, 6 surplus Fr Air Force 2000-5 used for conversion

trg pending arrival of 10 upgraded 2000 EG, 2 with F-4E

AEW 2 S100B Argus
RECCE 1 sqn with RF-4E
TPT 3 sqn with C-130H/B, YS-11, C-47, Do-28, *Gulfstream*
HEL 1 sqn with AB-205A, AB-212, Bell 47G
AD 1 bn with *Nike Hercules* SAM (36 launchers), 12 bty with *Skyguard/Sparrow* SAM, twin **35mm** guns

AIR TRAINING COMMAND

TRG 4 sqn
1 with T-41A, 1 with T-37B/C, 2 with T-2E (first of 45 T-6A in service to replace T-41 and T-37)

EQUIPMENT

458 cbt ac, no armed hel
AC 90 **A-7 H** (FGA), 4 **TA-7H** (FGA) • 87 **F-5A/B**, 10 **NF-5A**, 1 **NF-5B** • 95 **F-4E/RF-4E**, of which 39 being upgraded • 75 **F-16CG** (FGA)/**DG** (trg) • 27 *Mirage* **F-1 CG** (ftr) • 34 *Mirage* **2000** (**EG** (FGA)/ **BG*** (trg))-10 EG to be upgraded to 2000-5 from 2001 • (94 F-TF-104Gs in storage) • 2 S100B Argus (on loan from Swe AF pending delivery of 4 EMB-145/*Erieye* from 2002) • 4 **C-47** (tpt) • 10 **C-130H** (tpt) • 5 **C-130B** (tpt) • 10 **CL-215** (tpt, fire-fighting) • 2 **CL-415** (fire-fighting) - 8 more to follow by late 2001. 13 **Do-28** (lt tpt) • 1 *Gulfstream* I (VIP tpt) • 35* **T-2E** (trg) • 34 **T-37B/ C** (trg) • 20 **T-41D** (trg) • 1 **YS-11-200** (tpt)
HEL 13 **AB-205A** (SAR) • 1 **AB-206** • 4 **AB-212** (VIP, tpt) • 7 **Bell 47G** (liaison)

MISSILES

ASM AGM-65 *Maverick*, AGM-88 HARM
AAM AIM-7 *Sparrow*, AIM-9 *Sidewinder* L/P, R-550 *Magic* 2, AIM 120 AMRAAM, *Super* 530D
SAM 1 bn with 36 *Nike Hercules*, 3 *Patriot* PAC-2 for trg, prior to delivery of 4 PAC-3 bty from 2001, 12 bty with *Skyguard*, 40 *Sparrow*, 4 SA-15, 9 *Crotale*, **35mm** guns

Forces Abroad

CYPRUS 1,250: incl 1 mech bde and officers/NCO seconded to Greek-Cypriot forces
UN AND PEACEKEEPING
ADRIATIC (*Sharp Guard* if re-implemented): 2 MSC
BOSNIA (SFOR II): 250 **SFOR Air Component** 1 C-130
ETHIOPIA/ERITREA (UNMEE): 2 obs **GEORGIA** (UNOMIG): 4 obs **IRAQ/KUWAIT** (UNIKOM): 4 obs **WESTERN SAHARA** (MINURSO): 1 obs **YUGOSLA-VIA** (KFOR): 1,700

Paramilitary 4,000

COAST GUARD AND CUSTOMS 4,000
some 100 patrol craft, **ac** 2 Cessna *Cutlass*, 2 TB-20 *Trinidad*

Foreign Forces

NATO HQ Joint Command South-Centre (SOUTHCENT). (COMMZ(S)): ε18 spt tps from 6 countries for KFOR
US 480: **Navy** 240; facilities at Soudha Bay **Air Force** 240; air base gp; facilities at Iraklion

Hungary Hu

forint f		**1999**	**2000**	**2001**	**2002**
GDP	f	11.4tr	13.1tr		
	US$	47bn	47bn		
per capita	US$	8,000	8,528		
Growth	%	3.8	5.3		
Inflation	%	10.3	9.8		
Debt	US$	29.2bn	32.2bn		
Def exp	f	188bn	218bn		
	US$	768m	793m		
Def bdgt	f	182bn	189bn	236bn	
	US$	745m	689m	805m	
FMA (US)	US$	1.5m	1.6m	1.7m	
US$1=f		244	275	293	
Population				**10,002,000**	

Romany 4% **German** 3% **Serb** 2% **Romanian** 1% **Slovak** 1%

Age	13–17	18–22	23–32
Men	304,000	386,000	721,000
Women	288,000	362,000	675,000

Total Armed Forces

ACTIVE 33,810

(incl 450 Central HQ comd staff and 12,700 centrally controlled formations/units; 22,900 conscripts)
Terms of service 9 months

RESERVES 90,300

Army 74,900 **Air Force** 15,400 (to age 50)

Land Forces 13,160

(incl conscripts)
1 Land Forces HQ, 1 garrison comd
1 mob and trg comd (with 5 trg school/centre)
3 mech inf bde each 2 mech, 1 armd bn
1 mixed arty bde, 1 SAM regt
1 engr bde
1 lt mixed, 1 MP regt
2 recce bn
1 army maritime wing, 1 counter mine bn

RESERVES

4 mech inf bde

EQUIPMENT

MBT 753: 515 T-55 (108 in store), 238 T-72
RECCE 104 FUG D-442
AIFV 490 BMP-1, 12 BRM-1K, 178 BTR-80A
APC 459 BTR-80, 336 PSZH D-944 (83 in store), 4 MT-LB (plus 310 APC and AIFV 'look-a-like' types)
TOTAL ARTY 839
  TOWED 532: **122mm**: 230 M-1938 (M-30) (42 in store); **152mm**: 302 D-20 (108 in store)
  SP 122mm: 151 2S1
  MRL 122mm: 56 BM-21
  MOR 120mm: 100 M-120 (1 in store)
ATGW 369: 115 AT-3 *Sagger*, 30 AT-4 *Spigot* (incl BRDM-2 SP), 224 AT-5 *Spandrel*
ATK GUNS 85mm: 162 D-44 (all in store); **100mm**: 106 MT-12
AD GUNS 57mm: 186 S-60 (43 in store)
SAM 243 SA-7, 60 SA-14, 45 *Mistral*
SURV PSZNR-5B, SZNAR-10

Army Maritime Wing (270)

BASE Budapest

RIVER CRAFT 50

6 *Nestin* MSI (riverine), some 44 An-2 mine warfare/patrol boats

Air Force 7,500

(incl conscripts)
AIR DEFENCE COMMAND
46 cbt ac, 51 attack hel
Flying hours 50
FGA 1 tac ftr wg with 27 MiG-29A/UB
IN STORE 61 MiG-21, 9 MiG-23, 10 Su-22
ATTACK HEL 1 cbt hel wg with 51 Mi-24 (some in store)
SUPPORT HEL 23 Mi-8/17 (tpt/assault), 1 Mi-9 (Cmd Post), 2 Mi-17PP (EW)
TPT 1 mixed tpt wg, 1 mixed tpt sqn, ac 8 An-26, 4 Z-43, hel 20 Mi-2, 25 Mi-8/17
TRG 19 L-39*, 12 Yak-52
AAM AA-2 *Atoll*, AA-8 *Aphid*, AA-10 *Alamo*, AA-11 *Archer*
ASM AT-2 *Swatter*, AT-6 *Spiral*
SAM 2 mixed AD msl regt with 66 SA-2/-3/-5, 12 SA-4, 20 SA-6

Forces Abroad

UN AND PEACEKEEPING
BOSNIA (SFOR II): 4 obs **CROATIA** (SFOR II): 310; 1 engr bn **CYPRUS** (UNFICYP): 116 **EGYPT** (MFO): 41 mil pol **GEORGIA** (UNOMIG): 8 obs **IRAQ/KUWAIT** (UNIKOM): 6 obs **WESTERN SAHARA** (MINURSO): 6 obs **YUGOSLAVIA** (KFOR): 325

Paramilitary 14,000

BORDER GUARDS (Ministry of Interior) 12,000 (to reduce)

11 districts/regts plus 1 Budapest district (incl 7 rapid-reaction coy; 68 BTR-80 APC)

Iceland Icl

kronur K		1999	2000	2001	2002
GDP	K	638bn	668bn		
	US$	8.5bn	9bn		
per capita	US$	25,500	27,000		
Growth	%	6.0	3.6		
Inflation	%	3.2	5.0		
Publ debt	%	43.6	42.1		
Sy exp[a]	K	1.4bn	1.4bn		
	US$	19m	19m		
Sy bdgt[a]	K	1.4bn	1.4bn	1.5bn	
	US$	19m	19m	15.3m	
US$1=K		75.5	75.3	98.3	

[a] Icl has no Armed Forces. Sy bdgt is mainly for Coast Guard

Population				283,000
Age	13–17	18–22	23–32	
Men	11,000	11,000	22,000	
Women	10,000	10,000	20,000	

Total Armed Forces

ACTIVE Nil

Paramilitary 120

COAST GUARD 120
BASE Reykjavik
  PATROL CRAFT 4
  2 *Aegir* PCO with hel, 1 *Odinn* PCO with hel deck, 1 PCI<
  AVN ac 1 F-27, **hel** 1 SA-365N, 1 SA-332, 1 AS-350B

Foreign Forces

NATO Island Commander Iceland (ISCOMICE, responsible to CINCEASTLANT)
US 1,640: **Navy** 960; MR: 1 sqn with 4 P-3C **Marines** 80 **Air Force** 630; 6 F-15C/D, 1 HC-130, 1 KC-135, 4 HH-60G
NETHERLANDS 16: **Navy** 1 P-3C

Italy It

lira L		1999	2000	2001	2002
GDP	L	2,125tr	2,257tr		
	US$	1.1tr	1.1tr		
per capita	US$	22,000	23,436		
Growth	%	1.0	2.7		
Inflation	%	1.7	2.6		
Publ debt	%	116.6	110.8		
Def exp	L	41.8tr	43.0tr		
	US$	22bn	21bn		
Def bdgt	L	30.9tr	32.8tr	34.2tr	
	US$	16.2bn	16.0bn	15.5bn	
US$1=L		1,900	2,050	2,210	
Population				57,184,000	
Age		13–17	18–22	23–32	
Men		1,483,000	1,680,000	4,397,000	
Women		1,409,000	1,601,000	4,242,000	

Total Armed Forces

ACTIVE 230,350

(incl 86,760 conscripts)
Terms of service all services 10 months

RESERVES 65,200 (immediate mobilisation)
Army 11,900 (500,000 obligation to age 45) **Navy** 23,000
(to age 39 for men, variable for officers to 73) **Air Force**
30,300 (to age 25 or 45 (specialists))

Army 137,000

(incl 63,000 conscripts)
1 Op Comd HQ, 3 mil region HQ
1 Projection Force with 1 mech, 1 airmobile, 1 AB bde, 1
  amph, 1 engr regt
1 mtn force with 3 mtn bde, 1 engr, 1 avn regt, 1 alpine
  AB bn
2 div defence force
  1 with 1 armd, 1 mech, 1 armd cav bde, 1 engr regt
  1 with 3 mech, 1 armd bde, 1 engr, 1 avn regt
1 spt comd with
  1 AD div: 2 HAWK SAM, 2 SHORAD regt
  1 arty bde: 1 hy arty, 2 arty, 1 NBC regt
  1 engr bde (3 regt)
  1 avn div: 3 avn regt, 1 avn bn
EQUIPMENT
  MBT 1,349: 819 *Leopard* 1, 368 *Centauro* B-1, 162 *Ariete*
  AIFV 26 *Dardo*
  APC 827 M-113 (incl variants), 565 VCC-1, 1,228
    VCC-2, 157 Fiat 6614
  AAV 14 LVTP-7
  TOTAL ARTY 1,390
    TOWED 325: **105mm**: 157 Model 56 pack; **155mm**:
    164 FH-70, 4 M-114 (in store)

SP 155mm: 260 M-109G/L; **203mm**: 9 M-110
MRL 227mm: 22 MLRS
MOR 120mm: 774 Brandt; **81mm**: 1,200 (386 in
  store)
ATGW 426 TOW 2B, 432 I-TOW, 752 *Milan*
RL 1,860 *Panzerfaust* 3
RCL 80mm: 434 *Folgore*
AD GUNS 25mm: 208 SIDAM SP
SAM 60 HAWK, 112 *Stinger*, 32 *Skyguard/Aspide*
AC 6 SM-1019, 3 Do-228, 3 P-180
HELICOPTERS
  ATTACK 45 A-129
  ASLT 27 A-109, 62 AB-206
  SPT 86 AB-205A, 68 AB-206 (obs), 14 AB-212, 23
    AB-412, 36 CH-47C
UAV 5 *Mirach* 20

Navy 38,000

(incl 2,500 Naval Air, 1,200 Marines and 11,000 con-
scripts)
COMMANDS 1 Fleet Commander CINCNAV (also
NATO COMEDCENT) **Area Commands** 5 Upper
Tyrrhenian, Ionian and Strait of Otranto, Adriatic,
Sicily, Sardinia
BASES La Spezia (HQ), Taranto (HQ), Brindisi, Augusta
SUBMARINES 7
SSK 7
  4 *Pelosi* (imp *Sauro*) with Type 184 HWT
  3 *Sauro* with Type 184 HWT
PRINCIPAL SURFACE COMBATANTS 22
AIRCRAFT CARRIERS 1 *G. Garibaldi* CV with total ac
  capacity 16 AV-8B *Harrier* V/STOL or 18 SH-3 *Sea
  King* hel (usually a mix of both)
CRUISERS 1 *Vittorio Veneto* CGH with 4 *Teseo* SSM, 1 ×
  2 SM-1 ER SAM, 8 × 76mm gun, 2 × 3 ASTT, 6 AB-
  212 ASW hel (Mk 46 LWT)
DESTROYERS 4
DDG 4
  2 *Luigi Durand de la Penne* (ex-*Animoso*) with 8 *Teseo*
    SSM, 1 SM-1 MR SAM, 1 × 127mm gun, 6 ASTT, 2
    AB-312 hel
  2 *Audace* with 4 *Teseo* SSM, 1 SM-1 MR SAM, 1 ×
    127mm gun, 6 ASTT, 2 AB-212 hel
FRIGATES 16
FFG 16
  8 *Maestrale* with 4 *Teseo* SSM, *Aspide* SAM, 1 × 127mm
    gun, 2 × 533mm TT, 2 AB-212 hel
  4 *Lupo* with 8 *Teseo* SSM, *Sea Sparrow* SAM, 1 ×
    127mm gun, 2 × 3 ASTT, 1 AB-212 hel
  4 *Artigliere* with 8 *Teseo* SSM, 8 *Aspide* SAM, 1 ×
    127mm gun, 1 AB-212 hel
PATROL AND COASTAL COMBATANTS 15
CORVETTES 8 *Minerva* FS with *Aspide* SAM, 1 ×
  76mm gun, 6 × ASTT
PATROL, OFFSHORE 4
  4 *Cassiopea* PCO with 1 × 76mm gun, 1 AB-212 hel

PATROL, COASTAL 3

3 *Esplatore* PCC

MINE WARFARE 13

MINE COUNTERMEASURES 13

1 MCCS (ex *Alpino*)

4 *Lerici* MHC/MSC

8 *Gaeta* MHC/MSC

AMPHIBIOUS 3

2 *San Giorgio* LPD: capacity 350 tps, 30 trucks, 2 SH-3D or CH-47 hel, 7 craft

1 *San Giusto* LPD: capacity as above

Plus some 33 craft: about 3 LCU, 10 LCM and 20 LCVP

SUPPORT AND MISCELLANEOUS 29

2 *Stromboli* AO, 1 *Etna* AO; 7 AWT, 2 AR; 2 ARS, 7 sail trg, 7 AT (plus 44 coastal AT); 1 AGOR

SPECIAL FORCES (Special Forces Command – COMSUBIN)

4 gp; 1 diving op; 1 Navy SF op; 1 school; 1 research

MARINES (San Marco gp) (1,200)

1 bn gp, 1 trg gp, 1 log gp

EQUIPMENT

30 VCC-1 APC, 10 LVTP-7 AAV, 16 **81mm** mor, 8 **106mm** RCL, 6 *Milan* ATGW

NAVAL AVIATION (2,500)

EQUIPMENT

18 cbt ac; 80 armed hel

AIRCRAFT

FGA 16 AV-8B

TRG 2 TAV-8B*

HELICOPTERS

ASW 21 SH-3D, 45 AB-212

AMPH ASLT 8 SH-3D, 6 AB-212

MISSILES

ASM *Marte* Mk 2, AS-12, AGM-65 *Maverick*

AAM AIM-9L *Sidewinder*

Air Force 55,350

(incl 12,760 conscripts)

AFHO 2 Inspectorates (Naval Aviation, Flight Safety), 1 Op Cmd (responsible for 5 op bde), 1 Force Cmd, 1 Logs Cmd, 1 Trg Cmd

FGA 8 sqn

4 with *Tornado* IDS • 4 with AMX (50% of 1 sqn devoted to recce)

FTR 6 sqn

4 with F-104 ASA • 2 with *Tornado* ADV

MR 2 sqn with *Atlantic* (OPCON to Navy)

EW 1 ECM/recce sqn with G-222VS, PD-808, P-180, P-166DL-3

TPT 3 sqn

2 with G-222, C-130J • 1 with C-130H

TKR/TPT/CAL 1 sqn with B707-320, G-222 RM, PD-808

LIAISON/VIP 2 sqn with **ac** *Gulfstream* III, *Falcon* 50, *Falcon* 900, DC-9, A319 **hel** SH-3D

TRG

1 OCU with TF-104G

4 sqn with AMX-T, MB-339A, MB-339CD, SF-260M

1 sqn with MB-339A (aerobatic team)

1 sqn with NH-500

CSAR 1 sqn with HH-3F

SAR 3 det with HH-3F, 4 det with AB-212

AD 12 bty: 3 HSAM bty with *Nike Hercules*, 9 SAM bty with *Spada*

EQUIPMENT

329 cbt ac (plus 76 in store), 6 armed hel

AC 95 *Tornado* (75 IDS, 20 ADV) (plus 16 FGA and 4 ADV in store) • 55 **F-104ASA** (plus 14 in store) • 11 **TF-104G** (plus 7 in store) • 74 **AMX** (56 (FGA), 18 -**T** (trg)) (plus 32 FGA/5-T in store) • 70 **MB-339** (18 aero team, 52 trg) (plus 15 in store) • 14* **MB-339CD** (plus 1 in store) • 10* *Atlantic* (MR) (plus 8 in store) • 2 **Boeing-707-320** (tkr/tpt) (plus 2 in store) • 9 **C-130H** (plus 3 in store) • 5 **C-130J** (tpt/tkr) • 23 **G-222** (tpt/tac/calibration) (plus 18 in store) • 1 **DC9-32** (VIP) (plus 1 in store) • 2 **Airbus A319CJ** • 1 *Gulfstream* III (VIP) (plus 1 in store) • 3 *Falcon 50* (VIP) (plus 1 in store), 2 *Falcon* 900 (VIP) • 5 **P-166-DL3** (plus 1 in store) (liaison/trg) • 5 **P-180** (liaison) • 4 **PD-808** (ECM, cal, VIP, tpt) • 33 **SF-260M** (trg) (plus 5 in store) • 33 **SIAI-208** (liaison) (plus 6 in store)

HEL 23 **HH-3F** (17 SAR, 6*CSAR) (plus 10 in store) • 1 **SH-3D** (liaison/VIP) (plus 1 in store) • 31 **AB-212** (SAR) (plus 5 in store) • 51 **NH-500D** (trg)

UAV 4 *Predator* on order, first op by mid-2002

MISSILES

ASM AGM-88 HARM, *Kormoran*

AAM AIM-9L *Sky Flash*, *Aspide*

SAM *Nike Hercules*, *Aspide*

Forces Abroad

GERMANY 92: **Air Force, NAEW Force**

MALTA 16: **Air Force** with 2 AB-212

US 33: **Air Force** flying trg

CANADA 10: **Air Force** flying trg

UN AND PEACEKEEPING

ALBANIA (COMMZ-W): 1,160 spt tps for KFOR **BOSNIA** (SFOR II): 1,500: 1 mech inf bde gp **DROC** (MONUC): 2 **EGYPT** (MFO): 77 **ETHIOPIA/ERITREA** (UNMEE): 149 incl 5 obs **INDIA/PAKISTAN** (UNMOGIP): 6 obs **IRAQ/KUWAIT** (UNIKOM): 6 obs **LEBANON** (UNIFIL): 58; hel unit **MIDDLE EAST** (UNTSO): 8 obs **WESTERN SAHARA** (MINURSO): 5 obs **YUGOSLAVIA** (KFOR): 4,200

Paramilitary 252,200

CARABINIERI 109,700 (Ministry of Interior)

Territorial 5 inter-regional, 18 regional, 102 provincial
comd **Trg** HQ and 5 school **Mobile def** 1 div, 1 div
special units, 1 bde, 1 mounted cav regt, 1 special ops
gp, 13 mobile bn, 1 AB bn, avn and naval units
   EQUIPMENT 48 Fiat 6616 armd cars; 20 VCC2 APC
   hel 24 A-109, 38 AB-206, 30 AB-412 **craft** 72 PCC,
   74 PCI, 28 PCR<
PUBLIC SECURITY GUARD 79,000 (Ministry of Interior)
11 mobile units; 40 Fiat 6614 APC **ac** 5 P-68 **hel** 12 A-
   109, 20 AB-206, 9 AB-212
FINANCE GUARDS 63,500 (Treasury Department)
14 Zones, 20 Legions, 128 gp **ac** 5 P-166-DL3 **hel** 15 A-
   109, 65 Breda-Nardi NH-500M/MC/MD; 3 PCI; plus
   about 300 boats
HARBOUR CONTROL (*Capitanerie di Porto*)
(subordinated to Navy in emergencies): 11 PCI, 300+
   boats; 8 AB-412 (SAR) and 12 P166 DL3 hel

Foreign Forces

NATO HQ Allied Forces South Europe, HQ Allied Air
Forces South (AIRSOUTH), HQ Allied Naval Forces
South (NAVSOUTH), HQ Joint Command South
(JCSOUTH), HQ 5 Allied Tactical Air Force (5 ATAF)
US 10,850: **Army** 2,200; 1 inf bn gp **Navy** 4,400 **Air
Force** 4,140 **USMC** 110
DELIBERATE FORGE COMPONENTS Be 4 F-16A **Ca**
6 CF-18 **Da** 3 F-16A **Fr** 6 *Mirage* 2000C/D, 3 *Jaguar* **Nl** 4
F-16A **Sp** 5 EF-18, 1 KC-130 **Tu** 4 F-16C **UK** 4 *Harrier* GR-
7, 1 *Nimrod*, 1 K-1 *Tristar*, 2 E-3D *Sentry* **US** 32 F-16C/D,
1 AC-130, 1 KC-135, 6 UH-60, 2 U-2, 10 P-3C, 5 C-12, 2
C-21
SUPPORT COMPONENTS (for NATO ops in Kosovo)
Sp 1 CASA 212, **US** 4 C-12, 1 LJ-35, 1 BE-20, 4 C-130, 3
KC-135, 4 H-53, 2 H-3, 1 C-5, 3 P-3, 1 C-9, 2 C-2

Luxembourg Lu

franc fr		1999	2000	2001	2002
GDP	fr	708bn	727bn		
	US$	17.9bn	17.0bn		
per capita	US$	28,341	31,008		
Growth	%	5.1	8.5		
Inflation	%	1.0	3.2		
Publ debt	%	6.5	5.3		
Def exp	fr	5.3bn	5.5bn		
	US$	135m	128m		
Def bdgt	fr	4.0bn	4.3bn	4.3bn	
	US$	102m	100m	93.5m	
US$1=fr		39.6	42.7	46	
Population		436,000	foreign citizens ε124,000		
Age		13–17	18–22	23–32	
Men		12,000	12,000	27,000	
Women		12,000	12,200	28,000	

Total Armed Forces

ACTIVE 900

Army 900

1 lt inf bn, 2 recce coy (1 to Eurocorps/BE div, 1 to
AMF(L))
EQUIPMENT
   MOR 81mm: 6
   ATGW 6 TOW
   RL LAW

Air Force

(none, but for legal purposes NATO's E-3A AEW ac
have Lu registration)
1 sqn with 17 E-3A *Sentry* (NATO standard), 2 Boeing
   707 (trg)

Forces Abroad

UN AND PEACEKEEPING
BOSNIA (SFOR II): 23 **Deliberate Forge Air Component** 5 E-3A **YUGOSLAVIA** (KFOR): some

Paramilitary 612

GENDARMERIE 612

Netherlands Nl

guilder gld		1999	2000	2001	2002
GDP	gld	813bn	799bn		
	US$	375bn	347bn		
per capita	US$	23,800	25,171		
Growth	%	3.0	3.9		
Inflation	%	2.2	2.5		
Publ debt	%	67	63.7		
Def exp	gld	15bn	15bn		
	US$	6.9bn	6.5bn		
Def bdgt	gld	14.1bn	14.2bn	14.0bn	
	US$	6.5bn	6.2bn	5.6bn	
US$1=gld		2.16	2.30	2.51	
Population				15,854,000	
Age		13–17	18–22	23–32	
Men		447,000	439,000	1,112,000	
Women		428,000	419,000	1,053,000	

Total Armed Forces

ACTIVE 50,430

(incl 5,200 Royal Military Constabulary, 4,155 women; excl 20,000 civilians)

RESERVES 32,200

(men to age 35, NCOs to 40, officers to 45) **Army** 22,200 **Navy** some 5,000 **Air Force** 5,000 (immediate recall)

Army 23,100

(incl 1,630 women)
1 Corps HQ (Ge/Nl), 1 mech div HQ • 3 mech inf bde (2 cadre) • 1 lt bde • 1 air-mobile bde (3 inf bn) • 1 fd arty gp, 1 AD bn • 1 engr gp (2 bn)
Summary of cbt arm units
   3 tk bn • 6 armd inf bn • 3 air-mobile bn • 3 recce coy • 6 arty bn • 1 AD bn • 1 SF bn • 2 MLRS bty

RESERVES

(cadre bde and corps tps completed by call-up of reservists)
National Command (incl Territorial Comd): 6 inf bn, could be mob for territorial defence
Home Guard 3 sectors; lt inf wpns

EQUIPMENT

MBT 320 *Leopard* 2 (180 to be A5; 140 for sale)
AIFV 361 YPR-765
APC 258 YPR-765 (plus 549 look-a-likes), 66 XA-188 *Sisu*, 21 TPz-1 *Fuchs*
TOTAL ARTY 369
   TOWED 155mm: 20 M-114, 80 M-114/39, 12 FH-70 (trg)
   SP 155mm: 123 M-109A3
   MRL 227mm: 22 MLRS
   MOR 81mm: 40; **120mm**: 112 Brandt
ATGW 753 (incl 135 in store): 427 *Dragon*, 326 TOW (incl 96 YPR-765)
RL 84mm: AT-4
RCL 84mm: *Carl Gustav*
AD GUNS 35mm: 77 *Gepard* SP (60 to be upgraded); **40mm**: 60 L/70 towed
SAM 312 *Stinger*
SURV AN/TPQ-36 (arty, mor)
UAV *Sperwer*
MARINE 1 tk tpt, 3 coastal, 3 river patrol boats

Navy 12,130

(incl 950 Naval Aviation, 3,100 Marines; 1,150 women)
BASES Netherlands Den Helder (HQ). Nl and Be Navies under joint op comd based Den Helder. Valkenburg (MPA) De Kooy (hel) **Overseas** Willemstad (Curaçao)

SUBMARINES 4

SSK 4 *Walrus* with Mk 48 HWT; plus provision for *Harpoon* USGW

PRINCIPAL SURFACE COMBATANTS 12

DESTROYERS 2

DDG (Nl desig = FFG) 2

2 *Van Heemskerck* with 8 *Harpoon* SSM, 1 SM-1 MR SAM, 4 ASTT

FRIGATES 10

FFG 10

8 *Karel Doorman* with 8 *Harpoon* SSM, *Sea Sparrow* SAM, 1 × 76mm gun, 4 ASTT, 1 *Lynx* hel
2 *Kortenaer* with 8 × *Harpoon* SSM, 8 × *Sea Sparrow* SAM, 1 × 76mm gun, 4 ASTT, 2 *Lynx* hel

MINE WARFARE 12

MINELAYERS none, but *Mercuur*, listed under spt and misc, has capability
MINE COUNTERMEASURES 12
12 *Alkmaar* (tripartite) MHC
plus 4 diving vessels

AMPHIBIOUS 1

1 *Rotterdam* LPD: capacity 600 troops, 6 *Lynx* hel or 4 NH-90, 4 LCU or 6 LCA
plus craft: 5 LCU, 6 LCA

SUPPORT AND MISCELLANEOUS 8

1 *Amsterdam* AO (4 *Lynx* or 2 NH-90), 1 *Zuideruis* AO (2 *Lynx* or 2 NH-90), 1 *Pelikaan* spt; 1 *Mercuur* torpedo tender, 2 trg; 1 AGOR, 1 AGHS

NAVAL AVIATION (950)

EQUIPMENT

10 cbt ac, 21 armed hel
   AIRCRAFT
      MR/ASW 10 P-3C
   HELICOPTERS
      ASW/SAR 21 *Lynx*

MARINES (3,100)

3 Marine bn (1 cadre); 1 spt bn
(1 bn integrated with UK 3rd Cdo Bde to form UK/NL Amph Landing Force)

EQUIPMENT

APC 22 YPR-765 (incl 11 'look-a-likes'), 20 XA-188 *Sisu*
TOWED ARTY 105mm: 8 lt
MOR 81mm: 18; **120mm**: 14 Brandt
ATGW *Dragon*
RL AT-4
RCL 84mm: *Carl Gustav*
SAM *Stinger*

Air Force 10,000

(incl 975 women)
Flying hours 180
FTR/FGA/RECCE swing role. 6 sqn (with 18 F-16 AM (MLU) each) at 3 air bases. 1 trg sqn
TPT 1 sqn with F-50, F-60, C-130H-30, KDC-10 (tkr/tpt), *Gulfstream* IV
TRG 1 sqn with PC-7
HEL
   2 sqn with AH-64D
   1 sqn with BO-105
   1 sqn with AS-532U2, SA-316

1 sqn with CH-47D
1 SAR sqn with AB-412 SP
AD 4 sqns (TRIAD), each with 1 *Patriot* SAM bty
(TMD), 2 *Hawk* SAM bty, 7 *Stinger* teams

EQUIPMENT

157 cbt ac, 19 attack hel
AC 157 **F-16**: (138 - 92 F-16A, 21 F-16A(R) and 25 F-
16B - converted under European mid-life update
programme) • 2 **F-50** • 4 **F-60** • 2 **C-130H-30** • 2
KDC-10 (tkr/tpt) • 1 *Gulfstream* IV • 13 **PC-7** (trg)
HEL 3 **AB-412 SP** (SAR) • 4 **SA-316** • 15 **BO-105** •
19* **AH-64D** (30 by 2003) • 13 **CH-47D** • 17 **AS-
532U2**

MISSILES

AAM AIM-9/L/N *Sidewinder*, AIM-120B AMRAAM
ASM AGM-65G *Maverick*, AGM-114K *Hellfire*
SAM 48 HAWK, 5 *Patriot*, 100 *Stinger*
AD GUNS 25 VL 4/41 *Flycatcher* radar, 75 L/70 **40mm**
systems

Forces Abroad

GERMANY 2,600: **Army** 2,300; 1 lt bde (1 armd inf, 1
tk bn), plus spt elms **Air Force** 300
ICELAND 16: **Navy** 1 P-3C
NETHERLANDS ANTILLES Nl, Aruba and the
Netherlands Antilles operate a Coast Guard Force to
combat org crime and drug smuggling. Comd by
Netherlands Commander Caribbean. HQ Curaçao,
bases Aruba and St Maarten **Navy** 20 (to expand); 1
FFG, 1 amph cbt det, 3 P-3C, 1 Marine bn

UN AND PEACEKEEPING

BOSNIA (SFOR II): 1,100; 1 mech inf bn gp **ETHIO-
PIA/ERITREA** (UNMEE): 8 incl 1 obs **ITALY**: 80
(DELIBERATE FORGE) 4 F-16 **MIDDLE EAST**
(UNTSO): 11 obs **YUGOSLAVIA** (KFOR): 1,450

Paramilitary 5,200

ROYAL MILITARY CONSTABULARY (*Koninklijke
Marechaussee*) 5,200 (incl 400 women)
6 districts with 60 'bde'. Eqpt incl 24 YPR-765 APC

Foreign Forces

NATO HQ Allied Forces North Europe
US 665: **Army** 355 **Air Force** 290 **Navy** 10 **USMC** 10

Norway No

kroner kr		1999	2000	2001	2002
GDP	kr	1,192bn	1,423bn		
	US$	150bn	162bn		
per capita	US$	25,500	26,400		
Growth	%	0.6	2.2		
Inflation	%	2.4	3.1		
Publ debt	%	34.6	28.0		
Def exp	kr	25.8bn	25.7bn		
	US$	3.3bn	2.9bn		
Def bdgt	kr	26.3bn	25.3bn	25.8bn	
	US$	3.3bn	2.9bn	2.8bn	
US$1=kr		7.96	8.81		
Population				4,487,000	
Age		13–17	18–22		23–32
Men		138,000	134,000		327,000
Women		131,000	127,000		310,000

Total Armed Forces

ACTIVE 26,700

(incl 400 Joint Services org, 500 Home Guard permanent staff; 15,200 conscripts)
Terms of service **Army**, **Navy**, **Air Force**, 12 months, plus
4–5 refresher trg periods

RESERVES

222,000 on 24–72 hour readiness; obligation to 44
(conscripts remain with fd army units to age 35,
officers to age 55, regulars to age 60)
Army 89,000 **Navy** 25,000 **Air Force** 25,000 **Home
Guard** some 83,000 on mob

Army 14,700

(incl 8,700 conscripts)
2 Joint Comd, 4 Land Comd, 14 territorial regt
North Norway 1 ranger bn, border gd, cadre and trg
units for 1 div (1 armd, 2 mot inf bde) and 1 indep
mech inf bde
South Norway 2 inf bn (incl Royal Guard), indep units
plus cadre units for 1 mech inf and 1 armd bde

RESERVES

17 inf, 3 ranger, 1 arty bn; AD, engr, sigs and log units

LAND HOME GUARD 77,000

18 districts each divided into 2–6 sub-districts (bn)
comprising a total of 480 units (coy)

EQUIPMENT

MBT 170 *Leopard* (111 -1A5NO, 59 -1A1NO)
AIFV 53 NM-135 (M-113/**20mm**), ε104 CV 9030N
APC 109 M-113 (incl variants), ε80 XA-186/-200 *Sisu*
TOTAL ARTY 184
TOWED 155mm: 46 M-114/39

SP 155mm: 126 M-109A3GN
MRL 227mm: 12 MLRS
MOR 81mm: 450 (40 SP incl 24 M-106A1, 12 M-125A2)
ATGW 320 TOW-1/-2 incl 97 NM-142 (M-901), 424 *Eryx*
RCL 84mm: 2,517 *Carl Gustav*
AD GUNS 20mm: 252 Rh-202 (192 in store)
SAM 300 RBS-70 (120 in store)
SURV *Cymberline* (mor), 12 ARTHUR

Navy 6,100

(incl 160 Coastal Defence, 270 Coast Guard, 3,300 conscripts)
OPERATIONAL COMMANDS 2 Joint Operational Comds, COMNAVSONOR and COMNAVNON with regional naval commanders and 7 regional Naval districts
BASES Horten, Haakonsvern (Bergen), Olavsvern (Tromsø)
SUBMARINES 6
SSK 6 *Ula* with DM 2 A3 HWT
PRINCIPAL SURFACE COMBATANTS 3
FRIGATES 3
FFG 3 *Oslo* with 4 *Penguin 1* SSM, *Sea Sparrow* SAM, 1 × twin 76mm gun, 6 *Terne* ASW RL, *Stingray* LWT (1 in reserve)
PATROL AND COASTAL COMBATANTS 14
MISSILE CRAFT 14
14 *Hauk* PFM with 6 × *Penguin 2* SSM, 2 × *Mistral* SAM, 2 (Swe TP-613) HWT
plus 1 *Skjold* PFM (in development)
MINE WARFARE 12
MINELAYERS 3
2 *Vidar*, coastal (300–400 mines), 1 *Tyr* (amph craft also fitted for minelaying)
MINE COUNTERMEASURES 9
4 *Oskøy* MHC, 5 *Alta* MSC, plus 2 diver spt
AMPHIBIOUS craft only
5 LCT, 22 S90N LCA
SUPPORT AND MISCELLANEOUS 6
1 *Horten* sub/patrol craft depot ship; 1 *Valkyrien* TRV, 1 Royal Yacht, 2 *Hessa* trg, 1 *Mariata* AGI

NAVAL HOME GUARD 4,900
on mob assigned to 10 HQ sectors incl 31 areas; 235 vessels plus 77 boats

COASTAL DEFENCE
FORTRESS 6 **75mm**: 3; **120mm**: 3; **127mm**: 6; **150mm**: 2 guns; 3 cable mine and 3 torpedo bty

COAST GUARD (270)
PATROL AND COASTAL COMBATANTS 11
PATROL, OFFSHORE 4
3 *Nordkapp* with 1 *Lynx* hel (SAR/recce), fitted for 6 *Penguin* Mk 2 SSM, 1 *Nornen*

PATROL INSHSORE 7 PCI plus 7 cutters
AVN hel 6 *Lynx* Mk 86 (Air Force-manned)

Air Force 5,000

(incl 3,200 conscripts, 185 women)
Flying hours 180
OPERATIONAL COMMANDS 2 joint with COMSONOR and COMNON
FGA 4 sqn with F-16A/B
MR 1 sqn with 4 P-3C/2 P-3N *Orion*
TPT 1 sqn with C-130
CAL/ECM 1 sqn with 2 *Falcon* 20C (EW) and 1 *Falcon* 20C (Flight Inspection Service)
TRG MFI-15
SAR 1 sqn with *Sea King* Mk 43B
TAC HEL 2 sqn with Bell-412SP
EQUIPMENT
61 cbt ac (incl 4 MR), no armed hel
AC 57 **F-16A/B** • 6 **P-3** (4* **-C** UIP (MR), 2 **-N** (pilot trg)) • 6 **C-130H** (tpt) • 3 *Falcon* **20C** (EW/FIS) • 3 **DHC-6** (tpt) • 15 **MFI-15** (trg)
HEL 18 **Bell 412 SP** (tpt) • 12 *Sea King* **Mk 43B** (SAR) • 6 *Lynx* **Mk 86** (Coast Guard)
MISSILES
ASM CRV-7, *Penguin* Mk-3
AAM AIM-9L/N *Sidewinder*, AIM 120 AMRAAM
AIR DEFENCE
SAM 6 bty NASAMS, 10 bty RB-70
AAA 8 bty L70 (with Fire-Control System 2000) org into 5 gps

AA HOME GUARD
(on mob under comd of Air Force): 2,500; 2 bn (9 bty) AA **20mm** NM45

Forces Abroad

UN AND PEACEKEEPING
BOSNIA (SFOR II): 125 **CROATIA** (UNMOP): 1 obs
EAST TIMOR (UNTAET): 6 **EGYPT** (MFO): 5 Staff Officers **ETHIOPIA/ERITREA** (UNMEE): 5 obs
MIDDLE EAST (UNTSO): 11 obs **YUGOSLAVIA** (KFOR): 980

Foreign Forces

US 83: Prepo eqpt for **Marines**: 1 MEB **Army**: 1 arty bn
Air Force: ground handling eqpt
Ge prepositioned eqpt for 1 arty bn
NATO HQ Joint Command North Europe (JC North)

Poland Pl

zloty z		1999	2000	2001	2002
GDP	z	614bn	690bn		
	US$	157bn	160bn		
per capita	US$	7,941	8,422		
Growth	%	4.0	4.1		
Inflation	%	7.3	10.1		
Debt	US$	49bn	68bn		
Def exp	z	12.7bn	14.1bn		
	US$	3.2bn	3.3bn		
Def bdgt	z	12.6bn	13.2bn	14.8bn	
	US$	3.2bn	3.1bn	3.7bn	
FMA (US)	US$	1.6m	1.6m	1.7m	
US$1=z		3.91	4.32	3.99	
Population					38,819,000

German 1.3% **Ukrainian** 0.6% **Belarussian** 0.5%

Age	13–17	18–22	23–32
Men	1,640,000	1,688,000	2,792,000
Women	1,558,000	1,611,000	2,672,000

Total Armed Forces

ACTIVE 206,045

(incl 25,250 centrally controlled staffs, units/forma-
tions; 91,638 conscripts)
Terms of service 12 months

RESERVES 406,000

Army 343,000 **Navy** 14,000 (to age 50) **Air Force** 49,000
(to age 60)

Army 120,300

(incl 67,200 conscripts)
To reorg:
2 Mil Districts/Army HQ
1 Multi-national Corps HQ (Pl/Ge/Da)
1 Air-Mechanised Corps HQ
5 mech div (incl 1 coastal)
1 armd cav div
5 bde (incl 1 armd, 1 mech, 1 air aslt, 1 air cav, 1 mtn inf)
3 arty (incl 1 AD), 2 engr, 5 territorial def bde
1 recce, 1 SSM, 3 AD, 2 cbt hel regt
1 special ops, 1 gd regt
EQUIPMENT
 MBT 1,677: 786 T-55, 685 T-72, 206 PT-91
 RECCE 465 BRDM-2
 AIFV 1,404: 1,368 BMP-1, 36 BRM-1
 APC 33 OT-64 plus some 693 'look-a-like' types
 TOTAL ARTY 1,580
  TOWED 440: **122mm**: 280 M-1938 (M-30); **152mm**:
  160 M-1938 (ML-20)
  SP 652: **122mm**: 533 2S1; **152mm**: 111 *Dana* (M-77);
  203mm: 8 2S7
  MRL 258: **122mm**: 228 BM-21, 30 RM-70

 MOR 230: **120mm**: 214 M-120, 16 2B11/2S12
 SSM launchers: 32 FROG, SS-C-2B
 ATGW 403: 268 AT-3 *Sagger*, 110 AT-4 *Spigot*, 18 AT-5
  Spandrel, 7 AT-7 *Saxhorn*
 ATK GUNS 85mm: 723 D-44
 AD GUNS 686: **23mm**: 406 ZU-23-2, 56 ZSU-23-4 SP;
  57mm: 224 S-60
 SAM 1,012: 100 SA-6, 628 SA-7, 64 SA-8, 216 SA-9
  (*Grom*), 4 SA-13
 HELICOPTERS
  ATTACK 43 Mi-24D/V, 22 Mi-2URP
  SPT 8 Mi-2URN
  TPT 29 Mi-8, 3 Mi-17, 35 Mi-2, 34 Pzlw-3W
 SURV *Big Fred* ((SNAR-10) veh, arty)

Navy 16,760

(incl 2,500 Naval Aviation, 8,900 conscripts)
BASES Gdynia, Swinoujscie, Kolobrzeg, Hel, Gydnia-
Babie Doly (Naval Aviation Brigade)
SUBMARINES 3

SSK 3
 1 *Orzel* SS (RF *Kilo*) with 533mm TT
 2 *Wilk* (RF *Foxtrot*) with 533mm TT

PRINCIPAL SURFACE COMBATANTS 3

DESTROYERS 1
DDG 1 *Warszawa* (Sov mod *Kashin*) with 4 SS-N-2C
 Styx SSM, 2 × 2 SA-N-1 *Goa* SAM, 5 × 533mm TT, 2
 ASW RL
FRIGATES 2
FFG 1 *Pulawski* (US *Perry*) with *Harpoon* SSM, SM-1MR
 SAM, 1 × 76mm gun, 2 × 3 324mm ASTT (A 244 Mod
 3 LWT)
FF 1 *Kaszub* with SA-N-5 *Grail* SAM, 1 × 76mm gun, 2 ×
 2 533mm ASTT, 2 ASW RL

PATROL AND COASTAL COMBATANTS 23
CORVETTES 4 *Gornik* (Sov *Tarantul* I) FSG with 2 × 2
 SS-N-2C *Styx* SSM, 1 × 4 SA-N-5 *Grail* SAM, 1 ×
 76mm gun
MISSILE CRAFT 5 Sov *Osa* I PFM with 4 SS-N-2A SSM
PATROL CRAFT 14
 COASTAL 3 *Sassnitz* PCC with 1 × SA-N-5 *Grail*
 SAM, 1 × 76mm gun, 8 *Obluze* PCC
 INSHORE 11
 11 *Pilica* PCI<

MINE WARFARE 22
MINELAYERS none, but SSK, *Krogulec* MSC and
 Lublin LSM have minelaying capability
MINE COUNTERMEASURES 22
 3 *Krogulec* MHC/MSC, 13 *Goplo* (*Notec*) MSC, 4
 Mamry (*Notec*) MHC/MSC, 2 *Leniwka* MSI

AMPHIBIOUS 5
 5 *Lublin* LSM, capacity 135 tps, 9 tk
 Plus craft: 3 *Deba* LCU (none employed in amph role)

SUPPORT AND MISCELLANEOUS 18
 1 AOT; 5 ARS; 1 *Polochny C* AGF, 5 trg, 1 sail trg, 2

mod *Moma* AGI; 3 AGHS

NAVAL AVIATION (2,500)
ORGANISATION
Flying hours MiG-21: 60
AIRCRAFT
FTR 2 sqn with MiG-21 (all to transfer to Air Force in 2001)
RECCE 1 sqn with PZL TS-11 *Iskra*
SAR 1 sqn with PZL-3RM
TPT 1 sqn with PZL-W3, An-28
HELICOPTERS
ASW 1 sqn with Mi-14PL
SAR 1 sqn with Mi-14PS, Mi-2RM
TPT 1 sqn with Mi-2
EQUIPMENT
26 cbt ac, 11 armed hel
AIRCRAFT
26 **MiG-21** • 17 **PZL TS-11** *Iskra* • 5 **PZL-3RM** • 2 **PZL-W3** • 3 **An-28**
HELICOPTERS
11 **Mi-14PL** • 3 **Mi-14PS** • 3 **Mi-2RM** • 5 **Mi-2**

Air Force 43,735

(incl 15,538 conscripts); 212 cbt ac, no attack hel
Flying hours 60–120
2 AD Corps - North and South
FTR 1 sqn with 22 MiG-29 (18 -29U, 4 -29UB)
FGA/RECCE 5 sqn with 99 Su-22 (81 -22M4, 18 -22UM3K)
4 sqn with 91 MiG-21 (29 -21 bis, 34 -21MF/M, 28 -21UM)
TPT 1 regt and 3 sqn with 51 AT ac (10 An-26, 2 An-28, 12 Yak-40, 2 Tu-154, 25 An-2)
HEL 98 hel (68 Mi-2, 11 Mi-8, 18 W-3 *Sokol*, 1 Bell 412)
TRG 110 TS-11 *Iskra*, 11 PZL I-22 *Iryda*, 34 PZL-130 *Orlik*
AAM AA-2 *Atoll*, AA-3 *Anab*, AA-8 *Aphid*, AA-11 *Archer*
ASM AS-7 *Kerry*
SAM 4 bde and 1 indep regt with 28 btn (3 SA-2, 20 SA-3, 3 SA-4, 2 SA-5)

Forces Abroad

UN AND PEACEKEEPING
BOSNIA (SFOR II): 300; 2 inf coy; (UNMIBH): 1 obs
CROATIA (UNMOP): 1 obs **DROC** (MONUC): 1 obs
ETHIOPIA/ERITREA (UNMEE): 6 obs **GEORGIA** (UNOMIG): 4 obs **IRAQ/KUWAIT** (UNIKOM): 6 obs
LEBANON (UNIFIL): 598: 1 inf bn, mil hospital
SYRIA (UNDOF): 357: 1 inf bn **WESTERN SAHARA** (MINURSO): 6 obs **YUGOSLAVIA** (KFOR): 532; 1 inf bn

Paramilitary 22,000

BORDER GUARDS (Ministry of Interior and Administration) 14,500
11 district units, 2 trg centres

MARITIME BORDER GUARD
about 22 patrol craft: 2 PCC, 10 PCI and 10 PC1<
PREVENTION UNITS OF POLICE (OPP-Ministry of Interior) 7,500
(1,000 conscripts)

Foreign Forces

GERMANY ε70: elm Corps HQ (multinational)

Portugal Por

escudo esc		1999	2000	2001	2002
GDP	esc	21.5tr	22.1tr		
	US$	104bn	104bn		
per capita	US$	15,500	16,370		
Growth	%	3.1	3.3		
Inflation	%	2.3	2.9		
Publ debt	%	58.3	55.6		
Def exp	esc	448bn	475bn		
	US$	2.3bn	2.3bn		
Def bdgt	esc	262bn	274bn	301bn	
	US$	1.3bn	1.3bn	1.3bn	
FMA (US)	US$	0.7m	0.7m	0.75m	
US$1=esc		197	212	228	
Population				9,876,000	
Age		13–17	18–22	23–32	
Men		317,000	365,000	808,000	
Women		298,000	347,000	785,000	

Total Armed Forces

ACTIVE 43,600
(8,130 conscripts, 2,875 women)
Terms of service **Army** 4–8 months **Navy** and **Air Force** 4–12 months

RESERVES 210,930
(all services) (obligation to age 35) **Army** 210,000 **Navy** 930

Army 25,400

5 Territorial Comd (2 mil region, 1 mil district, 2 mil zone)
1 mech inf bde (2 mech inf bn, 1 tk gp, 1 recce sqn, 1 SP arty, 1 AA bty, 1 engr coy)
1 rapid reaction bde (lt intervention bde) (1 inf bn , 1 recce sqn, 1 fd arty gp, 1 AA bty, 1 engr coy)
1 AB bde (2 para bn, 1 recce sqn, 1 fd arty gp, 1 AA bty, 1 ATK, 1 engr coy)
1 composite regt (3 inf bn, 2 AA bty)
1 MP regt, 1 special ops centre

RESERVES

3 territorial def bde (on mob)

2 inf bn (on mob - for rapid reaction bde)

EQUIPMENT

MBT 187: 86 M-48A5, 101 M-60 (8 -A4, 86 -A3)

RECCE 15 V-150 *Chaimite*, 25 ULTRAV M-11

APC 245 M-113, 44 M-557, 81 V-200 *Chaimite*

TOTAL ARTY 318 (excl coastal)

  TOWED 134: **105mm**: 51 M-101, 24 M-56, 21 L119; **155mm**: 38 M-114A1

  SP 155mm: 6 M-109A2

  MOR 107mm: 62 M-30 (14 SP); **120mm**: 116 *Tampella*; **81mm**: incl 21 SP

  COASTAL 21: **150mm**: 9; **152mm**: 6; **234mm**: 6 (inactive)

  RCL 84mm: 162 *Carl Gustav*; **90mm**: 112; **106mm**: 128 M-40

  ATGW 131 TOW (incl 18 M-113, 4 M-901), 83 *Milan* (incl 6 ULTRAV-11)

  AD GUNS 95, incl **20mm**: Rh202; **40mm**: L/60

  SAM 15 *Stinger*, 37 *Chaparral*

DEPLOYMENT

AZORES AND MADEIRA 2,250; 1 composite regt (3 inf bn, 2 AA bty)

Navy 10,800

(incl 1,580 Marines; 360 conscripts, 130 recalled reserves)

COMMANDS Naval Area Comd, **4 Subordinate Comds** Azores, Madeira, North Continental, South Continental

BASES Lisbon (Alfeite), 4 spt bases Leca da Palmeira (North), Portimao (South), Funchal (Madeira), Ponta Delgada (Azores), Montido (naval aviation)

SUBMARINES 2

SSK 2 *Albacora* (Fr *Daphné*) with 12 × 550mm TT

PRINCIPAL SURFACE COMBATANTS 6

FRIGATES 6

FFG 3 *Vasco Da Gama* (MEKO 200) with 8 *Harpoon* SSM, 8 *Sea Sparrow* SAM, 1 × 100mm gun, 6 ASTT, some with 2 *Super Lynx* hel

FF 3 *Commandante João Belo* (Fr *Cdt Rivière*) with 2 × 100mm gun, 6 ASTT

PATROL AND COASTAL COMBATANTS 31

PATROL, OFFSHORE 10

  6 *João Coutinho* PCO with 2 × 76mm gun, hel deck

  4 *Baptista de Andrade* PCO with 1 × 100mm gun, hel deck

PATROL, COASTAL 8 *Cacine* PCC

PATROL, INSHORE 9

  5 *Argos* PCI<, 4 *Centauro* PCI<

RIVERINE 1 *Rio Minho* PCR, 3 *Albatros* PCR

AMPHIBIOUS craft only

  1 LCU

SUPPORT AND MISCELLANEOUS 13

  1 *Berrio* (UK *Green Rover*) AO; 2 trg, 1 ocean trg, 1 div spt; 8 AGHS

NAVAL AVIATION

EQUIPMENT

  HELICOPTERS

  5 *Super Lynx* Mk 95

MARINES (1,580)

2 bn, 1 police, 1 special ops det

1 fire spt coy

EQUIPMENT

  MOR 120mm: 36

Air Force 7,400

Flying hours F-16: 180

1 op air com (COFA), 5 op gps

FGA 2 sqn

  1 with F-16A/B, 1 with *Alpha Jet*

SURVEY 1 sqn with C-212

MR 1 sqn with P-3P

TPT 3 sqn

  1 with C-130H, 1 with C-212, 1 with *Falcon 20* and *Falcon 50*

SAR 2 sqn

  1 with SA-330 hel, 1 with SA-330 hel and C-212

LIAISON/UTILITY 1 sqn with Cessna FTB-337G, hel 1 sqn with SA-330

TRG 2 sqn

  1 with *Socata* TB-30 *Epsilon*, 1 with *Alpha Jet*

hel and multi-engine trg provided by SA-316 and one of C-212 sqns

EQUIPMENT

  51 cbt ac (plus 15 in store), no attack hel

  AC 25 *Alpha Jet* (FGA/trg) (plus 15 in store) • 20 **F-16A/B** (17 -A, 3 -B) • 6* **P-3P** (MR) • 6 **C-130H** (tpt/SAR) • 24 **C-212** (20 -A (12 tpt/SAR, 1 Nav trg, 2 ECM trg, 5 fisheries protection), 4 -B (survey)) • 12 **Cessna 337** (utility) • 1 *Falcon 20* (tpt, cal) • 3 *Falcon* **50** (tpt) • 16 *Epsilon* (trg)

  HEL 10 **SA-330** (SAR/tpt) • 18 **SA-316** (trg, utl)

  MISSILES

  ASM AGM-65B/G *Maverick*, AGM-84A *Harpoon*

  AAM AIM-9Li *Sidewinder*

Forces Abroad

SAO TOME & PRINCIPE

5 Air Force, 1 C-212

UN AND PEACEKEEPING

BOSNIA (SFOR II): 330; 1 inf bn(-) **CROATIA** (UNMOP): 1 obs **EAST TIMOR** (UNTAET): 924, 24 Air Force, 1 C-130H **WESTERN SAHARA** (MINURSO): 4 obs **YUGOSLAVIA** (KFOR): 313

Paramilitary 46,400

NATIONAL REPUBLICAN GUARD 25,600
Commando Mk III APC **hel** 7 SA-315
PUBLIC SECURITY POLICE 20,800

Foreign Forces

NATO HQ South Atlantic at Lisbon (Oeiras)
US 990: **Navy** 50 **Air Force** 940

Spain Sp

peseta pts		1999	2000	2001	2002
GDP	pts	93tr	100tr		
	US$	569bn	568bn		
per capita	US$	17,721	18,703		
Growth	%	3.7	3.7		
Inflation	%	2.3	3.4		
Publ debt	%	63.3	61.1		
Def exp	pts	1.2tr	1.3tr		
	US$	7.2bn	7.2bn		
Def bdgt	pts	1,201bn	1,231bn	1,303bn	
	US$	7.4bn	7.0bn	6.9bn	
US$1=pts		163	176	189	
Population					39,727,000
Age		13–17	18–22	23–32	
Men		1,156,000	1,435,000	3,326,000	
Women		1,084,000	1,355,000	3,166,000	

Total Armed Forces

ACTIVE 143,450

(incl 3,300 conscripts, some 9,400 women)
Terms of service 9 months (conscription ends 31 Dec 2001)

RESERVES 328,500

Army 265,000 **Navy** 18,500 **Air Force** 45,000

Army 92,000

6,600 women)
4 Area Defence Forces
1 rapid action div with 1 AB, 1 airmobile, 1 Legion lt
    inf bde, 1 Legion special ops unit
1 mech inf div with 2 mech inf, 1 armd bde, 1 lt armd
    cav, 1 SP arty, 1 AAA, 1 engr regt
1 mtn, 1 cav bde
1 army avn bde with 1 attack, 1 med tpt, 4 tac tpt bn
1 special ops comd with 3 special ops bn
1 fd arty comd with 4 SP arty regt and 2 AAA regt
1 engr comd with 4 engr bn
1 AD comd (2 HAWK SAM, 7 AD bn)
1 coast arty comd (2 coast arty regt)
2 Legion regt

RESERVES (cadre units)
1 cav bde, 3 inf bde, 1 fd arty regt, 1 engr regt

EQUIPMENT
MBT 688: 150 AMX-30 EM2, 164 M-48A5E, 244 M-
    60A3TTS, 108 *Leopard* 2 A4 (Ge tempy transfer), 22
    Centauro B-1
RECCE 318 BMR-VEC (78 **90mm**, 208 **25mm**, 32
    20mm gun)
AIFV 58 *Pizarro*
APC 2,023: 1,337 M-113 (incl variants), 686 BMR-600
    (incl variants)
TOTAL ARTY 931 (excluding coastal)
    TOWED 310: **105mm**: 170 M-56 pack, 56 L 118;
    155mm: 84 M-114
    SP 194: **105mm**: 34 M-108; **155mm**: 96 M-109A1/
    A5; **203mm**: 64 M-110A2
    COASTAL ARTY 53: **6in**: 44; **305mm**: 6; **381mm**: 3
    MRL 140mm: 18 *Teruel*
    MOR 120mm: 409 (incl 226 SP); plus **81mm**: 1,314
    (incl 102 SP)
ATGW 442 *Milan* (incl 106 SP), 28 HOT, 200 TOW
    (incl 68 SP)
RCL 106mm: 507
AD GUNS 20mm: 460 GAI-BO1; **35mm**: 92 GDF-002
    twin; **40mm**: 183 L/70
SAM 24 I HAWK, 18 *Roland*, 13 *Skyguard/Aspide*, 108
    Mistral
HELICOPTERS 153 (28 attack)
    27 HU-21C/HU-21L (AS-532UL), 48 HU-10B, 45
    HA/HR-15 (17 with **20mm** guns, 28 with HOT), 6
    HU-18, 10 HR-12B, 17 HT-17D
SURV 2 AN/TPQ-36 (arty, mor)

DEPLOYMENT
CEUTA AND MELILLA 8,100; 2 armd cav, 2 Spanish
    Legion, 2 mot inf, 2 engr, 2 arty regt; 2 lt AD bn, 1
    coast arty bn
BALEARIC ISLANDS 4,500; 1 mot inf regt: 3 mot inf
    bn; 1 mixed arty regt: 1 fd arty, 1 AD; 1 engr bn
CANARY ISLANDS 8,600; 3 mot inf regt each 2 mot
    inf bn; 1 mot inf bn, 2 mixed arty regt each: 1 fd arty,
    1 AD bn; 2 engr bn

Navy 26,950

(incl 700 Naval Aviation, 5,600 Marines; 1,600 women)
NAVAL ZONES Cantabrian, Strait (of Gibraltar),
Mediterranean, Canary (Islands)
BASES El Ferrol (La Coruña) (Cantabrian HQ), San
Fernando (Cadiz) (Strait HQ), Rota (Cadiz) (Fleet HQ),
Cartagena (Murcia) (Mediterranean HQ), Las Palmas
(Canary Islands HQ), Palma de Mallorca and Mahón
(Menorca)
SUBMARINES 8
SSK 8
    4 *Galerna* (Fr *Agosta*) with 20 *L-5* HWT
    4 *Delfin* (Fr *Daphné*) with 12 *L-5* HWT

PRINCIPAL SURFACE COMBATANTS 16

AIRCRAFT CARRIERS 1 (CVS) *Príncipe de Asturias*
(16,200t); air gp: typically 6 to 10 AV-8/AV-8B, 4 to 6
SH-3D ASW hel, 2 SH-3D AEW hel, 2 AB 212

FRIGATES 15

FFG 15

6 *Santa Maria* (US *Perry*) with 1 × 1 SM-1 MR
Standard SAM/*Harpoon* SSM launcher, 1 × 76mm
gun, 2 × 3 ASTT, 2 SH-60B hel

5 *Baleares* with 8 *Harpoon* SSM, 1 × 1 SM-1 MR
Standard SAM, 1 × 127mm gun, 2 × 2 ASTT, 8
ASROC SUGW

4 *Descubierta* with 8 *Harpoon* SSM, *Sea Sparrow* SAM,
1 × 76mm gun, 6 ASTT, 1 × 2 ASW RL

PATROL AND COASTAL COMBATANTS 37

PATROL, OFFSHORE 8

4 *Serviola* PCO with 1 × 76mm gun, 1 *Chilreu* PCO, 1
Descubierta PCO, 1 *Alboran* PCO, 1 *Arnomendi* PCO

PATROL, COASTAL 10 *Anaga* PCC

PATROL, INSHORE 19

6 *Barceló* PFI<, 4 *Conejera* PCI<, 2 *Toralla* PCI, 7 PCI<

MINE WARFARE 11

MINE COUNTERMEASURES 11

1 *Descubierta* MCCS

4 *Segura* MHO

6 *Júcar* (US *Adjutant*) MSC

AMPHIBIOUS 4

2 *Hernán Cortés* (US *Newport*) LST, capacity: 400 tps,
500t veh, 3 LCVPs, 1 LCPL, 1 hel

2 *Galicia* LPD, capacity 620 tps, 2500t veh, 6 LCVP/4
LCU, 4 hel

Plus 13 craft: 3 LCT, 2 LCU, 8 LCM

SUPPORT AND MISCELLANEOUS 27

2 AO; 3 AWT, 3 AK; 5 AT, 1 diver spt, 4 trg, 1 sail trg;
6 AGHS, 2 AGOR

NAVAL AVIATION (700)

ORGANISATION

Flying hours AV-8B: 160

AIRCRAFT

FGA 2 sqn with AV-8B/AV-8B plus

LIAISON 1 sqn with Cessna *Citation* II

HELICOPTERS

ASW 1 sqn with SH-3D/G *Sea King* (modified to
SH-3H standard), 1 sqn with SH-30B

EW 1 flt with SH-30B

COMD/TPT 1 sqn with AB-212

TRG 1 sqn with Hughes 500

EQUIPMENT

17 cbt ac; 37 armed hel

AIRCRAFT

9 **AV-8B** • 8 **AV-8B** plus • 3 **Cessna** *Citation* II

HELICOPTERS

10 **AB-212** • 11 **SH-3D** (8 -**H** ASW, 3 -**D** AEW) • 10
Hughes 500 • 6 **SH-60B**

MISSILES

AAM AIM-9 *Sidewinder*, *Maverick*, AMRAAM

ASW Mk 46 LWT

ASUW *Harpoon*

MARINES (5,600)

1 mne bde (3,000); 2 inf, 1 spt bn; 3 arty bty

5 mne garrison gp

EQUIPMENT

MBT 16 M-60A3

AFV 17 *Scorpion* lt tk, 16 LVTP-7 AAV, 4 BLR

TOWED ARTY 105mm: 12 M-56 pack

SP ARTY 155mm: 6 M-109A

ATGW 24 TOW-2, 18 *Dragon*

RL 90mm: C-90C

SAM 12 *Mistral*

Air Force 24,500

(incl 3,300 conscripts, 1,200 women)

Flying hours EF-18: 180; F-5: 220; *Mirage* F-1: 180

CENTRAL AIR COMMAND (Torrejon) 4 wg

FTR 2 sqn with EF-18 (F-18 *Hornet*)

RECCE 1 sqn with RF-4C

TPT 8 sqn

3 with C-212, 2 with CN-235, 1 with *Falcon* (20, 50,
900), 1 with Boeing 707 (tkr/tpt), 1 with AS-332 (tpt)

SPT 4 sqn

1 with CL-215, 1 with Boeing 707, C-212 (EW) and
Falcon 20, 1 with C-212, AS-332 (SAR), 1 with C-212
and Cessna *Citation*

TRG 3 sqn

1 with C-212, 1 with C-101, 1 with Beech *Bonanza*

EASTERN AIR COMMAND (Zaragosa) 2 wg

FTR 3 sqn

2 with EF-18, 1 OCU with EF-18

TPT 2 sqn

1 with C-130H, 1 tkr/tpt with KC-130H

SPT 1 sqn with **ac** C-212 (SAR) **hel** AS-330

STRAIT AIR COMMAND (Seville) 4 wg

FTR 3 sqn

2 with *Mirage* F-1 CE/BE

1 with EF/A-18

LEAD-IN TRG 2 sqn with F-5B

MP 1 sqn with P-3A/B

TRG 6 sqn

2 hel with *Hughes* 300C, S-76C, EC-120B *Colibri*, 1
with C-212, 1 with E-26 (*Tamiz*), 1 with C-101, 1
with C-212

CANARY ISLANDS AIR COMMAND (Gando) 1 wg

FGA 1 sqn with EF-18

TPT 1 sqn with C-212

SAR 1 sqn with **ac** F-27 **hel** AS-332 (SAR)

LOGISTIC SUPPORT COMMAND (MALOG)

1 trials sqn with C-101, C-212 and F-5A, EF/A-18, F-1

EQUIPMENT

211 cbt ac, no armed hel

AC 90 EF/A-18 A/B (ftr, OCU) • 35 **F-5B** (FGA) • 65

Mirage **F-1CF/-BE/-EE** of which 52 (48 FIC/CE/ EDA/EE and 4 FIB/BE) modernised • 14* **RF-4C** (recce) 7* **P-3** (2 **-A** (MR), 5 **-B** (MR)) • 4 **Boeing 707** (tkr/tpt) • 7 **C-130H/H-30** (tpt), 5 **KC-130H** (tkr) • 78 **C-212** (34 tpt, 9 SAR, 6 recce, 26 trg, 2 EW, 1 trials) • 2 **Cessna 560** *Citation* (recce) • 74 **C-101** (trg) • 15 **CL-215** (spt) • 5 *Falcon* **20** (3 VIP tpt, 2 EW) • 1 *Falcon* **50** (VIP tpt) • 2 *Falcon* **900** (VIP tpt) • 21 **Do-27** (U-9, liaison/trg) • 3 **F-27** (SAR) • 37 **E-26** (trg) • 20 **CN-235** (18 tpt, 2 VIP tpt) • 25 **E-24** (*Bonanza*) trg

HEL 5 **SA-330** (SAR) • 16 **AS-332** (10 SAR, 6 tpt) • 13 **Hughes 300C** (trg) • 8 **S-76C** (trg) • 3 **EC 120B** *Colibri* (a further 12 being delivered)

MISSILES

AAM AIM-7 *Sparrow*, AIM-9 *Sidewinder*, AIM-120 AMRAAM, R-530

ASM AGM-65G *Maverick*, AGM-84D *Harpoon*, AGM-88A HARM

SAM *Mistral*, *Skyguard/Aspide*

Forces Abroad

UN AND PEACEKEEPING

BOSNIA (SFOR II): 1,200; 2 inf coy, 1 cav sqn **ETHIOPIA/ERITREA** (UNMEE): 5 incl 3 obs **ITALY** (Deliberate Forge) 5 F/A-18, 1 KC-130 **YUGOSLAVIA** (KFOR): 1,300; 4 inf coy, 1 cav sqn

Paramilitary 71,260

GUARDIA CIVIL 70,500

(incl 2,200 conscripts); 9 regions, 19 inf *tercios* (regt) with 56 rural bn, 6 traffic security gp, 6 rural special ops gp, 1 special sy bn; 20 BLR APC, 18 Bo-105, 5 BK-117 hel

GUARDIA CIVIL DEL MAR 760

32 PCI

Foreign Forces

NATO HQ Joint Command South-West (JCSOUTHWEST)
US 2,190: **Navy** 1,760 **Air Force** 360 **USMC** 70

Turkey Tu

lira L		1999	2000	2001	2002
GDP	L	79,814tr	135,790tr		
	US$	186bn	210bn		
per capita	US$	5,733	6,101		
Growth	%	-2.3	6.0		
Inflation	%	64.8	54.9		
Debt	US$	111bn	110bn		
Def exp	L	4,367tr	6,999tr		
	US$	9.7bn	10.8bn		
Def bdgt	L	3,818tr	4,742tr	5,875tr	
	US$	8.9bn	7.3bn	5.1bn	
FMA (US)	US$	1.5m	1.5m	1.6m	
US$1=L		428,920	646,623	1,152	

Population			67,652,000	Kurds ε20%
Age		**13–17**	**18–22**	**23–32**
Men		3,924,000	3,251,000	6,242,000
Women		3,839,000	3,097,000	5,886,000

Total Armed Forces

ACTIVE 515,100

(incl ε391,000 conscripts) *Terms of service* 18 months

RESERVES 378,700

(all to age 41) **Army** 258,700 **Navy** 55,000 **Air Force** 65,000

Army ε402,000

(incl ε325,000 conscripts)
4 army HQ: 9 corps HQ • 1 mech div (1 mech, 1 armd bde) • 1 mech div HQ • 1 inf div • 14 armd bde (each 2 armd, 2 mech inf, 2 arty bn) • 17 mech bde (each 2 armd, 2 mech inf, 1 arty bn) • 9 inf bde (each 4 inf, 1 arty bn) • 4 cdo bde (each 4 cdo bn) • 1 inf regt • 1 Presidential Guard regt • 5 border def regt • 26 border def bn

RESERVES

4 coastal def regt • 23 coastal def bn

EQUIPMENT

Total figures in ( ) were reported to CFE on 1 Jan 2001
MBT 4,205 (2,478): 2,876 M-48 A5T1/T2 (1,300 to be stored), 932 M-60 (658 -A3, 274-A1), 397 *Leopard* (170-1A1, 227-1A3)
RECCE some *Akrep*, some ARSV (*Cobra*)
TOTAL AIFV/APC (2,966)
AIFV 650 AIFV
APC 830 AAPC, 2,813 M-113/-A1/-A2
TOTAL ARTY (2,953)
TOWED 105mm: M-101A1; **155mm**: 517 M-114A1\A2; **203mm**: 162 M-115
SP 105mm: 365 M-52T, 26 M-108T; **155mm**: 222 M-44T1; **175mm**: 36 M-107;

203mm: 219 M-110A2
MRL 70mm: 24; **107mm**: 48; **122mm**: T-122;
227mm: 12 MLRS (incl ATACMS)
MOR 2,021: **107mm**: 1,264 M-30 (some SP);
120mm: 757 (some 179 SP); plus **81mm**: 3,792
incl SP
ATGW 943: 186 *Cobra*, 365 TOW SP, 392 *Milan*
RL M-72
RCL 57mm: 923 M-18; **75mm**: 617; **106mm**: 2,329 M-
40A1
AD GUNS 1,664: **20mm**: 439 GAI-DO1; **35mm**: 120
GDF-001/-003; **40mm**: 803 L60/70, 40 T-1, 262 M-
42A1
SAM 108 *Stinger*, 789 *Redeye* (being withdrawn)
SURV AN/TPQ-36 (arty, mor)
AC 168: 3 Cessna 421, 34 *Citabria*, 4 B-200, 4 T-42A, 98
U-17B, 25 T-41D
HELICOPTERS
ATTACK 37 (26) AH-1W/P
SPT 50 S-70A, 19 AS-532UL, 12 AB-204B, 64 AB-
205A, 20 AB-206, 2 AB-212, 28 H-300C, 3 OH-58B,
94 UH-1H
UAV CL-89 (AN/USD-501), *Gnat* 750, *Falcon* 600

Navy 53,000

(incl 3,100 Marines, 1,050 Coast Guard, 34,500 con-
scripts)
BASES Ankara (Navy HQ and COMEDNOREAST),
Izmir (HQ Fleet, HQ Aegean), Istanbul (HQ Northern
area and Bosphorus), Antalya (HQ Southern area),
Eregli (HQ Black Sea), Mersin (HQ Mediterranean),
Aksaz Bay, Gölcük (HQ Fleet), Iskenderun

SUBMARINES 13

SSK 10
6 *Atilay* (Ge Type 209/1200) with 8 × 533mm TT (SST
4 HWT)
4 *Preveze* (Ge Type 209/1400) with *Harpoon* SSM, 8 ×
533mm TT
SSC 3
1 *Canakkale* (US *Guppy*)† with 10 × 533mm TT
2 *Hizirreis* (US *Tang*) with 8 × 533mm TT (Mk 37
HWT)

PRINCIPAL SURFACE COMBATANTS 23

FRIGATES 23
FFG 22
6 *Gaziantep* (US *Perry*) with 4 *Harpoon* SSM, 36 SM-1
MR SAM, 1 × 76mm gun, 2 × 3 ASTT
4 *Yavuz* (Ge MEKO 200) with 8 *Harpoon* SSM, *Sea
Sparrow* SAM, 2 × 3 ASTT, 1 AB-
212 hel
8 *Muavenet* (US *Knox*-class) with *Harpoon* SSM (from
ASROC launcher), 1 × 127mm gun, 4 ASTT, 8
ASROC SUGW, 1 AB 212 hel
4 *Barbaros* (MOD Ge MEKO 200) with 8 *Harpoon*
SSM, 8 *Sea Sparrow* SAM, 1 × 127mm gun, 6 ×
324mm TT, 1 AB-212 hel

FF 1 *Berk* with 4 × 76mm guns, 6 ASTT, 2 Mk 11
Hedgehog

PATROL AND COASTAL COMBATANTS 49

MISSILE CRAFT 21
3 *Kilic* PFM with 8 × *Harpoon* SSM, 1 × 76mm gun
8 *Dogan* (Ge Lürssen-57) PFM with 8 *Harpoon* SSM, 1
× 76mm gun
8 *Kartal* (Ge *Jaguar*) PFM with 4 *Penguin* 2 SSM, 2 ×
533mm TT
2 *Yildiz* PFM with 8 *Harpoon* SSM, 1 × 76mm gun
PATROL CRAFT 28
COASTAL 28
1 *Girne* PFC, 6 *Sultanhisar* PCC, 2 *Trabzon* PCC, 4
PGM-71 PCC, 1 *Bora* (US *Asheville*) PFC, 10 AB-25
PCC, 4 AB-21 PCC

MINE WARFARE 24

MINELAYERS 1
1 *Nusret* (400 mines) plus 3 ML tenders
(*Bayraktar*, *Sarucabey* and *Çakabey* LST have
minelaying capability)
MINE COUNTERMEASURES 23
5 *Edineik* (Fr *Circe*) MHC
8 *Samsun* (US *Adjutant*) MSC
6 *Karamürsel* (Ge *Vegesack*) MSC
4 *Foça* (US *Cape*) MSI (plus 8 MCM tenders)

AMPHIBIOUS 8

1 *Osman Gazi* LST: capacity 980 tps, 17 tk, 4 LCVP
2 *Ertugru* LST (US *Terrebonne Parish*): capacity 400 tps,
18 tk
2 *Bayraktar* LST (US LST-512): capacity 200 tps, 16 tk
2 *Sarucabey* LST: capacity 600 tps, 11 tk
1 *Çakabey* LSM: capacity 400 tps, 9 tk
Plus about 59 craft: 35 LCT, 2 LCU, 22 LCM

SUPPORT AND MISCELLANEOUS 27

1 *Akar* AO, 5 spt tkr, 2 Ge *Rhein* plus 3 other depot
ships, 3 tpt, 2 AR; 3 ARS, 5 AT, 1 div spt; 2 AGHS

NAVAL AVIATION

EQUIPMENT
16 armed hel
HELICOPTERS
ASW 3 AB-204AS, 13 AB-212
TRG 7 TB-20

MARINES (3,100)

1 regt, HQ, 3 bn, 1 arty bn (18 guns), spt units

Air Force 60,100

(incl 31,500 conscripts) 2 tac air forces (divided between
east and west), 1 tpt comd, 1 air trg comd, 1 air log comd
Flying hours 180
FGA 11 sqn
1 OCU with F-5A/B, 4 (1 OCU) with F-4E, 6 (1 OCU)
with F-16C/D
FTR 7 sqn
2 with F-5A/B, 2 with F-4E, 3 with F-16C/D

RECCE 2 sqn with RF-4E
TPT 5 sqn
  1 with C-130B/E, 1 with C-160D, 2 with CN-235, 1
  VIP tpt unit with *Gulfstream*, *Citation* and CN 235
TKR 2 KC-135R
LIAISON 10 base flts with **ac** T-33 **hel** UH-1H
SAR hel AS-532
TRG 3 sqn
  1 with T-41, 1 with SF-260D, 1 with T-37B/C and T-
  38A. Each base has a stn flt with **hel** UH-1H and in
  some cases, **ac** CN-235
SAM 4 sqn with 92 *Nike Hercules*, 2 sqn with 86 *Rapier*
EQUIPMENT
  505 cbt ac, no attack hel
  AC 240 **F-16C/D** (210 **-C**, 30 **-D**); further package of
  32, including 20 recce configuration, to be delivered by 2002) • 87 **F/NF-5A/B** (FGA) (48 being
  upgraded as lead-in trainers) • 178 **F-4E** (92 FGA,
  47 ftr, 39 **RF-4E** (recce)) (54 being upgraded to
  Phantom 2000) • 13 **C-130B/E** (tpt) • 7 **KC-135R** •
  19 **C-160D** (tpt) • 2 *Citation* VII (VIP) • 50 **CN-
  235** (tpt/EW) • 38 **SF-260D** (trg) • 34 **T-33** (trg) •
  60 **T-37** trg • 70 **T-38** (trg) • 28 **T-41** (trg)
  HEL 20 **UH-1H** (tpt, liaison, base flt, trg schools), 20
  AS-532 (14 SAR/6 CSAR) being delivered
MISSILES
  AAM AIM-7E *Sparrow*, AIM 9 S *Sidewinder*, AIM-120
  AMRAAM
  ASM AGM-65 *Maverick*, AGM-88 HARM, AGM-142,
  Popeye 1

Forces Abroad

TURKISH REPUBLIC OF NORTHERN CYPRUS
ε36,000; 1 corps; 386 M-48A5 MBT; 265 M-113, 211
AAPC APC; 72 **105mm**, 18 **155mm**, 12 **203mm** towed;
60 **155mm** SP; 127 **120mm**, 148 **107mm**, 175 **81mm** mor;
20mm, 16 **35mm**; 48 **40mm** AA guns; **ac** 3 **hel** 4 **Navy** 1
PCI

UN AND PEACEKEEPING
BOSNIA (SFOR II): 1,200; 1 inf bn gp; (UNMIBH): 1
obs **EAST TIMOR** (UNTAET): 2 obs **GEORGIA**
(UNOMIG): 5 obs **IRAQ/KUWAIT** (UNIKOM): 6 obs
ITALY (Deliberate Forge): 4 F-16 C **YUGOSLAVIA**
(KFOR): 940

Paramilitary

GENDARMERIE/NATIONAL GUARD ε150,000 (Ministry
of Interior, Ministry of Defence in war)
50,000 reserve; some *Akrep* recce, 535 BTR-60/-80, 25
Condor APC **ac** 2 Dornier 28D, 0-1E **hel** 19 Mi-17, 8
AB-240B, 6 AB-205A, 8 AB-206A, 1 AB-212, 14 S-70A
COAST GUARD 2,200
(incl 1,400 conscripts); 48 PCI, 16 PCI<, plus boats, 2 tpt

Foreign Forces

NATO HQ Joint Command South-East
(JCSOUTHEAST), HQ 6 Allied Tactical Air Force (6
ATAF)
OPERATION NORTHERN WATCH
UK Air Force 160; 4 *Jaguar* GR-3A/-B, 2 VC-10 (tkr)
US 2,040: **Navy** 20 **Air Force** 1,800; 1 wg (**ac** on det
only), numbers vary (incl F-16, F-15C, KC-135, E-3B/C,
C-12, HC-130, HH-60) **USMC** 220
US Installations for seismic monitoring
ISRAEL Periodic det of F-16 at Akinci

United Kingdom UK

pound £		1999	2000	2001	2002
GDP	£	890bn	934bn		
	US$	1.4tr	1.4tr		
per capita	US$	22,300	23,422		
Growth	%	1.7	3.0		
Inflation	%	1.6	2.9		
Publ debt	%	53	54.4		
Def exp	£	22.6bn	22.8bn		
	US$	36.4bn	34.6bn		
Def bdgt	£	22.3bn	23.3bn	23.8bn	
	US$	35.9bn	35.3bn	34.0bn	
US$1=£		0.64	0.66	0.7	

Population			58,938,000	

Northern Ireland 1,600,000 **Protestant** 56% **Roman
Catholic** 41%

Age	13–17	18–22	23–32
Men	1,926,000	1,772,000	3,997,000
Women	1,839,000	1,690,000	3,826,000

Total Armed Forces

ACTIVE 211,430
(incl 16,430 women, and 3,780 locally enlisted personnel)

RESERVES 247,100
Army 177,400 (Regular 137,100) **Territorial Army** (TA)
40,300 **Navy/Marines** 26,350 (Regular 22,300, Volunteer
Reserves 4,050) **Air Force** 43,350 (Regular 41,700,
Volunteer Reserves 1,650)

Strategic Forces (1,900)

SLBM 58 msl in 4 SSBN, fewer than 200 op available
warheads
  SSBN 4
  4 *Vanguard* SSBN each capable of carrying 16 *Trident*
  D5; will not deploy with more than 48 warheads per
  boat, but each msl could carry up to 12 MIRV (some
  Trident D5 msl loaded with single warheads for sub-
  strategic role)

EARLY WARNING

Ballistic-Missile Early-Warning System (BMEWS) station at Fylingdales

Army 113,950

(incl 7,750 women, 3,780 Gurkhas and 486 Full Time Reserve)

regt normally bn size

1 Land Comd HQ • 3 (regenerative) div HQ (former mil districts) and UK Spt Comd (Germany) • 1 armd div with 3 armd bde, 3 arty, 4 engr, 1 avn, 1 AD regt • 1 mech div with 3 mech bde (*Warrior/Saxon*), 3 arty, 4 engr, 1 AD regt • ARRC Corps tps: 3 armd recce, 2 MLRS, 2 AD, 1 engr regt (EOD) • 1 joint hel comd incorporating 1 air aslt bde • 1 AD bde • 2 log bde • 14 inf bde HQ (3 control ops in N. Ireland, remainder mixed regular and TA for trg/administrative purposes only)

1 joint NBC regt (Army/RAF)

Summary of combat arm units

6 armd regt • 4 armd recce regt • 6 mech inf bn (*Saxon*) • 9 armd inf bn (*Warrior*) • 25 lt inf bn (incl 3 AB bn (1 only in para role), 2 Gurkha) • 1 SF (SAS) regt • 11 arty regt (2 MLRS, 6 SP, 2 fd (1 cdo, 1 air aslt), 1 trg) • 4 AD regt (2 *Rapier*, 2 HVM) • 10 engr regt • 4 army avn regt

HOME SERVICE FORCES

N. Ireland 4,200: 6 inf bn (2,400 full-time)

Gibraltar 350: 1 regt (150 full-time)

Falkland Island Defence Force 60

RESERVES

Territorial Army 4 lt recce, 15 inf bn, 2 SF (SAS), 3 arty (1 MLRS, 1 fd, 1 obs), 4 AD, 5 engr, 1 avn regt

EQUIPMENT

MBT 636: 294 *Challenger* 2, 338 *Challenger*, 4 *Chieftain*

LT TK 1 *Scorpion*

RECCE 318 *Scimitar*, 138 *Sabre*, 11 *Fuchs*

TOTAL AIFV/APC 2,984 (incl 'look-a-likes')

   AIFV 575 *Warrior*, 11 AFV 432 *Rarden*

   APC 1,150 AFV 432, 597 FV 103 *Spartan*, 650 *Saxon*, 1 *Saracen*

TOTAL ARTY 475

   TOWED 233: **105mm**: 166 L-118/-119; **155mm**: 67 FH-70

   SP 155mm: 179 AS-90

   MRL 227mm: 63 MLRS

MOR 81mm: 543 (incl 110 SP)

ATGW 876 *Milan*, 60 *Swingfire* (FV 102 *Striker* SP), TOW

RL 94mm: LAW-80

SAM 135 HVM (SP), 147 *Starstreak* (LML), 335 *Javelin*, 72 *Rapier* (some 24 SP)

SURV 19 *Cymbeline* (mor)

AC 6 BN-2

ATTACK HEL 258: 133 SA-341, 125 *Lynx* AH-1/-7/-9

UAV *Phoenix*

LANDING CRAFT 6 RCL, 4 LCVP, 4 workboats

Navy (RN) 43,530

(incl 6,740 Naval Aviation, 6,740 Royal Marines Command; 3,330 women)

ROYAL FLEET AUXILIARY (RFA)

(2,400 civilians man major spt vessels)

MARINE SERVICES

(280 MoD civilians and 780 commercial contractors) 203 craft, provides harbour/coastal services

BASES UK Northwood (HQ Fleet, CINCEASTLANT), Devonport, Faslane, Portsmouth (HQ); Culdrose, Prestwick, Yeovilton (all Naval Aviation); **Overseas** Gibraltar

SUBMARINES 16

STRATEGIC SUBMARINES 4 SSBN

TACTICAL SUBMARINES 12

   SSN 12

   5 *Swiftsure* with *Spearfish* or *Tigerfish* HWT and *Sub-Harpoon* SSM (3 in refit); one (*Splendid*) with 12 *Tomahawk* Block III LAM

   7 *Trafalgar* with *Spearfish* and *Tigerfish* HWT and *Sub-Harpoon* SSM (2 in refit); two (*Triumph* and *Trafalgar*) with 12 *Tomahawk* Block III LAM

PRINCIPAL SURFACE COMBATANTS 34

AIRCRAFT CARRIERS 3: 2 mod *Invincible* CVS each with **ac** 8 FA-2 *Sea Harrier* V/STOL **hel** 12 *Sea King*, up to 9 ASW, 3 AEW; plus 1 *Invincible* in extended refit

   Full 'expeditionary air group' comprises 8 *Sea Harrier* FA-2, 8 RAF *Harrier* GR-7, 2 *Sea King* ASW, 4 *Sea King* AEW

DESTROYERS 11

   DDG 11

   7 Type 42 Batch 1/2 with 2 × *Sea Dart* SAM, 1 × 114mm gun, 6 × 324mm ASTT, 1 *Lynx* hel

   4 Type 42 Batch 3 with wpns as above

FRIGATES 20

   FFG 20

   4 *Cornwall* (Type 22 Batch 3) with 8 *Harpoon* SSM, *Seawolf* SAM, 1 × 114mm gun, 6 × 324mm ASTT (*Stingray* LWT)

   1 *Broadsword* (Type 22 Batch 2) with 4 × MM 38 *Exocet* SSM, *Seawolf* SAM, 6 × 324mm ASTT (*Stingray* LWT), 2 *Lynx* or 1 *Sea King* hel

   15 *Norfolk* (Type 23) with 8 *Harpoon* SSM, *Seawolf* VL SAM, 1 × 114mm gun, 4 × 324mm ASTT (*Stingray* LWT)

PATROL AND COASTAL COMBATANTS 23

PATROL, OFFSHORE 7

   2 *Castle* PCO, 5 *Island* PCO

PATROL, INSHORE 16

   16 *Archer* (incl 8 trg)

MINE WARFARE 23

MINELAYER no dedicated minelayer, but all SS have limited minelaying capability

MINE COUNTERMEASURES 23

11 *Hunt* MCC (4 mod *Hunt* MCC/PCC), 12 *Sandown* MHO (5 batch 1, 7 batch 2)

AMPHIBIOUS 6

1 *Fearless* LPD† with 4 LCU, 4 LCVP; capacity 350 tps, 15 tk, 3 hel

1 *Ocean* LPH with 4 LVCP, capacity 800 tps, 18 hel

4 *Sir Bedivere* LSL; capacity 340 tps, 16 tk, 1 hel (RFA manned)

Plus 23 craft: 9 LCU, 14 LCVP

(see Army for additional amph lift capability)

SUPPORT AND MISCELLANEOUS 20

UNDER WAY SUPPORT 8

2 *Fort Victoria* AO, 1 *Olwen* AO, 3 *Rover* AO, 2 *Fort Rosalie* AF (all RFA manned)

MAINTENANCE AND LOGISTIC 7

1 *Diligence* AR, 1 *Sea Crusader* AK, 1 *Sea Centurion* AK, 4 AOT (all RFA manned)

SPECIAL PURPOSE 2

1 *Argus* AVB (RFA manned), 1 *Endurance* (ice patrol)

SURVEY 3

1 *Scott* AGHS, 1 *Roebuck* AGHS, 1 *Gleaner* AGHS

NAVAL AVIATION (Fleet Air Arm)

(6,740 incl 330 women)

ORGANISATION

Flying hours *Harrier*: 275

A typical CVS air group consists of 8 *Sea Harrier* FA-2, 7 *Sea King* (ASW), 3 *Sea King* (AEW) (can carry 8 RAF *Harrier* GR-7 instead of 4 *Sea King*)

AIRCRAFT

FTR/ATK 2 sqn with *Sea Harrier* FA-2 plus 1 trg sqn with *Harrier* T-4/-8

TRG 1 sqn with *Jetstream*

HELICOPTER

ASW 4 sqn with *Sea King* Mk-6

ASW/ATK 2 sqn with *Lynx* HAS-3/HMA8 (in indep flt)

AEW 1 sqn with *Sea King* Mk-2

COMMANDO SPT 2 sqn with *Sea King* Mk-4

SAR 1 sqn with *Sea King* Mk-5

TRG 2 sqn with *Merlin* Mk-1, 1 sqn with *Sea King* Mk-4

FLEET SPT 13 *Mystère-Falcon* (civil registration), 1 Cessna *Conquest* (civil registration), 1 Beech *Baron* (civil registration) 5 GROB 115 (op under contract)

EQUIPMENT

34 cbt ac (plus 21 in store), 120 armed hel

AIRCRAFT

29 **Sea Harrier FA-2** (plus 19 in store) • 5* **T-4/T-8** (trg) plus 2 in store • 15 *Hawk* (spt) • 10 *Jetstream* • 7 **T-2** (trg) • 3 **T-3** (spt)

HELICOPTER

92 **Sea King** (49 **HAS-5/6**, 33 **HC-4**, 10 **AEW-2**) • 36 **Lynx** HAS-3 • 23 **Lynx** HAS-8, 12 **EH-101** *Merlin*

MISSILES

ASM *Sea Skua*

AAM AIM-9 *Sidewinder*, AIM-120C AMRAAM

ROYAL MARINES COMMAND (6,740, incl RN and Army)

1 cdo bde: 3 cdo; 1 cdo arty regt (Army); 1 cdo AD bty (Army), 2 cdo engr (1 Army, 1 TA), 1 LCA sqn. Serving with RN/Other comd: 1 sy gp, Special Boat Service, 1 cdo lt hel sqn, 2 LCA sqn, 3 dets/naval parties

EQUIPMENT

MOR 81mm

ATGW *Milan*

SAM *Javelin*

HEL 9 SA-341 (*Gazelle*); plus 3 in store, 6 *Lynx* AH-7

AMPH 24 RRC, 4 LACV

RESERVES

About 1,000

Air Force (RAF) 53,950

(incl 5,480 women)

Flying hours *Tornado* GRI/4: 188, F3: 181; *Harrier* GR-7: 204; *Jaguar*: 199

FGA/BBR 5 sqn with *Tornado* GRI/4

FGA 5 sqn

3 with *Harrier* GR-7, 2 with *Jaguar* GR-1A/GR-3/3A

FTR 5 sqn with *Tornado* F-3 plus 1 flt in the Falklands

RECCE 4 sqn

2 with *Tornado* GR-1A/4A, 1 with *Canberra* PR-9, 1 with *Jaguar* GR-1A/GR-3/3A

MR 3 sqn with *Nimrod* MR-2

AEW 2 sqn with E-3D *Sentry*

ELINT 1 sqn with *Nimrod* R-1

TPT/TKR 3 sqn

1 with VC-10 C1K, VC-10 K-3/-4, and 1 with *Tristar* K-1/KC-2A, plus 1 VC-10 flt in the Falklands

TPT 1 sqn with C-17, 4 sqn with *Hercules* C-130K/J, 1 comms sqn with **ac** BAe-125, BAe-146 **hel** AS-355 (*Twin Squirrel*)

TARGET FACILITY/CAL 1 sqn with *Hawk* T-1/T-1A

OCU 6: *Tornado* GR-1/4, *Tornado* F-3, *Jaguar* GR-3/3A/ T2A, *Harrier* GR-7/-T10, *Hercules* C-130K/J, *Nimrod* MR-2

TRG *Hawk* T-1/-1A/-1W, *Jetstream* T-1, *Bulldog* T-1, G.115E *Tutor*, HS-125 *Dominie* T-1, *Tucano* T-1, T-67 *Firefly*

TAC HEL 9 sqn

1 with CH-47 (*Chinook*) and SA-341 (*Gazelle* HT3), 1 with *Wessex* HC-2, 2 with SA-330 (*Puma*), 1 with CH-47 and *Sea King* HAR-3, 2 with CH-47, 1 with *Wessex* HC-2 and SA-330 (*Puma*), 1 with *Merlin* HC3

SAR 2 hel sqn with *Sea King* HAR-3/3A

TRG *Sea King* (including postgraduate training on 203(R) sqn), Tri-Service Defence Helicopter School with AS-350 (*Single Squirrel*) and Bell-412

EQUIPMENT

427 cbt ac (plus 121 in store), no armed hel

AC 217 *Tornado* (80 **GR-4/4A**, 43 **GR-1/1A**), 94 **F-3** (plus 50 **GR** and 19 **F-3** in store) • 53 *Jaguar* (43 **GR-1A/3/3A**, 10 **T-2A/B** (plus 26 in store)) • 60 *Harrier* (51 **GR-7**, 9 **T-10** (plus 24 **GR-7** and 2 **T-10** in store)) • 121 *Hawk* **T-1/1A-W** (incl 76* (**T1-A**)) (plus 16 in store) • 7 *Canberra* (2 **T-4**, 5 **PR-9**) • 24 *Nimrod* (3 **R-1** (ECM), 21* **MR-2** (MR) • 7 *Sentry* (**E-3D**) (AEW) • 4 **C-17A** • 9 *Tristar* (2 **K-1** (tkr/pax), 4 **KC-1** (tkr/pax/cgo), 2 **C-2** (pax), 1 **C-2A** (pax) • 20 **VC-10** (11 **C-1K** (tkr/cgo), 4 **K-3** (tkr), 5 **K-4** (tkr)) • 51 *Hercules* **C-130** (26 **-K**, 25 **-J**) • 6 **BAe-125 CC-3** (comms) • 2 *Islander* **CC-MK2** • 2 **BAe-146** Mk 2 (VIP tpt) • 88 *Tucano* (trg) (plus 40 in store) • 11 *Jetstream* (trg) • 10 *Dominie* (trg) • 88 *Tutor* (trg) • 46 *Firefly* 160 (trg)

HEL 15 *Wessex* • 38 **CH-47** (*Chinook*) • 6 *Merlin* HC3 (22 on order) • 39 **SA-330** (*Puma*) • 25 *Sea King* • 38 **AS-350B** (*Single Squirrel*) • 3 **AS-355** (*Twin Squirrel*) • 9 **Bell-412EP**

MISSILES

ASM AGM-65G2 *Maverick*, AGM-84D-1 *Harpoon*
AAM ASRAAM, AIM-9L/M *Sidewinder*, *Sky Flash* AMRAAM
ARM ALARM

ROYAL AIR FORCE REGIMENT

6 fd sqn, 4 gd based air defence sqns with 24 *Rapier* field standard C fire units; joint *Rapier* trg unit (with Army), 3 tactical Survival To Operate (STO) HQs

VOLUNTEER RESERVE AIR FORCES (Royal Auxiliary Air Force/RAF Reserve): 3 field sqns, 1 gd based AD sqn, 1 air movements sqn, 2 medical sqns, 2 intelligence sqns, 5 op support sqns covering STO duties, 1 C-130 Reserve Aircrew flt, 1 HQ augmentaion sqn, 1 mobile meteorological unit

Deployment

ARMY

LAND COMMAND

Assigned to ACE Rapid Reaction Corps **Germany** 1 armd div plus Corps cbt spt tps **UK** 1 mech inf div, 1 air aslt bde (assigned to MND(C)); additional TA units incl 8 inf bn, 2 SAS, 3 AD regt **Allied Command Europe Mobile Force** (*Land*) (AMF(L)): UK contribution 1 inf BG (incl 1 inf bn, 1 arty bty, 1 sigs sqn)

HQ NORTHERN IRELAND

(some 11,100 (incl 200 RN, 1,100 RAF), plus 3,900 Home Service committed to N. Ireland); 3 inf bde HQ, up to 15 major units in inf role (5 in province, 1 committed reserve, up to 4 roulement inf bn, 5 Home Service inf bn), 1 engr, 1 avn regt.

The roles of the remainder of Army regular and TA units incl Home Defence and the defence of Dependent Territories, the Cy Sovereign Base Areas and Bru.

NAVY

FLEET (CinC is also CINCEASTLANT and COMNAVNORTHWEST): almost all regular RN forces are declared to NATO, split between SACLANT and SACEUR

MARINES 1 cdo bde (declared to SACLANT)

AIR FORCE

STRIKE COMMAND responsible for all RAF front-line forces. Day-to-day control delegated to 3 Gps **No. 1** (All RAF front-line fast jet ac, excl *Harrier*) **No. 2** (AT, AAR, airborne C3I support and RAF regt) **No. 3** (Joint Force *Harrier* (all *Harrier* GR7s and RN *Sea Harrier*), maritime assets (*Nimrod* MR-2 and SAR hel force) and 1 HQ Augmentation sqn)

Forces Abroad

ANTARCTICA 1 ice patrol ship (in summer only)
ASCENSION ISLAND RAF 37
BELGIUM RAF 196
BELIZE Army 180
BRUNEI Army some 1,070: 1 Gurkha inf bn, 1 hel flt (3 hel)
CANADA Army 200 trg and liaison unit **RAF** 143; routine trg deployment of **ac** *Tornado, Harrier, Jaguar*
CYPRUS 3,250: **Army** 2,150; 2 inf bn, 1 engr spt sqn, 1 hel flt **RAF** 1,100; 1 hel sqn (4 *Wessex* HC-2), plus **ac** and 1 AD radar on det
FALKLAND ISLANDS 1,500: **Army** 1 inf coy on det **RN** 1 DDG/FFG, 1 PCO, 1 spt, 1 AR **RAF**, 4 *Tornado* F-3, 1 *Hercules* C-1, 1 VC-10 K (tkr), 2 *Sea King* HAR-3, 2 CH-47 hel, 1 sqn RAF regt (*Rapier* SAM)
GERMANY Army 17,100; 1 corps HQ (multinational), 1 armd div
GIBRALTAR 565: **Army** 60; Gibraltar regt 150 **RN/Marines** 240; 2 PCI; Marine det, base unit **RAF** some 115; periodic ac det
INDIAN OCEAN (*Armilla Patrol*): 1 DDG/FFG, 1 spt **Diego Garcia** 1 Marine/naval party
NEPAL Army 90 (Gurkha trg org)
NETHERLANDS RAF 137
OMAN & MUSCAT RAF 33
SIERRA LEONE 660: **Army** 370 incl Short term trg team (340), **RN** 68, International Mil Advisory and Trg Team 62, Tri-service HQ and spt 160
USA RAF 136
WEST INDIES 1 DDG/FFG, 1 spt

UN AND PEACEKEEPING

BAHRAIN (*Southern Watch*): RAF 50 1 VC-10 (tkr)
BOSNIA (SFOR II): 2,600 (incl log and spt tps in Croatia); 1 Augmented Brigade HQ (multinational) with 2 recce sqn, 1 armd inf bn, 1 tk sqn, 2 arty bty, 1 engr sqn, 1 hel det **hel** 2 *Sea King* MK4 (RN), 3 *Lynx* AH-7 (Army), 2 *Gazelle* (Army), 3 CH-47 *Chinook* (RAF)
CYPRUS (UNFICYP): 403: 1 inf bn, 1 hel flt, engr spt
EAST TIMOR (UNTAET): 4 obs **GEORGIA** (UNOMIG): 7 obs **IRAQ/KUWAIT** (*Southern Watch*):

RAF 300; 8 *Tornado* GRI; (UNIKOM): 11 obs **ITALY** (*Deliberate Forge*): 350; 4 *Harrier* GR-7, 1 K-1 *Tristar* (tkr), 2 E-3D *Sentry* (periodic) **SAUDI ARABIA** (*Southern Watch*): RAF 569; 6 *Tornado* F3 **SIERRA LEONE** (UNOMSIL): 24 incl 16 obs **TURKEY** (*Northern Watch*): RAF 185; 4 *Jaguar* GR-3/3A, 2 VC-10 (tkr) **YUGOSLAVIA** (KFOR): 3,900; 1 armd bde with 1 armd, 1 armd inf, 1 inf bn, 1 arty, 1 engr regt; hel 2 *Puma* **MILITARY ADVISERS** 458 in 26 countries

Foreign Forces

US 11,280: **Army** 380 **Navy** 1,220 **Air Force** 9,550; 1 Air Force HQ (3rd Air Force) 1 ftr wg (2 sqn with 27 F-15E, 1 sqn with 27 F-15C/D), 1 air refuelling wg with 15 KC-135, 1 Special Ops Gp with 5 MC-130P, 5 MC-130H, 1 C-130E, 8 MH-53J, 1 Recce sqn with 2 RC-135Js (ac not permanently assigned), 1 naval air flt with 2 C-12 **USMC** 120
NATO HQ Allied Naval Forces North (HQNAVNORTH), HQ East Atlantic (HQEASTLANT) Combined Air Operations Centre (CAOC) 9, High Wycombe

---

Albania Alb

leke		1999	2000	2001	2002
GDP	leke	460bn	523bn		
	US$	3.9bn	3.8bn		
per capita	US$	4,000	5,539		
Growth	%	8.0	7.8		
Inflation	%	0.4	-0.2		
Debt	US$	975m	1,100m		
Def exp	leke	ε18.7bn			
	US$	139m			
Def bdgt	leke	5.8bn			
	US$	43m			
FMAa (US)	US$	0.6m	0.6m		
FMA (Tu)	US$	5m			
US$1=leke		1.34	1.42	1.46	
Population					**3,028,000**

Muslim 70% Albanian Orthodox 20% Roman Catholic 10%; Greek ε3–8%

Age	13–17	18–22	23–32
Men	191,000	176,000	329,000
Women	174,000	161,000	304,000

Total Armed Forces

ACTIVE ε27,000

The Alb armed forces are being re-constituted. The army is to consist of 5 inf divs, a cdo bde of 3 bn, 10 inf bde, 1 mech inf bde, 4 tk bde and 4 arty bde. Restructuring is now

planned to be completed by 2010. Eqpt details are primarily those reported prior to the country-wide civil unrest of 1997 and should be treated with caution.

Army some 20,000

EQUIPMENT
MBT ε400: incl T-34 (in store), T-59
LT TK 35 Type-62
RECCE 15 BRDM-1
APC 103 PRC Type-531
TOWED ARTY 122mm: 425 M-1931/37, M-30, 208 PRC Type-60; **130mm**: 100 PRC Type-59-1; **152mm**: 90 PRC Type-66
MRL 107mm: 50 PRC Type-63
MOR 82mm: 259; **120mm**: 550 M-120; **160mm**: 100 M-43
RCL 82mm: T-21
ATK GUNS 45mm: M-1942; **57mm**: M-1943; **85mm**: 61 D-44 PRC Type-56; **100mm**: 50 Type-86
AD GUNS 125 incl **37mm**: M-1939; **57mm**: S-60

Navy ε2,500

BASES Durrës, Sarandë, Shëngjin, Vlorë
PATROL AND COASTAL COMBATANTS† 20
TORPEDO CRAFT 11 PRC *Huchuan* PHT with 2 533mm TT
PATROL CRAFT 9
  1 PRC *Shanghai* II PCC, 3 Sov Po-2 PFI<, 5 (US) PB Mk3 (for Coast Guard use)<
MINE WARFARE 3
MINE COUNTERMEASURES† 3
  3 Sov T-301 MSC, (plus 3 Sov T-43 MSO in reserve)
SUPPORT AND MISCELLANEOUS 2
  1 AGOR, 1 AT†

Air Force 4,500

98 cbt ac†, no armed hel
Flying hours 10–15
FGA 1 air regt with 10 J-2 (MiG-15), 14 J-6 (MiG-17), 23 J-6 (MiG-19)
FTR 2 air regt
  1 with 20 J-6 (MiG-19), 10 J-7 (MiG-21)
  1 with 21 J-6 (MiG-19)
TPT 1 sqn with 10 C-5 (An-2), 3 Il-14M, 6 Li-2 (C-47)
HEL 1 regt with 20 Z-5 (Mi-4), 4 SA-316, 1 Bell 222
TRG 8 CJ-5, 15 MiG-15UTI, 6 Yak-11
SAM† some 4 SA-2 sites, 22 launchers

Forces Abroad

UN AND PEACEKEEPING
BOSNIA (SFOR II): 100 **GEORGIA** (UNOMIG): 1 obs

Paramilitary

INTERNAL SECURITY FORCE 'SPECIAL POLICE': 1 bn
(Tirana) plus pl sized units in major towns

BORDER POLICE (Ministry of Public Order): e500

Foreign Forces

NATO (COMMZW): ε2,400 spt tps for KFOR

Armenia Arm

dram d		1999	2000	2001	2002
GDP	d	992bn	1,003bn		
	US$	1.85bn	1.9bn		
per capita	US$	2,900	3,703		
Growth	%	4.0	6.0		
Inflation	%	0.7	-0.8		
Debt	US$	870m	858m		
Def exp	d	ε85bn	ε80bn		
	US$	159m	151.5m		
Def bdgt	d	40bn	40bn	35.6bn	
	US$	75m	76m	65m	
US$1=d		536	528	548	
Population					3,464,000

Armenian Orthodox 94% **Russian** 2% **Kurd** 1%

Age	13–17	18–22	23–32
Men	186,000	180,000	297,000
Women	182,000	176,000	288,000

Total Armed Forces

ACTIVE 42,060

(incl 33,100 conscripts)
Terms of service conscription, 24 months

RESERVES

some mob reported, possibly 210,000 with mil service
within 15 years

Army 38,900

(incl conscripts)
5 Army Corps HQ
  1 with 2 MRR, 1 recce bn
  1 with 5 MRR, 1 tk bn, 1 recce, 1 arty, 1 MRL bn
  1 with 3 MRR, 1 tk bn, 1 SP arty regt
  1 with 1 MRR, 1 indep special rifle regt, 2 fortified
    areas
  1 with 2 MRR, 1 recce, 1 maint bn
1 mot rifle trg bde
2 arty regt (1 SP), 1 ATK regt
1 SAM bde, 2 SAM regt
1 mixed avn regt, 1 avn sqn
1 SF, 1 engr regt

EQUIPMENT
  MBT 8 T-54, 102 T-72
  AIFV 80 BMP-1, 7 BMP-1K, 5 BMP-2, 12 BRM-1K, 6
    BMD-1
  APC 11 BTR-60, 21 BTR-70, 4 BTR-80, plus 100 look-
    a-likes
  TOTAL ARTY 229
  TOWED 121: **122mm**: 59 D-30; **152mm**: 2 D-1, 34
    D-20, 26 2A36
  SP 38: **122mm**: 10 2S1; **152mm**: 28 2S3
  MRL 51: **122mm**: 47 BM-21, 4 WM-80
  MOR 120mm: 19 M-120
  ATK GUNS ε35: **85mm**: D-44; **100mm**: T-12
  ATGW 9 AT-3 *Sagger*, 13 AT-6 *Spiral*
  SAM 25 SA-2/-3, 27 SA-4, 20 SA-8, ε15 SA-9/-13
  SURV GS-13 (veh), *Long Trough* ((SNAR-1) arty), *Pork
    Trough* ((SNAR-2/-6) arty), *Small Fred/Small Yawn*
    (arty), *Big Fred* ((SNAR-10) veh/arty)

Air and Defence Aviation Forces 3,160

8 cbt ac, 12 armed hel
FGA 1 sqn with 5 Su-25, 1 MiG-25, 2 L-39
HEL 1 sqn with 7 Mi-24P* (attack), 3 Mi-24K*, 2 Mi-
  24R*, 6 Mi-8MT (combat support), 9 Mi-2 (utility)
TPT 1 An-24, 1 An-32
TRG CENTRE 6 An-2, 10 Yak-52, 6 Yak-55/Yak-18T

Paramilitary 1,000

MINISTRY OF INTERNAL AFFAIRS

4 bn: 44 BMP-1, 1 BMP-1K, 5 BRM-1K, 2 BMD-1, 24
BTR-60/-70/-152

MINISTRY OF NATIONAL SECURITY

35 BMP-1, 3 BRM-1K, 2 BMD-1, 23 BTR-60/-70

Foreign Forces

RUSSIA 2,900: **Army** 1 mil base (div) with 74 MBT, 17
APC, 129 ACV, 84 arty/MRL/mor **Air Defence** 1 sqn
18 MiG-29, 2 SA-12 (S-300) bty, SA-6 bty

Austria A

schilling ÖS		1999	2000	2001	2002
GDP	ÖS	2.7tr	2.8tr		
	US$	198bn	194bn		
per capita	US$	23,400	24,235		
Growth	%	2.2	3.2		
Inflation	%	0.9	2.4		
Publ Debt	%	64.9	62.9		
Def exp	ÖS	22.5bn	23.9bn		
	US$	1.7bn	1.6bn		
Def bdgt	ÖS	22.5bn	22.3bn	22.4bn	
	US$	1.7bn	1.5bn	1.5bn	
US$1=ÖS		13.5	14.6	14.6	

Population			8,257,000
Age	**13–17**	**18–22**	**23–32**
Men	245,000	237,000	576,000
Women	233,000	228,000	555,000

Total Armed Forces

(Air Service forms part of the Army)

ACTIVE some 34,600

(incl ε17,400 active and short term; ε17,200 conscripts; excl ε9,500 civilians; some 66,000 reservists a year undergo refresher trg, a proportion at a time) *Terms of service* 7 months recruit trg, 30 days reservist refresher trg during 8 years (or 8 months trg, no refresher); 60–90 days additional for officers, NCOs and specialists

RESERVES

72,000 ready (72 hrs) reserves; 990,000 with reserve trg, but no commitment. Officers, NCOs and specialists to age 65, remainder to age 50

Army 34,600

(incl ε17,200 conscripts)
2 corps
- 1 with 2 inf bde (each 3 inf bn), 1 mech inf bde (2 mech inf, 1 tk, 1 recce, 1 SP arty bn), 1 SP arty regt, 1 recce, 2 engr, 1 ATK bn
- 1 with 1 inf bde (3 inf bn), 1 mech inf bde (1 mech inf, 2 tk, 1 SP arty bn), 1 SP arty regt, 1 recce, 1 engr bn
- 1 Provincial mil comd with 1 inf regt (plus 5 inf bn on mob)
- 8 Provincial mil comd (15 inf bn on mob)

EQUIPMENT

MBT 163 M-60A3 (being withdrawn), 114 *Leopard* 2A4
LT TK 180 *Kuerassier* JPz SK (plus 133 in store)
APC 425 Saurer 4K4E/F (incl look-a-likes), 63 *Pandur*
TOWED ARTY 105mm: 104 IFH (M-101 deactivated); **155mm**: 20 M-2A1 (deactivated)
SP ARTY 155mm: 209 M-109A2/-A3/-A5ÖE
FORTRESS ARTY 155mm: 24 SFK M-2 (deactivated)
MOR 81mm: 498; **107mm**: 73; **120mm**: 241 M-43
ATGW 378 RBS-56 *Bill*, 88 RJPz-(HOT) *Jaguar* 1
RCL 84mm: 2,196 *Carl Gustav*; **106mm**: 374 M-40A1 (in store)
ANTI-TANK GUNS
  STATIC 105mm: some 227 L7A1 (*Centurion* tk – being deactivated)
AD GUNS 20mm: 145 (plus 323 in store)

MARINE WING

(under School of Military Engineering)
2 river patrol craft<; 10 unarmed boats

Air Force (6,500)

(ε3,400 conscripts); 52 cbt ac, 11 armed hel
Flying hours 120 ftr/FGA, 180 hel/tpt
1 air div HQ, 3 air regt, 3 AD regt, 1 air surv regt
FTR/FGA 1 wg with 23 SAAB J-35Oe
LIAISON 12 PC-6B
TPT 2 *Skyvan* 3M, 1 CASA 235-300 (on lease)
HEL
  LIAISON/RECCE 11 OH-58B*
  TPT 22 AB-212
  UTILITY/SAR 23 SA-319 *Alouette* III, 9 S-70A on order
TRG 16 PC-7, 29* SAAB 105Oe hel 11 AB-206A
MISSILES
  AAM AiM-9P3
AD 76 *Mistral* with Thomson RAC 3D radars; 89 **20mm** AA guns: 74 Twin **35mm** AA towed guns with 37 *Skyguard* radars; air surv *Goldhaube* with *Selenia* MRS-403 3D radars and Thomson RAC 3D. 1 3DLRR ordered

Forces Abroad

UN AND PEACEKEEPING
BOSNIA (SFOR II): 56 **CYPRUS** (UNFICYP): 62 **ETHIOPIA/ERITREA** (UNMEE): 7 incl 3 obs **GEORGIA** (UNOMIG): 3 obs **IRAQ/KUWAIT** (UNIKOM): 2 obs **MIDDLE EAST** (UNTSO): 3 obs **SYRIA** (UNDOF): 373; 1 inf bn **WESTERN SAHARA** (MINURSO): 3 obs **YUGOSLAVIA** (KFOR): 480

Azerbaijan Az

manat m		1999	2000	2001	2002
GDP	m	18.0tr	21tr		
	US$	4.5bn	4.8bn		
per capita	US$	1,950	2,181		
Growth	%	7.4	11.3		
Inflation	%	-8.5	1.8		
Debt	US$		1,158m		
Def exp	m	ε800bn	ε950bn		
	US$	203m	217m		
Def bdgt	m	472bn	520bn		
	US$	120m	119m		
FMA (Tu)	US$	3m			
US$1=m		3,950	4,378	4,579	
Population					7,752,000

Daghestani 3% **Russian** 2% **Armenian** 2–3% mostly in Nagorno-Karabakh

Age	13–17	18–22	23–32
Men	413,000	372,000	618,000
Women	393,000	345,000	610,000

Total Armed Forces

ACTIVE 72,100

Terms of service 17 months, but can be extended for ground forces

RESERVES

some mob 575,700 with mil service within 15 years

Army 62,000

4 Army Corps HQ • 22 MR bde • 2 arty bde, 1 ATK regt

EQUIPMENT

MBT 262: 136 T-72, 126 T-55

AIFV 253: 95 BMP-1, 91 BMP-2, 3 BMP-3, 41 BMD-1, 23 BRM-1

APC 25 BTR-60, 28 BTR-70, 11 BTR-80, 11 BTR-D, 306 MT-LB

TOTAL ARTY 303

TOWED 153: **122mm**: 97 D-30; **152mm**: 32 D-20, 24 2A36

SP 122mm: 14 2S1

COMBINED GUN/MOR 120mm: 28 2S9

MRL 122mm: 56 BM-21

MOR 120mm: 52 PM-38

ATGW ε250: AT-3 *Sagger*, AT-4 *Spigot*, AT-5 *Spandrel*, AT-7 *Saxhorn*

SAM ε40 SA-4/-8/-13

SURV GS-13 (veh); *Long Trough* ((SNAR-1) arty), *Pork Trough* ((SNAR-2/-6) arty), *Small Fred/Small Yawn* (veh, arty), *Big Fred* ((SNAR-10) veh, arty)

Navy 2,200

BASE Baku

PATROL AND COASTAL COMBATANTS 6

PATROL, CRAFT 6

1 *Turk*, 1 *Osa* II, 2 *Stenka* PFI<, 1 *Zhuk* PCI<, 1 *Svetlyak* PCI<

MINE WARFARE 5

MINE COUNTERMEASURES 5

3 *Sonya* MSC, 2 *Yevgenya* MSI

AMPHIBIOUS 2

2 *Polnochny* LSM capacity 180 tps

SUPPORT AND MISCELLANEOUS 3

1 *Vadim Popov* (research), 2 *Balerian Uryvayev* (research)

Air Force and Air Defence 7,900

35† cbt ac, 15 attack hel

FGA regt with 4 Su-17, 4 Su-24, 2 Su-25, 4 MiG-21

FTR sqn with 18* MiG-25, 3* MiG-25UB

TPT 4 ac (1 An-12, 3 Yak-40)

TRG 26 L-29, 12 L-39, 1 Su-17

HEL 1 regt with 7 Mi-2, 13 Mi-8, 15* Mi-24

IN STORE ac 27 MiG-25, 2 MiG-21, 1 Su-24, 2 L-29

SAM 100 SA-2/-3/-5

Forces Abroad

UN AND PEACEKEEPING

YUGOSLAVIA (KFOR II): 34

Paramilitary ε15,000+

MILITIA (Ministry of Internal Affairs) 10,000+

EQPT incl 7 BTR-60/-70/-80

BORDER GUARD (Ministry of Internal Affairs) ε5,000

EQPT incl 168 BMP-1/-2 AIFV, 19 BTR-60/-70/-80 APC, 2 US PCI<

Opposition

ARMENIAN ARMED GROUPS

ε18,000 in Nagorno-Karabakh, perhaps 40,000 on mob (incl ε8,000 personnel from Arm)

EQPT (reported) 316 incl T-72, T-55 MBT; 324 ACV incl BTR-70/-80, BMP-1/-2; 322 arty incl D-44, 102 D-30, 53 D-20, 99 2A36, 44 BM-21, KS-19

Belarus Bel

rubel r		1999	2000	2001	2002
GDP	r	2.9tr	9.1tr		
	US$	9.3bn	9.35bn		
per capita	US$	7,100	7,960		
Growth	%	3.0	6.0		
Inflation	%	293	169		
Debt	US$	1,312m	829m		
Def exp	r	ε145tr	364tr		
	US$	466m	373m		
Def bdgt	r	32.6tr	81.7bn	170.8bn	
	US$	105m	83.7m	125.7m	
FMAa (US) US$					
US$1=r		311	976	1,359	

a Excl US Cooperative Threat Reduction programme: **1992–96** US$119m budget, of which US$44m spent by Sept 1996. Programme continues through 1999

Population				10,208,000
Russian 13% Polish 4% Ukrainian 3%				
Age	13–17	18–22	23–32
Men	407,000	398,000	715,000
Women	393,000	387,000	711,000

Total Armed Forces

ACTIVE 82,900

(incl 17,100 in centrally controlled units and MoD staff; 4,000 women; 30,000 conscripts)
Terms of service 18 months

RESERVES some 289,500

with mil service within last 5 years

Army 43,600

MoD tps: 1 MRD (trg), 3 indep mob bde, 1 arty div (5 'bde'), 1 arty regt
2 SSM, 1 ATK, 1 *Spetsnaz*
3 Corps
 1 with 3 indep mech, 1 SAM bde, 1 arty, 1 MRL, 1 ATK regt
 1 with 1 SAM bde, 1 arty, 1 MRL regt
 1 with 1 SAM bde, 1 arty, 1 ATK, 1 MRL regt
EQUIPMENT (CFE declared totals as at 1 Jan 2001)
 MBT 1,683 (202 in store): 49 T-55, 1,539 T-72, 95 T-80
 AIFV 1,577 (63 in store): 98 BMP-1, 1,164 BMP-2, 161 BRM, 154 BMD-1
 APC 919 (258 in store): 188 BTR-60, 445 BTR-70, 194 BTR-80, 22 BTR-D, 70 MT-LB
 TOTAL ARTY 1,473 (151 in store) incl
 TOWED 428: **122mm**: 178 D-30; **152mm**: 6 M-1943 (D-1), 58 D-20, 136 2A65, 50 2A36
 SP 570: **122mm**: 236 2S1; **152mm**: 165 2S3, 120 2S5; **152mm**: 13 2S19; **203mm**: 36 2S7
 COMBINED GUN/MOR 120mm: 54 2S9
 MRL 344: **122mm**: 208 BM-21, 11 9P138; **130mm**: 1 BM-13; **220mm**: 84 9P140; **300mm**: 40 9A52
 MOR 120mm: 77 2S12
 ATGW 480: AT-4 *Spigot*, AT-5 *Spandrel* (some SP), AT-6 *Spiral* (some SP), AT-7 *Saxhorn*
 SSM 60 Scud, 36 FROG/SS-21
 SAM 350 SA-8/-11/-12/-13
 SURV GS-13 (arty), *Long Trough* ((SNAR-1) arty), *Pork Trough* ((SNAR-2/-6) arty), *Small Fred/Small Yawn* (veh, arty), *Big Fred* ((SNAR-10) veh, arty)

Air Force 12,000

177 cbt ac, 58 attack hel
Flying hours 15
FGA 29 Su-24, 80 Su-25
FTR 45 MiG-29, 23 Su-27
HELICOPTERS
 ATTACK 53 Mi-24, 4 Mi-24R, 1 Mi-24K
 CBT SPT 29 Mi-6, 125 Mi-8, 8 Mi-24K, 4 Mi-24R
TPT ac 4 Il-76 (plus 12 Il-76 civilian but available for mil use), 3 An-12, 1 An-24, 6 An-26, 1 Tu-134 **hel** 14 Mi-26
AWAITING DISPOSAL 3 MiG-23, 28 Su-17, 2 Su-25, 1 Mi-24

MISSILES
 AAM AA-7, AA-8, AA-10, AA-11
 ASM AS-10, AS-11, AS-14

Air Defence Force 10,200

Consists of SAM/AAA units, ECM/ECCM units
SAM 175 SA-3/-5/-10

Paramilitary 110,000

BORDER GUARDS (Ministry of Interior) 12,000
MINISTRY OF INTERIOR TROOPS 11,000
MILITIA (Ministry of Interior) 87,000

Bosnia-Herzegovina BiH

convertible mark		1999	2000	2001	2002
GDP	US$	ε4.4bn	ε5.1bn		
per capita	US$	ε7,000	ε8,557		
Growth	%	8	10		
Inflation	%	5	4.6		
Debt	US$	3.1bn	2.6bn		
Def exp[a]	US$	ε365m	186.7m		
Def bdgt[a]	US$	318m	163m	130m	
FMA[bc] (US)US$		0.6m	0.6m	0.8m	
$1=convertible mark		1.85	1.86	2.2	

[a] Excl Bosnian Serb def exp
[b] Eqpt and trg valued at εUS$450m from US, Sau, Kwt, UAE, Et and Tu in 1996–99
[c] UNMIBH **1997** US$190m **1998** US$190m; SFOR **1997** εUS$4bn **1998** US$4bn

Population			ε**3,889,000**
Bosnian Muslim 44% **Serb** 33% **Croat** 17%			
Age	13–17	18–22	23–32
Men	195,000	189,000	334,000
Women	185,000	178,000	313,000

Total Armed Forces

In accordance with the Dayton Peace Accords, **BiH** is composed of two **entities**:-
• the (Muslim-Croat) 'Federation of Bosnia and Herzegovina' and
• the (Serbian) 'Republika Srpska'.
The constitution has attributed all competencies regarding defence and military matters to the two entities. There are no armed forces (except for Border Guards and the Brcko-district police) at the State level. The two entities have kept the armed forces they had established throughout the armed conflict until the 1995 Dayton Peace Accord.
The armed forces of the entities are subject to an arms-limitation regime established under the Dayton Peace Accord. An agreement signed by BiH, its two entities, Cr and FRY on 14 June 1996, established ceilings for the armed forces of the parties. In 1999 and 2000 the international community

imposed 15% cuts (total 30%) on the entity armed forces. Further cuts are to be expected.

ACTIVE see individual entries below

Forces of the Federation of Bosnia and Herzegovina

The Armed Forces of the federation are composed of the (predominately Muslim) 'Army of Bosnia and Herzegovina' (VF-B formerly ABiH) and the Bosnian Croat 'Croatian Defence Council' (VF-H formerly HVO). The federation's defence law indicates that the forces are to have joint institutions at the level of Ministry of Defence, General Staff and some formations directly subordinated to the General Staff incl the air force, air defence command and arty div. Integration has been limited so far. Forces are separated from the corps level downwards. The Federation Army (VF) will probably have 4 Corps (3 Muslim, 1 Croat), 14 bde, 1 rapid reaction force (bde) and an arty div.

Army (VF) some 24,000
(VF-B 16,800; VF-H 7,200)

1 Joint HQ • 4 Corps HQ • 11 div HQ • 2 armd, 9 mot inf, 5 arty bde
RESERVES
VF-B: 150,000; 59 inf, 1 arty bde
VF-H: 40,000; 12 Home Guard inf regt, 6 Home Guard inf bn
EQUIPMENT (mostly held under SFOR control in weapon storage sites)
　MBT 205: T-34, T-54, T-55, M-84, AMX-30, M-60A3
　LT TK 8 PT-76
　RECCE 31 AML-90
　AIFV 25 AMX-10P, 10 M-80
　APC 160 incl 80 M-113A2, M-80
　TOTAL ARTY 919 (incl ATK guns)
　　TOWED incl **105mm**: 36 L-118, 28 M-2A1, 20 M-56; **122mm**: 116 D-30; **130mm**: 35 M-46; **152mm**: 18 D-20, M-84; **155mm**: 124 M-114 A2; **203mm**: 2 M-2
　　SP 122mm: 7 2S1
　　MRL 107mm: 31 Type 63; **122mm**: 41 APR-40; **128mm**: 34 M-91
　　MOR 82mm; **120mm**: 400 incl 343 M-75, 13 UBM-52, M-74, M-38
　ATGW 250 AT-3 *Sagger*, AT-4 *Fagot*, *Red Arrow* (TF-8) reported
　ATK GUNS 100mm: 27 T-12/MT-12
　AD GUNS 20mm: M-55, Bov-3; **23mm**: 19 ZU-23; **30mm**: M-53; **57mm**: S-60
　SAM SA-7/-9/-14/-16
　HEL 10 Mi-8/-17, 15 UH-1H
　AC 3 UTVA-75

Republika Srpska Armed Forces (VRS)

Army some 14,000

4 'Corps' HQ • 38 inf/armd/mot inf bde • 12 arty/ATK/AD regt
RESERVES 90,000
　EQUIPMENT (mostly held under SFOR control in weapon storage sites)
　MBT 137 incl T-55, M-84
　AIFV 75 M-80
　APC 64 incl M-60, BOV-M, BTR-50PK, MT-LB
　TOTAL ARTY 547 (incl ATK guns)
　　TOWED 105mm: 72 M-56; **122mm**: 148 D-30, M-1938 (M-30); **130mm**: 36 M-46; **152mm**: 12 D-20
　　SP 122mm: 24 2S1
　　MRL 128mm: 56 M-63; **262mm**: 1 M-87 *Orkan*
　　MOR 120mm: 70 incl M-75, M-52, M-74
　SSM FROG-7
　ATGW about 150 incl AT-3 *Sagger*
　ATK GUNS 100mm: 128 T-12
　AD GUNS 975: incl **20mm**, **23mm** incl ZSU 23-4; **30mm**: M53/59SP; **57mm**: ZSU-57-2; **90mm**
　SAM SA-2, some SA-6/-7B/-9
　AC 6 *Orao*, 13 *Jastreb*, 1 *Super Galeb*
　HEL 20 SA-341, 10 Mi-8

Forces Abroad

UN AND PEACEKEEPING
ETHIOPIA/ERITREA (UNMEE): 8 obs

Foreign Forces

NATO (SFOR II): about 20,000: Be, Ca, Cz, Da, Fr, Ge, Gr, Hu, It, Nl, No, Pl, Por, Sp, Tu, UK, US **Non-NATO** Alb, A, Ea, Lat, L, Mor, R, RF

Bulgaria Bg

leva L		1999	2000	2001	2002
GDP	L	23bn	26.3bn		
	US$	12.0bn	12.8bn		
per capita	US$	4,400	4,832		
Growth	%	2.5	5		
Inflation	%	2.6	10.4		
Debt	US$	9.9bn	10.4bn		
Def exp	L	750m	728m		
	US$	392m	353.7m		
Def bdgt	L	561m	729m	748m	
	US$	293m	354m	337m	
FMA (US)	US$	1.0m	1.0m		
US$1=L		1.91	2.06	2.22	
Population					8,187,000

Turkish 9% Macedonian 3% Romany 3%

Age	13–17	18–22	23–32
Men	277,000	303,000	598,000
Women	263,000	287,000	571,000

Total Armed Forces

ACTIVE ε77,260

(incl about 10,000 centrally controlled staff, 1,300 MoD staff, but excl some 10,000 construction tps; perhaps 49,000 conscripts). Being restructured. To be 45,000 by 2004

Terms of service 9 months

RESERVES 303,000

Army 250,500 **Navy** (to age 55, officers 60 or 65) 7,500
Air Force (to age 60) 45,000

Army 42,400

(incl ε33,300 conscripts)
3 Mil Districts/Corps HQ
   1 with 1 MRD, 1 tk, 2 mech bde • 1 with 1 MRD, 1
   Regional Training Centre (RTC), 1 tk bde • 1 with 2
   MRD, 2 tk, 1 mech bde
Army tps: 4 *Scud*, 1 SS-23, 1 SAM bde, 2 arty, 1 MRL, 3
   ATK, 3 AD arty, 1 SAM regt
1 AB bde
EQUIPMENT
   MBT 1,475: 1,042 T-55, 433 T-72
   ASLT GUN 68 SU-100
   RECCE 58 BRDM-1/-2
   AIFV 100 BMP-1, 114 BMP-23, BMP-30
   APC 1,750: 737 BTR-60, 1,013 MT-LB (plus 1,270
   'look-a-likes')
   TOWED ARTY 100mm: M-1944 (BS-3); **122mm**: 195
   M-30, M-1931/37 (A-19); **130mm**: 72 M-46;
   152mm: M-1937 (ML-20), 206 D-20
   SP ARTY 122mm: 692 2S1
   MRL 122mm: 222 BM-21
   MOR 120mm: M-38, 2S11, B-24, 359 *Tundzha* SP
   SSM launchers: 28 FROG-7, 36 *Scud*, 8 SS-23
   ATGW 200 AT-3 *Sagger*
   ATK GUNS 85mm: 150 D-44; **100mm**: 200 T-12
   AD GUNS 400: **23mm**: ZU-23, ZSU-23-4 SP; **57mm**:
   S-60; **85mm**: KS-12; **100mm**: KS-19
   SAM 20 SA-3, 27 SA-4, 20 SA-6
   SURV GS-13 (veh), *Long Trough* ((SNAR-1) arty), *Pork
   Trough* ((SNAR-2/-6) arty), *Small Fred/Small Yawn*
   (veh, arty), *Big Fred* ((SNAR-10) veh, arty)

Navy ε5,260

(incl ε2,000 conscripts)
BASES Coastal Varna (HQ), Atya **Danube** Vidin (HQ),
Balchik, Sozopol. Zones of operational control at Varna
and Burgas
SUBMARINES 1
SSK 1 *Pobeda* (Sov *Romeo*)-class with 533mm TT†
PRINCIPAL SURFACE COMBATANTS 1
FRIGATES 1

FF 1 *Smeli* (Sov *Koni*) with 1 × 2 SA-N-4 *Gecko* SAM, 2 ×
   twin 76mm guns, 2 × 12 ASW RL
PATROL AND COASTAL COMBATANTS 23
CORVETTES 7
   1 *Tarantul* II FSG with 2 × 2 SS-N-2C *Styx* SSM, 2 × 4
   SA-N-5 *Grail* SAM, 1 × 76mm gun
   4 *Poti* FS with 2 ASW RL, 4 ASTT
   2 *Pauk* I FS with 1 SA-N-5 *Grail* SAM, 2 × 5 ASW RL,
   4 × 406mm TT, 2 × 5 ASW RL
MISSILE CRAFT 6 *Osa* I/II PFM with 4 SS-N-2A/B
   Styx SSM
PATROL, INSHORE 10
   10 *Zhuk* PFI<
MINE WARFARE 20
MINE COUNTERMEASURES 20
   4 *Sonya* MSC, 4 *Vanya* MSC, 4 *Yevgenya* MSI<, 6 *Olya*
   MSI<, 2 PO-2 MSI<
AMPHIBIOUS 2 Sov *Polnocny A* LSM, capacity 150 tps,
   6 tk
   Plus 6 LCU
SUPPORT AND MISCELLANEOUS 16
   3 AO, 1 diving tender, 1 degaussing, 1 AT, 7 AG; 3
   AGHS

NAVAL AVIATION
EQUIPMENT
9 armed hel
   HELICOPTERS
   ASW 9 Mi-14
COASTAL ARTY 2 regt, 20 bty
GUNS 100mm: ε150; **130mm**: 4 SM-4-1
SSM SS-C-1B *Sepal*, SSC-3 *Styx*

NAVAL GUARD

3 coy

Air Force 18,300

181 cbt ac, 43 attack hel, 1 Tactical Aviation corps, 1 AD
corps
Flying hours 30–40
FGA 1 regt with 39 Su-25 (35 -A, 4 -UB)
FTR 3 regt with some 30 MiG-23 (being progressively
   withdrawn), 60 MiG-21 bis, 21 MiG-29 (17 -A, 4 -UB)
RECCE 1 regt with 21 Su-22* (18 -M4, 3 -UM3), 10
MiG-21MF/UM*
TARGET FACILITIES 12 L-29 operated by front-line
sqns
TPT 1 regt with 2 Tu-134, 2 An-24, 5 An-26, 6 L-410, 1
   Yak-40 (VIP)
SURVEY 1 An-30 (*Open Skies*)
HEL 2 regt
   1 with 43 Mi-24 (attack)
   1 with 8 Mi-8, 31 Mi-17, 6 Bell-206
TRG 2 trg schools with 12 L-29 (basic), 30 L-39ZA
   (advanced)

MISSILES
  ASM AS-7 *Kerry*, AS-14 *Kedge*
  AAM AA-2 *Atoll*, AA-7 *Apex*, AA-8 *Aphid*, AA-11
    Archer
  SAM SA-2/-3/-5/-10 (20 sites, some 110 launchers)

Forces Abroad

UN AND PEACEKEEPING
BOSNIA (SFOR II): 1 pl **ETHIOPIA/ERITREA**
(UNMEE): 6 incl 4 obs

Paramilitary 34,000

BORDER GUARDS (Ministry of Interior) 12,000
12 regt; some 50 craft incl about 12 Sov PO2 PCI<
SECURITY POLICE 4,000
RAILWAY AND CONSTRUCTION TROOPS 18,000

Croatia Cr

kuna k		1999	2000	2001	2002
GDP	k	142bn	157bn		
	US$	19.0bn	19.4bn		
per capita	US$	6,700	7,192		
Growth	%	-2.0	3.7		
Inflation	%	3.5	6.2		
Debt	US$	9.1bn	10.8bn		
Def exp	k	5.8bn	4.2bn		
	US$	776m	519.6m		
Def bdgt	k	6.1bn	4.8bn	4.3bn	
	US$	814m	590m	508m	
FMAa (US) US$		0.4m	0.6m	0.5m	
US$1=k		7.47	8.1	8.39	

a UNTAES **1997** US$266m; UNMOP (UNMIBH) **1997**
US$190m **1998** US$190m

Population		ε**4,410,000** Serb 3% Slovene 1%		
Age	13–17	18–22	23–32	
Men	163,000	169,000	328,000	
Women	153,000	159,000	314,000	

Total Armed Forces

ACTIVE ε58,300
(incl ε18–20,000 conscripts)
Terms of service 6 months (wef 1 Jan 01)

RESERVES 140,000
Army 100,000 **Home Defence** 40,000

Army ε50,700

(incl conscripts)

6 Mil Districts • 7 Guard bde (org varies) • 1 mixed
arty/MRL bde • 1 ATK bde • 4 AD bde • 1 engr bde

RESERVES
33 inf 'bde' (incl 1 trg), 8 mixed arty/MRL bde, 2 ATK
bde, 1 engr bde
EQUIPMENT
  MBT 301: 23 T-34, 222 T-55, 53 M-84, 3 T-72M
  RECCE 17 BRDM-2
  AIFV 106 M-80
  APC 15 BTR-50, 13 M-60PB, 9 BOV-VP plus 18 'look-
    a-likes'
  TOTAL ARTY some 1,200 incl
    TOWED 76mm: ZIS-3; **105mm**: 50 M-56, 6 M-
    56H1, 90 M-2A1; **122mm**: 45 M-1938, 42 D-30;
    130mm: 79 M-46; **152mm**: 20 D-20, 18 M-84, 3 M-
    84H1; **155mm**: 19 M-1, 18 M-1H1; **203mm**: 22 M-2
    SP 122mm: 8 2S1
    MRL 122mm: 42 BM-21; **128mm**: 8 M-63, 180 M-91;
    262mm: 2 M-87 *Orkan*
    MOR 1,000 incl: **82mm**: 489; **120mm**: 317 M-75, 6
    UBM-52
  ATGW AT-3 *Sagger* (10 on BRDM-2), AT-4 *Spigot*, AT-
    7 *Saxhorn*, *Milan* reported
  RL 73mm: RPG-7/-22. **90mm**: M-79
  ATK GUNS 100mm: 142 T-12
  AD GUNS 600+: **14.5mm**: ZPU-2/-4; **20mm**: BOV-1
    SP, M-55; **30mm**: M-53/59, BOV-3SP

Navy 3,000

BASES Split (HQ), Pula, Sibenik, Ploce, Dubrovnik
Minor facilities Lastovo, Vis
SUBMARINES 1
SSI 1 *Velebit* (Mod *Una*) for SF ops (4 SDV or 4 mines)
PATROL AND COASTAL COMBATANTS 8
MISSILE CRAFT 2
  1 *Kralj Petar* PFM with 4 or 8 RBS-15 SSM
  1 *Rade Koncar* PFM with 4 RBS-15 SSM
PATROL, COASTAL/INSHORE 6
  1 *Dubrovnik* (Mod Sov *Osa* 1) PFC, can lay mines
  4 *Mirna* PCC, 1 RLM-301 PCI< plus 5 PCR
AMPHIBIOUS craft only
  2 *Silba* LCT, and 9 LCU
SUPPORT AND MISCELLANEOUS 4
  2 AT, 1 *Spasilac* ARS, 1 Sov *Moma* AGHS

MARINES
2 indep inf coy

COASTAL DEFENCE
some 10 coast arty bty, 3 RBS-15 SSM bty

Air Force 4,600

(incl AD forces, conscripts)
44 cbt ac, 22 armed hel

Flying hours 50
FGA/FTR 2 sqn with 20 MiG-21 bis/4 MiG-21 UM
TPT 1 An-2, 2 An-32
HEL 6 Mi-8, 13* Mi-8MTV-1, 9* Mi-24
TRG 20* PC-9, 5 UTVA, 9 Bell 206B
AAM AA-2 *Atoll*, AA-8 *Aphid*
AIR DEFENCE FORCE (2,000)
SAM SA-7, SA-9, SA-10 (reportedly being returned), SA-14/-16

Forces Abroad

UN AND PEACEKEEPING
ETHIOPIA/ERITREA (UNMEE): 5 obs **SIERRA LEONE** (UNAMSIL): 10 obs

Paramilitary 10,000

POLICE 10,000 armed

COAST GUARD boats only

Foreign Forces

UN (UNMOP): 27 obs from 25 countries; (SFOR II): ε500

Cyprus Cy

pound C£		1999	2000	2001	2002
GDP	C£	4.9bn	5.5bn		
	US$	8.7bn	9.6bn		
per capita	US$	13,000	15,409		
Growth	%	4.5	5		
Inflation	%	1.5	4.2		
Debt	US$		11.1bn		
Def exp	C£	200m	266m		
	US$	353m	462m		
Def bdgt	C£	168m	224m	212m	
	US$	297m	389m	321m	
US$1=C£		0.57	0.6	0.66	

UNFICYP **1997** US$46m **1998** US$45m

Population			794,000	Turkish 23%	
Age		13–17	18–22	23–32	
Men		33,000	30,000	53,000	
Women		32,000	28,000	50,000	

Total Armed Forces

ACTIVE 10,000
(incl 8,700 conscripts; 423 women)
Terms of service conscription, 26 months, then reserve to age 50 (officers 65)

RESERVES
60,000 all services

National Guard 10,000

(incl 8,700 conscripts) (all units classified non-active under Vienna Document)
1 Corps HQ, 1 air comd, 1 naval comd • 2 lt inf div HQ • 2 lt inf bde HQ • 1 armd bde (3 bn) • 1 svc spt bde • 1 arty comd (regt) • 1 Home Guard comd • 1 SF comd (regt of 3 bn)
EQUIPMENT
　MBT 104 AMX-30 (incl 52 -B2), 41 T-80U
　RECCE 124 EE-9 *Cascavel*, 15 EE-3 *Jararaca*
　AIFV 27 VAB-VCI, 43 BMP-3
　APC 268 *Leonidas*, 118 VAB (incl variants), 16 AMX-VCI
　TOWED ARTY 75mm: 4 M-116A1 pack; **88mm**: 36 25-pdr (in store); **100mm**: 20 M-1944; **105mm**: 72 M-56; **155mm**: 12 TR F1
　SP ARTY 155mm: 12 F3
　MRL 128mm: 18 FRY M-63
　MOR 376+: **81mm**: 170 E-44, 70+ M1/M29 (in store); **107mm**: 20 M-30/M-2; **120mm**: 108 RT61
　ATGW 45 *Milan* (8 on EE-3 *Jararaca*), 22 HOT (18 on VAB)
　RL 66mm: M-72 LAW; **73mm**: 850 RPG-7; **112mm**: 1,000 *Apilas*
　RCL 90mm: 40 EM-67; **106mm**: 144 M-40A1
　AD GUNS 20mm: 36 M-55; **35mm**: 24 GDF-003 with *Skyguard*; **40mm**: 20 M-1 (in store)
　SAM 60 *Mistral* (some SP), 24 *Aspide*, 6 SA-15

MARITIME WING
1 *Kyrenia* (Gr *Dilos*) PCC
1 *Salamis* PCC< (plus 11 boats)
1 coastal def SSM bty with 3 MM-40 *Exocet*

AIR WING
AC 1 BN-2 *Islander*, 2 PC-9
HEL 2 Bell UH-1H, 3 Bell 206C, 4 SA-342 *Gazelle* (with HOT), 2 Mi-2 (in store)

Paramilitary some 750

ARMED POLICE about 500
1 mech rapid-reaction unit (350), 2 VAB/VTT APC, 1 BN-2A *Maritime Defender* ac, 2 Bell 412 hel
MARITIME POLICE 250
　2 *Evagoras* PFI, 1 *Shaltag* PFI, 5 SAB-12 PCC

Foreign Forces

GREECE 1,250: 1 mech inf bde incl 950 (ELDYK) (Army); 2 mech inf, 1 armd, 1 arty bn, plus ε200 officers/NCO seconded to Greek-Cypriot National Guard
　EQPT 61 M-48A5 MOLF MBT, 80 *Leonidas* APC (from National Guard), 12 M-114 155mm towed arty, 6 M-110A2 203mm SP arty
UK (in Sovereign Base Areas) 3,250: **Army** 2,150; 2 inf bn, 1 eng spt sqn, 1 hel flt **Air Force** 1,100; 1 hel sqn, plus ac on det

UN (UNFICYP) some 1,279; 3 inf bn (Arg, Slvk, UK), tps from Ca, SF, Hu, Irl, N, Nl, Slvn, plus 35 civ pol from 2 countries

'Turkish Republic of Northern Cyprus'

Data presented here represent the *de facto* situation on the island. This in no way implies international recognition as a sovereign state.

Population	ε**215,000**

Total Armed Forces

ACTIVE ε5,000

Terms of service conscription, 24 months, then reserve to age 50

RESERVES 26,000
11,000 **first-line** 10,000 **second-line** 5,000 **third-line**

Army ε5,000

7 inf bn
EQUIPMENT
  MOR 120mm: 73
  ATGW 6 *Milan*
  RCL 106mm: 36

Paramilitary

ARMED POLICE ε150
1 Police SF unit
COAST GUARD
(operated by TRNC Security Forces)
1 *Raif Denktash* PCC • 2 ex-US Mk5 PCC • 2 SG45/SG46 PCC • 1 PCI

Foreign Forces

TURKEY

ARMY ε36,000 (mainly conscripts)
  1 Corps HQ, 2 inf div, 1 armd bde, 1 indep mech inf bde
EQUIPMENT
  MBT 386 M-48A5 T1/T2, 8 M-48A2 (trg)
  APC 211 AAPC, 265 M-113
  TOWED ARTY 105mm: 72 M-101A1; **155mm**: 18 M-114A2; **203mm**: 12 M-115
  SP ARTY 105mm: 36 M-52A1; **155mm**: 24 M-44T
  MOR 81mm: 175; **107mm**: 148 M-30; **120mm**: 54 HY-12
  ATGW 66 *Milan*, 48 TOW
  RL 66mm: M-72 LAW
  RCL 90mm: M-67; **106mm**: 156 M-40A1

AD GUNS 20mm: Rh 202; **35mm**: 16 GDF-003; **40mm**: 48 M-1
SAM 50+ *Stinger*
SURV AN/TPQ-36
AC 3 U-17. Periodic det of F-16C/D, F-4E
HEL 4 UH-1H. Periodic det of S-70A, AS-532UL, AH-1P
NAVY
1 *Caner Goyneli* PCI

Estonia Ea

kroon kn		1999	2000	2001	2002
GDP	kn	75.4bn	91.9bn		
	US$	4.5bn	5.6bn		
per capita	US$	8,600	9,753		
Growth	%	-1.3	6.4		
Inflation	%	1.0	4.0		
Debt	US$	3,305m	3,092m		
Def expa	kn	1,083m	1,331m		
	US$	71m	80.7m		
Def bdgt	kn	1,134m	1,328m	1,657m	
	US$	74m	80m	92.4m	
FMA (US)	US$	0.7m	0.8m	0.8m	
US$1=kn		15.4	16.5	17.86	
a Incl exp on paramilitary forces					
Population					**1,375,000**

Russian 28% **Ukrainian** 3% **Belarussian** 2%

Age	13–17	18–22	23–32
Men	59,000	57,000	103,000
Women	56,000	55,000	100,000

Total Armed Forces

ACTIVE some 4,450

(incl 2,790 conscripts; excl some 390 civilians)
Terms of service 8 months, Navy and Border Guard 11 months

RESERVES some 14,000

Army some 4,040

(incl 2,600 conscripts)
4 Defence Regions, 14 Defence Districts, 5 inf, 1 arty • 1 guard, 1 recce bn • 1 peace ops centre, 1 peacekeeping bn (forming)

RESERVES
Militia 7,500, 15 *Kaitseliit* (Defence League) units
EQUIPMENT
  RECCE 7 BRDM-2
  APC 32 BTR-60/-70/-80
  TOWED ARTY 105mm: 19 M 61-37
  MOR 81mm: 44; **120mm**: 14 2S11

ATGW 10 *Mapats*, 3 RB-56 *Bill*
RL 82mm: 200 B-300
RCL 84mm: 109 *Carl Gustav*; **90mm**: 100 PV-1110;
  106mm: 30 M-40A1
AD GUNS 23mm: 100 ZU-23-2

Navy 300

(incl 140 conscripts)
Lat, Ea and L have set up a joint Naval unit BALTRON with bases at Liepaja, Riga, Ventspils (Lat), Tallinn (Ea), Klaipeda (L)
BASES Tallinn (HQ BALTRON), Miinisadam (Navy and BALTRON)
PATROL AND COASTAL COMBATANTS 3
  CORVETTE 1
  1 *Admiral Pitka* (Da *Beskytteren*) FS with 1 x 76mm gun
  PATROL CRAFT 2
  2 *Rihtiniemi* PCC
MINE WARFARE 3
MINELAYERS 0
  But *Rihtiniemi* can lay mines
MINE COUNTERMEASURES 3
  1 *Lindau* (Ge) MHC
  2 *Kalev* (Ge *Frauenlob*) MSI
SUPPORT AND MISCELLANEOUS 1
  1 *Laine* (Ru *Mayak*) AK

Air Force 110

(incl 50 conscripts)
1 air base and 1 air surv div
Flying hours 70
  ac 2 An-2 (another expected this year), 1 PZL-140
    Wilga **hel** 3 Mi-2, 4 Robinson R-44

Forces Abroad

UN AND PEACEKEEPING
BOSNIA (SFOR II): 46 **MIDDLE EAST** (UNTSO): 1 obs

Paramilitary 2,800

BORDER GUARD (Ministry of Internal Affairs) 2,800
(360 conscripts); 1 regt, 3 rescue coy; maritime elm of Border Guard also fulfils task of Coast Guard
  BASES Tallinn
  PATROL CRAFT 20
  PATROL, OFFSHORE 3
  1 *Kou* (*Silma*), 1 *Linda* (*Kemio*), 1 *Valvas* (US *Bittersweet*)
  PATROL, COASTAL 6
  3 PVL-100 (*Koskelo*), 1 *Pikker*, 1 *Torm* (*Arg*), 1 *Maru* (*Viima*)
  PATROL, INSHORE 11 PCI<
  AVN 2 L-410 UVP-1 *Turbolet*, 5 Mi-8 (In war, subordinated to Air Force staff)

MILITARY RESCUE SERVICES (incl ε250 conscripts)

Finland SF

markka m		1999	2000	2001	2002
GDP	m	718bn	775bn		
	US$	123bn	120bn		
per capita	US$	22,200	23,772		
Growth	%	3.6	5.2		
Inflation	%	1.2	3.4		
Publ debt	%	63.4	50		
Def exp	m	9.9bn	10bn		
	US$	1.7bn	1.5bn		
Def bdgt[a]	m	9.0bn	9.83bn	9.54bn	
	US$	1.7bn	1.5bn	1.4bn	
US$1=m		5.84	6.29	6.78	

[a] Excl supplementary multi-year budget for procurement of m6.1bn (US$1.1bn) approved in Apr 1998

Population			5,190,000
Age	13–17	18–22	23–32
Men	166,000	172,000	330,000
Women	157,000	163,000	316,000

Total Armed Forces

ACTIVE 32,250

(incl 15,500 conscripts, some 500 women)
Terms of service 6–9–12 months (12 months for officers, NCOs and soldiers with special duties)

RESERVES some 485,000 (to be 430,000)

Total str on mob some 485,000 (all services), with 100,000 op forces, 27,000 territorial forces and 75,000 in local forces. Some 35,000 reservists a year do refresher trg: total obligation 40 days (75 for NCOs, 100 for officers) between conscript service and age 50 (NCOs and officers to age 60)

Army 24,550 (to be 315,000 on mob)

(incl 11,500 conscripts)
(all bdes reserve, some with peacetime trg role; re-org underway to be complete by 2008)
3 Mil Comd
  1 with 6 mil provinces, 2 armd (1 trg), 2 *Jaeger* (trg), 7 inf bde
  1 with 2 mil provinces, 3 *Jaeger* (trg) bde
  1 with 4 mil provinces, 4 *Jaeger* (trg), 4 inf bde
Other units
  3 AD regt, 4 engr bn

RESERVES
some 150 local bn and coy
EQUIPMENT
  MBT 70 T-55M, 160 T-72

AIFV 156 BMP-1PS, 110 BMP-2 (incl 'look-a-likes')
APC 120 BTR-60PB, 500 XA-180/185/200 *Sisu*, 220 MT-LBV (incl 'look-a-likes')
TOWED ARTY 122mm: 486 H 63 (D-30); **130mm:** 36 K 54, **152mm:** 288 incl: H 55 (D-20), H 88-40, H 88-37 (ML-20), H 38 (M-10); **155mm:** 108 M-74 (K-83), 24 K 98
SP ARTY 122mm: 72 PsH 74 (2S1); **152mm:** 18 *Telak* 91 (2S5)
MRL 122mm: 58 Rak H 76 (BM-21), 36 Rak H 89 (RM-70)
MOR 81mm: 1,400; **120mm:** 954 (some SP): KRH 40, KRH 92
ATGW 178 M-82 (AT-4 *Spigot*), 5+ M-83 (BGM-71D TOW 2), M-82M (AT-5 *Spandrel*)
RL 112mm: APILAS
RCL 66mm: 66 KES-75, 66 KES-88; **95mm:** 100 SM-58-61
AD GUNS 23mm: 400 ZU-23; **30mm; 35mm:** GDF-005, *Marksman* GDF-005 SP; **57mm:** 12 S-60 towed, 12 ZSU-57-2 SP
SAM SAM-86M (SA-18), SAM-86 (SA-16), 20 SAM-90 (*Crotale* NG), 18 SAM-96 (SA-11)
SURV *Cymbeline* (mor)
HEL 4 Hughes 500D/E, 7 Mi-8

Navy 5,000

(incl 2,500 conscripts)
COMMANDS 2 major: Gulf of Finland, Archipelago Sea; minor: Kotka Coastal District
BASES Upinniemi (Helsinki), Turku
PATROL AND COASTAL COMBATANTS 10
CORVETTES 1 *Turunmaa* FS with 1 × 120mm gun, 2 × 5 ASW RL
MISSILE CRAFT 9
    4 *Helsinki* PFM with 4 × 2 MTO-85 (Swe RBS-15SF) SSM
    4 *Rauma* PFM with 2 × 2 and 2 × 1 MTO-85 (Swe RBS-15SF) SSM, 1 × 6 *Mistral* SAM
    1 *Hamina* PFM with 6 RBS 15 SF SSM, 1 × 6 *Mistal* SAM
MINE WARFARE 23
MINELAYERS 10
    2 *Hämeenmaa*, 150–200 mines, plus 1 × 6 Matra *Mistral* SAM
    1 *Pohjanmaa*, 100–150 mines; 2 × 5 ASW RL
    3 *Pansio* aux minelayer, 50 mines
    4 *Tuima* (ex-PFM), 20 mines
MINE COUNTERMEASURES 13
    6 *Kuha* MSI, 7 *Kiiski* MSI
AMPHIBIOUS craft only
    3 *Kampela* LCU tpt, 2 *Kala* LCU
SUPPORT AND MISCELLANEOUS 37
    1 *Kustaanmiekka* command ship, 5 *Valas* tpt, 6 *Hauki* tpt, 4 *Hila* tpt, 2 *Lohi* tpt, 1 *Aranda* AGOR (Ministry of Trade control), 9 *Prisma* AGS, 9 icebreakers (Board of Navigation control)

COASTAL DEFENCE
100mm: 61 D-10T (tank turrets); **130mm:** 190 K-54 (static) arty
COASTAL SSM 5 RBS-15

Air Force 2,700

(incl 1,500 conscripts) wartime strength 35,000; 64 cbt ac, no armed hel; 3 Air Comds: Satakunta (West), Karelia (East), Lapland (North). Each Air Comd assigned to one of the 3 AD areas into which SF is divided. 3 ftr wgs, one in each AD area.
Flying hours 120
FGA 3 wg with 57 F/A-18C, 7 F/A-18D
Advanced AD/Attack Trg/Recce
    20 *Hawk* 50/51A. One F-27 ESM/*Elint*
SURVEY 3 *Learjet* 35A (survey, ECM trg, target-towing)
TPT 1 **ac** sqn with 2 F-27, 3 Learjet-35A
TRG 22 *Hawk* Mk 51, 28 L-70 *Vinka*
LIAISON 14 Piper (8 *Cherokee Arrow*, 6 *Chieftain*), 9 L-90 *Redigo*
UAV Tactical (6 *Ranger* systems to be delivered)
AAM AA-8 *Aphid*, AIM-9 *Sidewinder*, RB-27, RB-28 (*Falcon*), AIM-120 AMRAAM

Forces Abroad

UN AND PEACEKEEPING
BOSNIA (SFOR II): 120; 1 inf coy **CROATIA** (UNMOP): 1 obs **CYPRUS** (UNFICYP): 6 **ETHIOPIA/ ERITREA** (UNMEE): 10 incl 7 obs **INDIA/PAKISTAN** (UNMOGIP): 5 obs **IRAQ/KUWAIT** (UNIKOM): 5 obs **LEBANON** (UNIFIL): 529; 1 inf bn **MIDDLE EAST** (UNTSO): 12 obs **YUGOSLAVIA** (KFOR): 800

Paramilitary 3,100

FRONTIER GUARD (Ministry of Interior) 3,100
(on mob 22,000); 4 frontier, 3 Coast Guard districts, 1 air patrol sqn; 6 offshore, 2 coastal (plus 60 boats and 4 ACVs); air patrol sqn with **hel** 3 AS-332, 4 AB-206L, 4 AB-412 **ac** 2 Do-228 (Maritime Surv)

Georgia Ga

lari		1999	2000	2001	2002
GDP	lari	5.6bn	9.4bn		
	US$	2.5bn	4.7bn		
per capita	US$	4,800	5,289		
Growth	%	3.0	-0.2		
Inflation	%	19.1	4.0		
Debt	US$	1.7bn	1.9bn		
Def exp	lari	250m	235m		
	US$	111m	118.7m		
Def bdgt[a]	lari	55m	43.7m	35.5m	
	US$	24m	22m	22m	

contd		1999	2000	2001	2002
FMA[b] (US) US$		0.4m	0.4m	0.4m	
FMA (Tu) US$		3.8m			
US$1=lari		2.25	1.98	1.97	

[a] Abkhazia def bdgt 1997 US$5m
[b] UNOMIG **1997** US$18m **1998** US$19m

Population					**4,891,000**

Armenian 8% **Azeri** 6% **Russian** 6% **Ossetian** 3%
Abkhaz 2%

Age	13–17	18–22	23–32
Men	214,000	209,000	381,000
Women	205,000	201,000	359,000

Total Armed Forces

ACTIVE 16,790
(incl 5,800 centrally controlled staff; 10,400 conscripts; excluding 1,500 civilians)
Terms of service conscription, 18 months

RESERVES up to 250,000
with mil service in last 15 years

Army some 8,620

(incl 1,578 National Guard; 5,572 conscripts)
2 comd HQ
2 MR 'bde', 1 national gd bde plus trg centre • 1 arty 'bde' (bn) • 1 recce bn, 1 marine inf bn, 1 peacekeeping bn
EQUIPMENT
  MBT 90: T-55, T-72
  AIFV/APC 185: 68 BMP-1, 13 BMP-2, 11 BRM-1K, 18 BTR-70, 3 BTR-80, 72 MT-LB
  TOWED ARTY 85mm: D-44; **100mm:** KS-19 (ground role); **122mm:** 60 D-30; **152mm:** 3 2A36, 10 2A65
  SP ARTY 152mm: 1 2S3, 1 2S19; **203mm:** 1 2S7
  MRL 122mm: 16 BM-21
  MOR 120mm: 17 M-120
  ATGW ε10
  ATK GUNS ε40
  SAM some SA-13

Navy 1,040

(incl 670 conscripts)
BASES Tbilisi (HQ), Poti
PATROL AND COASTAL COMBATANTS 11
PATROL CRAFT 11
  1 *Turk* PCC, 1 *Matka* PHM, 1 *Lindau* PCC, 2 *Dilos* PCC, 1 *Stenka* PCC, 1 *Zhuk* PCI<, plus 4 other PCI<
AMPHIBIOUS craft only
  2 LCT, 4 LCM

Air Force 1,330

(incl 560 conscripts)
7 cbt ac, 3 armed hel
ATTACK 7 Su-25 (1 -25, 5 - 25K, 1 -25UB), 5 Su-17 (non-operational)
TPT 6 An-2, 1 Yak-18T, 2 Yak-40, 1 Tu-134A (VIP)
HEL 3 Mi-24 (attack), 4 Mi-8/17, 10 UH-1H
TRG ac some Yak-52s and L-29 hel 2 Mi-2

AIR DEFENCE
SAM 75 SA-2/-3/-4/-5/-7

Forces Abroad

UN AND PEACEKEEPING
YUGOSLAVIA (KFOR): 34

Opposition

ABKHAZIA ε5,000
50+ T-72, T-55 MBT, 80+ AIFV/APC, 80+ arty
SOUTH OSSETIA ε2,000
5–10 MBT, 30 AIFV/APC, 25 arty incl BM-21

Paramilitary 11,700

MINISTRY OF INTERIOR TROOPS 6,300
BORDER GUARD 5,400
  COAST GUARD
  2 *Zhuk* PCI

Foreign Forces

RUSSIA 4,000: **Army** 3 mil bases (each = bde+); 65 T-72 MBT, 200 ACV, 139 arty incl **122mm:** D-30, 2S1; **152mm:** 2S3; **122mm:** BM-21 MRL; **120mm:** mor
PEACEKEEPING
Abkhazia 1,700 **South Ossetia** 530
UN (UNOMIG): 103 obs from 22 countries

Ireland Irl

pound I£		1999	2000	2001	2002
GDP	I£	67.3bn	81.3bn		
	US$	87bn	97.9bn		
per capita	US$	22,400	25,085		
Growth	%	8.6	10.7		
Inflation	%	1.6	5.5		
Publ debt	%	51.9	39.3		
Def exp	I£	576m	579m		
	US$	748m	697.6m		
Def bdgt	I£	576m	601m	707m	
	US$	748m	724m	794m	
US$1=I£		0.77	0.83	0.89	

Population			3,756,000
Age	13–17	18–22	23–32
Men	151,000	167,000	338,000
Women	142,000	158,000	319,000

Total Armed Forces

ACTIVE ε10,460

(incl 200 women)

RESERVES 14,800

(obligation to age 60, officers 57–65) **Army** first-line 500, second-line 14,000 **Navy** 300 **Air Corps** 75

Army ε8,500

3 inf bde each 3 inf bn, 1 arty regt, 1 cav recce sqn, 1 engr coy

Army tps: 1 lt tk sqn, 1 AD regt, 1 Ranger coy
Total units: 9 inf bn • 1 UNIFIL bn *ad hoc* with elm from other bn, 1 lt tk sqn, 3 recce sqn, 3 fd arty regt (each of 2 bty) • 1 indep bty, 1 AD regt (1 regular, 3 reserve bty), 4 fd engr coy, 1 Ranger coy

RESERVES

4 Army gp (garrisons), 18 inf bn, 6 fd arty regt, 3 cav sqn, 3 engr sqn, 3 AD bty

EQUIPMENT

LT TK 14 *Scorpion*
RECCE 15 AML-90, 18 AML-20
APC 47 Panhard VTT/M3, 5 *Timoney* Mk 6, 2 A-180 *Sisu*, some *Piranha* III
TOWED ARTY 88mm: 42 25-pdr; **105mm**: 24 L-118
MOR 81mm: 400; **120mm**: 64
ATGW 21 *Milan*
RL 84mm: AT-4
RCL 84mm: 444 *Carl Gustav*
AD GUNS 40mm: 24 L/60, 2 L/70
SAM 7 RBS-70

Naval Service 1,100

BASE Cork, Haulbowline
PATROL AND COASTAL COMBATANTS 8
PATROL OFFSHORE 8
1 *Eithne* with 1 *Dauphin* hel PCO, 3 *Emer* PCO, 2 *Orla* (UK *Peacock*) PCO with 1 × 76mm gun, 2 *Roisin* PCO with 1 × 76mm gun

Air Corps 860

17 FW ac, 13 hel; 3 wg (1 trg)
CCT 7 SF-260WE
MR 2 CN-235MP
TPT 1 *Super King Air* 200, 1 *Gulfstream* IV
LIAISON 1 sqn with 5 Cessna Reims FR-172H, 1 FR-172K

HEL 7 SA-316B (*Alouette* III), Army spt; 4 SA-365FI (*Dauphin*), Navy spt/SAR; 2 SA-342L (*Gazelle*), trg

Forces Abroad

UN AND PEACEKEEPING
BOSNIA (SFOR II): 50 **CROATIA** (UNMOP): 1 obs
CYPRUS (UNFICYP): 5 **EAST TIMOR** (UNTAET): 48 incl 2 obs **IRAQ/KUWAIT** (UNIKOM): 6 obs **LEBANON** (UNIFIL): 552; 1 bn; 4 AML-90 armd cars, 10 *Sisu* APC, 4 **120mm** mor **MIDDLE EAST** (UNTSO): 10 obs **WESTERN SAHARA** (MINURSO): 3 obs **YUGOSLAVIA** (KFOR): 104

Latvia Lat

lats L		1999	2000	2001	2002
GDP	L	3.7bn	4.3bn		
	US$	6.0bn	7.17bn		
per capita	US$	6,300	7,219		
Growth	%	0.8	5.5		
Inflation	%	2.4	2.7		
Debt	US$		4.73m		
Def exp[a]	L	ε35m	ε43m		
	US$	58m	72m		
Def bdgt	L	35.4m	43m	48m	
	US$	58m	72m	76m	
FMA (US)	US$	0.7m	0.7m	0.8m	
US$1=L		0.61	0.60	0.63	
[a] Incl exp on paramilitary forces.					

Population			2,308,000
Russian 34% Belarussian 5% Ukrainian 3% Polish 2%			
Age	13–17	18–22	23–32
Men	97,000	96,000	163,000
Women	94,000	92,000	160,000

Total Armed Forces

ACTIVE 6,500

(incl 2,350 National Guard; 2,050 conscripts)
Terms of service 12 months

RESERVES 14,400
National Guard

Army 3,100

(incl 1,050 conscripts)
1 mobile rifle bde with 1 inf bn • 1 recce bn • 1 HQ bn • 1 arty unit • 1 peacekeeping coy (bn to form) • 1 SF team

RESERVES
National Guard 5 bde, 32 territorial bn

EQUIPMENT

MBT 3 T-55 (trg)
RECCE 2 BRDM-2
APC 13 *Pskbil* m/42
TOWED ARTY 100mm: 26 K-53
MOR 82mm: 5; **120mm:** 32
RL 84mm: AT-4
AD GUNS 14.5mm: 12 ZPU-4; **40mm:** 18 L/70

Navy 840

(incl 260 conscripts, 250 Coastal Defence)
Lat, Ea and L have set up a joint Naval unit BALTRON with bases at Liepaja, Riga, Ventspils (Lat), Tallinn (Ea), Klaipeda (L)
BASES Liepaja, Riga, Ventspils

PATROL AND COASTAL COMBATANTS 4

PATROL COASTAL 4
　1 *Osa* PFM (unarmed), 3 *Storm* PCC (unarmed)
MINE WARFARE 3
MINE COUNTERMEASURES 3
　2 *Kondor* II MCC, 1 *Namejs* (Ge *Lindau*) MHC

SUPPORT AND MISCELLANEOUS 3
　1 *Nyrat* AT, 1 *Goliat* AT, 1 diving vessel

COASTAL DEFENCE (250)
1 coastal def bn
10 patrol craft: 2 *Ribnadzor* PCC, 5 KBV 236 PCI, 2 PCI<

Air Force 210

AC 13 An-2, 1 L-410, 5 PZL Wilga
HEL 3 Mi-2, 2 Mi-8

Forces Abroad

UN AND PEACEKEEPING
BOSNIA (SFOR II): 97 **YUGOSLAVIA** (KFOR): 10

Paramilitary 3,500

BORDER GUARD (Ministry of Internal Affairs) 3,500
1 bde (7 bn)

Lithuania L

litas L		1999	2000	2001	2002
GDP	L	42.6bn	44.8bn		
	US$	10.7bn	11.2bn		
per capita	US$	5,500	6,000		
Growth	%	-.3.3	3.4		
Inflation	%	0.8	1.0		
Debt	US$	2.4bn	2.5bn		

contd		1999	2000	2001	2002
Def exp	L	426m	795m		
	US$	106m	199m		
Def bdgt	L	716m	596m	737m	
	US$	179m	149m	184.3m	
FMA (US)	US$	0.7m	0.8m		
US$1=L		4.0	4.0	4.0	
Population					3,655,000

Russian 8% Polish 7% Belarussian 2%

Age	13–17	18–22	23–32
Men	142,000	139,000	253,000
Women	137,000	134,000	249,000

Total Armed Forces

ACTIVE 12,190
(incl 1,810 centrally controlled staff and support units, 1,500 Voluntary National Defence Force; 3,740 conscripts) *Terms of service* 12 months

RESERVES 336,000
27,800 **first line** (ready 72 hrs, incl 10,000 Voluntary National Defence Service), 308,200 **second line** (age up to 59)

Army 7,500

(incl 3,140 conscripts)
3 mil region, 1 motor rifle bde (4 bn), 1 motor rifle bde (3 bn) • 1 Jaeger, 1 trg regt (4 bn), 1 arty, 1 engr, 1 staff bn

EQUIPMENT
RECCE 10 BRDM-2
APC 11 BTR-60, 11 *Pskbil* m/42, 10 MT-LB, 49 M-113A1
MOR 120mm: 42 M-43
RL 73mm: RPG-7; **82mm:** 170 RPG-2
RCL 84mm: 119 *Carl Gustav*; **90mm:** PV-1110

RESERVES
Voluntary National Defence Service: 10 Territorial Defence regt, 36 territorial def bn with 130 territorial def coy, 2 air sqn

Navy 580

(incl 300 conscripts)
Lat, Ea and L have set up a joint Naval unit BALTRON with bases at Liepaja, Riga, Ventspils (Lat), Tallinn (Ea), Klaipeda (L)
BASE Klaipeda

PATROL AND COASTAL COMBATANTS 5

CORVETTES 2
2 Sov *Grisha* III FS, with 4 × 533mm TT, 2 × 12 ASW RL
PATROL COASTAL/INSHORE 3
　1 *Storm* PCC, 1 SK-21 PCI<, 1 SK-22 PCI<

MINE WARFARE 2
MINE COUNTERMEASURES 2
  2 *Suduvis* (Ge *Lindau*) MHC
SUPPORT AND MISCELLANEOUS 1
  1 *Valerian Uryvayev* AGOR/AG

Air Force 800

(no conscripts)
no cbt ac
Air Surveillance and Control Command, 2 air bases
Flying hours 90
TPT 2 L-410, 3 An-26, 22 An-2
TRG 6 L-39
HEL 8 Mi-8 (tpt/SAR), 5 Mi-2
AIRFIELD DEFENCE 1 AD bn with 18 40mm Bofors
  L/70. 1 reserve AD bn to be formed

Forces Abroad

UN AND PEACEKEEPING
BOSNIA (SFOR II): 2 **YUGOSLAVIA** (KFOR): 30

Paramilitary 12,450

STATE BORDER GUARD SERVICE (Ministry of Internal
Affairs) 4,400

COAST GUARD 550

RIFLEMEN UNION 7,500

Macedonia, Former Yugoslav Republic of FYROM

dinar d		1999	2000	2001	2002
GDP	US$	3.4bn	3.61bn		
per capita	US$	3,900	4,827		
Growth	%	2.5	5.1		
Inflation	%	-1.1	6.7		
Debt	US$	1.9bn	1.55bn		
Def exp	d	3.8bn	4.6bn		
	US$	67m	77.1m		
Def bdgt	d	3.8bn	4.6bn	4.6bn	
	US$	66m	77m	71.6m	
FMAab (US)US$		0.5m	0.5m	0.5m	
US$1=d		57.0	59.8	64.0	

a UNPREDEP **1997** US$45m **1998** US$21m
b UNPREDEP figures exclude US costs paid as voluntary
contributions

Population				1,983,000	

Albanian 22% Turkish 4% Romany 3% Serb 2%

Age	13–17	18–22	23–32
Men	97,000	95,000	173,000
Women	87,000	86,000	160,000

Total Armed Forces

ACTIVE ε16,000
(incl about 1,000 HQ staff; 8,000 conscripts) *Terms of
service* 9 months

RESERVES 60,000

Army ε15,000

2 Corps HQ (cadre), 3 bde incl 1 border gd bde
EQUIPMENT
  MBT 4 T-34, 94 T-55
  RECCE 10 BRDM-2, 41 HMMWV
  APC 60 BTR-70, 12 BTR-80, 30 M-113A, 10 *Leonidas*
  TOWED ARTY 76mm: 55 M-48, 72 M-1942; **105mm**:
    18 M-56, 18 M-2A1; **122mm**: 108 M-30
  MRL 128mm: 25 M-71 (single barrel), 12 M-77
  MOR 450: **60mm**; **82mm**; **120mm**
  ATGW AT-3 *Sagger*, 12 *Milan*
  RCL 57mm; **82mm**: M60A

  MARINE WING (400)
  5 river patrol craft

  ARMY AIR FORCE (800)
  4 cbt ac, 6 armed hel
  ATTACK 4 Su-25, incl 1 -25UB
  SURVEILLANCE 1 Cessna 337 (operated under
    contract)
  TPT/LIAISON ac 1 Learjet, 1 *Kingair* C-12, 3 An-2
  ARMED HEL 6 Mi-24V (4 more reportedly on
    order)
  TPT HEL 8 Mi-8/Mi-17, 5 UH-1H
  TRG 3 *Zlin*-242, some UTVA-75
  AD GUNS 50: **20mm**; **40mm**
  SAM 30 SA-7, SA-13

Paramilitary 10,000

POLICE 10,000 (some 4,500 armed)
Equipment incl ε100 TM-170 APC

Opposition

NATIONAL LIBERATION ARMY (NLA) ε500–1,000

Foreign Forces

UN (KFOR) about 5,000 providing logistic spt for tps
deployed in the FRY province of Kosovo

Malta M

lira ML		1999	2000	2001	2002
GDP	ML	1.4bn	1.5bn		
	US$	3.5bn	3.6bn		
per capita	US$	9,100	9,300		
Growth	%	3.5	3.4		
Inflation	%	2.1	2.5		
Debt	US$				
Def exp	ML	11.3m	11.3m		
	US$	27m	27m		
Def bdgt	ML	11.2m	11.3m	11.5m	
	US$	27.3m	27.6m	25.6m	
FMA (US)	US$	0.1m	0.1m	0.1m	
US$1=ML		0.41	0.41	0.45	
Population					393,000

Age	13–17	18–22	23–32
Men	14,000	15,000	26,000
Women	14,000	14,000	25,000

Total Armed Forces

ACTIVE 2,140

Armed Forces of Malta 2,140

Comd HQ, spt tps
No. 1 Regt (inf bn): 3 rifle, 1 spt coy
No. 2 Regt (composite regt):
  1 air wg (76) with **ac** 4 0-1 *Bird Dog*, 2 BN-2B *Islander*
  hel 5 SA-316B, 2 NH-369M Hughes, 2 AB-47G2
  1 maritime sqn (210) with 3 ex-GDR *Kondor* 1 PCC,
  4 PCI, 3 harbour craft, 1 LCVP
  1 AD bty; **14.5mm:** 50 ZPU-4; **40mm:** 40 Bofors
No. 3 Regt (Depot Regt): 1 engr sqn, 1 workshop, 1
  ordnance, 1 airport coy

Foreign Forces

ITALY 47: Air Force 2 AB-212

Moldova Mol

leu L		1999	2000	2001	2002
GDP	L	12.2bn	16bn		
	US$	1.1bn	1.26bn		
per capita	US$	3,200	3,343		
Growth	%	-5.0	1.9		
Inflation	%	46	31		
Debt	US$	972m	1.0bn		
Def exp[a]	L	305m	267m		
	US$	27.5m	21.1m		
Def bdgt	L	73.5m	64m	76.8m	
	US$	6.6m	5m	5.9m	

contd	1999	2000	2001	2002
FMA (US) US$	0.5m	0.6m	0.6m	
US$1=L	11.11	12.67	13.10	

[a] Incl exp on paramilitary forces

Population			4,384,000

Moldovan/Romanian 65% Ukrainian 14% Russian 13%
Gaguaz 4% Bulgarian 2% Jewish <1.5%

Age	13–17	18–22	23–32
Men	206,000	190,000	303,000
Women	187,000	187,000	299,000

Total Armed Forces

ACTIVE 8,220

(incl 300 Central HQ and Command staff; ε5,200
conscripts) *Terms of service* up to 18 months

RESERVES some 66,000

Army 7,120

(incl ε5,200 conscripts)
3 MR bde • 1 arty bde, 1 indep MR • 1 indep gd, 1 SF,
1 indep engr, 1 indep ATK bn
EQUIPMENT
  AIFV 53 BMD-1
  APC 11 BTR-80, 11 BTR-D, 1 BTR-60PB, 6 MT-LB, 127
    TAB-71, plus 149 'look-a-likes'
  TOTAL ARTY 151
  TOWED ARTY 122mm: 18 M-30; **152mm:** 32 D-20,
    21 2A36
  COMBINED GUN/MOR 120mm: 9 2S9
  MRL 220mm: 11 9P140 *Uragan*
  MOR 82mm: 54; **120mm:** 60 M-120
  ATGW 70 AT-4 *Spigot*, 19 AT-5 *Spandral*, 27 AT-6
    Spiral
  RCL 73mm: SPG-9
  ATK GUNS 100mm: 36 MT-12
  AD GUNS 23mm: 30 ZU-23; **57mm:** 12 S-60
  SURV GS-13 (arty), 1 L219/200 PARK-1 (arty), *Long
    Trough* ((SNAR-1) arty), *Pork Trough* ((SNAR-2/-6)
    veh, arty), *Small Fred/Small Yawn* (veh, arty), *Big
    Fred* ((SNAR-10) veh, arty)

Air Force 800

(incl Defence Aviation)
TPT 1 mixed sqn **ac** 3 An-72, 1 Tu-134, (6 MiG-29 in
  store) **hel** 11 Mi-8
SAM 1 bde with 25 SA-3/-5

Paramilitary 3,400

INTERNAL TROOPS (Ministry of Interior) 2,500
OPON (Ministry of Interior) 900 (riot police)

Opposition

DNIESTR ε5–10,000 (plus 15,000 on mob)
incl Republican Guard (Dniestr bn), Delta bn, ε1,000 Cossacks
Eqpt incl 18 tks; 40 APC; 122mm arty; BM-21MRL; 82mm and 120mm mor; 6 Mi-8, 2 Mi-2 hel

Foreign Forces

RUSSIA 1,500: 1 op gp
PEACEKEEPING
Russia 500: 1 MR bn

Romania R

lei		1999	2000	2001	2002
GDP	lei	521tr	796tr		
	US$	33bn	38.4bn		
per capita	US$	4,400	4,583		
Growth	%	-3.9	1.6		
Inflation	%	46	46		
Debt	US$	8.6bn			
Def exp	lei	9.6tr	17.1tr		
	US$	607m	941m	995m	
Def bdgt	lei	9.6tr	17.2tr	28.4tr	
	US$	607m	827.4m	1.0bn	
FMA (US)	US$	1.3m	1.2m	1.3m	
US$1=lei		15,835	20,750	28,430	
Population			22,231,000	Hungarian 9%	
Age		13–17	18–22	23–32	
Men		809,422	951,176	1,996,881	
Women		809,257	913,989	1,932,297	

Total Armed Forces

ACTIVE 103,000
(incl 21,000 in centrally controlled units; ε35,000 conscripts)
Terms of service All services 12 months

RESERVES 470,000
Army 400,000 **Navy** 30,000 **Air Force** 40,000

Army 52,900

(incl 21,000 conscripts)
3 Army Corps HQ each with 2–3 mech 1 tk, 1 mtn, 1 arty, 1 ATK bde, 2 para bde
Army tps: 1 arty, 1 ATK, 1 SAM bde, 1 engr regt
Defence Staff tps: 2 AB (Air Force), 1 gd bde
Land Force tps: 1 SAM, 2 engr regt
Determining the manning state of units is difficult. The following is based on the latest available information:

one-third at 100%, one-third at 50–70%, one-third at 10–20%.

EQUIPMENT
MBT 1,373: 821 T-55, 30 T-72, 314 TR-85 M1, 208 TR-580
ASLT GUN 84 SU-100
RECCE 121 BRDM-2
AIFV 177 MLI-84
APC 1,316: 170 TAB-77, 430 TABC-79, 1,058 TAB-71, 88 MLVM, 70 TAB ZIMBRU, plus 1,115 'look-a-likes'
TOTAL ARTY 1,381
   TOWED 788: **122mm**: 258 M-1938 (M-30) (A-19); **130mm**: 20 Gun 82; **150mm**: 12 Skoda (Model 1934); **152mm**: 114 Gun-how 85, 330 Model 81, 54 M-1937 (ML-20)
   SP 48: **122mm**: 6 2S1, 42 Model 89
   MLRS 122mm: 177 APR-40
   MOR 120mm: 368 M-1982
SSM launchers: 9 FROG
ATGM 53 9P122, 121 9P133, 54 9P148
ATK GUNS 57mm: 370; **85mm**: 130; **100mm**: 937 Gun 77, 75 Gun 75
AD GUNS 85mm caliber and above: 384
SAM 62 SA-6/-7/-8
SURV GS-13 (arty), 1 L219/200 PARK-1 (arty), *Long Trough* ((SNAR-1) arty), *Pork Trough* ((SNAR-2/-6) veh, arty), *Small Fred/Small Yawn* (veh, arty), *Big Fred* ((SNAR-10) veh, arty)
UAV 6 *Shadow*-600

Navy 10,200

(incl 5,000 conscripts)
Navy HQ with 1 Naval fleet, 1 Danube flotilla, 1 Naval inf corps
BASES Coastal Mangalia, Constanta **Danube** Braila, Giurgiu, Tulcea, Galati
SUBMARINES 1†
SSK 1 Sov *Kilo* with 6 × 533mm TT†
PRINCIPAL SURFACE COMBATANTS 7
DESTROYERS 1
   DDG 1 *Muntena* with 4 × 2 SS-N-2C *Styx* SSM, SA-N-5 *Grail* SAM, 4 × 76mm guns, 2 × 3 533mm ASTT, 2 IAR 316 *Alouette* III hel
FRIGATES 6
   FF 6
   4 *Tetal* 1 with 4 × 76mm guns, 4 ASTT, 2 ASW RL
   2 *Tetal* II with 1 × 76mm gun, 4 ASTT, 2 ASW RL, 1 IAR 316 *Alouette* III hel
PATROL AND COASTAL COMBATANTS 61
MISSILE CRAFT 6
   3 *Zborul* PFM (Sov *Tarantul* I) with 2 × 2 SS-N-2C *Styx* SSM, 1 × 76mm gun
   3 Sov *Osa* I PFM with 4 SS-N-2A *Styx* SSM
TORPEDO CRAFT 28
   12 *Epitrop* PFT with 4 × 533mm TT

16 PRC *Huchuan* PHT with 2 533mm TT†
PATROL CRAFT 27
  RIVERINE 27
  some 6 *Brutar* with 1 × 100mm gun, 1 × 122mm RL, 3
    Kogalniceanu with 2 × 100mm gun, 18 VB 76 PCR<
MINE WARFARE 17
MINELAYERS 2 *Cosar*, capacity 100 mines
MINE COUNTERMEASURES 15
  4 *Musca* MSO, 6 T-301 MSI, 5 VD141 MSI
SUPPORT AND MISCELLANEOUS 11
  2 *Constanta* log spt with 1 *Alouette* hel, 1 AK, 3 AOT; 1
  trg, 2 AT; 2 AGOR
NAVAL AVIATION
EQUIPMENT
7 armed hel
  HELICOPTERS
  3 IAR-316, 4 Mi-14 PL

NAVAL INFANTRY (10,200)
1 Corps HQ
2 mech, 1 mot inf, 1 arty bde, 1 ATK, 1 mne bn
EQUIPMENT
  MBT 120 TR-580
  APC 208: 172 TAB-71, 36 TABC-79 plus 100 'look-a-
    likes'
  TOTAL ARTY 138
    TOWED 90: **122mm**: 54 M-1938 (M-30); **152mm**: 36
      Model 81
    MRL 122mm: 12 APR-40
    MOR 120mm: 36 Model 1982
  ATK GUNS 100mm: 57 Gun 77

COASTAL DEFENCE
4 coastal arty bty with 32 **130mm**

Air Force 18,900

(incl 5,500 AB; 7,000 conscripts); 307 cbt ac, 18 attack
hel
Flying hours 40
Air Force comd: 2 Air Divs, 5–7 air bases, 4–6 air
  defence artillery bde or rgt
FGA 4 regt with 72 IAR-93, 5 regt with 180 MiG-21 (110
being upgraded to Lancer standard: 75 Lancer A (air-
to-gd), 25 Lancer C (AD), 10 Lancer B (two-seat
trainers))
FTR 1 regt with 18† MiG-29 (27 MiG-23 in store)
RECCE 1 sqn with 11* H-5 (recce/ECM/trg towing)
TPT ac 6 An-24, 11 An-26, 2 Boeing 707, 4 C-130B **hel** 5
  IAR-330, 9 Mi-8, 4 SA-365
SURVEY 3 An-30
HELICOPTERS
  ATTACK 15 IAR-316A, 3 IAR-330 SOCAT
  CBT SPT 71 IAR-330, 84 IAR-316, 23 Mi-8, 2 Mi-17
TRG ac 45 L-29, 21 L-39, 15 IAR-99
AAM AA-2 *Atoll*, AA-3 *Anab*, AA-7 *Apex*, AA-10b
  Alamo, AA-11 *Archer*
ASM AS-7 *Kerry*

UAV Shadow 600
AD 2 div bde
  20 SAM sites with 120 SA-2, SA-3

Forces Abroad

UN AND PEACEKEEPING
BOSNIA (SFOR II): ε60 **DROC** (MONUC): 17 obs
ETHIOPIA/ERITREA (UNMEE): 8 obs **IRAQ/
KUWAIT** (UNIKOM): 5 obs

Paramilitary 75,900

BORDER GUARDS (Ministry of Interior) 22,900
(incl conscripts) 9 regional formations, 3 regional
maritime dets
  33 TAB-71 APC, 18 SU-100 aslt gun, 12 M-1931/37
    (A19) **122mm** how, 18 M-38 **120mm** mor, 7 PRC
  Shanghai II PFI
GENDARMERIE (Ministry of Interior) 53,000

Slovakia Slvk

koruna Ks		1999	2000	2001	2002
GDP	Ks	779bn	887bn		
	US$	17.5bn	19.6bn		
per capita	US$	7,800	8,184		
Growth	%	1.0	2.1		
Inflation	%	10.6	12		
Debt	US$	10.4bn	10.8bn		
Def exp	Ks	13.5bn	15.7bn		
	US$	304.8m	347m		
Def bdgt	Ks	13.6bn	16.4bn	18.2bn	
	US$	311m	361.8m	369.2m	
FMA (US)	US$	0.6m	0.7m	0.7m	
US$1=Ks		44.4	45.3	49.3	
Population					5,384,000

Hungarian 11% Romany ε5% Czech 1%

Age	13–17	18–22	23–32
Men	219,000	238,000	425,000
Women	210,000	231,000	416,000

Total Armed Forces

ACTIVE 33,000
(incl 3,000 centrally controlled staffs, log and spt tps;
14,900 conscripts)
Terms of service 9 months

RESERVES ε20,000 on mob
National Guard Force

Army 19,800

(incl 10,400 conscripts)
1 Corps HQ
1 tk bde (2 tk, 1 mech, 1 recce, 1 arty bn)
1 mech inf bde (2 mech inf, 1 tk, 1 recce, 1 arty bn)
1 arty, 1 engr bde
1 SSM regt, 1 Rapid Reaction bn

RESERVES
1 Corps HQ, 2 mech bde, 1 arty bde
National Guard Force
EQUIPMENT
  MBT 272 T-72M
  RECCE 129 BRDM, 90 OT-65, 72 BPVZ
  AIFV 383 BMP-1, 93 BMP-2
  APC 175 OT-90
  TOTAL ARTY 390
    TOWED 122mm: 75 D-30
    SP 211: **122mm:** 51 2S1; **152mm:** 136 *Dana* (M-77);
    155mm: 24 *Zuzana* 2000
    MRL 122mm: 90 RM-70
    MOR 120mm: 14 M-1982
  SSM 9 FROG-7, SS-21
  ATGW 538 (incl BMP-1/-2 and BRDM mounted):
    AT-3 *Sagger*, AT-5 *Spandrel*
  AD GUNS 200: **30mm:** M-53/-59; **57mm:** S-60
  SAM SA-7, ε48 SA-13
  SURV GS-13 (veh), *Long Trough* (SNAR-1), *Pork
    Trough* ((SNAR-2/-6) arty), *Small Fred/Small Yawn*
    (veh, arty), *Big Fred* ((SNAR-10) veh, arty)

Air Force 10,200

56 cbt ac, 19 attack hel
Flying hours 45
1 Ftr wg with 24 MiG-29/UB, 12 MiG-21MF/UB
1 FGA/Recce wg 8 Su-22M4/UM3K, 12 Su-25K/UBK
1 Tpt wg 2 An-24, 2 An-26, 6 L410M, 2 Mi-8PS (VIP)
1 Hel wg 19* Mi-24V/D, 17 Mi-17, 6 Mi-2
Trg 20 L-29, 7 L-39
AAM AA-2 *Atoll*, AA-7 *Apex*, AA-8 *Aphid*, AA-10
  Alamo, AA-11 *Archer*
3 AD bde
AD SA-2, SA-3, SA-6, SA-10B

Forces Abroad

UN AND PEACEKEEPING
CYPRUS (UNFICYP): 272 **ETHIOPIA/ERITREA**
(UNMEE): 200 **MIDDLE EAST** (UNTSO): 2 obs
SIERRA LEONE (UNAMSIL): 2 obs **SYRIA** (UNDOF):
94 **YUGOSLAVIA** (KFOR): 40

Paramilitary 4,700

BORDER POLICE 1,700

GUARD TROOPS 250

CIVIL DEFENCE TROOPS 1,350
RAILWAY DEFENCE TROOPS 1,400

Slovenia Slvn

tolar t		1999	2000	2001	2002
GDP	t	3.6tr	4.1tr		
	US$	18.5bn	18.6bn		
per capita	US$	11,694	12,518		
Growth	%	3.8	4.7		
Inflation	%	6.6	8.9		
Debt	US$	5.5bn	6.2bn		
Def exp	t	65bn	49.5bn		
	US$	337m	227m		
Def bdgt	t	50bn	59bn	66.7bn	
	US$	259m	273m	269m	
FMA (US)	US$	0.7m	0.7m	0.7m	
US$1=t		192	218	248	
Population					1,981,000

Croat 3% **Serb** 2% **Muslim** 1%

Age	13–17	18–22	23–32
Men	67,000	75,000	148,000
Women	63,000	71,000	144,000

Total Armed Forces

ACTIVE 7,600
(incl ε4–5,000 conscripts) *Terms of service* 7 months

RESERVES 61,000
Army (incl 300 maritime)

Army 7,600

3 Force Comd • 7 inf bde (each 1 active, 3 reserve inf
bn) • 1 SF 'bde' • 1 SAM 'bde' (bn) • 2 indep mech bn
• 1 avn 'bde' • 1 arty bn

RESERVES
2 indep mech, 1 arty, 1 coast def, 1 ATK bn

EQUIPMENT
  MBT 46 M-84, 30 T-55S1
  RECCE 7 BRDM-2
  AIFV 52 M-80
  APC 10 *Valuk* (*Pandur*), 28 BOV-1
  TOWED ARTY 105mm: 18 M-2; **155mm:** 18 Model 845
  SP 122mm: 8 2S1
  MRL 128mm: 48 M-71 (single tube), 4 M-63
  MOR 120mm: 15 M-52, 101 M-74
  ATGW AT-3 *Sagger* (incl 1 BOV-3SP), AT-4 *Spigot*
    (incl 12 BOV-3SP)

MARITIME ELEMENT (100)
(effectively police)

BASE Koper
1 PCI

AIR ELEMENT (120)
8 armed hel
AC 12 PC-9, 8 Zlin-242, 1 LET L-410, 3 UTVA-75, 2 PC-6, 2 Z-143L
HEL 3 B-206, 8* B-412
SAM 9 SA-9
AD GUNS 20mm: 9 SP; **30mm**: 9 SP; **57mm**: 21 SP

Forces Abroad

UN AND PEACEKEEPING
BOSNIA (SFOR II): 78 **CYPRUS** (UNFICYP): 3
MIDDLE EAST (UNTSO): 2 obs **YUGOSLAVIA** (KFOR): 6

Paramilitary 4,500

POLICE 4,500
armed (plus 5,000 reserve) **hel** 2 AB-206 Jet Ranger, 1 AB-109A, 1 AB-212, 1 AB-412

Sweden Swe

kronor Skr		1999	2000	2001	2002
GDP	Skr	2.0tr	2.1tr		
	US$	230bn	238.6bn		
per capita	US$	23,000	24,032		
Growth	%	3.8	2.6		
Inflation	%	0.5	1.3		
Publ Debt	%	68.3	62.3		
Def exp	Skr	44.9bn	46.6bn		
	US$	5.2bn	5.3bn		
Def bdgt	Skr	38.7bn	39.6bn	42.7bn	
	US$	4.5bn	4.5bn	4.2bn	
US$1=Skr		8.56	8.8	10.26	
Population					8,935,000
Age		13–17	18–22	23–32	
Men		267,000	255,000	595,000	
Women		253,000	241,000	568,000	

Total Armed Forces

ACTIVE 33,900
(incl 15,900 conscripts and recalled reservists)
Terms of service **Army**, **Navy** 7–15 months **Air Force** 8–12 months

RESERVES 262,000
(obligation to age 47) **Army** (incl Local Defence and Home Guard) 225,000 **Navy** 20,000 **Air Force** 17,000

Army 19,100

(incl 9,900 conscripts and active reservists)
1 Joint Forces Comd
3 Mil Districts (incl Gotland)
1 div HQ
No active units (as defined by Vienna Document)
4 armd, 2 inf, 1 arty regt (trg establishments – on mob to form 6 mech bde with 16 mech inf, 6 rifle, 1 AB, 4 arty, 4 AA, 4 engr bn)
EQUIPMENT
MBT 70 Centurion, 40 Strv-103B (in store), 160 Strv-121 (Leopard 2), 98 Strv-122 (Leopard 2 (S))
LT TK 211 Ikv-91
AIFV 501 Pbv-302, 271 Strf-9040, 308 Pbv-501 (BMP-1)
APC 440 Pbv 401A (MT-LB), 100 Pskbil M/42, ε30 XA-203 (being delivered)
TOWED ARTY 105mm: 188 m/40; **155mm**: 206 FH-77A, 51 FH-77B, 140 Type F
SP ARTY 155mm: 23 BK-1C
MOR 81mm: 160; **120mm**: 575
ATGW 57 TOW (Pvrbv 551 SP), RB-55, RB-56 Bill
RL 84mm: AT-4
RCL 84mm: Carl Gustav; **90mm**: PV-1110
AD GUNS 40mm: 600 (incl 27 Strv 90LV)
SAM RBS-70 (incl 48 Lvrbv SP), RB-77 (I HAWK), RBS-90
SURV Green Archer (mor), ARTHUR (arty)
AC 1 C-212
HEL see under Air Force 'Armed Forces Helicopter Wing'
UAV 3 Sperwer systems

Navy 7,100

(incl 1,100 Coastal Defence, 320 Naval Aviation; 2,300 conscripts)
BASES Muskö, Karlskrona, Härnösand, Göteborg (spt only)
SUBMARINES 7
SSK 7
3 Gotland with 4 × 533mm TT, TP-613 HWT and TP-43/45 LWT (AIP powered)
4 Västergötland with 6 × 533mm TT, TP-613 HWT and TP-43/45 LWT (2 being fitted with AIP)
PATROL AND COASTAL COMBATANTS 45
MISSILE CRAFT 20 PFM
4 Göteborg with 4 × 2 RBS-15 SSM, 4 ASW torp, 4 ASW mor
2 Stockholm with 4 × 2 RBS-15 SSM, 2 Type 613 HWT, 4 ASW torp, 4 ASW mor (in refit until 2002)
8 Kaparen with 6 RBS-12 Penguin SSM, ASW mor
6 Norrköping with 4 × 2 RBS-15 SSM, 2–6 Type 613 HWT
PATROL CRAFT 25
About 25 PCI<

MINE WARFARE 22

MINELAYERS 2

1 *Carlskrona* (200 mines) trg, 1 *Visborg* (200 mines) (Mines can be laid by all SS classes)

MINE COUNTERMEASURES 20

4 *Styrsö* MCMV, 1 *Utö* MCMV spt, 1 *Skredsvic* MCM/ diver spt, 7 *Landsort* MHC, 2 *Gassten* MSO, 1 *Vicksten* MSO, 4 *Hisingen* diver spt

AMPHIBIOUS

craft only about 120 LCU

SUPPORT AND MISCELLANEOUS 23

1 AK, 1 AR; 1 AGI, 1 ARS, 2 TRV, 8 AT, 7 icebreakers, 2 sail trg

COASTAL DEFENCE (1,100)

2 amph regt (trg establishments - on mob to form 1 amph bde with 3 amph, 6 coast def bn)

EQUIPMENT

APC 3 *Piranha*

GUNS 40mm, incl L/70 AA; **75mm, 105mm, 120mm** 24 CD-80 *Karin* (mobile); **120mm** *Ersta* (static)

MOR 81mm, 120mm: 70

SSM 90 RBS-17 *Hellfire*, 6 RBS-15KA

SAM RBS-70

MINELAYERS 5 inshore

PATROL CRAFT 12 PCI<

AMPH 16 LCM, 52 LCU, 123 LCA

Air Force 7,700

(incl 1,900 conscripts and 1,800 active reservists); 206 cbt ac, no armed hel

Flying hours 110–140

1 Air Force Comd, 10 sqns

FGA/RECCE 1 sqn with 20 SAAB AJSH-37/AJSF-37, 1 OCU/EW trg with 12 SAAB SK-37E

MULTI-ROLE (FTR/FGA/RECCE) 4 sqn with 95 SAAB JAS-39 (5th sqn in 2002)

FTR 3 sqn + 2 trg units with 91 SAAB JA-37. (Two sqns from 2002, trg units to disband by 2003)

SIGINT 2 S-102B *Korpen* (*Gulfstream* IV)

AEW 6 S-100B *Argus* (SAAB-340B)

TPT 8 Tp-84 (C-130E/H), 3 Tp-101 (*King Air* 200), 1 Tp-100A (SAAB 340B) (VIP), 1 Tp-102A (*Gulfstream* IV) (VIP), 1 Tp-103 (Cessna 550)

ASW/MP 1 C-212

TRG 106 Sk-60

AAM RB-71 (*Skyflash*), RB-74 AIM 9L (*Sidewinder*), RB-99, AIM 120 (AMRAAM)

ASM RB-15F, RB-75 (*Maverick*), BK-39

AD semi-automatic control and surv system, *Stric*, coordinates all AD components

ARMED FORCES HELICOPTER WING

(1,000 personnel from all three services and 340 conscripts)

HEL 14 Hkp-4 (Vertol 107) ASW/tpt/SAR, 25 Hkp-5b (Hughes 300c) trg, 19 Hkp-6a (Bell-206) utl, 10 Hkp-6b, 20 Hkp-9a (BO-105) AT, 11 Hkp-10 (*Super Puma*) SAR, 5 Hkp-11 (Bell 412) SAR

Forces Abroad

UN AND PEACEKEEPING

BOSNIA (SFOR II): 41 **CROATIA** (UNMOP): 1 obs (SFOR): 1 **DROC** (MONUC): 1 obs **EAST TIMOR** (UNTAET): 2 obs **ETHIOPIA/ERITREA** (UNMEE): 13 incl 8 obs **GEORGIA** (UNOMIG): 5 obs **INDIA/PAKISTAN** (UNMOGIP): 8 obs **IRAQ/KUWAIT** (UNIKOM): 5 obs **MIDDLE EAST** (UNTSO): 11 obs **SIERRA LEONE** (UNAMSIL): 3 obs **YUGOSLAVIA** (KFOR): 751

Paramilitary 600

COAST GUARD 600

1 *Gotland* PCO and 1 KBV-171 PCC (fishery protection), some 65 PCI

AIR ARM 2 C-212 MR

CIVIL DEFENCE shelters for 6,300,000

All between ages 16–25 liable for civil defence duty

VOLUNTARY AUXILIARY ORGANISATIONS some 35,000

Switzerland CH

franc fr		1999	2000	2001	2002
GDP	fr	389bn	407bn		
	US$	247bn	245bn		
per capita	US$	29,600	30,017		
Growth	%	1.7	3.6		
Inflation	%	0.9	1.6		
Publ Debt	%	54.0			
Def exp	fr	4.9bn	4.9bn		
	US$	3.1bn	3.0bn		
Def bdgt	fr	5.0bn	4.9bn	4.7bn	
	US$	3.2bn	2.9bn	2.7bn	
US$1=fr		1.58	1.66	1.75	
Population					7,453,000
Age		13–17	18–22	23–32	
Men		203,000	205,000	477,000	
Women		194,000	198,000	468,000	

Total Armed Forces

ACTIVE about 3,600 (career officers and NCOs)

plus recruits (2 intakes in 2000 (total 23,270) each for 15 weeks only)

Terms of service 15 weeks compulsory recruit trg at age 19–20, followed by 10 refresher trg courses of 3 weeks over a 22-year period between ages 20–42. Some

181,000 attended trg in 2000

RESERVES 351,200

Army 320,600 (to be mobilised)

Armed Forces Comd (All units non-active/Reserve status)

Comd tps: 2 armd bde, 2 inf, 1 arty, 1 airport, 2 engr regt

3 fd Army Corps, each 2 fd div (3 inf, 1 arty regt), 1 armd bde, 1 engr, 1 cyclist, 1 fortress regt, 1 territorial div (5/6 regt)

1 mtn Army Corps with 3 mtn div (2 mtn inf, 1 arty regt), 3 fortress bde (each 1 mtn inf regt), 2 mtn inf, 2 fortress, 1 engr regt, 1 territorial div (6 regt), 2 territorial bde (1 regt)

EQUIPMENT

MBT 556: 186 Pz-68/88, 370 Pz-87 (*Leopard* 2)

RECCE 319 *Eagle*/II

AIFV 435 (incl 6 in store): 120 M-63/73, 315 M-63/89 (all M-113 with **20mm**)

APC 827 M-63/73 (M-113) incl variants, 353 *Piranha*

SP ARTY 155mm: 558 PzHb 66/74/-74/-79/-88 (M-109U)

MOR 81mm: 1,224 M-33, M-72; **120mm**: 534: 402 M-87, 132 M-64 (M-113)

ATGW 2,760 *Dragon*, 303 TOW-2 SP (MOWAG) *Piranha*

RL 12,512 incl: **60mm**: *Panzerfaust*; **83mm**: M-80

SAM *Stinger*

HEL 60 *Alouette* III

MARINE

10 *Aquarius* patrol boats

Air Force 30,600 (to be mobilised)

(incl AD units, mil airfield guard units); 138 cbt ac, no armed hel

1 Air Force bde, 1 AD bde, 1 Air-Base bde, 1 C³I bde, AF Maintenance Service

Flying hours: 150–200; reserves approx 50

FTR 9 (incl 1 trg) sqn

5 with 70 *Tiger* II/F-5E, 1 trg sqn with 3 *Tiger* II/F-5E and 12 *Tiger* II/F-5F

3 with 26 F/A-18 C and 7 F/A-18D

RECCE 2 sqn with 16* *Mirage* IIIRS 2, 4* *Mirage* IIIDS (pilot trg only)

TPT 1 sqn with 16 PC-6, 1 *Learjet* 35A, 2 Do-27, 1 *Falcon*-50

HEL 6 sqn with 15 AS-332 M-1 (*Super Puma*), 58 SA-316 (*Alouette* III)

TRG 19 *Hawk* Mk 66, 38 PC-7, 11 PC-9 (tgt towing)

UAV 4 systems ADS 95 *Ranger* operational 2003. 1 UAV bn in basic trg

AAM AIM-9 *Sidewinder*, AIM-120 AMRAAM

AIR DEFENCE

1 AD bde with

1 SAM regt (3 bn, each with 2 or 3 bty; B/L-84 *Rapier*)

5 AD Regt (each with 2 bn; each bn of 3 bty; 35mm guns, Skyguard fire control radar)

Forces Abroad

UN AND PEACEKEEPING

BOSNIA (OSCE): 50 **CROATIA** (UNMOP): 1 obs **DROC** (MONUC): 2 obs **ETHIOPIA/ERITREA** (UNMEE): 4 obs **GEORGIA** (UNOMIG): 4 obs **KOREA** (NNSC): 5 Staff **MIDDLE EAST** (UNTSO): 9 obs **YUGOSLAVIA** (KFOR): some 160; 1 coy

Paramilitary

CIVIL DEFENCE 280,000 (not part of Armed Forces)

Ukraine Ukr

hryvnia h		1999	2000	2001	2002
GDP	h	127bn	174bn		
	US$	49bn	32bn		
per capita	US$	4,550	4,762		
Growth	%	-0.4	6		
Inflation	%	22.7	25.8		
Debt	US$	12.6bn	10.4bn		
Def exp[a]	h	5.7bn	6bn		
	US$	1.4bn	1.1bn		
Def bdgt	h	1.5bn	2.4bn	3.15bn	
	US$	377m	441m	582m	
FMA[b] (US)	US$	2.2m	1.3m	1.5m	
US$1=h		3.97	5.44	5.41	

[a] Incl exp on paramilitary forces
[b] Excl US Cooperative Threat Reduction programme: **1992–96** US$395m, of which US$171m spent by Sep 1996. Programme continues through 2000

Population			50,387,000
Russian 22% Polish ε4% Jewish 1%			
Age	13–17	18–22	23–32
Men	1,901,000	1,877,000	3,595,000
Women	1,830,000	1,830,000	3,573,000

Total Armed Forces

ACTIVE ε303,800

(excl Strategic Nuclear Forces and Black Sea Fleet; incl 43,600 in central staffs and units not covered below)

Terms of service **Army**, **Air Force** 18 months **Navy** 2 years

RESERVES some 1,000,000

mil service within 5 years

Strategic Nuclear Forces

Elimination of Ukr's nuclear wpns on schedule to be completed by Dec 2001

Ground Forces 151,200

3 Op Comd (North, South, West)
MoD tps: 1 air mobile bde, 1 SSM bde (SS-21), 1 arty (trg), 1 engr bde
WESTERN OP COMD
Comd tps 1 arty div (1 arty, 1 MRL, 1 ATK bde), 3 SSM (SS-21) bde, 1 air mobile regt, 1 engr bde, 2 army avn bde
2 Army Corps
  1 with 2 mech div (each 3 mech, 1 tk, 1 SP arty regt), 2 mech bde, 1 arty bde, 1 MRL regt, 1 ATK regt
  1 with 2 mech div (each 3 mech, 1 tk, 1 SP arty regt), 1 mech bde, 1 arty regt, 1 MRL regt, 1 ATK regt
SOUTHERN OP COMD
Comd tps 1 mech div (2 mech bde), 1 air mobile div (1 air aslt, 1 airmobile bde, 1 arty regt), 1 arty div (1 arty, 1 MRL, 1 ATK bde), 1 air mobile, 1 SSM (Scud), 1 avn bde
2 Army Corps
  1 with 1 tank div (3 tk, 1 SP arty regt), 2 mech div (each 2 mech, 1 tk, 1 SP arty regt), 1 arty bde, 1 MRL regt, 1 ATK bde, 1 engr regt
  1 with 2 mech, 1 arty bde, 1 MRL, 1 ATK, 1 engr regt
NORTHERN OP COMD
Comd tps 2 mech div (3 mech, 1 SP arty regt), 1 tk trg centre, 1 tank, 2 SSM bde (1 Scud, 1 SS-21), 1 army avn bde, 1 engr regt
1 Army Corps with 1 tank div (3 tk, 1 SP arty regt), 1 mech div (2 mech, 1 SP arty regt), 1 mech trg centre, 1 arty bde, 1 MRL, 1 ATK, 1 engr regt
EQUIPMENT
  MBT 3,937: 149 T-55, 2,277 T-64, 1,238 T-72, 273 T-80
  RECCE some 600 BRDM-2
  AIFV 3,078: 1,011 BMP-1, 458 BRM-1K, 1,467 BMP-2, 3 BMP-3, 61 BMD-1, 78 BMD-2
  APC 1,782: 202 BTR-60, 1,087 BTR-70, 451 BTR-80, 42 BTR-D; plus 2,090 MT-LB, 4,700 'look-a-likes'
  TOTAL ARTY 3,702
    TOWED 1,130: **122mm**: 437 D-30; **152mm**: 219 D-20, 185 2A65, 289 2A36
    SP 1,301: **122mm**: 640 2S1; **152mm**: 496 2S3, 24 2S5, 40 2S19, **203mm**: 101 2S7
    COMBINED GUN/MOR 120mm: 62 2S9, 2 2B16
    MRL 603: **122mm**: 346 BM-21, 20 9P138; **132mm**: 4 BM-13; **220mm**: 139 9P140; **300mm**: 94 9A52
    MOR 604: **120mm**: 346 2S12, 257 PM-38; **160mm**: 1 M-160
  SSM 72 Scud B, 50 FROG, 90 SS-21
  ATGW AT-4 Spigot, AT-5 Spandrel, AT-6 Spiral
  ATK GUNS 100mm: ε500 T-12/MT-12
  AD GUNS 30mm: 70 2S6 SP; **57mm**: ε400 S-60
  SAM 100 SA-4, 125 SA-8, 60 SA-11, ε150 SA-13

ATTACK HEL 247 Mi-24
SPT HEL 4 Mi-2, 31 Mi-6, 162 Mi-8, 11 Mi-26
SURV SNAR-10 (Big Fred), Small Fred (arty)

Navy† ε13,000

(incl nearly 2,500 Naval Aviation, 1,500 Naval Infantry; 2,000 conscripts)
On 31 May 1997, RF President Boris Yeltsin and Ukr President Leonid Kuchma signed an inter-governmental agreement on the status and terms of the Black Sea Fleet's deployment on the territory of Ukr and parameters for the fleet's division. The RF Fleet will lease bases in Sevastopol for the next 20 years. It is based at Sevastopol and Karantinnaya Bays and jointly with Ukr warships at Streletskaya Bay. The overall serviceability of the fleet is very low

BASES Sevastopol, Donuzlav, Odessa, Kerch, Ochakov, Chernomorskoye (Balaklava, Nikolaev construction and repair yards)
SUBMARINES 1†
SSK 1 Foxtrot (Type 641) (non-op)
PRINCIPAL SURFACE COMBATANTS 3
CRUISERS 1†
CG 1 Ukraina (RF Slava) (in refit)
FRIGATES 2
FFG 1
  1 Mikolair (RF Krivak I) with 4 SS-N-14 Silex SSM/ASW, 2 SA-N-4 Gecko SAM, 4 × 76mm gun, 8 × 533mm TT†
FF 1
  1 Sagaidachny (RF Krivak III) 3 with 2 SA-N-4 Gecko SAM, 1 × 100mm gun, 8 × 533mm TT, 1 KA-27 hel
PATROL AND COASTAL COMBATANTS 8
CORVETTES 2
  2 Grisha II/V FS with 2 SA-N-4 Gecko SAM, 1 × 76mm gun, 4 × 533mm TT
TORPEDO CRAFT 2
  2 Pauk 1 PFT with 4 SA-N-5 Grail SAM, 1 × 76mm gun, 4 × 406mm TT
MISSILE CRAFT 3
  3 Matka PHM with 2 SS-N-2C Styx SSM, 1 × 76mm gun
PATROL CRAFT 1
  1 Zhuk PCI†
MINE WARFARE 5
MINE COUNTERMEASURES 5
  1 Yevgenya MHC, 2 Sonya MSC, 2 Natya MSC
AMPHIBIOUS 7
  4 Pomornik ACV with 2 SA-N-5 capacity 30 tps and crew
  1 Ropucha LST with 4 SA-N-5 SAM, 2 × 2 57mm gun, 92 mines; capacity 190 tps or 24 veh
  1 Alligator LST with 2/3 SA-N-5 SAM capacity 300 tps and 20 tk
  1 Polnocny LSM capacity 180 tps and 6 tk

SUPPORT AND MISCELLANEOUS 9

1 AO, 2 *Vytegrales* AK, 1 *Lama* msl spt, 1 Mod *Moma* AGI, 1 *Primore* AGI, 1 *Kashtan* buoytender, 1 *Elbrus* ASR; 1 AGOS

NAVAL AVIATION (2,500)

EQUIPMENT

13 armed hel

AIRCRAFT

TPT 8 An-26, 1 An-24, 5 An-12, 1 Il-18, 1 Tu-134

HELICOPTERS

ASW 11 Be-12, 2 Ka-27E

TPT 5 Mi-6

UTL 28 Ka-25, 42 Mi-14

NAVAL INFANTRY (1,500)

2 inf bn

Air Force 96,000

543 cbt ac, no attack hel

2 air corps (5th and 14th AVK), 1 multi-role rapid reaction air gp (35th AVG), 1 cbt trg centre, 1 trg institute

BBR 1 regt with 32 Tu-22M

FGA/BBR 2 div HQ, 5 regt (incl 1 trg) with 126 Su-24

FGA 2 regt with 63 Su-25

FTR 2 div, 8 regt with 224 MiG-29 (206 operational, 2 trg, 16 in store), 62 Su-27

RECCE 2 regt with 29* Su-24

CBT TRG 4* Su-24, 1* MiG-23, 2* MiG-29

TPT 78 Il-76, 45 An-12/An-24/An-26/An-30/Tu-134, Il-78 (tkr/tpt)

TRG 5 regt with 329 L-39 (plus 293 in store), 1 regt with 16 Mi-8

SPT HEL 111 Mi-2, 23 Mi-6, 170 Mi-8

AAM AA-7, AA-8., AA-9, AA-10, AA-11

ASM AS-7, AS-9, AS-10, AS-11, AS-12, AS-13, AS-14, AS-15

SAM 825: SA-2/-3/-5/-10/-12A/-300

Forces Abroad

UN AND PEACEKEEPING

CROATIA (UNMOP): 1 obs **DROC** (MONUC): 9 obs **ETHIOPIA/ERITREA** (UNMEE): 6 obs **LEBANON** (UNIFIL): 642 **YUGOSLAVIA** (KFOR): 240

Paramilitary

MVS (Ministry of Internal Affairs) 42,000, 4 regions, internal security tps, 85 ACV, 6 ac, 8 hel

NATIONAL GUARD 26,600 (to be disbanded)

4 div, 1 armd regt, 1 hel bde, 60 MBT, 500 ACV, 12 attack hel

BORDER GUARD 34,000

HQ and 3 regions, 200 ACV

MARITIME BORDER GUARD

The Maritime Border Guard is an independent subdivision of the State Commission for Border Guards, is not part of the Navy and is org with:

4 cutter, 2 river bde • 1 gunship, 1 MCM sqn • 1 aux ship gp • 1 trg div • 3 air sqn

PATROL AND COASTAL COMBATANTS 36

3 *Pauk* 1 with 4 SA-N-5 SAM, 1 76mm gun, 4 406mm TT

3 *Muravey* PHT with 1 76mm gun, 2 406mm TT

10 *Stenka* PFC with 4 30mm gun, 4 406mm TT

20 *Zhuk* PCI

AIRCRAFT

An-24, An-26, An-72, An-8, Ka-27

COAST GUARD 14,000

3 patrol boats, 1 water jet boat, 1 ACV, 1 landing ship, 1 OPV, 1 craft

CIVIL DEFENCE TROOPS (Ministry of Emergency Situations): some 9,500; 4 indep bde, 4 indep regt

Foreign Forces

Russia ε1,100 naval inf

Yugoslavia, Federal Republic of (Serbia–Montenegro) FRY

new dinar d		1999	2000	2001	2002
GDP	d	174bn	221bn		
	US$	13bn	18.3bn		
per capita	US$	4,300	4,931		
Growth	d	-20	10.7		
Inflation	d				
Debt	US$		12.2bn		
Def exp	d	ε19bn	22.1bn		
	US$	1.6bn	1.8bn		
Def bdgt	d	14.4bn	16.3bn	32.1bn	
	US$	1.3bn	1.3bn	479m	
US$1=d		11.5	12.1	66.9	
Population				ε**10,603,000**	

Serbia ε9,900,000 **Serb** 66% **Albanian** 17%, 90% in Kosovo **Hungarian** 4% mainly in Vojvodina

Montenegro ε700,000 **Montenegrin** 62% **Serb** 9% **Albanian** 7%

ε2,032,000 Serbs were living in the other Yugoslav republics before the civil war

Age	13–17	18–22	23–32
Men	412,000	425,000	837,000
Women	388,000	402,000	795,000

Total Armed Forces

ACTIVE 105,500

(43,000 conscripts) *Terms of service* 12–15 months

RESERVES some 400,000

Army (JA) some 79,000

(incl 4,000 naval ground tps; 37,000 conscripts)
3 Army, 7 Corps (incl 1 capital def) • 1 div HQ • 6 tk
bde • 1 gd bde (-), 1 SF bde • 2 mech bde • 1 AB bde •
12 mot inf bde (incl 1 protection) • 6 mixed arty bde •
7 AD bde • 1 SAM bde • 2 MP bn

RESERVES
ε350,000: 27 mot inf, 19 inf bde

EQUIPMENT
  MBT 721 T-55, 230 M-84 (T-74; mod T-72), 65 T-72
  AIFV 557 M-80
  APC 147 M-60P, 57 BOV VP M-86
  TOWED 105mm: 243 M-56; **122mm**: 54 M-38, 304 D-
      30; **130mm**: 238 M-46; **152mm**: 25 D-20, 52 M-84;
      155mm: 112 M-1, 6 M-65
  SP 122mm: 82 2S1
  MRL 128mm: 36 M-63, 51 M-77
  MOR 82mm: 1,100; **120mm**: 283 M-74, 802 M-75
  SSM 4 FROG
  ATGW 142 AT-3 *Sagger* incl SP (BOV-1, BRDM-1/2),
      AT-4 *Fagot*
  RCL 57mm: 1,550; **82mm**: 1,500 M-60PB SP; **105mm**:
      650 M-65
  ATK GUNS 725 incl: **90mm**: M-36B2 (incl SP), M-3;
      100mm: 138 T-12, MT-12
  AD GUNS 2,000: **20mm**: M-55/-75, BOV-3 SP triple;
      30mm: M-53, M-53/-59, BOV-30 SP; **57mm**: ZSU-
      57-2 SP
  SAM 60 SA-6/-9/-13, 900 SA-7/-14/-16/-18

Navy 7,000

(incl 3,000 conscripts and 900 Marines)
BASES Kumbor, Tivat, Bar, Novi Sad (River Comd)
(Most former Yugoslav bases are now in Cr hands)
SUBMARINES 4
SSK 1
  1 *Sava* with 533mm TT
  plus 3 *Una* SSI for SF ops (all non-op)
PRINCIPAL SURFACE COMBATANTS 3
FRIGATES 3
FFG 3
  2 *Kotor* with 4 SS-N-2C *Styx* SSM, 1 × 2 SA-N-4 *Gecko*
      SAM, 2 × 3 ASTT, 2 × 12 ASW RL
  1 *Split* (Sov *Koni*) with 4 SS-N-2C *Styx* SSM, 1 × 2 SA-
      N-4 *Gecko* SAM, 2 × 12 ASW RL
PATROL AND COASTAL COMBATANTS 31
MISSILE CRAFT 9
  5 *Rade Koncar* PFM with 2 SS-N-2B *Styx* SSM (some †)
  4 *Mitar Acev* (Sov *Osa* I) PFM with 4 SS-N-2A *Styx* SSM
PATROL CRAFT 22†

PATROL, INSHORE 4 *Mirna* PCI<
PATROL, RIVERINE about 18 < (some in reserve)
MINE WARFARE 10
MINE COUNTERMEASURES 10
  2 *Vukov Klanac* MHC, 1 UK *Ham* MSI, 7 *Nestin* MSI
AMPHIBIOUS 1
  1 *Silba* LCT/ML: capacity 6 tk or 300 tps, 1 × 4 SA-N-
      5 SAM, can lay 94 mines
  plus craft:
  8 Type 22 LCU, 6 Type 21 LCU, 4 Type 11 LCVP
SUPPORT AND MISCELLANEOUS 9
  1 PO-91 *Lubin* tpt, 1 water carrier, 4 AT, 2 AK, 1
      degaussing

MARINES (900)
2 mot inf 'bde' (2 regt each of 2 bn) • 1 lt inf bde
(reserve) • 1 coast arty bde • 1 MP bn

Air Force 19,500

(incl 3,000 conscripts); 111 cbt ac, 19 armed hel
2 Corps (1 AD)
FGA 5 sqn with 14 *Orao* 2, 36 *Super Galeb* G-4
FTR 4 sqn with 20 MiG-21F/PF/M/bis, 9 MiG-21U, 4
    MiG-29A, 1 MiG-29U
RECCE 2 sqn with 17* *Orao*, 10* MiG-21R
ARMED HEL 17 H-45 *Partizan* (*Gazelle*)
ASW 1 hel sqn with 2* Ka-25
TPT 8 An-26, 2 *Falcon* 50 (VIP), 6 Yak-40, 2 Do-28D
    Skyservant
LIAISON ac 32 UTVA-66 **hel** 27 HN-42 *Partizan*, 40+
    Mi-8
TRG ac 30 UTVA-75 **hel** 3 HI-42 (*Gazelle*)
AAM AA-2 *Atoll*, AA-8 *Aphid*, AA-10 *Alamo*, AA-11
    Archer
ASM AGM-65 *Maverick*, AS-7 *Kerry*
AD 8 SAM bn, 12 SA-3
  15 regt AD arty

Paramilitary

MINISTRY OF INTERIOR TROOPS ε80,000
internal security; eqpt incl 150 AFV, 170 mor, 16 hel
SPECIAL POLICE UNITS ε7,000
MONTENEGRIN MINISTRY OF INTERIOR TROOPS ε6,000

Opposition

**LIBERATION ARMY OF PRESEVO, MEDVEDJA AND
BUJANOVAC** ε800

UN and Peacekeeping

KFOR (Kosovo Peace Implementation Force): some
38,600 tps from 30 countries are deployed in Kosovo, a
further 7,500 provide rear area spt in Alb, FYROM and
Gr

MAIN DEVELOPMENTS

After years of false starts, Russian military reform appears to be getting underway. The new programme, adopted on 15 January 2001, covers the period up to 2005. President Vladimir Putin's active involvement and direction are key to this process. Economic growth is also having an impact, with more money available for defence spending. New senior appointments herald change and indicate the areas accorded priority. Restructuring is concentrated on re-balancing the force structure in favour of the ground forces, with an emphasis on combat training. At the same time, re-equipment and the wider issues relating to the military-industrial complex, such as research and development, and arms sales, are receiving much-needed attention. US missile-defence plans, NATO enlargement and lessons from Chechnya drive the debate over priorities. However, the ongoing conflict in Chechnya is draining resources and, with mounting casualties, has a debilitating effect on the reform process.

MILITARY REFORM

Defence leadership

The main change in the armed forces in 2001 has been in the leadership of the Ministry of Defence. By appointing Sergei Ivanov as the first civilian minister of defence in March, Putin achieved a primary aim of his reform programme: establishing civilian control over the military. He followed through by appointing a series of deputy defence ministers. The new deputy minister for finance, Lyubov Kudelina, is renowned for her tough stance on corruption and her belief in the need for secrecy in defence budgeting. Another key appointment is that of deputy minister for armaments, former intelligence officer from the External Intelligence Service (SVR), Mikhail Dmitriev, who is also the chairman of the Committee on Military-Technical Cooperation with Foreign States. His appointment is a clear indication that re-equipment is a high priority of the reform programme; also, that arms sales are regarded as an important source of revenue to fund new programmes. The appointment of Colonel General Aleksei Moskovsky – formerly a senior figure in the military-industrial complex – to the post of deputy minister and state secretary underscores this point. The serviceability figures for the Russian Air Force are a good example of the armed forces' urgent need to re-equip: of the air force's 2,000 aircraft, only 46% are estimated to be serviceable.

Changes have also been made in the area of international military cooperation. Colonel General Leonid Ivashov, former Head of the Main Directorate for International Military Cooperation and a known hardliner towards NATO, has been replaced by Lieutenant General Anatoly Mazurkeyevich, a former head of the External Relations Directorate of the Ministry of Defence, who has a background in diplomacy. Colonel General Yuri Baluevsky, former head of the Main Directorate for Operations, is now deputy chief of the general staff, with responsibility for US–Russia bilateral negotiations on missile defence.

Ground forces

Putin's next priority task was to raise the status of the ground forces, the largest part of the armed forces, putting them back on a par with the navy and the air force as a separate service, a position they lost in the Yeltsin reforms of 1993. To achieve this, Putin appointed Colonel General Nikolai Kormiltsev as the commander-in chief of the ground forces. Kormiltsev was also made deputy minister with responsibility for combat training. This dual appointment not only raises the status of the ground forces, but also places more emphasis on combat training, which has been lacking in recent years, as has been highlighted in Chechnya. Furthermore, it gives Kormiltsev a role in both the Ministry of Defence and the General Staff. Arguably, Kormiltsev, and by extension, the ground forces, now have greater influence than the other two services, by his having a voice in both organs.

Strategic forces

Under Putin's reforms the Strategic Rocket Forces (SRF) have lost their position as a separate service by being downgraded to be a branch of the armed forces, thus ending the argument between Chief of the General Staff Army General Anatoly Kvashnin and former Defence Minister Marshal Igor Sergeyev, over whether the SRF should retain its status. The former minister, who had argued in favour, is himself now an advisor to the president on strategic affairs.

A key change for the strategic forces is the creation of a new and independent arm, the Space and Space-Defence Force, comprising the former elements of the SRF that were responsible for launching and controlling spacecraft, as well as the missile-defence forces. This new organisation, created on 1 June 2001, is under the command of Colonel General Anatoly Perminov. Its responsibilities include:

- the technical elements of satellite communications;
- warning of missile attack;
- intercept of attack on the 'protected regions' as defined in the 1972 Anti-Ballistic Missile (ABM) Treaty;
- provision of intelligence;
- satellite navigation;
- meteorological and cartographical information; and
- control of outer space.

The remaining elements of the SRF may eventually pass to the air force, possibly by 2005. Meanwhile, the navy retains control of approximately 35% of nuclear delivery systems.

One result of downgrading the SRF is that its resources have been reduced. Production of TOPOL-M missiles, which was programmed to be as high as 20 a year, is now believed to be about five or six per annum. There is obvious reluctance in Moscow to increase this number despite pressure by some hardliners in the Ministry of Defence to do so caused by Moscow's argument with Washington over the US National Missile Defense plans.

Airborne forces

The airborne forces retain their status as an independent service but are to lose 2,000 soldiers in cuts announced in June 2001. This will reduce their strength to 30,000. To alleviate over-commitment of the airborne forces, it is believed that they will be relieved of their Balkan peacekeeping duties and will soon be replaced by motor-rifle troops, who are undergoing training for the task. A parallel manpower-saving measure is the reduction of the Russian military contingent in Bosnia-Herzegovina from 1,100 to 600 and its redesignation as 22 Airborne Regiment.

Volga–Ural Military District

The delayed merger of the Privolzhskiye and Ural Military Districts should be complete by 1 September 2001. The headquarters will be in Yekaterinburg and may serve as the rear headquarters for operations in the Central Asia region and, possibly, for peacekeeping operations. The 27 (Volga) Motor Rifle Division, based in the newly amalgamated military district, is being reconstituted, having been disbanded as part of an earlier defence cut, and may return to its traditional role as a peacekeeping formation.

Personnel

Improvements in pay and conditions of service are the leading contenders for scarce resources. It is no longer possible for Putin to stave off criticism on this issue. He has called for a 'compact, modern, well-paid professional army' and has authorised a 20% pay rise. One measure to help fund this increase is a further 365,000 reduction in personnel, to be completed by 2003. The army will be cut by 180,000, the navy by 50,000 and the air force by 40,000; the remaining reductions will be achieved by scaling down paramilitary and other security forces. However, to end years of conscription is not only expensive, but also requires a root-and-branch reform of current terms and conditions of service. It will be some time before this can be achieved. One option which has been tested, particularly in Chechnya, is contract service. However, the introduction of this type of engagement has alienated conscript soldiers receiving less pay than their contract counterparts, and has had a counterproductive effect on discipline.

Overall, the new reform programme is a step forward and for the first time the federal government has recognised the problems for personnel arising from the changes with a direct allocation of funds to assist redundant servicemen. Finance Minister Alexei Kudrin announced in August 2001 that R4.5bn is to be allocated this year and R16.6bn next year. However, it is noticeable that some of the new measures merely reverse reforms of previous programmes. For example, the re-establishment of the ground forces as a separate service, and the re-creation of the Space and Space-Defence Force.

CHECHNYA

The second military campaign in Chechnya, which started in August 1999, is now entering its third year. Until 2001, the emphasis was on old-style military operations. Motor-rifle and armoured troops, backed by air and artillery strikes, had difficulty coping with the complexities of the counter-terrorist campaign. The casualty figures, both military and civilian, were high, and collateral damage was extensive. However, a troop reduction in January 2001, estimated at 5,000, heralded a change in the conduct of the campaign. Some heavy equipment is being withdrawn gradually, and air and artillery strikes have reduced in quantity and scale, with a corresponding fall in collateral damage to civilian areas. The Federal Security Bureau (FSB)

Table 13 **Estimated Costs of the Chechnya Campaign**		US$m
	Total	**MOD**	**Other**
2000	940	710	230
2001	725	290	435

has been given the lead role in operations. However, the rebels continue to demonstrate considerable freedom of movement by carrying out attacks in the heart of the republic, and their resistance shows little sign of weakening. Their main *modus operandum* is to attack Russian federal forces by mining routes with conventional, radio-controlled and wire-operated explosive devices. Sniper attacks and intense small-arms attacks on checkpoints and other static locations are daily occurrences. The federal counter-strategy is to conduct extensive search-and-destroy operations to kill or capture rebel commanders. These tactics, carried out mainly by FSB and Special Force units, with MOD and Interior Troops in support, have had some success, but are limited in scope, and risk alienating an increasingly hostile population. Disproportionate use of force, and widespread human-rights abuses by federal forces in Chechnya have been heavily criticised by the Russian and foreign press, the Council of Europe, the Organisation for Security and Cooperation in Europe (OSCE) and non-governmental organisations. However, the federal authority has had little success in dealing with the problem. The armed forces themselves show little enthusiasm for carrying out internal investigations, despite some attempts by the military prosecutor's office to deal with the results of endemic poor discipline. Until this is done, the battle for the 'hearts and minds' of the civil population, which is crucial to the success of the campaign in Chechnya, will be lost.

The MOD-provided troops in Chechnya are based around the building-block formation of 42 Motor Rifle Division, which is permanently garrisoned in Chechnya. The division has been specially constructed for Chechnya and comprises 15,000 troops organised into four motor-rifle regiments, one of which is designated for operations in mountainous terrain. In addition, MOD troops from across the Russian Federation are deployed as *roulement* units, coming into the conflict area from other regions on a rotational basis as needed. The two main tasks of 42 Motor Rifle Division and the other MOD units are guarding key points and route security. Troops from these units and formations also man village garrisons in populated parts of the area of operations. The Interior Ministry's 46 Independent Brigade, which has about 10,800 troops, provides policing and plays a large part in 'cleansing' activities; that is, clearing rebels from populated areas by carrying out extensive house-to-house searches. The other major force element is a Border Guard contingent of 8,000 troops. Overall, the force ratio is approximately 1:18 in favour of the federal forces. However, the largely hostile population in the area of operations reduces this advantage.

Costs of the Chechnya Campaign

The financial cost of the campaign is high, with some Russian analysts quoting a total of R33bn ($940m) for the campaign in 2000. This figure is a combination of at least R25bn ($710m) spent on the military campaign and R14bn ($230m) spent on economic reconstruction. Officials claim that military operations are wholly financed from MOD sources and it is difficult to discern how much may have come from the federal budgetary surplus. This year's defence budget allocations are about R25m ($725m). With a total of R15bn ($435m) to be spent on reconstruction, the MOD's contribution is likely to be about R10bn ($290m). According to official estimates, restoring the Chechen Republic's civilian infrastructure in the next two years will require the Russian government to spend twice the amount allocated in 2001.

MILITARY COOPERATION/CENTRAL ASIA

A major development in Russian military reform at the strategic level has been the restructuring and reorientation of the armed forces to deal with threats from Central Asia. This has been carried out in cooperation with the countries in the region, mainly through the mechanism of the Commonwealth of Independent States (CIS) Collective Security Treaty. At the May 2001 CIS summit in Yerevan, a decision was taken to form a 'Collective Rapid Deployment Force' (CRDF) for regional contingencies, specifically to counter Islamic extremist insurgency emanating from Afghanistan. This force, which is not a standing force, is to consist of battalions from Kazakstan, Kyrgyzstan and Tajikistan, with a significant but undeclared Russian element. All elements remain in their home countries except when called upon. The CRDF will be under the command of a Russian general officer, Major General Sergei Chernomyrdin, with the command-and-control centre located in Bishkek, Kyrgyzstan.

RUSSIAN MILITARY AND THE WEST

NATO enlargement and the European Security and Defence Policy (ESDP)

The possibility of further NATO enlargement strengthens the case of those senior Russian military figures who argue that NATO remains a threat. Russian officials claim that enlargement is not necessary in the post-Cold War world and that if the Baltic states joined NATO, Kaliningrad would become the first part of the Russian Federation to be surrounded by NATO countries. To promote the idea that NATO expansion is unnecessary, and that European security is best dealt with by Europeans alone, Russia prefers to work through European mechanisms. Consequently, Russia's stated willingness to examine new ways of contributing to EU crisis-management operations suggests that MOD strategic planners view the ESDP as offering greater opportunities for cooperation than NATO. However, some officials in Moscow still believe that the ESDP is no more than an extension of NATO.

Missile defence

The outcome of Putin's meeting with US President George W. Bush at the July 2001 G-8 summit in Genoa was the opening of a dialogue linking the issues of missile defence and strategic nuclear reductions. This outcome indicates the importance assigned by Putin to a sound working relationship with the US on key security and economic issues. In taking this track, Putin has rejected, at least for the time being, the possibility of making common cause with the Chinese in opposing the US missile-defence plans outright. Since both Russia and the US want major reductions in their strategic forces, there are prospects for progress; however, the Russian president still faces the challenge of selling such reductions to his domestic military constituency. The impending negotiations will undoubtedly be a test of his authority and leadership in military and security issues.

DEFENCE SPENDING

After the financial crisis and resulting collapse of the rouble in August 1998, Russia is now experiencing robust economic growth. The higher price of oil and metals, together with lower interest rates, some fiscal stimulus and strong export performance, spurred growth to 7.7% in 2000.

The continuing recovery in the Russian economy and the associated rise in government revenues, largely from oil, supported another increase in the officially reported defence budget, which rose from R141bn in 2000 to R219bn in 2001. R14bn were added to the initial 2000 budget mainly to cover costs in Chechnya. Nevertheless, there is concern that, despite a somewhat better economic outlook, the recovery is hostage to oil price trends. Should the current positive situation change, the defence budget is likely to suffer. Meanwhile, there is a continuing need to rein in defence spending. As a result, Russia is extending the life of its existing intercontinental ballistic missiles (ICBMs) and slowing the introduction of new missiles. The current deployment rate of new *Topol-M* missiles, about five or six per annum, is less than one-third of the amount originally planned. This reflects in part the decision to increase funding for conventional forces at the expense of the strategic arm.

Defence industry and sales

At the end of 2000, the military-industrial complex underwent a major reorganisation. The previous export organisation, which had been split between *Rosvooruzheniye* and *Promexport*, was dismantled, and a new company, *Rosoboronexport*, emerged. Unlike its predecessors, which came under the Ministry of Science and Technology, *Rosoboronexport* was placed in the domain of the MOD. Moreover, it was announced on 19 July 2001 that the avionics industry is to gain a new state-controlled company. This move once again reinforces the Kremlin's view that the defence industry should be placed under tight state control. The new corporation, *Avionika*, will be formed under a presidential decree, to be signed by the end of 2001. The government is expected to have a 51% stake in the company.

Table 14 **Official Russian defence budgets and outlays, 1992–2001**				Rm
	Defence budget	Federal budget (%)	Defence outlay	Federal outlay (%)	GDP (%)
1992	384	16.0	855	16.4	4.7
1993	3,116	16.6	7,210	20.7	4.4
1993 Revised	8,327	n.a	7,210	20.7	4.4
1994	40,626	20.9	28,028	16.4	4.6
1995	48,577	19.6	47,800	12.2	3.1
1995 Revised	59,379	21.3	47,800	12.2	3.1
1996	80,185	18.4	63,900	14.2	3.0
1997	104,300	19.7	79,700	16.2	3.1
1997 Revised	83,000	19.7	79,700	16.2	3.1
1998	81,765	16.4	56,700	12.7	2.1
1999	93,702	16.3	116,000	17.2	2.6
1999 Revised	109,000	19.0	116,000	17.2	2.6
2000	140,850	16.7	n.a.	n.a.	2.6
2000 Revised	151,000	17.6	n.a.	n.a.	2.6
2001	218,940	18.4	n.a.	n.a.	2.9

Note Military pensions (R11bn) moved from the Defence Budget to the Social Budget in 1998

Table 15 **Estimated official Russian defence budget by function, 1999–2001**						Rm
	1999	%	2000	%	2001	%
Personnel	33,900	31.1	50,100	35.6	62,543	28.5
Operations & Maintenance	29,600	27.2	37,950	26.9	70,148	32.0
Procurement	23,800	21.8	27,300	19.4	43,788	20.0
R&D	14,000	12.8	15,600	11.1	21,894	10.0
Infrastructure	3,500	3.2	4,000	2.8	6,568	3.0
Nuclear	1,900	1.7	2,900	2.1	5,129	2.3
MoD	500	0.5	1,000	0.7	1,532	0.7
Other	1,800	1.7	2,000	1.4	7,338	3.3

Deputy Minister Dmitriev was appointed to oversee planned efforts to link sales, research and development, and domestic re-equipment. There have been immediate signs of an upward trend in sales: in 2000, Russia exported $3–4bn worth of arms, an increase of almost $1bn over 1999.

The geographical distribution of Russian exports remained largely unchanged, with India and China still the main customers. As of November 2000, the PRC accounted for 50% of deliveries and India accounted for 22%. China's acquisitions of the *Sovremenny*-class destroyer and of the *Kilo*-class submarine, as well as the transfer of the same class submarine to India, explain the high proportion of exports accounted for by naval equipment. At the end of 2000, Russia signed a series of agreements with India, worth more than $3.5bn, for the licensed production of 140 Su-30 MKI fighter jets, 310 T90 main battle tanks and the Soviet-era aircraft carrier *Admiral Gorshkov*. However, since the resignation of Indian Defence Minister George Fernandez in March 2001, the future of these deals is uncertain.

In contravention of the understanding stipulated in the 1995 Gore–Chernomyrdin agreement on arms sales to Iran, Russia is currently considering the resumption of arms deliveries to Iran.

An agreement was signed with Tehran in March 2001 to resume trade in conventional weapons, which had ceased in 1989. Fighter-ground attack (FGA) aircraft, helicopters and S-300 air-defence missiles are considered Iran's most likely purchases, and the total package may be worth as much as $4–5bn. Agreements have also been reached with both Libya and Algeria for the modernisation and re-equipment of their armed forces.

Table 16 Russian arms deliveries, 1993–2000

	Arms exports		Domestic procurement	Arms exports as % of domestic procurement	All merchandise exports	Arms exports as % of all exports	Russia's share of world arms market (%)
	US$bn	Rbn	Rbn		US$bn		
1993	3.4	3.4	2	170.0	44	7.7	10.6
1994	1.7	3.7	8	46.3	67	2.5	5.8
1995	3.5	16.0	10	160.0	83	4.2	9.7
1996	3.1	15.9	13	122.3	91	3.4	8.7
1997	2.6	23.1	21	110.0	89	2.9	6.3
1998	2.2	21.4	17	125.9	74	3.0	6.1
1999	3.1	76.6	24	319.2	73	4.3	8.5
2000	3.4	100.1	27.3	367	90	3.8	11.9

Table 17 Russian arms trade by service and destination, 2000[1]

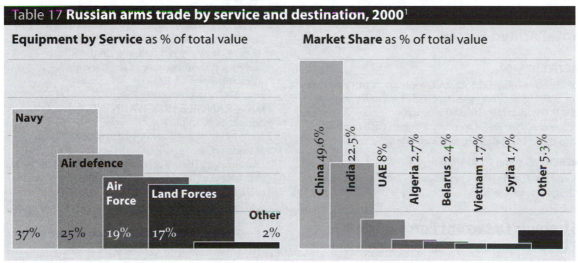

Equipment by Service as % of total value

Navy 37%   Air defence 25%   Air Force 19%   Land Forces 17%   Other 2%

Market Share as % of total value

China 49.6%   India 22.5%   UAE 8%   Algeria 2.7%   Belarus 2.4%   Vietnam 1.7%   Syria 1.7%   Other 5.3%

Note [1] As of November 2000

Russia RF

rouble r		1999	2000	2001	2002
GDP[1]	r	4,545bn	6,920bn		
	US$	1,100bn	1,200bn		
per capita	US$	7,000	7,600		
Growth	%	3.2	7.7		
Inflation	%	85.7	40		
Debt	US$	218bn			
Def exp[1]	US$	56bn	60bn		
Def bdgt[1]	r	112bn	143bn	218bn	
	US$	31bn	29bn	44bn	
FMA[2] (US)	US$	0.9m	0.9m	0.9m	
US$1=r		24.7	28.4	28.9	

[1] PPP est

[2] Under the US Cooperative Threat Reduction programme, $2.8bn has been authorised by the US to support START implementation and demilitarisation in RF, Ukr, Bel and Kaz. RF's share is 60–65%

Population				146,720,000
Tatar 4% Ukrainian 3% Chuvash 1% Bashkir 1%				
Belarussian 1% Moldovan 1% other 8%				
Age	13–17	18–22	23–32	
Men	5,967,000	5,684,000	10,034,000	
Women	5,735,000	5,538,000	9,852,000	

Total Armed Forces

ACTIVE 977,100

(incl about 200,000 MoD staff, centrally controlled units for EW, trg, rear services, not incl elsewhere; perhaps 330,000 conscripts, 100,000 women)
Terms of service 18–24 months. Women with medical and other special skills may volunteer

RESERVES some 20,000,000

some 2,400,000 with service within last 5 years; Reserve obligation to age 50

Strategic Deterrent Forces ε149,000

(incl 49,000 assigned from Air Force and Navy)

NAVY (ε13,000)

280 msl in 17 operational SSBN†
SSBN 17 declared operational (all based in RF ports)
6 *Delta* IV with 16 SS-N-23 *Skiff* (96 msl)
3 *Typhoon* with 20 SS-N-20 *Sturgeon* (60 msl)
7 *Delta* III with 16 SS-N-18 *Stingray* (112 msl)
1 *Delta* I with 12 SS-N-8 *Sawfly* (12 msl)
(The following non-op SSBNs remain START-accountable, with a total of 156 msl:
1 *Delta* IV with 16 SS-N-23 *Skiff* (16 msl)
2 *Typhoon* with 20 SS-N-20 *Sturgeon* (40 msl)
4 *Delta* III with 16 SS-N-18 *Stingray* (64 msl)
3 *Delta* I with 12 SS-N-8 *Sawfly* (36 msl)

In the 31 Jan START I declaration, RF declared a total of 436 'deployed' SLBMs. The above figures represent holdings as of 31 Jan 2001.)

STRATEGIC MISSILE FORCE TROOPS (ε100,000 incl 50,000 conscripts)

4 rocket armies equipped with silo and mobile msl launchers. 740 launchers with 3,380 nuclear warheads org in 19 div: launcher gp normally with 10 silos (6 for SS-18) and one control centre; 12 SS-24 rail, each with 3 launchers
ICBM 740
180 SS-18 *Satan* (RS-20) at 4 fields; mostly mod 4/5, 10 MIRV per msl
140 SS-19 *Stiletto* (RS-18) at 4 fields; mostly mod 3, 6 MIRV per msl
36 SS-24 *Scalpel* (RS-22) 10 MIRV; 36 rail
360 SS-25 *Sickle* (RS-12M); mobile, single-warhead; 10 bases with some 40 launch units
24 SS-27 (*Topol*-M2), 3 regts
ABM 100: 36 SH-11 (mod *Galosh*), 64 SH-08 *Gazelle*, S-400

WARNING SYSTEMS

ICBM/SLBM launch-detection capability, others include photo recce and ELINT
RADARS
OVER-THE-HORIZON-BACKSCATTER (OTH-B)
2 in Ukr, at Nikolaev and Mukachevo, covering US and polar areas. (While these facilities are functioning, they are not tied in with the RF air-defence system because of outstanding legal difficulties with Ukr.)
1 near Yeniseysk, covering PRC
LONG-RANGE EARLY-WARNING ABM-ASSOCIATED
7 long-range phased-array systems operational: Moscow, Olenegorsk (Kola), Gaballa (Az), Baranovichi (Bel), Pechora (Urals), Balkhash (Kaz), Mishelevka (Irkutsk)
11 *Hen House*-series; range 6,000km, 6 locations covering approaches from the west and south-west, north-east and south-east and (partially) south. Engagement, guidance, battle management: 1 *Pill Box* phased-array at Pushkino (Moscow)

SPACE FORCES

Formed 1 Jun 2001. Based on formations and units withdrawn from Strategic Missile and Air Defence Forces engaged in spacecraft launch and control

Army ε321,000

(incl ε190,000 conscripts)
7 Mil Districts (MD), 1 Op Strategic Gp
6 Army HQ, 3 Corps HQ
5 TD (3 tk, 1 motor rifle, 1 arty, 1 SAM regt; 1 armd recce bn; spt units)
18 MRD (3 motor rifle, 1 arty, 1 SAM regt; 1 indep tk, 1

Russia (sidebar)

ATK, 1 armd recce bn; spt units)

4 ABD (each 2/3 para, 1 arty regt) plus 1 AB trg centre (bde)

6 MG/arty div

5 arty div (each up to 6 bde incl 1 MRL, 1 ATK)

7 District trg centre (each = bde - 1 per MD)

14 indep bde (10 MR, 4 AB)

7 SF (*Spetsnaz*) bde

18 indep arty bde (incl MRL)

15 SSM bde (SS-21)

5 ATK bde, 3 ATK regt

19 SAM bde (incl 2 SA-4, 4 SA-11, 1 SA-12; all AD div disbanded)

20 hel regt (9 attack, 6 aslt tpt, 5 trg)

Other Front and Army tps

engr, pontoon-bridge, pipe-line, signals, EW, CW def, tpt, supply bde/regt/bn

RESERVES (cadre formations, on mobilisation form)

2 TD, 16 MRD, 1 hy arty bde, 4 indep arty bde, 6 MR bde, 2 tk bde

EQUIPMENT

Figures in () were reported to CFE on 1 Jan 2001 and include those held by Naval Infantry and Coastal Defence units

MBT about 21,820 (5,210), T-34 (1), 1,200 T-55 (15), 2,020 T-62 (265), 4,300 T-64A/-B (207), 9,700 T-72L/-M (1,798) 4,500 T-80/-U/UD/UM (2,921), 150 T-90 (3) (total incl ε8,000 in store - in RF)

LT TK 150 PT-76 (1)

RECCE some 2,000 BRDM-2

TOTAL AIFV/APC ε25,975 (8,923)

AIFV 14,700 (6,148): 7,500 BMP-1 (1,450), 4,600 BMP-2 (3,038), 100 BMP-3 (25), some 1,800 BMD incl BMD-1 (697), BMD-2 (336), BMD-3 (103), 700 BRM-1K (478), BTR-80A (21) (total incl 900 in store)

APC 11,275 (2,775): 1,000 BTR-50, 4,900 BTR-60/-70/-80 incl BTR-60 (25), BTR-70 (723), BTR-80 (934), 575 BTR-D (491); 4,800 MT-LB (602), plus 'look-alikes' (total incl 1,150 in store)

TOTAL ARTY 20,746 (5,991), with ε6,213 in store

TOWED 10,065 (1,972) incl: **122mm**: 1,200 M-30 (13); 3,050 D-30 (804); **130mm**: 50 M-46 (1); **152mm**: 100 ML-20 (1); 700 M-1943 (D1); 1,075 D-20 (185), 1,100 2A36 (536), 750 2A65 (432); **203mm**: 40 B-4M; incl ε2,000 mainly obsolete types

SP 4,705 (2,395) incl: **122mm**: 1,725 2S1 (395); **152mm**: 1,600 2S3 (1,101), 700 2S5 (451), 550 2S19 (418); **203mm**: 130 2S7 (30)

COMBINED GUN/MOR 820+ (349): **120mm**: 790 2S9 SP (318), 2B16 (22), 30 2S23 (9)

MRL 2,606 (921) incl: **122mm**: 50 BM-13/-14/-16 (6), 1,750 BM-21 (408), 25 9P138 (13); **220mm**: 675 (402) 9P140; **300mm**: 106 (92) 9A52

MOR 2,550 (354) incl: **120mm**: 920 2S12 (173), 900 PM-38 (145); **160mm**: 300 M-160; **240mm**: 430 2S4 SP (36)

SSM (nuclear-capable) ε200 SS-21 *Scarab* (*Tochka*), (all *Scud* and FROG in store)

ATGW AT-2 *Swatter*, AT-3 *Sagger*, AT-4 *Spigot*, AT-5 *Spandrel*, AT-6 *Spiral*, AT-7 *Saxhorn*, AT-9, AT-10

RL **64mm**: RPG-18; **73mm**: RPG-7/-16/-22/-26; **105mm**: RPG-27/-29

RCL **73mm**: SPG-9; **82mm**: B-10

ATK GUNS **57mm**: ASU-57 SP; **76mm**; **85mm**: D-44/SD-44, ASU-85 SP; **100mm**: 526 T-12/-12A/M-55 towed

AD GUNS **23mm**: ZU-23, ZSU-23-4 SP; **30mm**: 2S6 SP; **37mm**; **57mm**: S-60, ZSU-57-2 SP; **85mm**: M-1939; **100mm**: KS-19; **130mm**: KS-30

SAM about 2,300

450 SA-4 A/B *Ganef* (twin) (Army/Front wpn - most in store)

350 SA-6 *Gainful* (triple) (div wpn)

400 SA-8 *Gecko* (2 triple) (div wpn)

200 SA-9 *Gaskin* (2 twin) (regt wpn)

250 SA-11 *Gadfly* (quad) (replacing SA-4/-6)

100 SA-12A/B (*Gladiator/Giant*)

400 SA-13 *Gopher* (2 twin) (replacing SA-9)

120 SA-15 (replacing SA-6/SA-8)

SA-19 (2S6 SP) (8 SAM, plus twin **30mm** gun)

SA-7, SA-14 being replaced by SA-16, SA-18 (man-portable)

HELICOPTERS ε1,700 (with 600 in store)

ATTACK ε700 Mi-24 (583), 8 Ka-50 *Hokum* (4)

RECCE 140 Mi-24

TPT Mi-6, Mi-8/-17 (some armed), Mi-26 (hy)

Navy 171,500

(incl ε16,000 conscripts, ε13,000 Strategic Forces, ε35,000 Naval Aviation, 9,500 Coastal Defence Tps/Naval Infantry)

SUBMARINES 56

STRATEGIC 17 (see p. 113)

TACTICAL 34

SSGN 6 *Oscar* II with 24 SS-N-19 *Shipwreck* USGW (VLS); T-65 HWT

SSN 15

8 *Akula* with SS-N-21 *Sampson* SLCM, T-65 HWT

1 *Sierra* with SS-N-21 *Sampson* SLCM, T-65 HWT

1 *Yankee* 'Notch' with 20+ SS-N-21 *Sampson* SLCM

5 *Victor* III with SS-N-15 *Starfish* SSM, T-65 HWT

SSK 13

9 *Kilo*, 3 *Tango*, 1 *Foxtrot* (all with T-53 HWT)

OTHER ROLES 5

3 *Uniform* SSN, 1 *Yankee* SSN, 1 *X-Ray* SSK trials

RESERVE probably some *Foxtrot*, *Tango* and *Kilo*

PRINCIPAL SURFACE COMBATANTS 35

AIRCRAFT CARRIERS† 1 *Kuznetsov* CV (67,500t) capacity 20 ac Su-33 and 15–17 ASW hel or 36 Su-33 with 12 SS-N-19 *Shipwreck* SSM, 4 × 6 SA-N-9 *Gauntlet* SAM

CRUISERS 7

CGN 2 *Kirov* with 20 SS-N-19 *Shipwreck* SSM, 12 SA-N-6 *Grumble* SAM, SA-N-4 *Gecko* SAM, 2 × 130mm gun, 10 × 533mm ASTT, SS-N-15 *Starfish* SUGW, 3 Ka-25/-27 hel

CG 5

3 *Slava* with 8 × 2 SS-N-12 *Sandbox* SSM, 8 SA-N-6 *Grumble* SAM, 2 × 130mm gun, 8 × 533mm ASTT, 1 Ka-25/-27 hel

1 *Kara* with 2 × 2 SA-N-3 *Goblet* SAM, 2 SA-N-4 *Gecko* SAM, 10 × 533mm ASTT, 2 × 4 SS-N-14 *Silex* SUGW, 1 Ka-25 hel

1 *Kynda* with 8 SS-N-3B *Sepal* SSM, 2 SA-N-1 *Goa* SAM, 4 × 76mm gun, 6 × 533mm ASTT, 2 RBU 6000 mor

DESTROYERS 17

DDG 17

7 *Sovremennyy* with 2 × 4 SS-N-22 *Sunburn* SSM, 2 × 1 SA-N-7 *Gadfly* SAM, 2 × 2 130mm guns, 4 × 533mm TT, 1 Ka-25 hel

1 mod *Kashin* with 8 SS-N-25 *Svezda* SSM, 2 × 2 SA-N-1 *Goa* SAM, 2 × 76mm gun, 5 × 533mm ASTT

1 *Kashin* with 2 × 2 SA-N-1 *Goa* SAM, 2 × 76mm gun, 5 × 533mm ASTT, 2 ASW RL

7 *Udaloy* with 8 SA-N-9 *Gauntlet* SAM, 2 × 100mm gun, 8 × 533mm ASTT, 2 × 4 SS-N-14 *Silex* SUGW, 2 Ka-27 hel

1 *Udaloy* II with 8 × 4 SS-N-22 *Sunburn* SSM, 8 SA-N-9 *Gauntlet* SAM, 8 SA-N-11 *Grisson* SAM, 2 CADS-N-1 CIWS, 2 × 100mm gun, 10 × 533mm ASTT

FRIGATES 10

FFG 10

2 *Krivak* II with 2 SA-N-4 *Gecko* SAM, 2 × 100mm gun, 8 × 533mm ASTT, 1 × 4 SS-N-14 *Silex* SUGW, 2 × 12 ASW RL

7 *Krivak* I (wpn as *Krivak* II, but with 2 twin 76mm guns)

1 *Neustrashimyy* with SA-N-9 *Gauntlet* SAM, 1 × 100mm gun, 6 × 533mm ASTT, 2 × 12 ASW RL

PATROL AND COASTAL COMBATANTS 108

CORVETTES 27

27 *Grisha* I, -III, -IV, -V, with SA-N-14 *Gecko* SAM, 4 × 533mm ASTT, 2 × 12 ASW RL

LIGHT FRIGATES 12

12 *Parchim* II (ASW) with 2 SA-N-5 *Grail* SAM, 1 × 76mm gun, 4 × 406mm ASTT, 2 × 12 ASW RL

MISSILE CRAFT 54

29 *Tarantul* PFM, 1 -I, 5 -II, both with 2 × 2 SS-N-2C *Styx* SSM; 22 -III with 2 × 2 SS-N-22 *Sunburn* SSM

20 *Nanuchka* PFM 4 -I, 17 -III and 1 -IV with 2 × 3 SS-N-9 *Siren* SSM

2 *Dergach* PHM with 8 SS-N-22 *Sunburn* SSM, 1 SAN-4 *Gecko* SAM, 1 × 76mm gun

3 *Matka* PHM with 2 × 1 SS-N-2C *Styx* SSM

TORPEDO CRAFT 8 *Turya* PHT with 4 × 533mm TT

1 *Mukha* PHT with 8 × 406mm TT

PATROL CRAFT 6

COASTAL 6 *Pauk* PFC with 4 ASTT, 2 ASW RL

MINE WARFARE about 71

MINE COUNTERMEASURES about 71

OFFSHORE 14

2 *Gorya* MCO

12 *Natya* I and -II MSO

COASTAL 27 *Sonya* MSC

INSHORE 30 MSI<

AMPHIBIOUS about 25

LPD 1 *Ivan Rogov* with 4–5 Ka-27 hel, capacity 520 tps, 20 tk

LST 23

19 *Ropucha*, capacity 225 tps, 9 tk

4 *Alligator*, capacity 300 tps, 20 tk

LSM 1 *Polnocny*, capacity 180 tps, 6 tk

Plus about 21 craft: about 6 *Ondatra* LCM; about 15 LCAC (incl 4 *Pomornik*, 3 *Aist*, 3 *Tsaplya*, 1 *Lebed*, 1 *Utenok*, 2 *Orlan* WIG and 1 *Utka* (wing-in-ground-experimental))

Plus about 80 smaller craft

SUPPORT AND MISCELLANEOUS about 436

UNDER WAY SUPPORT 28

1 *Berezina*, 5 *Chilikin*, 22 other AO

MAINTENANCE AND LOGISTIC about 271

some 15 AS, 38 AR, 20 AOT, 8 msl spt/resupply, 90 AT, 9 special liquid carriers, 8 AWT, 17 AK, 46 AT/ARS, 13 ARS, 7 AR/C

SPECIAL PURPOSES about 57

some 17 AGI (some armed), 1 msl range instrumentation, 7 trg, about 24 icebreakers (civil-manned), 4 AH, 4 specialist spt vessels

SURVEY/RESEARCH about 80

some 19 naval, 61 civil AGOR

MERCHANT FLEET (aux/augmentation for sealift)

1,503 ocean-going veh over 1,000t: 275 AOT, 104 dry bulk; 24 AK, 8 ro-ro, 7 pax; 1,085 other (breakbulk, partial AK, refrigerated AK, specialised AK and LASH)

NAVAL AVIATION (ε35,000)

ORGANISATION

4 Fleet Air Forces, each organised in air div; each with 2-3 regt of HQ elm and 2 sqn of 9-10 ac each; recce, ASW, tpt/utl org in indep regt or sqn

Flying hours 40

EQUIPMENT

217 cbt ac; 80 armed hel

AIRCRAFT

BBR 45 Tu-22M

FGA 52 Su-24, 10 Su-25, 52 Su-27

ASW a0 Tu-142, 26 Il-38, 4 Be-12

MR/EW 18 An-12

TPT 37 An-12/An-24/An-26

HELICOPTERS

ASW 3 Mi-14, 72 Ka-27

MR/EW 8 Mi-8

CBT ASLT 12 Ka-29, 15 Mi-24

MISSILES
ASM AS-4 *Kitchen*, AS-7 *Kerry*, AS-10 *Karen*, AS-11, *Kelger*, AS-13 *Kingbolt*

COASTAL DEFENCE (9,500)

(incl Naval Infantry, Coastal Defence Troops)

NAVAL INFANTRY (Marines) (7,500)

1 inf 'div' (2,500: 3 inf, 1 tk, 1 arty bn) (Pacific Fleet)
3 indep bde (4 inf, 1 tk, 1 arty, 1 MRL, 1 ATK bn), 1 indep regt, 3 indep bn
3 fleet SF bde (1 op, 2 cadre): 2–3 underwater, 1 para bn, spt elm

EQUIPMENT
MBT 160: T-55M, T-72, T-80
RECCE 60 BRDM-2/*Sagger* ATGW
AIFV ε150 BMP-2, BMP-3, some BRM-1K
APC some 750: BTR-60/-70/-80, 250 MT-LB
TOTAL ARTY 321
    TOWED 122mm: 10 D-30
    SP 122mm: 102 2S1; **152mm**: 18 2S3
    MRL 122mm: 96 9P138
    COMBINED GUN/MOR 120mm: 70 2S9 SP, 14 2B16, 11 2S23 SP
ATGW 72 AT-3/-5
ATK GUNS 100mm: MT-12
AD GUNS 23mm: 60 ZSU-23-4 SP
SAM 250 SA-7, 20 SA-8, 50 SA-9/-13

COASTAL DEFENCE TROOPS (2,000)

(all units reserve status)
1 coastal defence div
1 coastal defence bde
1 arty regt
2 SAM regt

EQUIPMENT
MBT 350 T-64
AIFV 450 BMP
APC 280 BTR-60/-70/-80, 400 MT-LB
TOTAL ARTY 364 (152)
    TOWED 280: **122mm**: 140 D-30; **152mm**: 40 D-20, 50 2A65, 50 2A36
    SP 152mm: 48 2S5
    MRL 122mm: 36 BM-21

NAVAL DEPLOYMENT

NORTHERN FLEET (Arctic and Atlantic)

(HQ Severomorsk)
BASES Kola peninsula, Severodovinsk
SUBMARINES 34
  strategic 12 SSBN **tactical** 22 (4 SSGN, 12 SSN, 2 SSK, 4 SSN other roles)
PRINCIPAL SURFACE COMBATANTS 12
  1 CV, 3 CG/CGN, 6 DDG, 2 FFG
OTHER SURFACE SHIPS about 26 patrol and coastal combatants, 18 MCM, 8 amph, some 130 spt and misc
NAVAL AVIATION
EQUIPMENT
75 cbt ac; 30 armed hel

AIRCRAFT
BBR 25 Tu-22M • **FGA** 10 Su-25, 24 Su-27 • **ASW** 11 Il-38 • **MR/EW** 2 An-12 • **TPT** 25 An-12/An-24/An-26
HELICOPTERS
ASW 25 Ka-27 • **CBT ASLT** 5 Ka-29

BALTIC FLEET (HQ Kaliningrad)

BASES Kronstadt, Baltiysk
SUBMARINES 2 SSK
PRINCIPAL SURFACE COMBATANTS 6
  2 DDG, 4 FFG
OTHER SURFACE SHIPS about 26 patrol and coastal combatants, 13 MCM, 5 amph, some 130 spt and misc
NAVAL AVIATION
EQUIPMENT
55 cbt ac; 41 armed hel
AIRCRAFT
FGA 25 Su-24, 28 Su-27 • **MR/EW** 2 An-12 • **TPT** 12 An-12/An-24/An-26
HELICOPTERS
ASW 22 Ka-27 • **CBT ASLT** 4 Ka-29, 15 Mi-24

BLACK SEA FLEET (HQ Sevastopol)

The RF Fleet is leasing bases in Sevastopol for the next 20 years; it is based at Sevastopol and Karantinnaya Bays, and, jointly with Ukr warships, at Streletskaya Bay. The Fleet's overall serviceability is low.
BASES Sevastopol, Temryuk, Novorossiysk
SUBMARINES 10 (only one op)
  9 SSK, 1 SSK other roles
PRINCIPAL SURFACE COMBATANTS 7
  3 CG/CGN, 2 DDG, 2 FFG
OTHER SURFACE SHIPS about 15 patrol and coastal combatants, 14 MCM, 5 amph, some 90 spt and misc
NAVAL AVIATION
EQUIPMENT
35 cbt ac; 13 armed hel
AIRCRAFT
FGA 27 Su-24 • **ASW** 4 Be-12 • **MR/EW** 4 An-12
HELICOPTERS
ASW 5 Ka-27 • **MR/EW** 8 Mi-8

CASPIAN SEA FLOTILLA

BASE Astrakhan (RF)
The Caspian Sea Flotilla has been divided between Az (about 25%), RF, Kaz and Tkm, which are operating a joint flotilla under RF comd currently based at Astrakhan.
SURFACE COMBATANTS about 36
  10 patrol and coastal combatants, 5 MCM, some 6 amph, about 15 spt

PACIFIC FLEET (HQ Vladivostok)

BASES Vladivostok, Petropavlovsk Kamchatskiy, Magadan, Sovetskaya Gavan, Fokino
SUBMARINES 10
  strategic 5 SSBN **tactical** 5 (2 SSGN, 3 SSN)

PRINCIPAL SURFACE COMBATANTS 10
1 CG/CGN, 7 DDG, 2 FFG
OTHER SURFACE SHIPS about 30 patrol and coastal
combatants, 8 MCM, 4 amph, some 57 spt and misc
NAVAL AVIATION
EQUIPMENT
55 cbt ac; 26 armed hel
AIRCRAFT
BBR 20 Tu-22M • ASW 10 Tu-142, 15 Il-38 • MR/
EW 10 An-12
HELICOPTERS
ASW 20 Ka-27, 3 Mi-14 • CBT ASLT 3 Ka-29

Military Air Forces (VVS) ε184,600

The Military Air Forces comprise Long Range Aviation
Cmd (LRA), Military Transport Aviation Comd (VTA),
7 Tactical/Air Defence Armies comprising 77 air regts.
Tactical/Air Defence roles includes air defence,
interdiction, recce and tactical air spt. LRA (6 div) and
VTA (9 regt) are subordinated to central Air Force
comd. There is a Tactical/AD Army within each MD.
Each Air Force/AD Army is subordinated to Air Force
High Comd. A joint CIS Unified Air Defence System
covers RF, Arm, Bel, Ga, Kaz, Kgz, Tjk, Tkm, Ukr and
Uz.
Flying hours Average annual flying time for LRA and
Tactical/Air Defence is about 20 hours, and for VTA
approximately 44 hours

LONG-RANGE AVIATION COMMAND (37th Air Army)

5 hvy bbr aviation divs, plus 1 hy bbr trg centre
BBR (START-accountable) 74 Tu-95, 15 Tu-160 (Test ac:
7 Tu-95, 1 Tu-160)
117 Tu-22M/MR (plus others in store)
TKR 20 Il-78/Il-78M
TRG 8 Tu-22M-3, 30 Tu-134

TACTICAL AVIATION

Flying hours 20
BBR/FGA some 586: 359 Su-24, 227 Su-25
FTR some 952: 12 MiG-25, 237 MiG-29, 363 Su-27, 340
MiG-31
RECCE some 226: 70 MiG-25, 156 Su-24
AEW AND CONTROL 20 A-50/A-50U
ECM 60 Mi-8
TRG 2 centre for op conversion: some 90 ac incl 20
MiG-29, 35 Su-24, 15 Su-25
1 centre for instructor trg: 65 ac incl 10 MiG-25, 20
MiG-29, 15 Su-24, 10 Su-25, 10 Su-27
AAM AA-8 *Aphid*, AA-10 *Alamo*, AA-11 *Archer*
ASM AS-4 *Kitchen*, AS-7 *Kerry*, AS-10 *Karen*, AS-11
Kilter, AS-12 *Kegler*, AS-13 *Kingbolt*, AS-14 *Kedge*, AS-
15 *Kent*, AS-17 *Krypton*, AS-18 *Kazoo*
SAM 37 SAM regt
Some 1,900 SA-10/S-300. The first S-400 unit
reportedly to be deployed near Moscow by the
end of 2001.

MILITARY TRANSPORT AVIATION COMMAND (VTA)
(61st Air Army)

2 div, each 5 regt, each div has 150 ac; 4 indep regts, 37
ac
EQUIPMENT
some 354 ac, incl Il-76M/MD, An-12, An-22, An-124
CIVILIAN FLEET 1,500 medium- and long-range
passenger ac, incl some 350 An-12 and Il-76

AIR FORCE AVIATION TRAINING SCHOOLS

TRG 5 mil avn institutes subordinate to Air Force HQ:
some 980 ac incl L-39, Tu-134, Mig-23, MiG-29, Su-25,
Su-27

OPERATIONAL COMBAT AIRCRAFT

based west of Urals (CFE totals as at 1 Jan 2001 for all
air forces other than maritime)
ac 2,636: 194 Su-17 • 52 Su-22 • 432 Su-24 • 189 Su-
25 • 303 Su-27 • 1 MiG-21 • 402 MiG-23 • 127
MiG-25 • 149 MiG-27 • 448 MiG-29 • 247 MiG-31
• 63 Tu-22M • 29 Tu-22. No armed hel. Some of
these, including most MiG-23, are
decommissioned ac in store

Deployment

Deployment of formations within the Atlantic to the
Urals (ATTU) region is reported to be 2 TD, 8 MRD,
perhaps 4 AB, 1 arty div, 9 indep arty, 3 MRL, 7 MR, 8
SSM, 12 SAM bde.
The manning state of RF units is difficult to determine.
The following assessment of units within the ATTU
region is based on the latest available information.
Above 75% – possibly 3 ABD, all MR bde and 1 AB bde;
above 50% – possibly 1 TD, 6 MRD, 1 ABD, 1 arty bde.
The remainder are assessed as 20–50%. Units outside the
ATTU are likely to be at a lower level. All bde are
maintained at or above 50%. TLE in each MD includes
active and trg units and in store

KALININGRAD OPERATIONAL STRATEGIC GROUP

These forces are commanded by The Ground and
Coastal Defence Forces of the Baltic Fleet.
GROUND 12,770: 2 MRD (1 cadre), 1 SSM bde, 1 SAM
regt, 1 indep MRR (trg), 1 attack hel regt, 816 MBT,
869 ACV (plus 377 'look-a-likes'), 345 arty/MRL/
mor, 18 SS-21 *Scarab*, 51 attack hel
NAVAL INFANTRY (1,100)
1 regt (26 MBT, 220 ACV, 52 arty/MRL)(Kaliningrad)
COASTAL DEFENCE
2 arty regt (133 arty)
1 SSM regt: some 8 SS-C-1b *Sepal*
AD 1 regt: 28 Su-27 (Baltic Fleet)
SAM 50

RUSSIAN MILITARY DISTRICTS

LENINGRAD MD (HQ St Petersburg)
GROUND 32,500: 1 ABD; plus 2 indep MR bde, 2 arty
bde, 1 SSM, 1 SF, 4 SAM bde, 1 ATK, 1 MRL, 1 aslt

tpt hel regt, 183 MBT, 83 ACV (plus 950 'look-a-likes'), 419 arty/MRL/mor, 18 SS-21 *Scarab*, 35 attack hel

NAVAL INFANTRY (1,300 – subordinate to Northern Fleet)

1 regt (74 MBT, 209 ACV, 44 arty)

COASTAL DEFENCE

1 Coastal Defence (360 MT-LB, 134 arty), 1 SAM regt

AIR 6th Air Force and AD Army has 325 combat ac. It is divided into two PVO corps, 1 bbr div (79 Su-24), 1 recce regt (23 MiG-25, 20 Su-24), 1 ftr div (108 Su-27, 90 MiG-31, 5 MiG-25), 1 hel ECM sqn (35 Mi-8)

SAM 525

MOSCOW MD (HQ Moscow)

GROUND 74,000: 2 Army HQ, 2 TD, 2 MRD, 2 ABD, plus 1 arty div HQ, 4 arty bde (incl 1 trg), 3 indep arty, 3 SSM, 1 indep MR, 1 SF, 4 SAM bde, 2 attack hel regt, 2,000 MBT, 3,200 ACV (plus 1,600 'look-a-likes'), 2,450 arty/MRL/mor, 48 SS-21 *Scarab*, 120 attack hel

AIR Moscow AF and AD District has 2 PVO divs, one mixed div incl air aslt regt, one mil depot storing 43 MiG-25

469 cbt ac: 51 MiG-25, 105 MiG-29, 102 MiG-31, 79 Su-24, 16 Su-24MR, 47 Su-25, 69 Su-27 hel: 2 ECM sqn with 46 Mi-8

SAM 850

VOLGA MD (HQ Samara) (to merge with Ural MD by 1 Sep 01)

GROUND 32,600: 1 MRD, 1 arty bde, 1 SSM, 1 SF, 1 SAM bde, 1 MRL regt, 1 indep hel regt, 530 MBT, 1,000 ACV (plus 500 'look-alikes'), 690 arty/MRL/mor, 18 SS-21 *Scarab*, 45 attack hel

AIR 5th AF and AD Army has 1 regt attack/op trg, 48 MiG-29, 21 Su-25 **hel** Mi-8 comms

AD ad/op trg: incl 39 Su-27, 8 MiG-31

Air Force aviation schools (383 L-39, Mi-2), storage bases.

URAL MD (HQ Yekaterinburg) (to merge with Volga MD by 1 Sep 2001)

GROUND ε19,000: 1 TD, 1 MRD, 2 arty bde/regt, 1 SSM bde, 1,300 MBT, 1,600 ACV, 900 arty/MRL/mor, 18 SS-21 *Scarab*

AIR 5th AF and AD Army with avn and trg schools

AD Ural and Volga assets cover Siberian and Far East MDs: MiG-23s, MiG-29s, Su-27s

SAM 600

NORTH CAUCASUS MD (HQ Rostov-on-Don)

GROUND 76,000: 1 Army HQ, 1 Corps HQ, 3 MRD, 1 ABD, 3 indep MR, 1 AB, 1 SF, 2 arty bde, 2 indep MRR, 2 SSM, 3 SAM bde, 2 ATK, 2 attack hel, 1 aslt tpt hel regt, 650 MBT, 1,750 ACV (plus 1,200 'look-alikes'), 750 arty/MRL/mor, 18 SS-21 *Scarab*, 63 attack hel

NAVAL INFANTRY (ε1,400 - subordinate to Black Sea Fleet)

1 regt (59 ACV, 14 arty)

AIR 4th AF and AD Army has 345 cbt ac, 1 bbr div (61 Su-24), 1 recce regt (36 Su-24), 1 air aslt div (104 Su-25), 1 ftr corps of 4 regt (86 MiG-29, 58 Su-27), 1 hel ECM sqn with 52 Mi-8, trg regt of tac aviation and Air Force aviation schools

SAM 125

SIBERIAN MD (HQ Novosibirsk)

GROUND 2 Corps HQ, 2 TD, 2 MRD, 1 arty div, 2 MG/arty div, 3 MR, 1 AB, 10 arty bde/regt, 2 SSM, 2 SAM, 2 SF bde, 4 ATK, 1 attack hel, 4,468 MBT, 6,000 ACV, 4,300 arty/MRL/mor, 36 SS-21 *Scarab*, 35 attack hel

AIR 14th AF and AD Army:

BBR/FGA 56 Su-24M, 26 Su-25

FTR 46 MiG-29, 69 MiG-31

RECCE 29 Su-24MR

FAR EASTERN MD (HQ Khabarovsk) incl Pacific Fleet and Joint Command of Troops and Forces in the Russian Northeast (These forces are commanded by the Pacific Fleet)

GROUND 2 Army, 2 Corps HQ, 10 MRD (2 trg), plus 2 MG/arty div, 1 arty div, 9 arty bde/regt, 1 MR, 3 SSM, 5 SAM, 1 SF, 1 ATK bde, 2 attack hel, 2 aslt tpt hel regt, 3,900 MBT, 6,400 ACV, 3,000 arty/MRL/mor, 54 SS-21 *Scarab*, 85 attack hel

NAVAL INFANTRY (2,500; subordinate to Pacific Fleet)

1 div HQ, 3 inf, 1 tk and 1 arty bn

COASTAL DEFENCE

1 div

AIR 11th AF and AD Army:

BBR/FGA 90 Su-24M, 50 Su-25

FTR 147 Su-27

RECCE 55 Su-24MR

Forces Abroad

Declared str of forces deployed in Arm and Ga as at 1 Jan 2001 was 6,900. These forces are now subordinate to the North Caucasus MD. Total probably excludes locally enlisted personnel.

ARMENIA

GROUND 2,900; 1 mil base; 74 MBT, 17 APC, 129 ACV, 84 arty/MRL/mors

AD 1 sqn: 18 MiG-29, 2 SA-12 (S-300) bty, SA-6 bty

GEORGIA

GROUND 4,000; 3 mil bases (each = bde+); 65 T-72 MBT, 200 ACV, 139 arty incl **122mm** D-30, 2S1 SP; **152mm** 2S3; **122mm** BM-21 MRL; **120mm** mor, 5 attack hel

MOLDOVA (Dniestr)

GROUND 1,500; 1 op gp with 1 MR bde, 1 SAM regt; 108 MBT, 126 ACV, 125 arty/MRL/mor. These forces are now subordinate to the Moscow MD

TAJIKISTAN

GROUND ε8,000; 1 MRD, 128 MBT, 314 ACV, 180

arty/MRL/mor; plus 14,500 Frontier Forces (RF officers, Tjk conscripts)

UKRAINE

NAVAL INFANTRY 1,100; 1 regt (102 ACV, 24 arty)

AFRICA 100

CUBA some 800 SIGINT and ε10 mil advisers

SYRIA 150

VIETNAM 100; naval facility and SIGINT station. Used by RF ac and surface ships on reduced basis

Peacekeeping

BOSNIA (SFOR II): 600; 1 indep AB regt
GEORGIA/ABKHAZIA 1,700
GEORGIA/SOUTH OSSETIA 530
MOLDOVA/TRANSDNIESTR 500; 1 MR bn
YUGOSLAVIA (KFOR): 3,600

UNITED NATIONS

BOSNIA (UNMIBH): 1 **CROATIA** (UNMOP): 1 obs
DROC (MONUC): 10 obs **EAST TIMOR** (UNTAET): 2
obs **ETHIOPIA/ERITREA** (UNMEE): 6 obs **GEORGIA**
(UNOMIG): 3 obs **IRAQ/KUWAIT** (UNIKOM): 11 obs
MIDDLE EAST (UNTSO): 4 obs **SIERRA LEONE**
(UNAMSIL): 128 incl 15 obs; 4 Mi-24 **WESTERN**
SAHARA (MINURSO): 24 obs

Paramilitary ε409,100 active

FEDERAL BORDER GUARD SERVICE ε140,000

directly subordinate to the President; 10 regional directorates, 7 frontier gps

EQUIPMENT

1,000 ACV (incl BMP, BTR), 90 arty (incl 2S1, 2S9, 2S12)

ac some 70 Il-76, Tu-134, An-72, An-24, An-26, Yak-40, 16 SM-92 **hel** some 200+ Mi-8, Mi-24, Mi-26, Ku-27

PATROL AND COASTAL COMBATANTS about 237

PATROL, OFFSHORE 23
7 *Krivak*-III with 1 Ka-27 hel, 1 100mm gun, 12 *Grisha*-II, 4 *Grisha*-III

PATROL, COASTAL 35
20 *Pauk*, 15 *Svetlyak*

PATROL, INSHORE 95
65 *Stenka*, 10 *Muravey*, 20 *Zhuk*

RIVERINE MONITORS about 84
10 *Yaz*, 7 *Piyavka*, 7 *Vosh*, 60 *Shmel*

SUPPORT AND MISCELLANEOUS about 26
8 *Ivan Susanin* armed icebreakers, 18 *Sorum* armed AT/F

INTERIOR TROOPS 151,100

7 districts, some 11 'div' incl 5 indep special purpose div (ODON – 2 to 5 op regt), 29 indep bde incl 10 indep special designation bde (OBRON – 3 mech, 1 mor bn); 65 regt/bn incl special motorised units, avn

EQUIPMENT

incl 69 MBT, 1,700 ACV (incl BMP-1/-2, BTR-80), 20 D-30, 45 PM-38, 4 Mi-24

FEDERAL SECURITY SERVICE ε4,000 armed incl Alfa, Beta and Zenit cdo units

FEDERAL PROTECTION SERVICE ε10,000 to 30,000

org incl elm of Ground Forces (1 mech inf bde, 1 AB regt) and Presidential Guard regt

FEDERAL COMMUNICATIONS AND INFORMATION AGENCY ε54,000

RAILWAY TROOPS ε50,000 in 4 rly corps, 28 rly bde

MILITARY DEVELOPMENTS

The regional security situation in 2001 was dominated by the escalating violence between Israel and the Palestinians. The Israeli introduction of major weapon systems into the conflict – not simply main battle tanks, but air strikes by F-16 combat aircraft, which had not been used against Palestinian-controlled areas before – has moved the conflict to a higher level. In Algeria, fighting continues between the government and Islamic fundamentalist groups. A stalemate remains between the UN Security Council and Iraq. Iran continues to build up its military capabilities; however, the election of the reformist President Mohammad Khatami with a convincing majority gives hope of a more moderate foreign policy stand. The attack on the USS *Cole* in a Yemeni harbour by a group suspected to be sponsored by the international terrorist Osama bin Laden was a reminder of the continuing threat posed by international terrorism to the US and other Western countries.

The Middle East

Israel and the Palestinians The most recent wave of violence in the West Bank and Gaza was sparked by Ariel Sharon's provocative 28 September 2000 visit to the Temple Mount/Haram al-Sharif, where the al-Aqsa mosque compound is located. Sharon's defeat of former Prime Minister Ehud Barak in the February 2001 election guaranteed a continuation of this violence, which was by then developing rapidly into a full-scale *intifada* (uprising). A plan to end the violence was presented by Egypt and Jordan in April 2001, calling for a series of confidence-building measures that included the renewal of Israeli–Palestine security cooperation and the re-opening of the borders between Israel proper and the Palestinian Territories, which had been closed by Israel. The peace plan also called for a four-week cease-fire. This was strongly opposed by the Sharon government, which declared that it would not consider any political initiatives unless violence by the Palestinians stopped. A US-inspired initiative led to an investigation, headed by former US Senator George Mitchell, into the causes of the *intifada* following the al-Aqsa incident. The recommendations were released on 5 May 2001 and Palestinian leader Yasser Arafat said that he accepted them '100%'. Israel officially welcomed the Mitchell report but rejected one of its main recommendations: a freeze on further building in the Israeli settlements on the West Bank. On 22 May, Sharon called publicly for an immediate cease-fire. He ordered the Israeli Army to stop any further offensive actions and told them to shoot only if they were in real danger. He said that if the cease-fire held, he would be prepared to discuss the report's confidence-building measures. These positive developments were thrown into reverse on 1 June when 20 teenagers were killed and 120 wounded in the bombing of a Tel Aviv discotheque. The following day, Yasser Arafat announced a cease-fire. *Hamas* and *Islamic Jihad* leaders immediately rejected it. In an attempt to stem the violence, President George W. Bush sent George Tenet, director of the US Central Intelligence Agency, to develop a new cease-fire plan. Under Tenet's plan, the Palestinian Authority (PA) would make every effort to end attacks against Israelis, including arresting militants directing the terrorist operations from Gaza and the West Bank. Israel would end offensive operations against Palestinian controlled areas; the parties would withdraw to positions held in September 2000 before the *intifada*; and security cooperation and joint patrols should be restarted. A six-week timetable was set for the agreement to be put into effect. While both sides accepted the plan, Palestinian militants were not prepared to end their violence. The cease-fire was never effective and both sides escalated the violence. The Israelis responded to increased *Hamas* and *Islamic Jihad* bombings with air strikes by F-16s, and attack helicopters armed with laser-guided munitions on the offices and homes of the guerrilla groups. In particular, terrorist group leaders and senior members were targeted for assassination. This change in tactics brought international condemnation upon Israel, including that of its staunchest ally, the US. Likewise, the guerrilla groups' bomb attacks against civilians in restaurants and other public places in Israel itself also drew international condemnation, including that of Arab countries, such as Egypt, which are strong supporters of the Palestinian cause.

In August 2001, Sharon was still implacably insisting on the end of the violence as a precondition to any negotiations. This allowed those Palestinian militants opposed to any peace process with Israel to keep blocking the possibility of talks by committing further terrorist acts. Since the start of this round of violence in September 2000, approximately 700 people have been killed.

Lebanon and Syria

In June 2001, Syria started to withdraw some of its soldiers from positions in and around the Lebanese capital Beirut. It is estimated that up to 30,000 Syrian troops are on Lebanese territory, mostly in the Bekaa Valley. Some reports indicate that the move was more than redeployment and that as many as 5,000 troops may have returned to Syria, although this has not been confirmed. Since the Israeli withdrawal from South Lebanon in June 2000, *Hizbollah* attacks have, overall, been greatly reduced; however, on several occasions, *Hizbollah* have fired anti-tank missiles and mortars at Israeli positions in the Shebaa farms area. The Israeli Defence Force (IDF) has responded with attack helicopters and artillery. *Hizbollah's* tactics are not widely popular in Lebanon, not only because the general public do not share the armed group's main objective – the removal of Israeli forces from the Shebaa farms area now that Israel has withdrawn from South Lebanon – but also for fear of a violent response from Israel, such as the bombing in 2000 that cut off half the country's electricity supply. The Israeli Air Force has continued its attacks on Syrian air-defence radars in Lebanon to help preserve Israel's freedom of manoeuvre in Lebanese air space. The long-promised modernisation of the Syrian armed forces with Russian equipment has yet to happen: military spending is not a priority for President Bashar al-Assad.

The Gulf

Iraq and its neighbours The US and UK efforts in 2001 to develop a more focused sanctions regime to constrain Iraq came to naught. These two countries had taken the lead in drafting a UN Security Council resolution that would ease sanctions on a range of commercial goods, but would require a more rigorous application of the sanctions remaining on goods with a specific military application. The implementation of the proposed resolution would have required Iraq's neighbours to be much more assiduous in blocking illegal trade across their borders with Iraq. The resolution was vetoed by Russia. As a result, on 3 July 2001, the UN Security Council renewed the 'oil-for-food' arrangements for a further six months without any amendment to current sanctions arrangements.

Iraq's 2000 oil revenues are estimated at $18 billion, an increase of $14bn over 1997. It is channelling more trade through regional countries, making it harder for the US and UK to garner support for a robust policy against President Saddam Hussein. For example, according to UN records for the last six months of 2000, Egypt signed at least $740 million in contracts with Iraq and the United Arab Emirates (UAE) $703m. On 23 May 2001, Syria signed a cooperative trade agreement with Iraq, with the object of increasing the value of their trade from the 2000 figure of $500m to $1bn in 2001. In these circumstances, the prospect of an improved sanctions policy for Iraq is remote. Even more remote is the possibility of UN inspectors of the UN Monitoring, Verification and Inspection Commission (UNMOVIC) entering Iraq to seek out the remaining elements of the Iraqi weapons of mass destruction (WMD) programmes. It is likely that research and development work on these programmes is underway but the capacity to deploy the weapons as operational systems with appropriate delivery means remains constrained by sanctions (despite their inefficiencies) and the continuous US–UK aerial surveillance.

Since the end of *Operation Desert Storm* in 1991, US and British aircraft have flown more than 200,000 air patrols over Iraq to enforce the no-fly zones. This constant surveillance allows oversight of possible deployments of major systems such as surface-to-surface missiles (SSMs) and construction work on WMD facilities. The US and UK air forces continue to conduct air attacks in an effort to degrade the increasingly competent Iraqi air-defence system. There have been reports that Iraq has been supplied with advanced equipment to upgrade its air-defence capabilities, including its command-and-control system. This development has spurred the allied air forces to intensify their attacks. For example, on 9 August 2001, as many as 50 US and UK aircraft were deployed in attacks on air defence and command sites, mostly in the southern no-fly zone. Despite local political reluctance to take a tough line against Iraq, there is recognition in the region of the threat posed by the Baghdad regime.

The threat of attack by Iraq has been a powerful incentive for the significant improvements in regional air defences. In particular, in 2001, a radar identification and tracking network has been set up that links all six Gulf Cooperation Council (GCC) member states. The aircraft identification system *Hizam al Taawun* cost $85m and can track several hundred aircraft at once. The system can potentially be developed to give advance warning of missile attacks. In June 2001, US forces exercised with Egyptian, Jordanian and GCC forces in manoeuvres to test interoperability and rapid response to WMD attacks in the region. The leaders of the six GCC states signed a mutual defence agreement during their 30–31 December 2000 summit in Bahrain. The agreement is significant because for the first time it creates a legal framework for cooperation. It includes accelerated plans to expand the rapid reaction force, *Peninsular Shield,* which was formed by the GCC states in 1986 and is based at Hafr al-Batin. Under these plans, the force will be expanded from 5,000 to at least 25,000 personnel.

Domestic opposition to President Saddam Hussein's regime remains weak. A modest allocation of funds by the US Congress to Iraqi opposition groups has had no effect beyond indicating US political support. In December 2000, Saddam felt strong enough to begin a new campaign against the Iraqi Kurds, forcing thousands from their homes in government-controlled areas. However, the various Kurdish groups in Iraq remain bitterly divided. In late 2000, fighting broke out between the Patriotic Union of Kurdistan (PUK), which controls the southern third of the Iraqi-Kurdish enclave, and the Kurdistan Workers Party (PKK) near the Turkish border. These divisions were not only exploited by the Baghdad regime but also gave the opportunity for the Turkish armed forces to mount operations into Iraq against the PKK on several occasions in the first half of 2001.

Iran

Despite the re-election of reformist President Khatami in August 2001, the leadership of the armed forces remains loyal to the senior clerics. Ongoing political reform raises the prospect of improved relations with the Western powers; however, the upgrading and modernisation of the armed forces continues at pace, boosted in the past year by a major arms deal with Russian companies.

The Iranian ballistic missile programme continues. Iran started testing the *Shihab* 3 missile in July 1998. The last test – with the aim of checking the Russian-supplied subsystems – was believed to be in February 2000. It is thought that Iran recently decided to reduce its *Shihab* 3 and *Shihab* 4 programmes to focus on shorter-range missiles.

Iran has been trying to enhance its submarine capabilities. An indigenously built mini-submarine, the *Al-Sabiha* 15, was reported to have deployed for the first time in October 2000. It is doubtful, however, if the Iranian Navy has the trained personnel necessary to operate the mini-submarine to its full potential. Also, it is suspected that two of the navy's three Russian *Kilo*-class submarines are still not fully operational, due mainly to persistent battery problems.

The armed opposition presents little real threat to the current regime. The main group, the *Mojahedin-e Khalq* Organisation (MKO), continues to launch attacks against Iranian targets from its bases in Iraq and also within Tehran, as in a January 2001 mortar attack on a military base housing Iran's Islamic Revolutionary Guard Corps in the north of the city. In April 2001, the government stepped up its activities against the MKO, firing over 50 missiles at their camps in Iraq. In the same month, the government claimed that security forces had killed more than 70 terrorists linked to the MKO on the Iraqi border.

The unresolved issue of the division of Caspian Sea oil wealth is a potential cause of conflict among the states of the Caspian littoral. On 23 July, an Iranian aircraft and gunboat chased a BP oil-exploration team from the disputed Alov, Araz, and Sarq oilfields 150km south-west of the Azerbaijani capital Baku, sparking a diplomatic row between Iran and Azerbaijan. In this dispute, Russia and Kazakstan sided with Azerbaijan, which claims that these oilfields are its own. Turkmenistan, which also lays claim to the Sarq field, allied itself with Iran, which itself claims 20% of the Caspian seabed, including these three fields. The next round of talks on the issue, to be held in autumn 2001, is unlikely to resolve the argument. Unless agreement is reached in the near future, there is the danger of more serious incidents occurring, as the output of existing oil wells increases and with it the need for further exploration. The president of the Azerbaijan State Oil Company, Ilham Aliyev, who is the son of Azerbaijan's President Heydar Aliyev, is encouraging BP to resume its exploratory activities, which were being carried out as part of a joint agreement with his company.

Yemen

A terrorist attack on the USS *Cole* in Aden in October 2000 killed 17 US sailors and wounded almost 40. The US Navy's formal investigation into the bombing concluded in January 2001 that, although force-protection measures should be improved, it would be extremely difficult to have prevented or deterred the attack. Fear of further attacks caused the US and UK navies to stop their ships from passing through the Suez Canal for about a month.

In Yemen, at least 20 people were killed during the run-up to the 2001 election, which was the first since reunification of the country in 1990. Armed clashes broke out in two districts between supporters of the Islamic opposition *Islah* party and backers of President Ali Abdullah Saleh's ruling General People's Congress.

Algeria

Since December 2000, when 300 people were killed in a single month, there has been a major escalation of attacks by armed Islamic groups, in particular the *Groupe Islamique Armée* (GIA) on mostly civilian targets. It is estimated that 3,000 people have been killed in the year to 1 August 2001. The security situation has been further complicated by the Berber protests, which started in April 2001 and left around 90 people dead and 2,000 wounded, mainly in the Kabylie region of north-eastern Algeria. The Berbers, who make up a third of the population, have long opposed the military-backed government and want their language and culture to have equal status to Arabic. The riots were sparked by the death of a youth in police custody on 24 April 2001. Around 500,000 people joined the protests, which included a march on the capital Algiers, to demand the withdrawal of all paramilitary gendarmes from the Kabylie region. In response, the government has launched an official inquiry into the conduct of the paramilitary police during the unrest.

The level of foreign investment in Algeria – particularly in the oil and gas industry – means that international players have a close interest in Algerian stability. For example, the Algerian government has signed its first full partnership deal with a foreign corporation in a $2.5bn project to develop a second major Algerian gas field, deep in the Sahara Desert. The state gas corporation, Sonatrach, and British Petroleum-Amoco, the joint British and American hydrocarbons enterprise, signed the deal in Algiers in August 2001. Italy has already agreed to buy nearly half of the 9bn cubic metres of gas expected to come on stream by 2004. This interdependency between the Algerian government and some Western powers will heighten foreign concerns, particularly among EU countries, about stability in Algeria and the conduct of the current government and its security forces. Evidence of this increased concern was demonstrated at the 16 June 2001 EU summit in Sweden, when the leaders called on the Algerian government to begin a process of political dialogue to end the country's violent unrest.

DEFENCE SPENDING

Defence spending in the region in 2000 was $59bn, slightly lower than the $60bn in 1999, although initial budgets for 2000 had suggested that government spending would pick up by around 4%. Current estimates suggest that there will be a significant increase in defence expenditure, by as much as 10%, in 2001.

In 2000, high oil prices boosted the economies of regional oil-producing countries. For example, Saudi Arabia more than doubled its revenue from oil exports during the year, to around $68bn. Another factor in the strong economic growth enjoyed by Saudi Arabia and other Gulf and Middle Eastern countries is structural reform, aimed at stimulating the non-oil private sector, which was undertaken when oil prices were much lower. In 2001, it became clear that many regional countries would not be funnelling the additional oil revenues into new weapons but rather into other areas of government spending, such as infrastructure, the creation of new jobs and the discharge of national debt. Saudi Arabia has put off replacing its ageing F-5 aircraft fleet and is unlikely to announce any major new weapons purchases in the next three years. Kuwait has signalled that it is holding off the purchase of AH-64D *Apache* helicopters and self-propelled artillery, focusing instead on military training and recruitment needs. On the other hand, Iran has increased its defence spending and has placed major contracts with Russian companies.

Israel

Defence expenditure in 2000 increased by NS3bn, largely due to the new outbreak of violence in the West Bank and Gaza The budget increases included NS1bn to finance withdrawal from Lebanon, NS1bn for the protection of settler communities in the Palestinian Territories and the construction of new defences along the Lebanese border, and NS1bn to cover Israel Defense Force (IDF) expenses arising from the latest Palestinian uprising. The budget for 2001 has been increased to NS37.43bn ($9.1bn), including a $450m US congressional supplement. The budget had originally been set at NS34.63bn, but was revised in May and the extra money taken from other areas of the state budget and transferred to the Ministry of Defence, the Border Police, the General Security Service and other security organisations. The army cancelled plans to buy 12 used *Apache* helicopters and upgrade them to AH-64D *Longbow* standard; instead, it will buy nine new AH-64Ds. The air force acquired 24 Sikorsky S-70A *Black Hawk* utility helicopters to supplement the 25 UH-60s already in operation. Deliveries are scheduled for 2002. Another 50 F-16Is were ordered in June 1999. Cooperation with the US on the *Arrow* anti-missile system continued. During tests, the system successfully tracked and destroyed an incoming target missile fired at Israel from the coast. One *Arrow* battery is currently operational and there are plans to install another two. The navy received its third and last *Dolphin*-class submarine in 2000; these are considerably more capable than the two *Gal* submarines they replace. Israel also plans to order up to five improved *Sa'ar*-5 corvettes from the United States for US$1bn, primarily to improve the defence of its shipping routes.

Egypt

Partly in response to Israel's increased submarine capabilities, in late 2000 Egypt signed a letter of intent to buy two Dutch-designed *Moray*-class diesel submarines. The submarines will be built at Ingalls Shipyards in the United States and paid for by the US Foreign Military Funding programme. Their delivery in 2007–08 will significantly improve Egypt's submarine forces. Egypt has also ordered four *Ambassador* Mk 3 fast patrol craft armed with surface-to-surface missiles (PFMs) from the United States at a cost of $400m. These craft will be considerably better-equipped and more modern than Egypt's current fleet of 21 British- and Chinese-built patrol craft. Egypt is the first country to have its fleet of AH-64A helicopters remanufactured to AH-64D *Apache Longbow* configuration. In a deal worth $400m, the upgrade programme is scheduled to start in 2003.

Iran

Iran's official defence budget increased by 22% to r15.9bn in 2001. The allocations for defence, security and foreign affairs amount to 25% of the total government budget.

In 2001, Iran and Russia signed an agreement to resume trade in conventional weapons for the first time since 1979. It is thought that Iran would like to buy up to $7bn worth of weapons; likely purchases are fighter aircraft, helicopters and S-300 air-defence systems. As part of the package, Russia may be prepared to sell some of its anti-ship *Yakhont* air-launched cruise missiles If the sale goes ahead, the Iranians will probably also purchase Su-27 or Su-30 aircraft as the launch platforms for *Yakhont*. However, sales of the missile could be in violation of Moscow's obligations as a member Missile Technology Control Regime (MTCR). Iran reported success in testing a new domestically built anti-tank missile *Saeqeh*-1 (*Lightning*-1).

Kuwait

During a review of Kuwait's military readiness in early 2001, the defence ministry placed some major acquisition programmes on hold, including the purchase of US-built AH-64D *Apache Longbow* and UH-60A *Black Hawk* helicopters as well as the proposed *Paladin* self-propelled artillery and associated vehicles. Kuwait has signalled its intention to buy an Egyptian air-defence system and will go ahead with a plan, on hold since the Gulf War, to purchase two new *Amoun* units, thought to be valued at around $625m.

Oman

Unlike many of its neighbours, Oman increased its defence budget for 2001. It was higher by 30% at OR926m ($2.4bn), roughly 37% of the total state budget. The funds will be earmarked for a modernisation programme that was postponed when oil prices fell in 1998–99. Oman plans to acquire new weapons in line with the mutual defence agreement signed by the six GCC states in December 2000. These purchases include 80 *Piranha* armoured vehicles, *Mistral* SAM systems, F-16 aircraft, *Super Lynx* helicopters and upgrades to the fleet of *Scorpion* reconnaissance vehicles already in service. In 2001, Oman received the final ten of 38 British-made *Challenger* 2 main battle tanks.

Saudi Arabia

Saudi Arabia's defence budget rose from R88.4bn ($23.6bn) in 2000 to R102bn ($27bn) in 2001. The US approved a $2.7bn package for Saudi Arabia under the Foreign Military Sales programme. The largest component of the package is for continued technical support and spare parts for the Royal Saudi Air Force's entire fleet of F-15 aircraft. The remainder covers the supply of 132 light armoured vehicles, tube-launched optically tracked wire-guided (TOW) missiles and tactical communications systems for the National Guard. Saudi Arabia is expected to commission the first of three French-built *La Fayette*-class frigates in early 2002 that will be the most capable surface combatants in the Middle East and North Africa region.

Table 18 Arms orders and deliveries, Middle East and North Africa, 1998–2001

Country supplier ⇩	Classification ⇩	Designation	Quantity ⇩	Order date	Delivery date	Comment ⇩
Algeria Tu	LACV	**Scorpion**	700	1995	1996	Deliveries continuing
Ukr	MBT	**T-72**	27	1997	1998	
Ukr	AIFV	**BMP-2**	32	1997	1998	
Ukr	cbt hel	**Mi-24**	14	1997	1998	
Bel	FGA	**MiG-29**	36	1998	1999	Reportedly in exchange for 120 MiG-21s
RF	ASSM	**Kh-35**	96	1998	1999	For FACs. 2 batches of 48 ordered
RF	FGA	**Su-24**	22	2000	2001	
US	ESM	**Beech** 1900	6	2000		For SIGINT role
Bahrain US	FGA	**F-16C/D**	10	1998	2000	AMRAAM-equipped; option for 2 more
US	MRL	**ATACMS**	30	1999	2001	
US	AAM	**AMRAAM**		1999		
Egypt US	hel	**AH-64**	36	1990	1994	24 delivered by 1995; 12 more 1997–99
US	FF	**Perry**	4	1994	1996	Deliveries to 1998
US	hel	**SH-2G**	10	1994	1997	Deliveries to 1999
US	arty	**SP 122 SPG**	24	1996	2000	2nd order
US	FGA	**F-16C/D**	21	1996	1999	2 delivered per month until 2000
US	hel	**CH-47D**	4	1997	1999	Also updates for 6 CH-47Cs to D
US	SAM	**Avenger**	50	1998	2001	
US	ARV	**M88A2**	63	1998	2002	50 delivered in 2000
dom	APC	**Al-Akhbar**		1998	2001	Dev complete
US	SAM	**Patriot**	384	1998	2001	384 msl; 48 launchers
RF	SAM	**Pechora**	50	1999	2003	Upgrade to *Pechora*-2 aka SA-3A *Goa*
US	LST	**Newport**	1	1999	2000	
US	FGA	**F-16**	24	1999	2001	12 × 1 seater; 12 × 2 seater
PRC	trg	**K-8**		1999	2001	
US	AEW	**E-2C**	5	1999	2002	Upgrade
SF	arty	**GH-52**	1	1999		
US	MBT	**M1A1**	200	1999	2001	Kits for local assembly
Ge	trg	**G 115EG**	74	1999	2000	Deliveries to 2002
US	SAM	**AMRAAM**		2000		Ground launched variant
US	hel	**AH-64A**	35	2000		Upgrade to *Longbow* standard
It	FAC	**Ramadan**-class	6	2000		Upgraded Comd & Control systems
US	arty	**M109**	279	2000	2002	
Nl	SSK	**Moray**-class	2	2000	2007–08	
US	FM	**Ambassador** III	4	2001	2004	
A	UAV	**Camcopter**	2	2001	2002	
Iran dom	SSM	**Shihab-3**		1994	1999	Reportedly based on DPRK *No-dong* 1
dom	MRBM	**Shihab-4**		1994		Dev. Reportedly based on RF SS-4

	Country supplier ⇩	Classification ⇩ / Designation	Quantity ⇩	Order date	Delivery date	Comment ⇩
	dom	ICBM / *Shihab*-5		1994		Dev. Possibly based on *Taepo-dong*
	PRC	tpt / **Y-7**	14	1996	1998	Deliveries 1998–2006
	PRC	FGA / **F-7**	10	1996	1998	
	dom	hel / *Shahed*-5	20	1999		
	RF	hel / **Mi-17**	4	1999	2000	Potential for further 20
	dom	SSI / **Al-Sabehat 15**	1		2000	Mini-sub
	Ir	FGA / **MiG-29**	29	1999	1999	Held since 1990; returned by Ir 1999
Israel	col	BMD / *Arrow*	2	1986	1999	Deployment to begin 1999; with US
	dom	PFM / *Saar* **4.5**	6	1990	1994	Upgrade. 4th delivered 1998. Deliveries of last 2 pending
	dom	sat / *Ofek*-4	1	1990	1999	Launch failed
	dom	MBT / *Merkava* **4**		1991	2001	In dev
	dom	ATGW / **LAHAT**		1991	1999	Dev completed end-1999
	Ge	SSK / *Dolphin*	3	1991	1998	Final delivery 2000. Funded by Ge
	col	BMD / *Nautilus*		1992	2000	Joint dev with US
	Fr	hel / **AS-565**	8	1994	1997	5 delivered 1997
	US	FGA / **F-15I**	25	1994	1998	Deliveries: 4 in 1998, continue to 2000
	dom	sat / *Amos*-1	1	1995		Dev slowed by lack of funds
	US	tpt hel / **S-70A**	15	1995	1998	1st 2 deliveries complete
	dom	UAV / *Silver Arrow*		1997		Prototype unveiled April 1998
	US	AAM / **AIM-120B**	64	1998	1999	
	US	FGA / **F-16I**	50	1999	2003	With *Popeye* 2 and *Python* 4 AAM
	US	ASM / *Hellfire*	480	1999		
	US	cbt hel / **B200**	5	2000		
	US	AAM / **AMRAAM**	57	2000		
	US		JDAM	2000		
	US	hel / **AH-64D**	9	2000		New purchase rather than upgrading current fleet
	US	hel / **UH-60L**	35	2000		
	US	hel / **S-70A**	24	2001	2002	
	US	FGA / **F-16I**	50	2001		
Jordan	US	MBT / **M-60A3**	50	1996		38 delivered 1997
	UK	ASSM / *Sea Skua*	60	1997	1998	
	US	cbt hel / **AH-64**	16	1997	2000	*Longbow* radar not fitted
	US	SP arty / **M-109A6**	48	1998		Includes spt veh. Order frozen late 1998
	UK	MBT / *Challenger* **1**	288	1999	2001	Ex-British Army
	UK	recce / *Scorpion*		1999	2001	Upgrade
	US	APC / **M-113**		1999		
	Tu	tpt / **CN-235**	2	1999	2001	One year lease
	Ukr	APC / **BTR-94**	50	1999	2000	mod BTR-80
	Be	APC / *Spartan*	100	2001	2001	2nd-hand
Kuwait	US	ATGW / **TOW-2B**	728	1999		
	US	arty / **Paladin**		2000		To equip 3 battalions
	col	hel / **EC135**	2	1999	2001	
Libya	DPRK	SSM / **Nodong**	50	1999	2000	
Mauritania	It	trg / **SF360E**	5		2000	
Morocco	Fr	FF / *Floreal*	2	1998	2001	
	Bel	MBT / **T-72**	48	2001		

	Country supplier	Classification ⇩ / Designation	Quantity ⇩	Order date	Delivery date	Comment ⇩
Oman	UK	MBT *Challenger* 2	38	1997	1999	Final 10 delivered 2000
	UK	radar *S743D*		1999	2002	
	UK	SAM *Mistral* 2		2000	2001	
	UK	APC *Piranha* 2	80	2000	2001	In 7 versions
	UK	recce *Scorpion*	60	2000	2002	Upgrades
	US	FGA *F-16*	12	2001		
	col	hel *Super Lynx*	20	2001		
Qatar	UK	APC *Piranha* 2	40	1995	1997	2 delivered 1997, 26 1998
	UK	trg *Hawk* 100	15	1996	1999	
Saudi Arabia	Ca	LAV *LAV-25*	1,117	1990	1992	800 delivered by 1998
	UK	FGA *Tornado* IDS	48	1993	1996	Deliveries completed 1998
	Fr	FFG *F-3000*	3	1994	2001	1st delivery 2001, 2nd 2003, 3rd 2005
	US	Construction *Jizan*	1	1996	1999	Military city and port
	Fr	hel *AS-532*	12	1996	1998	4 delivered 1998
	US	AWACS *E-3*	5	1997	2000	Upgrade
	It	SAR hel *AB-412TP*	44	1998	2001	
	US	AAM *AMRAAM*	475	2000		
	US	ATGW *TOW 2A*	1,827	2000		
Syria	RF	ATGW *AT-14*	1,000	1997	1998	msl
	RF	SAM *S-300*		1997		Unconfirmed
	RF	FGA *Su-27*			2000	4 delivered
	RF	FGA *MiG-29*			2000	Deliveries from previously unnanounced order
Tunisia	Sau	MBT *AMX-30*	30	2000		2nd-hand
UAE	Fr	MBT *Leclerc*	390	1993	1994	Also 46 ARVs. Deliveries to 2003
	RF	tpt *Il-76*	4	1997	1998	On lease
	Tu	APC *M-113*	136	1997	1999	
	Indo	tpt *CN-235*	7	1997		
	US	cbt hel *AH-64A*	10	1997	1999	
	Fr	hel *Gazelle*	5	1997	1999	Option for further 5
	Fr	FGA *Mirage* 2000-09	30	1997	2000	
	Fr	FGA *Mirage* 2000	33	1997	2000	Upgrade to 2000-9 standard
	Fr	ALCM *Black Shahine*		1998	2000	For new and upgraded *Mirage* 2000-9
	UK	trg *Hawk-200*	18	1998	2001	Following delivery of 26 1992–6
	Indo	MPA *CN-235*	4	1998		
	UK	PFC *Protector*	2	1998	1999	
	Fr	trg *Alpha Jet*		1999		
	Fr	trg *AS 350B*	14	1999		
	US	FGA *F-16*	80	2000	2002	With AMRAAM, HARM and *Hakeem* msl
	Ge	APC *Fuchs*	64	2000		recce veh
	RF	SAM *Partzyr-S1*	50	2000	2002	
	col	MPA *C-295*	4	2001		
	Fr	FAC	6	2001		
Yemen	Fr	PCI *Vigilante*	6	1996	1997	Commissioning delayed
	Cz	trg *L-39C*	12	1999	1999	Deliveries began late 1999
	RF	FGA *Su-27*	14	1999	2001	
	Cz	MBT *T-55*	106		2000	
	RF	MBT *T-72*	30		2000	

Middle East and North Africa

Algeria Ag

dinar D		1999	2000	2001	2002
GDP	D	3.2tr	3.3tr		
	US$	46.8bn	44.2bn		
per capita	US$	7,000	7,300		
Growth	%	2.8	2.6		
Inflation	%	3.1	0.5		
Debt	US$	28.3bn	25bn		
Def exp	D	210bn	223bn		
	US$	3.1bn	3.0bn		
Def bdgt	D	121bn	138bn		
	US$	1.8bn	1.8bn		
FMA (US)	US$	100m	100m	100m	200m
US$1=D		68.0	74.6	77.8	

Population				32,136,000
Age	13–17	18–22	23–32	
Men	1,986,000	1,834,000	2,962,000	
Women	1,847,000	1,709,000	2,783,000	

Total Armed Forces

ACTIVE ε124,000

(incl ε75,000 conscripts)
Terms of service **Army** 18 months (6 months basic, 12 months civil projects)

RESERVES
Army some 150,000, to age 50

Army 107,000

(incl ε75,000 conscripts)
6 Mil Regions; re-org into div structure on hold
2 armd div (each 3 tk, 1 mech regt) • 2 mech div (each 3 mech, 1 tk regt) • 1 AB div (5 AB regt) • 1 indep armd bde • 4 indep mot/mech inf bde, 14 indep inf, 2 arty, 1 AD, 6 AAA bn

EQUIPMENT
  MBT 1,089: 288 T-54/-55, 334 T-62, 467 T-72
  RECCE 85 BRDM-2
  AIFV 700 BMP-1, 289 BMP-2, 100 BMP-3
  APC 530 BTR-50/-60, 150 OT-64, 80 BTR-80, 100 *Fahd*
  TOWED ARTY 122mm: 28 D-74, 100 M-1931/37, 60 M-30 (M-1938), 198 D-30; **130mm**: 10 M-46; **152mm**: 22 ML-20 (M-1937)
  SP ARTY 185: **122mm**: 150 2S1; **152mm**: 35 2S3
  MRL 122mm: 48 BM-21; **140mm**: 48 BM-14-16; **240mm**: 30 BM-24
  MOR 82mm: 150 M-37; **120mm**: 120 M-1943; **160mm**: 60 M-1943
  ATGW AT-3 *Sagger*, AT-4 *Spigot*, AT-5 *Spandrel*
  RCL 82mm: 120 B-10; **107mm**: 58 B-11
  ATK GUNS 57mm: 156 ZIS-2; **85mm**: 37 D-44; **100mm**: 3 T-12, 50 SU-100 SP

AD GUNS 14.5mm: 80 ZPU-2/-4; **20mm**: 100; **23mm**: 75 ZU-23 towed, 330 ZSU-23-4 SP; **37mm**: 145 M-1939; **57mm**: 70 S-60; **85mm**: 20 KS-12; **100mm**: 150 KS-19; **130mm**: 10 KS-30
SAM SA-7/-8/-9

Navy ε7,000

(incl ε500 Coast Guard)
BASES Mers el Kebir, Algiers, Annaba, Jijel
SUBMARINES 2
SSK 2 Sov *Kilo* with 533mm TT
PRINCIPAL SURFACE COMBATANTS 3
FRIGATES 3
FF 3 *Mourad Rais* (Sov *Koni*) with SA-N-4 *Gecko* SAM, 4 × 76mm gun, 2 × 12 ASW RL
PATROL AND COASTAL COMBATANTS 17
CORVETTES 5
  3 *Rais Hamidou* (Sov *Nanuchka* II) FSG with 4 SS-N-2C *Styx* SSM, SA-N-4 *Gecko* SAM
  2 *Djebel Chinoise* FS with 3 × 76mm gun
MISSILE CRAFT 9 *Osa* with 4 SS-N-2 *Styx* SSM (plus 2 non-op)
PATROL CRAFT 3
  COASTAL 3 *El Yadekh* PCC
AMPHIBIOUS 3
  2 *Kalaat beni Hammad* LST: capacity 240 tps, 10 tk, hel deck
  1 *Polnocny* LSM: capacity 180 tps, 6 tk
SUPPORT AND MISCELLANEOUS 3
  1 div spt, 1 *Poluchat* TRV, 1 *El Idrissi* AGHS
COAST GUARD (ε500)
  Some 7 PRC *Chui-E* PCC, about 6 *El Yadekh* PCC, 16 PCI<, 1 spt, plus boats

Air Force 10,000

ε176 cbt ac, 63 armed hel
Flying hours 50
FGA 3 sqn
  1 with 14 Su-24MK (8 more to arrive by 2002), 2 with 34 MiG-23BN
FTR 5 sqn
  1 with 14 MiG-25
  4 with some 30 MiG-23B/E, 70 MiG-21MF/bis (12+ MiG-29C/UB possibly serving with 1 sqn)
RECCE 1 sqn with 4* MiG-25R
SIGINT 1 sqn with 6 *Beech* 1900D
MR 2 sqn with 15 *Super King Air* B-200T
TPT 2 sqn with 10 C-130H, 8 C-130H-30, 3 Il-76MD, 6 Il-76TD
VIP 2 *Falcon* 900, 3 *Gulfstream* III, 3 F-27
HELICOPTERS
  ATTACK 33 Mi-24, 30 Mi-8/17
  TPT 2 Mi-4, 5 Mi-6, 16 Mi-8/17, 2 AS 355

TRG 5 T-34C, 30 ZLIN-142, 4* MiG-21U, 5* MiG-23U, 1* MiG-25U, 30 L-39 hel: 25 Mi-2
UAV *Seeker*
AAM AA-2, AA-6, AA-7
AD GUNS 3 bde+: 725 **85mm, 100mm, 130mm**
SAM 3 regt with 100 SA-3, SA-6, SA-8

Forces Abroad

UN AND PEACEKEEPING
DROC (MONUC): 13 obs **ETHIOPIA/ERITREA** (UNMEE): 8 obs

Paramilitary ε181,200

GENDARMERIE 60,000 (Ministry of Defence)

6 regions; 44 Panhard AML-60/M-3, BRDM-2 recce, 200 *Fahd* APC **hel** Mi-2

NATIONAL SECURITY FORCES 20,000 (Directorate of National Security)

small arms

REPUBLICAN GUARD 1,200

AML-60, M-3 recce

LEGITIMATE DEFENCE GROUPS ε100,000

self-defence militia, communal guards

Opposition

GROUPE ISLAMIQUE ARMÉE (GIA) small gps each ε50–100; total less than 1,500

GROUPE SALAFISTE POUR LA PRÉDICATION ET LE COMBAT small gps; total less than 500

Bahrain Brn

dinar D		1999	2000	2001	2002
GDP	D	2.2bn	2.6bn		
	US$	5.7bn	6.9bn		
per capita	US$	9,800	10,300		
Growth	%	5.0	4.0		
Inflation	%	1.0	1.5		
Debt	US$		2.6bn		
Def exp	D	166m	167m		
	US$	441m	444m		
Def bdgt[a]	D	115m	119m	119m	
	US$	306m	315m	315m	
FMA (US)	US$	200m	200m	200m	200m
US$1=D		0.38	0.38	0.38	
[a] Excl procurement					
Population					626,000

Nationals 63% **Asian** 13% **other Arab** 10% **Iranian** 8%
European 1%

Age	13–17	18–22	23–32
Men	35,000	26,000	40,000
Women	33,000	25,000	40,000

Total Armed Forces

ACTIVE 11,000

Army 8,500

1 armd bde (-) (2 tk, 1 recce bn) • 1 inf bde (2 mech, 1 mot inf bn) • 1 arty 'bde' (1 hy, 2 med, 1 lt, 1 MRL bty) • 1 SF, 1 *Amiri* gd bn • 1 AD bn (2 SAM, 1 AD gun bty)
EQUIPMENT
MBT 106 M-60A3
RECCE 22 AML-90, 8 *Saladin*, 8 *Ferret*, 8 Shorland
AIFV 25 YPR-765 (with **25mm**)
APC some 10 AT-105 *Saxon*, 110 Panhard M-3, 115 M-113A2
TOWED ARTY 105mm: 8 lt; **155mm**: 14 M-198
SP ARTY 203mm: 62 M-110
MRL 227mm: 9 MLRS (some ATACMS)
MOR 81mm: 12; **120mm**: 9
ATGW 15 TOW
RCL 106mm: 25 M-40A1; **120mm**: 6 MOBAT
AD GUNS 35mm: 15 Oerlikon; **40mm**: 12 L/70
SAM 60 RBS-70, 18 *Stinger*, 7 *Crotale*, 8 I HAWK

Navy 1,000

BASE Mina Salman
PRINCIPAL SURFACE COMBATANTS 1
FRIGATES
FFG 1 *Sabha* (US *OH Perry*) with 4 *Harpoon* SSM, 1 *Standard* SM-1MR SAM, 1 × 76mm gun, 2 × 3 ASTT
PATROL AND COASTAL COMBATANTS 10
CORVETTES 2 *Al Manama* (Ge Lürssen 62m) FSG with 2 × 2 MM-40 *Exocet* SSM, 1 × 76mm gun, hel deck
MISSILE CRAFT 4 *Ahmad el Fateh* (Ge Lürssen 45m) PFM with 2 × 2 MM-40 *Exocet* SSM, 1 × 76mm gun
PATROL CRAFT 4
COASTAL/INSHORE 4
2 *Al Riffa* (Ge Lürssen 38m) PFC
2 *Swift* FPB-20 PCI<
SUPPORT AND MISCELLANEOUS 5
4 *Ajeera* LCU-type spt
1 *Tiger* ACV, **hel** 2 B-105

Air Force 1,500

34 cbt ac, 40 armed hel
FGA 1 sqn with 8 F-5E, 4 F-5F
FTR 2 sqn with 18 F-16C, 4 F-16D
TPT 2 *Gulfstream* (1 -II, 1 -III; VIP), 1 Boeing 727
HEL 1 sqn with 12 AB-212 (10 armed), 3 sqn with 24* AH-1E, 6* TAH-1P, 1 VIP unit with 3 Bo-105, 1 UH-60L (VIP), 1 S-70A (VIP)
MISSILES
ASM AS-12, AGM-65D/G *Maverick*

AAM AIM-9P *Sidewinder*, AIM-7F *Sparrow*
ATGW BGM-71 TOW

Paramilitary ε10,160

POLICE 9,000 (Ministry of Interior)
2 Hughes 500, 2 Bell 412, 1 BO-105 hel
NATIONAL GUARD ε900
3 bn
COAST GUARD 260 (Ministry of Interior)
1 PCI, some 20 PCI<, 2 spt/landing craft, 1 hovercraft

Foreign Forces

US Air Force periodic detachments of ftr and spt ac
Navy (HQ CENTCOM and 5th Fleet): 680 **Marine** 45
UK RAF 40 (*Southern Watch*), 2 VC-10 tkr

Egypt Et

pound E£		**1999**	**2000**	**2001**	**2002**
GDP	E£	302bn	312bn		
	US$	89bn	90bn		
per capita	US$	4,400	5,000		
Growth	%	6.0	3.0		
Inflation	%	3.1	2.8		
Debt	US$	29bn	27bn		
Def exp	E£	ε10.1bn	9.9bn		
	US$	3.0bn	2.9bn		
Def bdgt	E£	8.7bn	8.1bn	7.9bn	
	US$	2.5bn	2.4bn	2.1bn	
FMA (US)	US$	2.1bn	2.0bn	2.0bn	2.0bn
US$1=E£		3.39	3.44	3.88	
Population				**70,615,000**	
Age		*13–17*	*18–22*	*23–32*	
Men		3,707,000	3,313,000	5,150,000	
Women		3,510,000	3,128,000	4,853,000	

Total Armed Forces

ACTIVE 443,000
(incl ε322,000+ conscripts)
Terms of service 18 months–3 years (selective)

RESERVES 254,000
Army 150,000 **Navy** 14,000 **Air Force** 20,000 **AD** 70,000

Army 320,000

(ε250,000+ conscripts)
4 Mil Districts, 2 Army HQ • 4 armd div (each with 2 armd, 1 mech, 1 arty bde) • 8 mech inf div (each with 2 mech, 1 armd, 1 arty bde) • 1 Republican Guard armd bde • 4 indep armd bde • 4 indep mech bde • 1 air-

mobile bde • 2 indep inf bde • 1 para bde • cdo gp • 1 SF group • 15 indep arty bde • 2 SSM bde (1 with FROG-7, 1 with *Scud*-B)
EQUIPMENT[a]
MBT 895 T-54/-55, 260 *Ramses* II (mod T-54/55), 550 T-62, 1,600 M-60 (400 M-60A1, 1,200 M-60A3), 555 M1A1 *Abrams*
RECCE 300 BRDM-2, 112 *Commando Scout*
AIFV 220 BMP-1 (in store), 265 BMR-600P, 310 YPR-765 (with **25mm**)
APC 600 *Walid*, 192 *Fahd*/-30, 1,075 BTR-50/OT-62 (most in store), 2,320 M-113A2 (incl variants), 100 YPR-765
TOWED ARTY 122mm: 36 M-1931/37, 359 M-1938, 156 D-30M; **130mm**: 420 M-46
SP ARTY 122mm: 124 SP 122, **155mm**: 354 M-109A2
MRL 122mm: 96 BM-11, 60 BM-21/*as-Saqr*-10/-18/-36
MOR 82mm: 540 (some 50 SP); **120mm**: 1,800 M-1938; **160mm**: 60 M-160
SSM 9 FROG-7, *Saqr*-80 (trials), 9 *Scud*-B
ATGW 1,400 AT-3 *Sagger* (incl BRDM-2); 220 *Milan*; 200 *Swingfire*; 530 TOW (incl I-TOW, TOW-2A (with 52 on M-901, 210 on YPR-765 SP))
RCL 107mm: 520 B-11
AD GUNS 14.5mm: 200 ZPU-4; **23mm**: 280 ZU-23-2, 118 ZSU-23-4 SP, 36 *Sinai*; **37mm**: 200 M-1939; **57mm**: some S-60, 40 ZSU-57-2 SP
SAM 600+ SA-7/'*Ayn as-Saqr*, 20 SA-9, 26 M-54 SP *Chaparral*, *Stinger*, 25 *Avenger*
SURV AN/TPQ-37 (arty/mor), RASIT (veh, arty), *Cymbeline* (mor)
UAV R4E-50 *Skyeye*
[a] Most Sov eqpt now in store, incl MBT and some cbt ac

Navy 19,000

(incl ε2,000 Coast Guard and ε12,000 conscripts)
BASES Mediterranean Alexandria (HQ), Port Said, Mersa Matruh, Port Tewfig **Red Sea** Safaqa (HQ), Berenice, Hurghada, Suez
SUBMARINES 4
SSK 4 *Romeo* with *Harpoon* SSM and 533mm TT
PRINCIPAL SURFACE COMBATANTS 11
DESTROYERS 1 DD *El Fateh* (UK 'Z') (trg) with 4 × 114mm guns, 5 × 533mm TT
FRIGATES 10
FFG 10
4 *Mubarak* (ex-US OH *Perry*) with 4 *Harpoon* SSM, *Standard* SM-1-MR SAM, 1 × 76mm gun, 2 hel
2 *El Suez* (Sp *Descubierta*) with 2 × 4 *Harpoon* SSM, 1 × 76mm gun, 2 × 3 ASTT, 1 × 2 ASW RL
2 *Al Zaffir* (PRC *Jianghu* I) with 2 CSS-N-2 (*HY* 2) SSM, 2 ASW RL
2 *Damyat* (US *Knox*) with 8 *Harpoon* SSM, 1 × 127mm gun, 4 × 324mm TT
PATROL AND COASTAL COMBATANTS 38
MISSILE CRAFT 23

6 *Ramadan* with 4 *Otomat* SSM

5 Sov *Osa* I with 4 SS-N-2A *Styx* SSM (1 may be non-op)

5 *6th October* with 2 *Otomat* SSM

2 Sov *Komar* with 2 SSN-2A *Styx* SSM

5 PRC *Hegu* (*Komar*-type) with 2 SSN-2A *Styx* SSM

PATROL CRAFT, COASTAL 15

4 PRC *Hainan* PFC with 6 × 324mm TT, 4 ASW RL (plus 4 in reserve)

6 Sov *Shershen* PFC; 2 with 4 × 533mm TT and BM-21 (8-tube) 122mm MRL; 4 with SA-N-5 SAM and 1 BM-24 (12-tube) 240mm MRL

5 PRC *Shanghai* II PFC

MINE WARFARE 13

MINE COUNTERMEASURES 13

6 *Assiout* (Sov T-43 class) MSO (op status doubtful)

4 *Aswan* (Sov *Yurka*) MSC

3 *Swiftship* MHI

plus 1 route survey boat

AMPHIBIOUS 3

3 Sov *Polnocny* LSM, capacity 100 tps, 5 tk

plus craft: 9 *Vydra* LCU

SUPPORT AND MISCELLANEOUS 20

7 AOT (small), 5 trg, 6 AT, 1 diving spt, 1 *Tariq* (ex-UK FF) trg

NAVAL AVIATION

EQUIPMENT

24 armed hel (operated by Air Force)

HELICOPTERS

5 *Sea King* Mk 47, 9 SA-342, 10 SH-2G *Super Sea-Sprite* with Mk 46 LWT

COASTAL DEFENCE (Army tps, Navy control)

GUNS 130mm: SM-4-1

SSM *Otomat*

Air Force 29,000

(incl 10,000 conscripts); 580 cbt ac, 129 armed hel

FGA 7 sqn

2 with 41 *Alpha Jet*, 2 with 44 PRC J-6, 2 with 28 F-4E, 1 with 20 *Mirage* 5E2

FTR 22 sqn

2 with 25 F-16A/10 F-16B, 6 with 40 MiG-21, 7 with 135 F-16C/29 F-16D, 3 with 53 *Mirage* 5D/E, 3 with 53 PRC J-7, 1 with 18 *Mirage* 2000C

RECCE 2 sqn with 6* *Mirage* 5SDR, 14* MiG-21R

EW ac 2 C-130H (ELINT), 4 Beech 1900 (ELINT) **hel** 4 *Commando* 2E (ECM)

AEW 5 E-2C

MR 2 Beech 1900C surv ac

TPT 19 C-130H, 5 DHC-5D, 1 *Super King Air*, 3 *Gulfstream* III, 1 *Gulfstream* IV, 3 *Falcon* 20

HELICOPTERS

ASW 9* SA-342L, 5* *Sea King* 47, 10* SH-2G (with Navy)

ATTACK 4 sqn with 69 SA-342K (44 with HOT, 25 with 20mm gun), 36 AH-64A

TAC TPT hy 15 CH-47C, 14 CH-47D **med** 66 Mi-8, 25 *Commando* (3 VIP), 2 S-70 (VIP) **lt** 12 Mi-4, 17 UH-12E (trg), 2 UH-60A, 2 UH-60L (VIP), 3 AS-61

TRG incl 4 DHC-5, 54 EMB-312, 36 *Gumhuria*, 16* JJ-6, 40 L-29, 48 L-39, 30* L-59E, first of 80 K-8 being delivered to replace L-29, 10* MiG-21U, 5* *Mirage* 5SDD, 3* *Mirage* 2000B

UAV 29 Teledyne-Ryan 324 *Scarab*

MISSILES

ASM AGM-65 *Maverick*, AGM-84 *Harpoon*, *Exocet* AM-39, AS-12, AS-30, AS-30L HOT, AGM-119 *Hellfire*

ARM *Armat*

AAM AA-2 *Atoll*, AIM-7E/F/M *Sparrow*, AIM-9F/L/P *Sidewinder*, MATRA R-530, MATRA R-550 *Magic*

Air Defence Command 75,000

(incl 50,000 conscripts)

4 div: regional bde, 100 AD arty bn, 40 SA-2, 53 SA-3, 14 SA-6 bn, 12 bty I HAWK, 12 bty *Chaparral*, 14 bty *Crotale*

EQUIPMENT

AD GUNS some 2,000: **20mm, 23mm, 37mm, 57mm, 85mm, 100mm**

SAM some 300 SA-2, 232 SA-3, 78 I HAWK, some 30 *Crotale*

AD SYSTEMS some 18 *Amoun* (*Skyguard*/RIM-7F *Sparrow*, some 36 twin **35mm** guns, some 36 quad SAM); *Sinai*-23 short-range AD (Dassault 6SD-20S radar, **23mm** guns, '*Ayn as-Saqr* SAM)

Forces Abroad

Advisers in O, Sau, DROC

UN AND PEACEKEEPING

CROATIA (UNMOP): 1 obs **DROC** (MONUC): 26 incl 25 obs **EAST TIMOR** (UNTAET): 75 incl 2 obs **GEORGIA** (UNOMIG): 3 obs **SIERRA LEONE** (UNAMSIL): 10 obs **WESTERN SAHARA** (MINURSO): 19 obs

Paramilitary ε325,000 active

CENTRAL SECURITY FORCES 250,000 (Ministry of Interior)

110 *Hotspur Hussar, Walid* APC

NATIONAL GUARD 60,000

8 bde (each of 3 bn; cadre status); lt wpns only

BORDER GUARD FORCES 15,000

19 Border Guard Regt; lt wpns only

COAST GUARD ε2,000 (incl in Naval entry)

PATROL, INSHORE 40

20 *Timsah* PCI<, 9 *Swiftships*, 5 *Nisr*†, 6 *Crestitalia*

PFI<, plus some 60 boats

Opposition

AL-JIHAD 1,000+

ISLAMIC GROUP 1,000+

Foreign Forces

PEACEKEEPING

MFO Sinai: some 1,896 from **Aus, Ca, Co, Fji, Fr, Hu, It, No, NZ, Ury, US**

Iran Ir

rial r		1999	2000	2001	2002
GDP[a]	r	401tr	540tr		
	US$	93bn	99bn		
per capita	US$	7,000	7,400		
Growth	%	5.5	4.5		
Inflation	%	22	30		
Debt	US$	12.1bn	12bn		
Def exp[a]	r	10.0tr	13.1tr		
	US$	5.7bn	7.5bn		
Def bdgt	r	10.0tr	13.1tr	15.9tr	
	US$	5.7bn	7.5bn	9.1bn	
US$1=r		1,753	1,753	1,753	

[a] Excl defence industry funding

Population			68,281,000

Persian 51% **Azeri** 24% **Gilaki/Mazandarani** 8%
Kurdish 7% **Arab** 3% **Lur** 2% **Baloch** 2% **Turkman** 2%

Age	13–17	18–22	23–32
Men	4,735,000	3,960,000	5,959,000
Women	4,531,000	3,835,000	5,613,000

Total Armed Forces

ACTIVE ε513,000

(perhaps 220,000 conscripts)
Terms of service 21 months

RESERVES

Army 350,000, ex-service volunteers

Army 325,000

(perhaps 220,000 conscripts)
4 Corps HQ • 4 armd div (each 3 armd, 1 mech bde, 4–5 arty bn) • 6 inf div (each 4 inf bde, 4–5 arty bn) • 2 cdo div • 1 AB bde • some indep armd, inf, cdo bde • 5 arty gps • Army avn

EQUIPMENT† (overall totals incl those held by Revolutionary Guard Corps Ground Forces)

MBT some 1,565 incl: 500 T-54/-55 and PRC Type-59, some 75 T-62, 480 T-72, 200 *Chieftain* Mk 3/5, 150 M-47/-48, 150 M-60A1, ε10 *Zulfiqar*

LT TK 80 *Scorpion, Towsan*

RECCE 35 EE-9 *Cascavel*

AIFV 350 BMP-1, 400 BMP-2

APC 300 BTR-50/-60, 250 M-113, ε40 *Boragh*

TOWED 2,085: **105mm**: 130 M-101A1; **122mm**: 500 D-30, 100 PRC Type-54; **130mm**: 1,100 M-46/Type-59; **152mm**: 30 D-20; **155mm**: 15 WAC-21, 70 M-114; 120 GHN-45; **203mm**: 20 M-115

SP 310: **122mm**: 60 2S1, *Thunder* 1; **155mm**: 180 M-109, *Thunder* 2; **170mm**: 10 M-1978; **175mm**: 30 M-107; **203mm**: 30 M-110

MRL 889+: **107mm**: 700 PRC Type-63; *Haseb, Fadjr* 1; **122mm**: 50 *Hadid/Arash/Noor*, 100 BM-21, 20 BM-11; **240mm**: 9 M-1985, ε10 *Fadjr* 3; **333mm**: *Fadjr* 5

MOR 5,000 incl: **60mm; 81mm; 82mm; 107mm**: 4.2in M-30; **120mm**: M-65

SSM ε17 *Scud*-B/-C (300 msl), ε30 CSS-8 (175 msl), *Arash/Noor, Oghab, Shahin* 1/-2, *Nazeat*, some *Shehab* 3 (20 msl)

ATGW 75: TOW, AT-3 *Sagger* (some SP), AT-4 *Spigot*, some AT-5 *Spandrel*

RL 73mm: RPG-7

RCL 75mm: M-20; **82mm**: B-10; **106mm**: ε200 M-40; **107mm**: B-11

AD GUNS 1,700: **14.5mm**: ZPU-2/-4; **23mm**: ZU-23 towed, ZSU-23-4 SP; **35mm; 37mm**: M-1939, PRC Type-55; **57mm**: ZSU-57-2 SP, S-60

SAM SA-7/-14/-16

UAV *Mohajer* II/III/IV

AC incl 50 Cessna (150, 180, 185, 310), 19 F-27, 8 *Falcon* 20

HEL 85 AH-1J **attack**; 40 CH-47C **hy tpt**; 180 Bell 214A; 50 AB-205A; 130 AB-206; 30 Bell 204; 5 Hughes 300C; 8 RH-53D; 17 SH-53D; 45 UH-1H, Mi-8/-17

Revolutionary Guard Corps (*Pasdaran Inqilab*) some 125,000

GROUND FORCES some 100,000

grouped into perhaps 16–20 div incl 2 armd, 5 mech, 10 inf, 1 SF and 15–20 indep bde, incl inf, armd, para, SF, 6 arty gp (incl SSM), engr, AD and border defence units, serve indep or with Army; eqpt incl 470 tk, 620 APC/ACV, 360 arty, 40 RL and 140 AD guns, all incl in army inventory; controls *Basij* (see *Paramilitary*) when mob

NAVAL FORCES some 20,000

BASES Al-Farsiyah, Halul (oil platform), Sirri, Abu Musa, Bandar-e-Abbas, Larak
some 40 Swe Boghammar Marin boats armed with ATGW, RCL, machine guns; 10 *Hudong* with C-802 SSM; controls coast-defence elm incl arty and CSSC-3 (*HY* 2) *Seersucker* SSM bty

MARINES some 5,000 1 bde

AIR FORCES

Few details known of this org, which is commanded by a Brig Gen

Navy 18,000

(incl Naval Air and 2,600 Marines)

BASES Bandar-e-Abbas (HQ), Bushehr, Kharg, Bandar-e-Anzelli, Bandar-e-Khomeini, Bandar-e-Mahshahr, Chah Bahar

SUBMARINES 6

SSK 3 *Kilo* (RF Type 877) with 6 × 533mm TT (TEST 71/96 HWT/LWT)

SSI 3

PRINCIPAL SURFACE COMBATANTS 3

FRIGATES

FFG 3 *Alvand* (UK Vosper Mk 5) with 2 × 2 C-802 SSM, 1 × 114mm gun, 1 × 3 *Limbo* ASW RL

PATROL AND COASTAL COMBATANTS 53

CORVETTES 2 *Bayandor* FS (US PF-103) with 2 × 76mm gun

MISSILE CRAFT 10

10 *Kaman* (Fr *Combattante* II) PFM; 5 of which have 2 or 4 C-802 SSM

PATROL, COASTAL 3

3 *Parvin* PCC

PATROL, INSHORE 38

3 *Zafar* PCI<, some 35 PFI<, plus some 14 hovercraft< (not all op), 200+ small craft

MINE WARFARE 7

MINE LAYERS 2

2 *Hejaz* LST

MINE COUNTERMEASURES 5†

1 *Shahrokh* MSC (in Caspian Sea as trg ship)

2 292 MSC

2 *Riazi* (US *Cape*) MSI

AMPHIBIOUS 9

4 *Hengam* LST, capacity 225 tps, 9 tk, 1 hel
3 *Iran Hormuz 24* (ROK) LSM, capacity 140 tps, 9 tk
2 *Fouque* LSL
Plus craft: 3 LCT, 6 ACV

SUPPORT AND MISCELLANEOUS 22

1 *Kharg* AO with 3 hel, 2 *Bandar Abbas* AO with 1 hel; 2 AWT, 3 *Delvar* spt, 12 *Hendijan* spt; 1 AT, 2 trg craft

NAVAL AVIATION (2,000)

5 cbt ac, 19 armed hel

MR 5 P-3F, 5 Do-228

ASW 1 hel sqn with ε10 SH-3D, 6 AB-212 ASW

MCM 1 hel sqn with 3 RH-53D

TPT 1 sqn with 4 *Commander*, 4 F-27, 3 *Falcon* 20 hel, 5 AB 205a, 4 Mi-171, 2 AB-206, 5 Mi-171

MARINES (2,600) 2 bde

Air Force ε45,000

(incl 15,000 Air Defence); some 283 cbt ac (serviceability probably about 60% for US ac types and about 80% for PRC/Russian ac); no armed hel

FGA 9 sqn

4 with some 66 F-4D/E, 4 with some 60 F-5E/F, 1 with 30 Su-24MK (including former Irq ac), 7 Su-25K (former Irq ac), some Mirage F1 (former Irq ac)

FTR 7 sqn

2 with 25 F-14, 1 with 24 F-7M, 2 with 25 MiG-29A/UB (incl former Irq ac)

(Some F-7 operated by Pasdaran air arm)

MR 5* C-130H-MP

AEW 1 Il-76 (former Irq ac)

RECCE 1 sqn (det) with some 6* RF-4E

TKR/TPT 1 sqn with 3 Boeing 707, 1 Boeing 747

TPT 5 sqn with 4 Boeing 747F, 1 Boeing 727, 18 C-130E/H, 3 *Commander* 690, 10 F-27, 1 *Falcon* 20, 2 *Jetstar*, 10 PC-6B, 2 Y-7, some Il-76 (former Irq ac), 9 Y-12(II)

HEL 2 AB-206A, 30 Bell 214C, Shabaviz 2061 and 2-75 (indigenous versions in production), 2 CH-47

TRG incl 20 Beech F-33A/C, 15 EMB-312, 40 PC-7, 7 T-33, 15* FT-7, 20* F-5B, 8 TB-21, 4 TB-200, 22 MFI-17 *Mushshaq*

MISSILES

ASM some 3,000 AGM-65A *Maverick*, AS-10, AS-11, AS-14, C-801

AAM AIM-7 *Sparrow*, AIM-9 *Sidewinder*, AIM-54 *Phoenix*, probably AA-8, AA-10, AA-11 for MiG-29, PL-2A, PL-7

SAM 16 bn with ε150 I HAWK, 5 sqn with 30 *Rapier*, 15 *Tigercat*, 45 HQ-2J (PRC version of SA-2), 10 SA-5, FM-80 (PRC version of *Crotale*), SA-7, *Stinger*

Forces Abroad

LEBANON ε150 Revolutionary Guard
SUDAN mil advisers

Paramilitary 40,000 active

BASIJ ('Popular Mobilisation Army') (R) ε300,000 peacetime volunteers, mostly youths; str up to 1,000,000 during periods of offensive ops. Small arms only; org into ε900 bn but not currently embodied for mil ops

LAW-ENFORCEMENT FORCES (Ministry of Interior) ε40,000

incl border-guard elm **ac** Cessna 185/310 lt **hel** ε24 AB-205/-206; about 90 patrol inshore, 40 harbour craft

Opposition

NATIONAL LIBERATION ARMY (NLA) some 6–8,000

Irq based; org in bde, armed with captured eqpt.
Perhaps 250+ T-54/-55, *Chieftain* MBT, BMP-1 AIFV,

D-30 **122mm** arty, BM-21 **122mm** MRL, Mi-8 hel
KURDISH DEMOCRATIC PARTY OF IRAN (KDP-Iran)
ε1,200–1,800

**KURDISTAN ORGANISATION OF THE COMMUNIST
PARTY OF IRAN** (KOMALA–Iran) based in Irq ε200

Foreign Forces

some 400 mil technicians/trg staff from PRC, DPRK, RF

Iraq Irq

dinar D		1999	2000	2001	2002
GDP	US$	ε20bn	ε15.4bn		
Growth	%		ε4		
Inflation	%	ε45	ε100		
Debt	US$		ε25bn		
Def exp	US$	ε1.4bn	ε1.4bn	ε1.4bn	
US$1=D		0.31	0.31	0.31	
Population					**22,300,000**

Arab 75–80% (of which Shi'a Muslim 55%, Sunni Muslim
45%) **Kurdish** 20–25%

Age	13–17	18–22	23–32
Men	1,538,000	1,324,000	1,960,000
Women	1,472,000	1,270,000	1,899,000

Total Armed Forces

ACTIVE ε424,000

Terms of service 18–24 months

RESERVES ε650,000

Army ε375,000

(incl ε100,000 recalled Reserves)
7 corps HQ • 3 armd div, 3 mech div[a] • 11 inf div[a] • 6
Republican Guard Force div (3 armd, 1 mech, 2 inf) • 4
Special Republican Guard bde • 5 cdo bde • 2 SF bde
EQUIPMENT[b]
  MBT perhaps 2,200, incl 1,500 T-55/-62 and PRC
  Type-59, 700 T-72
  RECCE 400: BRDM-2, AML-60/-90, EE-9 *Cascavel*,
  EE-3 *Jararaca*
  AIFV perhaps 900 BMP-1/-2
  APC perhaps 2,400, incl BTR-50/-60/-152, OT-62/-
  64, MTLB, YW-701, M-113A1/A2, EE-11 *Urutu*
  TOWED ARTY perhaps 1,900, incl **105mm**: incl M-56
  pack; **122mm**: D-74, D-30, M-1938; **130mm**: incl M-
  46, Type 59-1; **155mm**: some G-5, GHN-45, M-114
  SP ARTY 150, incl **122mm**: 2S1; **152mm**: 2S3; **155mm**:
  M-109A1/A2, AUF-1 (GCT)
  MRL perhaps 200, incl **107mm**; **122mm**: BM-21;

127mm: ASTROS II; **132mm**: BM-13/-16; **262mm**:
  Ababeel
MOR 81mm; 120mm; 160mm: M-1943; **240mm**
SSM up to 50 FROG and 6 *Scud* launchers (ε27 msl)
  reported
ATGW AT-3 *Sagger* (incl BRDM-2), AT-4 *Spigot*
  reported, SS-11, *Milan*, HOT (incl 100 VC-TH)
RCL 73mm: SPG-9; **82mm**: B-10; **107mm**: B-11
ATK GUNS 85mm; 100mm towed
HELICOPTERS ε375
  ATTACK ε100 Bo-105 with AS-11/HOT, Mi-24,
  SA-316 with AS-12, SA-321 (some with *Exocet*), SA-
  342
  TPT hy Mi-6 **med** AS-61, Bell 214 ST, Mi-4, Mi-8/-
  17, SA-330 **lt** AB-212, BK-117 (SAR), Hughes 300C,
  Hughes 500D, Hughes 530F
  SURV RASIT (veh, arty), *Cymbeline* (mor)

[a] All divisions other than Republican Guard at reported
50% cbt effectiveness
[b] 50% of all eqpt lacks spares

Navy ε2,000

BASES Basra (limited facilities), Al Zubayr, Umm Qasr
PATROL AND COASTAL COMBATANTS 6
MISSILE CRAFT 1 Sov *Osa* I PFM with 4 SS-N-2A
  Styx SSM
PATROL, INSHORE 5†
  1 Sov *Bogomol* PFI<, 3 PFI<, 1 PCI< (all non-op)
  plus 80 boats
MINE WARFARE 3
MINE COUNTERMEASURES 3
  1 Sov *Yevgenya*, 2 *Nestin* MSI
SUPPORT AND MISCELLANEOUS 2
  1 *Damen* AG, 1 yacht with hel deck

Air Force ε30,000

ε316 cbt ac, no armed hel
Serviceability of fixed-wg ac about 55%, serviceability
of hel poor
Flying hours snr pilots 90–120, jnr pilots as little as 20
BBR ε6, incl H-6D, Tu-22
FGA ε130, incl MiG-23BN, *Mirage* F1EQ5, Su-20, 40 Su-
  22 M, 2 Su-24 MK, 2 Su-25
FTR ε180 incl F-7, 40 MiG-21, 50 MiG-23, 12 MiG-25, 50
  Mirage F-1EQ, 10 MiG-29
RECCE ε5 incl MiG-25
TKR incl 2 Il-76
TPT incl An-2, 3 An-12, An-24, 6 An-26, Il-76
TRG incl 20 AS-202, 50 EMB-312, some 50 L-39, *Mirage*
  F-1BQ, 25 PC-7, 12 PC-9
MISSILES
  ASM AM-39, AS-4, AS-5, AS-11, AS-9, AS-12, AS-30L,
  C-601
  AAM AA-2/-6/-7/-8/-10, R-530, R-550

Air Defence Command ε17,000

AD Comd given priority since 1991. **HQ** Baghdad/Al-Muthanna **Four regional AD centres** Kirkuk (north), Kut al Hayy (east), Al Basra (south), Ramadia (west)

AD GUNS ε6,000: **23mm**: ZSU-23-4 SP; **37mm**: M-1939 and twin; **57mm**: incl ZSU-57-2 SP; **85mm**; **100mm**; **130mm**

SAM some 1,500 launchers SA-2/-3/-6/-7/-8/-9/-13/-14/-16, *Roland*, *Aspide*

Paramilitary 42–44,000

SECURITY TROOPS ε15,000

BORDER GUARDS ε9,000

lt wpns and mor only

SADDAM'S *FEDAYEEN* ε18–20,000

Opposition

KURDISH DEMOCRATIC PARTY (KDP) ε15,000

(plus 25,000 tribesmen); small arms, some Ir lt arty, MRL, mor, SAM-7

PATRIOTIC UNION OF KURDISTAN (PUK) ε10,000

(plus 22,000 tribesmen); 450 mor (**60mm**, **82mm**, **120mm**); **106mm** RCL; some 200 **14.5mm** AA guns; SA-7 SAM

SUPREME COUNCIL FOR ISLAMIC RESISTANCE IN IRAQ (SCIRI)

4–8,000; ε1 'bde'; Ir-based; Irq dissidents, ex-prisoners of war

Foreign Forces

UN (UNIKOM): some 904 tps and 195 mil obs from 32 countries

Israel II

new sheqalim NS		1999	2000	2001	2002
GDP	NS	410bn	444bn		
	US$	99bn	107bn		
per capita	US$	18,700	19,200		
Growth	%	2.2	3.8		
Inflation	%	7.0	1.7		
Debt	US$	56bn	61bn		
Def exp	NS	ε36.4bn	ε39.4bn		
	US$	8.9bn	9.5bn		
Def bdgt	NS	27.6bn	28.9bn	37.4bn	
	US$	6.7bn	7.0bn	9.0bn	
FMA (US)	US$	3bn	4bn	2.8bn	2.8bn
US$1=NS		4.12	4.12	4.14	
Population[b]					6,336,000

Jewish 82% Arab 19% (incl Christian 3%, Druze 2%)
Circassian ε3,000

Age	13–17	18–22	23–32
Men	284,000	272,000	525,000
Women	268,000	258,000	528,000

[b] Incl ε180,000 Jewish settlers in Gaza and the West Bank, ε217,000 in East Jerusalem and ε15,000 in Golan

Total Armed Forces

ACTIVE ε163,500

(107,500 conscripts)
Terms of service **officers** 48 months **other ranks** 36 months **women** 21 months (Jews and Druze only; Christians, Circassians and Muslims may volunteer). Annual trg as cbt reservists to age 41 (some specialists to age 54) for men, 24 (or marriage) for women

RESERVES 425,000

Army 400,000 **Navy** 5,000 **Air Force** 20,000. Reserve service can be followed by voluntary service in Civil Guard or Civil Defence

Strategic Forces

Il is widely believed to have a nuclear capability with up to 100 warheads. Delivery means could include ac, *Jericho* 1 SSM (range up to 500km), *Jericho* 2 (range ε1,500–2,000km)

Army 120,000

(85,000 conscripts, male and female); some 530,000 on mob
3 territorial, 1 home front comd • 3 corps HQ • 3 armd div (2 armd, 1 arty bde, plus 1 armd, 1 mech inf bde on mob) • 2 div HQ (op control of anti-*intifada* units) • 3 regional inf div HQ (border def) • 4 mech inf bde (incl 1 para trained) • 3 arty bn with MLRS

RESERVES

8 armd div (2 or 3 armd, 1 affiliated mech inf, 1 arty bde) • 1 air-mobile/mech inf div (3 bde manned by para trained reservists) • 10 regional inf bde (each with own border sector)

EQUIPMENT

MBT 3,930: 800 *Centurion*, 250 M-48A5, 300 M-60/A1, 600 M-60A3, 400 *Magach* 7, 200 Ti-67 (T-54/-55), 100 T-62, 1,280 *Merkava* I/II/III

RECCE about 400, incl RAMTA RBY, BRDM-2, ε8 *Fuchs*

APC 5,500 M-113A1/A2, ε200 *Nagmashot* (*Centurion*), ε200 *Achzarit*, *Puma*, BTR-50P, 4,000 M-2/-3 half-track (most in store)

TOWED ARTY 520: **105mm**: 70 M-101; **122mm**: 100 D-30; **130mm**: 100 M-46; **155mm**: 50 Soltam M-68/-71, 50 M-839P/-845P, 50 M-114A1, 100 Soltam M-46

SP ARTY 855: **155mm**: 150 L-33, 530 M-109A1/A2; **175mm**: 140 M-107; **203mm**: 35 M-110

MRL 198: **122mm**: 50 BM-21; **160mm**: 50 LAR-160; **227mm**: 48 MLRS; **240mm**: 30 BM-24; **290mm**: 20 LAR-290.

MOR 60mm: ε5,000; **81mm**: 700; **120mm**: 530; **160mm**: 240 (some SP)

SSM 20 *Lance* (in store), some *Jericho* 1/2

ATGW 300 TOW-2A/-B (incl *Ramta* (M-113) SP), 1,000 *Dragon*, AT-3 *Sagger*, 25 *Mapats*, *Gill/Spike*

RL 82mm: B-300

RCL 106mm: 250 M-40A1

AD GUNS 20mm: 850: incl TCM-20, M-167 *Vulcan*, 35 M-163 *Vulcan*/M-48 *Chaparral* gun/msl, *Machbet Vulcan/Stinger* gun/msl SP system; **23mm**: 150 ZU-23 and 60 ZSU-23-4 SP; **37mm**: M-39; **40mm**: 150 L-70

SAM 250 *Stinger*, 1,000 *Redeye*, 48 *Chaparral*

SURV EL/M-2140 (veh), AN/TPQ-37 (arty), AN/PPS-15 (arty)

Navy ε6,500

(incl 2,500 conscripts), 11,500 on mob
BASES Haifa, Ashdod, Eilat
SUBMARINES 3
SSK 3 *Dolphin* (Ge Type 212 variant) with *Sub-Harpoon* USGW, 4 × 650mm ASTT, 6 × 533mm ASTT
PATROL AND COASTAL COMBATANTS 47
CORVETTES 3
    3 *Eilat* (*Sa'ar* 5) FSG with 8 *Harpoon* SSM, 8 *Gabriel* II SSM, 2 *Barak* VLS SAM (2 × 32 mls), 1 × 76mm gun, 6 × 324mm ASTT, 1 SA-366G hel
MISSILE CRAFT 10
    2 *Aliya* PFM with 4 *Harpoon* SSM, 4 *Gabriel* SSM, 1 SA-366G *Dauphin* hel
    6 *Hetz* (*Sa'ar* 4.5) PFM with 8 *Harpoon* SSM, 6 *Gabriel* SSM, 6 *Barak* VLS SAM, 1 × 76mm gun
    2 *Reshef* (*Sa'ar* 4) PFM with 8 *Harpoon* SSM, 6 *Gabriel* SSM, 1 × 76mm gun
PATROL, INSHORE 34
    13 *Super Dvora* PFI<, some with 2 × 324mm TT
    3 *Nashal* PCI
    15 *Dabur* PFI< with 2 × 324mm TT
    3 Type-1012 *Bobcat* catamaran PCC
AMPHIBIOUS craft only
    1 *Ashdod* LCT, 1 US type LCM
NAVAL COMMANDOS ε300

Air Force 37,000

(20,000 conscripts, mainly in AD), 57,000 on mob; 446 cbt ac (plus perhaps 250 stored including significant number of *Kfir* C7), 133 armed hel
Flying hours regulars: 180; reserves: 80
FGA/FTR 12 sqn
    2 with 50 F-4E-2000, 20 F-4E
    2 with 73 F-15 (38 -A, 8 -B, 16 -C, 11 -D)
    1 with 25 F-15I
    7 with 237 F-16 (92 -A, 17 -B, 79 -C, 49 -D)

FGA 1 sqn with 25 A-4N
RECCE 10* RF-4E
AEW 6 Boeing 707 with *Phalcon* system
EW 3 Boeing 707 (ELINT/ECM), 6 RC-12D, 3 IAI-200, 15 Do-28, 10 *King Air* 2000
MR 3 IAI-1124 *Seascan*
TKR 3 KC-130H
TPT 1 wg incl 5 Boeing 707 (3 tpt/tkr), 12 C-47, 22 C-130H
LIAISON 2 *Islander*, 20 Cessna U-206, 10 *Queen Air* 80
TRG 77 CM-170 *Tzukit*, 28 *Super Cub*, 9* TA-4H, 17* TA-4J, 4 *Queen Air* 80
HELICOPTERS
    ATTACK 21 AH-1G, 36 AH-1F, 30 Hughes 500MD, 42 AH-64A
    ASW 4* AS-565A, 2 × SA-366G
    TPT 38 CH-53D, 10 UH-60; 15 S-70A *Blackhawk*, 54 Bell 212, 43 Bell 206
UAV *Scout*, *Pioneer*, *Searcher*, *Firebee*, *Samson*, *Delilah*, *Hunter Silver Arrow*
MISSILES
    ASM AGM-45 *Shrike*, AGM-62A *Walleye*, AGM-65 *Maverick*, AGM-78D *Standard*, AGM-114 *Hellfire*, TOW, *Popeye* I + II, (GBU-31 JDAM undergoing IAF op/integration tests)
    AAM AIM-7 *Sparrow*, AIM-9 *Sidewinder*, AIM-120B AMRAAM, R-530, *Shafrir*, *Python* III, *Python* IV
    SAM 17 bty with MIM-23 I HAWK, 3 bty *Patriot*, 1 bty Arrow 2, 8 bty *Chapparal*, *Stinger*

Forces Abroad

TURKEY occasional det of Air Force F-16 ac to Akinci air base

Paramilitary ε8,050

BORDER POLICE ε8,000
    some *Walid* 1, 600 BTR-152 APC
COAST GUARD ε50
    1 US PCR, 3 other patrol craft

Foreign Forces

UN (UNTSO): 144 mil obs from 21 countries

Jordan HKJ

dinar D		1999	2000	2001	2002
GDP	D	5.5bn	5.4bn		
	US$	7.7bn	7.6bn		
per capita	US$	3,200	3,200		
Growth	%	1.5	2.0		
Inflation	%	0.6	0.6		
Debt	US$	8.2bn	8.0bn		
Def exp	D	403m	370m		
	US$	569m	520m		

contd		1999	2000	2001	2002
Def bdgt	D	347m	350m	355m	
	US$	488m	492m	499m	
FMA (US)	US$	300m	425m	225m	225m
US$1=D		0.71	0.71	0.71	
Population		**6,869,000** Palestinian ε50–60%			
Age		13–17	18–22	23–32	
Men		280,000	247,000	454,000	
Women		272,000	240,000	443,000	

Total Armed Forces

ACTIVE 100,240

RESERVES 35,000 (all services)
Army 30,000 (obligation to age 40)

Army 84,700

2 armd div (each 2 tk, 1 mech inf, 1 arty, 1 AD bde)
2 mech inf div (each 2 mech inf, 1 tk, 1 arty, 1 AD bde)
1 indep Royal Guard bde
1 SF bde (2 SF, 2 AB, 1 arty bn)
1 fd arty bde (4 bn)
Southern Mil Area (3 inf, 1 recce bn)

EQUIPMENT

MBT 1,058: 78 M-47/-48A5 (in store), 305 M-60 (117 -A1, 188 -A3), 274 *Khalid/Chieftain*, 281 *Tariq* (*Centurion*), ε120 *Challenger* 1 (*Al Hussein* (288 to be delivered))
LT TKS 19 *Scorpion*
AIFV some 26 BMP-2
APC 1,080 M-113, 50 BTR-94 (BTR-80)
TOWED ARTY 113: **105mm**: 54 M-102; **155mm**: 38 M-114, 17 M-59/-M-1; **203mm**: 4 M-115
SP ARTY 418: **105mm**: 35 M-52; **155mm**: 29 M-44, 234 M-109A1/A2; **203mm**: 120 M-110A2
MOR 81mm: 450 (incl 130 SP); **107mm**: 50 M-30; **120mm**: 300 Brandt
ATGW 330 TOW/-2A (incl 70 M-901 ITV), 310 *Dragon*
RL 94mm: 2,500 LAW-80; **112mm**: 2,300 APILAS
AD GUNS 416: **20mm**: 100 M-163 *Vulcan* SP; **23mm**: 52 ZSU-23-4 SP
SAM SA-7B2, 52 SA-8, 92 SA-13, 300 SA-14, 240 SA-16, 260 *Redeye*
SURV AN-TPQ-36/-37 (arty, mor)

Navy ε540

BASE Aqaba
PATROL AND COASTAL COMBATANTS 3
PATROL CRAFT, INSHORE 3
3 *Al Hussein* (Vosper 30m) PFI
plus 3 *Al Hashim* (Rotork) boats, 4 Bertram boats

Air Force 15,000

(incl 3,400 AD); 101 cbt ac, 20 armed hel
Flying hours 180
FGA/RECCE 4 sqn
3 with 55 F-5E/F
1 with 15 *Mirage* F-1EJ
FTR 2 sqn
1 with 15 *Mirage* F-1 CJ/BJ
1 with 16 F-16A/B (12 -A, 4 -B)
TPT 1 sqn with 4 C-130H, 2 C-212A, 2 CN-235, 2 TB-20, 2 CL-604
VIP 1 royal flt with **ac** 2 *Gulfstream* IV, 1 L-1011, 1 Airbus A340-211 **hel** 4 S-70A
HELICOPTERS 3 sqn
ATTACK 2 with 20 AH-1F (with TOW ASM)
TPT 1 with 10 AS-332M, 36 UH-1H, 3 Bo-105 (operated on behalf of police)
TRG 3 sqn with ac: 15 *Bulldog*, 13 C-101, hel: 6 Hughes 500D
AD 2 bde: 14 bty with 80 I HAWK
MISSILES
ASM TOW, AGM-65D *Maverick*
AAM AIM-9 *Sidewinder*, MATRA R-530, MATRA R-550 *Magic*

Forces Abroad

UN AND PEACEKEEPING

CROATIA (UNMOP): 1 obs **DROC** (MONUC): 28 incl 22 obs **EAST TIMOR** (UNTAET): 774 incl 4 obs **ETHIOPIA/ERITREA** (UNMEE): 963 incl 6 obs **GEORGIA** (UNOMIG): 6 obs **SIERRA LEONE** (UNAMSIL): 130 incl 10 obs **YUGOSLAVIA** (KFOR): 99

Paramilitary ε10,000 active

PUBLIC SECURITY DIRECTORATE (Ministry of Interior) ε10,000
(incl Police Public Sy bde); some *Scorpion* lt tk, 25 EE-11 *Urutu*, 30 *Saracen* APC
CIVIL MILITIA 'PEOPLE'S ARMY' (R) ε35,000
(to be 5,000) **men** 16–65 **women** 16–45

Kuwait Kwt

dinar D		1999	2000	2001	2002
GDP	D	9.0bn	10.2bn		
	US$	29.5bn	33.4bn		
per capita	US$	14,600	15,000		
Growth	%	13.0	4.2		
Inflation	%	3.0	2.6		
Debt	US$		6.0bn		
Def exp	D	1.0bn	1.0bn		
	US$	3.2bn	3.3bn		

contd		1999	2000	2001	2002
Def bdgt	D	700m	800m	820m	
	US$	2.3bn	2.6bn	2.6bn	
US$1=D		0.31	0.31	0.31	
Population				2,065,000	

Nationals 35% **other Arab** 35% **South Asian** 9%
Iranian 4% **other** 17%

Age	13–17	18–22	23–32
Men	124,000	107,000	148,000
Women	92,000	80,000	114,000

Total Armed Forces

ACTIVE 15,500

(some conscripts)
Terms of service voluntary, conscripts 2 years

RESERVES 23,700

obligation to age 40; 1 month annual trg

Land Force 11,000

(incl 1,600 foreign personnel)
3 armd bde • 2 mech inf bde • 1 recce (mech) bde • 1
force arty bde • 1 force engr bde

ARMY
1 reserve bde • 1 Amiri gd bde • 1 cdo bn
EQUIPMENT
  MBT 150 M-84 (ε50% in store), 218 M-1A2, 17
    Chieftain (in store)
  AIFV 46 BMP-2, 55 BMP-3, 254 *Desert Warrior* (incl
    variants)
  APC 60 M-113, 40 M-577, 40 *Fahd* (in store), 11 TPz-1
    Fuchs
  SP ARTY 155mm: 23 M-109A3, 18 GCT (in store), 18
    F-3, 27 PLZ 45
  MRL 300mm: 27 *Smerch* 9A52
  MOR 81mm: 60; **107mm**: 6 M-30; **120mm**: ε12 RT-F1
  ATGW 118 TOW/TOW II (incl 8 M-901 ITV; 66
    HMMWV)

Navy ε2,000

(incl 400 Coast Guard)
BASE Ras al Qalaya
PATROL AND COASTAL COMBATANTS 10
MISSILE CRAFT 10
  8 *Um Almaradim* PFM (Fr P-37 BRL) with 4 *Sea Skua*
    SSM, 1 × 6 Sadral SAM
  1 *Istiqlal* (Ge Lürssen FPB-57) PFM with 2 × 2 MM-40
    Exocet SSM
  1 *Al Sanbouk* (Ge Lürssen TNC-45) PFM with 2 × 2
    MM-40 *Exocet* SSM
  plus about 30 boats

SUPPORT AND MISCELLANEOUS 6
  2 LCM, 4 spt

Air Force ε2,500

82 cbt ac, 20 armed hel
Flying hours 210
FTR/FGA 40 F/A-18 (-C 32, -D 8)
FTR 14 *Mirage* F1-CK/BK
CCT 1 sqn with 12 *Hawk* 64, 16 Shorts *Tucano*
TPT ac 3 L-100-30, 1 DC-9 **hel** 4 AS-332 (tpt/SAR/
    attack), 8 SA-330
TRG/ATK hel 16 SA-342 (with HOT)

AIR DEFENCE
4 *Hawk* Phase III bty with 24 launchers
6 bty *Amoun* (each bty, 1 *Skyguard* radar, 2 *Aspide*
    launchers, 2 twin **35mm** Oerlikon), 48 *Starburst*

Paramilitary 5,000 active

NATIONAL GUARD 5,000
3 gd, 1 armd car, 1 SF, 1 mil police bn; 20 VBL recce, 70
Pandur APC (incl variants)
COAST GUARD
4 *Inttisar* (Aust 31.5m) PCC, 1 *Al Shaheed* PCC, 3 LCU
Plus some 30 armed boats

Foreign Forces

UN (UNIKOM): some 904 tps and 195 obs from 32
countries
UK Air Force (Southern Watch): 12 Tornado-GR1/1A
US 4,690: **Army** 2,600; prepo eqpt for 1 armd bde (2 tk,
1 mech, 1 arty bn) **Air Force** 2,000 (Southern Watch);
Force structure varies with ac detachments **Navy** 10
USMC 80

Lebanon RL

pound LP		1999	2000	2001	2002
GDP	LP	25.2tr	24.1tr		
	US$	16.7bn	16.0bn		
per capita	US$	6,400	6,800		
Growth	%	-1.0	0		
Inflation	%	1.0	1.5		
Debt	US$	7.5bn	7.0bn		
Def exp	LP	852bn	ε850bn		
	US$	563m	564m		
Def bdgt	LP	901bn	ε850bn	900bn	
	US$	560m	564m	594m	
FMA (US)	US$	12m	15m	35m	32m
US$1=LP		1,515	1,512	1,514	

Population		**3,137,000**

Christian 30% **Druze** 6% **Armenian** 4%, excl ε300,000 Syrian nationals and ε350,000 Palestinian refugees

Age	13–17	18–22	23–32
Men	216,000	194,000	397,000
Women	220,000	200,000	406,000

Total Armed Forces

ACTIVE 71,830 (incl 22,600 conscripts)

Terms of Service 1 year

Army 70,000 (incl conscripts)

5 regional comd

11 mech inf bde (-) • 1 Presidential Guard bde, 1 MP bde, 1 cdo/Ranger, 5 SF regt • 1 air aslt regt • 1 mne cdo regt • 2 arty regt

EQUIPMENT

MBT 115 M-48A1/A5, 212 T-54/-55

LT TK 36 AMX-13

RECCE 67 AML, 22 *Saladin*

APC 1,164 M-113A1/A2, 81 VAB-VCI, 81 AMX-VCI, 12 Panhard M3/VTT

TOWED ARTY 105mm: 13 M-101A1; **122mm**: 36 M-1938, 26 D-30; **130mm**: 11 M-46; **155mm**: 12 Model 50, 18 M-114A1, 35 M-198

MRL 122mm: 23 BM-21

MOR 81mm: 158; **82mm**: 111; **120mm**: 108 Brandt

ATGW ENTAC, *Milan*, 20 BGM-71A TOW

RL 85mm: RPG-7; **89mm**: M-65

RCL 106mm: M-40A1

AD GUNS 20mm; 23mm: ZU-23; **40mm**: 10 M-42A1

Navy 830

BASES Jounieh, Beirut

PATROL AND COASTAL COMBATANTS 7

PATROL CRAFT, INSHORE 7

5 UK *Attacker* PCI<, 2 UK *Tracker* PCI<, plus 27 armed boats

AMPHIBIOUS 2

2 *Sour* (Fr *Edic*) LST, capacity 96 tps

Air Force 1,000

All ac grounded and in store

EQUIPMENT

HEL 16 UH-1H, 1 SA-318, 3 SA-316, 5 Bell-212, 3 SA-330, 2 SA-342

TRG 5 CM-170, 3 *Bulldog*

Paramilitary ε13,000 active

INTERNAL SECURITY FORCE ε13,000 (Ministry of Interior)

(incl Regional and Beirut *Gendarmerie* coy plus Judicial Police); 30 *Chaimite* APC

CUSTOMS

2 *Tracker* PCI<, 5 *Aztec* PCI<

Opposition

MILITIAS

Most militias, except *Hizbollah*, have been substantially disbanded and hy wpn handed over to the National Army.

HIZBOLLAH ('Party of God'; Shi'a, fundamentalist, pro-Ir): ε3–500 (-) active; about 2,000 in spt

EQUIPMENT arty, MRL, RL, RCL, ATGW (AT-3 *Sagger*, AT-4 *Spigot*), AA guns, SAM

Foreign Forces

UN (UNIFIL): 5,496; 7 inf bn, 1 each from **Fji**, **Gha**, **Ind**, **Irl**, **N**, **SF**, **Ukr**, plus spt units from **Fr**, **It**, **Pl**

IRAN ε150 Revolutionary Guard

SYRIA 18,000 **Beirut** elm 1 mech inf bde, 5 SF regt **Metn** elm 1 mech inf bde **Bekaa** 1 mech inf div HQ, elm 2 mech inf, elm 1 armd bde **Tripoli** 1 SF regt **Batrum** 1 SF Regt **Kpar Fallus** elm 3 SF regt

---

Libya LAR

dinar D		1999	2000	2001	2002
GDP	US$	ε35bn	ε38bn		
per capita	US$	5,700	6,200		
Growth	%	ε5.4	3.5		
Inflation	%	ε6.0	-3.0		
Debt	US$	ε3.8bn	3.8bn		
Def exp	D	ε590m	ε600m		
	US$	1.3bn	1.2bn		
Def bdgt	D	ε580m	ε600m	ε650m	
	US$	1.3bn	1.2bn	1.2bn	
US$1=D		0.45	0.5	0.5	
Population				**5,644,000**	
Age		13–17	18–22		23–32
Men		387,000	320,000		492,000
Women		372,000	309,000		473,000

Total Armed Forces

ACTIVE 76,000

(incl ε40,000 conscripts)

Terms of service selective conscription, 1–2 years

RESERVES some 40,000
People's Militia

Army 45,000

(ε25,000 conscripts)
11 Border Def and 4 Sy Zones • 1 élite bde (regime sy force) • 10 tk bn • 22 arty bn • 18 inf bn • 7 AD arty bn • 10 mech inf bn • 6 para/cdo bn • 4 SSM bde

EQUIPMENT
    MBT 560 T-55, 280 T-62, 145 T-72 (plus some 1,040 T-54/-55, 70 T-62, 115 T-72 in store†)
    RECCE 166 BRDM-2, 272 EE-9 *Cascavel*
    AIFV 1,000 BMP-1
    APC 750 BTR-50/-60, 67 OT-62/-64, 28 M-113, 100 EE-11 *Urutu*, some BMD
    TOWED ARTY some 647: **105mm**: some 42 M-101; **122mm**: 190 D-30, 60 D-74; **130mm**: 330 M-46; **152mm**: 25 M-1937
    SP ARTY 265: **122mm**: 90 2S1; **152mm**: 46 2S3, 80 DANA; **155mm**: 115 *Palmaria*, 14 M-109
    MRL 107mm: Type 63; **122mm**: 350 BM-21/RM-70, 214 BM-11
    MOR some 500 incl: **82mm; 120mm**: ε48 M-43; **160mm**: ε24 M-160
    SSM launchers: 40 FROG-7, 80 *Scud*-B (SSM msl totals ε450-500)
    ATGW 3,000: *Milan*, AT-3 *Sagger* (incl BRDM SP), AT-4 *Spigot*, AT-5 *Spandrel*
    RCL 84mm: *Carl Gustav*; **106mm**: 220 M-40A1
    AD GUNS 600: **23mm**: ZU-23, ZSU-23-4 SP; **30mm**: M-53/59 SP; **57mm**: S-60
    SAM SA-7/-9/-13, 24 quad *Crotale*
    SURV RASIT (veh, arty)

Navy 8,000

(incl Coast Guard)
BASES Major Tripoli, Benghazi, Tobruk, Khums
Minor Derna, Zuwurah, Misonhah
SUBMARINES 1†
SSK 1 *Al Badr* † (Sov *Foxtrot*) with 533mm and 406mm TT (plus 2 non-op)
FRIGATES 2
FFG 2 *Al Hani* (Sov *Koni*) with 4 SS-N-2C *Styx* SSM, 4 ASTT, 2 ASW RL
PATROL AND COASTAL COMBATANTS 16
CORVETTES 3
    3 *Ean al Gazala* (Sov *Nanuchka* II) FSG with 2 × 2 SS-N-2C *Styx* SSM
MISSILE CRAFT 13
    7 *Sharaba* (Fr *Combattante* II) PFM with 4 *Otomat* SSM, 1 × 76mm gun (plus 2 non-op)
    6 *Al Katum* (Sov *Osa* II) PFM with 4 SS-N-2C *Styx* SSM (plus 6 non-op)
MINE WARFARE 6

MINE COUNTERMEASURES 6
    6 *Ras al Gelais* (Sov *Natya*) MSO (plus 2 non-op)
    (*El Temsah* and about 5 other ro-ro tpt have mine-laying capability)
AMPHIBIOUS 4
    2 *Ibn Ouf* LST, capacity 240 tps, 11 tk, 1 SA-316B hel
    2 Sov *Polnocny* LSM, capacity 180 tps, 6 tk (plus 1 non-op)
Plus craft: 3 LCT
SUPPORT AND MISCELLANEOUS 9
    1 *El Temsah* tpt, about 5 other ro-ro tpt, 1 *Zeltin* log spt; 1 ARS, 1 diving spt

NAVAL AVIATION
EQUIPMENT
7 armed hel
    HELICOPTERS
        1 sqn with 7 SA-321 (Air Force assets)

COASTAL DEFENCE
1 SSC-3 *Styx* bty

Air Force 23,000

(incl Air Defence Command; ε15,000 conscripts) 372 cbt ac, 41 armed hel (many non-operational) (many ac in store) **Flying hours** 85
BBR 1 sqn with 6 Tu-22
FGA 7 sqn with 40 MiG-23BN, 15 MiG-23U, 30 *Mirage* 5D/DE, 14 *Mirage* 5DD, 14 *Mirage* F-1AD, 6 Su-24 MK, 53 Su-20/-22
FTR 9 sqn with 25 MiG-21, 75 MiG-23, 70 MiG-25, 3 -25U, 7 *Mirage* F-1ED, 3 -BD
RECCE 2 sqn with 4* *Mirage* 5DR, 7* MiG-25R
TPT 7 sqn with 23 An-26, 12 Lockheed (7 C-130H, 2 L-100-20, 3 L-100-30), 6 G-222, 25 Il-76, 15 L-410
ATTACK HEL 29 Mi-25, 12 Mi-35
TPT HEL hy 12 CH-47C **med** 34 Mi-8/17 **lt** 11 SA-316, 5 AB-206
TRG ac 102 *Galeb* G-2 **hel** 50 Mi-2 **other ac** incl 1 Tu-22, 115 L-39ZO, 20 SF-260WL
MISSILES
    ASM AT-2 *Swatter* ATGW (hel-borne), AS-7, AS-9, AS-11
    AAM AA-2 *Atoll*, AA-6 *Acrid*, AA-7 *Apex*, AA-8 *Aphid*, R-530, R-550 *Magic*

AIR DEFENCE COMMAND
Senezh AD comd and control system
4 bde with SA-5A: each 2 bn of 6 launchers, some 4 AD arty gun bn; radar coy
5 Regions: 5–6 bde each 18 SA-2; 2–3 bde each 12 twin SA-3; ε3 bde each 20–24 SA-6/-8

Forces Abroad

UN AND PEACEKEEPING
DROC (MONUC): 1 obs

Paramilitary

CUSTOMS/COAST GUARD (Naval control)
a few patrol craft incl in naval totals, plus armed boats

Mauritania RIM

ougiya OM		**1999**	**2000**	**2001**	**2002**
GDP	OM	203bn	205bn		
	US$	1.0bn	0.8bn		
per capita	US$	1,900	1,900		
Growth	%	4.1	5.0		
Inflation	%	4.0	4.5		
Debt	US$				
Def exp	OM	ε5.0bn	ε5.7bn		
	US$	26m	23.6m		
Def bdgt	OM	ε5.4bn	ε5.7bn	ε6.5bn	
	US$	26m	23.6m	25.6m	
FMA (Fr)	US$	1.2m			
US$1=OM		207	242	254	
Population					**2,753,000**
Age		*13–17*	*18–22*		*23–32*
Men		149,000	121,000		194,000
Women		147,000	117,000		188,000

Total Armed Forces

ACTIVE ε15,650

Terms of service conscription 24 months authorised

Army 15,000

6 Mil Regions • 7 mot inf bn • 8 inf bn • 1 para/cdo bn
• 1 Presidential sy bn • 2 Camel Corps bn • 3 arty bn •
4 AD arty bty • 1 engr coy • 1 armd recce sqn
EQUIPMENT
  MBT 35 T-54/-55
  RECCE 60 AML (20 -60, 40 -90), 40 *Saladin*, 5 *Saracen*
  TOWED ARTY 105mm: 35 M-101A1/HM-2;
    122mm: 20 D-30, 20 D-74
  MOR 81mm: 70; **120mm**: 30
  ATGW *Milan*
  RCL 75mm: M-20; **106mm**: M-40A1
  AD GUNS 23mm: 20 ZU-23-2; **37mm**: 15 M-1939;
    57mm: S-60; **100mm**: 12 KS-19
  SAM SA-7

Navy ε500

BASES Nouadhibou, Nouakchott
PATROL CRAFT 7
  OFFSHORE 2
  1 *Aboubekr Ben Amer* (Fr OPV 54) PCO
  1 *N'Madi* (UK *Jura*) PCO (fishery protection)

COASTAL 1
1 *El Nasr* (Fr *Patra*) PCC
INSHORE 4
4 *Mandovi* PCI<

Air Force 150

7 cbt ac, no armed hel
CCT 5 BN-2 *Defender*, 2 FTB-337 *Milirole*
MR 2 *Cheyenne* II
TPT 2 Cessna F-337, 1 DHC-5D, 1 *Gulfstream* II, 2 Y-12 (II)

Paramilitary ε5,000 active

GENDARMERIE (Ministry of Interior) ε3,000
6 regional coy
NATIONAL GUARD (Ministry of Interior) 2,000
plus 1,000 auxiliaries
CUSTOMS
  1 *Dah Ould Bah* (Fr *Amgram* 14)

Morocco Mor

dirham D		**1999**	**2000**	**2001**	**2002**
GDP	D	352bn	350bn		
	US$	35bn	33bn		
per capita	US$	3,900	4,200		
Growth	%	0.6	0.8		
Inflation	%	0.7	8.1		
Debt	US$	18bn	16.1bn		
Def exp	D	17.5bn	ε18bn		
	US$	1.8bn	1.7bn		
Def bdgt	D	17.3bn	ε18bn		
	US$	1.7bn	1.7bn		
FMA (US)	US$		14m	14m	16m
US$1=D		9.94	10.5	11.6	
Population					**28,476,000**
Age		*13–17*	*18–22*		*23–32*
Men		1,780,000	1,612,000		2,726,000
Women		1,722,000	1,559,000		2,628,000

Total Armed Forces

ACTIVE 198,500
(incl ε100,000 conscripts)
Terms of service conscription 18 months authorised;
most enlisted personnel are volunteers

RESERVES
Army 150,000; obligation to age 50

Army 175,000

(ε100,000 conscripts)

2 Comd (Northern Zone, Southern Zone) • 3 mech inf bde • 1 lt sy bde • 2 para bde • 8 mech/mot inf regt • Indep units

11 armd bn • 2 cav bn • 39 inf bn • 1 mtn inf bn • 2 para bn • 3 mot (camel corps) bn • 9 arty bn • 7 engr bn • 1 AD gp • 7 cdo units

ROYAL GUARD 1,500

1 bn, 1 cav sqn

EQUIPMENT

MBT 224 M-48A5, 420 M-60 (300 -A1, 120 -A3), 100 T-72

LT TK 100 SK-105 *Kuerassier*

RECCE 16 EBR-75, 80 AMX-10RC, 190 AML-90, 38 AML-60-7

AIFV 60 *Ratel* (30 -20, 30 -90), 45 VAB-VCI, 10 AMX-10P

APC 420 M-113A1, 320 VAB-VTT, some 45 OT-62/-64 may be op

TOWED ARTY 105mm: 30 L-118, 20 M-101, 36 M-1950; **130mm:** 18 M-46; **155mm:** 20 M-114, 35 FH-70, 26 M-198

SP ARTY 105mm: 5 Mk 61; **155mm:** 98 F-3, 44 M-109, 20 M-44; **203mm:** 60 M-110

MRL 122mm: 26 BM-21

MOR 81mm: 870; **120mm:** 600 (incl 20 VAB SP)

ATGW 440 *Dragon*, 80 *Milan*, 150 TOW (incl 80 on M-901), 50 AT-3 *Sagger*

RL 89mm: 150 3.5in M-20

RCL 106mm: 350 M-40A1

ATK GUNS 90mm: 28 M-56; **100mm:** 8 SU-100 SP

AD GUNS 14.5mm: 200 ZPU-2, 20 ZPU-4; **20mm:** 40 M-167, 60 M-163 *Vulcan* SP; **23mm:** 90 ZU-23-2; **100mm:** 15 KS-19 towed

SAM 37 M-54 SP *Chaparral*, 70 SA-7

SURV RASIT (veh, arty)

UAV R4E-50 *Skyeye*

Navy 10,000

(incl 1,500 Marines)

BASES Casablanca, Agadir, Al Hoceima, Dakhla, Tangier

PRINCIPAL SURFACE COMBATANTS 1

FRIGATES 1 *Lt Col. Errhamani* (Sp *Descubierta*) FFG with *Aspide* SAM, 1 × 76mm gun, 2 × 3 ASTT (Mk 46 LWT), 1 × 2 375mm AS mor (fitted for 4 MM-38 *Exocet* SSM)

PATROL AND COASTAL COMBATANTS 27

MISSILE CRAFT 4 *Cdt El Khattabi* (Sp *Lazaga* 58m) PFM with 4 MM-38 *Exocet* SSM, 1 × 76mm gun

PATROL CRAFT 23

COASTAL 17

2 *Okba* (Fr PR-72) PCC with 1 × 76mm gun

6 *LV Rabhi* (Sp 58m B-200D) PCC

4 *El Hahiq* (Dk *Osprey* 55) PCC (incl 2 with customs)

5 *Rais Bargach* (navy marine for fisheries dept)

INSHORE 6 *El Wacil* (Fr P-32) PFI< (incl 4 with customs)

AMPHIBIOUS 4

3 *Ben Aicha* (Fr *Champlain* BATRAL) LSM, capacity 140 tps, 7 tk

1 *Sidi Mohammed Ben Abdallah* (US Newport) LST, capacity 400 troops

Plus craft: 1 *Edic*-type LCT

SUPPORT AND MISCELLANEOUS 4

2 log spt, 1 tpt, 1 AGOR (US lease)

MARINES (1,500)

2 naval inf bn

Air Force 13,500

95 cbt ac, 24 armed hel

Flying hours F-5 and *Mirage*: over 100

FGA 8 F-5A, 3 F-5B, 24 F-5E, 4 F-5F, 14 *Mirage* F-1EH

FTR 1 sqn with 15 *Mirage* F-1CH

RECCE 2 C-130H (with side-looking radar), 4* 0V-10

EW 2 C-130 (ELINT), 1 *Falcon* 20 (ELINT)

TKR 1 Boeing 707, 2 KC-130H (tpt/tkr)

TPT 12 C-130H, 7 CN-235, 2 Do-28, 2 *Falcon* 20, 1 *Falcon* 50 (VIP), 2 *Gulfstream* II (VIP), 4 *King Air* 100, 3 *King Air* 200

HELICOPTERS

ATTACK 24 SA-342 (12 with HOT, 12 with cannon)

TPT hy 7 CH-47 **med** 29 SA-330, 30 AB-205A **lt** 20 AB-206, 3 AB-212

TRG 8 AS-202, 2 CAP-10, 4 CAP-230, 10 T-34C, 23* *Alpha Jet*

LIAISON 2 *King Air* 200, 2 UH-60 *Blackhawk*

AAM AIM-9B/D/J *Sidewinder*, R-530, R-550 *Magic*

ASM AGM-65B *Maverick* (for F-5E), HOT

Forces Abroad

UN AND PEACEKEEPING

BOSNIA (SFOR II): ε800; 1 mot inf bn **DROC** (MONUC): 618 **YUGOSLAVIA** (KFOR): 279

Paramilitary 48,000 active

GENDARMERIE ROYALE 18,000

1 bde, 4 mobile gp, 1 para sqn, air sqn, coast guard unit

EQPT 18 boats **ac** 2 *Rallye* **hel** 3 SA-315, 3 SA-316, 2 SA-318, 6 *Gazelle*, 6 SA-330, 2 SA-360

FORCE AUXILIAIRE 30,000

incl 5,000 Mobile Intervention Corps

CUSTOMS/COAST GUARD

4 *Erraid* PCI, 32 boats, 3 SAR craft

Opposition

POLISARIO FRONT ε3–6,000

Mil wing of Sahrawi People's Liberation Army, org in bn
EQPT 100 T-55, T-62 tk; 50+ BMP-1, 20–30 EE-9 *Cascavel* MICV; 25 D-30/M-30 **122mm** how; 15 BM-21 **122mm** MRL; 20 **120mm** mor; AT-3 *Sagger* ATGW; 50 ZSU-23-2, ZSU-23-4 **23mm** SP AA guns; SA-6/-7/-8/-9 SAM (Captured Mor eqpt incl AML-90, *Eland* armd recce, *Ratel* 20, Panhard APC, Steyr SK-105 *Kuerassier* lt tks)

Foreign Forces

UN (MINURSO): some 27 tps, 202 mil obs in Western Sahara from 25 countries

Oman O

rial R		1999	2000	2001	2002
GDP	R	5.8bn	6.8bn		
	US$	15.0bn	17.7bn		
per capita	US$	8,100	8,200		
Growth	%	5.5	4.7		
Inflation	%	0.3	1.5		
Debt	US$	3.9bn	5.7bn		
Def exp	R	627m	680m		
	US$	1.6bn	1.7bn		
Def bdgt[a]	R	613m	673m	926m	
	US$	1.6bn	1.75bn	2.4bn	
FMA[b] (US) US$		0.2m	0.3m	0.25m	0.3m
US$1=R		0.38	0.38	0.38	

[a] Five-year plan 2001–2005 allocates R3.4bn (US$9.05bn) for defence
[b] Excl εUS$100m over 1990–99 from US Access Agreement renewed in 1990

Population		**2,674,000** expatriates 27%	
Age	13–17	18–22	23–32
Men	136,000	110,000	159,000
Women	131,000	107,000	149,000

Total Armed Forces

ACTIVE 43,400

(incl Royal Household tps, and some 3,700 foreign personnel)

Army 25,000

(regt are bn size)
1 armd, 2 inf bde HQ • 2 armd regt (3 tk sqn) • 1 armd recce regt (3 sqn) • 4 arty (2 fd, 1 med (2 bty), 1 AD (2 bty)) regt • 1 inf recce regt (3 recce coy), 2 indep recce coy • 1 fd engr regt (3 sqn) • 1 AB regt • Musandam Security Force (indep rifle coy)
EQUIPMENT
   MBT 6 M-60A1, 73 M-60A3, 38 *Challenger* 2

LT TK 37 *Scorpion*
RECCE 41 VBL
APC 6 *Spartan*, 13 *Sultan*, 10 *Stormer*, 160 *Piranha*
TOWED ARTY 96: **105mm**: 42 ROF lt; **122mm**: 30 D-30; **130mm**: 12 M-46, 12 Type 59-1
SP ARTY 155mm: 24 G-6
MOR 81mm: 69; **107mm:** 20 4.2in M-30; **120mm:** 12
ATGW 18 TOW/-2A (some SP), 30 *Milan*
RL 73mm: RPG-7; **94mm:** LAW-80
AD GUNS 23mm: 4 ZU-23-2; **35mm:** 10 GDF-005 with *Skyguard*; **40mm:** 12 Bofors L/60
SAM *Blowpipe*, 14 *Javelin*, 34 SA-7

Navy 4,200

BASES Seeb (HQ), Wudam (main base), Salalah, Ghanam Island, Alwi
PATROL AND COASTAL COMBATANTS 13
CORVETTES 2 *Qahir Al Amwaj* FSG with 8 MM-40 *Exocet* SSM, 8 *Crotale* SAM, 1 76mm gun, 6 × 324mm TT, hel deck)
MISSILE CRAFT 4 *Dhofar* PFM, 1 with 2 × 3 MM-40 *Exocet* SSM, 3 with 2 × 4 MM-40 *Exocet* SSM
PATROL CRAFT, COASTAL/INSHORE 7
   3 *Al Bushra* (Fr P-400) PCC with 1 × 76m gun, 4 × 406mm TT
   4 *Seeb* (Vosper 25m) PCI<
AMPHIBIOUS 1
   1 *Nasr el Bahr* LST†, capacity 240 tps, 7 tk, hel deck Plus craft: 3 LCM, 1 LCU
SUPPORT AND MISCELLANEOUS 4
   1 *Al Sultana* AK, 1 *Al Mabrukah* trg with hel deck (also used in offshore patrol role), 1 supply, 1 AGHS

Air Force 4,100

40 cbt ac, no armed hel
FGA 2 sqn, each with 8 *Jaguar* S(O) Mk 1, 4 T-2 (being progressively upgraded to (S01) GR-3 standard)
FGA/RECCE 12 *Hawk* 203
CCT 1 sqn with 12* PC-9, 4* *Hawk* 103
TPT 3 sqn
   1 with 3 BAC-111
   2 with 10 *Skyvan* 3M (7 radar-equipped, for MR), 3 C-130H
HEL 2 med tpt sqn with 19 AB-205, 3 AB-206, 3 AB-212, 5 AB-214
TRG 4 AS-202-18, 7 MFI-17B *Mushshak*
AD 2 sqn with 40 *Rapier* SAM, *Martello* radar, 6 *Blindfire* radar
AAM AIM-9M *Sidewinder*

Royal Household 6,400

(incl HQ staff) 2 SF regt (1,000)
Royal Guard bde (5,000) 9 VBC-90 lt tk, 14 VAB-VCI APC, 9 VAB-VDAA, *Milan* ATGW, 14 *Javelin* SAM

Royal Yacht Squadron (based Muscat) (150) 1 Royal Yacht *Al Said*, 3,800t with hel deck, 1 *Fulk Al Salamah* tps and veh tpt with up to 2 AS-332C *Puma* hel, 1 *Zinat Al Bihaar Dhow*

Royal Flight (250) **ac** 2 Boeing-747 SP, 1 DC-8-73CF, 2 *Gulfstream* IV **hel** 3 AS-330, 2 AS-332C, 1 AS-332L

Paramilitary 4,400 active

TRIBAL HOME GUARD (*Firqat*) 4,000

org in teams of ε100

POLICE COAST GUARD 400

3 CG 29 PCI, plus 14 craft

POLICE AIR WING

ac 1 Do-228, 2 CN 235M, 1 BN-2T Islander **hel** 2 Bell 205A, 3 Bell 214ST

Foreign Forces

US 690 **Air Force** 200 **Navy** 60

Palestinian Autonomous Areas of Gaza and Jericho GzJ

		1999	2000	2001	2002
GDP	US$				
per capita	US$				
Growth	%				
Inflation	%				
Debt	US$				
Sy bdgt	US$				
FMA (US)	US$	100m	485m	85m	75m

Population ε**3,000,000**

West Bank and Gaza excluding East Jerusalem ε2,900,000 **Israeli** ε180,000 excl East Jerusalem **Gaza** ε1,200,000 **Israeli** ε6,100 **West Bank excl East Jerusalem** ε1,700,000 **Israeli** ε174,000 **East Jerusalem Israeli** ε217,000 **Palestinian** ε86–200,000

Age	13–17	18–22	23–32
Men	163,000	140,000	233,000
Women	158,000	134,000	222,000

Total Armed Forces

ACTIVE Nil

Paramilitary ε35,000

PUBLIC SECURITY 6,000 Gaza, 8,000 West Bank

CIVIL POLICE 4,000 Gaza, 6,000 West Bank

PREVENTIVE SECURITY 1,200 Gaza, 1,800 West Bank

GENERAL INTELLIGENCE 3,000

MILITARY INTELLIGENCE 500

PRESIDENTIAL SECURITY 1,000

Others include **Coastal Police, Civil Defence, Air Force, Customs and Excise Police Force, University Security Service**

EQPT incl small arms, 45 APC **ac** 1 Lockheed *Jet Star* **hel** 2 Mi-8, 2 Mi-17

PALESTINIAN GROUPS

All significant Palestinian factions are listed irrespective of where they are based. Est number of active 'fighters' are given; these could perhaps be doubled to give an all-told figure. In 1991, the Lebanon Armed Forces (LAF), backed by Syr, entered refugee camps in southern RL to disarm many Palestinian gps of their heavier wpns, such as tk, arty and APCs. The LAF conducted further disarming ops against *Fatah* Revolutionary Council (FRC) refugee camps in spring 1994.

PLO (Palestine Liberation Organisation) **Leader** Yasser Arafat

FATAH Political wing of the PLO

PLF (Palestine Liberation Front) ε300–400 **Leader** Al Abas; **Based** Irq

DFLP (Democratic Front for the Liberation of Palestine) ε100 **Leader** Nayef Hawatmah; **Based** Syr, RL, elsewhere **Abd Rabbu faction** ε150–200 **Based** HKJ

PFLP (Popular Front for the Liberation of Palestine) ε100 **Leader** n.k.; **Based** Syr, RL, Occupied Territories

PSF (Popular Struggle Front) ε50 **Leader** Samir Ghansha; **Based** Syr

ARAB LIBERATION FRONT ε300 **Based** RL, Irq

GROUPS OPPOSED TO THE PLO

FATAH **DISSIDENTS** (Abu Musa gp) ε1,000 **Based** Syr, RL

FRC (*Fatah* Revolutionary Council, Abu Nidal Organisation) ε300 **Based** RL, Syr, Irq, elsewhere

PFLP (GC) (Popular Front for the Liberation of Palestine (General Command)) ε300 **Leader** Ahmad Jibril

PFLP (SC) (Popular Front for the Liberation of Palestine – Special Command) str n.k. **Based** RL, Irq, Syr

AL SAIQA ε300 **Leader** al-Khadi; **Based** Syr

IZZ AL-DIN AL-QASSEM (HAMAS) ε500 **Based** Occupied Territories

PALESTINE ISLAMIC JIHAD (PIJ) ε500 all factions **Based** Occupied Territories

PALESTINE LIBERATION FRONT ε3–400 Abd al-Fatah Ghanim faction **Based** Syr

PLA (Palestine Liberation Army) ε2,000 **Based** Syr

Qatar Q

rial R		1999	2000	2001	2002
GDP	R	51.3bn	59.7bn		
	US$	10.7bn	12.4bn		
per capita	US$	21,000	23,800		
Growth	%	6.5	12.9		
Inflation	%	2.0	2.8		
Debt	US$	12.2bn	13bn		
Def exp	R	ε5.1bn	ε5.3bn		
	US$	1.4bn	1.4bn		
Def bdgt	R	ε4.7bn	ε5.0bn	ε5.3bn	
	US$	1.3bn	1.4bn	1.5bn	
US$1=R		3.64	3.64	3.64	
Population					610,000

nationals 25% **expatriates** 75% of which Indian 18%, Iranian 10%, Pakistani 18%

Age	13–17	18–22	23–32
Men	26,000	22,000	38,000
Women	29,000	24,000	33,000

Total Armed Forces

ACTIVE ε12,330

Army 8,500

1 Royal Guard regt • 1 tk bn • 4 mech inf bn • 1 fd arty regt • 1 mor bn • 1 ATK bn • 1 SF 'bn' (coy)

EQUIPMENT

MBT 35 AMX-30
RECCE 16 VBL, 12 AMX-10RC, 8 V-150
AIFV 40 AMX-10P
LAV 36 *Piranha* II
APC 160 VAB, 30 AMX-VCI
TOWED ARTY 155mm: 12 G5
SP ARTY 155mm: 28 F-3
MRL 4 ASTROS II
MOR 81mm: 30 L16 (some SP); **120mm:** 15 Brandt
ATGW 100 *Milan*, HOT (incl 24 VAB SP)
RCL 84mm: *Carl Gustav*

Navy ε1,730

(incl Marine Police)
BASE Doha (HQ), Halul Island
PATROL AND COASTAL COMBATANTS 7
MISSILE CRAFT 7
3 *Damsah* (Fr *Combattante* III) PFM with 2 × 4 MM-40 *Exocet* SSM
4 *Barzan* (UK *Vita*) PFM with 8 MM-40 *Exocet* SSM, 6 *Mistral* SAM, 1 × 76mm gun
Plus some 20 small craft operated by Marine Police

COASTAL DEFENCE

4 × 3 *quad* MM-40 *Exocet* SSM bty

Air Force 2,100

18 cbt ac, 19 armed hel
FGA/FTR 2 sqn
1 with 6 *Alpha* jets
1 with 12 *Mirage* 2000-5 (9 EDA, 3 DDA)
TPT 1 sqn with 2 Boeing 707, 1 Boeing 727, 2 *Falcon* 900, 1 *Airbus* A340
ATTACK HEL 11 SA-342L (with HOT), 8 *Commando* Mk 3 (*Exocet*)
TPT 4 *Commando* (3 Mk 2A tpt, 1 Mk 2C VIP)
MISSILES
ASM *Exocet* AM-39, HOT, *Apache*
AAM MATRA R550 *Magic*, MATRA *Mica*
SAM 9 *Roland* 2, 24 *Mistral*, 12 *Stinger*, 20 SA-7 *Grail*, 10 *Blowpipe*

Foreign Forces

US Army 37; prepo eqpt for 1 armd bde (forming)

Saudi Arabia Sau

rial R		1999	2000	2001	2002
GDP	R	529bn	694bn		
	US$	141bn	185bn		
per capita	US$	9,400	10,100		
Growth	%	9.0	7.6		
Inflation	%	-1.2	2.5		
Debt	US$	26bn	32bn		
Def exp	R	81bn	70bn		
	US$	21.8bn	18.7bn		
Def bdgt	R	69bn	70bn	102bn	
	US$	18.4bn	18.7bn	27.2bn	
US$1=R		3.75	3.75	3.75	
Population					22,205,000

nationals 73% of which Bedouin up to 10%, Shi'a 6%, **expatriates** 27% of which Asians 20%, Arabs 6%, Africans 1%, Europeans <1%

Age	13–17	18–22	23–32
Men	1,391,000	1,177,000	1,725,000
Women	1,246,000	1,051,000	1,494,000

Total Armed Forces

ACTIVE ε126,500
(plus 75,000 active National Guard)

Army 75,000

3 armd bde (each 3 tk, 1 mech, 1 fd arty, 1 recce, 1 AD, 1 ATK bn) • 5 mech bde (each 3 mech, 1 tk, 1 fd arty, 1 AD, 1 spt bn) • 1 AB bde (2 AB bn, 3 SF coy) • 1 Royal Guard regt (3 bn) • 8 arty bn • 1 army avn comd with 2 avn bde

EQUIPMENT

MBT 315 M-1A2 *Abrams* (ε200 in store), 290 AMX-30
(50% in store), 450 M60A3

RECCE 300 AML-60/-90

AIFV 570+ AMX-10P, 400 M-2 *Bradley*

APC 1,750 M-113 A1/A2/A3 (incl variants), 150
Panhard M-3

TOWED ARTY 105mm: 100 M-101/-102 (in store);
155mm: 40 FH-70 (in store), 40 M-198, 50 M-114;
203mm: 8 M-115 (in store)

SP ARTY 155mm: 110 M-109A1B/A2, 90 GCT

MRL 60 ASTROS II

MOR 400, incl: **81mm**: (incl 70 SP); **107mm**: 4.2in M-30
(incl 150 SP); **120mm**: 110 Brandt

SSM some 10 PRC CSS-2 (40 msl)

ATGW 950 TOW/-2 (incl 200 VCC-1 SP), 1,000 M-47
Dragon, HOT (incl 100 AMX-10P SP)

RCL 84mm: 300 *Carl Gustav*; **90mm**: 100 M-67;
106mm: 50 M-40A1

ATTACK HEL 12 AH-64

TPT HEL 12 S-70A-1, 22 UH-60A (4 medevac), 6 SA-
365N (medevac), 13 Bell 406CS

SAM *Crotale*, 500 *Stinger*, 500 *Redeye* **SURV** AN/
TPQ-36/-37 (arty, mor)

Navy 15,500

(incl 3,000 Marines)

BASES Riyadh (HQ Naval Forces) **Western Fleet**
Jeddah (HQ), Yanbu **Eastern Fleet** Jubail (HQ),
Dammam, Ras al Mishab, Ras al Ghar

PRINCIPAL SURFACE COMBATANTS 8

FRIGATES

FFG 4

4 *Madina* (Fr F-2000) with 8 *Otomat* 2 SSM, 8 *Crotale*
SAM, 1 × 100mm gun, 4 × 533mm ASTT, 1 SA 365F
hel

CORVETTES 4

4 *Badr* (US *Tacoma*) FSG with 2 × 4 *Harpoon* SSM, 1 ×
76mm gun, 2 × 3 ASTT (Mk 46 LWT)

PATROL AND COASTAL COMBATANTS 26

MISSILE CRAFT 9 *Al Siddiq* (US 58m) PFM with 2 × 2
Harpoon SSM, 1 × 76mm gun

PATROL CRAFT 17 US *Halter Marine* PCI< (some with
Coast Guard) plus 40 craft

MINE WARFARE 7

MINE COUNTERMEASURES 7

3 *Al Jawf* (UK *Sandown*) MHO

4 *Addriyah* (US *MSC-322*) MCC†

AMPHIBIOUS (craft only)

4 LCU, 4 LCM

SUPPORT AND MISCELLANEOUS 7

2 *Boraida* (mod Fr *Durance*) AO with 1 or 2 hel, 3 AT/
F, 1 ARS, 1 Royal Yacht with hel deck

NAVAL AVIATION

EQUIPMENT

21 armed hel

HELICOPTERS

19 AS-565 (4 SAR, 15 with AS-15TT ASM), 12 AS-
332B/F (6 tpt, 6 with AM-39 *Exocet*)

MARINES (3,000)

1 inf regt (2 bn) with 140 BMR-600P

Air Force 20,000

348 cbt ac, no armed hel

FGA 4 sqn

1 with 15 F-5B/F/RF, 53 F-5E on strength, but most
off-line

3 with 85 *Tornado* IDS (incl 10 IDS recce)

FTR 9 sqn

1 with 22 *Tornado* ADV

5 with 87 F-15 (67 -C, 20 -D)

3 with 72 F-15S

AEW 1 sqn with 5 E-3A

TKR 8 KE-3A, 8 KC-130H (tkr/tpt)

OCU 2 sqn with 14* F-5B

TPT 3 sqn with 38 C-130 (7 -E, 29 -H, 2 H-30), 3 L-100-
30HS (hospital ac), 4 CN-235

HEL 2 sqn with 22 AB-205, 13 AB-206A, 17 AB-212, 40
AB-41EP (SAR), 10 AS-532A2 (CSAR)

TRG 3 sqn with 45 *Hawk* (25 Mk 65, 20 Mk 65A) (incl
aerobatic team), 2 sqn with 45 PC-9, 1 sqn with 1
Jetstream 31, 1 sqn with 13 Cessna 172

ROYAL FLT ac 2 Boeing-747SP, 1 Boeing-737-200, 4
BAe 125–800, 2 *Gulfstream* III, 2 *Learjet* 35, 4 VC-130H,
1 Cessna 310 **hel** 3 AS-61, AB-212, 1 S-70

MISSILES

ASM AGM-65 *Maverick*, *Sea Eagle*, ALARM

AAM AIM-9J/L/M/P *Sidewinder*, AIM-7F *Sparrow*,
Skyflash

Air Defence Forces 16,000

33 SAM bty

16 with 128 I HAWK

17 with 68 *Shahine* fire units and AMX-30SA 30mm
SP AA guns

73 *Shahine/Crotale* fire units as static defence

EQUIPMENT

AD GUNS 20mm: 92 M-163 *Vulcan*; **30mm**: 50 AMX-
30SA; **35mm**: 128; **40mm**: 70 L/70 (in store)

SAM 141 *Shahine*, 128 MIM-23B I HAWK, 40 *Crotale*

National Guard 75,000

(75,000 active plus 25,000 tribal levies)

3 mech inf bde, each 4 all arms bn

5 inf bde

1 ceremonial cav sqn

EQUIPMENT

LAV 1,117 LAV (incl 384 LAV-25, 182 LAV-CP, 130 LAV-AG, 111 LAV-AT, 73 LAV-M, 47 LAV plus 190 spt vehs)
APC 290 V-150 *Commando* (plus 810 in store), 440 *Piranha*
TOWED ARTY 105mm: 40 M-102; **155mm**: 30 M-198
MOR 81mm; **120mm**: incl 73 on LAV-M
RCL 106mm: M-40A1
ATGW TOW incl 111 on LAV

Paramilitary 15,500+ active

FRONTIER FORCE 10,500

COAST GUARD 4,500 (base as Azizam)
  EQPT 4 *Al Jouf* PFI, about 30 PCI<, 16 hovercraft, 1 trg, 1 Royal Yacht (5,000t) with 1 Bell 206B hel, about 350 armed boats

GENERAL CIVIL DEFENCE ADMINISTRATION UNITS
10 KV-107 **hel**

SPECIAL SECURITY FORCE 500
UR-416 APC

Foreign Forces

PENINSULAR SHIELD FORCE ε7,000
1 inf bde (elm from all GCC states)
FRANCE (Southern Watch): 170; 5 *Mirage* 2000C, 3 F-1CR, 3 C 135FR
UK (Southern Watch): ε200; 6 *Tornado* GR-1A
US 5,110 **Army** 790 incl 1 *Patriot* SAM, 1 sigs unit and those on short-term duty (6 months) **Air Force** (Southern Watch) 4,050; units on rotational det, numbers vary (incl: F-15, F-16, F-117, C-130, KC-135, U-2, E-3) **Navy** 20 **USMC** 250

Syria Syr

pound S£		1999	2000	2001	2002
GDP	S£	802bn	800bn		
	US$	17.6bn	13.79bn		
per capita	US$	7,600	7,818		
Growth	%	2.0	3.2		
Inflation	%	2.5	3.5		
Debt	US$	16bn	22bn		
Def exp	S£	45bn	ε45bn		
	US$	989m	775m		
Def bdgt	S£	39bn	42bn	44bn	
	US$	868m	729m	838m	
US$1=S£		45	58	52.5	
Population				16,493,000	
Age		13–17	18–22	23–32	
Men		1,076,000	883,000	1,274,000	
Women		1,036,000	857,000	1,247,000	

Total Armed Forces

ACTIVE ε321,000
Terms of service conscription, 30 months

RESERVES (to age 45) 354,000
Army 280,000 **Navy** 4,000 **Air Force** 70,000

Army ε215,000

(incl conscripts)
3 corps HQ • 7 armd div (each 3 armd, 1 mech bde, 1 arty regt) • 3 mech div (-) (each 2 armd, 2 mech bde, 1 arty regt) • 1 Republican Guard div (3 armd, 1 mech bde, 1 arty regt) • 1 SF div (3 SF regt) • 4 indep inf bde • 1 Border Guard bde • 2 indep arty bde • 2 indep ATK bde • 1 indep tk regt • 10 indep SF regt • 3 SSM bde (each of 3 bn): 1 with FROG, 1 with *Scud*-B/-C, 1 with SS-21 • 1 coastal def SSM bde with SS-C-1B *Sepal* and SS-C-3 *Styx*

RESERVES
1 armd div HQ, 4 armd bde, 2 armd regt
31 inf, 3 arty regt

EQUIPMENT
  MBT 4,700 (incl some 1,200 in static positions and in store): 2,000 T-55/MV, 1,000 T-62M/K, 1,700 T-72/-72M
  RECCE 850 BRDM-2, 85 BRDM-2 Rkh
  AIFV 2,250 BMP-1, 100 BMP-2, BMP-3
  APC some 1,600 BTR-50/-60/-70/-152
  TOWED ARTY 1,630: **122mm**: 100 M-1931/-37 (in store), 150 M-1938, 500 D-30; **130mm**: 800 M-46; **152mm**: 20 D-20, 50 M-1937; **180mm**: 10 S23
  SP ARTY 122mm: 400 2S1; **152mm**: 50 2S3
  MRL 107mm: 200 Type-63; **122mm**: 280 BM-21
  MOR 82mm: 200; **120mm**: 350 M-1943; **160mm**: 100 M-160; **240mm**: ε8 M-240
  SSM launchers: 18 FROG-7, some 18 SS-21, 26 *Scud*-B/-C; 4 SS-C-1B *Sepal*, 6 SS-C-3 *Styx* coastal (SSM msl totals ε850)
  ATGW 3,500 AT-3 *Sagger* (incl 2,500 SP), 150 AT-4 *Spigot*, 200 AT-5 *Spandrel*, AT-7 *Saxhorn*, 2,000 AT-10, AT-14 *Kornet* and 200 *Milan*
  AD GUNS 2,060: **23mm**: 650 ZU-23-2 towed, 400 ZSU-23-4 SP; **37mm**: 300 M-1939; **57mm**: 675 S-60, 10 ZSU-57-2 SP; **100mm**: 25 KS-19
  SAM 4,000 SA-7, 20 SA-9, 35 SA-13

Navy 6,000

BASES Latakia, Tartus, Minet el-Baida
PRINCIPAL SURFACE COMBATANTS 2
FRIGATES 2
FF 2 Sov *Petya* III with 5 × 533mm TT, 4 ASW RL
PATROL AND COASTAL COMBATANTS 18

MISSILE CRAFT 10
  10 Sov *Osa* I and II PFM with 4 SS-N-2 *Styx* SSM
PATROL CRAFT, INSHORE 8
  8 Sov *Zhuk* PFI<
MINE WARFARE 5
MINE COUNTERMEASURES 5
  1 Sov T-43 MSO, 1 *Sonya* MSC, 3 *Yevgenya* MSI
AMPHIBIOUS 3
  3 *Polnocny* LSM, capacity 100 tps, 5 tk
SUPPORT AND MISCELLANEOUS 4
  1 spt, 1 trg, 1 div spt, 1 AGOR

NAVAL AVIATION
EQUIPMENT
16 armed hel
  HELICOPTERS
    ASW 12 Mi-14, 4 Ka-28 (Air Force manpower)

Air Force 40,000

589 cbt ac; 87 armed hel (some may be in store)
Flying hours 30
FGA 9/10 sqn
  5 with 90 Su-22, 2 with 44 MiG-23 BN, 2 with 20 Su-24, 1 possibly forming with Su-27
FTR 17 sqn
  8 with 170 MiG-21, 5 with 90 MiG-23, 2 with 30 MiG-25, 2 with 20 MiG-29
RECCE 6* MiG-25R, 8* MiG-21H/J
TPT ac 5 An-26, 2 *Falcon* 20, 4 Il-76, 7 Yak-40, 1 *Falcon* 900, 6 Tu-134 **hel** 10 Mi-2, 100 Mi-8/-17
ATTACK HEL 48 Mi-25, 39 SA-342L
TRG incl 80* L-39, 20 MBB-223, 20* MiG-21U, 6* MiG-23UM, 5* MiG-25U, 6 *Mashshak*
MISSILES
  ASM AT-2 *Swatter*, AS-7 *Kerry*, AS-12, HOT
  AAM AA-2 *Atoll*, AA-6 *Acrid*, AA-7 *Apex*, AA-8 *Aphid*, AA-10 *Alamo*

Air Defence Command ε60,000

25 AD bde (some 150 SAM bty)
Some 600 SA-2/-3, 200 SA-6 and 4,000 AD arty
2 SAM regt (each 2 bn of 2 bty) with some 48 SA-5, 60 SA-8, S-300 on order

Forces Abroad

LEBANON 18,000; 1 mech div HQ, elm 1 armd, 4 mech inf bde, elm 10 SF, 2 arty regt

Paramilitary ε108,000

GENDARMERIE 8,000 (Ministry of Interior)
WORKERS' MILITIA (PEOPLE'S ARMY) (*Ba'ath* Party) ε100,000

Foreign Forces

UN (UNDOF): 1,040 tps plus 80 obs; contingents from **A** 367 **Ca** 186 **J** 30 **Pl** 358 **Slvk** 93 **Swe** 1
RUSSIA ε150 advisers, mainly AD

Tunisia Tn

dinar D		1999	2000	2001	2002
GDP	D	25bn	27bn		
	US$	21bn	21bn		
per capita	US$	6,800	7,100		
Growth	%	6.2	5.0		
Inflation	%	2.7	3.0		
Debt	US$	12.5bn	10.4bn		
Def exp	D	ε417m	ε450m		
	US$	347m	356m		
Def bdgt	D	421m	461m		
	US$	351m	365m		
FMA (US)	US$	0.9m	3.9m	4.5m	4.5m
US$1=D		1.20	1.36	1.45	
Population					9,697,000
Age		13–17	18–22		23–32
Men		529,000	505,000		869,000
Women		507,000	484,000		843,000

Total Armed Forces

ACTIVE ε35,000
(incl ε23,400 conscripts)
Terms of service 12 months selective

Army 27,000

(incl 22,000 conscripts)
3 mech bde (each with 1 armd, 2 mech inf, 1 arty, 1 AD regt) • 1 Sahara bde • 1 SF bde • 1 engr regt
EQUIPMENT
  MBT 54 M-60A3, 30 M-60A1
  LT TK 54 SK-105 *Kuerassier*
  RECCE 24 *Saladin*, 45 AML-90
  APC 140 M-113A1/-A2, 18 EE-11 *Urutu*, 110 Fiat F-6614
  TOWED ARTY 105mm: 48 M-101A1/A2; **155mm**: 12 M-114A1, 57 M-198
  MOR 81mm: 95; **107mm**: 42 4.2in (some SP); **120mm**: 18 Brandt
  ATGW 100 TOW (incl 35 M-901 ITV), 500 *Milan*
  RL 89mm: 300 LRAC-89, 300 3.5in M-20
  RCL 57mm: 140 M-18; **106mm**: 70 M-40A1
  AD GUNS 20mm: 100 M-55; **37mm**: 15 Type-55/-65
  SAM 48 RBS-70, 25 M-48 *Chaparral*
  SURV RASIT (veh, arty)

Navy ε4,500

(incl ε700 conscripts)
BASES Bizerte, Sfax, Kelibia
PATROL AND COASTAL COMBATANTS 19
MISSILE CRAFT 6
   3 *La Galite* (Fr *Combattante* III) PFM with 8 MM-40 *Exocet* SSM, 1 × 76mm gun
   3 *Bizerte* (Fr *P-48*) PFM with 8 SS-12M SSM
PATROL, COASTAL/INSHORE 13
   3 *Utique* (mod PRC *Shanghai* II) PCC, some 10 PCI<
SUPPORT AND MISCELLANEOUS 2
   1 *Salambo* (US *Conrad*) survey/trg, 1 AGS

Air Force 3,500

(incl 700 conscripts); 51 cbt ac, 7 armed hel
FGA 15 F-5E/F
CCT 6 MB-326K, 6 MB-326L
TPT 5 C-130B, 2 C-130H, 1 *Falcon* 20, 3 LET-410, 2 G-222
LIAISON 1 S-208M
TRG 18 SF-260 (6 -C, 12* -W), 5 MB-326B, 12* L-59
ARMED HEL 5 SA-341 (attack) 2 HH-3 (ASW)
TPT HEL 1 wg with 15 AB-205, 6 AS-350B, 1 AS-365, 6 SA-313, 3 SA-316, 5 UH-1H, 2 UH-1N
AAM AIM-9J *Sidewinder*

Forces Abroad

UN AND PEACEKEEPING
DROC (MONUC): 243 incl 19 obs **ETHIOPIA/ ERITREA** (UNMEE): 6 incl 3 obs

Paramilitary 12,000

NATIONAL GUARD 12,000 (Ministry of Interior)
incl Coastal Patrol with 5 (ex-GDR) *Kondor* I-class PCC, 5 (ex-GDR) *Bremse*-class PCI<, 4 *Gabes* PCI<, plus some 10 other PCI< **ac** 5 P-6B **hel** 8 SA-318/SA-319

United Arab Emirates UAE

dirham D		1999	2000	2001	2002
GDP	D	190bn	213bn		
	US$	52bn	58bn		
per capita	US$	21,800	25,600		
Growth	%	10.0	6.5		
Inflation	%	2.4	4.0		
Debt	US$	15.5bn	16bn		
Def exp	D	ε11.3bn	ε12.5bn		
	US$	3.2bn	3.4bn		
Def bdgt[a]	D	ε14.0bn	ε14.5bn		
	US$	3.8bn	3.9bn		
US$1=D		3.67	3.67	3.67	

[a] Including extra-budgetary funding for procurement

Population			2,571,000

nationals 24% **expatriates** 76% of which Indian 30%, Pakistani 20%, other Arab 12%, other Asian 10%, UK 2%, other European 1%

Age	13–17	18–22	23–32
Men	87,000	87,000	143,000
Women	87,000	83,000	115,000

Total Armed Forces

The Union Defence Force and the armed forces of the UAE (Abu Dhabi, Dubai, Ras Al Khaimah and Sharjah) were formally merged in 1976 and centred on Abu Dhabi. Dubai still maintains its independence, as do other emirates to a smaller degree.

ACTIVE ε65,000 (perhaps 30% expatriates)

Army 59,000

(incl **Dubai** 15,000) **MoD** Dubai **GHQ** Abu Dhabi
INTEGRATED 1 Royal Guard 'bde' • 2 armd bde • 3 mech inf bde • 2 inf bde • 1 arty bde (3 regt)
NOT INTEGRATED 2 inf bde (Dubai)
EQUIPMENT
   MBT 45 AMX-30, 36 OF-40 Mk 2 (*Lion*), ε330 *Leclerc*
   LT TK 76 *Scorpion*
   RECCE 49 AML-90, 20 *Saladin* (in store), 20 *Ferret* (in store)
   AIFV 15 AMX-10P, 600 BMP-3
   APC 80 VCR (incl variants), 240 Panhard M-3, 100 EE-11 *Urutu*, 136 AAPC (incl 53 engr plus other variants), 64 TPz-1 *Fuchs*
   TOWED ARTY 105mm: 60 ROF lt; **130mm**: 20 PRC Type-59-1
   SP ARTY 155mm: 18 Mk F-3, 78 G-6, 85 M-109A3
   MRL 70mm: 18 LAU-97; **122mm**: 48 FIROS-25 (ε24 op); **300mm**: 6 *Smerch* 9A52
   MOR 81mm: 114 L16, 20 Brandt; **120mm**: 21 Brandt
   SSM 6 *Scud*-B (Dubai only)
   ATGW 230 *Milan*, *Vigilant*, 25 TOW, 50 HOT (20 SP)
   RCL 84mm: 250 *Carl Gustav*; **106mm**: 12 M-40
   AD GUNS 20mm: 42 M-3VDA SP; **30mm**: 20 GCF-BM2
   SAM 20+ *Blowpipe*, 20 *Mistral*

Navy ε2,000

BASE Abu Dhabi
NAVAL FACILITIES Dalma, Mina Zayed **Dubai** Mina Rashid, Mina Jabal **Ras al Khaimah** Mina Sakr **Sharjah** Mina Khalid, Khor Fakkan
PRINCIPAL SURFACE COMBATANTS 2
FRIGATES 2
FFG 2 *Abu Dhabi* (NL *Kortenaer*) with 8 *Harpoon* SSM, 8 *Sea Sparrow* SAM, 1 × 76mm gun, 4 × 324mm TT, 2 AS565 hel

Tn UAE
Middle East and North Africa

PATROL AND COASTAL COMBATANTS 16

CORVETTES 2 *Muray Jip* FSG (Ge Lürssen 62m) with 2 × 2 MM-40 *Exocet* SSM, 1 SA-316 hel

MISSILE CRAFT 8

6 *Ban Yas* (Ge Lürssen TNC-45) PFM with 2 × 2 MM-40 *Exocet* SSM, 1 × 76mm gun

2 *Mubarraz* (Ge Lürssen 45m) PFM with 2 × 2 MM-40 *Exocet* SSM, 1 × 76mm gun

PATROL, COASTAL 6

6 *Ardhana* (UK Vosper 33m) PCC

AMPHIBIOUS (craft only)

3 *Al Feyi* LCT, 2 other LCT

SUPPORT AND MISCELLANEOUS 2

1 div spt, 1 AT

NAVAL AVIATION

4 SA-316 *Alouette* hel, 6 AS 585 *Panther* hel

Air Force 4,000

(incl Police Air Wing) 101 cbt ac, 49 armed hel

Flying hours 110

FGA 3 sqn

1 with 9 *Mirage* 2000E

1 with 17 *Hawk* 102

1 with 17 *Hawk* Mk 63/63A/63C (FGA/trg)

FTR 1 sqn with 22 *Mirage* 2000 EAD

CCT 1 sqn with 8 MB-326 (2 -KD, 6 -LD), 5 MB-339A

OCU 5* *Hawk* Mk 61, 4* MB-339A, 6* *Mirage* 2000 DAD

RECCE 8* *Mirage* 2000 RAD

TPT incl 1 BN-2, 4 C-130H, 1 L-100-30, 4 C-212, 7 CN-235M-100, 4 Il-76 (on lease)

HELICOPTERS

ATTACK 5 AS-332F (anti-ship, 3 with *Exocet* AM-39), 10 SA-342K (with HOT), 7 SA-316/-319 (with AS-11/-12), 20 AH-64A, 7 AS-565 *Panther*

TPT 2 AS-332 (VIP), 1 AS-350, 30 Bell (8 -205, 9 -206, 5 -206L, 4 -214, 1 -407, 3 -412), 10 SA-330, 2 *King Air* 350 (VIP)

SAR 3 Bo-105, 3 *Agusta* -109 K2

TRG 30 PC-7, 5 SF-260 (4 -TP, 1 -W), 12 Grob G-115TA

MISSILES

ASM HOT, AS-11/-12, AS-15 *Exocet* AM-39, *Hellfire*, *Hydra*-70, PGM1, PGM2

AAM R-550 *Magic*, AIM 9L

AIR DEFENCE

1 AD bde (3 bn)

5 bty I HAWK

12 *Rapier*, 9 *Crotale*, 13 RBS-70, 100 *Mistral* SAM, *Javelin*, *Igla* (SA-16)

Forces Abroad

UN AND PEACEKEEPING

YUGOSLAVIA (KFOR): 1,250; 3 AIFV coy, 1 MBT sqn, 1 arty bty, 1 ATK hel flt

Paramilitary

COAST GUARD (Ministry of Interior)

some 40 PCI<, plus boats

Foreign Forces

US Air Force 390

Yemen, Republic of Ye

rial R		**1999**	**2000**	**2001**	**2002**
GDP	R	988bn	1,017bn		
	US$	6.7bn	6.4bn		
per capita	US$	1,500	1,500		
Growth	%	3.3	6.5		
Inflation	%	7.0	15		
Debt	US$	4.6bn	4.0bn		
Def exp	R	63bn	80bn		
	US$	429m	498m		
Def bdgt	R	55bn	70bn		
	US$	374m	435m		
FMA (US)	US$	0.1m	0.1m	0.1m	
US$1=R		148	159	166	
Population		**18,885,000**	North 79%	South 21%	
Age		13–17	18–22		23–32
Men		1,008,000	803,000		1,328,000
Women		982,000	778,000		1,213,000

Total Armed Forces

ACTIVE 54,000

(incl conscripts)

Terms of service conscription, 2 years

RESERVES perhaps 40,000

Army 49,000

(incl conscripts)

10 armd bde • 1 SF bde • 20 inf bde • 8 mech bde • 2 AB/cdo bde • 1 SSM bde • 7 arty bde • 1 central guard force • 2 AD bde: 4 AAA, 1 SAM bn

EQUIPMENT

MBT 910: 50 T-34, 500 T-54/-55, 250 T-62, 50 M-60A1, 60 T-72

RECCE 70 AML-90, 50 BRDM-2

AIFV 320 BMP-1/-2

APC 60 M-113, 380 BTR-40/-60/-152 (180 op)

TOWED ARTY 395: **105mm**: 35 M-101A1; **122mm**: 30 M-1931/37, 100 M-1938, 130 D-30; **130mm**: 75 M-46; **152mm**: 10 D-20; **155mm**: 15 M-114

SP ARTY 122mm: 25 2S1

ASLT GUNS 100mm: 30 SU-100

COASTAL ARTY 130mm: 36 SM-4-1
MRL 122mm: 150 BM-21; **140mm**: 14 BM-14
MOR ε502 incl **81mm**: 200; **82mm**: 90 M-43; **107mm**: 12; **120mm**: 100; **160mm**: ε100
SSM 12 FROG-7, 12 SS-21, 6 *Scud*-B
ATGW 12 TOW, 24 *Dragon*, 35 AT-3 *Sagger*
RL 66mm: M72 LAW; **73mm**: RPG-7
RCL 75mm: M-20; **82mm**: B-10; **107mm**: B-11
ATK GUNS 85mm: D-44; **100mm**: 20 M-1944
AD GUNS 20mm: 50 M-167, 20 M-163 *Vulcan* SP; **23mm**: 100 ZSU-23-2, 50 ZSU-23-4; **37mm**: 150 M-1939; **57mm**: 120 S-60; **85mm**: 40 KS-12
SAM ε800: SA-7/-9/-13/-14

Navy 1,500

BASES Aden, Hodeida
FACILITIES Al Mukalla, Perim Island, Socotra (these have naval spt eqpt)
PATROL AND COASTAL COMBATANTS 9
  MISSILE CRAFT 4
  3 *Huangfen* with C-801 SSM (only 4 C-801 between the 3 craft)
  1 *Tarantul* 1 PFM with 4 SS-N-2C *Styx* SSM (plus 1 non-op)
  plus 6 boats
  PATROL, INSHORE 5
  2 *Sana'a* (US *Broadsword* 32m) (1 non-op) PFI, 3 Sov *Zhuk* PFI<

MINE WARFARE 6
MINE COUNTERMEASURES 6
  1 Sov *Natya* MSO
  5 Sov *Yevgenya* MHC
AMPHIBIOUS 1
  1 *Ropucha* LST, capacity 190tps/10 tks
  plus craft: 2 Sov *Ondatra* LCM
  3 Pl NS-717 LCU
AUXILIARIES 2
  2 *Toplivo* AOT

Air Force 3,500

71 cbt ac (plus some 40 in store), 8 attack hel
FGA 10 F-5E, 30 Su-20/-22
FTR 20 MiG-21, 5 MiG-29
TPT 2 An-12, 6 An-26, 3 C-130H, 4 IL-14, 3 IL-76
HEL 2 AB-212, 14 Mi-8, 1 AB-47, 8 Mi-35 (attack)
TRG 2* F-5B,4* MiG-21U, 14 YAK-11, 12 L-39C

AIR DEFENCE 2,000
SAM some SA-2, SA-3, SA-6
AAM AA-2 *Atoll*, AIM-9 *Sidewinder*

Paramilitary 70,000

MINISTRY OF THE INTERIOR FORCES 50,000
TRIBAL LEVIES at least 20,000
COAST GUARD
(slowly being established)
5 Fr *Interceptor* PCI<

REGIONAL TRENDS

The tensions between India and Pakistan continue to be a major factor in regional military affairs. The optimism that preceded the July meeting between Indian Prime Minister Atal Behari Vajpayee and Pakistani President Pervez Musharraf in Agra diminished once it became clear that there could be no substantive progress on the Kashmir issue. An important development is the more cooperative relationship between the US and India that has developed since the Bush administration took office in January 2001. In Central Asia, Russian-led efforts to counter the threat of renewed incursions from Afghanistan by Islamic insurgents have led to strengthened regional cooperation, not only among the members of the Commonwealth of Independent States (CIS) but also including Uzbekistan and China. Afghanistan continues to cast a shadow over security through its support for Islamic groups in the region and beyond it, in areas such as Chechnya.

India and Pakistan

The July 2001 talks in Agra promised much, but delivered little, at least publicly. They were preceded by hopes of a breakthrough in the Kashmir conflict, but the result was a stalemate, followed immediately by an outburst of fighting in the disputed region. There is a commitment to return to talks at a future date; however, Musharraf is in a difficult position as a member of the Urdu-speaking minority in the military, a group heavily outnumbered by the Punjabi majority, which is unrelenting in its support for the continuation of the Kashmir conflict. Pakistani military intelligence is also reported to be giving active support to the Kashmir-based Muslim guerrilla movement, *Lashkar-e-Taiba*, as is the international terrorist Osama bin Laden. On the brighter side, there is the growing number of Kashmiri Muslims who are weary of the conflict and wish to reach an accord with India. In turn, India wants to cut down on its constant and heavy military commitment in Kashmir, which is a drain on resources that could be better directed to its military-modernisation plans.

India is embarking upon an ambitious programme to restructure, modernise and re-equip its armed forces. Its improved relationship with the US may result in financial assistance and thus some impetus to this process. As it is, resources are stretched and unless the government allocates substantially more money for equipment and spare parts, plans to modernise and strengthen ground forces in the period up to 2010 could be put on hold, at least in part. The commitment of a standing force of some 300,000 police and military to Kashmir is a heavy burden for a country that is trying to implement large-scale reforms. At risk is the purchase of S-300 air defence systems, 155mm howitzers, tactical missiles and ammunition, and spare parts. Nevertheless, some procurement is taking place, with the announcement that all *Vijayanta* tanks are to be retired and replaced by modernised T-72M1 and T-90S tanks. Delivery of the T-90S will almost certainly end further development and series production of the locally manufactured *Arjun* main battle tank (MBT). The first ever corps-level exercise to be carried out in a nuclear, biological and chemical scenario, *Absolute Victory*, took place in early May.

Economic pressures are forcing the Pakistani government to find ways of cutting defence expenditure. Islamabad is finding the cost of maintaining a large standing force with a strategic element hard to bear. In the past 12 months, Pakistan has not test-fired any ballistic missiles, despite the Indian test-firing of the *Agni* 2 medium-range ballistic missile (MRBM). This represents a change from the past pattern of one country carrying out a test in response to that of the other. This restraint may be as much to do with the state of the Pakistani economy as with the fact that Pakistan has no need to enhance its capability, having achieved minimum deterrence requirements – a situation underlined by the scaling-down of Pakistan's strategic weapons budget for 2001.

LOCAL CONFLICTS

Sri Lanka

On 24 December 2000, the Liberation Tigers of Tamil Eelam (LTTE) announced a unilateral cease-fire, but this lapsed on 24 April 2001. Just prior to this date, in March 2001, Erik Solheim, the Norwegian special envoy, went to Sri Lanka in a fresh bid to broker peace between the government and the LTTE. However, in late April, a large-scale battle erupted in the Jaffna Peninsula, resulting in more than 300 fatalities. Fatalities since October 2000 are estimated at 6,000 as at August 2001, down from 8,000 in the previous year.

The LTTE has recently transformed its military element, which is now more akin in structure and tactics to a quasi-conventional force than a guerrilla organisation. Nevertheless, the 23 July 2001 suicide bombing attack on Bandaranaika Airport showed that the movement still has the capability and will to adopt terrorist-style tactics where necessary. The attack, launched on the anniversary of the 23 July 1983 riots in which 300 Tamils died, was well-planned and carried out against a key target of economic and psychological significance. It showed all too clearly that this conflict is far from being resolved.

Nepal

Since the assassination of the king and other members of the Nepalese royal family on 4 June 2001, the militant Communist Party of Nepal (Maoist) (CPN(M)) has shown signs of increased activity. The assassination is not thought to have any direct connection to the Maoist movement, but the resulting instability has provided an opportunity for the CPN(M) to step up its campaign against the government. The group is reported to be in virtual control of seven out of 75 regions of Nepal, and Maoist fighters killed 41 policemen in three separate assaults immediately following the assassination. At the same time, an operation by army and police to free 70 police officers held hostage by the group resulted in the deaths of 150 rebels. This was the first time that Nepalese troops had been used directly in domestic counter-insurgency operations. The rebel leader, known as 'Prachanda', announced a temporary cease-fire following the killing of 16 policemen on 17 July. On 23 July, after the appointment of Sher Bahadur Deuba as prime minister, it was announced in the media that 'Prachanda' had agreed to consider holding talks with the new government

CENTRAL ASIA

Afghanistan's *Taleban* regime's continuing support of Islamic fundamentalist movements in Central Asia threatens the fragile stability of countries like Tajikistan, Kyrgyzstan and Uzbekistan. As such, opposing the *Taleban* is a unifying factor for the secular states of the region. Moreover, the *Taleban*'s assistance to Chechen fighters puts it in direct confrontation with Russia, which continues to support the Northern Alliance, led by General Ahmad Shah Masood, in its struggle against the *Taleban* in Afghanistan itself. Iran too is actively opposed to the *Taleban* and has been successful in interdicting the westward passage of drugs across its border with Afghanistan. Meanwhile, an estimated 25,000 Afghan refugees constitute a huge economic and humanitarian problem for Islamabad. Pakistan, one of three countries to recognise the *Taleban* government, has indicated that its support can no longer be relied upon. Reports in early May showed that Pakistan was attempting to seal its border to control the ingress of Afghan refugees and limit the *Taleban's* access to Islamic militants and supplies in Pakistan.

At a 15 June 2001 meeting of the Shanghai-5 (Russia, China, Kazakstan, Kyrgyzstan and Tajikistan) group in its namesake city, a decision was taken to admit Uzbekistan as a sixth member. This was a significant move, and a triumph for Russian diplomacy in the region: Uzbekistan, despite being the most powerful military regime in Central Asia, had until then stood outside all regional collective-security arrangements. Not being a member of the CIS collective security mechanism, the Uzbeks had not been part of the decision to form the Collective Rapid Deployment Force (CRDF) for a proposed Central Asian Collective Security Region, which had been taken at the May 2001 CIS meeting in Yerevan. But now, as a member of the newly named Shanghai Organisation for Cooperation, Uzbekistan has at least joined one element of the regional counter-terrorist effort. The organisation has declared its intention to set up a counter-terrorist centre in Bishkek, Kyrgyzstan.

The Command and Control Centre of the CRDF is to be set up in Bishkek by 1 August 2001, with a staff of 15 officers from each participating country. The force is to comprise one battalion from each of the three regional member states of the CIS Collective Security Treaty: Kyrgyzstan, Kazakstan and Tajikistan. This will not be a standing force – all elements will remain in their countries unless called upon. The specific capabilities of the national elements are not clear, except that the Kyrgyz element will be a battalion group designated and trained for operations in mountainous terrain. In total, the proposed number of troops from the CIS countries is between 1,300 and 1,700. In addition, there will be a sizeable Russian contingent. (A Russian, Major General Sergei Chernomyrdin, will command the force.) However, some countries have already said that insufficient forces have been earmarked, and more may be assigned in the future. The only country in the region now remaining outside all regional cooperative security arrangements is Turkmenistan.

Both the CIS and the Shanghai Organisation for Cooperation are designed to counter future incursions into the region from Afghanistan such as occurred first in August 1999 in the Batken region of Kyrgyzstan, and was repeated in 2000 on a wider scale, reaching deep into the Ferghana Valley region of Uzbekistan. A cause of increasing concern is the apparent coordination of effort between different Islamic fundamentalist groups. The emergence of a new group, the Islamic Movement of Turkestan, which may be a reorganisation of the Islamic Movement of Uzbekistan (IMU), suggests greater cohesion amongst such organisations operating from camps inside Afghanistan. Reports indicate that this group seeks to unite Chechen, Uzbek, Uighur and other separatist elements in their attempts to destabilise the secular Central Asian governments and to establish separatist regimes.

The increase in military-industrial cooperation between Russia and the Central Asian states shows a different aspect of the growing cooperation in the defence affairs of this region. For example, *Rosoboronexport*, the newly formed Russian arms-export agency, has proposed a five-year partnership programme with Turkmenistan. The preliminary agreement, reached between Turkmenistan President Saparmurad Niyasov and Sergei Cheremezov, first deputy general director of *Rosoboronexport*, involves *Itera*, the Turkmen gas-export corporation and is, in essence, an 'arms for gas' arrangement.

Regional naval trends

India's naval developments have been directed at achieving the major aim set out in its December 1999 naval doctrine. This called for ocean-going and forward-presence capabilities, in the form of two aircraft carriers and better-armed submarines, in both the western and eastern Indian Ocean by 2010. Progress towards this aim in the past year has been slowing. The two-year refit of the navy's lone aircraft carrier *Viraat*, now over 40 years old, was completed in January 2001; it is anticipated that the vessel will stay in service until at least 2006. Plans for *Viraat*'s successor – a 32,000 tonne indigenously built air-defence ship (ADS) operating 16 combat aircraft and 15 anti-submarine warfare (ASW) helicopters – are advancing. Building is slated to start in 2002, to meet an in-service date of 2010. However, India is still in negotiations with the Russian government about the transfer of the 45,000 tonne aircraft carrier *Admiral Gorshkov,* intended as the navy's second carrier. Although a memorandum of understanding was signed in December 1999, no further progress has been made. Also stalled is the planned acquisition of 40 MiG-29 fighter aircraft, intended for operation from both the *Gorshkov* and the ADS. Funding for both carriers and their aircraft remains in doubt.

Despite slow progress towards achieving the goals of the 1999 doctrine, the Indian Navy remains by far the most capable in the region. India's eagerness to expand its capabilities further shows the country's concern with potential naval threats from outside the South Asian region, in particular from East Asia. Indian naval officials have already expressed willingness to take action over the rising incidence of piracy in the Malacca Strait. In February 2001, Admiral Sushil Kumar, chief of the naval staff, offered Indian naval units to take part in combined multinational anti-piracy patrols in the strait, but no action has yet been taken.

The Pakistani Navy is awaiting delivery of its second advanced *Agosta B* diesel submarine early in 2002, with the third and final to follow in late 2002. Pakistan's defensive naval capabilities will be further improved if the planned $600m acquisition of four Chinese-designed *Jiangwei II* frigates, announced in January 2001, goes ahead. It is unlikely that the Chinese frigates will be as capable as the Indian Navy's Russian- and Indian-built equivalents; however, they will probably be better armed than the Pakistan Navy's current ageing British-built frigates.

DEFENCE SPENDING

Regional

Overall defence spending in the region was $22.5bn in 2000, up from $21bn in 1999. The rise was driven primarily by another increase in Indian spending. Economic growth in the region continued strong, fuelled by buoyant domestic demand and exports. In Bangladesh and Nepal, growth was at its highest since the mid-1990s, with Bangladesh achieving self-sufficiency in food for the first time in many years. The Russian Federation's economic recovery and the rise in international energy prices helped generate strong growth in many Central Asian countries and underpinned increased defence spending.

India

India's 2001 defence budget rose by 3.2% to Rs732bn, from Rs709bn in 2000. The defence budget has increased by nearly 70% (in local currency terms) since 1998, amounting to 3.1% of gross domestic product (GDP) in 2000. In 2001, procurement rose to 30% of the total defence budget as India began to replace obsolete weapon systems and build a nuclear force based on a platform of aircraft, mobile land-based missiles and sea-based assets. In December 2000, Russia and India signed a major licensed-production agreement for 140 Su-30MKI fighter aircraft. These are to be built over the next 17 years, at a cost of $3.5bn. In a further agreement, India is to buy 310 T-90S MBT from Russia to counter the 320 T-80UDs Pakistan acquired from Ukraine. About 124 of the tanks are to be purchased outright, with the remainder to be assembled under licence in India.

The Indian Air Force will receive Rs156bn to help fund the purchase of the new Su-30MKI aircraft, and continued upgrades to the MiG-21, MiG-27M, MiG-29 and *Mirage* 2000H fighters.

The *Mirage* is expected to form part of India's nuclear force. India still has to place the order to remedy its urgent need for an advanced trainer. It is believed that the British *Hawk* is the chosen aircraft, but export restrictions on US-made components in the navigation system is delaying completion of the order. Following a fatal accident in November, when a Mi-8 helicopter crashed killing a dozen Indian paramilitary troops, the Indian Air Force has decided to phase out the Mi-8, opting to buy 40 new Mi-17s and upgrade the older versions already in operation.

The Indian Navy was allocated Rs93bn, around 12.5% of the overall 2001 defence budget. The situation regarding the transfer of the 45,000 tonne carrier *Admiral Gorshkov* from Russia remains unclear. A memorandum of understanding between the two countries was signed in December 1999 and it is believed that the ship is currently being refitted in St Petersburg at India's expense. It is also believed that India wants to acquire at least 20 Russian MiG-29Ks for the carrier. Although the navy's allocation was increased by 11.5% in the 2001–2002 defence budget, it may still not be enough to cover the procurement costs of the ADS ($500m), the *Gorshkov* ($750m) and

Table 19 Indian defence budget by service/department, 1996–2001 constant 2000 US$m

	1996	%	1997	%	1998	%	1999	%	2000	%	2001	%
Army	4,719	53.4	5,772	57.2	5,318	52.2	5,928	48.5	7,685	52.3	7,832	51.2
Air Force	2,263	25.6	2,515	24.9	2,314	22.7	2,374	19.4	2,543	17.3	3,168	20.7
Navy	1,197	13.5	1,190	11.8	1,476	14.5	1,567	12.8	1,848	12.6	1,907	12.5
R&D	437	4.9	372	3.7	439	4.3	644	5.3	698	4.7	734	4.8
DP&S other	225	2.6	241	2.4	629	6.2	1,705	14.0	1,925	13.1	1,660	10.8
Total	8,841	100	10,090	100	10,176	100	12,218	100	14,699	100	15,301	100
% change		-1.6		14.1		0.9		20.1		20.3		4.1

Table 20 Indian defence and military-related spending by function, 1999–2001 US$m

	1999 outurn	2000 outurn	2001 budget
Personnel, Operations & Maintenance			
MoD	75	76	79
Defence pensions	2,560	2,373	2,296
Army	5,719	5,893	6,076
Navy	835	906	907
Air Force	1,430	1,642	1,644
Defence ordnance factories	1,173	1,383	1,354
Recoveries & receipts	-1,298	-1,449	-1,544
Sub-Total	10,494	10,824	10,812
R&D, Procurement and Construction			
Tri-Service Defence R&D	151	185	195
Army	1,446	1,792	1,918
Navy	781	942	1,040
Air Force	971	901	1,590
Other	52	55	65
Sub-Total	3,401	3,875	4,808
Total Defence Budget	13,895	14,699	15,620

the MiG-29 ($1.5bn). Lack of funding is also delaying progress on the navy's indigenous nuclear-powered submarine project, named ATV, which has been in existence for over twenty years. The project's success would have greatly enhanced the navy's forward-projection capabilities, but it has proved too expensive. Money is instead being spent on improving the armament on the navy's diesel submarines. One of the ten *Sindhughosh* (Russian *Kilo*) submarines has been refitted with Russian *Klub-S* anti-surface ship missiles (ASSMs), which have a range of 180km (compared with Pakistan's submarine ASSM range of 100km). Three more submarines of this class are being similarly upgraded in Russia. Escort forces are being renewed more slowly. Three *Kashmir* (*Krivak* 3)-class frigates are being built in Russia for delivery to India in 2002–03. India is building three more frigates, which will be based on the French *La Fayette* design and armed with Russian weapons, including *Klub-N* ASSMs. These frigates are due for delivery in 2006–08. Two more *Brahmaputra*-class frigates are in domestic production, for delivery in 2001–02. Initially, these frigates will be without their main weapon – the indigenously built *Trishul* surface-to-air missile (SAM) – which has not yet proved successful in its development phase.

The Indian Army received Rs374bn ($7.9bn) in the 2001 budget, 50% of the total and a minimal increase over 2000. A primary requirement remains the purchase of unmanned aerial vehicles from Israel and other surveillance devices for use along the border with China and Pakistan.

The allocation for ordnance factories is maintained at 8% of the total budget, signalling that India wishes to increase self-sufficiency and improve the output of its sluggish defence industry. Spending on research and development remains only 4.8% of the total budget.

India successfully test-fired the *Agni* 2 intermediate-range ballistic missile (IRBM) on 17 January 2001, and production has now begun. The missile has ranges of 3,000km with a 1,000kg payload and 3,700km with a 500kg payload. So far, 15 have been produced.

Kazakstan

Kazakstan doubled its official defence budget to t30.9bn ($211m), which is about 1% of GDP. The United States will donate $4m to the country's defence while the Russians will donate arms worth about $20m to help improve border security. Kazakstan's real spending on defence, including factors hidden under the heading of public order and security, is closer to 2% of GDP.

Pakistan

As in previous years, *The Military Balance* estimates that Pakistan's defence spending in 2000 was above budget, in this instance by approximately 21% at Rs190bn ($3.6bn). In 2001, reductions in government spending were announced in the face of the country's severe economic difficulties. As a result, the 2001 defence budget was frozen at R157bn; however, it is difficult to see how spending can be contained at this level and another overspend is likely. In 2000, Pakistan finalised a deal to purchase 30–40 *Chengdu* F-7MG fighter ground attack (FGA) aircraft from China to replace aircraft lost through attrition and to bridge the capability gap until the development of its new *Super*-7 multi-role light combat aircraft is completed. In further cooperation with China, Pakistan is embarking on the pre-production of a batch of 15 *Al-Khalid* MBT. The joint project between the two countries has been underway for 10 years and, once in service, the *Al-Khalid* will be the most powerful tank in Pakistan's arsenal.

The Pakistan Atomic Energy Commission's National Defence Complex began serial production of its indigenously built solid-fuel *Shaheen* 1 IRBM in February 2001. The *Shaheen* 1 has a declared range of 750km and it is thought that the *Shaheen* 2, with a range of 2,500km, is ready for testing. The shorter 100km-range *Hatf* 1 was successfully tested in February 2000.

Sri Lanka

The war between government forces and the LTTE resulted in defence spending of Rs65.9bn

($88om) in 2000, approximately Rs13.5bn ($182m) over budget. In a new equipment deal with the Czech Republic, Sri Lanka is to receive up to 40 T-55 MBT, eight MT-55A bridge layers and 16 VT-55 armoured recovery vehicles.

Table 21 Arms orders and deliveries, Central and South Asia, 1998–2001

	Country supplier ⇩	Classification ⇩ / Designation	Quantity ⇩	Order date	Delivery date	Comment ⇩
Bangladesh	PRC	FGA / **F-7**	24	1996	1997	Deliveries continuing through 1999
	PRC	trg / **FT-7B**	4	1997	1999	
	US	tpt / **C-130B**	4	1997	1999	
	RF	FGA / **MiG-29B**	8	1999	1999	Order placed 1999 after delay
	ROK	FF / **Ulsan**	1	1998	2002	
	Cz	trg / **L-39ZA**	4	1999	2000	Following delivery of 8 in 1995
	ROK	FAC / **PKM-200**	2		2000	
India	dom	SSN / **ATV**	1	1982	2007	
	dom	ICBM / **Surya**		1983		Dev. 5,000km range
	dom	SLCM / **Sagarika**		1983	2003	300km range. May be ballistic
	dom	MRBM / **Agni 2**	5	1983	2000	Range 2,000km
	dom	MRBM / **Agni 3**		1983	2000	Dev. Range 4,000km
	dom	SSM / **Prithvi SS150**	150	1983	1996	150km range. Low-vol prod
	dom	SSM / **Prithvi SS250**	50	1983	2001	Air force variant
	dom	SSM / **Prithvi**	100	1983	2001	Naval variant aka *Danush*
	dom	SAM / **Akash**		1983	1999	Dev. High-altitude SAM.
	dom	SAM / **Trishul**		1983	1999	Dev.
	dom	ATGW / **Nag**		1983	1999	Ready for prod mid-1999
	dom	AAM / **Astra**		1999	2002	Dev. 1st test planned Jul 1999
	dom	FGA / **LCA**		1983	2012	
	RF	SSK / **Kilo**	10	1983	2000	Last of 10 delivered in 2000
	dom	FFG / **Brahmaputra**	3	1989	2000	2nd delivered in 2001
	dom	hel / **ALH**	12	1984	2000	Tri-service requirement for 300.
	dom	ELINT / **HS-748**		1990		Dev
	dom	UAV / **Nishant**	14	1991	1999	Dev. 3 prototypes built. 14 pre-prod units on order
	dom	sat / **Ocean sat**	1	1995	1999	Remote sensing
	dom	AGHS / **Sandhayak**	2	1995	1999	Following delivery of 6 1981–93
	RF	tkr AC / **IL-78**	6	1996	1998	First 2 delivered early 1998
	RF	ASSM / **SS-N-25**	16	1996	1997	Deliveries continue
	RF	FGA / **Su-30MK**	18	1996	1997	To be upgraded to MKI standard
	RF	FGA / **Su-30MKI**	32	1996	2001	To be completed by 2003
	RF	FGA / **MiG-21BIS**	125	1996	2001	Upgrades
	Il	PFC / **Super Dvora MK3**	6	1996	1998	1st delivery 1998.
	RF	FF / **Krivak III**	3	1997	2002	1 for delivery by 2002, 2 by 2003.
	RF	hel / **KA-31**	12	1997	2001	To operate from *Krivak* III
	Ge	SS / **Type 209**	2	1997	2003	To be built in Ind
	UK	FGA / **Harrier TMk4**	2	1997	1999	2 ex-RN ac for delivery 1999
	RSA	APC / **Casspir**	90	1998	1999	10 delivered. 80 in 1999
	RF	SLCM / **SS-NX-27**		1998	2004	For *Krivak* 3 frigate. First export
	UK	FGA / **Jaguar**	18	1998	2001	Potential upgrade for up to 60
	RF	FGA / **MiG-21**	125	1999	2003	Upgrade. Fr and Il avionics
	dom	MBT / **Arjun**	124	1999	2001	
	dom	trg / **HJT-36**	200	1999	2004	

	Country supplier ⇩	Classification ⇩ Designation	Quantity ⇩	Order date	Delivery date ⇩	Comment
	Pl	trg **TS-11**	12	1999	2000	Option on 8 more
	dom	CV *Viraat*	1	1999	2001	Upgrade (ex-UK *Hermes*)
	RF	CV *Admiral Gorshkov*	1	1999	2003	
	RF	FGA *MiG-29K*	24	1999	2003	Possibly 60. To equip CV *Gorshkov*
	Slvk	ARV **T-72 VT**	42	1999	2001	Original order for 85. 43 from Pl
	Pl	ARV **WZT-3**	43	1999	2001	Original order for 85
	Swe	arty **155mm**	400	1999		
	Il	arty **M-46**	35	1999	2000	
	dom	AAM *Astra*		1999		Live firing due 2001
	dom	MPA **Do-228**	7	1999		Deliveries completed by 2003
	Il	arty **M-46**	35	1999	2000	Req for further 500
	RF	hel **Mi-17iB**	40	2000	2001	
	RF	MBT **T-90**	310	2000		186 to be built in Ind
	Il	UAV *Searcher* 2	20	2000		In addition to 8 delivered 1999
	Fr	FGA *Mirage* **2000**	10	2000	2003	Originally approved 1996
	RF	FGA **Su-30MKI**	140	2000		Licensed Production
	RF	recce **Tu-142F**	8	2000	2002	Upgrades
	Il	hel **Mi-8/17**	80	2001		Upgrades
	RF	hel **Ka-31**	10	2001	2001	
	dom	FGA **MiG-27M**	40	2001	2004	Upgrades
Kazakstan	RF	FGA **Su-27**	16	1997	1999	
	RF	SAM **S-300**		1997	2000	
Pakistan	US	APC **M113**	775	1989	1990	Licensed prod; deliveries to 1999
	dom	MBT *Al-Khalid*	15	1991	2000	Pre-prod batch
	PRC	FGA **FC-1/S-7**		1993	2005	In co-dev with PRC, req for up to 150
	dom	MRBM *Ghauri* 1		1993	1998	Range 1,500km. Aka *Hatf* 5
	dom	MRBM *Ghauri* 2		1993	1999	Dev. Aka *Hatf* 6
	dom	MRBM *Ghauri* 3		1993		Dev. Range 3,000km
	dom	SSM *Hatf* 2		1994	1996	Dev. Based on PRC M-11
	dom	SSM *Hatf* 3		1994		Dev. Range 600–800km. Based on M-9
	dom	SSM *Shaheen* 1		1994	1999	In prod mid-1999. Aka *Hatf* 4
	dom	SSM *Shaheen* 2		1994		Dev. Range 2,500km. Aka *Hatf* 7
	Fr	SSK *Khalid*	3	1994	1999	1st in 1999, 2nd 2001, 3rd 2002
	Fr	FGA *Mirage* III	40	1996	1998	Upgrade. 8 delivered by Apr 1999
	dom	PFM *Mod. Larkana*	1	1996	1997	Commissioned 14 Aug 1997
	PRC	PFM *Shujat* 2	1	1997	1999	
	PRC	FGA **F-7MG**	30	1999	2001	Stop gap until S-7 completed
	dom	UAV *Bravo*			2000	In service
	PRC	FFG *Jiangwei* II	4	2001	2006	
Sri Lanka	Il	UAV *Super Scout*				
	UK	ACV **M10**		1995	1999	Hovercraft
	RF	cbt hel **Mi-35**	2	1997	1999	May be 4. 5 delivered previously
	US	tpt **C-130**	3	1997	1999	
	Ukr	cbt hel **Mi-24**	2	1998	1999	
	PRC	arty **152mm**	36	1999	2000	
	UK	tpt **C-130**	2	1999		
	Il	FGA *Kfir*	8	2000		
	Ind	OPV *Sukanya Class*	2		2000	
	Cz	MBT **T-55**	11	2000	2000	New order up to total of 40 expected
	RF	AIFV **BMP-2**	36	2000	2001	Reconditioned

Afghanistan Afg

afghani Afs		1999	2000	2001	2002
GDP	US$	ε2.0bn			
per capita	US$	ε700			
Growth	%	ε6			
Inflation	%	ε14			
Debt	US$	5.8			
Def exp	US$	ε250m			
US$1=Afs		3,000	3,000	4,750	
Population[b]				ε**22,567,000**	

Pashtun 38% Tajik 25% **Hazara** 19% **Uzbek** 12% **Aimaq** 4% **Baluchi** 0.5%

Age	13–17	18–22	23–32
Men	1,499,000	1,194,000	2,053,000
Women	1,442,000	1,134,000	1,930,000

[b] Includes ε1,500,000 refugees in Pak, ε1,000,000 in Ir, ε150,000 in RF and ε50,000 in Kgz

Total Armed Forces

There are no state-constituted armed forces. The *Taleban* now controls 85–90% of Afg. It continues to mount mil ops against an alliance of Ahmad Shah Massoud, deposed President Burhanuddin Rabbani and the National Islamic Movement (NIM) of General Abdul Rashid Dostum.

EQUIPMENT

It is impossible to show the division of ground force eqpt among the different factions. The list below represents wpn known to be in the country in Apr 1992. Individual wpn quantities are unknown.

MBT ε1,000: T-54/-55, T-62
LT TK PT-76
RECCE BRDM-1/-2
AIFV BMP-1/-2
APC ε1,000: BTR-40/-60/-70/-80/-152
TOWED ARTY 76mm: M-1938, M-1942; **85mm**: D-48; **100mm**: M-1944; **122mm**: M-30, D-30; **130mm**: M-46; **152mm**: D-1, D-20, M-1937 (ML-20)
MRL ε125: **122mm**: BM-21; **140mm**: BM-14; **220mm**: 9P140 *Uragan*
MOR 82mm: M-37; **107mm; 120mm**: M-43
SSM ε20–30: *Scud*, FROG-7
ATGW AT-1 *Snapper*, AT-3 *Sagger*
RCL 73mm: SPG-9; **82mm**: B-10
AD GUNS: **14.5mm; 23mm**: ZU-23, ZSU-23-4 SP; **37mm**: M-1939; **57mm**: S-60; **85mm**: KS-12; **100mm**: KS-19
SAM SA-7/-13

Air Force

Only the *Taleban* and Gen Massoud's forces have ac

TALEBAN
 FGA some 20 MiG-21/Su-22, plus 5 L-39
 TPT some An-24
 HEL Mi-8/17 aslt tpt, Mi-24/-25/-35 attack hel
ISLAMIC SOCIETY
 2 Mi-35 attack hel, 6–7 Mi-17 airlift hel

Opposition Groups

In the midst of a civil war, this section lists armed gp operating in the country.

TALEBAN ε50,000 **Leader** Mullah Mohamed Omar **Area** now control 85–90% of Afg **Ethnic group** Pashtun. Formed originally from religious students in Madrassahs (mostly Pashtun)

Northern Alliance

The Northern Alliance represents the armed grouping of the 'United Islamic Front for the Salvation of Afghanistan', comprising:

ISLAMIC SOCIETY (*Jamia't-i-Islami*) ε20,000 **Leaders** Ahmad Shah Massoud and deposed President Burhanuddin Rabbani **Area** north of Kabul and Panshir Valley **Ethnic groups** Turkoman, Uzbek, Tajik
NATIONAL ISLAMIC MOVEMENT (NIM)[a] (*Jumbesh-i-Milli Islami*) str n.k. **Leader** General Abdul Rashid Dostum. Formed in Mar 1992, mainly from tps of former Afghan Army Northern Comd. Predominantly Uzbek, Tajik, Turkoman, Ismaili and Hazara Shi'a.
ISLAMIC UNITY PARTY (*Hizb-i Wahdat-i Islami - Khalili*) **Leader** Abdul Karim Khalili

Other Groups

ISLAMIC PARTY (*Hizb-i Islami-Gulbuddin*) Gulbuddin *Hekmatyar* faction
ISLAMIC PARTY (*Hizb-i Islami-Khalis*) Yunis Khalis faction
ISLAMIC UNION FOR THE LIBERATION OF AFGHANISTAN (*Ittihad-i-Islami Barai Azadi Afghanistan*) **Leader** Abdul Rasul Sayyaf
ISLAMIC REVOLUTIONARY MOVEMENT (*Harakat-Inqilab-i-Islami*) **Leader** Mohammed Nabi Mohammadi
AFGHANISTAN NATIONAL LIBERATION FRONT (*Jabha-i-Najat-i-Milli Afghanistan*) **Leader** Sibghatullad Mojaddedi
NATIONAL ISLAMIC FRONT (*Mahaz-i-Milli-Islami*) **Leader** Sayed Aha Gailani
ISLAMIC UNITY PARTY (*Hizb-i Wahdat-Akbari* faction) **Leader** Mohammed Akbar Akbari
ISLAMIC MOVEMENT (*Harakat-i-Islami*) **Leader** Mohammed Asif Mohseni
These smaller gps occasionally support the *Taleban* as well as at times supporting the Northern Alliance

HIZB-I WAHDAT-I (Unity Party) Shi'a umbrella party of which the main groups are:

Sazman-e-Nasr str n.k. **Ethnic group** Hazara
Shura-Itifaq-Islami str n.k. **Ethnic group** Hazara
Harakat-e-Islami str n.k. **Ethnic group** Pashtun, Tajik, Uzbek

These Shi'a groups have at times been allied with the Northern Alliance, at others were attacked by them. The Hazara group enjoy support from Ir.

ª Form the Supreme Coordination Council

Bangladesh Bng

taka Tk		1999	2000	2001	2002
GDP	Tk	1.7tr	1.9tr		
	US$	35.7bn	37bn		
per capita	US$	1,700	1,800		
Growth	%	4.4	5.3		
Inflation	%	6.3	4.7		
Debt	US$	15.1bn	15.8bn		
Def exp	Tk	32.7bn	34.8bn		
	US$	667m	684m		
Def bdgt	Tk	30bn	34.8bn	37.4bn	
	US$	612m	682m	692m	
FMA (US)	US$	0.4m	0.4m	0.4m	
US$1=taka		49	51	54	

Population			130,764,000 Hindu 12%	
Age	13–17	18–22	23–32
Men	8,107,000	7,738,000	12,341,000
Women	7,794,000	7,257,000	11,684,000

Total Armed Forces

ACTIVE 137,000

Army 120,000

7 inf div HQ • 17 inf bde (some 26 bn) • 1 armd bde (2 armd regt) • 2 armd regt • 1 arty div (6 arty regt) • 1 engr bde • 1 AD bde

EQUIPMENT†

MBT 100 PRC Type-59/-69, 100 T-54/-55
LT TK some 40 PRC Type-62
APC 60 BTR-70, 20 BTR-80, some MT-LB, ε50 YW531
TOWED ARTY 105mm: 30 Model 56 pack, 50 M-101; **122mm**: 20 PRC Type-54; **130mm**: 40+ PRC Type-59
MOR 81mm; 82mm: PRC Type-53; **120mm**: 50 PRC Type-53
RCL 106mm: 30 M-40A1
ATK GUNS 57mm: 18 6-pdr; **76mm**: 50 PRC Type-54
AD GUNS 37mm: 16 PRC Type-55; **57mm**: PRC Type-59

SAM some HN-5A

Navy† 10,500

BASES Chittagong (HQ), Dhaka, Khulna, Kaptai
PRINCIPAL SURFACE COMBATANTS 4

FRIGATES 4

FFG 1 *Osman* (PRC *Jianghu* I) with 2 × 2 CSS-N-2 *Hai Ying* 2 SSM, 2 × 2 100mm gun, 2 × 5 ASW mor
FF 3
1 *Umar Farooq* (UK *Salisbury*) with 1 × 2 115mm gun, 1 × 3 *Squid* ASW mor
2 *Abu Bakr* (UK *Leopard*) with 2 × 2 115mm guns

PATROL AND COASTAL COMBATANTS 33

MISSILE CRAFT 10
5 *Durdarsha* (PRC *Huangfeng*) PFM with 4 HY 2 SSM
5 *Durbar* (PRC *Hegu*) PFM< with 2 SY-1 SSM
TORPEDO CRAFT 4
4 PRC *Huchuan* PHT< with 2 × 533mm TT
PATROL, OFFSHORE 2
1 *Madhumati* (J *Sea Dragon*) PCO with 1 × 76mm gun
1 *Durjoy* (PRC *Hainan*) PCO with 4 × 5 ASW RL
PATROL, COASTAL 8
2 *Meghna* fishery protection
2 *Karnaphuli* PCC
4 *Shahead Daulat* PFC
PATROL, INSHORE 4
1 *Bishkali* PCI<, 1 *Bakarat* PCI<, 2 *Akshay* PCI<
PATROL, RIVERINE 5 *Pabna* PCR<

MINE WARFARE 4

MINE COUNTERMEASURES 4
3 *Shapla* (UK *River*) MSI, 1 *Sagar* MSO

AMPHIBIOUS craft only

7 LCU, 4 LCM, 3 LCVP

SUPPORT AND MISCELLANEOUS 8

1 coastal AOT, 1 AR, 1 AT/F, 1 AT, 2 *Yuch'in* AGHS, 1 *Shaibal* AGOR (UK *River*) (MCM capable), 1 *Shaheed Ruhul Amin* (trg)

Air Force† 6,500

83 cbt ac, no armed hel **Flying hours** 100–120
FGA/FTR 4 sqn with 8 MiG-29 (incl 2 -UB), 18 A-5C *Fantan*, 16 F-6, 23 F-7M/FT-7B *Airguard*, 1 OCU with 10 FT-6, 8 L-39ZA
TPT 3 An-32
HEL 3 sqn with 11 Bell 212, 1 Mi-8, 15 Mi-17
TRG 20 PT-6, 12 T-37B, 8 CM-170, 2 Bell 206L
AAM AA-2 *Atoll*

Forces Abroad

UN AND PEACEKEEPING

CROATIA (UNMOP): 1 obs **DROC** (MONUC): 16 incl 9 obs **EAST TIMOR** (UNTAET): 547 incl 7 obs

ETHIOPIA/ERITREA (UNMEE): 172 incl 6 obs
GEORGIA (UNOMIG): 7 obs **IRAQ/KUWAIT**
(UNIKOM): 816 incl 6 obs **SIERRA LEONE**
(UNAMSIL): 4,278 incl 12 obs **WESTERN SAHARA**
(MINURSO): 6 obs

Paramilitary 63,200

BANGLADESH RIFLES 38,000
border guard; 41 bn
ARMED POLICE 5,000
rapid action force (forming)
ANSARS (Security Guards) 20,000+
A further 180,000 unembodied

COAST GUARD 200
(HQ Chittagong and Khulma)
1 *Bishkhali* PCI<
(force in its infancy and expected to expand)

India Ind

rupee Rs		1999	2000	2001	2002
GDP	Rs	18.9tr	20.9tr		
	US$	440bn	471bn		
per capita	US$	1,800	1,900		
Growth	%	5.9	6.4		
Inflation	%	4.7	4.0		
Debt	US$	99bn	103bn		
Def exp[a]	Rs	610bn	655bn		
	US$	14.2bn	14.7bn		
Def bdgt	Rs	533bn	709bn	732bn	
	US$	12.4bn	15.9bn	15.6bn	
FMA (US)	US$	0.5m	0.5m	0.5m	
FMA (Aus)	US$	0.2m			
US$1=Rs		43.0	44.4	46.9	

[a] Incl exp on paramil org

Population			1,029,548,000
Hindu 80% Muslim 14% Christian 2% Sikh 2%			

Age	13–17	18–22	23–32
Men	54,638,000	49,922,000	88,478,000
Women	51,292,000	46,415,000	80,937,000

Total Armed Forces

ACTIVE 1,263,000

RESERVES 535,000

Army 300,000 (first-line reserves within 5 years' full-time service, a further 500,000 have commitment until age 50) **Territorial Army** (volunteers) 40,000 **Air Force** 140,000 **Navy** 55,000

Army 1,100,000

HQ: 5 Regional Comd, 4 Fd Army, 12 Corps
3 armd div (each 2–3 armed, 1 SP arty (2 SP fd, 1 med regt) bde) • 4 RAPID div (each 2 inf, 1 mech bde) • 18 inf div (each 2–5 inf, 1 arty bde; some have armd regt) • 9 mtn div (each 3–4 bde, 1 or more arty regt) • 1 arty div (3 bde) • 15 indep bde: 7 armd, 5 inf, 2 mtn, 1 AB/cdo • 1 SSM regt (*Prithvi*) • 4 AD bde (plus 14 cadre) • 3 engr bde
These formations comprise
  59 tk regt (bn) • 355 inf bn (incl 25 mech, 8 AB, 3 cdo) • 190 arty regt (bn) reported: incl 1 SSM, 2 MRL, 50 med (11 SP), 69 fd (3 SP), 39 mtn, 29 AD arty regt; perhaps 2 SAM gp (3–5 bty each) plus 15 SAM regt • 22 hel sqn: incl 5 ATK

RESERVES
Territorial Army 25 inf bn, plus 29 'departmental' units
EQUIPMENT
  MBT ε3,414 (ε1,100 in store): some 700 T-55 (450 op), ε1,500 T-72/M1, 1,200 *Vijayanta*, ε14 *Arjun*
  LT TK ε90 PT-76
  RECCE ε100 BRDM-2
  AIFV 350+ BMP-1, 1,000 BMP-2 (*Sarath*)
  APC 157 OT-62/-64 (in store), ε160 *Casspir*
  TOWED ARTY 4,175 (perhaps 600 in store) incl: **75mm**: 900 75/24 mtn, 215 FRY M-48; **105mm**: some 1,300 IFG Mk I/II, 50 M-56; **122mm**: some 550 D-30; **130mm**: 750+ M-46; **155mm**: 410 FH-77B
  SP ARTY 105mm: 80 *Abbot* (in store); **130mm**: 100 mod M-46 (ε70 in store); **152mm**: some 2S19
  MRL 122mm: ε100 incl BM-21, LRAR; **214mm**: *Pinacha* (being deployed)
  MOR 81mm: L16A1, E1; **120mm**: 500 Brandt AM-50, E1; **160mm**: 500 M-1943
  SSM *Prithvi* (3–5 launchers)
  ATGW *Milan*, AT-3 *Sagger*, AT-4 *Spigot* (some SP), AT-5 *Spandrel* (some SP)
  RCL 84mm: *Carl Gustav*; **106mm**: 1,000+ M-40A1
  AD GUNS some 2,424: **20mm**: Oerlikon (reported); **23mm**: 300 ZU 23-2, 100 ZSU-23-4 SP; **30mm**: 24 2S6 SP; **40mm**: 1,200 L40/60, 800 L40/70
  SAM 180 SA-6, 620 SA-7, 50 SA-8B, 400 SA-9, 45 SA-3, SA-13, 500 SA-16
  SURV MUFAR, *Green Archer* (mor)
  UAV *Searcher*, *Nishant*
  HEL 100 *Chetak*, 50 *Cheetah*
  LC 2 LCVP
DEPLOYMENT
  North 3 Corps with 8 inf, 2 mtn div **West** 3 Corps with 1 armd, 5 inf div, 3 RAPID **Central** 1 Corps with 1 armd, 1 inf, 1 RAPID **East** 3 Corps with 1 inf, 7 mtn div **South** 2 Corps with 1 armd, 3 inf div

Navy 53,000

(incl 5,000 Naval Aviation and 1,000 Marines; ε2,000 women)

PRINCIPAL COMMAND Western, Southern, Eastern (incl Far Eastern sub comd)

SUB-COMMAND SS, Naval Air

BASES Mumbai (Bombay) (HQ Western Comd), Kochi (Cochin) (HQ Southern Comd), Vishakhapatnam (HQ Eastern), Port Blair (Andaman Is, HQ Far Eastern sub Comd), Goa (HQ Naval Avn), Arakonam (Naval Avn), Calcutta, Madras, Karwar (under construction)

FLEETS Western base Bombay **Eastern base** Visakhapatnam

SUBMARINES 16

SSK 16

10 *Sindhughosh* (Sov *Kilo*) with 533mm TT (at least 1 with SS-NX-27 *Club* SSM)

4 *Shishumar* (Ge T-209/1500) with 533mm TT

2 *Kursura* (Sov *Foxtrot*)† with 533mm TT (plus 3 in reserve)

PRINCIPAL SURFACE COMBATANTS 27

AIRCRAFT CARRIERS 1 *Viraat* (UK *Hermes*) CV

Air group typically **ac** 6 *Sea Harrier* (*Sea Eagle* ASM) ftr/attack **hel** 6 *Sea King* ASW/ASUW

DESTROYERS 8

DDG 8

5 *Rajput* (Sov *Kashin*) with 4 SS-N-2C *Styx* SSM, 2 × 2 SA-N-1 *Goa* SAM, 2 × 76mm gun, 5 × 533mm ASTT, 2 ASW RL, 1 Ka-25 or 28 hel

3 *Delhi* with 16 SS-N-25 *Switchblade* SSM, 2 × SA-N-7 *Gadfly* SAM, 1 × 100mm gun, 5 × 533mm ASTT, 2 hel

FRIGATES 11

FFG 4

1 *Brahmaputra* with 16 × SS-N-25 *Switchblade* SSM, 20 SA-N-4 *Gecko* SAM, 1 × 76mm gun, 2 × 3 324mm ASTT, 1 hel

3 *Godavari* with SS-N-2D *Styx* SSM, 1 × 2 SA-N-4 *Gecko* SAM, 2 × 3 324mm ASTT, 1 *Sea King* hel

FF 7

4 *Nilgiri* (UK *Leander*) with 2 × 114mm guns, 2 × 3 ASTT, 1 × 3 *Limbo* ASW mor, 1 *Chetak* hel (2 with 1 *Sea King*)

1 *Krishna* (UK *Leander*) (trg role)

2 *Arnala* (Sov *Petya*) with 4 × 76mm gun, 3 × 533mm ASTT, 4 ASW RL

CORVETTES 7

4 *Khukri* FSG with 4 SS-N-2C *Styx* SSM, 1 × 76mm gun, hel deck

3 mod *Khukri* FSG with 16 × SS-N-25 *Switchblade* SSM, SA-N-5 *Grail* SAM, 1 × 76mm gun

PATROL AND COASTAL COMBATANTS 39

CORVETTES 17

1 *Vijay Durg* (Sov *Nanuchka* II) FSG with 4 SS-N-2C *Styx* SSM, SA-N-4 *Gecko* SAM (plus 1 non-op)

11 *Veer* (Sov *Tarantul*) FSG with 4 *Styx* SSM, SA-N-5 *Grail* SAM, 1 × 76mm gun

1 *Vibhuti* (mod *Veer*) FSG with 16 × SS-N-25 *Switchblade* SSM, SA-N-5 *Grail* SAM, 1 × 76mm gun

4 *Abhay* (Sov *Pauk* II) FS with SA-N-5 *Grail* SAM, 1 × 76mm gun, 4 × 533mm ASTT, 2 ASW mor

MISSILE CRAFT 6 *Vidyut* (Sov *Osa* II) with 4 *Styx* SSM†

PATROL, OFFSHORE 5 *Sukanya* PCO

PATROL, INSHORE 11

7 SDB Mk 3 PCI

4 *Super Dvora* PCF<

MINE WARFARE 18

MINELAYERS 0

none, but all SS and *Pondicherry* MSO have minelaying capability

MINE COUNTERMEASURES 18

12 *Pondicherry* (Sov *Natya*) MSO, 6 *Mahé* (Sov *Yevgenya*) MSI<

AMPHIBIOUS 7

2 *Magar* LST, capacity 500 tps, 18 tk, 1 hel

5 *Ghorpad* (Sov *Polnocny* C) LSM, capacity 140 tps, 6 tk

Plus craft: 10 *Vasco da Gama* LCU

SUPPORT AND MISCELLANEOUS 32

1 *Aditya* (mod *Deepak*) AO, 1 *Deepak* AO, 1 *Jyoti* AO, 6 small AOT; 3 YDT, 1 *Tir* trg, 2 AWT, 3 TRV, 1 AH; 8 *Sandhayak* AGHS, 4 *Makar* AGHS, 1 *Sagardhwani* AGOR

NAVAL AVIATION (5,000)

ORGANISATION

Flying hours Sea Harrier 180

AIRCRAFT

FTR 2 sqn with *Sea Harrier* FRS Mk-1, 1 T-60 trg*

MR 3 sqn with Il-38, Tu-142F *Bear*, Do-228, BN-2 *Defender*

COMMS 1 sqn with Do-228

TRG 1 sqn with HJT-16, 8 HPT-32

HELICOPTERS

ASW 6 sqn with *Chetak*, Ka-25, Ka-28, *Sea King* Mk-42A/B

SAR 1 sqn with *Sea King* Mk-42C

TRG 1 sqn with *Chetak**, Hughes 300

EQUIPMENT

37 cbt ac; 72 armed hel

AIRCRAFT

23 *Sea Harrier* FRS Mk-1 • 1 **T-60** trg* • 5 Il-38 • 5 **Tu-142F** *Bear* • 29 **Do-228** (18 -MR, 10 -COMMS) • 18 **BN-2** *Defender* • 6 **HJT-16** • 8 **HPT-32**

HELICOPTERS

26 *Chetak* (24 - ASW, 2 - TRG) • 7 **Ka-25** • 14 **Ka-28** • 25 *Sea King* **Mk-42A/B** • 6 *Sea King* **Mk-42C** • 4 **Hughes 300**

MISSILES

AAM R-550 *Magic* 1 and 2

ASM *Sea Eagle*, *Sea Skua*

MARINES (1,000)

1 regt (3 gp)

Air Force 110,000

738 cbt ac, 22+ armed hel **Flying hours** 150
Five regional air comds: **Central** (Allahabad), **Western** (New Delhi), **Eastern** (Shillong), **Southern** (Trivandrum), **South-Western** (Gandhinagar); 2 spt comds: trg and maint
FGA 21 sqn
  1 with 16 Su-30K/MK, 3 with 52 MiG-23 BN/UM, 4 with 84 *Jaguar* S(I), 6 with 135 MiG-27M, 5 with 55 MiG-21 MF/PFMA, 10 with 165 MiG-21bis/U (125 being upgraded), 2 with 40 *Mirage* 2000H/TH (secondary ECM role)
FTR 19 sqn
  5 with 66 MiG-21 FL/U, 1 with 26 MiG-23 MF/UM, 3 with 63 MiG-29
ECM 1 sqn with 4 *Canberra* B(I) 58 (ECM/target towing), 2 *Canberra* TT-18 (target towing), some MiG-21M (ECM)
ELINT 2 Boeing 707, 2 Boeing 737
TANKER 6 IL-78
MARITIME ATTACK 1 sqn with 6 *Jaguar* S(I) with *Sea Eagle*
ATTACK HEL 2 sqn with 20+ Mi-25/35
RECCE 2 sqn
  1 with 8 *Canberra* (6 PR-57, 2 PR-67)
  1 with 5* MiG-25R, 2* MiG-25U
MR/SURVEY 2 *Gulfstream* IV SRA, 2 *Learjet* 29
TRANSPORT
  ac 12 sqn
    6 with 105 An-32 *Sutlej*, 2 with 45 Do-228, 2 with 28 BAe-748, 2 with 25 Il-76 *Gajraj*
  hel 14 sqn with 73 Mi-8/50 Mi-17, 1 sqn with 10 Mi-26 (hy tpt), 8 sqn with *Cheetah/Chetak*
VIP 1 HQ sqn with 2 Boeing 737-200, 7 BAe-748, 6 Mi-8
TRG ac 28 BAe-748 (trg/tpt), 120 *Kiran* I, 56 *Kiran* II, 88 HPT-32, 38 *Hunter* (20 F-56, 18 T-66), 14* *Jaguar* B(1), 9* MiG-29UB, 44 TS-11 *Iskara* **hel** 20 *Chetak*, 2 Mi-24, 2* Mi-35
UAV *Searcher*-2
MISSILES
  ASM *Prithvi* SS250, AS-7 *Kerry*, AS-11B (ATGW), AS-12, AS-30, *Sea Eagle*, AM 39 *Exocet*, AS-17 *Krypton*
  AAM AA-7 *Apex*, AA-8 *Aphid*, AA-10 *Alamo*, AA-11 *Archer*, R-550 *Magic*, *Super* 530D
  SAM 38 sqn with 280 *Divina* V75SM/VK (SA-2), *Pechora* (SA-3), SA-5, SA-10

Forces Abroad

UN AND PEACEKEEPING
DROC (MONUC): 20 incl 18 obs **ETHIOPIA/ ERITREA** (UNMEE): 1,328 incl 5 obs **IRAQ/KUWAIT** (UNIKOM): 6 obs **LEBANON** (UNIFIL): 792

Paramilitary 1,089,700 active

NATIONAL SECURITY GUARDS 7,400

(Cabinet Secretariat)
Anti-terrorism contingency deployment force, comprising elements of the armed forces, CRPF and Border Security Force
SPECIAL PROTECTION GROUP 3,000
Protection of VVIP
SPECIAL FRONTIER FORCE 9,000
(Cabinet Secretariat)
mainly ethnic Tibetans
RASHTRIYA RIFLES 40,000 (Ministry of Defence)
36 bn in 12 Sector HQ
DEFENCE SECURITY CORPS 31,000
provides security at Defence Ministry sites
INDO-TIBETAN BORDER POLICE 32,400 (Ministry of Home Affairs)
29 bn, Tibetan border security
ASSAM RIFLES 52,500 (Ministry of Home Affairs)
7 HQ, 31 bn, security within north-eastern states, mainly Army-officered; better trained than BSF
RAILWAY PROTECTION FORCES 70,000
CENTRAL INDUSTRIAL SECURITY FORCE 95,000 (Ministry of Home Affairs)[a]
guards public-sector locations
CENTRAL RESERVE POLICE FORCE (CRPF) 167,400 (Ministry of Home Affairs)
137 bn incl 10 rapid action, 2 *Mahila* (women); internal security duties, only lightly armed, deployable throughout the country
BORDER SECURITY FORCE (BSF) 174,000 (Ministry of Home Affairs)
some 157 bn, small arms, some lt arty, tpt/liaison air spt
HOME GUARD (R) 574,000
authorised, actual str 399,800 in all states except Arunachal Pradesh and Kerala; men on lists, no trg
STATE ARMED POLICE 400,000
For duty primarily in home state only, but can be moved to other states, incl 24 bn India Reserve Police (commando-trained)
CIVIL DEFENCE 453,000 (R)
in 135 towns in 32 states
COAST GUARD over 8,000
  PATROL CRAFT 36
    3 *Samar* PCO, 9 *Vikram* PCO, 21 *Jija Bai*, 3 SDB-2 plus 16 boats
  AVIATION
    3 sqn with **ac** 14 Do-228, **hel** 15 *Chetak*

[a] Lightly armed security guards only

Opposition 2,000–2,500

HIZB-UL-MUJAHIDEEN str 1,000–1,200 Operates in Ind Kashmir

HARAKAT-UL-MUJAHIDEEN str 450–500 Operates from Pak Kashmir
LASHKAR-E-TAYYABA str 300–400 Operates from Pak Kashmir
JESH-E-MOHAMMADI str 300–400 Operates from Pak Kashmir
AL-BADR MUJAHIDEEN str 40–50 Operates in Ind Kashmir

Foreign Forces

UN (UNMOGIP): 43 mil obs from 8 countries

Kazakstan Kaz

tenge t		1999	2000	2001	2002
GDP	t	1.9tr	2.6tr		
	US$	14.5bn	18.2bn		
per capita	US$	3,300	3,700		
Growth	%	1.7	9.6		
Inflation	%	8.2	13.4		
Debt	US$	7.9bn	12.3		
Def exp[a]	t	37.5bn	51.9bn		
	US$	291m	364.2m		
Def bdgt	t	15.1bn	16.5bn	31bn	
	US$	117m	115m	211m	
FMA[b] (US)	US$	0.6m	0.6m	0.6m	
US$1=t		128.9	142.5	146.3	

[a] Incl exp on paramilitary forces
[b] Excl US Cooperative Threat Reduction Programme funds for nuclear dismantlement and demilitarisation. Bdgt 1993–99 εUS$300m. Programme continues through 2000.

Population			16,115,000

Kazak 51% **Russian** 32% **Ukrainian** 5% **German** 2%
Tatar 2% **Uzbek** 2%

Age	13–17	18–22	23–32
Men	919,000	826,000	1,379,000
Women	896,000	814,000	1,356,000

Total Armed Forces

ACTIVE 64,000
Terms of service 31 months

RESERVES ε237,000

Army 45,000

2 Mil District (plus 1 forming, 1 more to form)
2 Army Corps (third to form)
1 with 1 mech div, 2 MR bde, 1 arty regt
1 with 1 mech div, 1 MR bde, 1 arty bde, 1 trg centre
1 air aslt, 1 SSM, 1 arty bde
EQUIPMENT

MBT 650 T-72, 280 T-62
RECCE 140 BRDM
AIFV 508 BMP-1/-2, 65 BRM
APC 84 BTR-70/-80, 686 MT-LB APC (plus some 1,000 in store)
TOWED ARTY 505: **122mm**: 161 D-30; **152mm**: 74 D-20, 90 2A65, 180 2A36
SP ARTY 163: **122mm**: 74 2S1; **152mm**: 89 2S3
COMBINED GUN/MOR 120mm: 26 2S9
MRL 147: **122mm**: 57 BM-21; **220mm**: 90 9P140 *Uragan*
MOR 145: **120mm**: 2B11, M-120
SSM 12 SS-21
ATK GUNS 100mm: 68 T-12/MT-12

In 1991, the former Soviet Union transferred some 2,680 T-64/-72s, 2,428 ACVs and 6,900 arty to storage bases in Kaz. This eqpt is under Kaz control, but has deteriorated considerably. An eqpt destruction prog is about to begin.

Air Force 19,000

(incl Air Defence)
1 Air Force div, 164 cbt ac **Flying hours** 100
FTR 1 regt with 40 MiG-29
FGA 3 regt
1 with 14 Su-25
1 with 25 Su-24
1 with 14 Su-27
RECCE 1 regt with 12 Su-24*
ACP Tu-134, Tu-154
TRG 12 L-39, 4 Yak-18
HEL numerous Mi-8, Mi-29
STORAGE some 75 MiG-27/MiG-23/MiG-23UB/MiG-25/MiG-29/SU-27
AIR DEFENCE
FTR 1 regt with 43 MiG-31, 16 MiG-25
SAM 100 SA-2, SA-3, 27 SA-4, SA-5, 20 SA-6, S-300
MISSILES
ASM AS-7 *Kerry*, AS-9 *Kyle*, S-10 *Karen*, AS-11 *Killer*
AAM AA-6 *Acrid*, AA-7 *Apex*, AA *Aphid*

Paramilitary 34,500

STATE BORDER PROTECTION FORCES ε12,000 (Ministry of Interior) incl
MARITIME BORDER GUARD (3,000)
BASE Aktau (HQ) Bautino (Caspian)
PATROL AND COASTAL COMBATANTS 10
5 *Guardian* PCI<, 1 *Dauntless* PCI<, 4 *Almaty* PCI<, plus 5 boats†
INTERNAL SECURITY TROOPS ε20,000 (Ministry of Interior)
PRESIDENTIAL GUARD 2,000
GOVERNMENT GUARD 500

Kyrgyzstan Kgz

som s		1999	2000	2001	2002
GDP	s	43.5bn	62bn		
	US$	1.1bn	1.3bn		
per capita	US$	2,200	2,300		
Growth	%	3.6	5		
Inflation	%	39	18.7		
Debt	US$	1,193m	1,700m		
Def exp[a]	s	1,383m	1,500m		
	US$	35.5m	31.2m		
Def bdgt	s	950m	1,216m	2.0bn	
	US$	21.4m	25.3m	40.8m	
FMA (US)	US$	0.3m	0.4m	0.4m	
US$1=s		39.0	48.0	49	

[a] Incl exp on paramilitary forces

Population				4,733,000	
Kyrgyz 56% Russian 17% Uzbek 13% Ukrainian 3%					
Age		13–17	18–22	23–32	
Men		292,000	246,000	372,000	
Women		287,000	244,000	369,000	

Total Armed Forces

ACTIVE 9,000

Terms of service 18 months

RESERVES 57,000

Army 6,600

1 MRD
2 indep MR bde (mtn), 1 AD bde, 1 AAA regt, 3 SF bn
EQUIPMENT
  MBT 233 T-72
  RECCE 30 BRDM-2
  AIFV 274 BMP-1, 113 BMP-2
  APC 53 BTR-70, 10 BTR-80
  TOWED ARTY 141: **100mm**: 18 M-1944 (BS-3);
    122mm: 72 D-30, 35 M-30; **152mm**: 16 D-1
  SP ARTY 122mm: 18 2S1
  COMBINED GUN/MOR 120mm: 12 2S9
  MRL 122mm: 21 BM-21
  MOR 120mm: 6 2S12, 48 M-120
  ATGW 26 AT-3 *Sagger*
  ATK GUNS 100mm: 18 T-12/MT-12
  AD GUNS 23mm: 16 ZSU-23-4SP; **57mm**: 24 S-60
  SAM SA-7

Air Force 2,400

102 cbt ac, 9 attack hel
1 Ftr regt with 4 L-39, 48 MiG-21
1 Comp Avn regt with 2 An-12, 2 An-26
1 Hel regt with 9 Mi-24, 23 Mi-8
In store: 2 Mi-23, 24 L-39, 24 MiG-21

AIR DEFENCE
  SAM SA-2, SA-3, 12 SA-4

Forces Abroad

UN AND PEACEKEEPING
SIERRA LEONE (UNAMSIL): 2 obs

Paramilitary ε5,000

BORDER GUARDS ε5,000 (Kgz conscripts, RF officers)

Nepal N

rupee NR		1999	2000	2001	2002
GDP	NR	335bn	376bn		
	US$	5.0bn	5.4bn		
per capita	US$	1,500	1,500		
Growth	%	3.3	6		
Inflation	%	8.1	3.4		
Debt	US$	2.7bn	2.5bn		
Def exp	NR	2.8bn	3.5bn		
	US$	41.8m	50m		
Def bdgt	NR	3.5bn	3.5bn		
	US$	52m	50m		
FMA (US)	US$	0.2m	0.2m	0.2m	
US$1=NR		67.4	70.2	74.9	

Population				24,434,000	
Hindu 90% Buddhist 5% Muslim 3%					
Age		13–17	18–22	23–32	
Men		1,528,000	1,270,000	1,894,000	
Women		1,447,000	1,183,000	1,723,000	

Total Armed Forces

ACTIVE 46,000 (to be 50,000)

Army 46,000

1 Royal Guard bde (incl 1 MP bn) • 7 inf bde (16 inf bn)
• 44 indep inf coy • 1 SF bde (incl 1 AB bn, 2 indep SF
coy, 1 cav sqn (*Ferret*)) • 1 arty bde (1 arty, 1 AD regt) •
1 engr bde (4 bn)
EQUIPMENT
  RECCE 40 *Ferret*
  TOWED ARTY† **75mm**: 6 pack; **94mm**: 5 3.7in mtn
    (trg); **105mm**: 14 pack (ε6 op)
  MOR 81mm; **120mm**: 70 M-43 (ε12 op)
  AD GUNS 14.5mm: 30 PRC Type 56; **37mm**: PRC
    40mm: 2 L/60

AIR WING (215)

no cbt ac, or armed hel
TPT ac 1 BAe-748, 2 *Skyvan* **hel** 2 SA-316B *Chetak*, 1 SA-

Sri Lanka Ska

rupee Rs		1999	2000	2001	2002
GDP	Rs	1,113bn	1,255bn		
	US$	15.7bn	16.7bn		
per capita	US$	4,300	4,600		
Growth	%	4.2	5.4		
Inflation	%	4.7	6.2		
Debt	US$	8.9bn	9.5bn		
Def exp	Rs	57bn	66bn		
	US$	807m	880m		
Def bdgt	Rs	45bn	52bn		
	US$	635m	700m		
FMA (US)	US$	0.2m	0.2m	0.2m	
US$1=Rs		70.9	74.9	89.7	
Population					18,976,000

Sinhalese 74% Tamil 18% Moor 7%; Buddhist 69%
Hindu 15% Christian 8% Muslim 8%

Age	13–17	18–22	23–32
Men	927,000	930,000	1,601,000
Women	890,000	893,000	1,563,000

Total Armed Forces

ACTIVE ε118–123,000
(incl recalled reservists)

RESERVES 4,200
Army 1,100 **Navy** 1,100 **Air Force** 2,000
Obligation 7 years, post regular service

Army ε90–95,000

(incl 42,000 recalled reservists; ε1,000 women)
10 div • 3 mech inf bde • 1 air mobile bde • 23 inf bde
• 1 indep SF bde • 1 cdo bde • 1 armd regt • 3 armd
recce regt (bn) • 4 fd arty (1 reserve) • 4 fd engr regt (1
reserve)

EQUIPMENT
MBT ε65 T-55
RECCE 20 *Saladin*, 15 *Ferret*, 12 Daimler *Dingo*
AIFV 12 BMP-1, 40 BMP-2
APC 35 PRC Type-85, 10 BTR-152, 31 *Buffel*, 30
   Unicorn, 10 Shorland, 6 *Hotspur*, 30 *Saracen*, some
   BTR-80A
TOWED ARTY 76mm: 12 FRY M-48; **85mm**: 12 PRC
   Type-56; **88mm**: 12 25-pdr; **122mm**: some; **130mm**:
   12+ PRC Type-59-1; **152mm**: 33 PRC Type-66
MRL 122mm: 16 RM-70
MOR 81mm: 276; **82mm**: 100+; **107mm**: 12; **120mm**:
   36 M-43
RCL 105mm: 15 M-65; **106mm**: 34 M-40
AD GUNS 40mm: 24 L-40; **94mm**: 3 3.7in
SURV 2 AN/TPQ-36 (arty)
UAV 1 *Seeker*

Navy 18,000

(incl 2,100 recalled reservists)
BASES Colombo (HQ), Trincomalee (main base),
Karainagar, Tangalle, Kalpitiya, Galle, Welisara
PATROL AND COASTAL COMBATANTS 40
PATROL, OFFSHORE 3
   1 *Sukanya* PCO • 1 *Jayesagara* PCO • 1 *Parakrambahu*
   PCO
PATROL, COASTAL 5
   2 *Rana* PCC • 3 *Sooraya* PCC
PATROL, INSHORE 32
   3 *Dvora* PFI< • 8 *Super Dvora* PFI< • 3 ROC *Killer*
   PFI< • 10 *Colombo* PFI< • 6 *Trinity Marine* PFI< • 2
   Shaldag PFI< • plus some 36 boats
AMPHIBIOUS 1
   1 *Wuhu* LSM
   plus 7 craft: 2 LCM, 2 LCU, 1 ACV, 2 fast personnel
   carrier

Air Force 10,000

29 cbt ac, 20 armed hel **Flying hours** 420
FGA 4 F-7M, 1 FT-7, 2 FT-5, 12 *Kfir* (7 C-2, 1 TC-2, 4 C-
   7), 6 MiG-27M, 1 MiG-23UB (conversion trg), 2 FMA
   IA58A *Pucara*
ATTACK HEL 11 Bell 212, 6 Mi-24V, 3 Mi-35
TPT 1 sqn with **ac** 3 BAe 748, 2 C-130C, 1 Cessna 421C,
   1 *Super King Air*, 1 Y-8, 9 Y-12 (II), 4 An-24, 4 An-32B,
   1 Cessna 150 **hel** 3 Bell 412 (VIP)
HEL 9 Bell 206, 3 Mi-17 (plus 6 in store)
TRG ac 8 SF-260TP, 4 SF-260W (being replaced by 6 K-
   8), 10 CJ-6, 4 DHC-1, **hel** 3 Bell 206
RESERVES Air Force Regt, 3 sqn; Airfield
   Construction, 1 sqn
UAV 5 *Superhawk*

Paramilitary e88,600

POLICE FORCE (Ministry of Defence) 60,600
incl 30,400 reserves, 1,000 women and Special Task
Force: 3,000-strong anti-guerrilla unit
NATIONAL GUARD ε15,000
HOME GUARD 13,000

Opposition

LIBERATION TIGERS OF TAMIL EELAM (LTTE) ε6,000
Eqpt incl **122mm**, **152mm** arty, **120mm** mor; some
ATGW and SAM reported. 1 Robinson R-44 *Astro* lt hel
plus 2 lt ac for recce and liaison
Leader Velupillai Prabhakaran

Tajikistan Tjk

rouble Tr		1999	2000	2001	2002
GDP[a]	Tr	1,256bn	1,807bn		
	US$	1.2bn	1.3bn		
per capita	US$	1,000	1,000		
Growth	%	3.7	8.3		
Inflation	%	23	60		
Debt	US$	1.0bn	1.2bn		
Def exp	US$	ε92m	ε82m		
Def bdgt	US$	18m	19m		
US$1=Tr		1,035	1,436	2,350	
Population					6,225,000

Tajik 67% **Uzbek** 25% **Russian** 2% **Tatar** 2%

Age	13–17	18–22	23–32
Men	438,000	346,000	497,000
Women	424,000	338,000	484,000

Total Armed Forces

ACTIVE some 6,000

Terms of service 24 months
A number of potential officers are being trained at the Higher Army Officers and Engineers College, Dushanbe. It is planned to form an Air Force sqn and to acquire Su-25 from Bel; 5 Mi-24 and 10 Mi-8 have been procured.

Army some 6,000

2 MR bde (incl 1 trg), 1 mtn bde, 1 arty bde
1 SF bde, 1 SF det (εbn+)
1 SAM regt

EQUIPMENT
 MBT 33 T-72, 3 T-62
 AIFV 9 BMP-1, 25 BMP-2
 APC 1 BTR-60, 2 BTR-70, 26 BTR-80
 TOWED ARTY 122mm: 11 D-30
 MRL 122mm: 11 BM-21
 MOR 120mm: 9
 SAM 20 SA-2/-3/-7, *Stinger* (reported)
 HEL 10 Mi-24, 11 Mi-8

Paramilitary ε1,200

BORDER GUARDS ε1,200 (Ministry of Interior)

Opposition

ISLAMIC MOVEMENT OF TAJIKISTAN some 5,000
Signed peace accord with govt on 27 Jun 1997. Integration with govt forces slowly proceeding

Foreign Forces

RUSSIA Frontier Forces ε14,500 (Tjk conscripts, RF officers) **Army** 8,000; 1 MRD
 EQUIPMENT
  MBT 128 T-72
  AIFV/APC 314 BMP-2, BRM-1K, BTR-80
  SP ARTY 122mm: 66 2S1; **152mm:** 54 2S3
  MRL 122mm: 12 BM-21; **220mm:** 12 9P140
  MOR 120mm: 36 PM-38
 AIR DEFENCE
  SAM 20 SA-8

Turkmenistan Tkm

manat		1999	2000	2001	2002
GDP	US$	ε3.3bn	ε4.4bn		
per capita	US$	2,200	2,600		
Growth	%	18.5	17.6		
Inflation	%	27			
Debt	US$	2.0bn	2.4bn		
Def exp	US$	ε109m	ε176m		
Def bdgt	US$	108m	157m		
FMA (US)	US$	0.3m	0.3m	0.3m	
US$1=manat		5,350	5,350	5,200	
Population					4,450,000

Turkmen 77% **Uzbek** 9% **Russian** 7% **Kazak** 2%

Age	13–17	18–22	23–32
Men	275,000	228,000	361,000
Women	268,000	224,000	357,000

Total Armed Forces

ACTIVE 17,500

Terms of service 24 months

Army 14,500

5 Mil Districts • 4 MRD (1 trg) • 1 arty bde • 1 MRL regt • 1 ATK regt •1 engr regt • 2 SAM bde • 1 indep air aslt bn

EQUIPMENT
 MBT 702 T-72
 RECCE 170 BRDM/BRDM-2
 AIFV 930 BMP-1/-2, 12 BRM
 APC 829 BTR (-60/-70/-80)
 TOWED ARTY 122mm: 197 D-30; **152mm:** 17 D-1, 72 D-20
 SP ARTY 122mm: 40 2S1
 COMBINED GUN/MOR 120mm: 17 2S9
 MRL 122mm: 56 BM-21, 9 9P138
 MOR 82mm: 31; **120mm:** 66 PM-38
 ATGW 100 AT-3 *Sagger*, AT-4 *Spigot*, AT-5 *Spandrel*, AT-6 *Spiral*

MILITARY DEVELOPMENTS

The most significant issue for the region is US policy towards the Pacific area and particularly towards Taiwan. Missile defence, the boosting of arms sales to Taiwan, and the strengthening of the US–Japan alliance has placed the new US administration of President George W. Bush in a more challenging position towards China. While economic prosperity is Beijing's top priority, the Chinese government sees it as essential to increase defence spending and to modernise its military in order to counter the threats it perceives.

Driven by events in East Timor and elsewhere in the region, Australia is reconfiguring its defence priorities. The need to redefine defence and security policy has led to far-reaching reforms in the country's armed forces. The December 2000 White Paper *Defence 2000: Our Future Defence Force*, and the following discussion paper *Defence 2000 and the Defence of Australia*, set out strategy and priorities for the development of the three armed services. The document draws on experience in East Timor and places emphasis on a regional power-projection capability.

Considerable potential for instability in the region lies in South-east Asia. Indonesia and the Philippines continue to struggle with rebel movements intent on separatism. Maritime piracy is also increasing in the area.

Naval capabilities are being slowly expanded across the region. Six countries have acquired submarines and advanced surface ships to enhance their capability to carry out blue-water operations and sea-control strategies. However, no country in the region yet has firm plans to expand their navies further by acquiring significant power-projection assets such as aircraft carriers or sea-launched land-attack missiles in the short term. Therefore the United States' Pacific Fleet, although reduced in strength by about 40% since 1990, is still the overwhelming naval power in the region; with 135,000 personnel, 27 nuclear-powered attack submarines (SSN) and six carrier battle groups. The Russian Pacific Fleet, in contrast, is vastly reduced in strength and will almost certainly not renew its lease on Cam Ranh Bay naval base in Vietnam after 2004.

North-east Asia

China is aiming to restructure, re-equip, and modernise its armed forces. The strategy paper, *China's National Defence in 2000*, published in October 2000, lays down policy and restructuring priorities for the next five years.

The strategy document lacks any specific information on how its goals will be accomplished, but it emphasises the need for modernisation. As part of the restructuring process, the People's Liberation Army (PLA) has been striving to reduce its dependence on conscripts, with a goal of cutting them from 82% to 65% of military personnel. Recruitment is not believed to be a problem. It is currently only necessary to draft one eligible male in ten to fill the PLA's manpower requirements. However, funding a fully professional army may be difficult to achieve without significantly increased expenditure. Reform of the ground forces is also taking place with the creation of so-called 'Fist Formations' designed to react quickly to external and internal threats. The principle rationale for change is given as the need to respond to the strengthening US–Japan alliance, US weapon sales to Taiwan, and concerns about US missile defence plans in the region. A specific requirement indicated in *China's National Defence in 2000* is for strategies to combat US carrier groups. The purchase from Russia of two *Sovremenny*-class destroyers armed with SS-N-22 *Sunburn* missiles may indicate that this need is being addressed.

China continues to concentrate on gradually increasing the capabilities of its submarine fleet. The Type 093 SSN is in build in China and is a modified version of the Russian *Victor* 3 SSN; the

ATK GUNS 100mm: 72 T-12/MT-12
AD GUNS 23mm: 48 ZSU-23-4 SP; 57mm: 22 S-60
SAM 40 SA-8, 13 SA-13

Navy none

Has announced intention to form a Navy/Coast Guard and
has minor base at Turkmenbashy with 5 boats. Caspian Sea
Flotilla (see **Russia**) is operating as a joint RF, Kaz and Tkm
flotilla under RF comd based at Astrakhan.

Air Force 3,000

(incl Air Defence)
89 cbt ac (plus 200 in store)
FGA/FTR 2 avn sqns with 24 MiG-29 (incl 2 -U), 65 Su-
17
IN STORE 46 Su-25, 120 MiG-23, 10 MiG-23U, 24 MiG-
25
TPT/GENERAL PURPOSE 1 composite avn sqn with
1 An-26, 10 Mi-24, 8 Mi-8
TRG 1 unit with 3 Su-7B, 2 L-39
AIR DEFENCE
SAM 50 SA-2/-3/-5

Uzbekistan Uz

som s		1999	2000	2001	2002
GDP	s	1,942bn	2,523bn		
	US$	15.9bn	18.9bn		
per capita	US$	2,900	3,000		
Growth	%	4.4	4		
Inflation	%	20	28		
Debt	US$	4.2bn	4.5bn		
Def exp[a]	US$	1.3bn	1.5bn		
Def bdgt	US$	285m	300m		
FMA (US)	US$	0.5m	0.5m	0.5m	
US$1=s		122	133	337	

[a] Incl exp on paramilitary forces

Population			24,576,000

Uzbek 73% Russian 6% Tajik 5% Kazak 4% Karakalpak
2% Tatar 2% Korean <1% Ukrainian <1%

Age	13–17	18–22	23–32
Men	1,555,000	1,298,000	1,921,000
Women	1,520,000	1,281,000	1,962,000

Total Armed Forces

ACTIVE some 50–55,000
(incl MoD staff and centrally controlled units)
Terms of service conscription, 18 months

Army 40,000

4 Mil Districts, 2 op comd, 1 Tashkent comd

1 tk, 11 MR, 1 lt mtn, 1 AB, 3 air aslt, 5 engr bde
1 National Guard bde
EQUIPMENT
MBT 190 T-62, 100 T-64, 60 T-72
RECCE 13 BRDM-2
AIFV 160 BMP-2, 120 BMD-1, 9 BMD-2, 6 BRM
APC 25 BTR-70, 24 BTR-60, 210 BTR-80, 50 BTR-D
TOWED ARTY 122mm: 70 D-30; 152mm: 140 2A36
SP ARTY 122mm: 18 2S1; 152mm: 17 2S3, 2S5
(reported); 203mm: 48 2S7
COMBINED GUN/MOR 120mm: 54 2S9
MRL 122mm: 36 BM-21, 24 9P138; 220mm: 48 9P140
MOR 120mm: 18 PM-120, 19 2S12, 5 2B11
ATK GUNS 100mm: 36 T-12/MT-12

(In 1991 the former Soviet Union transferred some 2,000 tanks
(T-64), 1,200 ACV and 750 arty to storage bases in Uz. This eqpt
is under Uz control, but has deteriorated considerably.)

Air Force some 10–15,000

7 fixed wg and hel regts
135 cbt ac (plus 30 in store), 42 attack hel
BBR/FGA 1 regt with 20 Su-25/Su-25BM, 26 Su-
17MZ/Su-17UMZ, 1 regt with 23 Su-24, 11 Su-24MP
(recce)
FTR 1 regt with 30 MiG-29/MiG-29UB, 1 regt with 25
Su-27/Su-27UB
IN STORE 30 MiG-29/-29UB
TPT/ELINT 1 regt with 26 An-12/An-12PP, 13 An-26/
An-26RKR
TPT 1 Tu-134, 1 An-24
TRG 14 L-39 (9 in store), 1 Su-17
HELICOPTERS
1 regt with 42 Mi-24 (attack), 29 Mi-8 (aslt/tpt), 1 Mi-
26 (tpt)
1 regt with 26 Mi-6 (tpt), 2 Mi-6AYa (cmd post), 29
Mi-8 (aslt/tpt)
MISSILES
AAM AA-8, AA-10, AA-11
ASM AS-7, AS-9, AS-10, AS-11, AS-12
SAM 45 SA-2/-3/-5

Paramilitary ε18–20,000

INTERNAL SECURITY TROOPS (Ministry of Interior) ε17–
19,000

NATIONAL GUARD (Ministry of Defence) 1,000
1 bde

Opposition

ISLAMIC MOVEMENT OF UZBEKISTAN

ε2,000 **Leader** Tahir Yoldosh **Based** near Kunduz, Afg;
sometimes supported by Juma Numangoni, warlord,
based in Tjk or Afg

first of the class is not expected to be in service until 2005 at the earliest. The in-service date for the Type 094 nuclear-fuelled ballistic-missile submarine (SSBN) has been further delayed until the end of the decade. It will replace China's single *Xia*-class SSBN, and again be built in China with Russian help. Progress is being made towards bringing new diesel submarines (SSK) into service, with a second indigenous *Song*-class and a second improved *Ming* being commissioned in 2001. However, it is believed that both classes, as well as the four *Kilo*-class submarines already in service, have operational problems that have yet to be overcome.

Another priority area cited by the strategy paper is information warfare. This is highlighted as a key requirement in the policy document, and is an aspect of modern warfare that is being incorporated into the PLA's training exercises.

Development and testing of new submarine-launched ballistic missiles (SLBMs) and intercontinental ballistic missiles (ICBMs) continue slowly. The *Dong-feng* 31 (CSS-X-9) ICBM is believed to be undergoing testing as is the intermediate-range ballistic missile (IRBM) CSS-5 *Dong-feng* 21 which is due to replace the CSS-2 *Dong-feng* 3.

An increasing internal-security problem for China is Uighur separatism in Xinjiang province. The police and Interior Forces bear the brunt of dealing with the threat inside China, but there is concern that the problem is spreading and that the military in the province are vulnerable to terrorist attack. A mechanism under the Shanghai Agreement on Cooperation (formerly the Shanghai-5) has been set up for exchanging information with the countries of Central Asia on separatists on both sides of the Chinese border. This is part of China's strategy for containing the threat, as is military assistance to Central Asian countries, for example Kyrgyzstan, which is not only faced by the threat of insurgency from Tajikistan, but also has a substantial Uighur population, as does Kazakstan. Uighur fighters are now believed to be fighting in the ranks of the Islamic Movement of Uzbekistan (IMU).

Against a backdrop of Chinese criticism of US missile defence plans, **Taiwan** is improving its capability in this area with the acquisition of the US *Patriot* Advanced Capability (PAC) 3 missile system for defence against short-range ballistic missiles and cruise missiles. Taipei has also requested destroyers equipped with the *Aegis* radar system, which would enable use of the US *Navy Theater-Wide* (NTW) missile defence system when it becomes operational. The US is not offering this equipment in the short-term but the existing enhancements to Taiwan's defence still give grounds for increased tension between the US and China. The four *Kidd*-class destroyers being delivered to the Taiwanese navy provide it with an efficient counter to the *Sovremenny* destroyers that China acquired from Russia.

The gap between the Taiwanese and Chinese navies will narrow if Taiwan receives all the naval assets offered by the United States in April 2001 – including eight SSKs, the four *Kidd*-class destroyers, and 12 P-3 *Orion* maritime patrol aircraft (MPA) – but it is unlikely that all the equipment will be received. The United States does not produce its own-design diesel submarines, although it is about to produce four Dutch-designed *Moray*-class SSKs for Egypt under licence. The Dutch, German and Swedish governments have said that they will not cooperate with the Americans in building an SSK for Taiwan. No other major producer has offered to assist and so, at best, there will be a considerable delay in transferring the SSKs. There are also difficulties with the *Kidd* acquisition as Taiwan does not have a military port large enough to berth and maintain these vessels; it is thought probable that a civilian port will be adapted for the purpose.

Japan In December 2000, the Japanese Security Council and Cabinet adopted the Mid-Term Defence Programme (MTDP) for fiscal years (FY) 2001–05. The programme sets out priorities for defence development. Amongst these is the need to develop measures to counter cyber-attack

and to secure all means of information technology and communications. The programme also stipulates the need to develop measures to counter, and to cope with, attack by irregular forces, possibly armed with nuclear, biological, or chemical devices.

The Self-Defense Force (SDF) is to be reduced to about 166,000 under the programme. The structure of the Ground Self-Defense Force following the reorganisation, which is to be complete by the end of the MTDP period, will include ten divisions, four brigades and one combined-arms brigade. The programme also highlights the need to enhance air and sea defence.

The Japanese Air Defense Force has finally achieved funding for in-flight refuelling capability, provoking some concern in the region that Japan may be departing from its constitutional commitment to maintaining self-defence forces only. The four new tankers will allow coastal air patrols to remain airborne for longer as well as to reduce fuel costs by decreasing the current frequency of take-off and landing operations.

Japan is also expanding its naval capabilities. It has commissioned the fourth of a projected eight *Oyashio*-class SSK and the seventh of nine *Murasame*-class destroyers; although these will replace rather than extend capabilities. The MTDP, published in 2001, outlined plans for 15 new surface ships and development of a 13,500 tonne helicopter-carrying destroyer, similar in design to a small aircraft carrier, is underway. Even if, as Japan is keen to stress, the proposed ship is not a carrier, its entry into service would make it the Maritime Self-Defense Force's first asset with a capability for force projection. The Maritime Self-Defense Force is also carrying out training in a broader spectrum than before; for example, Exercise *Keen Sword* in November 2000 was the largest-ever combined US–Japan naval exercise.

Events in East Timor, and particularly the International Force in East Timor (INTERFET) and United Nations Transitional Administration in East Timor (UNTAET) missions, have stimulated debate over greater Japanese participation in Peace Support Operations (PSO). There is little sign of any imminent change to Article 9 of the country's constitution, which only allows deployment of non-combatant forces. However, regional pressures for greater Japanese involvement in multinational PSO are seen as making a revision more likely, particularly as this is an explicit objective of Japan's new prime minister, Junichiro Koizumi.

Stable relations have continued between **North Korea** and **South Korea** since the June 2000 summit meeting between their presidents Kim Jong Il and Kim Dae Jung. However, the engagement process lost some momentum in early 2001 as the new US administration reviewed policy towards Pyonyang, adopting a more cautious approach towards Kim Dae Jung's 'Sunshine Policy' towards the North. Little of note changed in the defence aspect of the bi-lateral relationship in the year to August 2001. South Korea is due to make a decision on which aircraft will replace its air force's ageing fighter component, but this decision may be delayed until after the presidential election in 2002. Paradoxically, improved relations with North Korea have not boosted Kim Dae Jung's popularity and he may prefer to delay this expensive re-equipment programme. South Korea is, however, going ahead with the expansion of its submarine and surface fleets.

Following Kim Jong Il's visit to Moscow in August 2001, a statement by the North Korean and Russian leaders underlined Pyongyang's intention to continue adherence to the 1999 moratorium on its missile programme. This is seen as a minor success for Russian President Vladimir Putin in the context of US missile defence plans. It is reported that, in return, Russia may be about to sell Su-24 and MiG-29 aircraft and naval equipment to North Korea.

Australasia and South-east Asia

Australia published its White Paper, *Our Future Defence Force* in December 2000, and the Department of Defence discussion document *Defence 2000 and the Defence of Australia* in April

2001. The papers set four distinct defence priorities:

- territorial defence;
- fostering the security of the neighbouring area;
- working with other powers to promote stability in South-east Asia; and
- contributing in appropriate ways to maintaining strategic stability in the wider Asia-Pacific region.

Many decisions in the paper are driven by Australia's experience in East Timor and by a sense that Australia is a natural leader in multi-national operations in the region. The US has made it clear that it regards Australia as its natural ally in the area, and it is also clear that the Australian military has drawn on the experience of US 'battlefield laboratories' in its force-development programmes.

A key difference between this White Paper and its predecessors is that it is tied to a Defence Capability Plan, designed to maintain a balanced force deployable at short notice. Capital equipment programmes outlined in the paper are aimed at improving force-projection and force-protection capabilities. The proposed acquisition of Airborne Early Warning (AEW) aircraft, and three amphibious ships, are clear indications of this principle in the new strategy. Another of the paper's conclusions is that Australia must enhance the compatibility of its military equipment with that of its allies to improve cooperation in multi-national operations. Naval surface capabilities are also being reinforced with the third of eight *Anzac*-class frigates commissioned in 2001. It is planned to upgrade this class by adding *Harpoon* surface-to-surface missiles. The planned procurement of at least three destroyers between 2010 and 2014 to replace the current *Adelaide*-class frigates will also considerably enhance naval capabilities. Current amphibious capabilities have been increased with the return to service of the two former *Newport* Landing Ship Tank (LST) vessels following their conversion to Landing Platforms Amphibious (LPA). The trimaran *Jervis Bay*, a temporary replacement for them, has consequently returned to merchant service.

The thrust of **New Zealand**'s defence policy has changed. During the 1990s, defence was seen as a foreign-policy tool. Naval, air, land and Special Forces all contributed to coalition operations, which maintained the country's international standing and reputation with key allies such as the US and Australia. However, the Labour/Alliance coalition government that took power in 1999 has adopted a less engaged approach in which the primary form of international involvement will be deployment of army formations on peacekeeping operations. There will be considerably less emphasis on air and naval combat capability. It appears that only maritime surveillance using surface ships and aircraft is given priority in the government's still-emerging defence policy. Strike capability based on frigates, attack aircraft, and long-range maritime patrol/anti-submarine warfare Lockheed P-3K *Orions* has been reduced. Press reports indicate that while the P-3s will be retained for the time being, civilian surveillance of the Exclusive Economic Zone is being considered as a policy option.

Meanwhile, New Zealand's only sealift ship, *Charles Upham,* has been scrapped, and there is no intention of replacing it. The two *Anzac*-class frigates may also be scrapped, leaving the country with hardly any naval capabilities. It has also been confirmed that the Royal New Zealand Air Force's air-combat role is to be dropped. However, reflecting the priority given to the army's ability to participate in peace-support operations, the New Zealand battalion group in East Timor was a highly-valued enhancement to the combat capability of INTERFET.

Singapore continues to build defence relations with international partners, working through The Association of South East Asian Nations (ASEAN), and also through the Five Power Defence Arrangement (FPDA) with the UK, New Zealand, Australia and Malaysia to strengthen its position in the region. The policy paper *Defending Singapore in the 21st Century*, published at the end of 2000, lays out Singapore's defence priorities. These are firstly, maintaining a credible deterrent against invasion and secondly, strengthening the concept of 'total defence' in which the entire population is involved in a response to crises. The policy paper also includes measures, including equipment enhancements, to tackle the problem of piracy in the neighbouring Strait of Malacca, which is a major concern to Singapore. Singapore has played a major role in INTERFET and UNTAET missions in East Timor to which it has contributed approximately 400 personnel, three LSTs and a C-130 *Hercules* aircraft.

Indonesia and the **Philippines** are the most unstable areas in South-east Asia. In the Philippines, the *Abu Sayyaf* group has continued its attempt to create a separate Islamic state in west Mindanao with a campaign characterised largely by terrorism and hostage-taking. Four other groups listed in table 39 on page 306 are also fighting the government. However, on 7 August 2001 the Moro Islamic Front, which has been seeking to create an independent Islamic state in Bangsa Moro, declared a cease-fire and formed an alliance with the more moderate Moro National Liberation Front (MNLF).

In Indonesia, the violence in Aceh province continues, and on 10 August 2001, 31 people believed to be plantation workers were the victims of a terrorist attack by the Free Aceh Movement. The new Indonesian president, Megawati Sukarnoputri, who replaced the ousted Abdurrahman Wahid in July 2001, is believed to be more likely to adopt a hardline approach to unrest in the provinces. The authorities are keen to eliminate independence movements in the Maluki Islands and West Papua, as well as Aceh in order to avoid a repetition of the crisis in East Timor. Megawati sees the military as an important power base, and may give the army a freer hand in quelling unrest than did her predecessor. She may also be less likely to bring in reforms that would put the armed forces under civilian control. The US has also indicated that it sees the Indonesian military as an important factor in re-establishing stability in the country. However, any US assistance to the government in Jakarta will be tempered by concerns over human rights.

In the **South-west Pacific**, area indigenous and cultural issues remain grounds for unrest. There is the possibility of renewed fighting in the Solomon Islands, and instability lingers below the surface in Fiji and Papua New Guinea.

The incidence of **maritime piracy** in the region, especially in South-east Asia, has risen rapidly in the past year. In 2000, Indonesian territorial waters accounted for 119 incidents, a quarter of the global total according to the International Maritime Bureau. The Malacca Strait accounted for a further 75, a substantial increase on the 37 incidents in 1999. The rise in piracy attacks has prompted some states to hold combined anti-piracy exercises – the most prominent being held in November 2000 with the Indian Navy, Japanese Maritime Self-Defense Force and the Malaysian Navy off the Indian eastern seaboard. However, despite separate offers by both the Indian and Japanese governments to mount anti-piracy patrols in the Malacca Strait, no regional agreement has yet been reached on such an operation.

DEFENCE SPENDING

Regional Trends Recovery from the financial crisis of 1997–98 strengthened in 2000 with a rise in regional gross domestic product (GDP) of over 7%. Several countries benefited from lower domestic interest rates and more competitive exchange rates together with action taken to reduce the impact of non-performing loans. The strength of the US economy and relatively benign inflation throughout the region saw several countries report double-figure export growth, particularly in the information and communications sectors.

Defence spending in the region increased from $135bn in 1999 to $142bn in 2000. However, early indications from budgets published for 2001 suggest that the rise in regional spending since the financial crisis will come to a halt, particularly if the US dollar strengthens.

However, in the first half of 2001, the economic outlook for East Asia has deteriorated palpably. Declining import demand in the United States, especially for the information-technology products in which many of the region's exporters specialise, will result in a significant slowdown in growth across the region for the year as a whole. Many countries will try to compensate by applying fiscal stimuli, but few have the resources to do so effectively. As export earnings fall and still-robust balance-of-payments positions start to deteriorate, local currencies could come under more pressure.

China showed continuing strong economic growth in 2000. Real GDP growth was 7.8%, up from 7.1% in 1999, driven by an acceleration in industrial growth. Further steps were taken towards liberalising the financial sector for entry into the World Trade Organisation and, with strong growth in the US and the recovery of Asian countries affected by the 1997–98 crisis, export growth surged 27%.

China's official defence budget increased by 17.7% from Y120bn to Y141bn. The increase in spending was intended to improve military salaries in order to attract and retain skilled personnel, who are becoming increasingly drawn to the private sector. Part of the personnel costs shown in the budget are believed to be compensation for the closure of commercial enterprises formerly run by the PLA. These businesses generated income for the PLA budget in the past, but have now been transferred to civilian control. Once compensation has been paid, it is possible, but by no means certain, that this aspect of expenditure could decrease over time. Meanwhile, the real size of China's defence spending remains a mystery. It is generally believed that the official budget accounts for little more than personnel and operational costs. Other significant items including procurement, military research and development and pensions for retired personnel are funded from elsewhere in the national budget. Therefore, purchases such as Russian built Su-27 and Su-30 fighter aircraft are not included in the official budget. *The Military Balance* estimates that real military spending in 2000 was around $42bn, approximately 5.3% of China's GDP.

During the year China signed a contract covering the procurement of KH-35 long-range anti-ship missiles to be integrated with the *Sukhoi* Su-30MKK, suggesting that the latest batch of 40 aircraft are to be deployed by China's naval aviation force.

Further progress was made on the development of China's first land-attack cruise missile, a terminally-guided development of the air-launched YJ-6C/C-601 anti-ship missile. The missile, known as the YJ-63, carries a 500kg warhead and would be more accurate than the short-range ballistic missiles China is currently deploying along the Taiwan Strait. It would join the *Hong Niao* family of cruise missiles that entered service for operational evaluation in 1992.

The army began fielding the new Type 98 main battle tank, the most advanced MBT to enter the service.

Japan Despite its fragile economy and a 2.7% cut in the federal budget, defence spending rose 0.4% in 2000 to ¥4,955bn. At the same time the Japanese government cleared a ¥25trn defence spending programme for the next five years. Included in the defence funds are ¥5.3bn to start development of a new maritime patrol aircraft and the new C-X military transport aircraft. The spending programme includes ¥90bn for four in-flight refuelling tankers, stirring controversy that Japan may be planning to depart from its constitutional commitment to self-defence only. The plan also covers procurement of 47 Mitsubishi F-2 fighters, the first of which was deployed at Misawa Air Base in late 2000 and a new 13,500-tonne helicopter-carrying destroyer.

South Korea increased its defence budget for 2001 by 6.5% to won15.4bn ($11.8bn) despite the continuing improvement in the political climate on the peninsula. However, the weakness of the won in 2001 means that the effective buying power of the Ministry of National Defence (MND) has decreased as most equipment is imported.

The MND plans to launch 20 new force-development projects in 2001, including four long awaited major programmes: the AHX combat helicopter, the SAM-X surface-to-air missile to replace the *Nike Hercules*, the F-X advanced fighter and the KDX-3 destroyer, which is expected to provide the navy with an *Aegis*-type capability.

The fate of the supersonic trainer/light combat aircraft, T/A-50 *Golden Eagle* programme (formerly known as the KTX-2) is less clear. The tight fiscal budget that is required in preparation for the cost of reunification could threaten certain defence programmes. In a move to keep open the manufacturing lines that would finally produce the aircraft, the MND has opted to build another 20 Block 52 advanced medium-range air-to-air missile (AMRAAM)-capable F-16s on top of the original order of 120, the last of which was delivered in 2000.

In the competition for a new fighter aircraft for the South Korean air force, Boeing was assumed to be front runner to win the $4bn contract for 40 multi-role aircraft. (Boeing needs to keep its F-15 line open pending a decision on who will build the Joint Strike Fighter.) Others in contention are Dassault, marketing the *Rafale*, and EADS, who see a South Korean order as critical for sales of *Eurofighter* to other modernising customers such as Singapore. In the end, the stable and traditional relationship with the US may prove a key factor. Nevertheless, the decision could be postponed to the end of 2002 after the presidential election.

Another major project is the development of an airborne early warning and control aircraft. The E-X project received the go-ahead in October after several years' hesitation over the cost. The contract is due to be awarded by 2002 with deliveries completed by 2008.

The navy has ordered three advanced German-designed AIP Type 214 SSKs for delivery by 2009 and will commission the ninth and final Type 209 *Chang Bogo* SSK in late 2001. Three KDX-2 destroyers are in build with an in-service date of 2003–05; three more could be ordered. In the 2002 defence budget, funding has been given for up to six follow-on KDX-3 destroyers, with the 100km-range US SM2 block VI-A TMD system. No other country in the region, including Japan, has a theatre missile defence capability. The South Korean navy has plans for a 12,500 tonne Landing Platform Dock (LPD) and a small short take-off and vertical-landing aircraft carrier, but these are unlikely to be ordered until the middle of the next decade.

Australia Following from the December 2000 White Paper, *Our Future Defence Force*, and the discussion document *Defence 2000 and the Defence of Australia* in April 2001, Australia's government confirmed that it would increase defence spending in line with the recommendations. An additional A$4.7bn ($2.46bn) will be injected into the defence budget over the next four years and a total of A$23.5bn ($12.3bn) over the next decade.

The defence budget is to increase at an average of 3% per year in real terms over the next decade and this will be supplemented by efficiency gains from the reform programme initiated two years ago.

The defence industry has been given a more certain basis for business planning and a total of 38 major capital equipment acquisition projects worth around A$5.5bn have been approved, including:

- options to acquire up to 100 new aircraft to replace the F/A-18 and the F-111
- five new air-to-air refuelling tankers
- four Airborne Early Warning and Communications (AEW&C) aircraft with an option on a further three

- an upgrade for the C-130 fleet
- two squadrons of armed reconnaissance helicopters to enter service by 2004
- one squadron of 12 troop-lift helicopters
- continuing upgrade of P-3C *Orion* maritime patrol aircraft
- major upgrade of the M113 fleet
- tactical unmanned aerial vehicles (UAV) to enter service from 2003
- *Anzac* frigates to be fitted with anti-ship missile systems
- new class of three air-defence capable ships.

Singapore's defence budget for 2001 is up from S$7.4bn (US$4.4bn) to S$7.8bn (US$4.3bn). Following the order in 2000 for six modified *La Fayette* frigates, the major order in 2001 was for a further 20 F-16C/D fighter aircraft. To meet its main defence tasks the navy received in 2001 the final *Sjoormen* SSK of its order of four from Sweden. Two of these are in service, although it will be several years before the Singaporean navy has the experience to operate them to their full potential. The navy is also awaiting the delivery of six French *La Fayette*-class frigates between 2005 and 2009. These will substantially increase its surface capabilities, as it has never had such a large class of surface ship before. Changi naval base has been opened and received the US Navy's aircraft carrier *Kitty Hawk* in March 2001.

In **Thailand** the defence budget was virtually unchanged at b77.2bn ($1.7bn). The navy requested further funds to buy more warships despite the fact that the helicopter carrier *Chakri Narubetr* was anchored for much of the year to save operating costs. Both **Malaysia** and Thailand are interested in acquiring diesel submarines, probably by means of short-term leases. Malaysia has received competing offers of second-hand SSKs from France, Germany and the Netherlands but has yet to place an order. It has, however, ordered six *Meko*-100 offshore patrol craft for delivery in 2004, mainly to patrol its Exclusive Economic Zone. The Thai navy is very anxious to acquire one or possibly two SSKs, probably German Type 206s, but still lacks the funds to do so. It also intends to order two, and possibly a further two, offshore patrol craft for an initial delivery date of 2003, but it has not yet placed an order.

The **Taiwan** defence budget for 2001 was originally projected at NT$320bn but was later cut to NT$271bn to ease pressure on government spending. Even so, defence still accounts for 16.9% of overall expenditure. This figure is not compatible with the 2000 defence budget, which covered an 18-month period; Taiwan switched to a calendar-based year for 2001. Officials also announced plans gradually to reduce the armed forces by almost 30% from 376,000 to 270,000 personnel over the next 10 years.

In April the Bush administration offered a major weapons package to Taiwan, although it stopped short of including the advanced *Aegis*-type destroyer. Included in the items available for purchase are eight diesel powered submarines, four *Kidd*-class destroyers, up to 12 P-3 *Orion* anti-submarine warfare aircraft, *Paladin* self-propelled artillery, MH-53 minesweeper helicopters, AAV7A1 amphibious-assault vehicles, *Harpoon* anti-ship missiles and MK-8 Mod-4 torpedoes. Whilst the *Kidd*-class destroyers lack the capabilities of the *Aegis* radar and cannot launch *Standard* air-defence missiles, they would provide a credible answer to the four *Sovremenny*-class destroyers that China is in the process of acquiring from Russia.

Also included in the deal are technical briefings on *Patriot* PAC-3, which would be the first step in upgrading Taiwan's current *Patriot* anti-missile force.

The **Philippines** would like to buy new patrol craft. Funds were set aside for this purpose in the July 2001 budget so a small order may be forthcoming. **Indonesia** cannot afford to replace its ageing fleet, which was estimated by former defence minister Juwono Sudarsono in early 2001 to be well-below the acceptable standard of readiness.

However, the Indonesian military is considering the purchase of Russian arms, including a quantity of Su-30 fighter-bombers. With scant financial resources it is difficult to see how a large deal such as this could be paid for.

Table 22 Arms orders and deliveries, East Asia and Australasia, 1998–2001

Country supplier	Classification ⇩	Designation	Quantity ⇩	Order date	Delivery date	Comment ⇩
Australia dom	SSK	Collins	6	1987	1996	Swe license. Deliveries to 2000
dom	FGA	F-111	71	1990	1999	Upgrade of F/RF-111C
Ca	LACV	ASLAV	276	1992	1996	2nd batch of 150 for delivery 2002–03
dom	MHC	Huon	6	1994	1999	Last delivery 2002
dom	FGA	F-111	36	1995	2000	Upgrade continuing
US	MPA	P-3C	17	1996	1999	Upgrade to AP-3C
US	tpt	C-130J	12	1996	1999	Deliveries to 2000. 2-year slippage
US	hel	SH-2G	11	1997	2000	Deliveries to 2002. Penguin ASSM (No)
UK	trg	Hawk-100	33	1997	1999	Final delivery 2006
US	hel	CH-47D	2	1997	1999	Follow-on; 4 D models delivered 1994
UK	FGA	F/A-18	71	1998	2005	Upgrade
dom	FF	Anzac	6	1999	2001	Upgrade to 2006
dom	LACV	Bushmaster	370	1999	2000	55 delivered in 2000
No	ASSM	Penguin		1999	2003	For use with SH-2G
US	AAM	AMRAAM		2000		
US	hel	S-70B2	16	2000		Upgrade
US	AEWAC	Boeing 737	4	2000	2007	Option on further 3
Brunei UK	FSG	FSG	3	1995	2001	Scaled-down version of Leiku FF
UK	trg	Hawk 100/20	10	1996	1999	
Indo	MPA	CN-235	3	1996	1999	Requirement for up to 12
Fr	SAM	Mistral	16	1997	1999	Launchers
Fr	ASSM	Exocet	59	1997	1999	
Fr	SAM	Mistral	16	1998	1999	16 launchers
China dom	ICBM	DF-41		1985	2005	Dev; range 12,000km
dom	ICBM	DF-31		1985	2005	Dev; range 8,000km. Tested Aug 1999
dom	SLBM	JL-2		1985	2008	Dev; range 8,000km
dom	SSGN	Type 093	1	1985	2006	Similar to RF Victor 3. Launch expected 2000
dom	SSBN	Type 094	4	1985	2009	Dev programme
dom	ASSM	C701			1999	Dev completed
dom	bbr	H-6			1998	Still in production
dom	MBT	Type-85-III	400	1985	1990	Dev complete 1997
Fr	hel	AS-365	50	1986	1989	Local production continues
dom	MBT	Type-90		1987		For export only. No prod by 1997
dom	FGA	JH-7	20	1988	1993	Upgrade to FBC-2 standard has begun
dom	SRBM	DF-11	100	1988	1996	Production continuing
dom	SRBM	DF-15	300	1988	1996	Production continuing
dom	FGA	FC-1		1990	2005	With Pak (150 units). 1st flight in 2000
col	hel	EC-120		1990		In dev with Fr and Sgp
RF	SAM	S-300	30	1990	1992	Continued in 1998
dom	FGA	F-8IIM		1993	1996	Modernisation completed 1999
dom	FGA	F-10		1993		Dev continues

Country supplier ⇩	Classification ⇩	Designation	Quantity ⇩	Order date	Delivery date	Comment ⇩
RF	SS	*Kilo*	4	1993	1995	Deliveries to 1999. 2 Type 877, 2 Type 636
dom	SS	*Song*	2	1994	2002	2 *Song* under construction at Wuhan
RF	SAM	**SA-15**	35	1995	1997	Orders: 15 (1995), 20 (1999). Deliveries to 2000
dom	AGI	*Shiyan* 970	1	1995	1999	Sea trials in 1999
RF	FGA	**SU-27**	200	1996	1998	15 units for production 1998–2000
dom	DDG	*Luhai*	2	1996	1999	
RF	DDG	*Sovremenny*	2	1996	2000	Possible further 2 to be ordered
RF	AIFV	**BMD-3**		1997		Could be BMD-1
dom	SLCM	**C-801(mod)**		1997		Dev (also known as YJ-82)
col	ASM	**KR-1**		1997		In dev with RF. Kh-31P variant
UK	MPA	*Jetstream*	2	1997	1998	For Hong Kong Government
Il	AEW	**Il-76**	4	1997		
RF	hel	**Ka-28**	12	1998	2000	For DDG operation
RF	SAM	**FT-2000**		1998		
RF	tkr ac	**Il-78**	4	1998		
RF	SSM	**SSN-24**	24	1998	2000	For *Sovremenny*
dom	FFG	*Jiangwei* II	8	1998	1998	6 delivered
RF	FGA	**SU-30MKK**	40	1999	2000	
dom	IRBM	**DF-21X**		1999		Modernised DF-15
RF	FGA	**Su-27UBK**	28	2000	2001	Trainers
dom	sat	*Zhongxing*-22	1		2000	Replaces *Dongfanghong*-3
RF	AEW	**A-50**	6	2000		Part of debt settlement
dom	lt tk	**Type 99**			2000	Replacement for Type 63?
RF	ASM	**Kh-35**		2001		To equip Su-30MKK
Indonesia UK	FGA	*Hawk* 209	16	1996	1999	12 were to be delivered in 1999
dom	MPA	**CN-235MP**	3	1996	1999	
RF	hel	**Mi-17**	2	1997	2000	
ROK	trg	**KT-1**	7	2001	2002	
RF	hel	**Mi-2**	8	2001		
Japan US	AEW	**B-767**	4	1991	1998	
dom	DD	*Murasame*	9	1991	1994	7 delivered by 2000
dom	SSK	*Oyashio-class*	8	1993	2000	4 delivered by 2001
dom	AAM	**XAAM-5**		1994	2001	Dev
dom	LST	*Oosumi-class*	3	1994	1997	1 delivered by 2000
dom	SP arty	**155mm**		1994	2000	Entered prod 1999. Replacing Type-75
dom	SAR			1996		US-1 replacement in dev
dom	BMD	**TMD**		1997		Joint dev with US from late 1998
dom	recce	**sat**	4	1998	2002	Dev Prog. 2 optical, 2 radar
dom	mor	**L16**	42	1999	2000	
dom	mor	**120mm**	27	1999	2000	
dom	SP arty	**Type-96**	3	1999	2000	
dom	SP arty	**155 mm**	4	1999	2000	Replacing Type-75. Entered prod 1999
col	arty	**FH70**		1999	2000	40 req under 1996–2000 MTDP
dom	MRL	**MLRS**	9	1999	2000	45 req under 1996–2000 MTDP
dom	AAA	**Type-87**	1	1999	2000	1 delivered 1998
dom	MBT	**Type 90**	17	1999	2000	90 req under 1996–2000 MTDP
dom	AIFV	**Type-89**	2	1999	2000	2 delivered 1998
dom	APC	**Type-96**	28	1999	2000	157 req under 1996–2000 MTDP
dom	APC	**Type-82**	1	1999	2000	1 delivered 1998

East Asia and Australasia

Country supplier	Classification ⇩	Designation	Quantity ⇩	Order date	Delivery date	Comment ⇩
dom	lt tk	**Type-87**	1	1999	2000	1 delivered 1998
dom	hel	**AH-1S**		1999	2000	3 req under 1996–2000 MTDP
dom	hel	**OH-1**	3	1999	2000	Cost $66m
dom	hel	**UH-60JA**	3	1999	2000	Cost $84m
dom	hel	**CH-47JA**	2	1999	2000	9 req under 1996–2000 MTDP
dom	recce	**LR-2**	1	1999	2000	Cost $24m
dom	SAM	*Hawk*		1999	2000	
dom	ASSM	**Type-88**	4	1999	2000	24 req under 1996–2000 MTDP
dom		**Type-96**	6	1999	2000	
dom	MCMV	*Sugashima*	4	1999	2008	
dom	FAC		2	1999	2000	
dom	AK		1	1999	2000	
dom	hel	**SH-60J**	9	1999	2000	37 req under 1996–2000 MTDP
dom	FGA	**F-2**	130	1999	2000	18 to be delivered by 2001
dom	hel	**CH-47J**	2	1999	2000	4 req under 1996–2000 MTDP
dom	SAR	**U-125A**	2	1999	2000	Cost $76m
dom	hel	**UH-60J**	2	1999	2000	Cost $59m
dom	trg	**T-4**	10	1999	2000	54 req under 1996–2000 MTDP
dom	trg	**T-400**		1999	2000	
dom	tpt	**U-4**		1999	2000	
dom	trg	**T-X**	50	2000		Dev Prog. Replacing *Fuji* T-3s. Delayed
dom	tpt	**C-X**		2000		Replacement for C-1A
dom	MPA	**MPA-X**		2000		Replacement for P3
US	SAM	**Standard**	16	2000		Block III
North Korea dom	MRBM	*Taepo-dong* **1**				Tested October 1998
dom	MRBM	*Taepo-dong* **2**				Test was expected August 1999
Kaz	FGA	**MiG-21**	30	1999	1999	Also spare parts for existing fleet
RF	FGA	**MiG-21**	10	1999	2000	
South Korea dom	APC	**KIFV**	2,000	1981	1985	Still producing in 1998, incl exports
dom	SSK	*Chang Bogo*	9	1987	2001	9th delivered in 2001
US	hel	**UH-60P**	138	1988	1990	Deliveries to 1999
US	FGA	**F-16C/D**	120	1992	1995	Licence. Deliveries to 1999.
dom	sat	**KITSAT-3**		1995	1999	
RF	AIFV	**BMP-3**	23	1995	1996	Deliveries to 1999
RF	MBT	**T-80**	33	1995	1996	Deliveries to 1999
US	sigint	*Hawker* 800	10	1996	1999	
Il	AAM	*Popeye*	100	1996	2000	Deliveries 2000–02
dom	DDG	*Okpo*	3	1996	1998	3 delivered by end of 1999
US	MRL	**MLRS**	29	1997	1999	Including 2,400 rockets
Il	UAV	*Harpy*	100	1997	2001	
dom	trg	**KTX-2**	94	1997	2005	Dev
Fr	utl	**F-406**	5	1997	1999	
dom	SAM	*Pegasus*		1997	1999	Dev
Il	UAV	*Searcher*	3	1997	1998	
RF	SAM	*Igla*		1997	1999	
RF	ATGW	*Metis*		1997	1999	
UK	hel	*Lynx*	13	1997	1999	
Indo	tpt	**CN-235**	8	1997	1999	Delivery delayed
US	AEW	**B-767**	4	1998		Delivery delayed
dom	DDG	**KDX-2**	3	1998	2003	

Country supplier ⇩	Classification Designation	Quantity ⇩	Order date	Delivery date ⇩	Comment
	dom	SAM	**M-SAM**		1998	2008	Dev
	Ge	hel	**BO-105**	12	1998	1999	
	US	AAV	**AAV7A1**	57	1998	2001	Licence. Following delivery of 103 from US
	dom	SPA	**XK9**	68	1998	1999	
	RF	tpt	**Be-200**	1	1998	2000	
	dom	SAM	**P-SAM**		1998	2003	Dev
	dom	SSM	*Hyonmu*		1999		300km and 500km variants
	US	FGA	**F-16C/D**	20	1999	2003	Follow on order after orders for 120
	RF	hel	**Ka-32**	31	1999	2000	Upgrades
	RF	hel	**Ka-32T**	3	1999	2000	Follow on order expected
	US	SAM	**ATACMS**	111	1999		
	US	SAM	**RAM**	64	1999		Block I
	US	SAM	*Standard*	110	2000		
	US	SSM	*Harpoon*	96	2000		
	US	SAM	**SM-2**		2000		
	US	SSK	**Type 214**	3	2000	2007	
	dom	DDG	**KDX-3**	5	2000	2009	In dev
Malaysia	UK	FF	*Lekiu*-class	2	1992	1999	2 delivered in 1999
	It	FSG	*Assad*	4	1995	1997	Originally for Irq. Deliveries 1997–99
	Indo	tpt	**CN-235**	6	1995	1999	
	Ge	OPV	*Meko* A 100	6	1997	2004	Licence built. Req for 27 over 20 yrs
	RF	FGA	**Mig-29**	18	1997	1999	Upgrade
	It	trg	**MB-339**	2	1998	1999	
	RF	hel	**Mi-17**	10	1998	1999	
	UK	hel	*Super Lynx*	6	1999	2001	
	Tu	AIFV		211	2000		
	RSA	arty	**G5 155mm**	22	2000		
Myanmar	PRC	FGA	**F-7**	21	1996	1998	Following deliveries of 36 1991–96
	PRC	trg	**K-8**	4	1998	2000	
	RF	FGA	**MiG-29**	10	2001		
New Zealand	Fr	SAM	*Mistral*	12	1996	1997	Delvery of 2 launchers in late 1997
	US	trg	**CT-4E**	13	1997	1998	11 delivered. Lease programme
	US	hel	**SH-2G**	5	1997	2000	
	US	tpt	**C-130J**	5	1999		Lease of 5 to 7. Delayed
	Ca	APC	**LAV III**	105	2000	2002	Deliveries 2002–04
	US	ATGW	*Javelin*	24	2000		
Papua New Guinea							
	Indo	hel	**BO-105**	1	1998	1999	
Philippines	ROC	FGA	**F-5E**	40	1999		
Singapore	dom	AIFV	**IFV**	500	1991	1999	Two batches: 300 then 200
	dom	OPV	*Fearless*	12	1993	1996	Deliveries to 1999
	US	FGA	**F-16C/D**	42	1995	1998	First order for 18, follow-on for 24
	Swe	SSK	*Sjoormen*	4	1995	2000	2nd delivery due 2001
	dom	LST	*Endurance*	4	1997	1999	Deliveries to 2000
	RF	SAM	**SA-16/SA-18**		1997	1998	
	US	tkr ac	**KC-135**	4	1997	2000	
	US	hel	**CH-47D**	8	1997	2000	Follow-on order after 1994 order for 6
	dom		**Naval Base**	1	1998	2000	In construction at Changi

Country supplier ⇩	Classification ⇩ / Designation	Quantity ⇩	Order date	Delivery date ⇩	Comment
US	cbt hel / **AH-64D**	12	2000	2003	
Fr	FFG / **Lafayette**	6	2000	2005	mod *Lafayette*. 1st to be built in Fr. Final delivery 2009
US	FGA / **F-16**	20	2000	2003	
Fr	SSM / **Exocet MM40**		2000		
US	AAM / **AMRAAM**	100	2000		Only to be delivered if under military threat
Taiwan US	FF / **Knox**	8	1989	1993	Final delivery in 1999
US	FGA / **F-16A/B**	150	1992	1997	60 delivered in 1997
dom	PFM / **Jin Chiang**	12	1992	1994	8 delivered
US	SAM / **Patriot**	6	1993	1997	Completed 1998. Upgrade to PAC-3 standard
US	tpt / **C-130**	12	1993	1995	Deliveries continue
US	MPA / **P-3**		1996		With *Harpoon* SSM
Sgp	recce / **RF-5E**		1996	1998	Unspecified number of F-5E entered service as RF-5E
dom	trg / **AT-3**	40	1997		Order resheduled
US	ASW hel / **S-70C**	11	1997	2000	
US	hel / **OH-58D**	13	1998	2001	Following deliveries of 26 1994–95
US	ASSM / **Harpoon**	58	1998		
US	hel / **CH-47SD**	9	1999	2002	Following deliveries of 7 1993–97
US	radar / **Pave Paws**		1999	2002	
US	LSD / **Anchorage**	1	1999	2000	USS *Pensacola* to replace existing 2 LSDs
dom	FF / **Chengkung**	1	1999	2003	Based on US *Perry*
US	AEW / **E-2T**	4	1999	2002	Following delivery of 4 in 1995
US	hel / **CH-47SD**	9	2000		3 plus long lead time for further 6
US	AAM / **AMRAAM**	200	2000		Only to be delivered if under military threat
US	arty / **M-109A5**	146	2000		
Thailand Indo	tpt / **CN-235**	2	1996		Delayed
It	MHC / **Lat Ya**	2	1996	1998	Deliveries to December 1999
dom	corvette	3	1996	2000	2 delivered by 2000
Il	UAV / **Searcher**	4	1997		
Fr	APC / **VAB NG**		1997		Selected to replace 300 M-113. Order delayed
Fr	sat		1997		Order for recce sat delayed late 1997
A	LCU	3	1997		
US	hel / **SH-2F**	10	1999	2002	
Ge	FGA / **Alpha Jet**		1999		Ex -Luftwaffe to replace OV-10
US	FGA / **F-16 A**	18	2000	2002	Replacing purchase of F/A-18
US	hel / **UH-60L**	2	2000		
Vietnam Il	FGA / **MiG-21**		1996		Upgrade
RF	corvette / **Taruntul 2**	2	1997	1999	Following delivery of 2 *Taruntul* 1995
DPRK	SSM / **Scud**		1999	1999	Probably *Scud*-Cs; quantity unknown

Australia Aus

dollar A$		1999	2000	2001	2002
GDP	AS$	610bn	655bn		
	US$	399bn	380bn		
per capita	US$	23,400	24,500		
Growth	%	3.0	3.7		
Inflation	%	1.5	4.5		
Publ Debt	%	26.1	26.6		
Def exp	AS$	11.9bn	12.2bn		
	US$	7.8bn	7.1bn		
Def bdgt	AS$	11.1bn	12.2bn	12.7bn	
	US$	7.2bn	7.1bn	6.6bn	
US$1=A$		1.53	1.72	1.91	
Population		**19,015,000** Asian 4% Aborigines <1%			
Age		13–17	18–22	23–32	
Men		697,000	680,000	1,497,000	
Women		660,000	646,000	1,452,000	

Total Armed Forces

ACTIVE 50,700

(incl 7,270 women)

RESERVES 21,340

Army 17,900 **Navy** 1,220 **Air Force** 2,220

Army 24,150

integrated = formation/unit comprising active and reserve personnel
(incl 2,600 women)
1 Land HQ, 1 Joint Force HQ, 1 Task Force HQ (integrated), 1 bde HQ
1 armd regt (integrated), 2 recce regt (1 integrated), 1 SF (SAS) regt, 6 inf bn (2 integrated), 1 cdo bn (integrated), 2 indep APC sqn (1 integrated), 1 med arty regt, 2 fd arty regt (1 integrated), 1 AD regt (integrated), 3 cbt engr regt (1 integrated), 2 avn regt

RESERVES

1 div HQ, 7 bde HQ, 1 cdo, 2 recce, 1 APC, 1 med arty, 3 fd arty, 3 cbt engr, 2 engr construction regt, 13 inf bn; 1 indep fd arty bty; 1 recce, 3 fd engr sqn; 3 regional force surv units

EQUIPMENT

MBT 71 *Leopard* 1A3 (excl variants)
LAV 111 ASLAV-25
APC 463 M-113 (excl variants, 364 being upgraded, 119 in store)
TOWED ARTY 105mm: 246 M2A2/L5, 104 *Hamel*; **155mm**: 35 M-198
MOR 81mm: 296
RCL 84mm: 577 *Carl Gustav*; **106mm**: 74 M-40A1
SAM 19 *Rapier*, 17 RBS-70
AC 3 *King Air* 200, 2 DHC-6 (all on lease)

HEL 35 S-70 A-9, 38 Bell 206 B-1 *Kiowa* (to be upgraded), 25 UH-1H (armed), 17 AS-350B, 6 CH-47D
MARINES 15 LCM
SURV 14 RASIT (veh, arty), AN-TPQ-36 (arty, mor)

Navy 12,500

(incl 990 Fleet Air Arm; 1,970 women)
Maritime Comd, Spt Comd, Trg Comd
BASES Sydney, (Maritime Comd HQ) Stirling, Cairns, Darwin

SUBMARINES 5

5 *Collins* SSK with *sub-Harpoon* USGW and Mk 48 HWT

PRINCIPAL SURFACE COMBATANTS 10

DESTROYERS DDG 1 *Perth* (US *Adams*) with 1 SM-1 MR SAM/*Harpoon* SSM launcher, 2 × 127mm guns, 2 × 3 ASTT (Mk 32 LWT)

FRIGATES 9
  FFG 6
  6 *Adelaide* (US *Perry*), with SM-1 MR SAM, *Harpoon* SSM, 1 × 76mm gun, 2 × 3 ASTT (Mk 32 LWT), 2 S-70B *Sea Hawk* hel
  FF 3
  3 *Anzac* (*Meko* 200) with *Sea Sparrow* VLS SAM, 1 × 127mm gun, 6 × 324mm ASTT (Mk 32 LWT), 1 S-70B-2 *Sea Hawk* hel (being replaced by SH-2GA *Super Seasprite*)

PATROL AND COASTAL COMBATANTS 15
PATROL, OFFSHORE 15 *Fremantle* PCO

MINE WARFARE 5

MINE COUNTERMEASURES 5
  2 *Rushcutter* MHI, 3 *Huon* MHC, plus 2 *Bandicoot* MSA, 1 *Brolga* MSA

AMPHIBIOUS 4
  1 *Jervis Bay* catamaran (leased until mid-2001)
  1 *Tobruk* LST, capacity 500 tps, 2 LCM, 2 LCVP
  2 *Kanimbla* (US *Newport*) LPH, capacity 450 tps, 2 LCM, hel 4 Army *Blackhawk* or 3 *Sea King*, no beach-landing capability
  plus 5 *Balikpapan* LCH and 4 LCM

SUPPORT AND MISCELLANEOUS 13
  1 *Success* AO, 1 *Westralia* AO; 1 sail trg, 5 AT, 3 TRV; 2 *Leuwin* AGHS plus 4 craft

NAVAL AVIATION (Fleet Air Arm) (990)
EQUIPMENT
no cbt ac, 16 armed hel
  AIRCRAFT
    EW 2 BAe-748
  HELICOPTERS
    ASW 1 sqn with 16 S-70B-2 *Sea Hawk*
    UTL/SAR 1 sqn with 6 AS-350B and 3 Bell 206B, 1 sqn with 7 *Sea King* Mk 50A

Air Force 14,050

(incl 2,700 women); 141 cbt ac incl MR, no armed hel
2 Comds – Air, Trg
Flying hours F-111, 200; F/A-18, 175
STK/RECCE GP 2 sqn with 35 F-111 (13 F-111C, 4 F-
111A (C), 14 F-111G, 4 RF-111C), 2 EP-3C
TAC/FTR GP 3 sqn (plus 1 OCU) with 71 F/A-18 (55 -
A, 16 -B)
TAC TRG 2 sqn with 33 *Hawk* 127 lead-in ftr trainers
FAC 1 flt with 3 PC-9A
MP GP 2 sqn with 17* P-3C, 3 TAP-3B
AIRLIFT GP 7 TPT/TKR sqn
   2 with 24 C-130 (12 -H, 12 -J)
   1 with 5 Boeing 707 (4 tkr)
   2 with 14 DHC-4 (*Caribou*)
   1 VIP with 5 *Falcon* 900
   1 with 10 HS-748 (8 for navigation trg, 2 for VIP tpt),
     2 Beech-200 *Super King Air*, 1 Beech 1900-D
TRG 59 PC-9
AD *Jindalee* OTH radar: Radar 1 at Longreach (N.
Queensland), Radar 2 at Laverton (W. Australia),
third development site at Alice Springs, 3 control
and reporting units (1 mobile)
MISSILES
   ASM AGM-84A, AGM-142
   AAM AIM-7 *Sparrow*, AIM-9M *Sidewinder*, ASRAAM

Forces Abroad

Advisers in **Fji**, **Indo**, **Solomon Islands**, **Th**, **Vanuatu**,
Tonga, **Western Samoa**, **Kiribati**
MALAYSIA Army: ε115; 1 inf coy (on 3-month
rotational tours) **Air Force**: 33; det with 2 P-3C **ac**
PAPUA NEW GUINEA: 38; trg unit
UN AND PEACEKEEPING
EAST TIMOR (UNTAET): 1,474 incl 17 obs and 4 SA-
70A hel **ETHIOPIA/ERITREA** (UNMEE): 2 **EGYPT**
(MFO): 26 obs **MIDDLE EAST** (UNTSO): 12 obs
PAPUA NEW GUINEA: 149 (Bougainville Peace
Monitoring Group)

Paramilitary

AUSTRALIAN CUSTOMS SERVICE
   ac 3 DHC-8, 3 *Reims* F406, 6 BN-2B-20, 1 *Strike
Aerocommander* 500 **hel** 1 Bell 206L-4; about 6 boats

Foreign Forces

US Air Force 260; **Navy** 40; joint facilities at NW Cape,
Pine Gap and Nurrungar
NEW ZEALAND Air Force 9 navigation trg
SINGAPORE 230; Flying Training School with 27 S-211
ac

Brunei Bru

dollar B$		1999	2000	2001	2002
GDP	B$		10.2bn	10.5bn	
	US$		6.0bn	6.1bn	
per capita	US$		7,800	8,100	
Growth	%		1.8	2.5	
Inflation	%		3.2	3.2	
Debt	US$				
Def exp	B$		684m	610m	
	US$		402m	354m	
Def bdgt	B$		ε620m	ε600m	ε484m
	US$		365m	348m	267m
US$1=B$			1.7	1.7	1.8
Population					**334,000**

Muslim 71%; **Malay** 67% **Chinese** 16% **non-Malay
indigenous** 6%

Age	13–17	18–22	23–32
Men	16,000	14,000	28,000
Women	15,000	15,000	26,000

Total Armed Forces

ACTIVE 5,900
(incl 700 women)

RESERVES 700
Army 700

Army 3,900

(incl 250 women)
3 inf bn • 1 spt bn with 1 armd recce, 1 engr sqn

EQUIPMENT
   LT TK 20 *Scorpion*
   APC 39 VAB
   MOR 81mm: 24
   RL *Armbrust*

RESERVES
1 bn

Navy 900

(inc 80 women)
BASE Muara
PATROL AND COASTAL COMBATANTS 6
MISSILE CRAFT 3 *Waspada* PFM with 2 MM-38 *Exocet*
   SSM
PATROL, INSHORE 3 *Perwira* PFI†
PATROL, RIVERINE boats
AMPHIBIOUS craft only
    4 LCU; 1 SF sqn plus boats

Air Force 1,100

(incl 75 women)
no cbt ac, 5 armed hel
HEL 2 sqn
  1 with 10 Bell 212, 1 Bell 214 (SAR), 4 S-70A, 1 S-70C
    (VIP)
  1 with 5 Bo-105 armed hel (**81mm** rockets)
TPT 1 sqn with 1 CN-235M
TRG 1 sqn with 2 SF-260W, 4 PC-7, 2 Bell 206B
AIR DEFENCE 2 sqn with 12 *Rapier* (incl *Blindfire*), 16
  Mistral

Paramilitary ε3,750

GURKHA RESERVE UNIT ε2,000+
2 bn
ROYAL BRUNEI POLICE 1,750
7 PCI<

Foreign Forces

UK Army some 1,070; 1 Gurkha inf bn, 1 hel flt, trg
school
SINGAPORE 500; trg school incl hel det (5 UH-1)

Cambodia Cam

riel r		1999	2000	2001	2002
GDP	r	ε13.2tr	ε12.2tr		
	US$	3.5bn	3.2bn		
per capita	US$	725	730		
Growth	%	4.0	4.0		
Inflation	%	4.1	1.0		
Debt	US$	2.0bn	2.0bn		
Def exp	r	ε670bn	ε750bn		
	US$	176m	195m		
Def bdgt	r	ε330bn	ε460bn	ε500bn	
	US$	87m	120m	128m	
FMA (US)	US$	1.5m	2.6m	2.7m	
FMA (Aus)	US$	0.1m			
US$1=r		3,807	3,836	3,901	
Population					**11,450,000**
Khmer 90% **Vietnamese** 5% **Chinese** 1%					
Age		13–17	18–22	23–32	
Men		645,000	501,000	888,000	
Women		631,000	493,000	865,000	

Total Armed Forces

ACTIVE ε140,000 (to reduce)

(incl Provincial Forces, perhaps only 19,000 cbt capable)
Terms of service conscription authorised but not
implemented since 1993

Army ε90,000

6 Mil Regions (incl 1 special zone for capital) • 22 inf
div[a] • 3 indep inf bde • 1 protection bde (4 bn) • 9
indep inf regt • 3 armd bn • 1 AB/SF regt • 4 engr regt
(3 fd, 1 construction) • some indep recce, arty, AD bn
EQUIPMENT
  MBT 100+ T-54/-55, 50 PRC Type-59
  LT TK PRC Type 62, 20 PRC Type 64
  RECCE BRDM-2
  APC 160 BTR-60/-152, M-113, 30 OT-64 (SKOT)
  TOWED ARTY some 400: **76mm**: M-1942; **122mm**:
    M-1938, D-30; **130mm**: Type 59
  MRL 107mm: Type-63; **122mm**: 8 BM-21; **132mm**:
    BM-13-16; **140mm**: 20 BM-14-16
  MOR 82mm: M-37; **120mm**: M-43; **160mm**: M-160
  RCL 82mm: B-10; **107mm**: B-11
  AD GUNS 14.5mm: ZPU 1/-2/-4; **37mm**: M-1939;
    57mm: S-60

[a] Inf div established str 3,500, actual str some 1,500 or less

Navy ε3,000

(incl 1,500 Naval Infantry)
BASES Ream (maritime), Prek Ta Ten (river)
PATROL AND COASTAL COMBATANTS 4
PATROL, COASTAL 2
  2 Sov *Stenka* PFC
RIVERINE 2
  2 *Kaoh Chhlam* PCR<

NAVAL INFANTRY (1,500)
  7 inf, 1 arty bn

Air Force 2,000

24 cbt ac†; no armed hel
FTR 1 sqn with 19† MiG-21 (14 -bis, 5 -UM) (up to 9 to
  be upgraded by IAI: 2 returned but status unclear)
TPT 1 sqn with 2 Y-12, 1 BN-2. 1 VIP sqn (reporting to
  Council of Ministry) with 2 An-24RV, 1 Cessna 401, 1
  Cessna 421, 1 Falcon, 1 AS-350, 1 AS-365
HEL 1 sqn with 14 Mi-8/Mi-17 (incl 1 VIP Mi-8P), 2
  Mi-26
RECCE/TRG 5* L-39 for MiG-21 lead-in trg, 5 *Tecnam*
  P-92 for pilot trg/recce

Provincial Forces some 45,000

Reports of at least 1 inf regt per province, with varying
numbers of inf bn with lt wpn

Paramilitary

POLICE 67,000 (incl *gendarmerie*)

China, People's Republic of PRC

yuan Y		1999	2000	2001	2002
GDP[a]	Y	8.2tr	8.9tr		
	US$	732bn	794bn		
per capita	US$	4,000	4,300		
Growth	%	7.1	7.8		
Inflation	%	-1.3	0.4		
Debt	US$	154bn	160bn		
Def exp[a]	US$	ε39.5bn	ε42bn		
Def bdgt[b]	Y	104.7bn	120.5bn	141.0bn	
	US$	12.6bn	14.5bn	17.0bn	
US$1=Y		8.28	8.28	8.28	

[a] PPP est incl extra-budgetary mil exp
[b] Def bdgt shows official figures at market rates

Population				1,293,239,000

Tibetan, Uighur and other non-Han 8% Xinjiang
Muslim ε60% of which Uighur ε44% Tibet Chinese
ε60% Tibetan ε40%

Age	13–17	18–22	23–32
Men	52,707,000	46,251,000	119,898,000
Women	50,049,000	43,196,000	112,665,000

Total Armed Forces

ACTIVE some 2,310,000 (being reduced)
(incl about 130,000 MOD staff, centrally-controlled
units not included elsewhere; perhaps 1,000,000
conscripts, some 136,000 women)
Terms of service selective conscription; all services 2 years

RESERVES some 500–600,000
militia reserves being formed on a province-wide basis

Strategic Missile Forces

OFFENSIVE (100,000)+
org as 18 launch bdes within 6 msl armies; org varies
by msl type; one testing and one trg base
ICBM 20+
    20+ DF-5A (CSS-4)
    First DF-31 (CSS-9) bde reportedly operational
IRBM 130-150
    20+ DF-4 (CSS-3)
    60-80 DF-3A (CSS-2)
    50 DF-21 (CSS-5). At least 3 bde deployed
SLBM 1 *Xia* SSBN with 12 CSS-N-3 (JL-1)
SRBM about 25 DF-15 launchers with 160+ msl (CSS-
    6/M-9) (range 600km). 1 bde deployed
    25 DF-11 (CSS-7/M-11) launchers with 175 msl
    (range 120–300+km). 2 bde deployed
DEFENSIVE
Tracking stations Xinjiang (covers Central Asia) and
    Shanxi (northern border)
Phased-array radar complex ballistic-msl early-warning

Army ε1,600,000

(perhaps 800,000 conscripts) (reductions continue)
7 Mil Regions, 28 Provinicial Mil Districts, 4 Garrison
Comd
21 Integrated Group Armies (3 possibly to disband)
    GA: from 40–89,000, equivalent to Western corps,
    org varies, normally with 2–3 inf div/bde, 1 armd, 1
    arty, 1 AAA bde or 2–3 inf, 1 armd div/bde, 1 arty, 1
    AAA bde, cbt readiness category varies with 10 GA
    at Category A and 11 at Category B (reorg to bde
    structure in progress)
Summary of cbt units
Group Army 44 inf div (incl 7 mech inf) 3 with national
    level rapid-reaction role and at least 9 with regional
    rapid-reaction role ready to mobilise in 24–48 hours;
    9 armd div, 12 armd bde, 13 inf bde, 6 arty div, 3 ATK
    bde, 20 arty bde, 12 avn regt
Independent 5 inf div, 1 armd, 2 inf bde, 1 arty div, 3
    arty bde, 4 AAA bde
Local Forces (Garrison, Border, Coastal) 12 inf div, 1
    mtn bde, 4 inf bde, 87 inf regt/bn
AB (manned by Air Force) ε35,000: 1 corps of 3 div
Support Troops incl 50 engr, 50 sigs regt
EQUIPMENT
    MBT incl ε8,000 Type-59-I/-II, Type-79, Type-88B, Type-
      88C, Type-98
    LT TK ε1,200 incl Type-63, Type-63A, Type-62/62I
    AIFV/APC 5,000 incl 4,000 Type-63A/I/II, some
      Type-77 (BTR-50PK), Type-89I/II (mod Type-85),
      WZ-523, Type-92 (WZ-551), Type-86/86A (WZ-
      501), 100 BMD-3
    TOWED ARTY 13,000: **100mm**: Type-59 (fd/ATK);
      122mm: Type-54-1, Type-60, Type-83; **130mm**:
      Type-59/-59-1; **152mm**: Type-54, Type-66, Type-83;
      155mm: 300+ Type-88 (WAC-21)
    SP ARTY 122mm: ε1,000 incl Type-70/-70I, Type-89;
      152mm: Type-83
    COMBINED GUN/MOR 100 2S23 *Nona-SVK*
    MRL 3,000: **122mm**: Type-81, Type-89 SP; **130mm**:
      Type-70 SP, Type-82; **273mm**: Type-83; **320mm**:
      Type-96
    MOR 82mm: Type-53/-67/-W87/-82 (incl SP);
      100mm: Type-71 reported; **120mm**: Type-55 (incl
      SP); **160mm**: Type-56
    ATGW 6,500: HJ-73 (*Sagger*-type), HJ-8 (TOW/
      Milan-type), HJ-9
    RL 62mm: Type-70-1
    RCL 75mm: Type-56; **82mm**: Type-65, Type-78;
      105mm: Type-75
    ATK GUNS 100mm: Type-73, Type-86; **120mm**: 300+
      Type-89 SP
    AD GUNS 23mm: Type-80; **25mm**: Type-85; **35mm**:
      50+ Type-90; **37mm**: Type-88SP, Type-55/-65/-74;
      57mm: Type-59, -80 SP; **85mm**: Type-56; **100mm**:
      Type-59
    SAM HN-5A/-B/-C (SA-7 type), HN-6, HQ-61A,
      HQ-7, 26 SA-15 (Tor-M1)

SURV *Cheetah* (arty), Type-378 (veh), RASIT (veh, arty)
AC 2 Y-8
HEL 24 Mi-17, 30 Mi-171, 3 Mi-6, 4 Z-8A, 73 Z-9/-WZ-9, 8 SA-342 (with HOT), 20 S-70C2, 20 Z-11
UAV ASN-104/-105

RESERVES

(undergoing major re-org on provincial basis): some 500–600,000: 70 inf, arty and AD div, 100 indep inf, arty regt

DEPLOYMENT

(GA units only)

North-east Shenyang MR (Heilongjiang, Jilin, Liaoning MD): ε250,000: 4 GA, 1 armd, 10 inf div, 1 armd bde, 1 arty div, some arty bde, 1 ATK bde

North Beijing MR (Beijing, Tianjin Garrison, Nei Mongol, Hebei, Shanxi MD): ε300,000: 5 GA, 2 armd, 12 inf div, 3 armd, 3 inf bde, 1 arty div, 1 ATK bde

West Lanzhou MR (incl Ningxia, Shaanxi, Gansu, Qing-hai, Xinjiang, South Xinjiang MD): ε220,000: 2 GA, 1 armd, 4 inf div, 1 armd bde

South-west Chengdu MR (incl Chongqing Garrison, Sichuan, Guizhou, Yunnan, Xizang MD): ε180,000: 2 GA, 4 inf, 1 arty div plus 2 armd bde

South Guangzhou MR (Hubei, Hunan, Guangdong, Guangxi, Hainan MD): ε180,000: 2 GA, 1 armd div, 4 inf bde, 1 arty div. Hong Kong: ε7,000: 1 inf bde (3 inf, 1 mech inf, 1 arty regt, 1 engr bn), 1 hel unit

Centre Jinan MR (Shandong, Henan MD): ε190,000: 3 GA, 2 armd, 7 inf div, 4 inf bde, 1 arty div, some arty bde

East Nanjing MR (Shanghai Garrison, Jiangsu, Zhejiang, Fujian, Jiangxi, Anhui MD): ε250,000: 3 GA, 2 armd, 5 inf div, 3 inf bde, 1 arty div, 1 ATK bde

Navy ε250,000

(incl Coastal Regional Defence Forces, 26,000 Naval Aviation, some 10,000 Marines; some 40,000 conscripts)

SUBMARINES 69

STRATEGIC 1 *Xia* SSBN
TACTICAL 67
  SSN 5 *Han* (Type 091)
  SSG 1 mod *Romeo* (Type S5G), with 6 C-801 (YJ-6, *Exocet* derivative) ASSM; 533mm TT (test platform)
  SSK 61
    3 *Song* with YJ 8-2 ASSM (C-802 derivative), 6 × 533mm TT
    2 *Kilo*-class (RF Type EKM 877) with 533mm TT
    2 *Kilo*-class (RF Type EKM 636) with 533mm TT
    3 *Ming* (Type ES5C/D) with 533mm TT
    16 imp *Ming* (Type ES5E) with 533mm TT
    35 *Romeo* (Type ES3B)† with 533mm TT
OTHER ROLES 1 *Golf* (SLBM trials) SS

PRINCIPAL SURFACE COMBATANTS 62

DESTROYERS 21

DDG 21
  2 RF *Sovremenny* with 2 × 4 SS-N-22 *Sunburn* SSM, 2

SA-N-7 *Gadfly* SAM, 2 × 2 130mm guns, 2 × 2 533mm ASTT, 2 ASW mor, 1 Ka-28 hel
1 *Luhai* with 4 × 4 CSS-N-4 SSM, 1 × 8 Crotale SAM, 1 × 2 100mm guns, 2 × 3 ASTT, 2 Ka-28 hel
2 *Luhu* with 4 × 2 YJ-8/CSS-N-4 SSM, 1 × 8 *Crotale* SAM, 2 × 100mm guns, 2 × 3 ASTT, 2 Z-9A (Fr *Panther*) hel
1 *Luda* III with 4 × 2 YJ-8/CSS-N-4 SSM, 2 × 2 130mm gun, 2 × 3 ASTT
2 mod *Luda* with 2 × 3 HY-1/CSS-N-2 SSM, 1 × 2 130mm guns, 2 × 3 ASTT, 2 Z-9C (Fr *Panther*) hel
13 *Luda* (Type-051) with 2 × 3 CSS-N-2 or CSS-N-4 SSM, 2 × 2 130mm guns, 6 × 324mm ASTT, 2 × 12 ASW RL (2 also with 1 × 8 *Crotale* SAM)

FRIGATES about 41 FFG

7 *Jiangwei* II with CSS-N-4 *Sardine* SSM, 1 × 8 *Croatale* SAM, 1 × 2 100mm guns, 2 × 6 ASW mor, 1 Z-9A (Fr *Dauphin*) hel
4 *Jiangwei* I with 2 × 3 C-801 SSM, 1 × 6 × HQ-61/CSA-N-1 SAM, 1 × 2 100mm guns, 2 × 6 ASW mor, 1 Z-9C (Fr *Panther*) hel
About 30 *Jianghu*; 3 variants:
  About 26 Type I, with 2 × 2 SY-1/CSS-N-1 SSM, 2 × 100mm guns, 4 × 5 ASW mor
  About 1 Type II, with 1 × 2 SY-1/CSS-N-1 SSM, 1 × 2 × 100mm guns, 2 × 5 ASW RL, 1 Z-9C (Fr *Panther*) hel
  About 3 Type III, with 8 CSS-N-4 SSM, 2 × 2 100mm guns, 4 × 5 ASW RL

PATROL AND COASTAL COMBATANTS about 368

MISSILE CRAFT 93

5 *Huang* PFM with 6 YJ-8/CSS-N-4 SSM
20 *Houxin* PFM with 4 YJ-8/CSS-N-4 SSM
Some 38 *Huangfeng/Hola* (Sov *Osa* I-Type) PFM with 4 SY-1 SSM
30 *Houku* (*Komar*-Type) PFM with 2 SY-1 SSM

TORPEDO CRAFT about 16

16 *Huchuan* PHT

PATROL CRAFT about 259

COASTAL about 118
  2 *Haijui* PCC with 3 × 5 ASW RL
  About 96 *Hainan* PCC with 4 ASW RL
  20 *Haiqing* PCC with 2 × 6 ASW mor
INSHORE about 111
  100 *Shanghai* PCI<, 11 *Haizhui* PCI<
RIVERINE about 30<

MINE WARFARE about 39

MINELAYERS 1

1 *Wolei*
In addition, *Luda* class DDG, *Hainan*, *Shanghai* PC and T-43 MSO have minelaying capability

MINE COUNTERMEASURES about 38

27 Sov T-43 MSO
7 *Wosao* MSC
3 *Wochang* and 1 *Shanghai* II MSI
plus about 50 *Lienyun* aux MSC, 4 drone MSI and 42 reserve drone MSI

AMPHIBIOUS 56

7 *Yukan* LST, capacity about 200 tps, 10 tk
3 *Shan* (US LST-1) LST, capacity about 165 tps, 16 tk
9 *Yuting* LST, capacity about 250 tps, 10 tk, 2 hel
1 *Yudeng* LSM, capacity about 500 tps, 9 tk
22 *Yuliang* LSM, capacity about 100 tps, 3 tk
13 *Yuhai* LSM, capacity 250 tps, 2tk
1 *Yudao* LSM
craft: 45 LCU, 10 LCAC plus over 230 LCU in reserve

SUPPORT AND MISCELLANEOUS about 163

1 *Nanchang* AO, 2 *Fuqing* AO, 33 AOT, 14 AF, 10 AS, 1 ASR, 2 AR; 6 *Qiongsha* AH, 30 tpt, 4 icebreakers, 25 AT/F, 1 hel trg, 1 trg; 33 AGOR/AGOS

NAVAL AVIATION (26,000)

EQUIPMENT
471 shore-based cbt ac, 35 armed hel

AIRCRAFT
BBR 7 H-6, 18 H-6D reported with 2 YJ-6/61 anti-ship ALCM; about 50 H-5 torpedo-carrying lt bbr
FGA some 30 Q-5, 10 JH-7
FTR some 250 J-6, 40 J-7, 18 J-8/8A, 12 J-8B, 12 J-8D
RECCE 7 HZ-5
MR/ASW 4 PS-5 (SH-5), 4 Y-8X
AEW 4 Y-8
TRG 53 PT-6, 16* JJ-6, 4* JJ-7
TPT 12 Mi-8

HELICOPTERS
ASW 12 SA-321, 3 Z-8, 12 Z-9C, 8 Ka-28
TPT 50 Y-5, 4 Y-7, 4 Y-8, 2 YAK-42, 6 An-26

MISSILES
ALCM YJ-6/C-601, YJ-61/C-611, YJ-81/C-801K

(Naval ftr integrated into national AD system)

MERCHANT FLEET

1,449 ocean-going ships over 1,000t (incl 252 AOT, 335 dry bulk, 94 container, 15 ro-ro, 4 pax, 749 other)

COASTAL REGIONAL DEFENCE FORCES

ε40 indep arty and ε10 SSM regt deployed to protect naval bases, offshore islands and other vulnerable points
SSM HY-2/C-201/CSS-C-3, HY-4/C-401/CSS-C-7
AD GUNS 37mm, 57mm

MARINES (some 10,000)

2 bde (3 marine, 1 mech inf, 1 lt tk, 1 arty bn); special recce units (third bde reported)
3 Army div also have amph role

EQUIPMENT
LT TK Type-63, Type-63A
APC Type-77-II
ARTY 122mm: Type-83
MRL 107mm: Type-63
ATGW HJ-8
SAM HN-5

DEPLOYMENT AND BASES

NORTH SEA FLEET
coastal defence from DPRK border (Yalu River) to south of Lianyungang (approx 35°10′N); equates to Shenyang, Beijing and Jinan MR, and to seaward
BASES Qingdao (HQ), Dalian (Luda), Huludao, Weihai, Chengshan, Yuchi; 9 coastal defence districts
FORCES under review

EAST SEA FLEET
coastal defence from south of Lianyungang to Dongshan (approx 35°10′N to 23°30′N); equates to Nanjing Military Region, and to seaward
BASES HQ Dongqian Lake (Ninbo), Shanghai Naval base, Dinghai, Hangzhou, Xiangshan; 7 coastal defence districts

SOUTH SEA FLEET
coastal defence from Dongshan (approx 23°30′N) to Vn border; equates to Guangzhou MR, and to seaward (including Paracel and Spratly Islands)
BASE Hong Kong, Yulin, Guangzhou

Air Force 420,000

(incl strategic forces, 220,000 AD personnel and 160,000 conscripts); some 2,900 cbt ac, some armed hel **Flying hours** H-6: 80; J-7 and J-8: 100; Su-27: 120

HQ Beijing. 4 Air Corps, each equivalent to a PLA Group Army - 1 Corps (Changchun), 7 Corps (Nanning), 8 Corps (Fuzhou), 10 Corps (Datong). Eight PLAAF Comd Centres, one per Mil Region plus one in Xinjian District. 44 air divs (32 ftr, 5 bbr, 7 attack, 2 tpt). Up to 4 sqn, each with 10–15 ac, 1 maint unit, some tpt and trg ac, make up an air regt; 3 air regt form an air div. Varying numbers of air divs in the Mil Regions – many in the south-east

BBR 1-2 regt with 40 H-5, 3 regt with 110 H-6E/F (some may be nuclear-capable/30 modified to carry YJ-6/C-601 ASUWM), H-6H (could carry future YJ-63)
FTR 300 J-7II/IIA, 50 J-7IIH, 24 J-7 IIM, 100 J-7III, 150 J-7E, 70 J-8A/E, 100 J-8B/D, 70 Su-27, 20 more -27UBK to be delivered by 2002
FGA First 20 of 40 Su-30MKK delivered. 300 Q-5, some 60 regt with 1,500+ J-6/B/D/E
RECCE/ELINT ε290: ε40 HZ-5, 100 JZ-6, some JZ-7, 4 Tu-154M
TPT ε513: incl some 15 Tu-154M, 2 Il-18, 14 Il-76MD, 300 Y-5, 100 Y-7/An-24/An-26, 48 Y-8/An-12, 15 Y-11, 8 Y-12, 6 Boeing 737-200 (VIP), 5 CL-601 *Challenger*
TKR 10+ HY-6
HEL some 170: incl 6 AS-332 (VIP), 4 Bell 214, 40 Mi-8, 20 Z-9
TRG ε200: incl HJ-5, JJ-6, 50+ JJ-7, 8+ JL-8, PT-6 (CJ-6)
MISSILES
AAM PL-2, PL-5, PL-8, 250+ AA-10, 250+ AA-11, *Python* 3, 100 AA-12 on order for Su-30MKK
ASM YJ-6/C-601, YJ-61/C-611, YJ-63 expected, YJ-

81K/C-801K
UAV *Chang Hong* 1
AD 10 AD bde (6 mixed AAA/SAM, 4 AAA), 16,000 **85mm** and **100mm** guns; 100+ SAM units with 500+ HQ-2/2A/2B, 100+ HQ-7, 120 SA-10, 20+ HQ-15 FT-2000

Forces Abroad

UN AND PEACEKEEPING
DROC (MONUC): 10 obs **ETHIOPIA/ERITREA** (UNMEE): 5 obs **MIDDLE EAST** (UNTSO): 5 obs **IRAQ/KUWAIT** (UNIKOM): 11 obs **SIERRA LEONE** (UNAMSIL): 6 obs **WESTERN SAHARA** (MINURSO): 16 obs

Paramilitary ε1,500,000 active

PEOPLE'S ARMED POLICE (Ministry of Public Security) ε1,500,000

45 div (14 each with 4 regt, remainder no standard org; with 1–2 div per province) incl **Internal security** ε800,000 **Border defence** some 100,000 **Guards, Comms** ε69,000

Fiji Fji

dollar F$		1999	2000	2001	2002
GDP	F$	3.5bn	3.3bn		
	US$	1.8bn	1.5bn		
per capita	US$	6,100	6,400		
Growth	%	7.0	4.9		
Inflation	%	2.0	2.4		
Debt	US$	262m			
Def exp	F$	68m	70m		
	US$	35m	32m		
Def bdgt	F$	54m	58m	58m	
	US$	27m	27m	25m	
FMA (US)	US$		0.2m	0.2m	
FMA (Aus)	US$	3m			
US$1=F$		1.98	2.14	2.26	
Population					825,000

Fijian 51% Indian 44% European/other 5%

Age	13–17	18–22	23–32
Men	46,000	46,000	67,000
Women	44,000	43,000	64,000

Total Armed Forces

ACTIVE some 3,500
(incl recalled reserves)
RESERVES some 6,000
(to age 45)

Army 3,200

(incl 300 recalled reserves)
7 inf bn (incl 4 cadre) • 1 engr bn • 1 arty bty • 1 special ops coy
EQUIPMENT
   TOWED ARTY 88mm: 4 25-pdr (ceremonial)
   MOR 81mm: 12
   HEL 1 AS-355, 1 SA-365

Navy 300

BASES Walu Bay, Viti (trg)
PATROL AND COASTAL COMBATANTS 9
PATROL, COASTAL/INSHORE 9
   3 *Kula* (*Pacific Forum*) PCC, 4 *Vai* (*Il Dabur*) PCI<, 2 *Levuka* PCI<
SUPPORT AND MISCELLANEOUS 2
   1 *Cagi Donu* presidential yacht (trg), 1 *Tovutu* AGHS

Forces Abroad

UN AND PEACEKEEPING
EAST TIMOR (UNTAET): 194 **EGYPT** (MFO): 339; 1 inf bn(-) **IRAQ/KUWAIT** (UNIKOM): 7 obs **LEBANON** (UNIFIL): 587; 1 inf bn **PAPUA NEW GUINEA**: 6 (Bougainville Peace Monitoring Group)

Indonesia Indo

rupiah Rp		1999	2000	2001	2002
GDP	Rp	1,107tr	1,332tr		
	US$	140bn	160bn		
per capita	US$	3,900	4,000		
Growth	%	1.8	4.5		
Inflation	%	20.5	3.8		
Debt	US$	150bn	144bn		
Def exp	Rp	ε11.8tr	12.7tr		
	US$	1.5bn	1.5bn		
Def bdgt	Rp	12.2tr	13.0tr	14.3tr	
	US$	1,553m	2,271m	1,268m	
FMA (US)	US$	0.5m	0.6m	0.4m	
FMA (Aus)	US$	4.0m	5.2m		
US$1=Rp		7,855	8,320	11,277	
Population					216,213,000

Muslim 87%; Javanese 45% Sundanese 14% Madurese 8% Malay 8% Chinese 3% other 22%

Age	13–17	18–22	23–32
Men	11,037,000	11,208,000	18,278,000
Women	10,556,000	10,712,000	18,275,000

Total Armed Forces

ACTIVE 297,000

Terms of service 2 years selective conscription authorised

RESERVES 400,000

Army cadre units; numbers, str n.k., obligation to age 45 for officers

Army ε230,000

Strategic Reserve (KOSTRAD) (30,000)
2 inf div HQ • 3 inf bde (9 bn) • 3 AB bde (9 bn) • 2 fd arty regt (6 bn) • 1 AD arty regt (2 bn) • 2 armd bn • 2 engr bn

11 Mil Area Comd (KODAM) (150,000) (Provincial (KOREM) and District (KODIM) comd)
2 inf bde (6 bn) • 65 inf bn (incl 5 AB) • 8 cav bn • 11 fd arty, 10 AD bn • 8 engr bn • 1 composite avn sqn, 1 hel sqn

Special Forces (KOPASSUS) (ε5,000); 3 SF gp (incl 2 para-cdo, 1 int, 8 counter-terrorist, 1 trg unit)

EQUIPMENT
LT TK some 275 AMX-13 (to be upgraded), 30 PT-76, 50 *Scorpion*-90
RECCE 69 *Saladin* (16 upgraded), 55 *Ferret* (13 upgraded), 18 VBL
AIFV 11 BMP-2
APC 200 AMX-VCI, 45 *Saracen* (14 upgraded), 60 V-150 *Commando*, 22 *Commando Ranger*, 80 BTR-40, 34 BTR-50PK, 40 *Stormer* (incl variants)
TOWED ARTY 76mm: 100 M-48; **105mm**: 170 M-101, 10 M-56; **155mm**: 5 FH 2000
MOR 81mm: 800; **120mm**: 75 Brandt
RCL 90mm: 90 M-67; **106mm**: 45 M-40A1
RL 89mm: 700 LRAC
AD GUNS 20mm: 125; **40mm**: 90 L/70; **57mm**: 200 S-60
SAM 51 *Rapier*, 42 RBS-70
AC 10 NC-212, 2 *Commander* 680, 3 DHC-5, 18 Pzl-104
HEL 30 Bell 205A, 17 Bo-105, 28 NB-412, 15 Hughes 300C (trg)

Navy 40,000

(incl ε1,000 Naval Aviation and 12,000 Marines) (overall serviceability of whole fleet is low)

PRINCIPAL COMMAND
WESTERN FLEET HQ Teluk Ratai (Jakarta)
BASES Primary Teluk Ratai, Belawan **Other** 10 plus minor facilities
EASTERN FLEET HQ Surabaya
BASES Primary Surabaya, Ujung Pandang, Jayapura **Other** 13 plus minor facilities

MILITARY SEALIFT COMMAND (KOLINLAMIL)
controls some amph and tpt ships used for inter-island comms and log spt for Navy and Army (assets incl in Navy and Army listings)

SUBMARINES 2
SSK 2 *Cakra* (Ge *T-209*) with 8 × 533mm TT (Ge HWT)

PRINCIPAL SURFACE COMBATANTS 17

FRIGATES 17
FFG 10
6 *Ahmad Yani* (Nl *Van Speijk*) with 2 × 4 *Harpoon* SSM, 2 × 2 *Mistral* SAM, 1 × 76mm gun, 2 × 3 ASTT, 1 *Wasp* hel
3 *Fatahillah* with 2 × 2 MM-38 *Exocet* SSM, 1 × 120mm gun, 2 × 3 ASTT (not *Nala*), 1 × 2 ASW mor, 1 *Wasp* hel (*Nala* only)
1 *Hajar Dewantara* (trg) with 2 × 2 MM-38 *Exocet* SSM, 2 × 533mm ASTT, 1 ASW mor
FF 7
4 *Samadikun* (US *Claud Jones*) with 1 × 76mm gun, 2 × 3 324mm ASTT
3 *M. K. Tiyahahu* (UK *Tribal*) with *Mistral* SAM, 2 × 114mm guns, 1 × 3 *Limbo* ASW mor, 1 *Wasp* hel

PATROL AND COASTAL COMBATANTS 36

CORVETTES 16 *Kapitan Patimura* (GDR *Parchim*) FS with SA-N-5 *Gecko* SAM (in some), 1 × 57mm gun, 4 × 400mm ASTT, 2 ASW RL
MISSILE CRAFT 4 *Mandau* (Ko *Dagger*) PFM with 4 MM-38 *Exocet* SSM
TORPEDO CRAFT 4 *Singa* (Ge Lürssen 57m) with 2 × 533mm TT
PATROL CRAFT 12
OFFSHORE 4
4 *Kakap* (Ge Lürssen 57m) PCO with hel deck
COASTAL/INSHORE 8
8 *Sibarau* (Aust *Attack*) PCC
plus 18 craft

MINE WARFARE 12

MINE COUNTERMEASURES 12
2 *Pulau Rengat* (mod Nl *Tripartite*) MCC (sometimes used for coastal patrol)
2 *Pulau Rani* (Sov *T-43*) MCC (mainly used for coastal patrol)
8 *Palau Rote* (GDR *Kondor* II)† MSC (mainly used for coastal patrol, 7 non-op)

AMPHIBIOUS 26
6 *Teluk Semangka* (SK *Tacoma*) LST, capacity about 200 tps, 17 tk, 2 with 3 hel (1 fitted as AH)
1 *Teluk Amboina* LST, capacity about 200 tps, 16 tk
7 *Teluk Langsa* (US *LST-512*) LST, capacity 200 tps, 16 tks
12 *Teluk Gilimanuk* (GDR *Frosch* I/II) LST
Plus about 65 LCM and LCVP

SUPPORT AND MISCELLANEOUS 15
1 *Sorong* AO, 1 *Arun* AO (UK *Rover*), 2 Sov *Khobi* AOT, 1 cmd/spt/replenish; 1 AR, 2 AT/F, 1 *Barakuda* (Ge Lürssen Nav IV) presidential yacht; 6 AGOR/AGOS

NAVAL AVIATION (ε1,000)
EQUIPMENT
no cbt ac, 18 armed hel

AIRCRAFT
MR 9 N-22 *Searchmaster* B, 6 *Searchmaster* L, 10 NC-212 (MR/ELINT), 14 N-22B, 6 N-24, 3 CN-235 MP
TPT 4 *Commander*, 10 NC-212, 2 DHC-5, 20 *Nomad* (6 VIP)
TRG 2 *Bonanza* F33, 6 PA-38
HELICOPTERS
ASW 6 *Wasp* HAS-1
UTL 3* NAS-332F (2 non-op), 5* NBo-105, 4* Bell-412, 2 Mi-17, 8 Mi-2

MARINES (KORMAR) (12,000)

1 mne corps gp with 1 mne inf bde, 1 indep mne inf bde • 1 SF bn(-) • 1 cbt spt regt (arty, AD)
EQUIPMENT
LT TK 100 PT-76†
RECCE 14 BRDM
AIFV 10 AMX-10 PAC 90
APC 24 AMX-10P, 60 BTR-50P
TOWED ARTY 48: **105mm**: 20 LG-1 Mk II; **122mm**: 28 M-38
MOR 81mm
MRL 140mm: 15 BM-14
AD GUNS 50+: **40mm**: 5 L60/70; **57mm**: S-60

Air Force 27,000

108 cbt ac, no armed hel; 2 operational cmds (East and West Indo) plus trg cmd
FGA 5 sqn
 1 with 21 A-4 (18 -E, 1 TA-4H, 2 TA-4J)
 1 with 10 F-16 (7 -A, 3 -B)
 2 with 7 *Hawk* Mk 109 and 32 *Hawk* Mk 209 (FGA/ftr)
 1 with 14 *Hawk* Mk 53 (FGA/trg)
FTR 1 sqn with 12 F-5 (8 -E, 4 -F)
RECCE 1 flt with 12* OV-10F (only a few op)
MR 1 sqn with 3 Boeing 737-200
TKR 2 KC-130B
TPT 4 sqn with 19 C-130 (9 -B, 3 -H, 7 -H-30), 3 L100-30, 1 Boeing 707, 4 Cessna 207, 5 Cessna 401, 2 C-402, 6 F-27-400M, 1 F-28-1000, 2 F-28-3000, 10 NC-212, 1 *Skyvan* (survey), 23 CN-235-110
HEL 3 sqn with 10 S-58T, 10 Hughes 500, 11 NAS-330, 5 NAS-332L (VIP/CSAR), 4 NBO-105CD, 2 Bell 204B
TRG 3 sqn with 39 AS-202, 2 Cessna 172, 22 T-34C, 6 T-41D
MISSILES
AIM-9P *Sidewinder*, AGM-65G *Maverick*

Forces Abroad

UN AND PEACEKEEPING
CROATIA (UNMOP): 2 obs **DROC** (MONUC): 5 incl 2 obs **GEORGIA** (UNOMIG): 4 obs **IRAQ/KUWAIT** (UNIKOM): 6 obs **SIERRA LEONE** (UNAMSIL): 10 obs

Paramilitary ε195,000 active

POLICE (Ministry of Interior) ε195,000
incl 14,000 police 'mobile bde' (BRIMOB) org in 56 coy, incl counter-terrorism unit (*Gegana*)
 EQPT APC 34 *Tactica*; **ac** 1 *Commander*, 2 Beech 18, 1 PA-31T, 1 Cessna-U206, 2 NC-212 **hel** 19 NBO-105, 3 Bell 206
MARINE POLICE (12,000)
 about 10 PCC, 9 PCI and 6 PCI< (all armed)
KAMRA (People's Security) (R)
ε40,000 report for 3 weeks' basic trg each year; part-time police auxiliary
CUSTOMS
 about 72 PFI<, armed
SEA COMMUNICATIONS AGENCY (responsible to Department of Communications)
 5 Kujang PCI, 4 Golok PCI (SAR), plus boats

Opposition

ORGANISASI PAPUA MERDEKA (OPM) ε150 (100 armed)
FREE ACEH MOVEMENT (*Gerakan Aceh Merdeka*) armed wing (AGAM) ε2,000–5,000

Other Forces

Militia gps operating in some provinces include:
a. Muslim
 Laskar Jihad (Holy war soldiers) Java-based. With ε2,000–3,000 to Ambon in Maluku
 Laskar Sabillah based west/central Java, south Sumatra
 Front to Defend Islam based Java/Sumatra
 Muslim Brotherhood, Laskar Mujahidin, Banser plus eight other gps
b. Non-Muslim
 Laskar Kristus based Ambon
 Satgas Golkar plus 4 other gps

East Timor

In accordance with UN Security Council resolution 1272 of 25 Oct 1999 the United Nations Transitional Administration in East Timor (UNTAET) was established to administer the territory and exercise legislative and executive authority during the transition towards independence.

Total UN Transitional Authority (UNTAET) budget in FY2000/01: US$563m

Population   ε**600,000** plus 200,000 in Indonesia

Total Armed Forces

Trg began in Jan 2001 with the aim of deploying 1,500 full time personnel and 1,500 reservists by Jan 2004

Foreign Forces

UN (UNTAET): some 8,077 tps incl 124 obs from 30 countries

Japan J

yen ¥		1999	2000	2001	2002
GDP	¥	495tr	512tr		
	US$	4.3tr	4.7tr		
per capita	US$	23,800	24,600		
Growth	%	-1.4	1.7		
Inflation	%	-0.3	-0.6		
Publ Debt	%	115	123		
Def exp	¥	4.6tr	4.9tr		
	US$	40.8bn	45.6bn		
Def bdgt	¥	4.9tr	4.9tr	4.9tr	
	US$	43.2bn	45.6bn	40.4bn	
US$1=¥		113	108	122	
Population			127,014,000	Korean <1%	
Age	13–17		18–22		23–32
Men	3,585,000		3,991,000		9,647,000
Women	3,417,000		3,800,000		9,205,000

Total Armed Forces

ACTIVE some 239,800

(incl 1,500 Central Staffs; some 10,200 women)

RESERVES some 47,400

READY RESERVE Army (GSDF) some 4,300
GENERAL RESERVE Army (GSDF) some 41,300 **Navy** (MSDF) some 1,000 **Air Force** (ASDF) some 800

Ground Self-Defence Force
some 148,700

5 Army HQ (Regional Comds) • 1 armd div • 10 inf div (6 at 7,000, 5 at 9,000 each); 2 inf bde • 2 composite bde • 1 AB bde • 1 arty bde; 2 arty gp • 2 AD bde; 3 AD gp • 4 trg bde (incl 1 spt) • 5 engr bde •1 hel bde • 5 ATK hel sqn

EQUIPMENT
  MBT some 840 Type-74, some 210 Type-90
  RECCE some 90 Type-87
  AIFV some 60 Type-89
  APC some 180 Type-60, some 340 Type-73, some 230 Type-82

TOWED ARTY 155mm: some 480 FH-70
SP ARTY 155mm: some 200 Type-75; **203mm**: some 90 M-110A2
MRL 130mm: some 50 Type-75 SP; **227mm**: some 60 MLRS
MOR incl **81mm**: some 710; **107mm**: some 230; **120mm**: some 340 (some SP)
SSM some 90 Type-88 coastal
ATGW some 130 Type-64, some 240 Type-79, some 310 Type-87
RL 89mm: some 1,510
RCL 84mm: some 2,720 *Carl Gustav*; **106mm**: some 220 (incl Type 60 SP)
AD GUNS 35mm: some 30 twin, some 50 Type-87 SP
SAM some 310 *Stinger*, some 60 Type 81, some 140 Type 91, some 60 Type 93, some 200 I HAWK
AC some 10 LR-1, some LR-2
ATTACK HEL some 90 AH-1S
TPT HEL 3 AS-332L (VIP), some 50 CH-47J/JA, some V-107, some 160 OH-6D, some 140 UH-1H/J, some 20 UH-60JA
SURV Type-92 (mor), J/MPQ-P7 (arty)

Maritime Self-Defence Force some 44,200

(incl some 9,800 Naval Aviation; and some 1,800 women)
BASES Yokosuka, Kure, Sasebo, Maizuru, Ominato
FLEET Surface units org into 4 escort flotillas of 8 DD/ FF each **Bases** Yokosuka, Kure, Sasebo, Maizuru
SS org into 2 flotillas **Bases** Kure, Yokosuka
Remainder assigned to 5 regional districts
SUBMARINES 16
SSK 16
  6 *Harushio* with *Harpoon* USGW, 6 × 533mm TT (J Type-89 HWT)
  6 *Yuushio* with *Harpoon* USGW, 6 × 533mm TT (J Type-89 HWT)
  4 *Oyashio* with *Harpoon* USGW, 6 × 533mm TT
PRINCIPAL SURFACE COMBATANTS some 54
DESTROYERS 42
  DDG 30
  4 *Kongou* with 2 × 4 *Harpoon* SSM, 2 VLS for *Standard* SAM and ASROC SUGW, 1 × 127mm gun, 2 × 3 ASTT, hel deck
  2 *Hatakaze* with 2 × 4 *Harpoon* SSM, 1 SM-1-MR SAM, 2 × 127mm guns, 2 × 3 ASTT, 1 × 8 ASROC SUGW
  3 *Tachikaze* with 2 × 4 *Harpoon* SSM, 1 SM-1-MR SAM, 1 × 127mm guns, 2 × 3 ASTT, 1 × 8 ASROC SUGW
  2 *Takatsuki* (J DD) with 2 × 4 *Harpoon* SSM, *Sea Sparrow* SAM, 1 × 127mm gun, 2 × 3 ASTT, 1 × 8 ASROC SUGW, 1 × 4 ASW RL
  8 *Asagiri* (J DD) with 2 × 4 *Harpoon* SSM, *Sea Sparrow* SAM, 2 × 3 ASTT, 1 × 8 ASROC SUGW, 1 SH-60J hel

11 *Hatsuyuki* (J DD) with 2 × 4 *Harpoon* SSM, *Sea Sparrow* SAM, 2 × 3 ASTT, 1 × 8 ASROC SUGW, 1 SH-60J hel

DD 12

7 *Murasame* with 1 VLS *Sea Sparrow* SAM, 2 × 3 ASTT, 1 VLS ASROC SUGW, 1 SH-60J hel

2 *Shirane* (J DDH) with *Sea Sparrow* SAM, 2 × 127mm guns, 2 × 3 ASTT, 1 × 8 ASROC SUGW, 3 SH-60J hel

2 *Haruna* (J DDH) with 1 x *Sea Sparrow* SAM, 2 × 127mm guns, 2 × 3 ASTT, 1 × 8 ASROC SUGW, 3 SH-60J hel

1 *Yamagumo* (J DDH) with 4 × 76mm gun, 2 × 3 ASTT, 1 × 8 ASROC SUGW, 1 × 4 ASW RL

FRIGATES 12

FFG 9

6 *Abukuma* (J DE) with 2 × 4 *Harpoon* SSM, 1 × 76mm gun, 2 × 3 ASTT, 1 × 8 ASROC SUGW

2 *Yubari* (J DE) with 2 × 4 *Harpoon* SSM, 2 × 3 ASTT, 1 × 4 ASW RL

1 *Ishikari* (J DE) with 2 × 4 *Harpoon* SSM, 2 × 3 ASTT, 1 × 4 ASW RL

FF 3

3 *Chikugo* (J DE) with 2 × 76mm guns, 2 × 3 ASTT, 1 × 8 ASROC SUGW

PATROL AND COASTAL COMBATANTS 3

MISSILE CRAFT 3 *Ichi-Go* (J PG) PHM with 4 SSM-1B

MINE WARFARE 30

MINE COUNTERMEASURES 30

2 *Uraga* MCM spt (J MST) with hel deck; can lay mines

3 *Yaeyama* MSO

12 *Hatsushima* MSC

9 *Uwajima* MSC

2 *Sugashima* MSC

2 *Nijma* coastal MCM spt

AMPHIBIOUS 8

1 *Osumi* LST, capacity 330 tps, 10 tk, 2 LCAC, (large flight deck)

2 *Miura* LST, capacity 200 tps, 10 tk

1 *Atsumi* LST, capacity 130 tps, 5 tk

2 *Yura* and 2 *Ichi-Go* LSM

Plus craft: 2 LCAC, 11 LCM

SUPPORT AND MISCELLANEOUS 20

3 *Towada* AOE, 1 *Sagami* AOE (all with hel deck), 2 AS/ARS, 1 *Minegumo* trg, 1 *Kashima* (trg), 1 *Shimayuki* (trg), 2 trg spt, 8 AGHS/AGOS, 1 icebreaker

NAVAL AVIATION (ε9,800)

ORGANISATION

7 Air Groups

AIRCRAFT

MR 10 sqn (1 trg) with P-3C

EW 1 sqn with EP-3

TPT 1 sqn with YS-11M

SAR 1 sqn with US-1A

TRG 4 sqn with T-5, TC-90, YS-11T

HELICOPTERS

ASW 6 land-based sqn (1 trg) with HSS-2B, 4 shipboard sqn with SH-60J

MCM 1 sqn with MH-53E

SAR 2 sqn with S-61, UH-60J

TRG 1 sqn with OH-6D, OH-6DA

EQUIPMENT

80 cbt ac; 90 armed hel

AIRCRAFT

80 **P-3C** • several **EP-3** • several **YS-11M** • some 6 **YS-11T** • 7 **US-1A** • 36 **T-5** • 28 **TC-90**

HELICOPTERS

20 **HSS-2B** • 60 **SH-60J** • 10 **MH-53E** • 3 **S-61** • 18 **UH-60J** • 10 **OH-6D** • several **OH-6DA**

Air Self-Defence Force some 45,400

some 297 cbt ac, no armed hel, 7 cbt air wings

Flying hours 150

FGA 1 sqn with some 35 F-I, 2 sqn with some 20 F-2

FTR 9 sqn

7 with some 130 F-15J/DJ

2 with some 50 F-4EJ

RECCE 1 sqn with some 20* RF-4E/EJ

AEW 1 sqn with some 10 E-2C, 4 Boeing E-767 (AWACS)

EW 2 sqn with 1 EC-1, some 5 YS-11 E

COMBAT TRG 1 sqn with some 10 F-15DJ

TPT 4 sqn, 4 flt

3 with some 25 C-1, some 15 C-130H, a few YS-11

1 with a few 747-400 (VIP)

4 flt hy-lift hel with some 15 CH-47J

SAR 1 wg (10 det) with **ac** some 10 MU-2, some 10 U-125A **hel** some 10 KV-107, some 20 UH-60J

CAL 1 sqn with a few YS-11, a few U-125-800

TRG 5 wg, 12 sqn with some 32* T-2, some 43 T-3, some 76 T-4, some 10 T-400

LIAISON some 90 T-4, a few U-4

TEST 1 wg with a few F-15J, some 7 T-4

AIR DEFENCE

ac control and warning: 4 wg, 28 radar sites

6 SAM gp (24 sqn) with some 140 *Patriot*

Air Base Defence Gp with **20mm** *Vulcan* AA guns, Type 81 short-range SAM, Type 91 portable SAM, *Stinger* SAM

ASM ASM-1, ASM-2

AAM AAM-3, AIM-7 *Sparrow*, AIM-9 *Sidewinder*

Forces Abroad

UN AND PEACEKEEPING

SYRIA/ISRAEL (UNDOF): 30

Paramilitary 12,250

COAST GUARD 12,250 (Ministry of Transport, no cbt role)

PATROL VESSELS some 343

Offshore (over 1,000 tons) 52, incl 1 *Shikishima* with 2 *Super Puma* hel, 2 *Mizuho* with 2 Bell 212, 8 *Soya* with 1 Bell 212 hel, 2 *Izu*, 28 *Shiretok* and 1 *Kojima* (trg)
Coastal (under 1,000 tons) 66 **Inshore** some 225 patrol craft most<

MISC 93: 12 AGHS, 60 nav tender, 14 fire fighting boats, 4 buoy tenders, 3 trg

AC 5 NAMC YS-11A, 2 Saab 340, 19 *King Air*, 1 Cessna U-206G

HEL 26 Bell 212, 4 Bell 206B, 6 Bell 412, 4 *Super Puma*, 4 Sikorsky S76C

Foreign Forces

US 38,330: **Army** 1,600; 1 Corps HQ **Navy** 5,200; bases at Yokosuka (HQ 7th Fleet) and Sasebo **Marines** 18,050; 1 MEF in Okinawa **Air Force** 13,480; 1 Air Force HQ (5th Air Force), 90 cbt ac, 1 ftr wg, 2 sqn with 36 F-16, 1 wg, 3 sqn with 54 F-15C/D, 1 sqn with 15 KC-135, 1 SAR sqn with 8 HH-60, 1 sqn with 2 E-3 AWACS; 1 airlift wg with 16 C-130E/H, 4 C-21, 3 C-9; 1 special ops gp with 4 MC-130P, 4 MC-130E

Korea, Democratic People's Republic of (North) DPRK

won		1999	2000	2001	2002
GNP[a]	US$	ε14.7bn	ε15bn		
per capita	US$	1,000	1,000		
Growth	%				
Inflation	%				
Debt	US$	ε12bn			
Def exp	US$	ε2.1bn	ε2.1bn		
Def bdgt	won	ε2.96bn	ε2.96bn	ε2.96bn	
	US$	1.3bn	1.3bn	1.3bn	
US$1=won		2.2	2.2	2.2	

[a] PPP est. GNP is larger than GDP because of remitted earnings of DPRK expatriates in J and ROK

Population				ε24,500,000
Age	13–17	18–22	23–32	
Men	1,074,000	908,000	2,504,000	
Women	1,117,000	1,004,000	2,048,000	

Total Armed Forces

ACTIVE ε1,082,000

Terms of service **Army** 5–8 years **Navy** 5–10 years **Air Force** 3–4 years, followed by compulsory part-time service to age 40. Thereafter service in the Worker/Peasant Red Guard to age 60

RESERVES 4,700,000 of which
Army 600,000 **Navy** 65,000 are assigned to units (see also *Paramilitary*)

Army ε950,000

20 Corps (1 armd, 4 mech, 12 inf, 2 arty, 1 capital defence) • 27 inf div • 15 armd bde • 14 inf • 21 arty • 9 MRL bde

Special Purpose Forces Comd (88,000): 10 *Sniper* bde (incl 2 amph, 2 AB), 12 lt inf bde (incl 3 AB), 17 recce, 1 AB bn, 'Bureau of Reconnaissance SF' (8 bn)

Army tps: 6 hy arty bde (incl MRL), 1 *Scud* SSM bde, 1 FROG SSM regt

Corps tps: 14 arty bde incl 122mm, 152mm SP, MRL

RESERVES

40 inf div, 18 inf bde

EQUIPMENT

MBT some 3,500: T-34, T-54/-55, T-62, Type-59
LT TK 560 PT-76, M-1985
APC 2,500 BTR-40/-50/-60/-152, PRC Type-531, VTT-323 (M-1973), some BTR-80A
TOTAL ARTY (excl mor) 10,400
  TOWED ARTY 3,500: **122mm**: M-1931/-37, D-74, D-30; **130mm**: M-46; **152mm**: M-1937, M-1938, M-1943
  SP ARTY 4,400: **122mm**: M-1977, M-1981, M-1985, M-1991; **130mm**: M-1975, M-1981, M-1991; **152mm**: M-1974, M-1977; **170mm**: M-1978, M-1989
  COMBINED GUN/MOR: 120mm (reported)
  MRL 2,500: **107mm**: Type-63; **122mm**: BM-21, BM-11, M-1977/-1985/-1992/-1993; **240mm**: M-1985/-1989/-1991
  MOR 7,500: **82mm**: M-37; **120mm**: M-43 (some SP); **160mm**: M-43
SSM 24 FROG-3/-5/-7; some 30 *Scud*-C, *No-dong*
ATGW: AT-1 *Snapper*, AT-3 *Sagger* (some SP), AT-4 *Spigot*, AT-5 *Spandrel*
RCL 82mm: 1,700 B-10
AD GUNS 11,000: **14.5mm**: ZPU-1/-2/-4 SP, M-1984 SP; **23mm**: ZU-23, M-1992 SP; **37mm**: M-1939, M-1992; **57mm**: S-60, M-1985 SP; **85mm**: KS-12; **100mm**: KS-19
SAM ε10,000+ SA-7/-16

Navy ε46,000

BASES East Coast Toejo (HQ), Changjon, Munchon, Songjon-pardo, Mugye-po, Mayang-do, Chaho Nodongjagu, Puam-Dong, Najin **West Coast** Nampo (HQ), Pipa Got, Sagon-ni, Chodo-ri, Koampo, Tasa-ri 2 Fleet HQ

SUBMARINES 26

SSK 26
  22 PRC Type-031/Sov *Romeo* with 533mm TT
  4 Sov *Whiskey*† with 533mm and 406mm TT
  (Plus some 45 SSI and 21 *Sang-O* SSC mainly used for SF ops, but some with 2 TT, all †)

PRINCIPAL SURFACE COMBATANTS 3

FRIGATES 3
  FF 3

1 *Soho* with 4 SS-N-2 *Styx* SSM, 1 × 100mm gun and hel deck, 4 ASW RL

2 *Najin* with 2 SS-N-2 *Styx* SSM, 2 × 100mm guns, 2 × 5 ASW RL

PATROL AND COASTAL COMBATANTS some 310

CORVETTES 6

4 *Sariwon* FS with 1 × 85mm gun

2 *Tral* FS with 1 × 85mm gun

MISSILE CRAFT 43

15 *Soju*, 8 Sov *Osa*, 4 PRC *Huangfeng* PFM with 4 SS-N-2 *Styx* SSM, 6 *Sohung*, 10 Sov *Komar* PFM with 2 SS-N-2 *Styx* SSM

TORPEDO CRAFT some 103

3 Sov *Shershen* PFT with 4 × 533mm TT

60 *Ku Song* PHT

40 *Sin Hung* PHT

PATROL CRAFT 158

COASTAL 25

6 *Hainan* PFC with 4 ASW RL, 13 *Taechong* PFC with 2 ASW RL, 6 *Chong-Ju* with 1 85mm gun, (2 ASW mor)

INSHORE some 133

18 SO-1<, 12 *Shanghai* II<, 3 *Chodo*<, some 100<

MINE WARFARE 23

MINE COUNTERMEASURES about 23 MSI<

AMPHIBIOUS 10

10 *Hantae* LSM, capacity 350 tps, 3 tk

plus craft 15 LCM, 15 LCU, about 100 Nampo LCVP, plus about 130 hovercraft

SUPPORT AND MISCELLANEOUS 7

2 AT/F, 1 AS, 1 ocean and 3 inshore AGHS

COASTAL DEFENCE

2 SSM regt: *Silkworm* in 6 sites, and probably some mobile launchers

GUNS 122mm: M-1931/-37; **130mm**: SM-4-1, M-1992; **152mm**: M-1937

Air Force 86,000

6 air divs, one per mil district:

3 bbr and ftr divs, 2 support ac divs, 1 trg div

Approx 70 full time/contingency air bases

621 cbt ac, ε24 armed hel

Flying hours 30 or less

BBR 3 lt regt with 80 H-5 (Il-28)

FGA/FTR 15 regt

3 with 107 J-5 (MiG-17), 4 with 159 J-6 (MiG-19), 4 with 130 J-7 (MiG-21), 1 with 46 MiG-23, 1 with 16 MiG-29, 1 with 18 Su-7, 1 with 35 Su-25, 30 MiG-29 (25 -As, 5 -Us), and 10 more being assembled, to start replacing J-5/J-6

TPT ac ε300 An-2/Y-5 (to infiltrate 2 air force sniper brigades deep into ROK rear areas), 6 An-24, 2 Il-18, 4 Il-62M, 2 Tu-134, 4 Tu-154

HEL ε320. Large hel aslt force spearheaded by 24 Mi-24*. Tpt/utility: 80 Hughes 500D, 139 Mi-2, 15 Mi-8/

-17, 48 Z-5

TRG incl 10 CJ-5, 7 CJ-6, 6 MiG-21, 170 Yak-18, 35 FT-2 (MiG-15UTI)

MISSILES

AAM AA-2 *Atoll*, AA-7 *Apex*

SAM ε45 SA-2 bty, 7 SA-3, 2 SA-5, many thousands of SA-7/14/16

Forces Abroad

advisers in some 12 African countries

Paramilitary 189,000 active

SECURITY TROOPS (Ministry of Public Security) 189,000 incl border guards, public safety personnel

WORKER/PEASANT RED GUARD some 3,500,000 (R)

Org on a provincial/town/village basis; comd structure is bde – bn – coy – pl; small arms with some mor and AD guns (but many units unarmed)

Korea, Republic of (South) ROK

won		1999	2000	2001	2002
GDP	won	484tr	516tr		
	US$	407bn	457bn		
per capita	US$	13,700	15,000		
Growth	%	10.7	8.8		
Inflation	%	0.8	2.3		
Debt	US$	141bn	136bn		
Def exp	won	14.3tr	ε14.4tr		
	US$	12.0bn	12.8bn		
Def bdgt	won	13.7tr	14.4tr	15.3tr	
	US$	11.6bn	12.8bn	11.8bn	
US$1=won		1,186	1,129	1,297	
Population				47,295,000	
Age		13–17	18–22	23–32	
Men		1,780,000	1,916,000	4,359,000	
Women		1,672,000	1,784,000	4,088,000	

Total Armed Forces

ACTIVE 683,000

(incl ε159,000 conscripts)

Terms of service conscription **Army** 26 months **Navy** and **Air Force** 30 months; First Combat Forces (Mobilisation Reserve Forces) or Regional Combat Forces (Homeland Defence Forces) to age 33

RESERVES 4,500,000

being re-org

DPRK ROK

East Asia and Australasia

Army 560,000

(incl 140,000 conscripts)
HQ: 3 Army, 11 Corps (two to be disbanded)
3 mech inf div (each 3 bde: 3 mech inf, 3 tk, 1 recce, 1 engr bn; 1 fd arty bde) • 19 inf div (each 3 inf regt, 1 recce, 1 tk, 1 engr bn; 1 arty regt (4 bn)) • 2 indep inf bde • 7 SF bde • 3 counter-infiltration bde • 3 SSM bn with NHK-I/-II (*Honest John*) • 3 AD arty bde • 3 I HAWK bn (24 sites), 2 *Nike Hercules* bn (10 sites) • 1 avn comd with 1 air aslt bde

RESERVES

1 Army HQ, 23 inf div

EQUIPMENT

MBT 1,000 Type 88, 80 T-80U, 400 M-47, 850 M-48
AIFV 40 BMP-3
APC incl 1,700 KIFV, 420 M-113, 140 M-577, 200 Fiat 6614/KM-900/-901, 20 BTR-80
TOWED ARTY some 3,500: **105mm**: 1,700 M-101, KH-178; **155mm**: M-53, M-114, KH-179; **203mm**: M-115
SP ARTY 155mm: 1,040 M-109A2, some K-9; **175mm**: M-107; **203mm**: 13 M-110
MRL 130mm: 156 *Kooryong* (36-tube); **227mm**: 29 MLRS (all ATACM capable)
MOR 6,000: **81mm**: KM-29; **107mm**: M-30
SSM 12 NHK-I/-II
ATGW TOW-2A, *Panzerfaust*, AT-7
RCL 57mm, 75mm, 90mm: M67; **106mm**: M40A2
ATK GUNS 58: **76mm**: 8 M-18; **90mm**: 50 M-36 SP
AD GUNS 600: **20mm**: incl KIFV (AD variant), 60 M-167 *Vulcan*; **30mm**: 20 B1 HO SP; **35mm**: 20 GDF-003; **40mm**: 80 L60/70, M-1
SAM 350 *Javelin*, 60 *Redeye*, ε200 *Stinger*, 170 *Mistral*, SA-16, 110 I HAWK, 200 *Nike Hercules*, *Chun Ma* (reported)
SURV RASIT (veh, arty), AN/TPQ-36 (arty, mor), AN/TPQ-37 (arty)
AC 5 O-1A
HEL
  ATTACK 60 AH-1F/-J, 45 Hughes 500 MD, 12 BO-105
  TPT 18 CH-47D, 6 MH-47E
  UTL 130 Hughes 500, 20 UH-1H, 116 UH-60P, 3 AS-332L

Navy 60,000

(incl 25,000 Marines and ε19,000 conscripts)
BASES Chinhae (HQ), Cheju, Mokpo, Mukho, Pohang, Pusan, Pyongtaek, Tonghae
FLEET COMMANDS 3
1st Tonghae (Sea of Japan); **2nd** Pyongtaek (Yellow Sea); **3rd** Chinhae (Korean Strait)
SUBMARINES 19
SSK 8 *Chang Bogo* (Ge T-209/1200) with 8 × 533 TT
SSI 11

3 KSS-1 *Dolgorae* (175t) with 2 × 406mm TT
8 *Dolphin* (175t) with 2 × 406mm TT
PRINCIPAL SURFACE COMBATANTS 39
DESTROYERS 6
  DDG 6
  3 *King Kwanggaeto* with 8 *Harpoon* SSM, 1 *Sea Sparrow* SAM, 1 × 127mm gun, 1 *Super Lynx* hel
  3 *Kwang Ju* (US *Gearing*) with 2 × 4 *Harpoon* SSM, 2 × 2 × 127mm guns, 2 × 3 ASTT, 1 × 8 ASROC SUGW, 1 *Alouette* III hel
FRIGATES 9
  FFG 9 *Ulsan* with 2 × 4 *Harpoon* SSM, 2 × 76mm gun, 2 × 3 ASTT (Mk 46 LWT)
CORVETTES 24
  24 *Po Hang* FS with 2 × 3 ASTT; some with 2 × 1 MM-38 *Exocet* SSM
PATROL AND COASTAL COMBATANTS 84
CORVETTES 4 *Dong Hae* (ASW) FS with 2 × 3 ASTT
MISSILE CRAFT 5
  5 *Pae Ku*-52 (US *Asheville*) PFM, 2 × 2 *Harpoon* SSM, 1 × 76mm gun
PATROL, INSHORE 75
  75 *Kilurki*-11 (*Sea Dolphin*) 37m PFI
MINE WARFARE 15
MINELAYERS 1
  1 *Won San* ML
MINE COUNTERMEASURES 14
  6 *Kan Keong* (mod It *Lerici*) MHC
  8 *Kum San* (US MSC-268/289) MSC
AMPHIBIOUS 14
  4 *Alligator* (RF) LST, capacity 700
  7 *Un Bong* (US LST-511) LST, capacity 200 tps, 16 tk
  3 *Ko Mun* (US LSM-1) LSM, capacity 50 tps, 4 tk
  Plus about 36 craft; 6 LCT, 10 LCM, about 20 LCVP
SUPPORT AND MISCELLANEOUS 14
  3 AOE, 2 spt AK, 2 AT/F, 2 salv/div spt, 1 ASR, about 4 AGHS (civil-manned, Ministry of Transport-funded)

NAVAL AVIATION
EQUIPMENT
16 cbt ac; 36 armed hel
  AIRCRAFT
    ASW 8 S-2E, 8 P-3C *Orion*
    MR 5 *Cessna* F406
  HELICOPTERS
    13 *Super Lynx* Mk 100, 17 *Super Lynx* Mk 99, 6 SA 316 *Alouette* III

MARINES (25,000)
2 div, 1 bde • spt units
  EQUIPMENT
  MBT 60 M-47
  AAV 60 LVTP-7, 42 AAV-7A1
  TOWED ARTY 105mm, 155mm
  SSM *Harpoon* (truck-mounted)

Air Force 63,000

3 Cmds (Ops, Logs, Trg), Tac Airlift Wg and Composite Wg are all responsible to ROK Air Force HQ. Ops Comd controls Anti-Aircraft Artillery Cmd, Air Traffic Centre and tac ftr wgs.

555 cbt ac, no armed hel

FTR/FGA 7 tac ftr wgs

2 with 160 F-16C/D

3 with 195 F-5E/F

2 with 130 F-4D/E

CCT 1 wg with 22* A-37B

FAC 1 wg with 20 O-1A, 10 O-2A

RECCE 1 gp with 18* RF-4C, 5* RF-5A

SAR 1 hel sqn, 5 UH-1H, 4 Bell-212

TAC AIRLIFT WG ac 2 BAe 748 (VIP), 1 Boeing 737-300 (VIP), 1 C-118, 10 C-130H, 15 CN-235M **hel** 6 CH-47, 3 AS-332, 3 VH-60

TRG 25* F-5B, 50 T-37, 30 T-38, 25 T-41B, 18 *Hawk* Mk-67

UAV 3 *Searcher*, 100 *Harpy*

MISSILES

ASM AGM-65A *Maverick*, AGM-88 HARM, AGM-130, AGM-142

AAM AIM-7 *Sparrow*, AIM-9 *Sidewinder*, AIM-120B AMRAAM

SAM *Nike-Hercules*, I HAWK, *Javelin*, *Mistral*

Forces Abroad

UN AND PEACEKEEPING

EAST TIMOR (UNTAET): 440 **GEORGIA** (UNOMIG): 3 obs **INDIA/PAKISTAN** (UNMOGIP): 9 obs **WESTERN SAHARA** (MINURSO): 20

Paramilitary ε4,500 active

CIVILIAN DEFENCE CORPS 3,500,000 (R) (to age 50)

MARITIME POLICE ε4,500

PATROL CRAFT 81

OFFSHORE 10

3 *Mazinger* (HDP-1000) (1 CG flagship), 1 *Han Kang* (HDC-1150), 6 *Sea Dragon/Whale* (HDP-600)

COASTAL 33

22 *Sea Wolf/Shark*, 2 *Bukhansan*, 7 *Hyundai*-type, 2 *Bukhansan*

INSHORE 38

18 *Seagull*, about 20<, plus numerous boats

SUPPORT AND MISCELLANEOUS 3 salvage

HEL 9 Hughes 500

Foreign Forces

US 36,520: **Army** 27,200; 1 Army HQ, 1 inf div **Navy** 300 **Air Force** 8,920: 1 HQ (7th Air Force); 90 cbt ac, 2 ftr wg; 3 sqn with 72 F-16, 1 sqn with 6 A-10, 12 OA-10, 1 special ops sqn with 5 MH -53J **USMC** 100

Laos Lao

kip		1999	2000	2001	2002
GDP	kip	6.8tr	13.4tr		
	US$	1.0bn	1.7bn		
per capita	US$	2,600	2,800		
Growth	%	3.8	6.5		
Inflation	%	128	27.1		
Debt	US$	2.5bn			
Def exp	kip	ε156bn	ε150bn		
	US$	22m	19.7m		
Def bdgt	kip	ε110bn	ε107bn	ε120bn	
	US$	15m	15.5m	15.8m	
FMA (US)	US$	4.0m	1.5m	1.5m	
US$1=kip		7,102	7,600	7,600	

Population			5,564,000

lowland Lao Loum 68% **upland** Lao Theung 22% **highland** Lao Soung incl **Hmong** and **Yao** 9%; **Chinese** and **Vietnamese** 1%

Age	13–17	18–22	23–32
Men	325,000	253,000	389,000
Women	319,000	249,000	388,000

Total Armed Forces

ACTIVE ε29,100

Terms of service conscription, 18 months minimum

Army 25,600

4 Mil Regions • 5 inf div • 7 indep inf regt • 1 armd, 5 arty, 9 AD arty bn • 3 engr (2 construction) regt • 65 indep inf coy • 1 lt ac liaison flt

EQUIPMENT

MBT 30 T-54/-55, T-34/85

LT TK 25 PT-76

APC 30 BTR-40/-60, 40 BTR-152

TOWED ARTY 75mm: M-116 pack; **105mm**: 25 M-101; **122mm**: 40 M-1938 and D-30; **130mm**: 10 M-46; **155mm**: M-114

MOR 81mm; 82mm; 107mm: M-2A1, M-1938; **120mm**: M-43

RCL 57mm: M-18/A1; **75mm**: M-20; **106mm**: M-40; **107mm**: B-11

AD GUNS 14.5mm: ZPU-1/-4; **23mm**: ZU-23, ZSU-23-4 SP; **37mm**: M-1939; **57mm**: S-60

(Army Marine Section ε600)

PATROL AND COASTAL COMBATANTS some 16

PATROL, RIVERINE some 16

some 12 PCR<, 4 LCM, plus about 40 boats

Lao

East Asia and Australasia

Air Force 3,500

14† cbt ac; no armed hel
FGA 2 sqn with some 12 MiG-21bis/2-UMs (service-ability in doubt)
TPT 1 sqn with 4 An-2, 5 An-24, 3 An-26, 1 Yak-40 (VIP), 1 An-74
HEL 1 sqn with 1 Mi-6, 9 Mi-8, 12 Mi-17, 3 SA-360, 1 Ka-32T (5 more on order), 1 Mi-26
TRG 8 Yak-18
AAM AA-2 *Atoll*†

Paramilitary

MILITIA SELF-DEFENCE FORCES 100,000+
village 'home-guard' org for local defence

Opposition

Numerous factions/groups; total armed str: ε2,000
United Lao National Liberation Front (ULNLF) largest group

Malaysia Mal

ringgit RM		1999	2000	2001	2002
GDP	RM	299bn	337bn		
	US$	78bn	88bn		
per capita	US$	10,600	12,900		
Growth	%	5.4	5.7		
Inflation	%	2.8	1.5		
Debt	US$	48bn	41bn		
Def exp[a]	RM	12.0bn	10.5bn		
	US$	3.2bn	2.8bn		
Def bdgt[b]	RM	6.9bn	6.0bn	7.3bn	
	US$	1.8bn	1.6bn	1.9bn	
FMA (US)	US$	0.7m	0.7m	0.7m	
FMA (Aus)	US$	4.2m			
US$1=RM		3.8	3.8	3.8	

[a] Incl procurement and def industry exp
[b] Excl procurement allocation in 1999 and 2000

Population			22,092,000

Muslim 54%; Malay and other indigenous 64%
Chinese 27% Indian 9%; Sabah and Sarawak non-Muslim Bumiputras form the majority of the population; 1,000,000+ Indonesian and Filipino illegal immigrants in 1997

Age	13–17	18–22	23–32
Men	1,293,000	1,056,000	1,791,000
Women	1,230,000	1,007,000	1,730,000

Total Armed Forces

ACTIVE 100,500

RESERVES 42,800

Army 40,000 **Navy** 2,200 **Air Force** 600

Army 80,000

2 Mil Regions • 1 HQ fd comd, 4 area comd (div) • 1 mech inf, 11 inf bde • 1 AB bde (3 AB bn, 1 lt arty regt, 1 lt tk sqn – forms Rapid Deployment Force)
Summary of combat units
    5 armd regt • 36 inf bn • 3 AB bn • 5 fd arty, 1 AD arty, 5 engr regt
1 SF regt (3 bn)
AVN 1 hel sqn

RESERVES

Territorial Army 1 bde HQ; 12 inf regt, 4 highway sy bn
EQUIPMENT
    LT TK 26 *Scorpion* (**90mm**)
    RECCE 162 SIBMAS, 140 AML-60/-90, 92 *Ferret* (60 mod)
    APC 111 KIFV (incl variants), 184 V-100/-150 *Commando*, 25 *Stormer*, 459 *Condor* (150 upgraded), 37 M-3 Panhard
    TOWED ARTY 105mm: 130 Model 56 pack, 40 M-102A1 († in store); **155mm**: 12 FH-70, some G5 (being delivered)
    MOR 81mm: 300
    ATGW SS-11, *Eryx*
    RL 89mm: M-20; **92mm**: FT5
    RCL 84mm: *Carl Gustav*; **106mm**: 150 M-40
    AD GUNS 35mm: 24 GDF-005; **40mm**: 36 L40/70
    SAM 48 *Javelin*, *Starburst*
    HEL 9 SA-316B
    ASLT CRAFT 165 *Damen*

Navy 12,500

(incl 160 Naval Air)
Fleet Operations Comd (HQ Lumut)
Naval Area 1 Kuantan **Naval Area 2** Labuan plus trg base at Pengelih (new base being built at Sepanggar Bay, Sabah)

SUBMARINES 0

but 2 *Zwaarduis* (NL) SSK in Mal but not in service
PRINCIPAL SURFACE COMBATANTS 4
FRIGATES 4
    FFG 2 *Lekiu* with 8 × MM-40 *Exocet* SSM, 1 × 16 VLS *Seawolf* SAM, 6 × 324mm ASTT
    FF 2 (both used for training)
    1 *Hang Tuah* (UK *Mermaid*) with 1 × 57mm gun, 1 × 3 *Limbo* ASW mor, hel deck
    1 *Rahmat* with 1 × 114mm gun, 1 × 3 ASW mor, hel deck
PATROL AND COASTAL COMBATANTS 41
CORVETTES 6
    4 *Laksamana* (It *Assad*) FSG with 6 OTO *Melara* SSM, 1 *Selenia* SAM, 1 × 76mm gun, 6 × 324mm ASTT

2 *Kasturi* (FS 1500) FS with 4 MM-38 *Exocet* SSM, 1 × 100mm gun, 2 × 2 ASW mor, hel deck

MISSILE CRAFT 8

4 *Handalan* (Swe *Spica*) PFM with 4 MM-38 *Exocet* SSM, 1 × 57mm gun

4 *Perdana* (Fr *Combattante* II) PFM with 2 *Exocet* SSM, 1 × 57mm gun

PATROL CRAFT 27

OFFSHORE 2 *Musytari* PCO with 1 × 100mm gun, hel deck

COASTAL/INSHORE 25

6 *Jerong* PFC, 4 *Sabah* PCC, 14 *Kris* PCC, 1 *Kedah* PCI<

MINE WARFARE 4

MINE COUNTERMEASURES 4

4 *Mahamiru* (mod It *Lerici*) MCO

plus 1 diving tender (inshore)

AMPHIBIOUS 1

1 *Sri Inderapura* (US *Newport*) LST, capacity 400 tps, 10 tk

Plus 115 craft: LCM/LCP/LCU

SUPPORT AND MISCELLANEOUS 4

2 log/fuel spt, 2 AGOR/AGOS

NAVAL AVIATION (160)

EQUIPMENT

9 armed hel

HELICOPTERS

6 *Wasp* HAS-1, 3 *Super Lynx*

SPECIAL FORCES

1 Naval Commando Unit

Air Force 8,000

71 cbt ac, no armed hel; 4 Air Div

Flying hours 60

FGA 4 sqn

3 with 8 *Hawk* 108, 17 *Hawk* 208, 9 MB-339

1 with 8 F/A-18D

FTR 2 sqn with 15 MiG-29N, 2 MiG-29U

MR 1 sqn with 4 Beech-200T

TRANSPORT 4 sqn

1 with 6 CN-235

1 with 5 C-130H

1 with 6 C-130H-30, 1 C-130H-MP, 2 KC-130H (tkr), 9 Cessna 402B (2 modified for aerial survey)

1 with ac 1 *Falcon*-900 (VIP), 1 Bombardier Global Express, 1 F-28 **hel** 2 S-61N, 1 Agusta-109, 2 S-70A

HEL 3 tpt/SAR sqn with 31 S-61A, 15 SA-316A/B, 2 Mi-17 (firefighting)

TRAINING

AC 20 MD3-160, 34 PC-7 (12* wpn trg)

HEL 8 SA-316

MISSILES

AAM AIM-7 *Sparrow*, AIM-9 *Sidewinder*, AA-10 *Alamo*, AA-11 *Archer*

ASM AGM-65 *Maverick*, AGM-84D *Harpoon*

AIRFIELD DEFENCE

1 field sqn

SAM 1 sqn with *Starburst*

Forces Abroad

UN AND PEACEKEEPING

EAST TIMOR (UNTAET): 35 incl 15 obs **ETHIOPIA/ ERITREA** (UNMEE): 12 incl 7 obs **DROC** (MONUC): 18 incl 7 obs **IRAQ/KUWAIT** (UNIKOM): 6 obs **SIERRA LEONE** (UNAMSIL): 10 obs **WESTERN SAHARA** (MINURSO): 13 obs

Paramilitary ε20,100

POLICE-GENERAL OPS FORCE 18,000

5 bde HQ: 21 bn (incl 2 Aboriginal, 1 Special Ops Force), 4 indep coy

EQPT ε100 Shorland armd cars, 140 AT-105 *Saxon*, ε30 SB-301 APC

MARINE POLICE about 2,100

BASES Kuala Kemaman, Penang, Tampoi, Kuching, Sandakan

PATROL CRAFT, INSHORE 30

15 *Lang Hitam* (38m) PFI, 6 *Sangitan* (29m) PFI, 9 improved PX PFI, plus 6 tpt, 2 tugs, 120 boats

POLICE AIR UNIT

ac 6 Cessna *Caravan* I, 4 Cessna 206, 7 PC-6 **hel** 1 Bell 206L, 2 AS-355F

AREA SECURITY UNITS (aux General Ops Force) 3,500

89 units

BORDER SCOUTS (in Sabah, Sarawak) 1,200

PEOPLE'S VOLUNTEER CORPS (RELA) 240,000

some 17,500 armed

CUSTOMS SERVICE

PATROL CRAFT, INSHORE 8

6 *Perak* (Vosper 32m) armed PFI, 2 *Combatboat 90H* PFI, plus about 36 craft

Foreign Forces

AUSTRALIA 148: **Army** 115; 1 inf coy **Air Force** 33; det with 2 P-3C **ac**

Mongolia Mgl

tugrik t		1999	2000	2001	2002
GDP	t	1.0tr	1.0tr		
	US$	980m	1.0bn		
per capita	US$	2,100	2,200		
Growth	%	3.5	3.5		
Inflation	%	7.3	11.6		
Debt	US$	890m	935m		

contd		1999	2000	2001	2002
Def exp	t	19.3bn	ε20bn		
	US$	19m	19.6m		
Def bdgt	t	19.7bn	25.1bn	33.3bn	
	US$	21m	24.6m	30.2m	
FMA (US)	US$	0.4m	0.5m	0.5m	
US$1=t		1,021	1,018	1,091	
Population					**2,731,000**

Kazak 4% Russian 2% Chinese 2%

Age	13–17	18–22	23–32
Men	161,000	142,000	237,000
Women	155,000	136,000	228,000

Total Armed Forces

ACTIVE 9,100

(incl 300 construction tps and 500 Civil Defence (see *Paramilitary*); 4,000 conscripts)
Terms of service conscription: males 18–28 years, 1 year

RESERVES 137,000
Army 137,000

Army 7,500

(incl 4,000 conscripts)
7 MR bde (all under str) • 1 arty bde • 1 lt inf bn (rapid-deployment) • 1 AB bn
EQUIPMENT
   MBT 650 T-54/-55/-62
   RECCE 120 BRDM-2
   AIFV 400+ BMP-1
   APC 250+ BTR-60
   TOTAL ARTY ε920 (incl ATK and AD Guns)
     TOWED ARTY ε300: **122mm**: M-1938/D-30; **130mm**: M-46; **152mm**: ML-20
     MRL 122mm: 130 BM-21
   MOR 140: **82mm, 120mm, 160mm**
   ATK GUNS 200 incl: **85mm**: D-44/D-48; **100mm**: BS-3, MT-12

Air Defence 800

9 cbt ac; 11 armed hel
Flying hours 22
2 AD regt
FTR 1 sqn with 8 MiG-21, 1 Mig-21U
ATTACK HEL 11 Mi-24
TPT (Civil Registration) 15 An-2, 12 An-24, 3 An-26, 1 An-30, 2 Boeing 727, 1 Airbus A310-300
AD GUNS: 150: **14.5mm**: ZPU-4; **23mm**: ZU-23, ZSU-23-4; **57mm**: S-60
SAM 250 SA-7

Paramilitary 7,200 active

BORDER GUARD 6,000 (incl 4,700 conscripts)
INTERNAL SECURITY TROOPS 1,200 (incl 800 conscripts) 4 gd units
CIVIL DEFENCE TROOPS (500)
CONSTRUCTION TROOPS (300)

Myanmar My

kyat K		1999	2000	2001	2002
GDP[a]	K	1,559bn	2,330bn		
	US$	29bn	37bn		
per capita	US$	1,200	1,400		
Growth	%	7.0	5.5		
Inflation	%	18.4	10.3		
Debt	US$	6.0bn	5.7bn		
Def exp[a]	K	31bn	32bn		
	US$	2.0bn	2.1bn		
Def bdgt[a]	K	31.8bn			
	US$	1.7bn	ε1.7bn	ε1.7bn	
US$1=K		6.35	6.25	6.6	

[a] PPP est

Population					**45,381,000**

Burmese 68% Shan 9% Karen 7% Rakhine 4% Chinese 3+% Other Chin, Kachin, Kayan, Lahu, Mon, Palaung, Pao, Wa, 9%

Age	13–17	18–22	23–32
Men	2,760,000	2,426,000	4,414,000
Women	2,685,000	2,386,000	4,343,000

Total Armed Forces

ACTIVE some 444,000 reported (incl People's Police Force and People's Militia – see *Paramilitary*)

Army 325,000

10 lt inf div (each 3 tac op comd (TOC))
12 Regional Comd (each with 10 regt)
32 TOC with 145 garrison inf bn
Summary of cbt units
   245 inf bn • 7 arty bn • 4 armd bn • 2 AA arty bn
EQUIPMENT†
   MBT 100 PRC Type-69II
   LT TK 105 Type-63 (ε60 serviceable)
   RECCE 45 *Ferret*, 40 *Humber*, 30 *Mazda* (local manufacture)
   APC 20 *Hino* (local manufacture), 250 Type-85
   TOWED ARTY 76mm: 100 M-1948; **88mm**: 50 25-pdr; **105mm**: 96 M-101; **122mm**; **130mm**: 16 M-46; **140mm**: 5.5in; **155mm**: 16 Soltam
   MRL 107mm: 30 Type-63

MOR **81mm; 82mm**: Type-53; **120mm**: Type-53, 80 Soltam
RCL **84mm**: 500 *Carl Gustav*; **106mm**: M40A1
ATK GUNS 60: **57mm**: 6-pdr; **76.2mm**: 17-pdr
AD GUNS **37mm**: 24 Type-74; **40mm**: 10 M-1; **57mm**: 12 Type-80
SAM HN-5A (reported), SA-16

Navy† 10,000

(incl 800 Naval Infantry)
BASES Bassein, Mergui, Moulmein, Seikyi, Yangon (Monkey Point), Sittwe
PATROL AND COASTAL COMBATANTS 68
CORVETTES 2†
1 *Yan Taing Aung* (US PCE-827) FS† with 1 × 76mm gun
1 *Yan Gyi Aung* (US *Admirable* MSF) FS† with 1 × 76mm gun
MISSILE CRAFT 6 *Houxin* PFM with 4 C-801 SSM
PATROL, OFFSHORE 3 *In Daw* (UK *Osprey*) PCO
PATROL, COASTAL 10 *Yan Sit Aung* (PRC *Hainan*) PCC
PATROL, INSHORE 18
12 US PGM-401/412, 3 FRY PB-90 PFI<, 3 *Swift* PCI 421
PATROL, RIVERINE about 29
2 *Nawarat*, 2 imp FRY Y-301 and 10 FRY Y-301, about 15<, plus some 25 boats
AMPHIBIOUS craft only
1 LCU, 10 LCM
SUPPORT 9
6 coastal tpt, 1 AOT, 1 diving spt, 1 buoy tender, plus 6 boats
NAVAL INFANTRY (800) 1 bn

Air Force 9,000

113 cbt ac, 29 armed hel
FTR 3 sqn with 50 F-7, 10 FT-7 (10 MiG-29 (incl 2 29-UB) or order)
FGA 2 sqn with 22 A-5M
CCT 2 sqn with 12 PC-7, 9 PC-9, 10 *Super Galeb* G4
TPT 1 sqn with 3 F-27, 4 FH-227, 5 PC-6A/-B, 2 Y-8D
LIAISON/TRG 4 Cessna 180, 1 Cessna *Citation* II, 12 K-8
HEL 4 sqn with 12 Bell 205, 6 Bell 206, 9 SA-316, 18* Mi-2, 11* Mi-17, 10 PZL W-3 *Sokol*

Paramilitary ε100,250

PEOPLE'S POLICE FORCE 65,000
PEOPLE'S MILITIA 35,000
PEOPLE'S PEARL AND FISHERY MINISTRY ε250
11 patrol boats (3 *Indaw* (Dk *Osprey*) PCC, 3 US *Swift* PGM PCI, 5 Aus *Carpentaria* PCI<)

Opposition and Former Opposition

GROUPS WITH CEASE-FIRE AGREEMENTS

UNITED WA STATE ARMY (UWSA) ε12,000 **Area** Wa hills between Salween river and PRC border; formerly part of Communist Party of Burma (CPB)
KACHIN INDEPENDENCE ARMY (KIA) some 8,000 **Area** northern My, incl Kuman range. Reached cease-fire agreement with govt in Oct 1993
MONG THAI ARMY (MTA) (formerly Shan United Army) ε3,000+ **Area** along Th border and between Lashio and PRC border
NATIONAL DEMOCRATIC ALLIANCE ARMY (NDAA) 1,000 **Area** north-east Shan state
MON NATIONAL LIBERATION ARMY (MNLA) ε1,000 **Area** on Th border in Mon state
NATIONAL DEMOCRATIC ALLIANCE ARMY (NDAA) ε1,000 **Area** eastern corner of Shan state on PRC–Lao border; formerly part of CPB
PALAUNG STATE LIBERATION ARMY (PSLA) ε700 **Area** hill tribesmen north of Hsipaw
NEW DEMOCRATIC ARMY (NDA) ε500 **Area** along PRC border in Kachin state; former CPB
DEMOCRATIC KAREN BUDDHIST ORGANISATION (DKBO) ε100–500 armed

GROUPS STILL IN OPPOSITION

SHAN STATE ARMY (SSA) ε3,000 **Area** Shan state
KAREN NATIONAL LIBERATION ARMY (KNLA) ε4,000 **Area** based in Th border area; political wg is Karen National Union (KNU)
ALL BURMA STUDENTS DEMOCRATIC FRONT ε2,000
KARENNI ARMY (KA) >1,000 **Area** Kayah state, Th border

New Zealand NZ

dollar NZ$		1999	2000	2001	2002
GDP	NZ$	99bn	107bn		
	US$	51bn	53bn		
per capita	US$	18,400	19,100		
Growth	%	4.5	3.5		
Inflation	%	-0.1	2.6		
Publ debt	%	36.7	31		
Def exp	NZ$	1.6bn	1.6bn		
	US$	824m	804m		
Def bdgt	NZ$	1.6bn	1.6bn	1.6bn	
	US$	824m	804m	678m	
US$1=NZ$		1.92	1.99	2.36	
Population					3,928,000
Maori 15% **Pacific Islander** 6%					

Age	13–17	18–22	23–32
Men	132,000	126,000	290,000
Women	124,000	122,000	278,000

Total Armed Forces

ACTIVE 9,230
(incl some 1,340 women)
RESERVES some 5,490
Regular some 2,410 **Army** 1,550 **Navy** 850 **Air Force** 10
Territorial 3,080 **Army** 2,650 **Navy** 390 **Air Force** 40

Army 4,450

(incl 550 women)
1 Land Force Comd HQ • 2 Land Force Gp HQ • 1
APC/Recce regt (-) • 2 inf bn • 1 arty regt (2 fd bty, 1
AD tp) • 1 engr regt (-) • 2 SF sqn (incl 1 reserve)

RESERVES

Territorial Force 6 Territorial Force Regional Trg regt
(each responsible for providing trained individuals for
top-up and round-out of deployed forces)

EQUIPMENT

LT TK 8 *Scorpion* (for disposal)
APC 56 M-113 (plus 21 variants)
TOWED ARTY 105mm: 24 *Hamel*
MOR 81mm: 50
ATGW some *Javelin*
RL 94mm: LAW
RCL 84mm: 63 *Carl Gustav*
SAM 12 *Mistral*
SURV *Cymbeline* (mor)

Navy 1,980

(incl 360 women)
BASE Auckland (Fleet HQ)

PRINCIPAL SURFACE COMBATANTS 3

FRIGATES 3

FF 3
2 *Anzac* with 8 *Sea Sparrow* VLS SAM, 1 × 127mm
gun, 6 × 324mm TT, 1 SH-2F hel
1 *Canterbury* (UK *Leander*) with 2 × 114mm guns, 6 ×
324mm ASTT, 1 SH-2F hel

PATROL AND COASTAL COMBATANTS 4

4 *Moa* PCI (reserve trg)

SUPPORT AND MISCELLANEOUS 7

1 *Endeavour* AO; 1 trg, 1 sail trg, 1 diving spt; 1
Resolution (US *Stalwart*) AGHS, 2 inshore AGHS

NAVAL AVIATION

EQUIPMENT

3 armed hel
HELICOPTERS
3 SH-2F *Sea Sprite* (see Air Force)

Air Force 2,800

(incl 430 women); 40 cbt ac, no armed hel

Flying hours A-4: 180

AIR COMMAND

FGA 2 sqn with 17 A-4K/TA-4K. To disband by Dec
2001
MR 1 sqn with 6* P-3K *Orion*
LIGHT ATTACK/TRG 1 sqn for *ab initio* and ftr lead-
in trg with 17* MB-339C. To disband by Dec 2001
ASW/ASUW 3 SH-2F (Navy-assigned)
TPT 2 sqn
ac 1 with 5 C-130H, 2 Boeing 727
hel 1 with 14 UH-1H, 5 Bell 47G (trg)
TRG 1 sqn with 13 CT-4E
MISSILES
ASM AGM-65B/G *Maverick*
AAM AIM-9L *Sidewinder*

Forces Abroad

AUSTRALIA 9 navigation trg
SINGAPORE 11; spt unit
UN AND PEACEKEEPING
BOSNIA (SFOR II): 27 **CAMBODIA** (CMAC): 2
CROATIA (UNMOP): 2 obs **EAST TIMOR**
(UNTAET): 669 incl 8 obs **EGYPT** (MFO): 26 **MIDDLE
EAST** (UNTSO): 7 obs **PAPUA NEW GUINEA**: 19
(Bougainville Peace Monitoring Group) **SIERRA
LEONE** (UNAMSIL): 2 obs

Papua New Guinea PNG

kina K		1999	2000	2001	2002
GDP	K	8.7bn	11bn		
	US$	3.2bn	4.5bn		
per capita	US$	2,800	2,800		
Growth	%	6.1	0.8		
Inflation	%	14.9	16.2		
Debt	US$	2.3bn	2.7bn		
Def exp	K	126m	ε135m		
	US$	46m	56m		
Def bdgt	K	80m	88m	ε90m	
	US$	29m	36m	30m	
FMA (US)	US$	0.2m	0.2m	0.2m	
FMA (Aus)	US$	6.7m			
US$1=K		2.73	2.41	2.95	
Population					**4,899,000**
Age		13–17	18–22		23–32
Men		278,000	247,000		427,000
Women		265,000	232,000		392,000

Total Armed Forces

ACTIVE ε4,400

Army ε3,800

2 inf bn • 1 engr bn
EQUIPMENT
 MOR 81mm; 120mm: 3

Maritime Element 400

BASES Port Moresby (HQ), Lombrum (Manus Island)
(patrol boat sqn); forward bases at Kieta and Alotau
PATROL AND COASTAL COMBATANTS 4
PATROL, COASTAL 4 *Tarangau* (Aust *Pacific Forum*
 32-m) PCC
AMPHIBIOUS 2
 2 *Salamaua* (Aust *Balikpapan*) LCH, plus 4 landing
 craft, manned and op by the civil administration

Air Force 200

no cbt ac, no armed hel
TPT 2 CN-235, 3 IAI-201 *Arava*, 1 CN-212
HEL †4 UH-1H

Foreign Forces

AUSTRALIA 38; trg unit
BOUGAINVILLE PEACE MONITORING GROUP
some 180 tps from Aus (149), NZ (19), Fiji (6), Vanuatu
(6)

Philippines Pi

peso P		1999	2000	2001	2002
GDP	P	3.0tr	3.3tr		
	US$	78.5bn	82.4bn		
per capita	US$	3,300	3,400		
Growth	%	3.2	4.0		
Inflation	%	6.7	4.3		
Debt	US$	52bn	51bn		
Def exp[a]	P	62bn	ε62bn		
	US$	1.6bn	1.5bn		
Def bdgt[b]	P	52bn	54bn	ε54bn	
	US$	1.4bn	1.3bn	1.1bn	
FMA (US)	US$	1.4m	1.4m	1.4m	
FMA (Aus)	US$	3.8m			
US$1=P		38.1	42.5	50	

[a] Incl paramil exp
[b] A five-year supplementary procurement budget of P50bn
(US$1.9bn) for 1996–2000 was approved in Dec 1996

Population				**77,318,000**	

Muslim 5–8%; **Mindanao provinces** Muslim 40–90%;
Chinese 2%

Age	13–17	18–22	23–32
Men	4,366,000	3,873,000	6,424,000
Women	4,219,000	3,737,000	6,200,000

Total Armed Forces

ACTIVE 107,000

RESERVES 131,000
Army 100,000 (some 75,000 more have commitments)
Navy 15,000 **Air Force** 16,000 (to age 49)

Army 67,000

5 Area Unified Comd (joint service) • 8 inf div (each
with 3 inf bde, 1 arty bn) • 1 special ops comd with 1 lt
armd bde ('regt'), 1 scout ranger, 1 SF regt • 5 engr bn
• 1 arty regt HQ • 1 Presidential Security Group

EQUIPMENT
 LT TK 40 *Scorpion*
 AIFV 85 YPR-765 PRI
 APC 100 M-113, 20 *Chaimite*, 100 V-150, 150 *Simba*
 TOWED ARTY 105mm: 230 M-101, M-102, M-26
  and M-56; 155mm: 12 M-114 and M-68
 MOR 81mm: M-29; 107mm: 40 M-30
 RCL 75mm: M-20; 90mm: M-67; 106mm: M-40 A1
 AC 2 Cessna (P-206, U-206)

Navy† ε24,000

(incl 7,500 Marines and 3,500 Coast Guard)
6 Naval Districts
BASES Sangley Point/Cavite, Zamboanga, Cebu
PRINCIPAL SURFACE COMBATANTS 1
FRIGATES
FF 1 *Rajah Humabon* (US *Cannon*) with 3 × 76mm gun,
 ASW mor
PATROL AND COASTAL COMBATANTS 58
PATROL, OFFSHORE 13
 2 *Rizal* (US *Auk*) PCO with 2 × 76mm gun, 3 × 2
  ASTT, hel deck
 3 *Emilio Jacinto* (ex-UK *Peacock*) PCO with 1 × 76mm
  gun
 8 *Miguel Malvar* (US PCE-827) PCO with 1 × 76mm
  gun
PATROL, COASTAL 11
 3 *Aguinaldo* PCC, 3 *Kagitingan* PCC, 5 *Thomas Batilo*
  (ROK *Sea Dolphin*) PCC
PATROL, INSHORE 34
 22 *José Andrada* PCI< and about 12 other PCI<
AMPHIBIOUS 7
 2 US *F. S. Besson*-class LST, capacity 32 tk plus 150
  tps, hel deck
 5 *Zamboanga del Sur* (US LST-1/511/542) LST,
  capacity either 16 tk or 10 tk plus 200 tps
 Plus about 39 craft: 30 LCM, 3 LCU, some 6 LCVP
SUPPORT AND MISCELLANEOUS 11
 2 AOT (small), 1 AR, 3 spt, 2 AWT, 3 AGOR/AGOS

NAVAL AVIATION

EQUIPMENT

no cbt ac, no armed hel

AIRCRAFT

MR/SAR 7 *Islander*

HELICOPTER

SAR 7 Bo-105

MARINES (7,500)

3 bde (10 bn) to be 2 bde (6 bn)

EQUIPMENT

AAV 30 LVTP-5, 55 LVTP-7

LAV 24 LAV-300

TOWED ARTY 105mm: 150 M-101

MOR 4.2in (**107mm**): M-30

Air Force ε16,000

44 cbt ac, some 97 armed hel

FTR 1 sqn with 8 F-5A/B

ARMED HEL 3 sqn with 60 Bell UH-1H/M, 16 AUH-76 (S-76 gunship conversion), 21 Hughes 500/520MD

MR 1 F-27M

RECCE 4 RT-33A, 21* OV-10 *Broncos*

SAR ac 4 HU-16 **hel** 10 Bo-105C

PRESIDENTIAL AC WG ac 1 F-27, 1 F-28 **hel** 2 Bell 212, 4 Bell-412, 2 S-70A, 2 SA-330

TPT 3 sqn

1 with 2 C-130B, 3 C-130H, 3 L-100-20, 7 F-27

2 with 2 BN-2 *Islander*, 14 N-22B *Nomad Missionmaster*

HEL 2 sqn with 55 Bell 205, 16 UH-1H, 33 MD-520

LIAISON 10 Cessna (7 -180, 2 -210, 1 -310), 5 DHC-2, 12 U-17A/B

TRG 4 sqn

1 with 4 T-33A, 1 with 14 T-41D, 1 with 28 SF-260TP, 1 with 15* S-211

AAM AIM-9B *Sidewinder*

Forces Abroad

UN AND PEACEKEEPING

EAST TIMOR (UNTAET): 617 incl 8 obs

Paramilitary 44,000 active

PHILIPPINE NATIONAL POLICE 40,500 (Department of Interior and Local Government)

62,000 active aux; 15 Regional, 73 Provincial Comd

COAST GUARD 3,500

Part of Department of Transport; but mainly funded, manned and run by the Navy

EQPT 1 *San Juan* PCO, 3 *De Haviland* PCI, 4 *Basilan* (US PGM-39/42) PCI, plus some 35 *Swift* PCI, 3 SAR hel (by 2000)

CITIZEN ARMED FORCE GEOGRAPHICAL UNITS (CAFGU) 40,000

Militia, 56 bn; part-time units which can be called up for extended periods

Opposition and Former Opposition

Groups with Peace Agreements

BANGSA MORO ARMY (armed wing of Moro National Liberation Front (MNLF); Muslim) ε5,700 integrated into national army

MORO ISLAMIC LIBERATION FRONT (breakaway from MNLF; Muslim) 10,000 (up to 15,000 reported)

Groups Still in Opposition

NEW PEOPLE'S ARMY (NPA; communist) ε9,500

MORO ISLAMIC REFORMIST GROUP (breakaway from MNLF; Muslim) 900

ABU SAYYAF GROUP ε1,500

Singapore Sgp

dollar S$		1999	2000	2001	2002
GDP	S$	144bn	162bn		
	US$	84bn	97bn		
per capita	US$	24,400	26,000		
Growth	%	5.4	10.1		
Inflation	%	0.5	1.8		
Debt	US$		9.7bn		
Def exp	S$	8.1bn	8.0bn		
	US$	4.7bn	4.8bn		
Def bdgt	S$	7.3bn	7.4bn	7.8bn	
	US$	4.2bn	4.4bn	4.3bn	
FMA (Aus) US$		0.5m			
US$1=S$		1.72	1.72	1.81	
Population					**3,691,000**
Chinese 76% Malay 15% Indian 6%					
Age		13–17	18–22		23–32
Men		122,000	108,000		240,000
Women		117,000	102,000		234,000

Total Armed Forces

ACTIVE 60,500

(incl 39,800 conscripts)

Terms of service conscription 24–30 months

RESERVES ε312,500

Army ε300,000; annual trg to age 40 for men, 50 for officers **Navy** ε5,000 **Air Force** ε7,500

Army 50,000

(35,000 conscripts)

3 combined arms div (mixed active/reserve forma-

tions) each with 2 inf bde (each 3 inf bn), 1 armd bde, 1 recce, 2 arty, 1 AD, 1 engr bn
1 Rapid Deployment div (mixed active/reserve formation) with 3 inf bde (incl 1 air mob, 1 amph – each 3 bn)
1 mech bde
Summary of active units
9 inf bn • 4 lt armd/recce bn • 4 arty bn • 1 cdo (SF) bn • 4 engr bn

RESERVES
9 inf bde incl in mixed active/reserve formations listed above • 1 op reserve div with additional inf bde • 2 People's Defence Force cmd with 12 inf bn • Total cbt units ε60 inf, ε8 lt armd/recce, ε12 arty, 1 cdo (SF), ε8 engr bn

EQUIPMENT
MBT 80-100 *Centurion* (trg only)
LT TK ε350 AMX-13SM1
RECCE 22 AMX-10 PAC 90
AIFV 22 AMX-10P, some IFV-25
APC 750+ M-113A1/A2 (some with 40mm AGL, some with 25mm gun), 30 V-100, 250 V-150/-200 *Commando*, some IFV-40/50
TOWED ARTY 105mm: 37 LG1; **155mm**: 38 Soltam M-71S, 16 M-114A1 (may be in store), 45 M-68 (may be in store), 52 FH-88, 18 FH-2000
MOR 81mm (some SP); **120mm**: 50 (some SP in M-113); **160mm**: 12 Tampella
ATGW 30+ *Milan, Spike*
RL *Armbrust*; **89mm**: 3.5in M-20
RCL 84mm: ε200 *Carl Gustav*; **106mm**: 90 M-40A1 (in store)
AD GUNS 20mm: 30 GAI-CO1 (some SP)
SAM 75+: RBS-70 (some SP in V-200) (Air Force), *Mistral* (Air Force), SA-18 (Air Force)
SURV AN/TPQ-36/-37 (arty, mor)

Navy 4,500
(incl 1,800 conscripts)
COMMANDS Fleet (1st, 3rd Flotillas and sub sqn)
Coastal and **Naval Logistic** and **Training Command**
BASES Tuas (Jurong), Changi
SUBMARINES 1
1 *Challenger* (Swe *Sjoormen*) SSK with 4 × 533 TT (2 more in trials in Sgp plus 1 awaiting delivery in late 2001 from Swe)
PATROL AND COASTAL COMBATANTS 24
CORVETTES 6 *Victory* (Ge Lürssen 62m) FSG with 8 *Harpoon* SSM, 1 × 2 *Barak* SAM, 1 × 76mm gun, 2 × 3 ASTT
MISSILE CRAFT 6
6 *Sea Wolf* (Ge Lürssen 45m) PFM with 2 × 4 *Harpoon* SSM, 4 × 2 *Gabriel* SSM, 1 × 2 *Mistral/Simbad* SAM, 1 × 57mm gun
PATOL CRAFT 12

12 *Fearless* PCO with 2 *Mistral/Sadral* SAM, 1 × 76mm gun (6 with 6 × 324mm TT)
MINE WARFARE 4
MINE COUNTERMEASURES 4
4 *Bedok* (SW *Landsort*) MHC
AMPHIBIOUS 5
1 *Perseverance* (UK *Sir Lancelot*) LSL with 1 × 2 *Mistral/Simbad* SAM, capacity 340 tps, 16 tk, hel deck
4 *Endurance* LST with 2 × 2 *Mistral/Simbad* SAM, 1 × 76mm gun; capacity: 350 tps, 18 tk, 4 LCVP, 2 hel
Plus craft: 6 LCM, 30 LCU, and boats
SUPPORT AND MISCELLANEOUS 3
1 *Jupiter* diving spt and salvage, 1 *Kendrick* sub spt ship, 1 trg

Air Force 6,000
(incl 3,000 conscripts); 150 cbt ac, 20 armed hel
FGA 6 sqn
2 with 64 A-4SU
1 with 3 F-16A, 4 F-16B
1 with 8 F-16C, 10 F-16D (some SEAD), plus 24 F-16C/D in US
2 with 28 F-5S, 9 F-5T (secondary GA role)
RECCE 1 sqn with 8 RF-5S
AEW 1 sqn with 4 E-2C
TKR 1 sqn with 1 KC-135. 1 more in US, another 2 to be delivered
TPT/TKR/RECCE 2 sqn
1 with 4 KC-130B (tkr/tpt), 5 C-130H (2 ELINT), 1 KC-130H
1 with 9 F-50 *Enforcer* (4 tpt, 5 MR)
ARMED HEL 2 sqn with 20 AS 550A2/C2 (8 AH-64D to be delivered from 2002)
HEL 4 sqn
1 with 19 UH-1H, 6 AB-205A, 2 with 20 AS-332AL (incl 5 SAR), 24 AS-532M
1 with 6 CH-47D
TRG
1 sqn with 27 SIAI S-211
1 trg detachment with 16 TA-4SU
UAV 1 sqn with 40 *Searcher* Mk 2, 24 *Chukar* III
AIR DEFENCE SYSTEMS DIVISION
4 field def sqn
Air Defence Bde 1 sqn with **35mm** Oerlikon, 1 sqn with 18 I-HAWK, 1 sqn with Blindfire *Rapier*
Air Force Systems Bde 1 sqn mobile radar, 1 sqn LORADS
Divisional Air Def Arty Bde (attached to Army divs) 1 bn with 36 *Mistral* (SAM), 3 bn with RBS 70 (SAM), 1 bn with SA-18 *Igla*
MISSILES
AAM AIM-7P *Sparrow*, AIM-9 N/P *Sidewinder* AIM-120 AMRAAM stored in US
ASM AGM-45 *Shrike*, AGM-65B *Maverick*, AGM-65G *Maverick*, AGM-84 *Harpoon*

Forces Abroad

AUSTRALIA 230; flying trg schools at Oakey (12 AS-332/532), and Pearce (27 S-211)
BRUNEI 500; trg school, incl hel det (with 5 UH-1H)
FRANCE 200; trg 8 A-4SU/10 TA-4SU (Cazaux AFB)
TAIWAN 3 trg camps (incl inf, arty and armd)
THAILAND 1 trg camp (arty, cbt engr)
US trg detachment some 6 CH-47D (ANG facility Grand Prairie, TX); 12 F-16C/D (leased from USAF at Luke AFB, AZ), 12 F-16C/D (at Cannon AFB, NM); 1 KC-135 trg det at McConnell AFB, KS

UN AND PEACEKEEPING

EAST TIMOR (UNTAET): 87 **ETHIOPIA/ERITREA** (UNMEE): 2 obs **IRAQ/KUWAIT** (UNIKOM): 5 obs

Paramilitary ε94,000+ active

SINGAPORE POLICE FORCE ε12,000 (incl 3,500 conscripts, 21,000 reservists)
incl Police Coast Guard
12 *Swift* PCI< and about 60 boats
Singapore Gurkha Contingent (1,500: 6 coy)
CIVIL DEFENCE FORCE 84,300
(incl 1,600 regulars, 3,200 conscripts, 23,000 reservists, 54,000+ volunteers); 1 construction bde (2,500 conscripts)

Foreign Forces

US 150: **Air Force** 40 **Navy** 90 **USMC** 20
NEW ZEALAND 11; spt unit

Taiwan (Republic of China) ROC

new Taiwan dollar NT$

		1999	2000	2001	2002
GNP	NT$	9.4tr	9.7tr		
	US$	288bn	314bn		
per capita	US$	15,600	16,800		
Growth	%	5.5	6.3		
Inflation	%	0.8	1.7		
Debt	US$		40bn		
Def exp[a]	NT$	490bn	542bn		
	US$	15.0bn	17.6bn		
Def bdgt[b]	NT$	357bn	395bn	271bn	
	US$	10.9bn	12.8bn	8.2bn	
US$1=NT$		32.7	30.8	32.9	

[a] Incl special appropriations for procurement and infrastructure amounting to NT$301bn (US$11bn) 1993–2001. Between 1993–98, NT$208bn (US$8bn) was spent out of NT$289bn (US$11bn) appropriated for these years.
[b] 1999 def bdgt covers 18-month period Jul 1999–Dec 2000.

Population			22,124,000
Taiwanese 84% mainland Chinese 14%			
Age	13–17	18–22	23–32
Men	966,000	1,021,000	1,816,000
Women	928,000	967,000	1,713,000

Total Armed Forces

ACTIVE ε370,000 (to be 350,000)
Terms of service 22 months

RESERVES 1,657,500
Army 1,500,000 with some obligation to age 30 **Navy** 32,500 **Marines** 35,000 **Air Force** 90,000

Army ε240,000 (to be 200,000)

(incl mil police)
3 Army, 1 AB Special Ops HQ • 10 inf div • 2 mech inf div • 2 AB bde • 6 indep armd bde • 1 tk gp • 2 AD SAM gp with 6 SAM bn: 2 with *Nike Hercules*, 4 with I HAWK • 2 avn gp, 6 avn sqn

RESERVES
7 lt inf div

EQUIPMENT
MBT 100 M-48A5, 450+ M-48H, 376 M-60A3
LT TK 230 M-24 (**90mm** gun), 675 M-41/Type 64
AIFV 225 M-113 with **20–30mm** cannon
APC 650 M-113, 300 V-150 *Commando*
TOWED ARTY 105mm: 650 M-101 (T-64); **155mm**: M-44, 90 M-59, 250 M-114 (T-65); **203mm**: 70 M-115
SP ARTY 105mm: 100 M-108; **155mm**: 20 T-69, 225 M-109A2/A5; **203mm**: 60 M-110
COASTAL ARTY 127mm: US Mk 32 (reported)
MRL 300+ incl **117mm**: KF VI; **126mm**: KF III/IV towed and SP
MOR 81mm: M-29 (some SP); **107mm**
SSM *Ching Feng*
ATGW 1,000 TOW (some SP)
RCL 90mm: M-67; **106mm**: 500 M-40A1, Type 51
AD GUNS 40mm: 400 (incl M-42 SP, Bofors)
SAM 40 *Nike Hercules* (to be retired), 100 HAWK, *Tien Kung* (*Sky Bow*) -1/-2, *Stinger*, 74 *Avenger*, 2 *Chaparral*, 25 *Patriot*
AC 20 O-1
HEL 100 UH-1H, 50 AH-1W, 10 TH-67, 30 OH-58D
UAV *Mastiff* III

DEPLOYMENT
Quemoy 15–20,000; 4 inf div **Matsu** 8–10,000; 1 inf div

Navy ε62,000

(incl 30,000 Marines)
3 Naval Districts
BASES Tsoying (HQ), Makung (Pescadores), Keelung,

Hualien (ASW HQ) (New East Coast fleet set up and based at Suo)

SUBMARINES 4

SSK 4

2 *Hai Lung* (Nl mod *Zwaardvis*) with 533mm TT

2 *Hai Shih* (US *Guppy* II) with 533mm TT (trg only)

PRINCIPAL SURFACE COMBATANTS 32

DESTROYERS 11

DDG 11

7 *Chien Yang* (US *Gearing*) (*Wu Chin* III conversion) with 4 *Hsiung Feng* SSM, SM-1-MR SAM, 2 × 3 ASTT, 1 × 8 ASROC SUGW, 1 *Hughes* MD-500 hel

3 *Fu Yang* (US *Gearing*) with 5 *Hsiung Feng* I/*Gabriel* II SSM, 1 or 2 × 127mm guns, 2 × 3 ASTT, 1 *Hughes* MD-500 hel (1 also with 1 × 8 ASROC SUGW)

1 *Po Yang* (US *Sumner*)† with *Hsiung Feng* SSM, 1 or 2 × 127mm guns, 2 × 3 ASTT, 1 *Hughes* MD-500 hel

FRIGATES 21

FFG 21

7 *Cheng Kung* (US *Perry*) with 8 *Hsiung Feng* II SSM, 1 SM-1 MR SAM, 1 × 76mm gun, 2 × 3 ASTT, 2 S-70C hel

6 *Kang Ding* (Fr *La Fayette*) with 8 *Hsiung Feng* SSM, 4 *Sea Chaparral* SAM, 1 × 76mm gun, 6 × 324mm ASTT, 1 S-70C hel

8 *Chin Yang* (US *Knox*) with *Harpoon* SSM, 1 × 127mm gun, 4 ASTT, 1 × 8 ASROC SUGW, 1 SH-2F hel

PATROL AND COASTAL COMBATANTS 59

MISSILE CRAFT 59

2 *Lung Chiang*† PFM with 2 *Hsiung Feng* I SSM

9 *Jinn Chiang* PFM with 4 *Hsiung Feng* I SSM

48 *Hai Ou* (mod II *Dvora*) PFM< with 2 *Hsiung Feng* I SSM

MINE WARFARE 12

MINE COUNTERMEASURES 12

4 (ex-US) *Aggressive* MSO

4 *Yung Chou* (US *Adjutant*) MSC

4 *Yung Feng* MSC converted from oil-rig spt ships

AMPHIBIOUS 18

1 *Shiu Hai* (US *Anchorage*) LSD

2 *Chung Ho* (US *Newport*) LST capacity 400 tps, 500 tons veh, 4 LCVP

1 *Kao Hsiung* (US LST 511) LCC

10 *Chung Hai* (US LST 511) LST, capacity 16 tk, 200 tps

4 *Mei Lo* (US LSM-1) LSM, capacity about 4 tk

Plus about 325 craft; some 20 LCU, 205 LCM, 100 LCVP and assault LCVP

SUPPORT AND MISCELLANEOUS 20

3 AO, 2 AR, 1 *Wu Yi* combat spt with hel deck, 2 *Yuen Feng* and 2 *Wu Kang* attack tpt with hel deck, 2 tpt, 7 AT/F, 1 *Te Kuan* AGOR

COASTAL DEFENCE 1

1 SSM coastal def bn with *Hsiung Feng* (*Gabriel*-type)

NAVAL AVIATION

EQUIPMENT

32 cbt ac; 20 armed hel

AIRCRAFT

MR 1 sqn with 32 S-2 (24 -E, 8 -G)

HELICOPTERS

20* S-70C ASW *Defender*

MARINES (30,000)

2 div, spt elm

EQUIPMENT

AAV LVTP-4/-5

TOWED ARTY 105mm, 155mm

RCL 106mm

Air Force 68,000

482 cbt ac, no armed hel

Flying hours 180

FTR 3 sqn with 58 *Mirage* 2000-5 (47 -5EI, 11 -5DI)

FGA/FTR 20 sqn

6 with 90 F-5E/F (plus many in store)

6 with 128 *Ching-Kuo*

7 with 146 F-16A/B (incl one sqn recce capable)

1 with 22 AT-3

RECCE 1 with 8 RF-5E

AEW 4 E-2T

EW 1 with 2 C-130HE, 2 CC-47

SAR 1 sqn with 17 S-70C

TPT 3 ac sqn

2 with 19 C-130H (1 EW)

1 VIP with 4 Boeing 727-100, 1 Boeing 737-800, 10 Beech 1900, 3 *Fokker* F-50

HEL 1 S-62A (VIP), 14 S-70, 3 CH-47

TRG ac incl 36* AT-3A/B, 42 T-34C

MISSILES

ASM AGM-65A *Maverick*

AAM AIM-4D *Falcon*, AIM-9J/P *Sidewinder*, *Shafrir*, *Sky Sword* I and II, MATRA *Mica*, MATRA R550 *Magic* 2

ARM *Sky Sword* IIA

Forces Abroad

US F-16 conversion unit at Luke AFB

Paramilitary ε26,650

SECURITY GROUPS 25,000

National Police Administration (Ministry of Interior); **Bureau of Investigation** (Ministry of Justice); **Military Police** (Ministry of Defence); **Coast Guard Administration**

MARITIME POLICE ε1,000

about 38 armed patrol boats

CUSTOMS SERVICE (Ministry of Finance) 650

5 PCO, 2 PCC, 1 PCI, 5 PCI<; most armed

COAST GUARD ADMINISTRATION 22,000 (all civilians)

responsible for guarding the Spratly and Pratas island groups, and to enforce law and order

Foreign Forces

SINGAPORE 3 trg camps

Thailand Th

baht b		1999	2000	2001	2002
GDP	b	5.0tr	4.8tr		
	US$	135bn	123bn		
per capita	US$	7,800	8,500		
Growth	%	4.2	4.4		
Inflation	%	0.2	1.5		
Debt	US$	95.6bn	80bn		
Def exp	b	98bn	97.8bn		
	US$	2.6bn	2.5bn		
Def bdgt	b	77.4bn	77.3bn	77.2bn	
	US$	2.1bn	2.0bn	1.7bn	
FMA (US)	US$	4.6m	$1.6m	$2.8m	
FMA (Aus)	US$	3.0m			
US$1=b		37.2	38.9	45.4	
Population					61,586,000

Thai 75% **Chinese** 14% **Muslim** 4%

Age	13–17	18–22	23–32
Men	3,135,000	3,184,000	6,203,000
Women	3,027,000	3,092,000	6,036,000

Total Armed Forces

ACTIVE ε306,000

Terms of service 2 years

RESERVES 200,000

Army 190,000

(incl ε70,000 conscripts)
4 Regional Army HQ, 2 Corps HQ • 2 cav div • 3
armd inf div • 2 mech inf div • 1 lt inf div • 2 SF div •
1 arty div, 1 AD arty div (6 AD arty bn) • 1 engr div • 4
economic development div • 1 indep cav regt • 8
indep inf bn • 4 recce coy • armd air cav regt with 3
air-mobile coy • Some hel flt • Rapid Reaction Force (1
bn per region forming)

RESERVES

4 inf div HQ

EQUIPMENT

  MBT 50 PRC Type-69 (trg/in store), 105 M-48A5, 178
    M-60 (125 A3, 53 A1)
  LT TK 154 *Scorpion* (ε50 in store), 200 M-41, 106
    Stingray
  RECCE 32 Shorland Mk 3, HMMWV
  APC 340 M-113A1/A3, 162 V-150 *Commando*, 18
    Condor, 450 PRC Type-85 (YW-531H)

  TOWED ARTY 105mm: 24 LG1 Mk 2, 285 M-101/-
    101 mod, 12 M-102, 32 M-618A2 (local manufac-
    ture); **130mm**: 15 PRC Type-59; **155mm**: 56 M-114,
    62 M-198, 32 M-71, 42 GHN-45A1
  SP ARTY 155mm: 20 M-109A2
  MOR 1,900 incl **81mm** (incl 21 M-125A3 SP), **107mm**
    incl M-106A1 SP; **120mm**: 12 M-1064A3 SP
  ATGW TOW (incl 18 M-901A5), 300 *Dragon*
  RL M-72 LAW
  RCL 75mm: 30 M-20; **106mm**: 150 M-40
  AD GUNS 20mm: 24 M-163 *Vulcan*, 24 M-167
    Vulcan; **37mm**: 122 Type-74; **40mm**: 80 M-1/M-42
    SP, 48 L/70; **57mm**: 24+ PRC Type-59 (ε6 op)
  SAM *Redeye*, some *Aspide*, HN-5A
  UAV *Searcher*
  AIRCRAFT
    TPT 2 C-212, 2 Beech 1900C, 1 Beech 99, 2 Short
    330UTT, 1 *Beech King Air*, 2 *Jetstream* 41, 10 Cessna
    208
    LIAISON 25 O-1A, 10 T-41A, 4 U-17B
    TRG 10 T-41D, 18 MX-7-235
  HELICOPTERS
    ATTACK 5 AH-1F
    TPT 10 CH-47D, 60 Bell (incl -206, -212, -214, -412), 69
    UH-1H
    TRG 40 Hughes 300C
  SURV RASIT (veh, arty), AN-TPQ-36 (arty, mor)

Navy 68,000

(incl 1,700 Naval Aviation, 18,000 Marines, 7,000
Coastal Defence; incl 27,000 conscripts)
FLEETS 1st North Thai Gulf **2nd** South Thai Gulf **3rd**
Andaman Sea
1 Naval Air Division
BASES Bangkok, Sattahip (Fleet HQ), Songkhla, Phang
Nga, Nakhon Phanom (HQ Mekong River Operating
Unit)

PRINCIPAL SURFACE COMBATANTS 13

  AIRCRAFT CARRIER 1 *Chakri Naruebet* CVS with 7
    AV-8B *Matador* (*Harrier*)†, 6 S-70B *Seahawk* hel
  FRIGATES 12
    FFG 8
    2 *Naresuan* with 2 × 4 *Harpoon* SSM, 8 cell *Sea Sparrow*
      SAM, 1 × 127mm gun, 6 × 324mm TT, 1 SH-2G hel
    2 *Chao Phraya* (PRC *Jianghu* III) with 8 C-801 SSM, 2 ×
      2 × 100mm guns, 2 × 5 ASW RL, 1 Bell 212 hel
    2 *Kraburi* (PRC *Jianghu* IV type) with 8 C-801 SSM, 1
      × 2 100mm guns, 2 × 5 ASW RL and 1 Bell 212 hel
    2 *Phutthayotfa Chulalok* (US *Knox*) (leased from US)
      with 8 *Harpoon* SSM, 1 × 127mm gun, 4 × 324
      ASTT, 1 Bell 212 hel
    FF 4
    1 *Makut Rajakumarn* with 2 × 114mm guns, 2 × 3
      ASTT
    2 *Tapi* (US PF-103) with 1 × 76mm gun, 6 × 324mm
      ASTT (Mk 46 LWT)

1 *Pin Klao* (US *Cannon*) with 3 × 76mm gun, 6 × 324mm ASTT

PATROL AND COASTAL COMBATANTS 88

CORVETTES 5

2 *Rattanakosin* FSG with 2 × 4 *Harpoon* SSM, 8 *Aspide* SAM, 1 × 76mm gun, 2 × 3 ASTT

3 *Khamronsin* FS with 1 × 76mm gun, 2 × 3 ASTT

MISSILE CRAFT 6

3 *Ratcharit* (It Breda 50m) PFM with 4 MM-38 *Exocet* SSM

3 *Prabparapak* (Ge Lürssen 45m) PFM with 5 *Gabriel* SSM

PATROL CRAFT 77

OFFSHORE

1 *Kua Hin* PCO with 1 × 76mm gun

COASTAL 12

3 *Chon Buri* PFC, 6 *Sattahip*, 3 PCC

INSHORE 64

7 T-11 (US PGM-71), 9 T-91, about 33 PCF and 15 PCR plus boats

MINE WARFARE 7

MINE COUNTERMEASURES 7

2 *Lat Ya* (It *Gaeta*) MCMV

2 *Bang Rachan* (Ge Lürssen T-48) MCC

2 *Bangkeo* (US *Bluebird*) MSC

1 *Thalang* MCM spt with minesweeping capability (Plus some 12 MSB)

AMPHIBIOUS 9

2 *Sichang* (Fr PS-700) LST, capacity 14 tk, 300 tps with hel deck (trg)

5 *Angthong* (US LST-511) LST, capacity 16 tk, 200 tps

2 *Kut* (US LSM-1) LSM, capacity about 4 tk

Plus about 51 craft: 9 LCU, about 24 LCM, 1 LCG, 2 LSIL, 3 hovercraft, 12 LCVP

SUPPORT AND MISCELLANEOUS 16

1 *Similan* AO (1 hel) , 1 *Chula* AO, 5 AO, 3 AGHS, 6 trg

NAVAL AVIATION (1,700)

(incl 300 conscripts)

EQUIPMENT

44 cbt ac; 5 armed hel

AIRCRAFT

FTR 9 *Harrier* (7 AV-8B, 2 TAV-8*)

MR/ATTACK 5 Cessna T-337 *Skymasters*, 14 A-7E, 4 TA-7C, 5 O-1G, 4 U-17B

MR/ASW 3 P-3T *Orion* (plus 2 P-3A in store), 6 Do-228, 3 F-27, 8 S-2F, 5 N-24A *Nomad*

SAR 2 CL-215

HELICOPTERS

ASW 5 S-70B

SAR 8 Bell 212, 5 Bell 214, 4 UH-1H, 5 S-76N

MISSILES

ASM AGM-84 *Harpoon*

MARINES (18,000)

1 div HQ, 2 inf regt, 1 arty regt (3 fd, 1 AA bn); 1 amph aslt bn; recce bn

EQUIPMENT

AAV 33 LVTP-7

TOWED ARTY 155mm: 12 GC-45

ATGW TOW, *Dragon*

Air Force ε48,000

4 air divs, one flying trg school

153 cbt ac, no armed hel

Flying hours 100

FGA 3 sqn

1 with 14 F-5A/B, 2 with 34 F-16 (26 -A, 8 -B) (16 ex-USAF F-16A/B to be delivered early 2002)

FTR/AGGRESSOR 2 sqn with 36 F-5E/F (being upgraded)

ARMED AC 5 sqn

1 with 4 AC-47, 3 with 22 AU-23A, 1 with 19 N-22B *Missionmaster* (tpt/armed), 1 with 19 OV-10C (coin/obs) – to be replaced by 25 Alphajets (first 5 delivered)

ELINT 1 sqn with 3 IAI-201

RECCE 3 RF-5A

SURVEY 2 *Learjet* 35A, 3 *Merlin* IVA, 3 GAF N-22B *Nomads*

TPT 3 sqn

1 with 6 C-130H, 6 C-130H-30, 3 DC-8-62F

1 with 3 C-123-K, 4 BAe-748

1 with 6 G-222

VIP Royal flight **ac** 1 Airbus A-310-324, 1 Boeing 737-200, 3 *King Air* 200, 2 BAe-748, 3 *Merlin* IV **hel** 2 Bell 412, 3 AS-532A2

TRG 24 CT-4, 29 *Fantrainer*-400, 13 *Fantrainer*-600, 10 SF-260, 15 T-33A/RT-33A, 22 PC-9, 6 -C, 12 T-37, 34 L-39ZA/MP

LIAISON 3 *Commander*, 1 *King Air* E90, 2 O-1 *Bird Dog*, 2 *Queen Air*, 3 *Basler Turbo*-67

HEL 2 sqn

1 with 17 S-58T, 1 with 25 UH-1H

AAM AIM-9B/J *Sidewinder*, *Python* 3

AIR DEFENCE

1 AA arty bty: 4 *Skyguard*, 1 *Flycatcher* radars, each with 4 fire units of 2 30mm Mauser/Kuka guns

SAM *Blowpipe*, *Aspide*, RBS NS-70, *Starburst*

Forces Abroad

UN AND PEACEKEEPING

EAST TIMOR (UNTAET): 742 incl 6 obs **IRAQ/KUWAIT** (UNIKOM): 5 obs **SIERRA LEONE** (UNAMSIL): 5 obs

Paramilitary ε104,000 active

THAHAN PHRAN (Hunter Soldiers) ε11,000 volunteer irregular force; 13 regt of some 100+ coy

PROVINCIAL POLICE ε50,000 incl ε500 Special Action Force

MARINE POLICE 2,500

3 PCO, 3 PCC, 8 PFI, some 110 PCI<

POLICE AVIATION 500

ac 1 *Airtourer*, 6 AU-23, 2 Cessna 310, 1 Fokker 50, 1 CT-4, 2 CN 235, 8 PC-6, 2 Short 330 **hel** 27 Bell 205A, 14 Bell 206, 3 Bell 212, 6 UH-12, 5 KH-4

BORDER PATROL POLICE 40,000

NATIONAL SECURITY VOLUNTEER CORPS 50,000

Foreign Forces

SINGAPORE 1 trg camp (arty, cbt engr)
US Army 40 **Air Force** 30 **Navy** 10 **USMC** 370

Vietnam Vn

dong d		**1999**	**2000**	**2001**	**2002**
GDP	d	416tr	442tr		
	US$	30bn	31bn		
per capita	US$	1,200	1,300		
Growth	%	3.5	5.8		
Inflation	%	7.6	-0.6		
Debt	US$	22bn			
Def exp	US$	ε890m	ε950m		
Def bdgt	US$	ε891m	ε1.0bn	ε1.8bn	
US$1=d		13,893	14,081	14,588	

Population			**80,976,000** Chinese 3%	
Age	**13–17**	**18–22**	**23–32**
Men	4,557,000	4,132,000	7,149,000
Women	4,403,000	3,993,000	6,950,000

Total Armed Forces

ACTIVE ε484,000

(referred to as 'Main Force')
Terms of service 2 years Army and Air Defence, 3 years Air Force and Navy, specialists 3 years, some ethnic minorities 2 years

RESERVES some 3–4,000,000

'**Strategic Rear Force**' (see also *Paramilitary*)

Army ε412,000

8 Mil Regions (incl capital) • 14 Corps HQ • 58 inf div[a] • 3 mech inf div • 10 armd bde • 15 indep inf regt • SF incl AB bde, demolition engr regt • Some 10 fd arty bde • 8 engr div • 10–16 economic construction div • 20 indep engr bde

EQUIPMENT

MBT 45 T-34, 850 T-54/-55, 70 T-62, 350 PRC Type-59
LT TK 300 PT-76, 320 PRC Type-62/63
RECCE 100 BRDM-1/-2

AIFV 300 BMP-1/-2
APC 1,100 BTR-40/-50/-60/-152, 80 YW-531, M-113
TOWED ARTY 2,300: **76mm; 85mm; 100mm:** M-1944, T-12; **105mm:** M-101/-102; **122mm:** Type-54, Type-60, M-1938, D-30, D-74; **130mm:** M-46; **152mm:** D-20; **155mm:** M-114
SP ARTY 152mm: 30 2S3; **175mm:** M-107
COMBINED GUN/MOR 120mm: 2S9 reported
ASLT GUNS 100mm: SU-100; **122mm:** ISU-122
MRL 107mm: 360 Type 63; **122mm:** 350 BM-21; 140mm: BM-14-16
MOR 82mm, 120mm: M-43; **160mm:** M-43
SSM *Scud* B/C (reported)
ATGW AT-3 *Sagger*
RCL 75mm: PRC Type-56; **82mm:** PRC Type-65, B-10; **87mm:** PRC Type-51
AD GUNS 12,000: **14.5mm; 23mm:** incl ZSU-23-4 SP; **30mm; 37mm; 57mm; 85mm; 100mm**
SAM SA-7/-16

[a] Inf div str varies from 5,000 to 12,500

Navy ε42,000

(incl 27,000 Naval Infantry)
Four Naval Regions
BASES Hanoi, Cam Ranh Bay, Da Nang, Haiphong (HQ), Ha Tou, Ho Chi Minh City, Can Tho, plus several smaller bases

SUBMARINES 2

SSI 2 DPRK *Yugo*

PRINCIPAL SURFACE COMBATANTS 6

FRIGATES 6

FF 6
1 *Barnegat* (US *Cutter*) with 1 × 127mm gun
3 Sov *Petya* II with 4 × 76mm gun, 10 × 406mm ASTT, 2 ASW RL
2 Sov *Petya* III with 4 × 76mm gun, 3 × 533mm ASTT, 2 ASW RL

PATROL AND COASTAL COMBATANTS 42

CORVETTES 1 HO-A (Type 124A) FSG with 8 SS-N-25 *Zvezda* SSM, SA-N-5 *Gecko* SAM

MISSILE CRAFT 12
8 Sov *Osa* II with 4 SS-N-2 *Styx* SSM
4 Sov *Tarantul* with 4 SS-N-2D *Styx* SSM

TORPEDO CRAFT 10
5 Sov *Turya* PHT with 4 × 533mm TT (2 without TT)
5 Sov *Shershen* PFT with 4 × 533mm TT

PATROL, INSHORE 19
4 Sov SO-1, 3 US PGM-59/71, 10 *Zhuk*<, 2 Sov *Poluchat* PCI; plus large numbers of river patrol boats

MINE WARFARE 10

MINE COUNTERMEASURES 10
2 *Yurka* MSC, 3 *Sonya* MSC, 2 PRC *Lienyun* MSC, 1 *Vanya* MSI, 2 *Yevgenya* MSI, plus 5 K-8 boats

AMPHIBIOUS 6

3 US LST-510-511 LST, capacity 200 tps, 16 tk
3 Sov *Polnocny* LSM, capacity 180 tps, 6 tk
Plus about 30 craft: 12 LCM, 18 LCU

SUPPORT AND MISCELLANEOUS 30+

incl 1 trg, 1 AGHS, 4 AO, about 12 small tpt, 2 ex-Sov floating docks and 3 div spt. Significant numbers of small merchant ships and trawlers are taken into naval service for patrol and resupply duties. Some of these may be lightly armed

NAVAL INFANTRY (27,000)

(amph, cdo)

People's Air Force 30,000

3 air divs (each with 3 regts), a tpt bde, an Air Force Academy
189 cbt ac, 26 armed hel
FGA 2 regt with 53 Su-22 M-3/M-4/MR (recce dedicated) and UM-3; 12 Su-27 SK/UBK
FTR 6 regt with 124 MiG-21bis/PF
ATTACK HEL 26 Mi-24
MR 4 Be-12
TPT 3 regt with ac: 12 An-2, 12 An-26, 4 Yak-40 (VIP) hel: 30 Mi-8/Mi-17, 4 Mi-6
ASW The PAF also maintains Vn naval air arm, operating 3 Ka-25s, 10 Ka-28s and 2 Ka-32s.

TRG 10 Yak-18, 10 BT-6, 18 L-39, some MiG-21UM
AAM AA-2 *Atoll*, AA-8 *Aphid*, AA-10 *Alamo*
ASM AS-9 *Kyle*
SAM some 66 sites with SA-2/-3/-6/-7/-16
AD 4 arty bde: **37mm, 57mm, 85mm, 100mm, 130mm**
People's Regional Force: ε1,000 units, 6 radar bde: 100 sites

Paramilitary 40,000 active

BORDER DEFENCE CORPS ε40,000

COAST GUARD

came into effect on 1 Sep 1998

LOCAL FORCES some 4–5,000,000

incl **People's Self-Defence Force** (urban units), **People's Militia** (rural units); these comprise static and mobile cbt units, log spt and village protection pl; some arty, mor and AD guns; acts as reserve

Foreign Forces

RUSSIA 100: naval facilities (Cam Ranh Bay, lease expires 2004); ELINT station

MILITARY DEVELOPMENTS

The region's most serious conflict is still raging in Colombia, despite the efforts of President Andres Pastrana to reach a deal with the principal armed groups. The fighting continues to spill over into the territories of Colombia's neighbours. By contrast, the violence in Mexico's Chiapas province has ended with the accession of President Vincente Fox, although a formal peace accord has yet to be signed between his government and the principal armed group, the *Ejército Zapatista de Liberación Nacional* (EZLN). Military spending in the region remains constrained, apart from the impact of the US aid package for Colombia's anti-narcotics efforts and Brazil's plans to modernise its air force and naval capabilities. This is due partly to armed-forces reform by major regional powers such as Argentina, Brazil and Chile, and partly to the economic difficulties experienced in parts of the region in 2001, particularly in Argentina. These problems have meant that the increase in defence spending that might have been expected after the region's economic upturn in 2000 has been limited.

Insurgency and Terrorism

Colombia's President Pastrana continued his effort to make peace with the principal rebel groups in his country but with little success. He held talks with Manuel Marulanda, leader of the *Fuerzas Armadas Revolucionarias de Colombia* (FARC) in February 2001, but came away with little to show in return for his earlier ceding of control over territory to the FARC. His experience with the other major rebel group, the *Ejército de Liberación Nacional de Colombia* (ELN) has been similar. This failure has sharply eroded his domestic popularity in 2001, which is hardly surprising given that there were over 750 civilian casualties in the first half of the year, more than at any time since the conflict started 37 years ago. One of the main reasons for the higher civilian death toll is that the competing rebel groups, FARC and ELN on the one hand and the right-wing paramilitary *Autodefensas Unidas de Colombia* (AUC) on the other, are targeting each other's civilian-support base in the struggle for control of territory and resources.

The US aid package of $1.3bn, which is part of *Plan Colombia*, is programmed to run from 2000 to 2003, but has yet to yield results. US-supported efforts to combat the drugs trade in the northern Andean region suffered two major setbacks in 2001. The first of these was the accidental shooting-down in Peruvian air space of a civilian aircraft carrying American missionaries. As a result of this, the US has suspended support for Peruvian air force action against the light aircraft used by drug-smugglers. In Colombia, resistance is building to the US-inspired plans to use government aircraft to spray coca-growing areas with herbicides. A Colombian court ruled such activities illegal in July 2001, mainly on the grounds that the herbicide is indiscriminate, damaging legal agricultural activities and harming the environment. Although the spraying has continued, its unpopularity has been enhanced by this challenge to the government's authority. The only positive development for security in the area was FARC's release of over 300 captured police and soldiers in June 2001, in exchange for 14 rebels released from state jails. There was hope that this could lead to progress in the slow-moving peace negotiations between Pastrana and FARC.

While the violence in the Chiapas province of **Mexico** has all but ended, there has not been a formal peace accord. Although the EZLN, which began its military campaign in 1994, has achieved no military victory, it has increased pressure on the legislators to respond to its demands for constitutional recognition of Indian rights and culture. In March 2001, the guerrillas led a demonstration in Mexico City, with the blessing of President Fox, calling for the rights of all indigenous groups throughout Mexico to be recognised. This wider appeal prevented the Mexican Congress from responding positively. The EZLN wants Congress to pass a package of laws that would give Indian communities a degree of self-determination, including the right to set up local administrations based on traditional systems of government. Despite Fox's support for this demand, the Congress could not accept such sweeping reforms in areas such as land rights for the indigenous people who compose nearly 10% of Mexico's population of some 104 million. The marchers returned to Chiapas empty-handed. Nevertheless, it appears that the armed conflict has ended for the time being.

DEFENCE SPENDING

Despite the strength of the dollar against local currencies, defence budgets in 2000 showed an increase of 9% in dollar terms over 1999, reflecting the relaxation of the austerity measures imposed in the wake of the 1998 financial crisis, and strong growth in regional economies. Across the region, there was a 4% improvement in economic performance in 2000, following negligible growth in 1999. This resulted from a combination of the continued expansion of the US economy, higher prices for commodities, particularly oil, and a fall in inflation, which greatly aided military planners. However, the current outlook for the region's economies is uncertain, particularly given the risk of Argentina defaulting on its substantial debt burden, with repercussions particularly for Brazil, but also throughout the region and beyond.

The financial position of **Argentina** is precarious, with the International Monetary Fund (IMF) having to step in with a $40bn crisis package, payable in instalments, approved in April 2001, to help the country meet interest and maturing debt obligations of some $128bn. As a result, Argentina cut its military spending in 2000 back to $4.5bn. Procurement programmes were particularly hard hit and, with over 90% of military expenditure going on personnel costs (including pensions), and operations and maintenance, there are unlikely to be any significant new acquisitions in the foreseeable future.

Brazil's economy grew by 4% in 2000, helped primarily by stronger export growth following the depreciation of the Brazilian real in early 1999. Defence spending remains a very small part of the total state budget (in the region of 3%). Although the 2000 defence budget was increased by R1.9bn to R18.5bn, this was only to cover programmes that were transferred to the military budget from other spending areas. Despite the lack of fresh funds, the air force reconstruction project, *Plan Phoenix*, was approved by the Brazilian government in July 2000. The modernisation plan, on which $3.35bn is to be spent over eight years, is badly needed as nearly half the air force fleet is grounded because of budget restrictions and lack of spare parts. Most of the principal combat aircraft are at least 30 years old with among them *Mirages* (F-103E/D and IIIE/IV DBR) in the Air Defence Command and similarly ageing US-made F-5s in the fighter, ground-attack role. Included in *Plan Phoenix* is $700m for the acquisition of up to 24 modern fighter aircraft. The existing F-5 fleet is to be upgraded as are the light ground-attack AMXs, of which there are some 47 on inventory. Also included in the plan is the procurement of at least 12 P-3C *Orion* surveillance aircraft and a similar number of medium-range transport aircraft. Most of the transport requirement is likely to be met by an order for C-130H aircraft withdrawn from service in the Italian Air Force. Competition for the fast-jet portion of the plan, potentially the most lucrative, is intense, with American (F-16), French (*Mirage*) and Swedish (*Gripen*) companies in contention. The French are in a strong position, with Dassault and other French partners having a 20% stake in the Brazilian company Embraer, which would manufacture the aircraft under licence. Originally set up by the Brazilian air force in 1969, Embraer was privatised in 1994. The prospect of becoming the regional supplier of this type of aircraft is a powerful attraction of the French bid for the Brazilians.

The US competitors are hindered, by the 1977 congressional embargo on the sale of advanced military equipment, despite some easing of the constraints in 1999. The sale of ten F-16s to Chile has been held up because of concerns about the level of technology to be transferred, particularly the inclusion of air-to-air missiles, radar and navigation systems. If the *Mirage* wins the Brazilian contract, Chile may be tempted to join forces with Brazil in order to obtain a more capable aircraft than a stripped-down F-16. However, while the French seemed to be the leading contender for the Brazilian order in August 2001, this could change as political pressures mount in advance of the decision, which is not likely to be made until December 2001. At one time for example, French companies were the leading contenders for the aerial surveillance system for the Amazon basin (SIVAM), only to be trumped at the last minute by a US supplier when the US government exerted heavy political pressure. The prospect of losing ground in a small but important market in the Americas may motivate the US Congress to further ease constraints on technology transfer.

Brazil is the only country in the region to have made significant naval acquisitions in 2000–01. The major purchase is the decommissioned French aircraft carrier *Foch* to replace the navy's existing carrier the *Minais Gerais*. The acquisition of the *Foch* (renamed *Sao Paolo*) will increase Brazil's power-projection capabilities, as it carries 15 A-4 *Skyhawk* fighter aircraft as opposed to the ten carried by the *Minais*. However, being 18,000 tonnes larger than the *Minais* and almost 40 years old, the *Sao Paolo* will be considerably more expensive to maintain and operate. Largely due to this increased expense, plans to convert the *Minais* into a helicopter carrier are very unlikely to be implemented. Brazil's research project to develop an indigenous nuclear-powered submarine (SSN) continues. The project demonstrates that Brazil intends to present itself not only as a naval power with global reach, but also as the industrial and technological leader in the region. However, even if this effort remains fully funded, Brazil will be unlikely to have an SSN capability until at least 2015, and military spending plans for 2002 and beyond may prove too ambitious in the light of the country's economic problems. By August 2001, the IMF had to provide a $15bn emergency credit line to enable Brazil to meet its debt obligations, principally due to the impact of Argentina's debt problems. And if the regional economic difficulties persist the military spending plans for 2002 and beyond may prove to be too ambitious

Defence spending in **Chile** increased in 2000 although, as in the recent past, this was due to meeting increased personnel and pension costs. This was made possible in

Table 23 **Chile: defence and security funding by service, 2000–01** US$m				
	2000	**%**	**2001**	**%**
Army	492	16.7	489	17.1
Navy	458	15.5	455	15.9
Air Force	241	8.2	236	8.2
Sub-total	1,191	40.4	1,180	41.1
Military Pensions	763	25.9	624	21.8
Other	165	5.6	160	5.6
Sub-total	2,119	71.9	1,964	68.5
Paramilitary	830	28.1	904	31.5
Total	2,949	100.0	2,868	100.0

part by the 16% increase in earnings from the copper industry from which the Ministry of Defence benefits directly for the purpose of procuring equipment. The long-awaited order for 10 F-16s to replace the ageing F-15 was finally agreed by the government only to find that, as noted above, US export controls prevented the inclusion of air-to-air missiles and more advanced avionics in the deal. The purchase has been postponed until 2002 amid much domestic wrangling

Colombia The US has announced the addition of $500m to the $1.3bn of assistance to Colombia's counter-narcotics efforts agreed in 2000 for the period 2000–03. The most expensive part of the package, the delivery of 18 UH-60 *Black Hawk* utility helicopters, was due to take place between July and December 2001.

Mexico The Mexican economy was boosted by increased oil exports to the US in 2000, however Mexico's strong trade links with its northern neighbour make it more vulnerable than other Latin American states to the US economic slowdown in 2001. Mexico's major order for military equipment in 2001 was the contract signed with Embraer of Brazil for an EMB-145 Airborne Early Warning & Control (AEW&C) aircraft and two EMB-145 maritime patrol aircraft.

Table 24 Arms orders and deliveries, Caribbean and Latin America, 1998–2001

Country supplier	Classification ⇩	Designation	Quantity ⇩	Order date	Delivery date ⇩	Comment ⇩
Argentina	US	hel	**UH-1H**	8	1996	1998	Acquired ex US
	US	MPA	**P-3B**	8	1996	1997	Deliveries to 1999
	US	LAW	**M72**	900	1997	1999	
	US	FGA	**A-4M**	8	1997	1999	Further 11 for spares
	US	hel	**UH-1H**	8	1997	1998	
	US	tkr ac	**KC-135**	1	1998	2000	
	Fr	AO	***Durance***	1	1998	1999	
	dom	trg	**IA-63**	1	1999	1999	
	US	APC	**M113A2**	90	1999		Ex-US Army
Bahamas	US	tpt	**C-26**	2	1997	1998	
	US	PCO	***Bahamas***	2	1997	1999	Contract options for 4 more
Bolivia	dom	PCR	**PCR**	23	1997	1999	
	US	FGA	**TA-4J**	18	1997	1998	12 for op and 6 for spare parts. Ex-USN ac
Brazil	dom	AAM	**MAA-1**	40	1976	1998	Under test since mid-1998
	col	FGA	**AM-X**	54	1980	1989	Deliveries continue. 2 delivered 1997
	Fr	hel	**AS-350**	77	1985	1988	Prod under licence continues at low rate
	Ge	SSK	**Type 209**	4	1985	1989	Last delivered 2000
	Ge	PCC	***Grauna***	12	1986	1993	Last 2 delivered 1999
	dom	MRL	***Astros* 2**	20	1994	1998	4 ordered 1996, 16 1998
	Be	MBT	***Leopard* 1**	87	1995	1997	55 delivered 1998–99
	dom	FF	***Niteroi***	6	1995	1999	Upgrade to 2001
	dom	trg	**AL-X**	99	1995	1999	First 33 to be delivered 1999
	dom	AEW	**EMB-145**	8	1997	2001	5 AEW, 3 Remote Sensing
	Fr	tpt	**F-406**	5	1997	1999	For delivery 1999–2001
	dom	ATGW	**MSS-1.2**	40	1997	2001	Dev
	col	FGA	**AM-X**	13	1998	2001	3rd batch
	Kwt	FGA	**A-4**	23	1998	1998	Ex-Kwt Air Force. Includes 3 TA-4
	Il	FGA	**F-5**	48	1998	2000	Upgrade
	UK	arty	**105mm**	18	1999	2001	
	Swe	HWT	**Tp-62**	50	1999	2000	For *Tupi* SSK
	US	MPA	**P-3A/B**	12	1999	2002	Plus a further 4
	col	hel	**AS532**	8	2000	2002	Surv and border patrol
	Fr	CV	***Foch***	1	2000	2001	
	It	tpt	**C-130H**	10	2001	2001	Second-hand
Chile	Ge	FAC	**Type 148**	6	1995	1997	2 delivered 1997, 4 1998
	Be	APC	**M-113**	128	1995	1998	

Country supplier ⇩	Classification ⇩	Designation	Quantity ⇩	Order date	Delivery date ⇩	Comment ⇩
UK	ASSM	**MM-38 Exocet**	4	1996	1998	*Excalibur* ASSM; refurbished in Fr
Fr	MBT	**AMX-30B**	60	1996	1998	Ex-Fr Army
US	recce	**Caravan 1**	3	1996	1998	
UK	arty	**M101**	100	1996	1998	Upgrade
col	MRL	**Rayo**		1996	1999	Dev Programme
US	tpt	**R-182**	8	1997	1998	
RSA	arty	**M71**	24	1997	1998	
Ge	PFM	**Tiger**	2	1997	1998	
Fr	SSK	**Scorpene**	2	1997	2003	1st delivery 2003, 2nd 2005
US	hel	**UH-60**	12	1998	1998	First delivery Jul 1998
dom	MPA	**P-3**	2	1998	1999	Upgrade for up to 8
Nl	MBT	**Leopard 1**	200	1998	1999	Deliveries completed in 2000
US	FGA	**F-16**	10	2000	2004	Possibly up to 12 req. Postponed to 2002
Colombia Sp	tpt	**CN-235**	3	1996	1998	
dom	utl	**Gavilan**	12	1997	1998	
US	hel	**B-212**	6	1998	1998	First 3 to arrive in Jul/Aug 1998
US	hel	**UH-60L**	6	1998	1999	For delivery Sep 1999–Jan 2000
US	hel	**UH-1H**	25	1998	1999	For delivery 1999
US	hel	**MD-530F**	2	1998	1999	National Police
US	hel	**Black Hawk**	18	2000	2001	For counter drug operations
US	hel	**UH-1H**	42	2000	2001	For counter drug operations
RF	hel	**Mi-17MD**	6	2001	2002	
Ecuador Il	AAM	**Python 3**	100	1996	1999	
US	ASW hel	**Bell 412EP**	2	1996	1998	1st delivered late 1998, 2nd early 1999
RF	hel	**Mi-17**	7	1997	1998	
Il	FGA	**Kfir**	2	1998	1999	Ex-IAF; also upgrade of 11
El Salvador US	ACV	**Hummer**	2			
US	hel	**MD-520N**	2	1997	1998	
Guatemala dom	APC	**Danto**		1994	1998	For internal security duties
Chl	trg	**T-35B**	10	1997	1998	Ex-Chl Air Force
Guyana UK	PCO	**Orwell**	1	2000	2001	
Honduras US	FGA	**Super Mystere**	11	1997	1998	
Jamaica Fr	hel	**AS-555**	4	1997	1999	
Mexico RF	tpt	**An-32**	2			
dom	PCO	**Holzinger 2000**	8	1997	1997	Final delivery 2001
Be	lt tk	**AMX 13**	136	1994	1995	97 delivered 1995, 5 1996 and 34 1998
Ukr	hel	**Mi-17**	12	1995	1997	*Erint* delivered 1998
US	FF	**Knox**	3	1996	1998	Third for delivery 1999
US	LST	**Newport**	1	1998	1999	Excess Defense Articles (EDA)
US	hel	**MD-520N**	8	1998	1999	
RF	hel	**Mi-26**	1	2000	2000	
Br	MPA	**EMB-145**	3	2001		Including 1 AEW&C
Paraguay ROC	FGA	**F-5E**	4	1997	1998	Total of 12 in all
ROC	PCI		2	1998	1999	Free transfer
Peru Bel	FGA	**Su-25**	18	1995	1998	
Bel	FGA	**MiG-29**	18	1995	1996	Deliveries 1996–97

Country	Classification ⇩	Designation	Quantity ⇩	Order date	Delivery date ⇩	Comment ⇩
supplier						
Fr	ASSM	*Exocet*	8	1995	1997	Deliveries to 1998
It	ASSM	*Otomat*	12	1995	1997	Deliveries to 1998
RF	FGA	**MiG-29**	3	1998	1998	Plus spares
Cz	arty	**D-30**	6	1998	1998	
Cz	trg	**ZLIN-242L**	18	1998	1998	
RF	tpt	**Il-103**	6	1999	1999	
US	PCI		6	2000	2000	For coastguard
Suriname Sp	MPA	**C-212-400**	2	1997	1998	Second delivered 1999
Uruguay Il	MBT	**T-55**	11	1996	1997	Deliveries to 1998
Cz	MRL	**RM-70**	1	1998	1998	
Cz	SPA	**2S1**	6	1998	1998	
Venezuela Pl	tpt	**M-28**	12	1996	1996	Deliveries 1996–98
Sp	MPA	**C-212**	3	1997	1998	Plus modernisation of existing C-212-200
US	FGA	**F-16B**	2	1997	1999	
US	hel	**B-212**	2	1997	1999	US grant aid for counter-drug op
Fr	hel	**AS-532**	6	1997	2000	
US	hel	**UH-1H**	5	1997	1999	
Swe	ATGW	**AT-4**		1997	1999	
US	FF	*Lupo*	2	1998	2001	Upgrade and modernisation
Swe	radar	*Giraffe*	4	1998	1999	4 truck-mounted systems
It	trg	**SF-260E**	12	1998	1999	2nd batch of 12 possible
US	PCI	**PCI**	12	1998	1999	Aluminium 80 foot craft
US	PCI	**PCI**	10	1998	1999	Aluminium 54 foot craft
It	trg	**MB-339FD**	10	1998	2000	Req for up to 24. Deliveries to 2001
It	FGA	**AMX**	8	1998	2001	In cooperation with Br. Up to 24 req
US	SAR hel	**AB-412EP**	4	1998	1999	Option for a further 2
Il	SAM	*Barak*-1	6	1999	2000	Part of Guardian Air Defence modernisation
Swe	SAM	**RBS-70**	500	1999	2000	Includes AT-4 ATGW
Fr	radar	*Flycatcher*	3	1999	2000	Deliveries to early 2002. Part of Guardian

Dollar GDP figures for several countries in Latin America are based on Inter-American Development Bank estimates. In some cases, the dollar conversion rates are different from the average exchange rate values shown under the country entry. Dollar GDP figures may vary from those cited in *The Military Balance* in previous years. Defence budgets and expenditures have been converted at the dollar exchange rate used to calculate GDP.

Antigua and Barbuda AB

East Caribbean dollar EC$

		1999	2000	2001	2002
GDP	EC$	1.8bn	1.3bn		
	US$	653m	670m		
per capita	US$	6,437	6,797		
Growth	%	4.6	3.5		
Inflation	%	3.0	2.0		
Ext Debt	US$	350m			
Def exp	EC$	11m	11m		
	US$	4m	4m		
Def bdgt	EC$	11m	12m	12m	
	US$	4m	4m	4m	
FMA	US$	0.1m	0.1m	0.1m	
US$1=EC$		2.7	2.7	2.7	
Population					68,000

Age	13–17	18–22	23–32
Men	5,000	5,000	6,000
Women	5,000	5,000	8,000

Total Armed Forces

ACTIVE 170 (all services form combined **Antigua and Barbuda Defence Force**)

RESERVES 75

Army 125

Navy 45

BASE St Johns
PATROL CRAFT 3
   PATROL, INSHORE 3
   1 *Swift* PCI< • 1 *Dauntless* PCI< • 1 *Point* PCI<

Argentina Arg

peso P

		1999	2000	2001	2002
GDP	P	283.2bn	282.8bn		
	US$	283bn	282bn		
per capita	US$	9,996	10,106		
Growth	%	-3.0	0.6		
Inflation	%	-1.2	-0.7		
Debt	US$	145bn	158bn		
Def exp	P	5.4bn	4.8bn		
	US$	5.4bn	4.8bn		

contd		1999	2000	2001	2002
Def bdgt	P	3.5bn	3.1bn		
	US$	3.5bn	3.1bn		
FMA (US)	US$	1.4m	0.7m	1.8m	
US$1=P		1.0	1.0		
Population				37,587,000	

Age	13–17	18–22	23–32
Men	1,631,000	1,651,000	2,824,000
Women	1,578,000	1,602,000	2,756,000

Total Armed Forces

ACTIVE 70,100

RESERVES none formally established or trained

Army 41,400

3 Corps
   1 with 1 mtn, 1 mech, 1 jungle bde
   1 with 1 mtn, 2 mech bde
   1 with 2 armd, 1 trg bde
STRATEGIC RESERVE
   1 mech, 1 AB bde
Army tps
   1 mot inf bn (Army HQ Escort Regt), 1 mot cav regt (Presidential Escort), 1 AD arty, 3 avn, 2 engr bn, 2 SF coy
EQUIPMENT
   MBT 200 TAM
   LT TK 50 AMX-13, 100 SK-105 *Kuerassier*
   RECCE 75 AML-90
   AIFV 160 VCTP (incl variants)
   APC 126 M-5 half-track, 323 M-113
   TOWED ARTY 105mm: 100 M 56 *Oto Melara*; **155mm**: 100 CITEFA Models 77/-81
   SP ARTY 155mm: 20 Mk F3, 15 VCA (*Palmaria*)
   MRL 105mm: 5 SLAM *Pampero*; **127mm**: 5 SLAM SAPBA-1
   MOR 81mm: 1,100; **120mm**: 360 Brandt (37 SP in VCTM AIFV)
   ATGW 600 SS-11/-12, *Cobra* (*Mamba*)
   RL 66mm: M-72
   RCL 75mm: 75 M-20; **90mm**: 100 M-67; **105mm**: 930 M-1968
   AD GUNS 30mm: 21; **40mm**: 76 L/60/-70
   SAM <40† *Tigercat*, <40† *Blowpipe*
   SURV RASIT also RATRAS (veh, arty), *Green Archer* (mor), *Skyguard*
   AC 1 C212-200, 3 Cessna 207, 1 Cessna 500, 2 DHC-6, 2 G-222, 3 *Merlin* IIIA, 3 *Merlin* IV, 1 *Queen Air*, 1 *Sabreliner*, 5 T-41, 21 OV-1D

HEL 4 A-109, 3 AS-332B, 1 Bell 212, 4 FH-1100, 2 SA-315B, 50 UH-1H, 8 UH-12

Navy 16,200

(incl 2,000 Naval Aviation and 2,800 Marines)
NAVAL AREAS Centre from River Plate to 42°45'S **South** from 42°45'S to Cape Horn **Antarctica**
BASES Buenos Aires, Puerto Belgrano (HQ Centre), Ushuaio (HQ South), Mar del Plata (SS and HQ Atlantic), Trelew, Punta Indio (naval air trg), Rio Santiago (shipbuilding)

SUBMARINES 3
SSK 3
2 *Santa Cruz* (Ge TR-1700) with 6 × 533mm TT (SST-4 HWT)
1 *Salta* (Ge T-209/1200) with 8 × 533mm TT (SST-4 HWT)

PRINCIPAL SURFACE COMBATANTS 13
DESTROYERS 5
DDG 1
2 *Hercules* (UK Type 42) with 4 MM-38 *Exocet* SSM, 1 × 114mm gun, 2 × 3 ASTT, 1 *Sea King* hel
4 *Almirante Brown* (Ge MEKO 360) with 8 MM-40 *Exocet* SSM, 1 × 127mm gun, 2 × 3 ASTT, 1 AS-555 hel
FRIGATES 8
FFG 8
5 *Espora* (Ge MEKO 140) with 4 MM-38 *Exocet* SSM, 1 × 76mm gun, 2 × 3 ASTT, 1 SA 319B hel
3 *Drummond* (Fr A-69) with 4 MM-38 *Exocet* SSM, 1 × 100mm gun, 2 × 3 ASTT

PATROL AND COASTAL COMBATANTS 15
TORPEDO CRAFT 2 *Intrepida* (Ge Lürssen 45m) PFT with 2 × 533mm TT (SST-4 HWT) (one with 2 MM-38 SSM)
PATROL, OFFSHORE 8
1 *Teniente Olivieri* (ex-US oilfield tug) PCO
3 *Irigoyen* (US *Cherokee* AT) PCO
2 *King* (trg) with 3 × 105mm guns PCO
2 *Sobral* (US *Sotoyomo* AT) PCO
PATROL, INSHORE 5
4 *Baradero* (*Dabur*) PCI<
1 *Point* PCI<
MINE WARFARE 2
MINE COUNTERMEASURES 2
2 *Neuquen* (UK *Ton*) MHC
AMPHIBIOUS craft only
4 LCM, 16 LCVP
SUPPORT AND MISCELLANEOUS 11
1 *Durance* AO, 3 *Costa* tpt; 3 *Red* buoy tenders, 1 icebreaker, 1 sail trg, 1 AGOR, 1 AGHS (plus 2 craft)

NAVAL AVIATION (2,000)

EQUIPMENT
25 cbt ac, 22 armed hel
AIRCRAFT
ATTACK 11 *Super Etendard*
MR/ASW 5 S-2T, 4 P-3B, 5 BE-200M/G
EW 1 L-188E
TRG 10 T-34C
HELICOPTERS
ASW 5 ASH-3H *Sea King*, 4 AS-555 *Fennec*
CBT SPT 5 SA-319B, 8 UH-1H
TPT 3 F-28
SURVEY 2 B-200F, 1 PL-6A
TRG 8 MC-32
MISSILES
ASM AM-39 *Exocet*, AS-12, *Martín Pescador*
AAM R-550 *Magic*

MARINES (2,800)
FLEET FORCES 2
1 with 1 marine inf, 1 AAV, 1 arty, 1 AAA bn, 1 cdo gp
1 with 2 marine inf bn, 2 naval det
AMPH SPT FORCE 1 marine inf bn
6 marine sy coy
EQUIPMENT
RECCE 12 ERC-90 *Lynx*
AAV 21 LVTP-7, 13 LARC-5
APC 6 MOWAG *Grenadier*, 36 Panhard VCR
TOWED ARTY 105mm: 6 M-101, 12 Model 56
MOR 81mm: 70; **120mm:** 12
ATGW 50 *Bantam*, *Cobra* (*Mamba*)
RL 89mm: 60 M-20
RCL 105mm: 30 1974 FMK1
AD GUNS 30mm: 12 HS-816; **35mm:** GDF-001
SAM 6 RBS-70

Air Force 12,500

130 cbt ac, 27 armed hel, 4 Major Comds – Air Operations, Personnel, Air Regions, Logistics
AIR OPERATIONS COMMAND (8 bde, 2 Air Mil Bases, 1 Airspace Surv and Control Gp, 1 EW Gp)
STRATEGIC AIR 5 sqn
2 with 23 *Dagger Nesher*
1 with 6 *Mirage* V Mara
2 with 36 A-4AR *Fightinghawk*
AIRSPACE DEFENCE 1 sqn with 13 *Mirage* III/EA, 6 TPS-43 field radars, SAM -3 *Roland*
AD GUNS 35mm: 1; 200mm: 86
TAC AIR 2 sqn
2 with 29 IA-58 *Pucara*
SURVEY/RECCE 1 sqn with 1 Boeing 707, 3 *Learjet* 35A, 2 IA-50
TPT/TKR 6 sqn
1 with 4 Boeing 707
2 with 13 C-130 *Hercules* (5 -B, 5 -H, 2 KC-H, 1 L-100-30)
1 with 7 F-27
1 with 4 F-28

1 with 6 DHC-6 *Twin Otter*
plus 3 IA-50 for misc comms
SAR
4 Bell 212, 10* UH-1H, 17* MD-500 hel
PERSONNEL COMMAND
TRG
30 *Mentor* B-45 (basic), 27 *Tucano* EMB-312 (primary), 13* *Pampa* IA-63, 10* *MS-760* (advanced), 8 Su-29AR **hel** 3 Hughes MD-500
MISSILES
ASM ASM-2 *Martín Pescador*
AAM AIM-9M *Sidewinder*, R-530, R-550, *Shafrir*

Forces Abroad

UN AND PEACEKEEPING
CROATIA (UNMOP): 1 obs **CYPRUS** (UNFICYP) 409: 1 inf bn **IRAQ/KUWAIT** (UNIKOM): 80 engr, 4 obs **MIDDLE EAST** (UNTSO): 1 obs **WESTERN SAHARA** (MINURSO): 1 obs **YUGOSLAVIA** (KFOR): 113

Paramilitary 31,240

GENDARMERIE (Ministry of Interior) 18,000
5 Regional Comd, 16 bn
   EQPT Shorland recce, 40 UR-416, 47 MOWAG *Grenadier*; **81mm** mor; **ac** 3 *Piper*, 3 PC-6, 1 Cessna *Stationair* **hel** 3 AS-350, 3 MD-500C/D
PREFECTURA NAVAL (Coast Guard) 13,240
7 comd
   SERVICEABILITY better than Navy
   EQPT 5 *Mantilla*, 1 *Delfin* PCO, 1 *Mandubi* PCO, 4 PCI, 21 PCI< plus boats; **ac** 5 C-212 **hel** 1 AS-330L, 2 AS-365, 4 AS-565MA, 2 Bell-47, 2 Schweizer-300C

Bahamas Bs

dollar B$		1999	2000	2001	2002
GDP	B$	3.8bn	4.7bn		
	US$	3.8bn	4.7bn		
per capita	US$	13,822	14,428		
Growth	%	6.0	3.0		
Inflation	%	1.5	1.4		
Debt	US$	315m			
Def exp	B$	26m	26m		
	US$	26m	26m		
Def bdgt	B$	26m	26m	26m	
	US$	26m	26m	26m	
FMA (US)	US$	1.3m	1.2m	1.5m	
US$1=B$		1.0	1.0		
Population					313,000
Age		13–17	18–22		23–32
Men		17,000	15,000		32,000
Women		13,000	14,000		30,000

Total Armed Forces

ACTIVE 860

Navy (Royal Bahamian Defence Force) 860

(incl 70 women)
BASE Coral Harbour, New Providence Island
MILITARY OPERATIONS PLATOON 1
   ε120; Marines with internal and base sy duties
PATROL AND COASTAL COMBATANTS 7
PATROL, OFFSHORE 2 *Bahamas* PCO
PATROL, INSHORE 5
   3 *Protector* PFC, 1 *Cape* PCI<, 1 *Keith Nelson* PCI<
SUPPORT AND MISCELLANEOUS 3
   1 *Fort Montague* (AG)<, 2 *Dauntless* (AG)<
HARBOUR PATROL UNITS 4
   4 *Boston* whaler<
AIRCRAFT 4
   1 Cessna 404, 1 Cessna 421C, 2 C-26

Barbados Bds

dollar B$		1999	2000	2001	2002
GDP	B$	5.0bn	5.3bn		
	US$	2.5bn	2.6bn		
per capita	US$	8,051	8,486		
Growth	%	3.5	3.7		
Inflation	%	1.6	3.8		
Debt	US$	490m	684m		
Def exp	B$	24m	26m		
	US$	12m	13m		
Def bdgt	B$	24m	26m	26m	
	US$	12m	13m	13m	
FMA	US$	0.1m	0.1m	0.1m	
US$1=B$		2.0	2.0	2.0	
Population					271,000
Age		13–17	18–22		23–32
Men		11,000	11,000		23,000
Women		11,000	10,000		22,000

Total Armed Forces

ACTIVE 610

RESERVES 430

Army 500

Navy 110

BASES St Ann's Fort Garrison (HQ), Bridgetown

PATROL AND COASTAL COMBATANTS 5
PATROL, COASTAL 1
  1 *Kebir* PCC
PATROL, INSHORE 4
  1 *Dauntless* PCI< • 3 *Guardian* PCI< • plus boats

Belize Bze

dollar BZ$		1999	2000	2001	2002
GDP	BZ$	1.3bn	1.3bn		
	US$	674m	674m		
per capita	US$	2,800	2,978		
Growth	%	4.6	6.0		
Inflation	%	-1.2	2.0		
Debt	US$	260m			
Def exp	BZ$	34m	34m		
	US$	17m	17m		
Def bdgt	BZ$	17m	17m	15m	
	US$	8m	9m	8m	
FMA (US)	US$	0.3m	0.4m	0.5m	
US$1=BZ$		2.0	2.0	2.0	
Population					246,000

Age	13–17	18–22	23–32
Men	14,000	13,000	20,000
Women	14,000	13,000	20,000

Total Armed Forces

ACTIVE ε1,050

RESERVES 700

Army ε1,050

3 inf bn (each 3 inf coy), 1 spt gp, 3 Reserve coy
EQUIPMENT
  MOR 81mm: 6
  RCL 84mm: 8 *Carl Gustav*

MARITIME WING
  PATROL CRAFT some 14 armed boats

AIR WING
No cbt ac or armed hel
  MR/TPT 1 BN-2B *Defender*
  TRG 1 T67-200 *Firefly*, 1 Cessna 182

Foreign Forces

UK Army 180

Bolivia Bol

boliviano B		1999	2000	2001	2002
GDP	B	51bn	52bn		
	US$	8.8bn	9.4bn		
per capita	US$	3,100	3,313		
Growth	%	1.0	3.8		
Inflation	%	2.1	3.4		
Debt	US$	5.8bn	4.3bn		
Def exp	B	864m	796m		
	US$	149m	130m		
Def bdgt	B	942m	796m		
	US$	162m	130m		
FMA[a] (US)	US$	55m	49m	53m	
US$1=B		5.8	6.1	6.5	

[a] Excl Plan Colombia allocation for 2001

Population			8,379,000
Age	13–17	18–22	23–32
Men	511,000	463,000	725,000
Women	502,000	460,000	744,000

Total Armed Forces

ACTIVE 31,500 (to be 35,000)
(incl some 20,000 conscripts)
Terms of service 12 months, selective

Army 25,000

(incl some 18,000 conscripts)
HQ: 6 Mil Regions
Army HQ direct control
  2 armd bn • 1 mech cav regt • 1 Presidential Guard
  inf regt
10 'div'; org, composition varies; comprise
  8 cav gp (5 horsed, 2 mot, 1 aslt) • 1 mot inf 'regt'
  with 2 bn • 22 inf bn (incl 5 inf aslt bn) • 10 arty
  'regt' (bn) • 1 AB 'regt' (bn) • 6 engr bn
EQUIPMENT
  LT TK 36 SK-105 *Kuerassier*
  RECCE 24 EE-9 *Cascavel*
  APC 18 M-113, 10 V-100 *Commando*, 20 MOWAG
    Roland, 24 EE-11 *Urutu*
  TOWED ARTY 75mm: 70 incl M-116 pack, ε10
    Bofors M-1935; **105mm**: 30 incl M-101, FH-18;
    122mm: 18 PRC Type-54
  MOR 81mm: 50; **107mm**: M-30
  AC 1 C-212, 1 *King Air* B90, 1 *King Air* 200, 1 Cessna

Navy 3,500

(incl 1,700 Marines)
NAVAL AREAS 3 (Strategic Logistic Support)
NAVAL DISTRICTS 6, covering Lake Titicaca and the
rivers; each 1 flotilla

BASES Riberalta (HQ), Tiquina (HQ), Puerto Busch, Puerto Guayaramerín (HQ), Puerto Villaroel, Trinidad (HQ), Puerto Suárez (HQ), Cobija (HQ), Santa Cruz (HQ), Bermejo (HQ), Cochabamba (HQ), Puerto Villarroel

PATROL AND COASTAL COMBATANTS ε60<

PATROL CRAFT, RIVERINE some 60 riverine craft/ boats, all<

SUPPORT AND MISCELLANEOUS some 18 logistic spt and patrol craft

MARINES (1,700)
6 bn (1 in each District)

Air Force 3,000

(incl perhaps 2,000 conscripts); 37 cbt ac, 16 armed hel
FGA 2 sqn with 18 AT-33AN
ADVANCED WPNS TRG/COIN 19 PC-7
ARMED HEL 1 anti-drug sqn with 16 Hughes 500M (UH-1H), plus 2 500M (VIP)
COMMS/SAR 1 hel sqn with 4 HB-315B, 2 SA-315B
SURVEY 1 sqn with 5 Cessna 206, 1 C-210, 1 C-402, 2 *Learjet* 25A/25D (secondary VIP role)
TPT 3 sqn with 1 *Sabreliner* 60, 9 C-130A/B/H, 3 F-27-400, 1 IAI-201, 3 *King Air*, 2 C-47, 3 *Convair* 580, 1 CASA 212, 1 L-188 in store
LIAISON 9 Cessna 152, 1 C-185, 13 C-206, 1 C-208, 2 C-402, 1 Beech *Bonanza*, 1 Beech *Baron*, 1 PA-32, 3 PA-34
TRG 1 Cessna 152, 2 C-172, 4 SF-260CB, 6 T-23, 10 T-34A, 1 *Lancair* 320
AD 1 air-base def regt† (Oerlikon twin **20mm**, 18 PRC Type-65 **37mm**, some truck-mounted guns)

Forces Abroad

UN AND PEACEKEEPING
DROC (MONUC): 1 obs **EAST TIMOR** (UNTAET): 2 obs **SIERRA LEONE** (UNAMSIL): 6 obs

Paramilitary 37,100

NATIONAL POLICE some 31,100
9 bde, 2 rapid action regt, 27 frontier units

NARCOTICS POLICE some 6,000

Brazil Br

real R		1999	2000	2001	2002
GDP	R	1,089bn	1,131bn		
	US$	600bn	643bn		
per capita	US$	6,300	6,700		
Growth	%	1.1	4.0		
Inflation	%	4.9	6.0		
Debt	US$	240bn	235bn		
Def exp[a]	R	ε29.0bn	32.3bn		
	US$	16.0bn	17.9bn		
Def bdgt	R	16.6bn	18.5bn	20.1bn	
	US$	9.1bn	9.9bn	8.8bn	
FMA (US)	US$	1.4m	1.7m	2.3m	
US$1=R		1.82	1.80	2.28	

[a] Incl spending on paramilitary forces

Population			171,863,000	
Age	13–17	18–22		23–32
Men	8,873,000	8,494,000		14,685,000
Women	8,773,000	8,483,000		14,835,000

Total Armed Forces

ACTIVE 287,600

(incl 48,200 conscripts)
Terms of service 12 months (can be extended to 18)

RESERVES

Trained first-line 1,115,000; 400,000 subject to immediate recall **Second-line** 225,000

Army 189,000

(incl 40,000 conscripts)
HQ: 7 Mil Comd, 12 Mil Regions; 8 div (3 with Regional HQ)
1 armd cav bde (2 armd cav, 1 armd, 1 arty bn), 3 armd inf bde (each 2 armd inf, 1 armd cav, 1 arty bn), 4 mech cav bde (each 2 mech cav, 1 armd cav, 1 arty bn) • 10 motor inf bde (26 bn) • 1 lt inf bde (3 bn) • 4 jungle bde • 1 frontier bde (6 bn) • 1 AB bde (3 AB, 1 arty bn) • 1 coast and AD arty bde (6 bn) • 3 cav guard regt • 10 arty gp (4 SP, 6 med) • 2 engr gp (9 bn) • 10 engr bn (incl 2 railway) (to be increased to 34 bn)
AVN 1 hel bde (2 bn each of 2 sqn)
EQUIPMENT
MBT 87 *Leopard* 1, 91 M-60A3
LT TK 286 M-41B/C
RECCE 409 EE-9 *Cascavel*
APC 219 EE-11 *Urutu*, 584 M-113
TOWED ARTY 105mm: 319 M-101/-102, 56 pack, 22 L118; **155mm**: 92 M-114
SP ARTY 105mm: 72 M-7/-108; **155mm**: 40 M-109A3
MRL 108mm: SS-06; 16 ASTROS II
MOR 81mm: 707; **107mm**: 236 M-30; **120mm**: 77 K6A3

ATGW 4 *Milan*, 18 *Eryx*
RL 84mm: 115 AT-4
RCL 84mm: 127 *Carl Gustav*; **106mm**: 163 M-40A1
AD GUNS 134 incl **35mm**: GDF-001; **40mm**: L-60/-70 (some with BOFI)
SAM 4 *Roland* II, 40 SA-18
HEL 4 S-70A, 33 SA-365, 18 AS-550 *Fennec*, 15 AS-350 (armed)

Navy 48,600

(incl 1,150 Naval Aviation, 13,900 Marines and 3,200 conscripts)
OCEANIC NAVAL DISTRICTS 5 plus 1 Riverine; 1 Comd
BASES Ocean Rio de Janeiro (HQ I Naval District), Salvador (HQ II District), Recife (HQ III District), Belém (HQ IV District), Floriancholis (HQ V District)
River Ladario (HQ VI District)
SUBMARINES 4
SSK 4
4 *Tupi* (Ge T-209/1400) with 8 × 533mm TT (UK *Tigerfish* HWT)
PRINCIPAL SURFACE COMBATANTS 19
AIRCRAFT CARRIERS 1 *Minas Gerais* (UK *Colossus*) CV, typically ASW **hel** 4–6 ASH-3H, 3 AS-332 and 2 AS-355; has been used by Arg for embarked ac trg (to be decommissioned in 2002)
plus 1 *Sao Paolo* (Fr *Clemenceau*) CV to enter service in 2002
FRIGATES 14
FFG 10
4 *Greenhaigh* (ex-UK *Broadsword*) with 4 MM-38 *Exocet* SSM, GWS 25 *Seawolf* SAM, 6 × 324mm ASTT (Mk 46 LWT), 2 *Super Lynx* hel
6 *Niteroi* with 2 × 2 MM 40 *Exocet* SSM, 2 × 3 *Seacat* SAM, 1 × 115mm gun, 6 × 324mm ASTT (Mk 46 LWT), 1 × 2 ASW mor, 1 *Super Lynx* hel
FF 4
4 *Para* (US *Garcia*) with 2 × 127mm guns, 2 × 3 ASTT, 1 × 8 ASROC SUGW, 1 *Super Lynx* hel
CORVETTES 4
4 *Inhauma* FSG, with 4 MM-40 *Exocet* SSM, 1 × 114mm gun, 2 × 3 ASTT, 1 *Super Lynx* hel
PATROL AND COASTAL COMBATANTS 50
PATROL, OFFSHORE 19
7 *Imperial Marinheiro* PCO with 1 × 76mm gun, 12 *Grajaü* PCO
PATROL, COASTAL 10
6 *Piratini* (US PGM) PCC, 4 *Bracui* (UK *River*) PCC
PATROL, INSHORE 16
16 *Tracker* PCI<
PATROL, RIVERINE 5
3 *Roraima* PCR and 2 *Pedro Teixeira* PCR
MINE WARFARE
MINELAYERS 0 but SSK class can lay mines

MINE COUNTERMEASURES 6
6 *Aratü* (Ge *Schütze*) MSC
AMPHIBIOUS 3
2 *Ceara* (US *Thomaston*) LSD capacity 345 tps, 21 LCM or 6 LCM and 3 LCUs
1 *Mattoso Maia* (US *Newport* LST) capacity 400 tps, 500 tons veh, 3 LCVP, 1 LCPL
Plus some 48 craft: 3 LCU, 10 LCM, 35 LCVP
SUPPORT AND MISCELLANEOUS 25
1 AO; 1 river gp of 1 AOT, 1 AK, 1 AF; 1 AK, 3 trp tpt; 2 AH, 1 ASR, 5 ATF, 4 AG; 2 polar AGOR, 2 AGOR, 1 AGHS plus 6 craft

NAVAL AVIATION (1,150)
EQUIPMENT
24 cbt ac, 54 armed hel
AIRCRAFT
FGA 24 A-4/TA-4*
HELICOPTERS
ASW 6 SH-3B, 7 SH-3D, 6 SH-3G/H
ATTACK 14 *Lynx* MK-21A
UTL 5 AS-332, 12 AS-350 (armed), 9 AS-355 (armed)
TRG 13 TH-57
MISSILES
ASM AS-11, AS-12, *Sea Skua*

MARINES (13,900)
FLEET FORCE 1 amph div (1 comd, 3 inf bn, 1 arty gp)
REINFORCEMENT COMD 5 bn incl 1 engr, 1 SF
INTERNAL SECURITY FORCE 8+ regional gp
EQUIPMENT
RECCE 6 EE-9 Mk IV *Cascavel*
AAV 11 LVTP-7A1, 13 AAV-7A1
APC 28 M-113, 5 EE-11 *Urutu*
TOWED ARTY 105mm: 15 M-101, 18 L-118; **155mm**: 6 M-114
MOR 81mm; **120mm**: 8 K 6A3
ATGW RB-56 *Bill*
RL 89mm: 3.5in M-20
RCL 106mm: 8 M-40A1
AD GUNS 40mm: 6 L/70 with BOFI

Air Force 50,000

(incl 5,000 conscripts); 281 cbt ac, 29 armed hel
AIR DEFENCE COMMAND 1 gp
FTR 2 sqn with 18 *Mirage* F-103E/D (14 *Mirage* IIIE/4 DBR)
TACTICAL COMMAND 10 gp
FGA 3 sqn with 47 F-5E/-B/-F (all being upgraded), 50 AMX (33 to be upgraded)
CCT 2 sqn with 53 AT-26 (EMB-326) - 33 to be upgraded
RECCE 2 sqn with 4 RC-95, 10 RT-26, 12 *Learjet* 35 recce/VIP, 3 RC-130E
AEW/SURVEILLANCE
5 R-99A and 3 R-99B being delivered

Br

Caribbean and Latin America

SURVEILLANCE/CALIBRATION 4 *Hawker* 800XP
for Amazon inspection/ATC calibration
LIAISON/OBS 7 sqn
1 with **ac** 8 T-27
5 with **ac** 31 U-7
1 with **hel** 29 UH-1H (armed)

MARITIME COMMAND 4 gp
MR/SAR 3 sqn with 10 EMB-110B, 20 EMB-111

TRANSPORT COMMAND
6 gp (6 sqn)
1 with 9 C-130H (delivery of 10 C-130H in
progress), 2 KC-130H • 1 with 4 KC-137 (tpt/tkr)
• 1 with 12 C-91 • 1 with 17 C-95A/B/C • 1 with
17 C-115 • 1 (VIP) with **ac** 1 VC-91, 12 VC/VU-93,
2 VC-96, 5 VC-97, 5 VU-9, 2 Boeing 737-200 **hel** 3
VH-4
7 regional sqn with 7 C-115, 86 C-95A/B/C, 6 EC-9
(VU-9)
HEL 6 AS-332, 8 AS-355, 4 Bell 206, 27 HB-350B
LIAISON 50 C-42, 3 C-98 Caravan (Cessna 205), 30
U-42

TRAINING COMMAND
AC 38* AT-26, 97 C-95 A/B/C, 25 T-23, 98 T-25, 61* T-
27 (*Tucano*), 14* AMX-T
HEL 4 OH-6A, 25 OH-13
CAL 1 unit with 2 C-95, 1 EC-93, 4 EC-95, 1 U-93

MISSILES
AAM AIM-9B *Sidewinder*, R-530, *Magic* 2,
MAA-1 *Piranha*

Forces Abroad

UN AND PEACEKEEPING
CROATIA (UNMOP): 1 obs **EAST TIMOR**
(UNTAET): 13 obs, 74 tps

Paramilitary

PUBLIC SECURITY FORCES (R) some 385,600
in state mil pol org (state militias) under Army control
and considered Army Reserve

Chile Chl

peso pCh		1999	2000	2001	2002
GDP	pCh	34.3tr	37.8tr		
	US$	80bn	87bn		
per capita	US$	12,200	12,800		
Growth	%	-1.1	5.5		
Inflation	%	3.3	4.5		
Debt	US$	34bn	37bn		
Def expª	pCh	1,371bn	1,689bn		
	US$	2.7bn	2.9bn		

contd		1999	2000	2001	2002
Def bdgt	pCh	1,033bn	1,096bn	1,265bn	
	US$	2.0bn	2.1bn	2.1bn	
FMA (US)	US$	0.5m	0.5m	0.5m	
US$1=pCh		509	515	602	

ª Incl spending on paramilitary forces

Population			15,405,000
Age	13–17	18–22	23–32
Men	725,000	640,000	1,218,000
Women	698,000	617,000	1,188,000

Total Armed Forces

ACTIVE 87,500
(incl 30,600 conscripts)
Terms of service **Army** 1 year **Navy** and **Air Force** 22
months. To be voluntary from 2002

RESERVES 50,000
Army 50,000

Army 51,000

(incl 27,000 conscripts)
7 Mil Regions, 2 Corps HQ
7 div; org, composition varies; comprise
23 inf (incl 10 mtn, 13 mot), 10 armd cav, 8 arty, 6
engr regt
Army tps: 1 avn bde, 1 engr, 1 AB regt (1 AB, 1 SF bn)

EQUIPMENT
MBT 40 AMX-30, 250 *Leopard* 1
RECCE 157 EE-9 *Cascavel*
AIFV 20 MOWAG *Piranha* with **90mm** gun, some M-
113C/-R
APC 144 M-113, 118 Cardoen/MOWAG *Piranha*,
ε290 EE-11 *Urutu*
TOWED ARTY 105mm: 66 M-101, 54 Model 56;
155mm: 8 M-71, 11 M-68, 24 G-4
SP ARTY 155mm: 12 Mk F3
MOR 81mm: 300 M-29; **107mm**: 15 M-30; **120mm**:
125 FAMAE (incl 50 SP)
ATGW *Milan/Mamba, Mapats*
RL 89mm: 3.5in M-20
RCL 150 incl: **57mm**: M-18; **106mm**: M-40A1
AD GUNS 20mm: 60 incl some SP (Cardoen/
MOWAG)
SAM 50 *Blowpipe, Javelin*, 12 *Mistral*

AIRCRAFT
TPT 6 C-212, 1 *Citation* (VIP), 5 CN-235, 1 Beech
Baron, 1 Beech *King Air*, 3 Cessna-208 *Caravan*
TRG 16 Cessna R-172
HEL 2 AS-332, 15 Enstrom 280 FX, 5 Hughes MD-530F
(armed), 16 SA-315B, 14 SA-330

Navy 24,000

(incl 600 Naval Aviation, 2,700 Marines, 1,300 Coast Guard and 2,100 conscripts)

DEPLOYMENT AND BASES

MAIN COMMAND Fleet (includes DD and FF), SS flotilla, tpt. Remaining forces allocated to 4 Naval Zones **1st** 26°S–36°S approx: Valparaiso (HQ) **2nd** 36°S–43°S approx: Talcahuano (HQ), Puerto Montt **3rd** 43°S to Antarctica: Punta Arenas (HQ), Puerto Williams **4th** north of 26°S approx: Iquique (HQ)

SUBMARINES 3

SSK 3

1 *O'Brien* (UK *Oberon*) with 8 × 533mm TT (Ge HWT)

2 *Thompson* (Ge T-209/1300) with 8 × 533mm TT (HWT)

PRINCIPAL SURFACE COMBATANTS 6

DESTROYERS 3

DDG 3

2 *Prat* (UK *Norfolk*) with 4 MM-38 *Exocet* SSM, 1 × 2 *Seaslug* SAM, 1 × 2 × 114mm guns, 2 × 3 ASTT (Mk 44 LWT), 1 AB-206B hel

1 *Blanco Encalada* (UK *Norfolk*) with 2 × 8 *Barak* 1 SAM, 2 × 114mm guns, 2 × 3 ASTT (Mk 44 LWT), 2 AS-332F hel

FRIGATES 3

FFG 3 *Condell* (mod UK *Leander*), with 2 × 114mm guns, 2 × 3 ASTT (Mk 44 LWT); 1 with 2 × 2 MM 38 *Exocet* SSM and 1 AB 206B hel; 2 with 2 × 2 MM 40 *Exocet* SSM and AS-332F hel

PATROL AND COASTAL COMBATANTS 27

MISSILE CRAFT 7

3 *Casma* (Il *Sa'ar* 4) PFM with 8 *Gabriel* SSM, 2 × 76mm gun

4 *Tiger* (Ge Type 148) PFM with 4 *Exocet* SSM, 1 × 6mm gun

PATROL, OFFSHORE 6

6 *Micalvi* PCO

PATROL, COASTAL 4

4 *Guacolda* (Ge Lürssen 36m) PCC

PATROL, INSHORE 10

10 *Grumete Diaz* (Il *Dabur*) PCI<

AMPHIBIOUS 3

2 *Maipo* (Fr *Batral*) LST, capacity 140 tps, 7 tk

1 *Valdivia* (US *Newport*) LST, capacity 400 tps, 500t veh

Plus craft: 2 *Elicura* LSM, 1 *Pisagua* LCU

SUPPORT AND MISCELLANEOUS 11

1 *Araucano* AO, 1 AK; 1 tpt, 2 AG; 1 trg ship, 3 ATF; 1 AGOR, 1 AGHS

NAVAL AVIATION (600)

EQUIPMENT

5 cbt ac, 20 armed hel

AIRCRAFT

MR 3* EMB-110, 2* P-3A *Orion*, 8 Cessna *Skymaster* (plus 2 in store)

LIAISON 3 C-212A

TPT 2 P-3A *Orion*

HELICOPTER

UTL 8 BO-105, 6 UH-57

ASW HEL 6 AS-532 (4 with AM-39 *Exocet*, 2 with torp)

TRG 10 PC-7

MISSILES

ASM AM-39 *Exocet*

MARINES (2,700)

4 gp: 4 inf, 2 trg bn, 4 cdo coy, 4 fd arty, 1 SSM bty, 4 AD arty bty • 1 amph bn

EQUIPMENT

LT TK 30 *Scorpion*

APC 40 MOWAG *Roland*

TOWED ARTY 105mm: 16 KH-178, **155mm**: 28 G-5

MOR 81mm: 50

SSM *Excalibur*

RCL 106mm: ε30 M-40A1

SAM *Blowpipe*

COAST GUARD (1,300)

(integral part of the Navy)

PATROL CRAFT 23

2 *Alacalufe* PCC, 15 *Rodman* PCI, 6 PCI, plus about 30 boats

Air Force 12,500

(incl 1,200 conscripts); 77 cbt ac, no armed hel

Flying hours: 100

5 Air Bde, 5 wg, 13 sqns

FGA 1 sqn with 14 *Mirage* 50 (12 M50M, 2 DCM)

FTR 1 sqn with 16 F-5 III (13 -E, 3 -F)

CCT 2 sqn with 14 A-37B, 12 A-36

FTR/RECCE 1 sqn with 21 *Mirage* 5 (16 M5MA, 4 M5MD, 1 M5BR)

RECCE 1 photo unit with 1 *King Air* A-100, 2 *Learjet* 35A, 3 DHC-6-100

AEW 1 IAI-707 *Phalcon* ('Condor')

TPT ac 3 Boeing 707(2 tpt, 1 tkr), 1 Boeing 737-500 (VIP), 2 C-130H, 3 C-130B, 4 C-212, 9 Beech 99 (ELINT, tpt, trg), 12 DHC-6 (2 -100, 10 -300), 1 *Gulfstream* IV (VIP), 1 *Beechcraft* 200 (VIP), 1 Cessna 206 (amph), 11 Piper PA-28

HEL 11 UH-1H (5 of which abandoned in Irq), 4 Bell 412 (first of 10–12 planned to replace UH-1H), 1 UH-60, 6 Bo-105, 3 SA-315B

TRG 1 wg, 3 flying schools **ac** 35 T-35A/B, 23 T-36, 5 *Extra* 300 **hel** 2 Bell 206A

MISSILES

AAM AIM-9B/J *Sidewinder, Shafrir, Python* III

AD 1 regt (5 gp) with **35mm**: Oerlikon GDF-005, MATRA *Mistral, Mygalle, Vulcan* 163/167

Forces Abroad

UN AND PEACEKEEPING

EAST TIMOR (UNTAET): 34 **INDIA/PAKISTAN** (UNMOGIP): 5 obs **MIDDLE EAST** (UNTSO): 3 obs

Paramilitary 34,700

CARABINEROS (Ministry of Defence) 34,700

13 zones, 39 districts, 174 *comisarias*
  APC 20 MOWAG *Roland*
  MOR 60mm, 81mm
  AC 1 PA-31, PA-31T, *Citation*, Cessna 182/206/210
  HEL 2 Bell 206, 8 Bo-105, EC-135, BK-117

Opposition

FRENTE PATRIOTICO MANUEL RODRIGUEZ – AUTONOMOUS FACTION (FPMR–A) ε800
leftist

Colombia Co

peso pC		1999	2000	2001	2002
GDP	pC	160tr	166tr		
	US$	77bn	81bn		
per capita	US$	5,300	5,400		
Growth	%	-5.0	3.0		
Inflation	%	11.2	8.8		
Debt	US$	34.4bn	33bn		
Def exp	pC	3.8tr	ε4.0tr		
	US$	2.2bn	2.0bn		
Def bdgt	pC	3.7tr	4.0tr	5.0tr	
	US$	2.1bn	2.0bn	2.1bn	
FMA (US)	US$	210m	820m	265m	
US$1=pC		1,756	2,005	2,369	
Population				43,765,000	
Age		13–17	18–22	23–32	
Men		1,965,000	1,916,000	3,325,000	
Women		1,873,000	1,840,000	3,263,000	

Total Armed Forces

ACTIVE 158,000

(incl some 74,700 conscripts)
Terms of service 12–18 months, varies (all services)

RESERVES 60,700

(incl 2,000 first-line) **Army** 54,700 **Navy** 4,800 **Air Force** 1,200

Army 136,000

(incl 63,800 conscripts)

5 div HQ
17 bde
  6 mech each with 3 inf, 1 mech cav, 1 arty, 1 engr bn
  2 air-portable each with 2 inf bn
  9 inf (8 with 2 inf bn, 1 with 4 inf bn)
2 arty bn
Army tps
  3 Mobile Counter Guerrilla Force (bde) (each with 1 cdo unit, 4 bn) – 2 more forming
  2 trg bde with 1 Presidential Guard, 1 SF, 1 AB, 1 mech, 1 arty, 1 engr bn
  1 AD arty bn
  1 army avn 'bde'
  3 counter-narcotics bn

EQUIPMENT

LT TK 12 M-3A1 (in store)
RECCE 12 M-8, 8 M-20, 119 EE-9 *Cascavel*
APC 100+ M-113, 76 EE-11 *Urutu*, 4 RG-31 *Nyala*
TOWED ARTY 75mm: 30 M-116; **105mm:** 72 M-101
MOR 81mm: 125 M-1; **107mm:** 148 M-2; **120mm:** 123 Brandt
ATGW 20 TOW (incl 8 SP)
RL 66mm: M-72; **89mm:** 15 M-20
RCL 106mm: 36 M-40A1
AD GUNS 40mm: 30 M-1A1
HEL some 100 incl 6 OH-6A, 11 UH-60, MD500/530, Bell 205/206/212, Bell 412, UH-1B, Hughes 300/500

Navy (incl Coast Guard) 15,000

(incl 10,000 Marines, 100 Naval Aviation and 7,000 conscripts)
BASES Ocean Cartagena (main), Buenaventura, Málaga (Pacific) **River** Puerto Leguízamo, Barrancabermeja, Puerto Carreño (tri-Service Unified Eastern Command HQ), Leticia, Puerto Orocue, Puerto Inirida

SUBMARINES 4

SSK 2 *Pijao* (Ge T-209/1200) with 8 × 533mm TT (Ge HWT)
SSI 2 *Intrepido* (It SX-506) (SF delivery)

PRINCIPAL SURFACE COMBATANTS 4

CORVETTES 4
  4 *Almirante Padilla* FSG with 8 MM-40 *Exocet* SSM, 1 × 76mm gun, 2 × 3 ASTT, 1 Bo-105 hel

PATROL AND COASTAL COMBATANTS 27

PATROL, OFFSHORE 5
  2 *Pedro de Heredia* (ex-US tugs) PCO with 1 × 76mm gun, 2 *Lazaga* PCO, 1 *Esperanta* (Sp *Cormoran*) PFO
PATROL, COASTAL/INSHORE 9
  1 *Quito Sueno* (US *Asheville*) PFC with 1 × 76mm gun, 2 *Castillo Y Rada* PCC, 2 *José Garcia* PCC, 2 *José Palas* PCI, 2 *Jaime Gomez* PCI
PATROL, RIVERINE 13
  3 *Arauca* PCR, 10 *Diligente* PCR, plus 76 craft: 9 *Tenerife*, 5 *Rio Magdalena*, 20 *Delfin*, 42 *Pirana*

SUPPORT AND MISCELLANEOUS 7

1 tpt; 1 AH, 1 sail trg; 2 AGOR, 2 AGHS

MARINES (10,000)

2 bde (each of 2 bn), 1 amph aslt, 1 river ops (15 amph patrol units), 1 SF, 1 sy bn
No hy eqpt (to get EE-9 *Cascavel* recce, EE-11 *Urutu* APC)

NAVAL AVIATION (100)
EQUIPMENT
  AIRCRAFT
  2 *Commander*, 2 PA-28, 2 PA-31, 2 *Cessna* 206
HELICOPTER
  2 Bo-105, 2 AS 555SN *Fennec*

Air Force 7,000

(some 3,900 conscripts); 58 cbt ac, 55 armed hel
AIR COMBAT COMMAND

FGA 2 sqn
  1 with 7 *Mirage* 5, 1 with 11 *Kfir* (10 -C2, 1 -TC2)

TACTICAL AIR SUPPORT COMMAND

CBT ac 4 AC-47T, 3 IA-58A, 20 A-37B, 13 OV-10
UTILITY/ARMED HEL 5 Bell 205, 13 Bell 212, 2 Bell 412, 12 UH-60A/L, 7 S-70 being delivered, 11 MD-500ME, 2 MD-500D, 3 MD-530F
RECCE 2 *Schweizer* SA 2-37A, 3 C-26

MILITARY AIR TRANSPORT COMMAND

  AC 1 Boeing 707, 2 Boeing 727, 7 C-130B, 2 C-130H, 1 C-117, 2 C-47, 2 CASA 212, 2 *Bandeirante*, 1 F-28, 3 CN-235
  HEL 17 UH-1H

AIR TRAINING COMMAND

  AC 12 T-27 (*Tucano*), 9 T-34M, 12 T-37, 8 T-41
  HEL 2 UH-1B, 4 UH-1H, 12 F-28F
MISSILES
AAM AIM-9 *Sidewinder*, R-530, *Python* III

Forces Abroad

UN AND PEACEKEEPING
EGYPT (MFO) 358: 1 inf bn

Paramilitary 104,600

NATIONAL POLICE FORCE 104,600
  ac 5 OV-10A, 12 Gavilan, 11 *Turbo Thrush* **hel** 10 Bell-206L, 9 Bell-212, 2 Hughes 500D, 49 UH-1H, 6 UH-60L

COAST GUARD (400)
integral part of Navy

Opposition

COORDINADORA NACIONAL GUERRILLERA SIMON

BOLIVAR **(CNGSB)** loose coalition of guerrilla gp incl *Fuerzas Armadas Revolucionarias de Colombia* **(FARC)** up to 17,000 reported active plus 5,000 urban militia; *Ejercito de Liberacion Nacional* **(ELN)** ε3,500 plus urban militia, pro-Cuban; *Ejercito Popular de Liberacion* **(EPL)** ε500

Other Forces

AUTODEFENSAS UNIDAS DE COLOMBIA **(AUC)** ε8,000 right-wing paramilitary gp

Foreign Forces

US Army 160

Costa Rica CR

colon C		1999	2000	2001	2002
GDP	C	3.2tr	3.3tr		
	US$	10.6bn	11.1bn		
per capita	US$	6,900	7,000		
Growth	%	8.3	1.5		
Inflation	%	10.0	11.5		
Debt	US$	3.8bn	3.5bn		
Sy exp[a]	C	19.8bn	25.6bn		
	US$	69m	86m		
Sy bdgt[a]	C	19.8bn	25.6bn		
	US$	69m	86m		
FMA (US)	US$	0.2m	0.2m	0.2m	
US$1=C		286	297	324	

[a] No defence forces. Budgetary data are for border and maritime policing and internal security.

Population				4,146,000
Age	13–17	18–22	23–32	
Men	198,000	180,000	301,000	
Women	190,000	174,000	292,000	

Total Armed Forces

ACTIVE Nil

Paramilitary 8,400

CIVIL GUARD 4,400
7 urban *comisaria* (reinforced coy) • 1 tac police *comisaria* • 1 special ops unit • 6 provincial *comisaria*

BORDER SECURITY POLICE 2,000
2 Border Sy Comd (8 *comisaria*)
MARITIME SURVEILLANCE UNIT (300)
  BASES Pacific Golfito, Punta Arenas, Cuajiniquil, Quepos **Atlantic** Limon, Moin
  PATROL CRAFT, COASTAL/INSHORE 8

1 *Isla del Coco* (US *Swift* 32m) PFC
1 *Astronauta* (US *Cape*) PCC
2 *Point* PCI<
4 PCI<; plus about 10 boats
AIR SURVEILLANCE UNIT (300)
No cbt ac
ac 1 Cessna O-2A, 1 DHC-4, 1 PA-31, 1 PA-34, 4
U206G **hel** 2 MD-500E, 1 Mi-17

RURAL GUARD (Ministry of Government and Police)
2,000

8 comd; small arms only

Cuba C

peso P		1999	2000	2001	2002
GDP	US$	ε15bn	ε16.8bn		
per capita	US$	2,400	2,600		
Growth	%	6.2	5.5		
Inflation	%	7.0			
Debt	US$	12bn	11.9bn		
Def exp	US$	ε750m	ε750m		
Def bdgt	P	630m	650m	ε692m	
	US$	27m	31m	33m	
US$1=P		23	21	21	
Population					11,242,000
Age		13–17	18–22	23–32	
Men		419,000	358,000	1,029,000	
Women		392,000	335,000	966,000	

Total Armed Forces

ACTIVE 46,000

Terms of service 2 years

RESERVES

Army 39,000 **Ready Reserves** (serve 45 days per year)
to fill out Active and Reserve units; see also *Paramilitary*

Army ε35,000

(incl conscripts and Ready Reserves)
HQ: 3 Regional Comd, 3 Army
4–5 armd bde • 9 mech inf bde (3 mech inf, 1 armd, 1
arty, 1 AD arty regt) • 1 AB bde • 14 reserve bde • 1
frontier bde
AD arty regt and SAM bde
EQUIPMENT † (some 75% in store)
MBT ε900 incl: T-34, T-54/-55, T-62
LT TK some PT-76
RECCE some BRDM-1/-2
AIFV some BMP-1
APC ε700 BTR-40/-50/-60/-152
TOWED ARTY 500: **76mm**: ZIS-3; **122mm**: M-1938,
D-30; **130mm**: M-46; **152mm**: M-1937, D-1

SP ARTY 40: **122mm**: 2S1; **152mm**: 2S3
MRL 175: **122mm**: BM-21; **140mm**: BM-14
MOR 1,000: **82mm**: M-41/-43; **120mm**: M-38/-43
STATIC DEF ARTY JS-2 (**122mm**) hy tk, T-34 (**85mm**)
ATGW AT-1 *Snapper*, AT-3 *Sagger*
ATK GUNS 85mm: D-44; **100mm**: SU-100 SP, T-12
AD GUNS 400 incl: **23mm**: ZU-23, ZSU-23-4 SP;
30mm: M-53 (twin)/BTR-60P SP; **37mm**: M-1939;
57mm: S-60 towed, ZSU-57-2 SP; **85mm**: KS-12;
100mm: KS-19
SAM some 300 incl: SA-6/-7/-8/-9/-13/-14/-16

Navy ε3,000

(incl 550+ Naval Infantry)
NAVAL DISTRICTS Western HQ Cabanas **Eastern**
HQ Holquin
BASES Cienfuegos, Cabanas, Havana, Mariel, Punta
Movida, Nicaro
PATROL AND COASTAL COMBATANTS 5†
MISSILE CRAFT 4 Sov *Osa* II PFM
PATROL, COASTAL 1 Sov *Pauk* II PFC with 1 × 76mm
gun, 4 ASTT, 2 ASW RL
MINE WARFARE 6
MINE COUNTERMEASURES 6†
2 Sov *Sonya* MSC, 4 Sov *Yevgenya* MHC
SUPPORT AND MISCELLANEOUS 1
1 AGHS†
NAVAL INFANTRY (550+)
2 amph aslt bn
COASTAL DEFENCE
ARTY 122mm: M-1931/37; **130mm**: M-46; **152mm**:
M-1937
SSM 2 SS-C-3 systems, some mobile *Bandera* IV
(reported)

Air Force ε8,000

(incl AD and conscripts); 130† cbt ac of which only
some 25 are operational, 45 armed hel
Flying hours less than 50
FGA 2 sqn with 10 MiG-23BN
FTR 4 sqn
2 with 30 MiG-21F, 1 with 50 MiG-21bis, 1 with 20
MiG-23MF, 6 MiG-29
(Probably only some 3 MiG-29, 10 MiG-23, 5 MiG-
21bis in operation)
ATTACK HEL 45 Mi-8/-17, Mi-25/35
ASW 5 Mi-14 hel
TPT 4 sqn with 8 An-2, 1 An-24, 15 An-26, 1 An-30, 2
An-32, 4 Yak-40, 2 Il-76 (Air Force ac in civilian
markings)
HEL 40 Mi-8/-17
TRG 25 L-39, 8* MiG-21U, 4* MiG-23U, 2* MiG-29UB,
20 Z-326

MISSILES

ASM AS-7

AAM AA-2, AA-7, AA-8, AA-10, AA-11

SAM 13 active SA-2, SA-3 sites

CIVIL AIRLINE

10 Il-62, 7 Tu-154, 12 Yak-42, 1 An-30 used as tp tpt

Paramilitary 26,500 active

STATE SECURITY (Ministry of Interior) 20,000

BORDER GUARDS (Ministry of Interior) 6,500

about 20 Sov *Zhuk* and 3 Sov *Stenka* PFI<, plus boats

YOUTH LABOUR ARMY 70,000

CIVIL DEFENCE FORCE 50,000

TERRITORIAL MILITIA (R) ε1,000,000

Foreign Forces

US 790: **Navy** 590 **Marines** 200

RUSSIA 810: 800 SIGINT, ε10 mil advisers

Dominican Republic DR

peso pRD		1999	2000	2001	2002
GDP	pRD	279bn	328bn		
	US$	12.2bn	13.6bn		
per capita	US$	5,500	5,800		
Growth	%	8.2	8.5		
Inflation	%	6.6	7.7		
Debt	US$	3.5bn			
Def exp	pRD	ε2.5bn	ε2.6bn		
	US$	114m	114m		
Def bdgt	pRD	2.1bn	2.4bn	2.5bn	
	US$	92m	105m	103m	
FMA (US)	US$	0.9m	1.0m	1.1m	
US$1=pRD		16.0	16.3	16.3	
Population					8,653,000
Age		13–17	18–22		23–32
Men		465,000	419,000		726,000
Women		453,000	410,000		717,000

Total Armed Forces

ACTIVE 24,500

Army 15,000

3 Defence Zones • 4 inf bde (with 8 inf, 1 arty bn, 2 recce sqn) • 1 armd, 1 Presidential Guard, 1 SF, 1 arty, 1 engr bn

EQUIPMENT

LT TK 12 AMX-13 (**75mm**), 12 M-41A1 (**76mm**)

RECCE 8 V-150 *Commando*

APC 20 M-2/M-3 half-track

TOWED ARTY 105mm: 22 M-101

MOR 81mm: M-1; **120mm**: 24 ECIA

Navy 4,000

(incl marine security unit and 1 SEAL unit)

BASES Santo Domingo (HQ), Las Calderas

PATROL AND COASTAL COMBATANTS 15

PATROL, OFFSHORE 5

2 *Cohoes* PCO with 2 × 76mm gun, 1 *Prestol* (US *Admirable*) with 1 × 76mm gun, 1 *Sotoyoma* PCO with 1 × 76mm gun, 1 *Balsam* PCO

PATROL, COASTAL/INSHORE 10

1 *Betelgeuse* (US PGM-71) PCC, 2 *Canopus* PCI<, 7 PCI<

SUPPORT AND MISCELLANEOUS 4

1 AOT (small harbour), 3 AT

Air Force 5,500

6 cbt ac, no armed hel

Flying hours probably less than 60

CCT 1 sqn with 6 A-37B

TPT 1 sqn with 1 Beech 60, 1 Beech 200, 1 Cessna 207, 2 C-212-400, 1 PA-31

MPA/SAR 1 sqn with 5 T-34B

HEL 1 Liaison/Casevac/SAR sqn with 6 UH-1H, 1 SA-365C, 1 SA-365N (VIP); trg, 1 SE-3130, 1 OH-6A

TRG 3 T-41D, 8 T-35B

AB 1 SF (AB) bn

AD 1 bn with 4 **20mm** guns

Paramilitary 15,000

NATIONAL POLICE 15,000

Ecuador Ec

sucre ES		1999	2000	2001	2002
GDP	ES	170tr	357tr		
	US$	19bn	20bn		
per capita	US$	4,300	4,500		
Growth	%	-7.0	2.0		
Inflation	%	52.3	91		
Debt	US$	16.1bn	13.5bn		
Def exp[a]	ES	ε4.0tr	ε8tr		
	US$	339m	320m		
Def bdgt[a]	ES	ε4.0tr	ε10.0tr		
	US$	339m	400m		
FMA (US)	US$	2.8m	2.7m	4.0m	
US$1=ES		11,787	25,000	25,000	

[a] incl extra-budgetary funding

Population			**12,831,000**
Age	13–17	18–22	23–32
Men	721,000	667,000	1,147,000
Women	700,000	650,000	1,123,000

Total Armed Forces

ACTIVE 59,500

Terms of service conscription 1 year, selective

RESERVES 100,000

Ages 18–55

Army 50,000

4 Defence Zones
  5 inf bde (each 3 inf, 1 armd, 1 arty bn) • 1 armd bde
  (3 armd, 1 mech inf, 1 SP arty bn) • 3 jungle bde (2
  with 3 jungle, 1 SF bn, 1 with 4 jungle bn)
Army tps: 1 SF (AB) bde (4 bn), 1 special ops gp, 1 AD
  arty gp, 1 avn gp (4 bn), 1 engr bde: 3 engr bn

EQUIPMENT
  MBT 30+ T-55
  LT TK 108 AMX-13
  RECCE 27 AML-60/-90, 30 EE-9 *Cascavel*, 10 EE-3
    Jararaca
  APC 20 M-113, 80 AMX-VCI, 30 EE-11 *Urutu*
  TOWED ARTY 175 incl: **105mm**: 50 M2A2, 30 M-
    101, 24 Model 56; **155mm**: 12 M-198, 12 M-114
  SP ARTY 155mm: 10 Mk F3
  MRL 122mm: 6 RM-70
  MOR 81mm: M-29; **107mm**: 4.2in M-30; **160mm**: 12
    Soltam
  RCL 90mm: 380 M-67; **106mm**: 24 M-40A1
  AD GUNS 14.5mm: 128 ZPU-1/-2; **20mm**: 20 M-
    1935; **23mm**: 34 ZU-23; **35mm**: 30 GDF-002 twin;
    37mm: 18 Ch; **40mm**: 30 L/70
  SAM 75 *Blowpipe*, *Chaparral*, SA-7/-8/-16, 90 SA-18
    (reported)

AIRCRAFT
  SURVEY 1 Cessna 206, 1 Cessna *Citation*
  TPT 1 CN-235, 1 DHC-5, 5 IAI-201, 1 *King Air* 200, 2
    PC-6

HELICOPTERS
  TPT/LIAISON 4 AS-332, 2 AS-350B, 1 Bell 214B, 1
    SA-315B, 1 SA-330, 20 SA-342, 4 Mi-17 (reported)

Navy 5,500

(incl 250 Naval Aviation and 1,700 Marines)
BASES Guayaquil (main base), Jaramijo, Galápagos
Islands

SUBMARINES 2
SSK 2 *Shyri* (Ge T-209/1300) with 8 × 533mm TT (Ge
  SUT HWT)

PRINCIPAL SURFACE COMBATANTS 2

FRIGATES 2
FFG 2 *Presidente Eloy Alfaro* (ex-UK *Leander* batch II)
  with 4 MM-38 *Exocet* SSM, 1 206B hel

PATROL AND COASTAL COMBATANTS 11
CORVETTES 6 *Esmeraldas* FSG with 2 × 3 MM-40
  Exocet SSM, 1 × 4 *Albatros* SAM, 1 × 76mm gun, 6 ×
  324mm ASTT, hel deck
MISSILE CRAFT 5
  3 *Quito* (Ge Lürssen 45m) PFM with 4 MM-38 *Exocet*
    SSM, 1 × 76mm gun
  2 *Manta*† (Ge Lürssen 36m) PFM with 4 *Gabriel* II SSM

AMPHIBIOUS 1
  1 *Hualcopo* (US LST-512-1152) LST, capacity 150 tps

SUPPORT AND MISCELLANEOUS 7
  2 AOT (small); 1 AE; 2 ATF, 1 sail trg; 1 AGOR

NAVAL AVIATION (250)
EQUIPMENT
  AIRCRAFT
    LIAISON 3 *Super King Air* 200, 1 *Super King Air*
      300, 1 CN-235
    TRG 3 T-34C
  HELICOPTER
    UTL 4 Bell 206, 2 Bell 412 EP, 4 Bell TH-57

MARINES (1,700)
3 bn: 2 on garrison duties, 1 cdo (no hy wpn/veh)

Air Force 4,000

79 cbt ac, no armed hel

OPERATIONAL COMMAND
2 wg, 4 sqn
  FGA 3 sqn
    1 with 8 *Jaguar* S (6 -A(E), 2 -B(E))
    1 with 10 *Kfir* C-2 (being modernised to CE
      standard), 2 TC-2
    1 with 20 A-37B
  FTR 1 sqn with 13 *Mirage* F-1JE, 1 F-1JB
  CCT 4 *Strikemaster* Mk 89A

MILITARY AIR TRANSPORT GROUP
  2 civil/mil airlines:
  TAME 6 Boeing 727, 2 BAe-748, 2 C-130B, 1 C-130H,
    1 DHC-6, 1 F-28, 1 L-100-30
  ECUATORIANA 3 Boeing 707-320, 1 DC-10-30, 2 A-310
  LIAISON 1 *King Air* E90, 1 *Sabreliner*
  LIAISON/SAR hel 2 AS-332, 1 Bell 212, 6 Bell-206B, 5
    SA-316B, 1 SA-330
  TRG incl 22 AT-33*, 20 Cessna 150, 5 C-172, 17 T-34C, 1
    T-41

MISSILES
  AAM R-550 *Magic*, *Super* 530, *Shafrir*, *Python* 3, *Python* 4
  AB 1 AB sqn

Paramilitary 270

COAST GUARD 270

PATROL, COASTAL/INSHORE 4

2 *5 De Agosto* PCC, 1 PGM-71 PCI, 1 *Point* PCI plus some 8 boats

---

El Salvador EIS

colon C		1999	2000	2001	2002
GDP	C	103bn	105bn		
	US$	10bn	10.6bn		
per capita	US$	2,900	3,000		
Growth	%	2.6	2.5		
Inflation	%	0.5	2.5		
Debt	US$	2.7bn	2.7bn		
Def exp	C	ε1.5bn	ε1.5bn		
	US$	171m	171m		
Def bdgt	C	983m	980m	ε980m	
	US$	112m	112m	112m	
FMA (US)	US$	0.5m	0.5m	0.5m	
US$1=C		8.76	8.76	8.76	
Population					**6,386,000**
Age		13–17	18–22	23–32	
Men		370,000	360,000	560,000	
Women		357,000	347,000	572,000	

Total Armed Forces

ACTIVE 16,800

Terms of service selective conscription, 1 year

RESERVES

Ex-soldiers registered

Army ε15,000

(incl 4,000 conscripts)
6 Mil Zones • 6 inf bde (each of 2 inf bn) • 1 special sy bde (4 MP, 2 border gd bn) • 8 inf det (bn) • 1 engr comd (2 engr bn) • 1 arty bde (2 fd, 1 AD bn) • 1 mech cav regt (2 bn) • 1 special ops gp (1 para bn, 1 naval inf, 1 SF coy)

EQUIPMENT

RECCE 10 AML-90 (2 in store)
APC 40 M-37B1 (mod), 8 UR-416
TOWED ARTY 105mm: 24 M-101 (in store), 36 M-102, 18 M-56
MOR 81mm: incl 300 M-29; **120mm**: 60 UB-M52, M-74 (in store)
RL 94mm: LAW; **82mm**: B-300
RCL 90mm: 400 M-67; **106mm**: 20+ M-40A1 (incl 16 SP)
AD GUNS 20mm: 36 FRY M-55, 4 TCM-20

Navy 700

(incl some 90 Naval Infantry and spt forces)
BASES La Unión, La Libertad, Acajutla, El Triunfo, Guija Lake
PATROL AND COASTAL COMBATANTS 5
PATROL, COASTAL/INSHORE 5
3 *Camcraft* 30m PCC, 2 PCI<, plus 22 river boats

NAVAL INFANTRY (Marines) (some 90)

1 sy coy

Air Force 1,100

(incl AD and ε200 conscripts); 23 cbt ac, 21 armed hel
Flying hours A-37: 90
CBT AC 1 sqn with 5 A-37B, 4 OA-37B, 1 *Ouragan*, 9 O-2A, 2 O-2B (psyops), 2 CM-170 in store
ARMED HEL 1 sqn with 1 MD-500D, 6 MD-500E, 3 UH-1M, (11 UH-1H in store)
TPT 1 sqn with ac 2 C-47, 6 Basler Turbo-67 (3 capable of being converted back to AC-47 gunships), 1 T-41D, 1 Cessna 337G, 1 *Merlin* IIIB, (1 C-123K and 1 OC-6B in store) **hel** 1 sqn with 18 UH-1H tpt hel (incl 4 SAR), (15 UH-1H in store)
TRG 5 *Rallye*, 5 T-35 *Pillan*, **hel** 6 Hughes 269A (of which 4 stored)
AAM *Shafrir*

Forces Abroad

UN AND PEACEKEEPING

WESTERN SAHARA (MINURSO): 2 obs

Paramilitary 12,000

NATIONAL CIVILIAN POLICE (Ministry of Public Security) some 12,000 (to be 16,000)

small arms; **ac** 1 Cessna O-2A **hel** 1 UH-1H, 2 Hughes-520N, 1 MD-500D
10 river boats

Guatemala Gua

quetzal q		1999	2000	2001	2002
GDP	q	133bn	138bn		
	US$	14.1bn	14.8bn		
per capita	US$	4,300	4,500		
Growth	%	3.5	3.5		
Inflation	%	4.9	7.0		
Debt	US$	4.0bn	4.7bn		
Def exp	q	ε1.1bn	ε1.2bn		
	US$	149m	155m		
Def bdgt	q	845m	950m	836m	
	US$	114m	123m	108.4m	

contd		1999	2000	2001	2002
FMA (US) US$		3.3m	3.2m	3.3m	
US$1=q		7.39	7.71	7.71	
Population					11,541,000
Age		13–17	18–22		23–32
Men		750,000	647,000		974,000
Women		729,000	630,000		960,000

Total Armed Forces

(National Armed Forces are combined; the Army provides log spt for Navy and Air Force)

ACTIVE ε31,400

(ε23,000 conscripts)
Terms of service conscription; selective, 30 months

RESERVES

Army ε35,000 (trained) **Navy** (some) **Air Force** 200

Army 29,200

(incl ε23,000 conscripts)
15 Mil Zones (22 inf, 1 trg bn, 6 armd sqn) • 2 strategic bde (4 inf, 1 lt armd bn, 1 recce sqn, 2 arty bty) • 1 SF gp (3 coy incl 1 trg) • 2 AB bn • 5 inf bn gp (each 1 inf bn, 1 recce sqn, 1 arty bty) • 1 Presidential Guard bn • 1 engr bn • 1 Frontier Detachment
RESERVES ε19 inf bn
EQUIPMENT
   RECCE 7 M-8 (in store), 9 RBY-1
   APC 10 M-113 (plus 5 in store), 7 V-100 *Commando*, 30 *Armadillo*
   TOWED ARTY 105mm: 12 M-101, 8 M-102, 56 M-56
   MOR 81mm: 55 M-1; **107mm**: 12 M-30 (in store);
     120mm: 18 ECIA
   RL 89mm: 3.5in M-20 (in store)
   RCL 57mm: M-20; **105mm**: 64 Arg M-1974 FMK-1;
     106mm: 56 M-40A1
   AD GUNS 20mm: 16 M-55, 16 GAI-DO1

Navy ε1,500

(incl some 650 Marines)
BASES Atlantic Santo Tomás de Castilla **Pacific** Puerto Quetzal
PATROL AND COASTAL COMBATANTS 9
PATROL CRAFT, COASTAL/INSHORE 9
   1 *Kukulkan* (US Broadsword 32m) PCI<, 2 *Stewart* PCI<, 6 *Cutlas* PCI<, plus 6 *Vigilante* boats
PATROL CRAFT, RIVERINE 20 boats

MARINES (some 650)
2 bn (-)

Air Force 700

10† cbt ac, 12 armed hel. Serviceability of ac is less than 50%
CBT AC 1 sqn with 4 Cessna A-37B, 1 sqn with 6 PC-7
TPT 1 sqn with 4 T-67 (mod C-47 *Turbo*), 2 F-27, 1 *Super King Air* (VIP), 1 PA 301 *Navajo*, 4 Arava 201
LIAISON 1 sqn with 2 Cessna 206, 1 Cessna 310
HEL 1 sqn with 12 armed hel (9 Bell 212, 3 Bell 412), 9 Bell 206, 3 UH-1H, 3 S-76
TRG 6 T-41, 5 T-35B, 5 Cessna R172K
TACTICAL SECURITY GROUP (Air Military Police)
   3 CCT coy, 1 armd sqn, 1 AD bty (Army units for air-base sy)

Paramilitary 19,000 active

NATIONAL POLICE 19,000
21 departments, 1 SF bn, 1 integrated task force (incl mil and treasury police)
TREASURY POLICE (2,500)

Guyana Guy

dollar G$		1999	2000	2001	2002
GDP	G$	119bn	133bn		
	US$	774m	800m		
per capita	US$	3,300	3,400		
Growth	%	2.0	3.0		
Inflation	%	5.0	6.6		
Debt	US$	1.7bn	1.8bn		
Def exp	G$	1.2bn	1.2bn		
	US$	7m	7m		
Def bdgt	G$	ε900m	ε950m	ε1,000m	
	US$	5m	5m	5m	
FMA (US) US$		0.3m	0.3m	0.3m	
US$1=G$		178	181	181	
Population					868,000
Age		13–17	18–22		23–32
Men		43,000	39,000		78,000
Women		41,000	37,000		74,000

Total Armed Forces

ACTIVE (combined **Guyana Defence Force**) some 1,600

RESERVES some 1,500
People's Militia (see *Paramilitary*)

Army 1,400

(incl 500 Reserves)
1 inf bn, 1 SF, 1 spt wpn, 1 engr coy

EQUIPMENT
RECCE 3 Shorland, 6 EE-9 *Cascavel* (reported)
TOWED ARTY 130mm: 6 M-46
MOR 81mm: 12 L16A1; **82mm**: 18 M-43; **120mm**: 18 M-43

Navy 100

(plus 170 reserves)
BASES Georgetown, New Amsterdam
PATROL AND COASTAL COMBATANTS 1
1 *Orwell* PCC plus 2 boats

Air Force 100

no cbt ac, no armed hel
TPT ac 1 Y-12, 1 *Skyvan* 3M **hel** 1 Bell 206, 1 Bell 412

Paramilitary

GUYANA PEOPLE'S MILITIA (GPM) some 1,500

Haiti RH

gourde G		**1999**	**2000**	**2001**	**2002**
GDP	G	66bn	76bn		
	US$	3.9bn	3.3bn		
per capita	US$	1,100	1,100		
Growth	%	2.5	1.0		
Inflation	%	8.7	10.0		
Debt	US$	1,195m			
Sy exp	G	ε850m	ε900m		
	US$	50m	49m		
Sy bdgt	G	ε850m	ε900m	ε900m	
	US$	50m	49m	37m	
FMAᵃ (US)	US$	4.0m	7.3m	4.8m	
US$1=G		16.9	18.3	24	
ᵃ UN **1999** US$19m					
Population					**8,448,000**
Age		*13–17*	*18–22*	*23–32*	
Men		431,000	380,000	626,000	
Women		420,000	374,000	623,000	

Total Armed Forces

ACTIVE Nil

Paramilitary

In 1994, the mil govt of Haiti was replaced by a civilian administration. The former armed forces and police were disbanded and an Interim Public Security Force (IPSF) of 3,000 formed. A National Police Force of ε5,300 personnel has now been formed. All Army eqpt has been destroyed.

The United Nations Civilian Police Mission in Haiti (MIPONUH) tasked to assist the govt of Haiti by supporting and contributing to the professionalisation of the National Police Force, completed its mandate on 15 Mar 2000

COAST GUARD 30
BASE Port-au-Prince
    PATROL CRAFT boats only

Honduras Hr

lempira L		**1999**	**2000**	**2001**	**2002**
GDP	L	76.6bn	85.7bn		
	US$	5.4bn	5.8bn		
per capita	US$	2,200	2,300		
Growth	%	-1.9	4.0		
Inflation	%	11.6	10.5		
Debt	US$	4.5bn	5.5bn		
Def exp	L	ε1,350m	ε1,400m		
	US$	95m	95m		
Def bdgt	L	ε500m	ε520m	ε550m	
	US$	35m	35m	35m	
FMA (US)	US$	0.5m	0.5m	0.5m	
US$1=L		14.2	14.7	15.3	
Population				**6,597,000**	
Age		*13–17*	*18–22*	*23–32*	
Men		412,000	352,000	573,000	
Women		398,000	343,000	562,000	

Total Armed Forces

ACTIVE 8,300

RESERVES 60,000
Ex-servicemen registered

Army 5,500

6 Mil Zones
4 inf bde
    3 with 3 inf, 1 arty bn • 1 with 3 inf bn
1 special tac gp with 1 inf (AB), 1 SF bn
1 armd cav regt (2 mech bn, 1 lt tk, 1 recce sqn, 1 arty, 1 AD arty bty)
1 engr bn
1 Presidential Guard coy
RESERVES
1 inf bde
EQUIPMENT
LT TK 12 *Scorpion*
RECCE 3 *Scimitar*, 1 *Sultan*, 50 *Saladin*, 13 RBY-1
TOWED ARTY 105mm: 24 M-102; **155mm**: 4 M-198
MOR 60mm; **81mm**; **120mm**: 60 FMK; **160mm**: 30 *Soltam*
RL 84mm: 120 *Carl Gustav*

RCL 106mm: 80 M-40A1
AD Guns 20mm: 24 M-55A2, 24 TCM-20

Navy 1,000

(incl 400 Marines)
BASES Atlantic Puerto Cortés, Puerto Castilla **Pacific** Amapala
PATROL AND COASTAL COMBATANTS 10
PATROL CRAFT, COASTAL/INSHORE 10
   3 *Guaymuras* (US *Swiftship* 31m) PFC
   2 *Copan* (US *Guardian* 32m) PFI<
   5 PCI<, plus 28 riverine boats
AMPHIBIOUS craft only
   1 *Punta Caxinas* LCT

MARINES (400)
3 indep coy (-)

Air Force 1,800

49 cbt ac, no armed hel
FGA 2 sqn
   1 with 13 A-37B
   1 with 11 F-5E/F
IN STORE 10 *Super Mystère* B2
TPT 5 C-47, 3 C-130A, 2 IAI-201, 1 IAI-1124, 1 L-188 *Electra*
LIAISON 6 C-185, 1 *Commander*, 1 PA-31, 1 PA-31T, 1 Cessna 401
HEL 9 Bell 412SP, 2 Hughes 500, 4 UH-1H, 1 A-109 (VIP)
TRG/COIN 4* C-101CC, 11* EMB-312, 6 T-41A, 2 Cessna 182
AAM *Shafrir*

Forces Abroad

UN AND PEACEKEEPING
WESTERN SAHARA (MINURSO): 12 obs

Paramilitary 6,000

PUBLIC SECURITY FORCES (Ministry of Public Security and Defence) 6,000
11 regional comd

Foreign Forces

US 1,120: **Army** 850 **Marines** 70 **Air Force** 200

Jamaica Ja

dollar J$		1999	2000	2001	2002
GDP	J$	259bn	286bn		
	US$	6.6bn	6.9bn		
per capita	US$	3,500	3,500		
Growth	%	-1.0	0.5		
Inflation	%	5.9	6.1		
Debt	US$	3.8bn	4.1bn		
Def exp	J$	2.0bn	2.1bn		
	US$	51m	50m		
Def bdgt	J$	2.0bn	2.1bn	2.2bn	
	US$	51m	50m	48m	
FMA (US)	US$	1.7m	1.7m	2.3m	
US$1=J$		39.0	41.8	45.5	
Population				2,608,000	
Age		13–17	18–22	23–32	
Men		121,000	119,000	226,000	
Women		121,000	116,000	226,000	

Total Armed Forces

ACTIVE (combined **Jamaican Defence Force**) some 2,830

RESERVES some 953
Army 877 **Coast Guard** 60 **Air Wing** 16

Army 2,500

2 inf, 1 spt bn, 1 engr regt (4 sqn)
EQUIPMENT
   APC 13 V-150 *Commando* (some non-op)
   MOR 81mm: 12 L16A1

RESERVES
1 inf bn

Coast Guard 190

BASE Port Royal, out stations at Discovery Bay and Pedro Cays
PATROL AND COASTAL COMBATANTS 4
PATROL COASTAL/INSHORE 4
   1 *Fort Charles* (US 34m) PFC, 1 *Paul Bogle* (US-31m) PFI<, 2 *Point* PCI<
   plus 7 craft and boats

Air Wing 140

3 flts plus National Reserve
no cbt ac, no armed hel. All apart from 4 AS-355 and 3 Bell 412 reported as grounded
AC 1 TPT/MPA flt with 1 BN-2A, 1 Cessna 210, 1 *King Air*
HEL 2 TPT/SAR flts with 4 Bell 206, 3 Bell 412, 4 AS-355

Mexico Mex

new peso NP		1999	2000	2001	2002
GDP	NP	4.6tr	5.2tr		
	US$	484bn	554bn		
per capita	US$	8,200	8,800		
Growth	%	3.7	7.0		
Inflation	%	16.6	9.5		
Debt	US$	162bn	172bn		
Def exp[a]	NP	41bn	50bn		
	US$	4.3bn	5.3bn		
Def bdgt	NP	23.2bn	28.4bn		
	US$	2.4bn	3.0bn		
FMA (US)	US$	6m	9m	11m	
US$1=NP		9.56	9.41	9.22	

[a] Incl spending on paramilitary forces.

Population		100,564,000	**Chiapas** region 4%	
Age	*13–17*	*18–22*	*23–32*	
Men	5,348,000	4,901,000	9,171,000	
Women	5,193,000	4,795,000	9,166,000	

Total Armed Forces

ACTIVE 192,770

(60,000 conscripts)
Terms of service 1 year conscription (4 hours per week)
by lottery

RESERVES 300,000

Army 144,000

(incl ε60,000 conscripts)
12 Mil Regions
44 Zonal Garrisons with 81 inf bn (1 mech), 19 mot cav, 3 arty regt plus 1 air-mobile SF unit per Garrison
3 Corps HQ each with 3 inf bde

STRATEGIC RESERVE

4 armd bde (each 2 armd recce, 1 arty regt, 1 mech inf bn, 1 ATK gp)
1 AB bde (3 bn)
1 MP bde (3 MP bn, 1 mech cav regt)

EQUIPMENT

RECCE 40 M-8, 119 ERC-90F *Lynx*, 40 VBL, 25 MOWAG, 40 MAC-1
APC 40 HWK-11, 32 M-2A1 half-track, 40 VCR/TT, 24 DN-3, 40 DN-4 *Caballo*, 70 DN-5 *Toro*, 495 AMX-VCI, 95 BDX, 26 LAV-150 ST, some BTR-60 (reported)
TOWED ARTY 75mm: 18 M-116 pack; **105mm**: 16 M-2A1/M-3, 80 M-101, 80 M-56
SP ARTY 75mm: 5 DN-5 *Bufalo*
MOR 81mm: 1,500; **120mm**: 75 Brandt
ATGW *Milan* (incl 8 VBL)
RL 82mm: B-300

ATK GUNS 37mm: 30 M-3
AD GUNS 12.7mm: 40 M-55; **20mm**: 40 GAI-BO1
SAM RBS-70

Navy 37,000

(incl 1,100 Naval Aviation and 8,700 Marines)
NAVAL COMMANDS Gulf, Pacific
NAVAL ZONES Gulf 6 **Pacific** 11
BASES Gulf Vera Cruz (HQ), Tampico, Chetumal, Ciudad del Carmen, Yukalpetén, Lerna, Frontera, Coatzacoalcos, Isla Mujéres **Pacific** Acapulco (HQ), Ensenada, La Paz, San Blas, Guaymas, Mazatlán, Manzanillo, Salina Cruz, Puerto Madero, Lázaro Cárdenas, Puerto Vallarta

PRINCIPAL SURFACE COMBATANTS 11

DESTROYERS 3

DD 3
2 *Ilhuicamina* (ex-*Quetzalcoatl*) (US *Gearing*) with 2 × 2 127mm guns, 1 Bo-105 hel
1 *Cuitlahuac* (US *Fletcher*) with 5 × 127mm guns, 5 × 533mm ASTT

FRIGATES 8

FF 8
2 *Knox* with 1 × 127mm gun, 4 × 324mm ASTT, 2 × 8 ASROC SUGW, 1 × Bo 105 hel
2 *H. Galeana* (US *Bronstein*) with 6 × 324mm ASTT, ASROC SUGW
3 *Hidalgo* (US *Lawrence/Crosley*) with 1 × 127mm gun
1 *Comodoro Manuel Azueta* (US *Edsall*) (trg) with 2 × 76mm gun

PATROL AND COASTAL COMBATANTS 109

PATROL, OFFSHORE 44

4 *Holzinger* 2000 PCO with MD 902 hel
4 *S. J. Holzinger* (ex-*Uxmal*) (imp *Uribe*) PCO with Bo-105 hel
6 *Uribe* (Sp 'Halcon') PCO with Bo-105 hel
11 *Negrete* (US *Admirable* MSF) PCO with 1 Bo-105 hel
17 *Leandro Valle* (US *Auk* MSF) PCO
1 *Guanajuato* PCO with 2 × 102mm gun
1 *Centenario* PCO

PATROL, COASTAL 41

31 *Azteca* PCC
3 *Cabo* (US *Cape Higgon*) PCC
7 *Tamiahua* (US *Polimar*) PCC

PATROL, INSHORE 6

4 *Isla* (US *Halter*) XFPCI<
2 *Punta* (US *Point*) PCI<

PATROL, RIVERINE 18<, plus boats

AMPHIBIOUS 3

2 *Panuco* (US-511) LST
1 *Grijalva* (US-511) LST

SUPPORT AND MISCELLANEOUS 19

1 AOT; 4 AK, 2 log spt; 6 AT/F, 1 sail trg; 2 AGHS, 3 AGOR

NAVAL AVIATION (1,100)

EQUIPMENT
8 cbt ac, no armed hel
AIRCRAFT
MR 1 sqn with 8* C-212-200M
TPT 1 C-212, 2 C-180, 3 C-310, 1 DHC-5, 1 FH-227, 1 *King Air* 90, 1 *Learjet* 24, 1 *Commander*, 2 C-337, 2 C-402, 5 An-32, 1 Mu-2F
TRG 12 *Maule* MX-7, 10 F-33C *Bonanza*, 10 L-90 *Redigo*
HELICOPTER
UTL 3 Bell 47, 4 SA-319, 20 Mi-8/17, 4 AS-555, 2 R-22 *Mariner*, 1 R-44
MR 12 Bo-105 (8 afloat), 10 MD-902 Explorer
TRG 4 MD-500E

MARINES (8,700)

3 marine bde (each 3 bn), 1 AB regt (2 bn) • 1 Presidential Guard bn • 11 regional bn • 1 Coast def gp: 2 coast arty bn • 1 indep sy coy
EQUIPMENT
AAV 25 VAP-3550
TOWED ARTY 105mm: 16 M-56
MRL 51mm: 6 *Firos*
MOR 100 incl **60mm, 81mm**
RCL 106mm: M-40A1
AD GUNS 20mm: Mk 38; **40mm**: Bofors
plus 60 Swe assault craft

Air Force 11,770

107 cbt ac, 71 armed hel
FTR 1 sqn with 8 F-5E, 2 -F
CCT 9 sqn
7 with 70 PC-7
2 with 17 AT-33
ARMED HEL 1 sqn with 1 Bell 205A, 15 Bell 206B, 7 Bell 206L-3, 24 Bell 212
RECCE 1 photo sqn with 10* *Commander* 500S, 2 SA 2-37A, 4 C-26
TPT 5 sqn with 1 Convair CV-580, 1 Lockheed L-1329 *Jetstar*, 1 Cessna 500 *Citation*, 1 C-118, 7 C-130A, 1 L-100 *Hercules*, 10 *Commander* 500S, 1 sqn with 9 IAI-201 (tpt/SAR)
HEL 6 S-70A, 1 Mi-2, 11 Mi-8, 24 Mi-17, 1 Mi-26T
PRESIDENTIAL TPT ac 1 Boeing 757, 3 Boeing 727-100
LIAISON/UTL 9 IAI *Arava*, 1 *King Air* A90, 3 *King Air* C90, 1 *Super King* 300, 1 *Musketeer*, 29 Beech *Bonanza* F-33C, 73 Cessna 182S, 11 Cessna 206, 11 Cessna 210, 4 PC-6, 6 Turbo Commander
TRG ac 6 Maule M-7, 21 Maule MXT-7-180, 12 PT-17 Stearman, 30 SF-260 **hel** 24* MD 530F (SAR/paramilitary/trg)

Paramilitary ε11,000

FEDERAL PREVENTIVE POLICE (Ministry of Interior) ε11,000

RURAL DEFENCE MILITIA (R) 14,000

COAST GUARD
4 *Mako* 295 PCI<

Opposition

ZAPATISTA ARMY OF NATIONAL LIBERATION str n.k.
POPULAR INSURGENT REVOLUTIONARY ARMY str n.k.
MEXICAN PEASANT WORKERS FRONT OF THE SOUTH EAST str n.k.
POPULAR MOVEMENT OF NATIONAL LIBERATION str n.k.
REVOLUTIONARY INSURGENT ARMY OF THE SOUTH EAST str n.k.

Nicaragua Nic

Cordoba oro Co		1999	2000	2001	2002
GDP	Co	28.0bn	28.9bn		
	US$	2.9bn	3.1bn		
per capita	US$	2,100	2,200		
Growth	%	6.0	5.5		
Inflation	%	10.9	9.7		
Debt	US$	6.7bn	7.0bn		
Def exp	Co	294m	329m		
	US$	25m	26m		
Def bdgt	Co	294m	329m	360m	
	US$	25m	26m	27m	
FMA (US)	US$	0.2m	0.2m	0.2m	
US$1=Co		11.9	12.5	13.2	
Population					**5,246,000**
Age		13–17	18–22		23–32
Men		339,000	287,000		366,000
Women		299,000	254,000		396,000

Total Armed Forces

ACTIVE ε16,000
Terms of service voluntary, 18–36 months

Army 14,000

Reorganisation in progress
5 Regional Comd (10 inf, 1 tk coy) • 2 mil det (2 inf bn) • 1 lt mech bde (1 mech inf, 1 tk, 1 recce bn, 1 fd arty gp (2 bn), 1 atk gp), 1 comd regt (1 inf, 1 sy bn) • 1 SF bde (3 SF bn) • 1 tpt regt (incl 1 APC bn) • 1 engr bn
EQUIPMENT
MBT some 127 T-55 (42 op remainder in store)
LT TK 10 PT-76 (in store)
RECCE 20 BRDM-2
APC 102 BTR-152 (in store), 64 BTR-60

TOWED ARTY 122mm: 12 D-30, 100 *Grad* 1P (single-tube rocket launcher); **152mm**: 30 D-20 (in store)
MRL 107mm: 33 Type-63; **122mm**: 18 BM-21
MOR 82mm: 579; **120mm**: 24 M-43; **160mm**: 4 M-160 (in store)
ATGW AT-3 *Sagger* (12 on BRDM-2)
RCL 82mm: B-10
ATK GUNS 57mm: 354 ZIS-2 (90 in store); **76mm**: 83 ZIS-3; **100mm**: 24 M-1944
SAM 200+ SA-7/-14/-16

Navy ε800

BASES Corinto, Puerto Cabezzas, El Bluff

PATROL AND COASTAL COMBATANTS 5
PATROL, INSHORE 5
  2 Sov *Zhuk* PFI<, 3 *Dabur* PCI<, plus boats

MINE WARFARE 2
MINE COUNTERMEASURES 2
  2 *Yevgenya* MHI

Air Force 1,200

no cbt ac, 15 armed hel
TPT 1 An-2, 4 An-26, 1 Cessna 404 Titan (VIP)
HEL 15 Mi-17 (tpt/armed) (3 serviceable), 1 Mi-17 (VIP)
UTL/TRG ac 1 Cessna T-41D
ASM AT-2 *Swatter* ATGW
AD GUNS 1 air def gp, 18 ZU-23, 18 C3-*Morigla* M1

Panama Pan

balboa B		1999	2000	2001	2002
GDP	B	9.7bn	10.2bn		
	US$	9.7bn	10.2bn		
per capita	US$	6,900	7,100		
Growth	%	3.2	2.5		
Inflation	%	1.3	1.4		
Debt	US$	5.4bn			
Sy bdgt	B	128m	135m		
	US$	128m	135m		
FMA (US)	US$	0.7m	0.1m	0.1m	
US$1=B		1.0	1.0	1.0	
Population					2,845,000
Age		13–17	18–22	23–32	
Men		146,000	137,000	261,000	
Women		139,000	131,000	252,000	

Total Armed Forces

ACTIVE Nil

Paramilitary ε11,800

NATIONAL POLICE FORCE 11,000
Presidential Guard bn (-), 1 MP bn plus 8 coys, 18 Police coy, 1 SF unit (reported); no hy mil eqpt, small arms only

NATIONAL MARITIME SERVICE ε400
BASES Amador (HQ), Balboa, Colón
PATROL AND COASTAL COMBATANTS 14
  PATROL CRAFT, COASTAL 5
  2 *Panquiaco* (UK *Vosper* 31.5m) PCC, 3 other PCC
  PATROL CRAFT, INSHORE 9
  3 *Tres de Noviembre* (ex-US *Point*) PCI<, 1 *Swiftships* 65ft PCI<, 1 ex-US MSB 5 class, 1 *Negrita* PCI<, 3 ex-US PCI< (plus some 25 boats)

NATIONAL AIR SERVICE 400
  TPT 1 CN-235-2A, 1 BN-2B, 1 PA-34, 3 CASA-212M *Aviocar*
  TRG 6 T-35D
  HEL 2 Bell 205, 6 Bell 212, 13 UH-1H

Paraguay Py

guarani Pg		1999	2000	2001	2002
GDP	Pg	28.4tr	28.4tr		
	US$	9.3bn	9.5bn		
per capita	US$	3,700	3,800		
Growth	%	-1.5	1.5		
Inflation	%	6.8	9.2		
Debt	US$	2.3bn	2.4bn		
Def exp	Pg	ε400bn	ε430bn		
	US$	128m	123m		
Def bdgt	Pg	262bn	290bn	310bn	
	US$	84m	83m	80.9m	
FMA (US)	US$	0.2m	0.2m	0.2m	
US$1=Pg		3,119	3,495	3,830	
Population				5,607,000	
Age		13–17	18–22	23–32	
Men		315,000	271,000	446,000	
Women		304,000	262,000	432,000	

Total Armed Forces

ACTIVE 18,600 (to reduce)
(incl 11,200 conscripts)
Terms of service 12 months **Navy** 2 years

RESERVES some 164,500

Army 14,900

(incl 10,400 conscripts)

3 corps HQ • 9 div HQ (6 inf, 3 cav) • 9 inf regt (bn) •
3 cav regt (horse) • 3 mech cav regt • Presidential
Guard (1 inf, 1 MP bn, 1 arty bty) • 20 frontier det • 3
arty gp (bn) • 1 AD arty gp • 4 engr bn

RESERVES

14 inf, 4 cav regt

EQUIPMENT

MBT 12 M-4A3
RECCE 8 M-8, 5 M-3, 30 EE-9 *Cascavel*
APC 10 EE-11 *Urutu*
TOWED ARTY 75mm: 20 Model 1927/1934;
  105mm: 15 M-101; **152mm**: 6 Vickers 6in (coast)
MOR 81mm: 80
RCL 75mm: M-20
AD GUNS 30: **20mm**: 20 Bofors; **40mm**: 10 M-1A1

Navy 2,000

(incl 900 Marines, 100 Naval Aviation)
BASES Asunción (Puerto Sajonia), Bahía Negra,
Ciudad Del Este

PATROL AND COASTAL COMBATANTS 10
PATROL, RIVERINE 10
  2 *Paraguais* PCR with 4 × 120mm guns†
  2 *Nanawa* PCR
  1 *Itapu* PCR
  1 *Capitan Cabral* PCR
  2 *Capitan Ortiz* PCR (ROC *Hai Ou*) PCR<
  2 ROC PCR
  plus some 20 craft
SUPPORT AND MISCELLANEOUS 5
  1 tpt, 1 trg/tpt, 1 AGHS<, 2 LCT

MARINES (900)
(incl 200 conscripts); 4 bn(-)

NAVAL AVIATION (100)
EQUIPMENT
  AIRCRAFT
    CCT 2 AT-6G
    LIAISON 2 Cessna 150, 2 C-206, 1 C-210
  HELICOPTER
    UTL 2 HB-350, 1 OH-13

Air Force 1,700

(incl 600 conscripts); 28 cbt ac, no armed hel
  FTR/FGA 8 F-5E, 4 F-5F
  CCT 6 AT-33, 6 EMB-326, 4 T-27
  LIAISON 1 Cessna 185, 4 C-206, 2 C-402, 2 T-41
  HEL 3 HB-350, 1 UH-1B, 2 UH-1H, 4 UH-12, 4 Bell
    47G
  TPT 1 sqn with 5 C-47, 4 C-212, 3 DC-6B, 1 DHC-6
    (VIP), 1 C-131D
  TRG 6 T-6, 10 T-23, 5 T-25, 10 T-35, 1 T-41

Forces Abroad

UN AND PEACEKEEPING
ETHIOPIA/ERITREA (UNMEE): 12 obs

Paramilitary 14,800

SPECIAL POLICE SERVICE 14,800
(incl 4,000 conscripts)

Peru Pe

new sol NS		1999	2000	2001	2002
GDP	NS	193bn	189bn		
	US$	62bn	66bn		
per capita	US$	4,500	4,700		
Growth	%	3.8	3.5		
Inflation	%	3.5	3.8		
Debt	US$	29bn	29.5bn		
Def exp	NS	ε3.0bn	3.1bn		
	US$	888m	878m		
Def bdgt	NS	2.7bn	2.9bn	3.0bn	
	US$	820m	825m	827m	
FMA (US)	US$	79m	50m	50m	
US$1=NS		3.38	3.48	3.6	
Population				26,058,000	
Age		13–17	18–22	23–32	
Men		1,369,000	1,309,000	2,314,000	
Women		1,356,000	1,300,000	2,304,000	

Total Armed Forces

ACTIVE 100,000
(incl 64,000 conscripts)
Terms of service 2 years, selective

RESERVES 188,000
Army only

Army 60,000

(incl 52,000 conscripts)
6 Mil Regions
Army tps
  1 AB div (3 cdo, 1 para bn, 1 arty gp) • 1 Presidential
  Escort regt • 1 AD arty gp
Regional tps
  3 armd div (each 2 tk, 1 armd inf bn,1 arty gp, 1 engr
  bn) • 1 armd gp (3 indep armd cav, 1 fd arty, 1 AD
  arty, 1 engr bn) • 1 cav div (3 mech regt, 1 arty gp) •
  7 inf div (each 3 inf bn, 1 arty gp) • 1 jungle div • 2
  med arty gp • 2 fd arty gp • 1 indep inf bn • 1 indep
  engr bn • 3 hel sqn

EQUIPMENT
    MBT 275 T-54/-55 (ε50 serviceable)
    LT TK 110 AMX-13 (ε30 serviceable)
    RECCE 60 M-8/-20, 10 M-3A1, 50 M-9A1, 15 Fiat
      6616, 30 BRDM-2
    APC 130 M-113, 12 BTR-60, 130 UR-416, Fiat 6614,
      Casspir, 4 *Repontec*
    TOWED ARTY 105mm: 20 Model 56 pack, 130 M-
      101; **122mm**: 42 D-30; **130mm**: 36 M-46; **155mm**: 36
      M-114
    SP ARTY 155mm: 12 M-109A2, 12 Mk F3
    MRL 122mm: 14 BM-21
    MOR 700 incl: **81mm**: incl some SP; **107mm**: incl
      some SP; **120mm**: 300 Brandt, ECIA
    ATGW 400 SS-11
    RCL 106mm: M40A1
    AD GUNS 23mm: 80 ZSU-23-2, 35 ZSU-23-4 SP;
      30mm: 10 2S6 SP; **40mm**: 45 M-1, 80 L60/70
    SAM some 450 incl SA-7, SA-16/-18, *Javelin*
    AC 13 Cessna incl 1 C-337, 1 *Queen Air* 65, 5 U-10, 3
      U-17, 1 U-150, 2 U-206, 4 AN-32B
    HEL 2 Bell 412, 3 Mi-26, 26 Mi-8, 13 Mi-17, 5 SA-315,
      8 F-28F, 10 *Agusta* A-109

Navy 25,000

(incl some 800 Naval Aviation, 4,000 Marines, 1,000
Coast Guard and 10,000 conscripts)
NAVAL AREAS Pacific, Lake Titicaca, Amazon River
BASES Ocean Callao, San Lorenzo Island, Paita, Talara
Lake Puno **River** Iquitos, Puerto Maldonado
SUBMARINES 6
SSK 6 *Casma* (Ge T-209/1200) with 533mm TT (It A184
    HWT) (2 in refit)

PRINCIPAL SURFACE COMBATANTS 5
CRUISERS 1
    CG 1 *Almirante Grau* (Nl *De Ruyter*) with 8 Otomat
      SSM, 4 × 2 152mm guns
FRIGATES 4
    FFG 4 *Carvajal* (mod It *Lupo*) CG with 8 Otomat SSM,
      Albatros SAM, 1 × 127mm gun, 2 × 3 324mm ASTT
      (Mk 32 HWT), 1 AB-212 or SH-3D hel

PATROL AND COASTAL COMBATANTS 10
MISSILE CRAFT 6 *Velarde* PFM (Fr PR-72 64m) with 4
    MM-38 *Exocet* SSM, 1 × 76mm gun
PATROL CRAFT, RIVERINE 4
    2 *Marañon* PCR with 2 × 76 mm gun
    2 *Amazonas* PCR with 1 × 76 mm gun
    (plus 3 craft for lake patrol)

AMPHIBIOUS 3
    3 *Paita* (US *Terrebonne Parish*) LST, capacity 395 tps,
    2,000t

SUPPORT AND MISCELLANEOUS 9
    3 AO, 1 AOT, 1 tpt; 1 AT/F (SAR); 1 AGOR, 2 AGHS

NAVAL AVIATION (some 800)
EQUIPMENT
9 cbt ac, 9 armed hel
    AIRCRAFT
      ASW/MR 5 *Super King Air* B 200T, 3 EMB-111A, 1 F-
      27
      TPT 2 An-32B, 1 Y-12
      TRG 1 Cessna 150, 5 T-34C
    HELICOPTER
      ASW/MR 5 AB-212, 4 SH-3D
      LIAISON 4 Bell 206B, 6 UH-1D, 3 Mi-8
    MISSILES
      ASM *Exocet* AM-39

MARINES (4,000)
1 Marine bde (2 inf, 1 amph veh, 1 recce bn, 1 arty gp, 1
special ops gp)
3 indep inf bn (incl 1 jungle), 1 inf gp, 1 cdo gp
EQUIPMENT
    RECCE V-100
    APC 15 V-200 *Chaimite*, 20 BMR-600
    TOWED ARTY 122mm: D-30
    MOR 81mm; **120mm** ε18
    RCL 84mm: *Carl Gustav*; **106mm**: M-40A1
    AD GUNS twin 20mm SP

COASTAL DEFENCE 3 bty with 18 **155mm** how

Air Force 15,000

(incl 2,000 conscripts); 116 cbt ac†, 19 armed hel
BBR 8 *Canberra*
FGA 2 gp, 6 sqn
    3 with 28 Su-22 (incl 4* Su-22U), 18 Su-25 (incl 8* Su-
      25UB)
    3 with 23 Cessna A-37B
FTR 3 sqn
    1 with 10 *Mirage* 2000P, 2 -DP
    2 with 9 *Mirage* 5P, 2 -DP
    1 with 16 MiG-29SE (incl 2 MiG-29UB)
ATTACK/ASSAULT HEL 1 sqn with 10 Mi-24/-25, 8
    Mi-17TM, 1 Ka-50 (under evaluation)
RECCE 3 MiG-25RB, 1 photo-survey unit with 2 *Learjet*
25B, 2 -36A
TKR 1 Boeing KC 707-323C
TPT 3 gp, 7 sqn
    ac 17 An-32, 3 AN-72, 4 C-130A, 6 -D, 5 L-100-20, 2
    DC-8-62F, 12 DHC-5, 8 DHC-6, 1 FH-227, 9 PC-6, 6 Y-
    12 (II), 1 Boeing 737 **hel** 3 sqn with 8 Bell 206, 14 B-
    212, 5 B-214, 1 B-412, 10 Bo-105C, 5 Mi-6, 3 Mi-8, 35
    Mi-17, 5 SA-316
PRESIDENTIAL FLT 1 F-28, 1 *Falcon* 20F
LIAISON ac 2 Beech 99, 3 Cessna 185, 1 Cessna 320, 15
    Queen Air 80, 3 *King Air* 90, 1 PA-31T **hel** 8 UH-1D
TRG ac 2 Cessna 150, 25 EMB-312, 6 Il-103, 13 MB-
    339A, 20 T-37B/C, 15 T-41A/-D **hel** 12 Bell 47G
MISSILES
    ASM AS-30

AAM AA-2 *Atoll*, AA-8 *Aphid*, AA-10 *Alemo*, R-550 *Magic*, AA-12 *Adder*
AD 3 SA-2, 6 SA-3 bn

Forces Abroad

UN AND PEACEKEEPING
DROC (MONUC): 4 obs **EAST TIMOR** (UNTAET): 18
ETHIOPIA/ERITREA (UNMEE): 2 obs

Paramilitary 77,000

NATIONAL POLICE 77,000 (100,000 reported)
General Police 43,000 **Security Police** 21,000 **Technical Police** 13,000
100+ MOWAG *Roland* APC

COAST GUARD (1,000)
5 *Rio Nepena* PCC, 3 *Dauntless* PCI<, 3 PCI, 10 riverine PCI<

RONDAS CAMPESINAS (peasant self-defence force)
perhaps 2,000 *rondas* 'gp', up to pl strength, some with small arms. Deployed mainly in emergency zone.

Opposition

SENDERO LUMINOSO (Shining Path) ε1,000
Maoist
MOVIMIENTO REVOLUCIONARIO TUPAC AMARU (MRTA) ε600
mainly urban gp

Suriname Sme

guilder gld		1999	2000	2001	2002
GDP	gld	344bn	360bn		
	US$	409m	409m		
per capita	US$	5,100	5,200		
Growth	%	4.0			
Inflation	%	28.7	16.8		
Debt	US$	160m			
Def exp	gld	ε9.0bn	ε9.0bn		
	US$	11m	11m		
Def bdgt	gld	ε9.0bn	ε9.0bn	ε9.0bn	
	US$	11m	11m	11m	
FMA (US)	US$	0.1m	0.1m	0.1m	
US$1=gld		810	810	810	
Population					419,000
Age		13–17	18–22	23–32	
Men		22,000	18,000	34,000	
Women		22,000	18,000	34,000	

Total Armed Forces

ACTIVE ε2,040
(all services form part of the Army)

Army 1,600

1 inf bn (4 inf coy) • 1 mech cav sqn • 1 MP 'bde' (coy)
EQUIPMENT
RECCE 6 EE-9 *Cascavel*
APC 15 EE-11 *Urutu*
MOR 81mm: 6
RCL 106mm: M-40A1

Navy 240

BASE Paramaribo

PATROL AND COASTAL COMBATANTS 3

PATROL CRAFT, INSHORE 3
3 *Rodman* 100 PCI<, plus 5 boats

Air Force ε200

7 cbt ac, no armed hel
MPA 2 C-212-400
TPT/TRG 4* BN-2 *Defender*, 1* PC-7
LIAISON 1 Cessna U206
HEL 2 SA-316, 1 AB-205

Trinidad and Tobago TT

dollar TT$		1999	2000	2001	2002
GDP	TT$	42.5bn	45.7bn		
	US$	6.8bn	7.3bn		
per capita	US$	11,900	12,800		
Growth	%	7.0	5.0		
Inflation	%	2.6	5.6		
Debt	US$	2.6bn	2.9bn		
Def exp	TT$	392m	ε390m		
	US$	62m	62m		
Def bdgt	TT$	372m	390m	400m	
	US$	59m	62m	64m	
FMA (US)	US$	0.4m	0.4m	0.4m	
US$1=TT$		6.3	6.3	6.2	
Population					1,293,000
Age		13–17	18–22		23–32
Men		73,000	65,000		103,000
Women		72,000	64,000		107,000

Total Armed Forces

ACTIVE ε2,700 (all services form part of the **Trinidad and Tobago Defence Force**)

Army ε2,000

2 inf bn • 1 spt bn
EQUIPMENT
  MOR 60mm: ε40; **81mm**: 6 L16A1
  RL 82mm: 13 B-300
  RCL 82mm: B-300

Coast Guard 700

(incl 50 Air Wing)
BASE Staubles Bay (HQ), Hart's Cut, Point Fortin, Tobago, Galeota

PATROL AND COASTAL COMBATANTS 12†

PATROL CRAFT, OFFSHORE 1
  1 *Nelson* (UK *Island*) PCO

PATROL CRAFT, COASTAL 2
  2 *Barracuda* PFC (Sw *Karlskrona* 40m) (non-op)

PATROL CRAFT, INSHORE 9
  4 *Plymouth* PCI<
  3 *Point* PCI<
  2 *Wasp* PCI<
  plus 10 boats and 2 aux vessels
AIR WING
  2 C-26, 1 Cessna 310, 1 C-402, 1 C-172, 2 *Navajos*

Uruguay Ury

peso pU		1999	2000	2001	2002
GDP	pU	239bn	231bn		
	US$	13.7bn	14.1bn		
per capita	US$	9,000	9,000		
Growth	%	-3.2	-1.0		
Inflation	%	5.6	4.8		
Debt	US$	6.7bn	6.8bn		
Def exp	pU	ε3.6bn	4.3bn		
	US$	318m	364m		
Def bdgt	pU	2.6bn	4.6bn	4.8bn	
	US$	232m	384m	367m	
FMA (US)	US$	0.3m	0.3m	0.3m	
US$1=pU		10.47	11.34	13.0	
Population					**3,368,000**
Age		13–17	18–22	23–32	
Men		129,000	136,000	254,000	
Women		126,000	131,000	247,000	

Total Armed Forces

ACTIVE 23,900

Army 15,200

4 Mil Regions/div HQ • 5 inf bde (4 of 3 inf bn, 1 of 1 mech, 1 mot, 1 para bn) • 3 cav bde (10 cav bn (4 horsed, 3 mech, 2 mot, 1 armd)) • 1 arty bde (2 arty, 1 AD arty bn) • 1 engr bde (3 bn) • 3 arty, 4 cbt engr bn
EQUIPMENT
  MBT 15 T-55
  LT TK 17 M-24, 29 M-3A1, 22 M-41A1
  RECCE 16 EE-3 *Jararaca*, 15 EE-9 *Cascavel*
  AIFV 15 BMP-1
  APC 15 M-113, 44 *Condor*, 43 OT-64 SKOT, 32 M-93 (MT-LB)
  TOWED ARTY 75mm: 10 Bofors M-1902; **105mm**: 48 M-101A/M-102; **155mm**: 8 M-114A1
  SP ARTY 122mm: 2 2S1
  MRL 122mm: 3 RM-70
  MOR 81mm: 93; **107mm**: 9 M-30; **120mm**: 34
  ATGW 5 *Milan*
  RCL 57mm: 67 M-18; **75mm**: 3; **106mm**: 30 M-40A1
  AD GUNS 20mm: 9 TCM-20, 6 M-167 *Vulcan*; **40mm**: 8 L/60

Navy 5,700

(incl 300 Naval Aviation, 450 Naval Infantry, 1,950 *Prefectura Naval* (Coast Guard))
BASES Montevideo (HQ), Paysando (river), La Paloma (naval avn), Laguna del Sauce (naval avn)
PRINCIPAL SURFACE COMBATANTS 3

FRIGATES 3
FFG 3 *General Artigas* (Fr *Cdt Rivière*) with 4 MM-38 *Exocet* SSM, 2 × 100mm guns, 2 × 3 ASTT, 1 × 2 ASW mor
PATROL AND COASTAL COMBATANTS 8
PATROL, COASTAL/INSHORE 8
  3 *15 de Noviembre* PCC (Fr *Vigilante* 42m), 2 *Colonia* PCI< (US *Cape*), 1 *Paysandu* PCI<, 2 other PCI< plus 9 craft
MINE WARFARE 3
MINE COUNTERMEASURES 3
  3 *Temerario* MSC (Ge *Kondor* II)
AMPHIBIOUS craft only
  2 LCM, 2 LCVP
SUPPORT AND MISCELLANEOUS 6
  1 *Vanguardia* ARS, 1 *Campbell* (US *Auk* MSF) PCO (Antarctic patrol/research), 1 AT (ex-GDR *Elbe*-Class), 1 trg, 1 AGHS, 1 AGOR

NAVAL AVIATION (300)

EQUIPMENT

1 cbt ac, no armed hel
  AIRCRAFT
    ASW 1 *Super King Air* 200T
    TRG/LIAISON 1 *Jet Stream* TMK 2, 3 S-2G *Tracrer*,
    2 T-34C
  HELICOPTER
    UTL 1 Wessex Mk60, 4 Wessex HC2, 1 Bell 47G

NAVAL INFANTRY (450)

1 bn

Air Force 3,000

28 cbt ac, no armed hel
Flying hours 120
CBT AC 2 sqn
  1 with 10 A-37B, 1 with 5 IA-58B
SURVEY 1 EMB-110B1
HEL 1 sqn with 2 Bell 212, 6 UH-1H, 6 *Wessex* HC2
TPT 3 sqn with 3 C-212 (tpt/SAR), 3 EMB-110C, 1 F-27,
  3 C-130B, 1 Cessna 310 (VIP), 1 Cessna 206
LIAISON 2 Cessna 182, 2 *Queen Air* 80, 5 U-17, 1 T-34A
TRG 13 SF-260EU*, 5 T-41D, 5 PC-7U

Forces Abroad

UN AND PEACEKEEPING

DROC (MONUC): 444 incl 24 obs **EAST TIMOR**
(UNTAET): 5 obs **EGYPT** (MFO): 60 **ETHIOPIA/
ERITREA** (UNMEE): 6 obs **GEORGIA** (UNOMIG): 3
obs **INDIA/PAKISTAN** (UNMOGIP): 2 obs **IRAQ/
KUWAIT** (UNIKOM): 6 obs **SIERRA LEONE**
(UNAMSIL): 11 obs **WESTERN SAHARA**
(MINURSO): 13 obs

Paramilitary 920

GUARDIA DE GRANADEROS 450

GUARDIA DE CORACEROS 470

COAST GUARD (1,950)

Prefectura Naval (PNN) is part of the Navy
operates 3 PCC, 2 LCMs plus 9 boats

Venezuela Ve

bolivar Bs		1999	2000	2001	2002
GDP	Bs	62bn	72bn		
	US$	85bn	91bn		
per capita	US$	8,000	8,300		
Growth	%	-7.2	3.5		
Inflation	%	23.6	12.5		
Debt	US$	32bn	33.5bn		
Def exp	Bs	805bn	949bn		
	US$	1,329m	1,405m		

contd		1999	2000	2001	2002
Def bdgt	Bs	805bn	949bn	1,400bn	
	US$	1,329m	1,404m	1,962m	
FMA (US)	US$	1.1m	1.1m	1.6m	
US$1=Bs		605	677	713	
Population					**24,627,000**
Age		13–17	18–22		23–32
Men		1,255,000	1,200,000		2,067,000
Women		1,207,000	1,159,000		2,010,000

Total Armed Forces

ACTIVE 82,300

(incl National Guard; ε31,000 conscripts)
Terms of service 30 months selective, varies by region for
all services

RESERVES

Army ε8,000

Army 34,000

(incl 27,000 conscripts)
6 inf div HQ • 1 armd bde • 1 cav bde • 7 inf bde (18
inf, 1 mech inf, 4 fd arty bn) • 1 AB bde • 2 Ranger bde
(1 with 4 bn, 1 with 2 bn) • 1 mobile counter guerrilla
bde (2 SF, 1 mot inf, 1 Civil Affairs bn) • 1 avn regt
RESERVES ε6 inf, 1 armd, 1 arty bn
EQUIPMENT
  MBT 81 AMX-30
  LT TK 75 M-18, 36 AMX-13, 80 *Scorpion* 90
  RECCE 30 M-8
  APC 25 AMX-VCI, 100 V-100, 30 V-150, 100 *Dragoon*
    (some with **90mm** gun), 35 EE-11 *Urutu*
  TOWED ARTY 105mm: 40 Model 56, 40 M-101;
    155mm: 12 M-114
  SP ARTY 155mm: 10 Mk F3
  MRL 160mm: 20 LAR SP
  MOR 81mm: 165; **120mm**: 60 Brandt
  ATGW AS-11, 24 *Mapats*
  RL 84mm: AT-4
  RCL 84mm: *Carl Gustav*; **106mm**: 175 M-40A1
  SURV RASIT (veh, arty)
  AC 5 IAI-202, 2 Cessna 182, 2 C-206, 1 C-207, 1 M-28
    Skytruck
  ATTACK HEL 7 A-109 (ATK)
  TPT HEL 4 AS-61A, 3 Bell 205, 2 Bell 412, 4 UH-1H
  SPT 2 Bell 206, 4 AS-532

Navy 18,300

(incl 500 Naval Aviation, 7,800 Marines, 1,000 Coast
Guard and ε4,000 conscripts)
NAVAL COMMANDS Fleet, Marines, Naval Avn,
Coast Guard, Fluvial (River Forces)
NAVAL FLEET SQN SS, FF, patrol, amph, service

BASES Main bases Caracas (HQ), Puerto Cabello (SS, FF, amph and service sqn), Punto Fijo (patrol sqn)
Minor bases Puerto de Hierro (naval avn), La Orchila (naval avn), Turiamo (naval avn), El Amparo (HQ Arauca River), Ciudad Bolivar (HQ Fluvial Forces), Maracaibo (Coast Guard), La Guaira (Coast Guard)

SUBMARINES 2

SSK 2 *Sabalo* (Ge T-209/1300) with 8 × 533mm TT (SST-4 HWT)

PRINCIPAL SURFACE COMBATANTS 6

FRIGATES 6

FFG 6 *Mariscal Sucre* (It mod *Lupo*) with 8 *Teseo* SSM, *Albatros* SAM, 1 × 127mm gun, 2 × 3 ASTT (A-244S LWT), 1 AB-212 hel

PATROL AND COASTAL COMBATANTS 6

MISSILE CRAFT 3

3 *Constitución* PFM (UK Vosper 37m), with 2 *Teseo* SSM

PATROL CRAFT, OFFSHORE 3

3 *Constitución* PCO (UK Vosper 37m) with 1 × 76mm gun

AMPHIBIOUS 4

4 *Capana* LST (Sov *Alligator*), capacity 200 tps, 12 tk
Plus craft: 2 LCU (river comd), 12 LCVP

SUPPORT AND MISCELLANEOUS 5

1 log spt; 1 *Punta Brava* AGOR, 2 AGHS; 1 sail trg

NAVAL AVIATION (500)

EQUIPMENT

3 cbt ac, 9 armed hel

   AIRCRAFT

     MR 1 sqn with 3 C-212-200 MPA
     TPT 3 C-212, 2 C-212 *Aviocar*, 1 *Super King Air*, 1 *King Air*, 1 *Aerocommander* 980C, 1 DHC-7
     TRG 2 Cessna 402, 1 Cessna 210, 2 Cessna 310Q

   HELICOPTER

     ASW 1 sqn with 8 AB-212, 1 Bell 212
     SPT 4 Bell 412-EP
     TRG 1 Bell 206B

MARINES (ε7,800)

1 div HQ, 2 landing, 1 river, 1 engr bde • cbt units incl: 8 inf bn (incl 2 river) • 1 arty bn (3 fd, 1 AD bty) • 1 amph veh bn • 4 engr

   EQUIPMENT

   AAV 11 LVTP-7 (to be mod to -7A1)
   APC 25 EE-11 *Urutu*, 10 *Fuchs/Transportpanzer* 1
   TOWED ARTY 105mm: 18 Model 56
   AD GUNS 40mm: 6 M-42 twin SP

COAST GUARD (1,000)

BASE La Guaira; operates under Naval Comd and Control, but organisationally separate

   PATROL, OFFSHORE 2

   2 *Almirante Clemente* FS with 2 × 76mm guns, 3 × 2 ASTT

PATROL, INSHORE 16

4 *Petrel* (USCG *Point*-class) PCI, 12 Gairon PCI< plus 27 river patrol craft and boats
plus 1 spt ship

Air Force 7,000

(some conscripts); 125 cbt ac, 31 armed hel
Flying hours 155
FTR/FGA 6 air gp
   1 with 16 CF-5A/B (12 A, 4 B), 7 NF-5A/B
   1 with 16 *Mirage* 50EV/DV
   2 with 22 F-16A/B (18 A, 4 B)
   2 with 20 EMB-312
RECCE 15* OV-10A
ECM 3 *Falcon* 20DC
ARMED HEL 1 air gp with 10 SA-316, 12 UH-1D, 5 UH-1H, 4 AS-532
TPT ac 7 C-123, 5 C-130H, 8 G-222, 2 HS-748, 2 B-707 (tkr) **hel** 2 Bell 214, 4 Bell 412, 8 AS-332B, 2 UH-1N, 18 Mi-8/17
PRESIDENTIAL FLT 1 Boeing 737, 1 *Gulfstream* III, 1 *Gulfstream* IV, 1 *Learjet* 24D **hel** 1 Bell 412
LIAISON 9 Cessna 182, 1 *Citation* I, 1 *Citation* II, 2 *Queen Air* 65, 5 *Queen Air* 80, 5 *Super King Air* 200, 9 SA-316B *Alouette* III
TRG 1 air gp: 12* EMB-312, 20 T-34, 17* T-2D, 12 SF-260E
MISSILES
AAM R-530 *Magic*, AIM-9L *Sidewinder*, AIM-9P *Sidewinder*
ASM *Exocet*
AD GUNS 20mm: some IAI TC-20; **35mm**; **40mm**: 114: Bofors L/70 towed, Otobreda 40L70 towed
SAM 10 *Roland*, RBS-70

National Guard (*Fuerzas Armadas de Cooperación*) 23,000

(internal sy, customs)
8 regional comd
EQUIPMENT
   20 UR-416 AIFV, 24 Fiat-6614 APC, 100 **60mm** mor, 50 **81mm** mor **ac** 1 *Baron*, 1 BN-2A, 2 Cessna 185, 5 -U206, 4 IAI-201, 1 *King Air* 90, 1 *King Air* 200C, 2 *Queen Air* 80, 6 M-28 *Skytruck* **hel** 4 A-109, 20 Bell 206, 2 Bell 212
PATROL CRAFT, INSHORE 52 craft/boats

Forces Abroad

UN AND PEACEKEEPING
IRAQ/KUWAIT (UNIKOM): 3 obs

Ve

Caribbean and Latin America

MILITARY DEVELOPMENTS

Many more lives are lost in sub-Saharan Africa as a result of malnutrition and disease, in particular HIV/AIDS, than as a direct result of armed conflict. Nonetheless, the region accounted for about half of the 60,000 people killed worldwide as a direct result of armed conflict in the year to August 2001. A decline in casualties in countries such as Sierra Leone, Sudan and the Democratic Republic of Congo was counterbalanced by a surge in fighting amongst the factions in Somalia. There has been a general increase in military spending by regional governments, which has been helped, at least among the oil-producing countries, by higher oil revenues resulting mainly from increased production, rather than rising prices. South Africa has the region's most ambitious defence procurement programme. Given its cost, doubt remains whether it will be implemented fully. However, the resulting benefits to industry may be an important element in the programme being sustained for some time.

Horn of Africa

The conflict between Eritrea and Ethiopia was formally brought to an end by a peace treaty signed by both parties on 12 December 2000. It is estimated that 30,000 people were killed as a direct result of the conflict, which lasted two and a half years until a cease-fire was signed after the Cessation of Hostilities Agreement (CHA) of 14 June 2000. As a consequence, both sides announced on 24 February 2001 that they had withdrawn from an agreed 25,000 square-kilometre Temporary Security Zone (TSZ) on the border. A UN observer force, the nearly 4,000-strong UN Mission in Ethiopia and Eritrea (UNMEE), has been deployed in the TSZ, and on 21 May 2001, a UN mediator was appointed to facilitate agreement on delineating the disputed border areas. Meanwhile, a prisoner exchange has proceeded hesitantly. By 1 August 2001, 629 Ethiopian and 856 Eritrean prisoners had been exchanged, with an estimated 400 Ethiopian and 1,800 Eritrean prisoners then remaining in detention camps.

Somalia's transitional government, established in August 2000 with international backing, raised hopes for a resolution of the ongoing conflict in which at least 1,000 people have died, mostly in or near Mogadishu, in the year to August 2001. These hopes have since been dashed by escalating fighting, engendered by clan leaders opposed to the transitional government. The clan leaders have been trying to establish control over the port of Kismayo, south of Mogadishu, and its surrounding fertile agricultural resources. In March 2001, they established the Somali Reconciliation and Restoration Council (SRRC), announcing that they will form a national government in opposition to the transitional government. In the same month, the government accused Ethiopia of helping the SRRC – this statement was later retracted. On 19 June 2001, Addis Ababa announced that it would mediate between the transitional Somali government and the clan leaders. Somalia has accepted the terms of this mediation.

In April 2001, the Sudanese government announced its intention to seek a comprehensive and permanent ceasefire with the Sudanese People's Liberation Movement (SPLM), according to a plan jointly mediated by Egypt and Libya. Under this arrangement, a committee has been set up to try to organise a conference on national reconciliation. The plan also calls for constitutional reform and a transitional government. Despite peace efforts, fighting has continued, with an estimated 1,000 casualties in southern Sudan in the year to August 2001. Despite some financial backing from US sources, operations by the Sudanese Peoples Liberation Army (SPLA), the military arm of the SPLM, have had little impact on the growing economy in the northern part of the country, in particular oil production. The development of the Sudanese oil industry, involving companies from Austria, Canada, China, France, Malaysia and Sweden, has made the government of President Umar al-Bashir more sensitive to its international image. International respectability has been enhanced by the further marginalisation of the former parliament speaker and main ideologue of Sudan's militant Islamists, Hasan al-Turabi. With these factors at play, the conditions are more propitious for at least an interim agreement to end the fighting than for some years.

Central Africa

In the Congo, the assassination of President Laurent Kabila on 16 January 2001 and the succession of his son Joseph to the presidency has, up to August 2001, been followed by a marked decline in the level of conflict. In February 2001, Joseph Kabila met Rwandan President Paul Kigame and in April, he held his first meeting with the Ugandan President Yoweri Museveni. Both meetings are part of an effort to push forward the delayed implementation of the December 2000 Harare Disengagement and Redeployment Plan. Under this accord, foreign forces in the Congo are to withdraw 15km from their front line positions, eventually leading to a complete withdrawal, and a UN force was to be deployed to help oversee the accord's implementation. Some withdrawals had begun by August 2001, but forces from Angola, Namibia, Rwanda, Uganda and Zimbabwe still remained in the Congo. The 2,000-strong Namibian contingent had been scheduled for complete withdrawal by the end of August. Rwandan forces have withdrawn from their positions deep in Congolese territory, but their president has said that a complete withdrawal will not be carried out until the security threat from the *Interahamwe* Hutu militia along the Rwandan border with the Congo is halted. Under the 1999 Lusaka Cease-fire Agreement, the *Interahamwe*, most of whom were involved in the 1994 massacres of the Rwandan Tutsi population, are supposed to be disarmed and repatriated. Kigame accuses the Congolese government of dragging its feet on implementing this part of the accord. Kinshasa has indeed set up camps to which the militia and their families can report and hand in their weapons; the government claimed that by August 2001 at least 4,000 militia and their dependents had reported to the camps. However, the strength of the *Interahamwe*, excluding dependents, is thought to remain about 15,000. Although originally mandated following the 1999 Lusaka agreement, it took until March 2001 for the first contingent (apart from HQ personnel and liaison officers) of the UN Mission in the Democratic Republic of the Congo (known as MONUC from its French title) to deploy. Of the 5,537 military personnel, including up to 500 military observers, projected for the UN deployment, by 1 August just over 2,000 were in the field. In the year to August 2001 it is estimated that 10,000 people were killed as a direct result of military operations in the Congo.

Burundi saw a surge in fighting in August 2000. This was followed a month later by the failure of an attempt to negotiate a cease-fire between government forces and the main rebel groups in the country, the National Liberation Front (NLF) and the Forces for the Defence of Democracy (FDD). This failure was due primarily to an offensive launched by reinforced government forces in eastern Burundi aimed at preventing FDD forces from obtaining a secure base in Tanzania. There are also political difficulties over the Arusha Agreement (the draft cease-fire document). The NLF declared that they were not prepared to sign the agreement unless the government were prepared to discuss political issues relating to the national constitution and representation in the national legislature. In an attempt to broker a peace settlement, former President Nelson Mandela of South Africa mediated at a ministerial meeting comprising the heads of government of Burundi, Rwanda, Uganda and Kenya, together with the Tanzanian foreign minister, Dr Aron Chiduo, on the fringes of the Organisation of African Unity (OAU)'s Lusaka summit in July 2001.

Since the rebel groups were not represented, this effort is unlikely to yield early results. Meanwhile, with an estimated 2,000 people killed in the year to August 2001, the fighting continues, although at a reduced level.

In Angola, the rebel forces of the *União Nacional para a Independência Total de Angola* (UNITA) have regrouped after a severe setback in conventional military operations in 1999; by 2001 they had become an increasingly effective guerrilla force. UNITA are adopting raiding tactics and avoiding direct confrontation with government forces. This has led to the movement's presence, and attacks, in 15 of Angola's 18 provinces. As of mid-2001, one of UNITA's main objectives appears to be to strike the government heartland of Bie Province and near the capital, Luanda. An example of this tactical change was seen early on 11 August 2001 with an attack on a train 150km south-east of Luanda which left more than 100 people dead. This incident coincided with a visit to Angola by a US delegation that was trying to assess whether conditions were right for a general election tentatively scheduled for 2002. The attack was an attempt by UNITA to embarrass the government by reminding the visitors that Angola, where 5,000 people were killed in fighting in the year to August 2001, is still far from stable and also that UNITA is not a spent force. The Angolan government offered peace talks to the rebels to restore the 1994 peace agreement, possibly as a result of the escalating violence. This is likely to be unacceptable to Jonas Savimbi, UNITA's leader, who has said that he will only resume talks with Luanda if the government stops attacking UNITA positions. It is likely, therefore, that any future negotiations would have to be on the basis of a new agreement. The secondary effects of the conflict continue to take their toll on the civilian population. Hundreds of thousands of anti-personnel mines are scattered throughout the country and the continuing fighting severely hampers serious attempts at mine clearance; landmine accidents are estimated to have killed over 800 people during 2000. Meanwhile, the exodus of refugees from the conflict zones causes further disruption. Health programmes are disrupted, and damage to the national economy is increasing as it becomes harder and more expensive to control the large numbers now scattered across the area. More than 430,000 Angolan refugees are registered with international aid agencies in southern Africa, and probably many more go unregistered, with the majority seeking refuge in Zambia and the Congo.

West Africa

In Sierra Leone, an agreement signed on 11 November 2000 between the Revolutionary United Front (RUF) and the government brought the fighting virtually to an end. The cease-fire has been monitored by the United Nations Mission in Sierra Leone (UNAMSIL), first authorised by the UN Security Council in October 1999, which was increased to a mandated strength of 17,500 in March 2001. This increase was inspired by the desire to avoid the serious setbacks UN forces had suffered in 2000 when, at one point, 500 UN soldiers were held hostage by the RUF. However, by August 2001, UNAMSIL was only about 12,500 strong, due to the difficulty in finding countries willing to contribute troops. The UK retains a force of some 800 troops in Sierra Leone, along with a training mission in support of government forces. In May 2001, the government held talks with the RUF and the *Kamajor* (civil defence militia) in Freetown as a result of which the rebels agreed to start disarming. Less than a week after the agreement, over 1,000 RUF members had turned in weapons at UN disarmament centres. As a result the government agreed to release up to 20 RUF prisoners in order to maintain the momentum of the peace process. The RUF, which controls seven out of twelve districts, wants legal recognition so that it can contest forthcoming elections. These were scheduled originally for December 2001, but are likely to be delayed until 2002, since the disarmament process may not have made sufficient progress to assure a safe election at that time. Despite the relative calm in Sierra Leone, hostile activities by RUF dissidents and other armed groups have spilled into Guinea and Liberia, with Guinea claiming that up to 1,000 people have been killed near its border with Sierra Leone and Liberia. A UN report, the *Eighth report of the Secretary-General on the United Nations Mission in Sierra Leone,* dated 15 December 2000, accuses Liberia's President Charles Taylor of being actively involved in fuelling violence in the region. He is alleged to have provided weapons, training, logistical support and a safe haven for RUF rebels in return for diamonds.

In Senegal the main rebel group, the *Mouvement des Forces Democratiques de Casamance* (MFDC), and the government signed a peace accord on 16 March 2001. The agreement provides, among other things, for the release of prisoners on both sides and mine clearance. However, the cease-fire is tenuous because of the MFDC's internal divisions, with some wishing to continue the fight. Ongoing differences between rival separatist factions resulted in an upsurge of fighting between the rival groups in June 2001. This forced the postponement of planned talks between the leaders of the MFDC factions.

Southern Africa

The dominant regional power in military and economic terms, South Africa, is still not in a position to flex its military muscle beyond its borders. This is partly due to continuing thorough reform of the armed forces both in terms of structure and modernisation of equipment. South African Defence Force (SANDF) personnel are participating in the Congo as part of MONUC, and with UNMEE in Eritrea/Ethiopia. These deployments boost the force's morale by giving a greater sense of purpose, as well as bringing valuable experience through operations with the armed forces of other countries. However, a shortage of funds for training, operations and maintenance will continue to hold back the development of the force. Part of the reason for this shortage is the ambitious procurement programme, which is taking up a far higher proportion of the defence budget, 40%, than is usual, even for advanced industrial economies. However, the eight-year 'Defence Renewal' programme, if fully realised, will result in a SANDF better organised and equipped for the kind of mission, principally peacekeeping, on which it is most likely to be deployed in the future.

In Zimbabwe, domestic violence related to the seizure of white-owned farms increased in 2001, with President Robert Mugabe seeming determined to press ahead with his plans to takeover 96% of white-owned farmland for distribution, he maintains, principally to veterans of the former guerrilla forces. These events have had little impact on the armed forces whose major commitment in 2001 remained the Congo, where numbers deployed may be in excess of 11,000. It seems certain that, in the areas in which they have been deployed, the Zimbabwean armed forces have been involved in the commercial exploitation of natural resources. These interests could have the effect of delaying their withdrawal under the terms of the peace agreement for eastern Congo.

As if to demonstrate that a year cannot pass without a coup south of the Sahara, the military took control of the island of Anjouan in the Comoros Islands in August 2001. This was the nineteenth coup in the Comoros since independence 25 years ago. Anjouan had unilaterally seceded from the Islamic Republic of the Comoros in 1997. After nearly four years of instability it seemed that the signing of a framework agreement in February 2001 would lead to reconciliation between Said Abeid Abderemane, the leader of Anjouan since 1999, and the central government. This agreement was not implemented. Soldiers dissatisfied with their pay and conditions, poor because of the island's economic difficulties, decided to act to break the impasse. This action may result in a deal with the central government whereby Anjouan will enjoy a high degree of autonomy but enjoy some of the economic benefits of being part of the federation.

DEFENCE SPENDING

Military spending in sub-Saharan Africa rose 4% in real terms in 2000, from $9.0bn in 1999 to $9.4bn (in constant 2000 dollars). As ever in the region, it is difficult to account for the real total of arms spending due to the high proportion of it made by guerrilla groups. Some of the increase in government spending was made possible by regional economic growth due to higher oil prices together with the benefits of improved macroeconomic policy and structural reform, particularly in the larger economies such as Nigeria and South Africa. Sudan, meanwhile, is an example of an oil producer that has benefited greatly from improved economic circumstances and has consequently been able to boost military spending. However, many countries were held back by drought, weak commodity prices and armed conflict and, if they are not oil producers, the higher cost of oil.

Nigeria

Higher oil prices boosted economic growth in Nigeria to around 3% in 2000. Improving government revenues enabled defence spending to be increased by 6% to N52.3bn ($2.4bn) during the year from N49bn ($2.2bn) in 1999, maintaining Nigeria's position as the largest military spender in West Africa. The official Ministry of Defence budget of only N34bn ($1.5bn) does not include items such as procurement, funding for military construction, military pensions, state-level funding for military governors or funding for paramilitary forces. The Nigerian government estimates that it has spent $13bn on regional peacekeeping and conflict resolution in the West African region in the last 12 years. Although the lack of accurate data covering the period of General Sani Abacha's rule in the country makes this figure difficult to verify, it seems reasonable given the number of troops deployed and the tempo of operations.

South Africa

South Africa's economy grew by 3% in 2000 as it responded to greater external demand and growing international competitiveness. The defence budget increased from R13.7bn ($1.9bn) in 2000 to R15.8bn ($2.0bn) in 2001. This follows last year's adoption of an eight-year procurement plan for the SANDF under which equipment purchases will take-up around 40% of the budget over the next three years, in order to maintain funding for the 11-year R43bn defence acquisition programme. The programme, which projects the acquisition of four corvettes, three submarines, 30 Augusta A-109M light attack helicopters, 24 *Hawk* trainers and 28 *Gripen* fighters, has become increasingly controversial. Allegations of corruption in the procurement process and in the awarding of contracts were followed in January 2001 by the establishment of a multi-agency investigation into the issue. Meanwhile, fluctuations in the rand and loan interest charges mean that by August 2001, the cost of the whole procurement package may have risen by up to 70%, from $3.7bn to $6.35bn. In October, the South African Navy (SAN) signed a contract to take over six Type 351 *Lindau*-class mine hunters from the German navy to supplement the current fleet of four *Ton*-class minesweepers, only two of which are currently in service. The SAN expects to keep the Type 351s in service for ten years until a new class of mine-countermeasure vessel replaces them. The navy has also decided to arm the four new *Meko* A-200 corvettes currently on order from Germany with *Exocet* MM40 anti-ship missiles. The ships are due to be delivered from 2002–04. The keel-laying ceremony for the first of these corvettes took place in Hamburg, Germany on 2 August 2001. The ships are being built by the European–South African Corvette Consortium (ESACC), comprising the German Frigate Consortium (GFC), Thales Navale of France and a number of South African companies. Some 33 South African companies will benefit from the planned offset arrangements under the National Industry Participation (NIP) plan, worth a total of $450m to South African businesses. Of this total, offset requirements worth $265m had been discharged by August 2001, according to ESACC. South African industrial involvement in the ESACC contract ranges from the supply of ship-building components and steel work to the design and manufacture of high-technology systems. This demonstration of South Africa's industrial potential will bring benefits beyond this particular defence contract by increasing opportunities for the companies involved. In another major industrial project, the defence procurement agency, Armscor, will start work on upgrading South Africa's *Mirage* F-1s and *Mirage* IIIs, in a joint programme with Russian companies. The planes will receive new RD-33 turbo-jet bypass engines, which power the MiG-29 and R-73 (AA-11 *Archer*) short-range air-to-air missiles.

The industrial advantage accruing from the ESACC and Armscor–Russian deals, will be an important element in keeping the ambitious procurement programme, based on the 1998 defence review, alive. However, this procurement drive means that at present, individual services will have to struggle hard to maintain their capabilities within budgetary constraints. For example, the South African Air Force (SAAF) has to close bases and reduce its inventory to bring it into line with goals set out in the 1998 defence review. In most instances, surplus airframes will be stored as attrition reserves, but some will be sold. By 2010, the SAAF aims to be able to sustain six core capabilities: air-defence, close air-support, maritime operations, search and rescue, air transport and aerial surveillance and reconnaissance.

Sudan

From 1998 to 2000, Sudan's defence budget increased from an estimated $248m to some $425m. This increase was made possible in part by increased oil production. Sudan has become the fifth largest oil producer in sub-Saharan Africa and by 2000 was producing 200,000 barrels a day, up from 10,000 in 1998. Oil remittances to the government are estimated to be around $500m per year. This figure will increase sharply after 2002, when the investing companies will have covered their exploration costs. Sudan's indigenous defence industry has continued to develop, and reports indicate that the government can meet its small arms, light weapons and ammunition requirements domestically. A modest, but growing, mid-level technological capability exists, which produces electronics and information technology equipment. This is adding to Sudan's military capabilities and bringing revenue through regional exports.

Zimbabwe

In November 2000, Zimbabwe announced that it would be cutting its operational defence budget for 2001 by 33%, in anticipation of the end of the conflict in the Congo. Zimbabwe has committed over a third of its troops and over $200m in defence spending to the Congo since 1998. The announcement formed part of an overall budgetary plan designed to address repeated demands from the International Monetary Fund (IMF) for debt scheduling, and to attract international funds after the IMF suspended credit facilities in 1999. However, in 2000, Harare's actual defence expenditure is calculated to be around $400m, against the official budget of $235m. Early estimates suggest that defence spending in 2001, although lower in total, will be far in excess of the official budget.

Uganda

Uganda continued to spend well over budget on defence. The official budget for 2000 was Ush210bn ($132m) falling to Ush207bn ($115m) in 2001, but it is likely that the actual amount spent in 2000 was closer to Ush400bn ($251m). Whatever the true figure, Uganda continues to commit over 50% of all government expenditure to defence, compared to only 2% allocated to its Poverty Eradication Action Plan (PEAP). In addition to its two internal conflicts, the war in the Congo has cost the government approximately $60m a year.

Table 25 South African Defence Budget by Programme, 1995–2001 — Rand m, US$m

	1995		1996		1997		1998		1999		2000		2001	
	Rm	$m	Rm	$m	Rm	$m	Rm	$m	Rm	$m	Rm	$m	Rm	$m
Administration and General Support														
	745	205	1,095	255	1,104	240	1,089	197	1,456	235	2,123	297	2,234	283
Army	3,980	1,097	4,214	980	4,288	931	3,924	710	3,619	584	3,210	450	3,650	462
Air Force														
	1,753	483	2,104	489	2,083	452	1,903	344	1,944	314	1,850	259	1,950	247
Navy	778	215	781	182	802	174	833	151	842	136	884	124	945	120
Medical Support														
	739	204	873	203	887	192	910	165	939	151	973	136	1,090	138
Special Defence Account and other														
	3,525	972	1,854	431	1,942	421	1,591	288	1,829	295	4,720	661	5,931	751
Total defence budget														
	11,521	3,176	10,922	2,540	11,106	2,410	10,250	1,853	10,628	1,714	13,760	1,927	15,800	2,000
R/$ Exchange rate														
	3.6		4.3		4.6		5.5		6.2		7.1		7.9	

Table 26 Arms orders and deliveries, Sub-Saharan Africa, 1998–2001

	Country supplier ⇩	Classification	Designation	Quantity ⇩	Order date	Delivery date	Comment ⇩
Angola	RF	MBT	**T-72**		1997	1999	
	RF	FGA	**MiG-23**	18	1997	1997	Deliveries into 1998
	Kaz	MRL	**BM-21**	4	1997	1998	RF state of origin
	Bel	APC	**BMP-1**	7	1998	1999	
	Bel	MRL	**BM-21**		1998	1999	RF state of origin
	Ukr	cbt hel	**Mi-24**	6	1998	1998	For UNITA
	Ukr	FGA	**MiG-23**	6	1998	1998	For UNITA
	Slvk	MBT	**T-55**	55		2001	
Botswana	A	lt tk	**SK-105**	50	1997	1999	30 in 1999, 20 in 2000
Burundi	RSA	APC	**RG-31**	12	1997	1998	
Cameroon	Il	arty	**155mm**	8	1996	1997	4 in 1997, 4 in 1998
Côte d'Ivoire	PRC	AF	**Atchan**	1	1994	1998	Logistic support ship
Democratic Republic of Congo							
	Pl	mor	**120mm**	18	1997	1998	With 1,000 rounds of ammunition
Eritrea	Il	tpt	**IAI-1125**	1	1997	1998	
	RF	FGA	**MiG-29**	6	1998	1998	
	SF	trg	**Rodrigo**	8	1998	1999	
	It	cbt hel	**Augusta**		1998	1998	
	Bg	MRL	**BM-21**		1998	1998	
	RF	hel	**Mi-17**	4	1998	1999	
	RF	SAM	**SA-18**	200	1999	1999	
	Mol	FGA	**MiG-21**	6	1999	1999	
	Ga	FGA	**Su-25**	8	1999	1999	
	Pl	LCU	**NS-717**	3	2001	2001	

Country supplier	Classification ⇩	Designation	Quantity ⇩	Order date	Delivery date	Comment ⇩
Ethiopia US	tpt	C-130B	4	1995	1998	Ex-USAF
RF	cbt hel	Mi-24	4	1998	1998	
RF	hel	Mi-17	8	1998	1998	
Bg	MBT	T-55	140	1998	1995	50 delivered 1998. Deliveries to 1999
R	FGA	MiG-21/23	10	1998	1999	
RF	FGA	Su-27	9	1998	1998	2 delivered 2000
RF	FGA	MiG-29			2000	
RF	SPA	152mm	10	1999	1999	
Kenya Fr	LACV		4	1997	1998	Riot control armoured cars
Mali PRC	hel	Zhi-9	2		2000	
Namibia Br	PCI			1996	1999	
RSA	arty	140mm	24	1997	1998	Free transfer
dom	APC	Werewolf MK2	30	1998	2000	Anti-mine vehicle
PRC	trg	K-8	4	1999	2000	
LAR	hel	Mi-24	2	2001	2001	
LAR	hel	Mi-8	2	2001	2001	
Rwanda RSA	APC	RG-31	14	1995	1997	4 in 1997, 10 in 1998
Senegal Fr	LACV		10	1997	1998	Fr donated to MISAB
Sierra Leone Ukr	cbt hel	Mi-24	2	1996	1999	
South Africa dom	AAM	R-Darter		1988	1998	Dev prog continuing, user trials 1998
dom	FGA	Cheetah-C	38	1988	1991	Upgrade with Il assistance through 1994, continuing to 1996
dom	APC	Mamba	586	1993	1995	Prod ended 1998. Mk 2 in dev
US	tpt	C-130	5	1995	1997	5 C-130 from US, upgrades for 12 C-130s through 2002
dom	cbt hel	Rooivalk	12	1996	1999	Deliveries to 2000
dom	arty	155mm		1997	2006	Dev
Ge	FSG	Meko A-200	4	1998	2002	Deliveries through 2004
dom	arty	LIW 35 DPG		1998		Dev. Twin 35mm gun completed first trials
dom	SSK	Daphne	2	1998	1999	Upgrade 1999–2000
Ge	SSK	Type 209	3	2000	2004	Deliveries 2004–06
It	hel	A109	30	2000	2003	option on further 10
Swe	FGA	JAS-39	9	2000	2007	Option on further 19
UK	FGA	Hawk	12	2000	2005	Option on further 12
UK	cbt hel	Lynx	4	2000	2002	
Ge	MSC	Type 351	6	2000	2001	Second hand
Tanzania RSA	hel	SA-316	4	1998	1998	Free transfer
Uganda RF	FGA	MiG-21/23	28	1998	1998	
Bg	MBT	T-54	90	1998	1998	All delivered 1998
RSA	APC	Chubby		1998		Mine Clearing veh
Pl	FGA	MiG-21	7	1999	1999	
Zambia PRC	trg	K-8	8	1999	2000	Purchased in kit form
Zimbabwe Fr	ACV	ACMAT	23	1992	1999	
It	trg	SF-260F	6	1997	1999	

Dollar GDP figures in Sub-Saharan Africa are usually based on African Development Bank estimates. In several cases, the dollar GDP values do not reflect the exchange rates shown in the country entry.

Angola Ang

kwanza		1999	2000	2001	2002
GDP	US$	ε6.1bn	ε6.6bn		
per capita	US$	1,500	1,600		
Growth	%	2.7	2.1		
Inflation	%	124.9	325		
Debt	US$	12.6bn	10.8bn		
Def exp	US$	ε1,005m	ε1,100m		
Def bdgt	US$	574m	ε542m		
FMA (Fr)	US$	0.5m	0.1m		
FMA (US)	US$	3.6m	3.4m		
US$1=kwanza		696,500	7.4	18.2	
Population					13,326,000

Ovimbundu 37% **Kimbundu** 25% **Bakongo** 13%

Age	13–17	18–22	23–32
Men	689,000	583,000	888,000
Women	691,000	587,000	906,000

Total Armed Forces

ACTIVE 130,500

Army ε120,000

35 regts/dets/gps (armd and inf – str vary)

EQUIPMENT†

MBT 400 T-54/-55, ε230 T-62, ε30 T-72
RECCE some 40+ BRDM-2
AIFV ε400 BMP-1/-2
APC ε170 BTR-60/-80/-152
TOWED ARTY 400: incl **76mm**: M-1942 (ZIS-3); **85mm**: D-44; **122mm**: 24 D-30; **130mm**: 48 M-46; **152mm**: 4 D-20
SP ARTY **152mm**: 4 2S3
ASLT GUNS **100mm**: SU-100
MRL **122mm**: 50 BM-21, 40 RM-70; **240mm**: some BM-24
MOR **82mm**: 250; **120mm**: 40+ M-43
ATGW AT-3 *Sagger*
RCL 500: **82mm**: B-10; **107mm**: B-11
AD GUNS 450+: **14.5mm**: ZPU-4; **23mm**: ZU-23-2, 20 ZSU-23-4 SP; **37mm**: M-1939; **57mm**: S-60 towed, 40 ZSU-57-2 SP
SAM ε575 SA-7/-14

Navy 2,500

BASE Luanda (HQ)
PATROL AND COASTAL COMBATANTS 7
PATROL, INSHORE 7†

4 *Mandume* Type 31.6m PCI<, 3 *Patrulheiro* PCI< (all non-op)
plus 1 amph spt ship

COASTAL DEFENCE†

SS-C-1 *Sepal* at Luanda (non-op)

Air Force/Air Defence 8,000

104 cbt ac, 40 armed hel
FGA 30 MiG-23, 12 Su-22 (a further 9 Su-22M4 being delivered), 22 Su-25, 2 Su-27
FTR 20 MiG-21 MF/bis
CCT/RECCE 9* PC-7/9
MR 2 EMB-111, 1 F-27MPA, 1 *King Air* B-200B
ATTACK HEL 15 Mi-25/35, 5 SA-365M (guns), 6 SA-342 (HOT), 14 Mi-24B
TPT 2 An-2, 9 An-26, 6 BN-2, 2 C-212, 4 PC-6B, 2 L-100-20, 2 C-130, 8 An-12 and Il-76 leased from Ukr
HEL 8 AS-565, 30 IAR-316, 25 Mi-8/17
TRG 3 Cessna 172, 6 Yak-11, Emb-312
AD 5 SAM bn, 10 bty with 40 SA-2, 12 SA-3, 25 SA-6, 15 SA-8, 20 SA-9, 10 SA-13 (mostly unserviceable)
MISSILES
   ASM HOT, AT-2 *Swatter*
   AAM AA-2 *Atoll*

Forces Abroad

DROC: ε8,000 reported **CONGO**: 500 reported

Paramilitary 15,000

RAPID-REACTION POLICE 15,000

Opposition

UNIÃO NACIONAL PARA INDEPENDENCIA TOTAL DE ANGOLA (UNITA)

ε20,000 fully equipped tps plus 30,000 spt militia reported
   EQPT T-34/-85, T-55, T-62 MBT; BMP-1, BMP-2 AIFV; misc APC; **75mm, 76mm, 100mm, 122mm, 130mm, 155mm** fd guns; BM-21 **122mm** MRL; **81mm, 82mm, 120mm** mor; **85mm** RPG-7 RL; **75mm** RCL; **12.7mm** hy machine guns; **14.5mm, 20mm,** ZU-23-2 **23mm** AA guns; SAM-7 (much eqpt is unserviceable)
No cbt ac or armed hel

FRENTE DE LIBERTAÇÃO DO ENCLAVE DE CABINDA (FLEC) ε600 (claims 5,000)
Small arms only

Benin Bn

CFA fr		1999	2000	2001	2002
GDP	fr	1.5tr	1.6tr		
	US$	2.4bn	2.6bn		
per capita	US$	2,000	2,200		
Growth	%	5.0	5.0		
Inflation	%	0.3	3.5		
Debt	US$	1.4bn			
Def exp	fr	ε21bn	ε26bn		
	US$	34m	37m		
Def bdgt	fr	ε21bn	ε26bn	ε31bn	
	US$	34m	37m	41m	
FMA (Fr)	US$	4m	4m		
FMA (US)	US$	0.4m	0.4m	0.4m	
US$1=fr		616	708	748	
Population					6,222,000

Age	13–17	18–22	23–32
Men	386,000	320,000	449,000
Women	393,000	333,000	486,000

Total Armed Forces

ACTIVE ε4,750

Terms of service conscription (selective), 18 months

Army 4,500

3 inf, 1 AB/cdo, 1 engr bn, 1 armd sqn, 1 arty bty

EQUIPMENT
LT TK 20 PT-76 (op status uncertain)
RECCE 9 M-8, 14 BRDM-2, 10 VBL
TOWED ARTY 105mm: 4 M-101, 12 L-118
MOR 81mm
RL 89mm: LRAC

Navy† ε100

BASE Cotonou
PATROL AND COASTAL COMBATANTS 1
PATROL, INSHORE 1
1 *Patriote* PFI (Fr 38m)<

Air Force† 150

no cbt ac
AC 2 An-26, 2 C-47, 1 *Commander* 500B, 2 Do-128, 1
Boeing 707-320 (VIP), 1 F-28 (VIP), 1 DHC-6
HEL 2 AS-350B, 1 SE-3130

Forces Abroad

UN AND PEACEKEEPING
DROC (MONUC): 20 incl 18 obs
ETHIOPIA/ERITREA (UNMEE): 8 incl 5 obs

Paramilitary 2,500

GENDARMERIE 2,500
4 mobile coy

Botswana Btwa

pula P		1999	2000	2001	2002
GDP	P	23.3bn	25.4bn		
	US$	5.0bn	4.5bn		
per capita	US$	6,600	7,200		
Growth	%	4.0	8.9		
Inflation	%	7.1	8.6		
Debt	US$	583m	385m		
Def exp	P	ε1,200m	ε1,400m		
	US$	260m	249.6m		
Def bdgt	P	990m	1,243m	1,196m	
	US$	214m	221m	221m	
FMA (US)	US$	0.5m	0.5m	0.5m	
US$1=P		4.62	5.61	5.4	
Population					1,649,000

Age	13–17	18–22	23–32
Men	107,000	90,000	140,000
Women	110,000	93,000	143,000

Total Armed Forces

ACTIVE 9,000

Army 8,500 (to be 10,000)

1 armd bde(-), 2 inf bde: 4 inf bn, 1 armd recce, 2 AD
arty, 1 engr regt, 1 cdo unit • 1 arty bde, 1 AD bde(-)

EQUIPMENT
LT TK 36 *Scorpion* (incl variants), 50 SK-105 *Kuerassier*
RECCE 12 V-150 *Commando* (some with **90mm** gun),
RAM-V
APC 30 BTR-60, 6 *Spartan*, ε8 RAM-V-2
TOWED ARTY 105mm: 12 L-118, 6 Model 56 pack;
155mm: Soltam (reported)
MOR 81mm: 12; **120mm**: 6 M-43
ATGW 6 TOW (some SP on V-150)
RCL 84mm: 30 Carl Gustav
AD GUNS 20mm: 7 M-167
SAM 12 SA-7, 10 SA-16, 6 *Javelin*

Air Wing 500

30 cbt ac, no armed hel
FTR/FGA 10 F-5A, 3 F-5B
TPT 2 CN-235, 2 *Skyvan* 3M, 1 BAe 125-800, 3 C-130, 2
CN-212 (VIP), 1 *Gulfstream* IV, 10* BN-2 *Defender*
TRG 2 sqn with 2 Cessna 152, 7* PC-7

HEL 4 AS-350B, 5 Bell 412

Paramilitary 1,000

POLICE MOBILE UNIT 1,000
(org in territorial coy)

Burkina Faso BF

CFA fr		**1999**	**2000**	**2001**	**2002**
GDP	fr	1.6tr	1.75tr		
	US$	3.5bn	3.8bn		
per capita	US$	1,000	1,000		
Growth	%	5.3	5.7		
Inflation	%	-1.1	0.3		
Debt	US$	1.6bn			
Def exp	fr	ε46bn	ε49bn		
	US$	75m	69m		
Def bdgt	fr	ε46bn	ε49bn	ε52bn	
	US$	75m	69m	69m	
FMA (Fr)	US$	4m	3m		
FMA (US)	US$			0.1m	
US$1=fr		616	708	748	
Population					12,236,000
Age		13–17	18–22	23–32	
Men		730,000	595,000	859,000	
Women		702,000	575,000	888,000	

Total Armed Forces

ACTIVE 10,000
(incl *Gendarmerie*)

Army 5,600

6 Mil Regions • 5 inf 'regt': HQ, 3 'bn' (each 1 coy of 5
pl) • 1 AB 'regt': HQ, 1 'bn', 2 coy • 1 tk 'bn': 2 pl • 1
arty 'bn': 2 tp • 1 engr 'bn'
EQUIPMENT
    RECCE 15 AML-60/-90, 24 EE-9 *Cascavel*, 10 M-8, 4
      M-20, 30 *Ferret*
    APC 13 M-3
    TOWED ARTY 105mm: 8 M-101; **122mm**: 6
    MRL 107mm: ε4 PRC Type-63
    MOR 81mm: Brandt
    RL 89mm: LRAC, M-20
    RCL 75mm: PRC Type-52
    AD GUNS 14.5mm: 30 ZPU
    SAM SA-7

Air Force 200

5 cbt ac, no armed hel
TPT 1 *Beech Super King*, 1 *Commander* 500B, 2 HS-748, 2

N-262, 1 Boeing 727 (VIP)
LIAISON 2 Cessna 150/172, 1 SA-316B, 1 AS-350, 3
  Mi-8/17
TRG 5* SF-260W/WL

Forces Abroad

UN AND PEACEKEEPING
DROC (MONUC): 10 obs

Paramilitary

GENDARMERIE 4,200
SECURITY COMPANY (CRG) 250
PEOPLE'S MILITIA (R) 45,000 trained

Burundi Bu

franc fr		**1999**	**2000**	**2001**	**2002**
GDP	fr	460bn	576bn		
	US$	1.1bn	1.2bn		
per capita	US$	600	600		
Growth	%	-0.8	1.8		
Inflation	%	3.4	22		
Debt	US$	1.1bn	1.1bn		
Def exp	fr	ε39bn	ε45bn		
	US$	69m	67m		
Def bdgt	fr	35bn	ε42bn	ε42bn	
	US$	62m	62m	50m	
FMA (US)	US$			0.1m	
US$1=fr		564	674	833	
Population		ε**6,773,000** Hutu 85% Tutsi 14%			
Age		13–17	18–22	23–32	
Men		455,000	364,000	541,000	
Women		414,000	334,000	502,000	

Total Armed Forces

ACTIVE 45,500
(incl *Gendarmerie*)

Army ε40,000

7 inf bn • 2 lt armd 'bn' (sqn), 1 arty bn • 1 engr bn •
some indep inf coy • 1 AD bn
RESERVES
    10 bn (reported)
EQUIPMENT
    RECCE 85 incl 18 AML (6-60, 12-90), 7 Shorland, 30
      BRDM-2
    APC 9 Panhard M-3, 20 BTR-40
    TOWED ARTY 122mm: 18 D-30
    MRL 122mm: 12 BM-21

MOR ε90+ incl **82mm**: M-43; **120mm**
RL 83mm: *Blindicide*
RCL 75mm: 15 PRC Type-52
AD GUNS some 150: **14.5mm**: 15 ZPU-4; **23mm**: ZU-23; **37mm**: Type-54
SAM ε30 SA-7

AIR WING (200)

4 cbt ac, no armed hel
TRG 4* SF-260W/TP
TP 2 DC-3
HEL 3 SA-316B, 2 Mi-8

Forces Abroad

DROC ε1,000 reported

Paramilitary

GENDARMERIE ε5,500 (incl ε50 Marine Police): 16 territorial districts
BASE Bujumbura
3 *Huchan* (PRC Type 026) PHT† plus 1 LCT, 1 spt, 4 boats

GENERAL ADMINISTRATION OF STATE SECURITY
ε1,000

Opposition

FORCES POUR LA DÉFENSE DE LA DEMOCRATIE (FDD) up to 16,000 reported
FORCES FOR NATIONAL LIBERATION (FNL)
ε2–3,000

Cameroon Crn

CFA fr		1999	2000	2001	2002
GDP	fr	6.3bn	6.3bn		
	US$	10.2bn	11.0bn		
per capita	US$	2,400	2,500		
Growth	%	4.4	5.4		
Inflation	%	2.0	-0.6		
Debt	US$	7.9bn	10.9bn		
Def exp	fr	ε95bn	ε111bn		
	US$	154m	155m		
Def bdgt	fr	95bn	ε111bn	ε120bn	
	US$	154m	155m	160m	
FMA (US)	US$	0.2m	0.2m	0.2m	
FMA (Fr)	US$	9m	8m		
US$1=fr		616	708	748	
Population					15,428,000
Age		13–17	18–22	23–32	
Men		886,000	766,000	1,157,000	
Women		884,000	768,000	1,175,000	

Total Armed Forces

ACTIVE ε22,100
(incl *Gendarmerie*)

Army 11,500

8 Mil Regions each 1 inf bn under comd • Presidential Guard: 1 guard, 1 armd recce bn, 3 inf coy • 1 AB/cdo bn • 1 arty bn (5 bty) • 5 inf bn (1 trg) • 1 AA bn (6 bty) • 1 engr bn
EQUIPMENT
RECCE 8 M-8, *Ferret*, 8 V-150 *Commando* (**20mm** gun), 5 VBL
AIFV 14 V-150 *Commando* (**90mm** gun)
APC 21 V-150 *Commando*, 12 M-3 half-track
TOWED ARTY 75mm: 6 M-116 pack; **105mm**: 16 M-101; **130mm**: 12 Type-59, 12 Gun 82 (reported); **155mm**: 8 I1
MRL 122mm: 20 BM-21
MOR 81mm (some SP); **120mm**: 16 Brandt
ATGW *Milan*, TOW (reported)
RL 89mm: LRAC
RCL 57mm: 13 PRC Type-52; **106mm**: 40 M-40A2
AD GUNS 14.5mm: 18 PRC Type-58; **35mm**: 18 GDF-002; **37mm**: 18 PRC Type-63

Navy ε1,300

BASES Douala (HQ), Limbe, Kribi
PATROL AND COASTAL COMBATANTS 3
PATROL, COASTAL 2
1 *Bakassi* (Fr P-48) PCC, 1 *L'Audacieux* (Fr P-48) PCC
PATROL, INSHORE 1
1 *Quartier* PCI<
PATROL, RIVERINE craft only
6 US *Swift*-38†, 6 *Simonneau*†

Air Force 300

15 cbt ac, 4 armed hel
1 composite sqn, 1 Presidential Fleet
FGA 4† *Alpha Jet*, 5 CM-170, 6 MB-326
MR 2 Do-128D-6
ATTACK HEL 4 SA-342L (with HOT)
TPT ac 3 C-130H/-H-30, 1 DHC-4, 4 DHC-5D, 1 IAI-201, 2 PA-23, 1 *Gulfstream* III, 1 Do-128, 1 Boeing 707 **hel** 3 Bell 206, 3 SE-3130, 1 SA-318, 3 SA-319, 2 AS-332, 1 SA-365

Paramilitary

GENDARMERIE 9,000
10 regional gp; about 10 US *Swift*-38 (see Navy)

Cape Verde CV

escudo E		1999	2000	2001	2002
GDP	E	26bn	28bn		
	US$	257m	280m		
per capita	US$	2,500	2,800		
Growth	%	6.0	8.0		
Inflation	%	4.0	2.4		
Debt	US$	261m	300m		
Def exp	E	700m	925m		
	US$	7m	7.6m		
Def bdgt	E	700m	925m	1,100m	
	US$	7m	8m	9m	
FMA (US)	US$	0.1m	0.1m	0.1m	
FMA (Fr)	US$				
US$1=E		103	122	122	
Population					430,000

Age	13–17	18–22	23–32
Men	27,000	24,000	37,000
Women	28,000	25,000	41,000

Total Armed Forces

ACTIVE ε1,200

Terms of service conscription (selective)

Army 1,000

2 inf bn gp
EQUIPMENT
  RECCE 10 BRDM-2
  TOWED ARTY 75mm: 12; **76mm**: 12
  MOR 82mm: 12; **120mm**: 6 M-1943
  RL 89mm: 3.5in
  AD GUNS 14.5mm: 18 ZPU-1; **23mm**: 12 ZU-23
  SAM 50 SA-7

Coast Guard ε100

1 *Kondor* I PCC
1 *Zhuk* PCI<†, 1 *Espadarte* PCI<

Air Force under 100

no cbt ac
MR 1 Do-228

Central African Republic CAR

CFA fr		1999	2000	2001	2002
GDP	fr	696bn	715bn		
	US$	1.1bn	1.2bn		
per capita	US$	1,400	1,400		
Growth	%	3.6	3.3		
Inflation	%	2.4	3.1		
Debt	US$	835m			
Def exp	fr	ε28bn	ε31bn		
	US$	46m	44m		
Def bdgt	fr	ε28bn	ε31bn	ε33bn	
	US$	46m	44m	44m	
FMAᵃ (US)	US$	0.1m	0.1m	0.1m	
FMA (Fr)	US$	5.0m	4.0m		
US$1=fr		616	708	748	

ᵃ MISAB **1997–98** US$102m; MINURCA **1998** US$52m
1999 US$34m

Population			3,657,000
Age	13–17	18–22	23–32
Men	216,000	170,000	304,000
Women	214,000	176,000	302,000

Total Armed Forces

ACTIVE ε4,150

(incl *Gendarmerie*)
Terms of service conscription (selective), 2 years; reserve
obligation thereafter, term n.k.

Army ε3,000

1 territorial defence regt (bn) • 1 combined arms regt
(1 mech, 1 inf bn) • 1 spt/HQ regt
EQUIPMENT†
  MBT 4 T-55
  RECCE 16 *Ferret*
  APC 4 BTR-152, some 10 VAB, 25+ ACMAT
  MOR 81mm; **120mm**: 12 M-1943
  RL 89mm: LRAC
  RCL 106mm: 14 M-40
  RIVER PATROL CRAFT 9<

Air Force 150

no cbt ac, no armed hel
TPT 1 Cessna 337, 1 *Mystère Falcon* 20, 1 *Caravelle*
LIAISON 6 AL-60, 6 MH-1521
HEL 1 AS-350, 1 SE-3130

Paramilitary

GENDARMERIE ε1,000
3 regional legions, 8 'bde'

Chad Cha

CFA fr		**1999**	**2000**	**2001**	**2002**
GDP	fr	958bn	991bn		
	US$	1.66bn	1.7bn		
per capita	US$	800	800		
Growth	%	-1.1	-0.5		
Inflation	%	-6.8	3.8		
Debt	US$	1,127m			
Def exp	fr	ε29bn	ε34bn		
	US$	47m	48m		
Def bdgt	fr	ε29bn	ε34bn	ε36bn	
	US$	47m	48m	48m	
FMA (Fr)	US$	10m	8m		
FMA (US)	US$	0.8m	0.7m	0.7m	
US$1=fr		616	708	748	
Population					7,891,000
Age		13–17	18–22		23–32
Men		408,000	332,000		518,000
Women		407,000	332,000		527,000

Total Armed Forces

ACTIVE ε30,350

(incl Republican Guard)
Terms of service conscription authorised

Army ε25,000

(being re-organised)
7 Mil Regions
1 armd, 7 inf, 1 arty, 1 engr bn

EQUIPMENT
  MBT 60 T-55
  RECCE ε100 BRDM-2
  AFV 4 ERC-90, some 50 AML-60/-90, 9 V-150 with **90mm**, 20 EE-9 *Cascavel*, ε20 BTR-60
  TOWED ARTY 105mm: 5 M-2
  MOR 81mm; 120mm: AM-50
  ATGW *Milan*
  RL 89mm: LRAC
  RCL 106mm: M-40A1; **112mm**: APILAS
  AD GUNS 20mm, 30mm

Air Force 350

2 cbt ac, 2 armed hel
ARMED HEL 2 Mi-25V
TPT ac 2 C-130, 1 An-26 **hel** 2 SA-316
LIAISON 2 PC-6B, 5 Reims-Cessna FTB 337
TRG 2* PC-7

Paramilitary 4,500 active

REPUBLICAN GUARD 5,000

GENDARMERIE 4,500

Opposition

WESTERN ARMED FORCES str n.k.

Foreign Forces

FRANCE 900: 2 inf coy; 1 AML sqn(-); 1 C-160, 1 C-130, 3 F-ICT, 2 F-ICR, 3 SA-330 hel

Congo RC

CFA fr		**1999**	**2000**	**2001**	**2002**
GDP	fr	1.3tr	2.1tr		
	US$	2.7bn	2.9bn		
per capita	US$	1,800	1,900		
Growth	%	-3.0	3.8		
Inflation	%	2.4	3		
Debt	US$	8.8bn			
Def exp	fr	ε45bn	ε52bn		
	US$	73m	73m		
Def bdgt	fr	ε45bn	ε52bn	ε52bn	
	US$	73m	73m	69m	
FMA (US)	US$			0.1m	
FMA (Fr)	US$	1.0m	1.0m		
US$1=fr		616	708	748	
Population					2,997,000
Kongo 48% Sangha 20% Teke 17% M'Bochi 12%					
European mostly French 3%					
Age		13–17	18–22		23–32
Men		187,000	148,000		234,000
Women		177,000	140,000		226,000

Total Armed Forces

ACTIVE ε10,000

Army 8,000

2 armd bn • 2 inf bn gp (each with lt tk tp, 76mm gun bty) • 1 inf bn • 1 arty gp (how, MRL) • 1 engr bn • 1 AB/cdo bn

EQUIPMENT†
  MBT 25 T-54/-55, 15 PRC Type-59 (some T-34 in store)
  LT TK 10 PRC Type-62, 3 PT-76
  RECCE 25 BRDM-1/-2
  APC M-3, 50 BTR (30 -60, 20 -152), 18 Mamba
  TOWED ARTY 76mm: M-1942; **100mm**: 10 M-1944; **122mm**: 10 D-30; **130mm**: 5 M-46; **152mm**: some D-20
  SP ARTY 122mm: 3 2S1
  MRL 122mm: 10 BM-21; **140mm**: BM-14-16
  MOR 82mm; 120mm: 28 M-43

RCL 57mm: M-18
ATK GUNS 57mm: 5 M-1943
AD GUNS 14.5mm: ZPU-2/-4; **23mm**: ZSU-23-4 SP;
  37mm: 28 M-1939; **57mm**: S-60; **100mm**: KS-19

Navy† ε800

BASE Pointe Noire
PATROL AND COASTAL COMBATANTS 3†
PATROL, INSHORE 3†
  3 Sov *Zhuk* PFI< (all non-op)
PATROL, RIVERINE
  boats only

Air Force† 1,200

12 cbt ac, no armed hel
FGA 12 MiG-21
TPT 5 An-24, 1 An-26, 1 Boeing 727, 1 N-2501
TRG 4 L-39
HEL 2 SA-316, 2 SA-318, 1 SA-365, 2 Mi-8
MISSILES
AAM AA-2 *Atoll*

Paramilitary 2,000 active

GENDARMERIE 2,000
20 coy
PEOPLE'S MILITIA 3,000
being absorbed into national Army
PRESIDENTIAL GUARD
(forming)

Foreign Forces

ANGOLA: 500 reported

Côte D'Ivoire CI

CFA fr		1999	2000	2001	2002
GDP	fr	8.0tr	10.1tr		
	US$	13.1bn	14.3bn		
per capita	US$	1,900	2,000		
Growth	%	1.4	5.0		
Inflation	%	0.8	2.4		
Debt	US$	15.1bn	13.3bn		
Def exp	fr	ε80bn	ε95bn		
	US$	130m	134m		
Def bdgt	fr	ε80bn	ε95bn	ε102bn	
	US$	130m	134m	136m	
FMA (US)	US$	0.2m	0.2m	0.1m	
FMA (Fr)	US$	6.0m	5.0m		
US$1=fr		616	708	748	

Population			**14,987,000**
Age	13–17	18–22	23–32
Men	1,068,000	842,000	1,212,000
Women	1,063,000	845,000	1,208,000

Total Armed Forces

ACTIVE ε13,900
(incl Presidential Guard, *Gendarmerie*)
Terms of service conscription (selective), 6 months

RESERVES 12,000

Army 6,800

4 Mil Regions • 1 armd, 3 inf bn, 1 arty gp • 1 AB, 1 AAA, 1 engr coy
EQUIPMENT
  LT TK 5 AMX-13
  RECCE 7 ERC-90 *Sagaie*, 16 AML-60/-90, 10 *Mamba*
  APC 16 M-3, 13 VAB
  TOWED ARTY 105mm: 4 M-1950
  MOR 81mm; **120mm**: 16 AM-50
  RL 89mm: LRAC
  RCL 106mm: ε12 M-40A1
  AD GUNS 20mm: 16, incl 6 M-3 VDA SP; **40mm**: 5 L/60

Navy ε900

BASE Locodjo (Abidjan)
PATROL AND COASTAL COMBATANTS 2
PATROL, COASTAL 2
  2 *L'Ardent* (Fr *Patra*) PCC†
AMPHIBIOUS 1
  1 *L'Eléphant* (Fr *Batral*) LST, capacity 140 tps, 7 tk, hel deck, plus some 8 craft†

Air Force 700

5† cbt ac, no armed hel
FGA 1 sqn with 5† *Alpha Jet*
TPT 1 hel sqn with 1 SA-318, 1 SA-319, 1 SA-330, 4 SA 365C
PRESIDENTIAL FLT ac 1 F-28, 1 *Gulfstream* IV, 3 Fokker 100 **hel** 1 SA-330
TRG 3 Beech F-33C, 2 Reims Cessna 150H
LIAISON 1 Cessna 421, 1 *Super King Air* 200

Paramilitary

PRESIDENTIAL GUARD 1,100
GENDARMERIE 4,400
VAB APC, 4 patrol boats
MILITIA 1,500

Foreign Forces

FRANCE 680: 1 marine inf bn (18 AML 601/90); 1 AS-555 hel

Democratic Republic of Congo
DROC

congolese franc fr		1999	2000	2001	2002
GDP	US$	4.8bn	4.7bn		
per capita	US$	400	400		
Growth	%	-14	-4.9		
Inflation	%	12.0	540		
Debt	US$	16bn			
Def exp	US$	ε411m	ε400m		
Def bdgt	US$	ε400m	ε400m		
FMA (US)	US$		0.04m	0.1m	
US$1=fr[a]		4.5	9.0	4.5	

[a] Congolese franc became sole legal tender in July 1999

Population				ε**53,297,000**

Bantu and Hamitic 45%; minority groups include Hutus and Tutsis

Age	13–17	18–22	23–32
Men	3,150,000	2,510,000	3,620,000
Women	3,112,000	2,502,000	3,652,000

Total Armed Forces

ACTIVE ε81,400

Army ε79,000

10+ inf, 1 Presidential Guard bde
1 mech inf bde, 1 cdo bde (reported)

EQUIPMENT†

MBT 20 PRC Type-59 (being refurbished), some 40 PRC Type-62
RECCE some 140 AML-60/-90
APC M-113, YW-531, Panhard M-3, some *Casspir*, *Wolf* Turbo 2, *Fahd*
TOWED ARTY 100+: **75mm**: M-116 pack; **85mm**: Type-56; **122mm**: M-1938/D-30, Type-60; **130mm**: Type-59
MRL ε30: **107mm**: Type 63; **122mm**: BM-21
MOR 81mm; 107mm: M-30; **120mm**: Brandt
RCL 57mm: M-18; **75mm**: M-20; **106mm**: M-40A1
AD GUNS ε50: **14.5mm**: ZPU-4; **37mm**: M-1939/Type; **40mm**: L/60
SAM SA-7

Navy ε900

BASES Coastal Matadi **River** Kinshasa, Boma **Lake** Tanganyika (4 boats)

PATROL AND COASTAL COMBATANTS 2†
PATROL, COASTAL/INSHORE 2
2 *Swiftships* PCI<, plus about 6 armed boats (most non-op)

Air Force ε1,500

Only a handful of utility and comms ac remain serviceable. **ac** 4 Su-25, with a further 6 reported on order **hel** 6-10 Mi-24

Paramilitary

NATIONAL POLICE incl Rapid Intervention Police (National and Provincial forces)
PEOPLE'S DEFENCE FORCE

Opposition

THE RALLY FOR CONGOLESE DEMOCRACY
ε23,000; split into two factions:
a. **Congolese Rally for Democracy – Liberation Movement** (RCD–ML) ε2-3,000
b. **Congolese Rally for Democracy – Goma** (RCD–Goma) up to 20,000 reported
MOVEMENT FOR THE LIBERATION OF THE CONGO (MLC) ε18,000
(The MLC and most of the RCD–ML formed an umbrella group on 16 Jan 2001: The Front for the Liberation of Congo (FLC) ε20,000)

Foreign Forces

In support of government:
  ANGOLA: ε8,000 **NAMIBIA**: 1,400 **ZIMBABWE**: up to 8,000 reported
In support of opposition:
  ANGOLA (UNITA): ε2,000 **BURUNDI**: ε1,000 reported **RWANDA**: 15–20,000 reported **UGANDA**: some 2,000
UN (MONUC): 282 obs and 928 tps from 41 countries

Djibouti Dj

franc fr		1999	2000	2001	2002
GDP	fr	79bn	96bn		
	US$	442m	460m		
per capita	US$	900	924		
Growth	US$	3.9	2.3		
Inflation	US$	2.0	2.0		
Debt	US$	309m			
Def exp	fr	ε3.9bn	ε4.0bn		
	US$	22m	23m		
Def bdgt	fr	ε3.9bn	ε4.0bn	4.0bn	
	US$	22m	23m	23m	

contd		1999	2000	2001	2002
FMA (US)	US$	0.1m	0.4m	0.9m	
FMA (Fr)	US$	6.0m	5.0m		
US$1=fr		178	178	175	
Population		783,000	Somali 60%	Afar 35%	
Age		13–17	18–22		23–32
Men		42,000	35,000		57,000
Women		40,000	35,000		60,000

Total Armed Forces

ACTIVE ε9,600

(incl *Gendarmerie*)

Army ε8,000

3 Comd (North, Central, South) • 1 inf bn, incl mor, ATK pl • 1 arty bty • 1 armd sqn • 1 border cdo bn • 1 AB coy • 1 spt bn

EQUIPMENT
    RECCE 15 VBL, 4 AML-60†
    APC 12 BTR-60 (op status uncertain)
    TOWED ARTY 122mm: 6 D-30
    MOR 81mm: 25; **120mm**: 20 Brandt
    RL 73mm; 89mm: LRAC
    RCL 106mm: 16 M-40A1
    AD GUNS 20mm: 5 M-693 SP; **23mm**: 5 ZU-23;
      40mm: 5 L/70

Navy ε200

BASE Djibouti
PATROL AND COASTAL COMBATANTS 7
PATROL CRAFT, INSHORE 7
    5 *Sawari* PCI<, 2 *Moussa Ali* PCI<, plus boats

Air Force 200

no cbt ac or armed hel
TPT 2 C-212, 2 N-2501F, 2 Cessna U206G, 1 *Socata* 235GT
HEL 3 AS-355, 1 AS-350; Mi-8, Mi-24 hel from **Eth**

Paramilitary ε3,000 active

GENDARMERIE (Ministry of Defence) 1,200

1 bn, 1 patrol boat

NATIONAL SECURITY FORCE (Ministry of Interior) ε3,000

Foreign Forces

FRANCE 3,200: incl 2 inf coy, 2 AMX sqn, 26 ERC90 recce, 6 155mm arty, 16 AA arty, 3 amph craft: 1 sqn: **ac** 6 *Mirage* F-1C (plus 4 in store), 1 C-160 **hel** 2 SA-330, 1 AS-555

Opposition

FRONT FOR THE RESTORATION OF UNITY AND DEMOCRACY (FRUD) str n.k.

Equatorial Guinea EG

CFA fr		1999	2000	2001	2002
GDP	fr	415bn	463bn		
	US$	527m	800m		
per capita	US$	3,100	3,346		
Growth	%	10.1	48.2		
Inflation	%	3.0	6.0		
Debt	US$	215m			
Def exp	fr	ε6bn	ε9bn		
	US$	10m	12.7m		
Def bdgt	fr	ε5bn	ε8bn	ε120m	
	US$	8m	11m	16m	
FMA (Fr)	US$	1.0m	1.0m		
US$1=fr		616	708	748	
Population					535,000
Age		13–17	18–22		23–32
Men		28,000	22,000		37,000
Women		28,000	23,000		37,000

Total Armed Forces

ACTIVE 1,320

Army 1,100

3 inf bn
EQUIPMENT
    RECCE 6 BRDM-2
    APC 10 BTR-152

Navy† 120

BASES Malabo (Santa Isabel), Bata
PATROL AND COASTAL COMBATANTS 2
PATROL CRAFT, INSHORE 2 PCI<†

Air Force 100

no cbt ac or armed hel
TPT ac 1 Yak-40, 3 C-212, 1 Cessna-337 **hel** 2 SA-316

Paramilitary

GUARDIA CIVIL

2 coy
COAST GUARD
1 PCI<

Eritrea Er

nakfa		1999	2000	2001	2002
GDP	US$	ε700m	ε710m		
per capita	US$	443	441		
Growth	%	0.8	-9.0		
Inflation	%	9	14		
Debt	US$		281m		
Def exp	US$	ε309m	ε360m		
Def bdgt	US$	ε210m	ε263m		
FMA (US)	US$	0.4m	1.4m	1.4m	
US$1=nakfa		ε8.1	ε9.5	ε9.5	
Population					**ε3,905,000**

Tigrinya 50% Tigre and Kunama 40% Afar 4% Saho 3%

Age	13–17	18–22	23–32
Men	252,000	210,000	319,000
Women	249,000	209,000	318,000

Total Armed Forces

ACTIVE ε171,900

Terms of service 16 months (4 month mil trg)
RESERVES ε120,000 (reported)
Total holdings of army assets n.k.

Army ε170,000

4 Corps
18 inf (incl 1 reserve), 1 cdo div, 1 mech bde
EQUIPMENT
  MBT ε100 T-54/-55
  RECCE 30 BRDM-1/-2
  AIFV/APC 50: BMP-1, BTR-60
  TOWED ARTY 100: **85mm**: D-44; **122mm**: D-30;
    130mm: 30 M-46
  SP ARTY 25: **122mm**: 12 2S1; **152mm**: 2S5
  MRL 122mm: 30 BM-21
  MOR 100+: **120mm**; **160mm**
  RL 73mm: RPG-7
  ATGW 200: AT-3 *Sagger*, AT-*Spandrel*
  AD GUNS 70+ incl **23mm**: ZU-23, ZSU-23-4
  SAM SA-7

Navy 1,400

BASES Massawa (HQ), Assab, Dahlak
PATROL AND COASTAL COMBATANTS 8
MISSILE CRAFT 1
  1 *Osa* II PFM with 4 SS-N-2B *Styx* SSM
PATROL, INSHORE 7
  4 *Super Dvora* PFI<, 3 *Swiftships* PCI
AMPHIBIOUS 2
  2 *Chamo* LST (Ministry of Transport)
  plus 2 *Soviet* LCU†

Air Force ε800

17† cbt ac, some armed hel
Current types and numbers are assessed as follows:
FTR/FGA 3† MiG-23, 3† MiG-21, 4 MiG-29 (1-UB)
TPT 3 Y-12(II), 1 IAI-1125
TRG 6 L-90 *Redigo*, 5* MB-339CE
HEL 5 Mi-8/-17, 1 Mi-35

Opposition

ALLIANCE OF ERITREAN FORCES
str ε3,000 incl **Eritrean Liberation Front of Abdullah Idris (ELF-AI)** and **Eritrean Liberation Front – National Congress (ELF–NC)** str n.k.

AFAR RED SEA FRONT str n.k.

Foreign Forces

UN (UNMEE): 216 obs and 3,643 tps from 44 countries

Ethiopia Eth

birr EB		1999	2000	2001	2002
GDP	EB	51bn	53.4bn		
	US$	6.2bn	6.7bn		
per capita	US$	554	571		
Growth	%	-3.5	4.6		
Inflation	%	3.6	4.0		
Debt	US$	11bn			
Def exp	EB	ε3,600m	ε3,700m		
	US$	444m	457m		
Def bdgt	EB	3,500m	3,700m		
	US$	432m	457m		
FMA (US)	US$	0.5m	1.5m	1.4m	
FMA (Fr)	US$	0.5m	0.5m		
US$1=EB		8.1	8.1	8.3	
Population					**ε63,659,000**

Oromo 40% Amhara and Tigrean 32% Sidamo 9%
Shankella 6% Somali 6% Afar 4%

Age	13–17	18–22	23–32
Men	3,976,000	3,172,000	4,780,000
Women	3,867,000	3,031,000	4,607,000

Total Armed Forces

ACTIVE ε252,500

The Eth armed forces were formed following Er's declaration of independence in Apr 1993. Extensive demobilisation of former members of the Tigray People's Liberation Front (TPLF) has taken place. Eth auctioned off its naval assets in Sep 1996. Currently 17 div reported. Peacetime re-org outlined below.

Army ε250,000

Re-org to consist of 3 Mil Regions each with corps HQ (each corps 2 divs, 1 reinforced mech bde); strategic reserve div of 6 bde will be located at Addis Ababa.

   MBT 300+: T-54/-55, T-62

   RECCE/AIFV/APC ε200, incl BRDM, BMP, BTR-60/-152

   TOWED ARTY ε300: **76mm**: ZIS-3; **85mm**: D-44; **122mm**: D-30/M-30; **130mm**: M-46

   SP ARTY 122mm: 2S1; **152mm**: 10 2S19

   MRL ε50 BM-21

   MOR 81mm: M-1/M-29; **82mm**: M-1937; **120mm**: M-1944

   ATGW AT-3 *Sagger*

   RCL 82mm: B-10; **107mm**: B-11

   AD GUNS 23mm: ZU-23, ZSU-23-4 SP; **37mm**: M-1939; **57mm**: S-60

   SAM ε370: SA-2, SA-3, SA-7

Air Force ε2,500

51 cbt ac, 26 armed hel
Air Force operability improved as it played an active role in the war with Er. Types and numbers of ac are assessed as follows:
FGA 24 MiG-21MF, 17 MiG-23BN, 4 Su-25 (2 -25T, 2 -25UB), 6 Su-27
TPT 4 C-130B, 7 An-12, 2 DH-6, 1 Yak-40 (VIP), 2 Y-12
TRG 13 L-39, 10 SF-260
ATTACK HEL 26 Mi-24
TPT HEL 26 Mi-8/17

Opposition

THE UNITED LIBERATION FORCES OF OROMIA str n.k.
An alliance of six groups

OGADEN NATIONAL LIBERATION FRONT str n.k.

Foreign Forces

UN (UNMEE): 216 obs and 3,643 tps from 44 countries

Gabon Gbn				

CFA fr		1999	2000	2001	2002
GDP	fr	4.0tr	4.5tr		
	US$	6.4bn	6.4bn		
per capita	US$	5,600	5,400		
Growth	%	-9.6	-2.9		
Inflation	%	2.0	1.0		
Debt	US$	4.4bn	3.7bn		
Def exp	fr	ε83bn	ε89bn		
	US$	135m	126m		
Def bdgt	fr	ε77bn	ε89bn	ε93bn	
	US$	125m	126m	125m	

contd		1999	2000	2001	2002
FMA (Fr)	US$	7.0m	6.0m		
FMA (US)	US$	0.05m	0.1m	0.1m	
US$1=fr		616	708	748	
Population					1,556,000

Age	13–17	18–22	23–32
Men	78,000	60,000	96,000
Women	78,000	61,000	101,000

Total Armed Forces

ACTIVE ε4,700

Army 3,200

Presidential Guard bn gp (1 recce/armd, 3 inf coy, arty, AA bty), under direct presidential control
8 inf, 1 AB/cdo, 1 engr coy
EQUIPMENT
   RECCE 14 EE-9 *Cascavel*, 24 AML-60/-90, 6 ERC-90 *Sagaie*, 12 EE-3 *Jararaca*, 14 VBL
   AIFV 12 EE-11 *Urutu* with **20mm** gun
   APC 9 V-150 *Commando*, Panhard M-3, 12 VXB-170
   TOWED ARTY 105mm: 4 M-101
   MRL 140mm: 8 *Teruel*
   MORS 81mm: 35; **120mm**: 4 Brandt
   ATGW 4 *Milan*
   RL 89mm: LRAC
   RCL 106mm: M40A1
   AD GUNS 20mm: 4 ERC-20 SP; **23mm**: 24 ZU-23-2; **37mm**: 10 M-1939; **40mm**: 3 L/70

Navy ε500

BASE Port Gentil (HQ)
PATROL AND COASTAL COMBATANTS 2
PATROL, COASTAL 2 *General Ba'Oumar* (Fr P-400 55m) PCC
AMPHIBIOUS 1
   1 *President Omar Bongo* (Fr *Batral*) LST, capacity 140 tps, 7 tk; plus craft 1 LCM

Air Force 1,000

10 cbt ac, 5 armed hel
FGA 9 *Mirage* 5 (2 -G, 4 -GII, 3 -DG)
MR 1 EMB-111
TPT 1 C-130H, 3 L-100-30, 1 EMB-110, 2 YS-11A, 1 CN-235
HELICOPTERS 5 SA-342*, 3 SA-330C/-H, 3 SA-316/-319
PRESIDENTIAL GUARD
   CCT 4 CM-170, 3 T-34
   TPT ac 1 ATR-42F, 1 EMB-110, 1 *Falcon* 900 **hel** 1 AS-332

Paramilitary 2,000

GENDARMERIE 2,000

3 'bde', 11 coy, 2 armd sqn, air unit with 1 AS-355, 2 AS-350

Foreign Forces

FRANCE 750: 1 mne inf bn (4 AML 60) **ac** 2 C-160 **hel** 1 AS-555, 13 AS-532

The Gambia Gam

dalasi D		1999	2000	2001	2002
GDP	D	5.0bn	5.1bn		
	US$	446m	470m		
per capita	US$	1,200	1,200		
Growth	%	4.2	3.4		
Inflation	%	3.8	0.9		
Debt	US$	441m			
Def exp	D	ε180m	ε190m		
	US$	16m	15m		
Def bdgt	D	ε180m	ε190m	ε200m	
	US$	16m	15m	13m	
US$1=D		11.4	12.6	15.5	
Population					1,351,000
Age		13–17	18–22		23–32
Men		69,000	57,000		88,000
Women		69,000	54,000		84,000

Total Armed Forces

ACTIVE 800

Gambian National Army 800

2 inf bn • Presidential Guard coy • 1 engr sqn

MARINE UNIT (about 70)

BASE Banjul

PATROL CRAFT, INSHORE 3

3 PCI<, boats

Forces Abroad

UN AND PEACEKEEPING

ETHIOPIA/ERITREA (UNMEE): 4 obs **SIERRA LEONE** (UNAMSIL): 26 obs

Ghana Gha

cedi C		1999	2000	2001	2002
GDP	C	26.7tr	25.5tr		
	US$	10.1bn	10.7bn		
per capita	US$	2,400	2,400		
Growth	%	4.5	3.6		
Inflation	%	10.0	16.5		
Debt	US$	6.6bn			
Def exp[a]	C	ε320bn	ε450bn		
	US$	121m	96m		
Def bdgt	C	150bn	ε210bn	ε260bn	
	US$	57m	45m	34m	
FMA (US)	US$	0.4m	0.4m	0.4m	
US$1=C		2,647	4,660	7,550	

[a] Defence and security bdgt including police

Population			20,807,000	
Age	13–17	18–22	23–32	
Men	1,227,000	1,015,000	1,511,000	
Women	1,221,000	1,013,000	1,523,000	

Total Armed Forces

ACTIVE 7,000

Army 5,000

2 Comd HQ • 2 bde (6 inf bn (incl 1 UNIFIL, 1 ECOMOG), spt unit) • 1 Presidential Guard, 1 trg bn • 1 recce regt (3 sqn) • 1 arty 'regt' (1 arty, 2 mor bty) • 2 AB/ SF coy • 1 fd engr regt (bn)

EQUIPMENT

RECCE 3 EE-9 *Cascavel*

AIFV 50 MOWAG *Piranha*

TOWED ARTY 122mm: 6 D-30

MOR 81mm: 50; **120mm**: 28 Tampella

RCL 84mm: 50 *Carl Gustav*

AD GUNS 14.5mm: 4 ZPU-2, ZPU-4; **23mm**: 4 ZU-23-2

SAM SA-7

Navy 1,000

COMMANDS Western and **Eastern**

BASES HQ Western Sekondi **HQ Eastern** Tema

PATROL AND COASTAL COMBATANTS 4

PATROL, COASTAL 4

2 *Achimota* (Ge *Lürssen* 57m) PFC

2 *Dzata* (Ge *Lürssen* 45m) PCC

Air Force 1,000

19 cbt ac, no armed hel

TPT 5 Fokker (4 F-27, 1 F-28 (VIP)); 1 C-212, 6 *Skyvan*, 1 *Gulfstream*

HEL 4 AB-212 (1 VIP, 3 utl), 2 Mi-2, 4 SA-319
TRG 12* L-29, 2* L-39, 2* MB 339F, 3* MB-326K

Forces Abroad

UN AND PEACEKEEPING
CROATIA (UNMOP): 1 obs **DROC** (MONUC): 6 obs
ETHIOPIA/ERITREA (UNMEE): 18 incl 11 obs **IRAQ/
KUWAIT** (UNIKOM): 1 obs **LEBANON** (UNIFIL): 785;
1 inf bn **SIERRA LEONE** (UNAMSIL): 869 incl 4 obs
WESTERN SAHARA (MINURSO): 13 incl 6 obs

Guinea Gui

franc fr		1999	2000	2001	2002
GDP	fr	4.5tr	6.2tr		
	US$	3.6bn	3.9bn		
per capita	US$	900	992		
Growth	%	3.7	5.0		
Inflation	%	4.0	7.7		
Debt	US$	3.0bn			
Def exp	fr	ε87bn	ε95bn		
	US$	59m	58m		
Def bdg	fr	ε75bn	ε90bn	ε100bn	
	US$	57m	55m	52m	
FMA (US)	US$	0.2m	0.2m	0.2m	
FMA (Fr)	US$	5m	4m		
US$1=fr		1,458	1,645	1,918	
Population					**7,592,000**
Age		13–17	18–22	23–32	
Men		449,000	371,000	554,000	
Women		458,000	375,000	559,000	

Total Armed Forces

ACTIVE 9,700

(perhaps 7,500 conscripts)
Terms of service conscription, 2 years

Army 8,500

1 armd bn • 5 inf bn • 1 cdo bn • 1 arty bn • 1 engr bn
• 1 AD bn • 1 SF bn
EQUIPMENT†
  MBT 30 T-34, 8 T-54
  LT TK 15 PT-76
  RECCE 25 BRDM-1/-2, 2 AML-90
  APC 40 BTR (16 -40, 10 -50, 8 -60, 6 -152)
  TOWED ARTY 76mm: 8 M-1942; **85mm**: 6 D-44;
    122mm: 12 M-1931/37
  MOR 82mm: M-43; **120mm**: 20 M-1938/43
  RCL 82mm: B-10
  ATK GUNS 57mm: M-1943
  AD GUNS 30mm: twin M-53; **37mm**: 8 M-1939;

57mm: 12 S-60, PRC Type-59; **100mm**: 4 KS-19
SAM SA-7

Navy† 400

BASES Conakry, Kakanda
PATROL AND COASTAL COMBATANTS 2†
  PATROL, INSHORE 2†
  2 US *Swiftships* 77 PCI†

Air Force† 800

8 cbt ac, no armed hel
FGA 4 MiG-17F, 4 MiG-21
TPT 4 An-14, 1 An-24
TRG 2 MiG-15UTI
HEL 1 IAR-330, 1 Mi-8, 1 SA-316B, 1 SA-330, 1 SA-342K
MISSILES
  AAM AA-2 *Atoll*

Forces Abroad

UN AND PEACEKEEPING
SIERRA LEONE (UNAMSIL): 789 incl 12 obs
WESTERN SAHARA (MINURSO): 3 obs

Paramilitary 2,600 active

GENDARMERIE 1,000
REPUBLICAN GUARD 1,600
PEOPLE'S MILITIA 7,000

Opposition

MOVEMENT OF THE DEMOCRATIC FORCES OF
GUINEA str n.k.

Guinea-Bissau GuB

CFA fr		1999	2000	2001	2002
GDP	fr	186bn	190bn		
	US$	303m	340m		
per capita	US$	1,000	1,100		
Growth	%	8.9	9.3		
Inflation	%	6.0	9.1		
Debt	US$	790m			
Def exp	US$	6m	6m		
Def bdgt	US$	3m	3m	3m	
FMA (Fr)	US$				
FMA (US)	US$	–	0.4m	0.6m	
US$1=fr		616	708	748	
Population					**1,238,000**
Age		13–17	18–22	23–32	
Men		67,000	59,000	94,000	
Women		66,000	55,000	87,000	

Total Armed Forces

ACTIVE ε9,250 (all services, incl *Gendarmerie,* form part of the armed forces)

Terms of service conscription (selective)

As a result of the 1998 revolt by dissident army tps, manpower and eqpt totals should be treated with caution.

Army 6,800

1 armd 'bn' (sqn) • 5 inf, 1 arty bn • 1 recce, 1 engr coy
EQUIPMENT†
    MBT 10 T-34
    LT TK 15 PT-76
    RECCE 10 BRDM-2
    APC 35 BTR-40/-60/-152, 20 PRC Type-56
    TOWED ARTY 85mm: 8 D-44; **122mm:** 18 M-1938/D-30
    MOR 82mm: M-43; **120mm:** 8 M-1943
    RL 89mm: M-20
    RCL 75mm: PRC Type-52; **82mm:** B-10
    AD GUNS 23mm: 18 ZU-23; **37mm:** 6 M-1939; **57mm:** 10 S-60
    SAM SA-7

Navy ε350

BASE Bissau
PATROL AND COASTAL COMBATANTS 3
PATROL, INSHORE 3
    2 *Alfeite* PCI<, 1 PCI<

Air Force 100

3 cbt ac, no armed hel
FTR/FGA 3 MiG-17
HEL 1 SA-318, 2 SA-319

Paramilitary

GENDARMERIE 2,000

Kenya Kya

shilling sh		**1999**	**2000**	**2001**	**2002**
GDP	sh	737bn	776bn		
	US$	10.5bn	10.7bn		
per capita	US$	1,500	1,500		
Growth	%	1.3	-0.4		
Inflation	%	2.6	5.8		
Debt	US$	5.8bn	6.0bn		
Def exp	sh	ε23bn	ε24bn		
	US$	327m	313m		
Def bdgt	sh	ε16bn	ε18bn		
	US$	228m	235m		
FMA (US)[a]	US$	0.5m	0.4m	0.4m	
US$1=sh		70.3	76.7	78.4	

[a] Excl ACRI and East Africa Regional funding

Population		**30,545,000** Kikuyu ε22–32%		
Age	**13–17**	**18–22**	**23–32**
Men	2,073,000	1,791,000	2,588,000
Women	2,065,000	1,794,000	2,616,000

Total Armed Forces

ACTIVE 24,400
(incl HQ staff)

Army 20,000

1 armd bde (3 armd bn) • 2 inf bde (1 with 2, 1 with 3 inf bn) • 1 indep inf bn • 1 arty bde (2 bn) • 1 AD arty bn • 1 engr bde • 2 engr bn • 1 AB bn • 1 indep air cav bn
EQUIPMENT
    MBT 78 Vickers Mk 3
    RECCE 72 AML-60/-90, 12 *Ferret*, 8 Shorland
    APC 52 UR-416, 10 Panhard M-3 (in store)
    TOWED ARTY 105mm: 40 lt, 8 pack
    MOR 81mm: 50; **120mm:** 12 Brandt
    ATGW 40 *Milan*, 14 *Swingfire*
    RCL 84mm: 80 *Carl Gustav*
    AD GUNS 20mm: ε70 TCM-20, 11 Oerlikon; **40mm:** 13 L/70

Navy 1,400

BASE Mombasa
PATROL AND COASTAL COMBATANTS 4
MISSILE CRAFT 2
    2 *Nyayo* (UK Vosper 57m) PFM with 4 *Ottomat* SSM, 1 × 76mm gun
PATROL, OFFSHORE 2
    2 *Shujaa* PCO with 1 × 76mm gun
AMPHIBIOUS craft only
    2 *Galana* LCM
SUPPORT AND MISCELLANEOUS 1
    1 AT

Air Force 3,000

29 cbt ac, 34 armed hel
FGA 9 F-5E/F
TPT 7 DHC-5D, 12 Y-12 (II), 1 PA-31, 3 DHC-8, 1 Fokker 70 (VIP) (6 Do-28D-2 in store)
ATTACK HEL 11 Hughes 500MD (with TOW), 8 Hughes 500ME, 15 Hughes 500M
TPT HEL 9 IAR-330, 3 SA-330, 1 SA-342

TRG some 6 *Bulldog* 103/127, 8* *Hawk* Mk 52, 12* *Tucano*, **hel** 2 Hughes 500D

MISSILES

    ASM AGM-65 *Maverick*, TOW

    AAM AIM-9 *Sidewinder*

Forces Abroad

UN AND PEACEKEEPING

CROATIA (UNMOP): 1 obs **DROC** (MONUC): 26 incl 14 obs **ETHIOPIA/ERITREA** (UNMEE): 625 incl 10 obs **EAST TIMOR** (UNTAET): 268 **IRAQ/KUWAIT** (UNIKOM): 3 obs **SIERRA LEONE** (UNAMSIL): 1,085 incl 11 obs **WESTERN SAHARA** (MINURSO): 8 obs

Paramilitary 5,000

POLICE GENERAL SERVICE UNIT 5,000

    AIR WING ac 7 Cessna lt **hel** 3 Bell (1 206L, 2 47G)

    POLICE NAVAL SQN/CUSTOMS about 5 PCI< (2 Lake Victoria), some 12 boats

Lesotho Ls

maloti M		1999	2000	2001	2002
GDP	M	5.0bn	5.2bn		
	US$	820m	730m		
per capita	US$	2,300	2,400		
Growth	%	0.5	2.5		
Inflation	%	7.2	6.1		
Debt	US$	830m	700m		
Def exp	M	210m	ε210m		
	US$	34m	30m		
Def bdgt	M	210m	170m	ε170m	
	US$	34m	26m	21m	
FMA (US)	US$	0.1m	0.1m	0.1m	
US$1=M		6.1	7.1	7.9	
Population					2,186,000
Age		13–17	18–22		23–32
Men		132,000	115,000		172,000
Women		130,000	115,000		172,000

Total Armed Forces

ACTIVE ε2,000

Army ε2,000

7 inf coy • 1 recce coy, 1 arty bty(-), 1 spt coy (with 81mm mor) • 1 air sqn

EQUIPMENT

    RECCE 10 Il *Ramta*, 8 Shorland, 4 AML-90

    TOWED ARTY 105mm: 2

MOR 81mm: 10

RCL 106mm: 6 M-40

AC 3 C-212 *Aviocar* 300, 1 Cessna 182Q

HEL 2 Bo-105 CBS, 1 Bell 47G, 1 Bell 412 SP, 1 Bell 412EP

Liberia Lb

dollar L$		1999	2000	2001	2002
GDP	US$	ε450m	ε450m		
per capita	US$	ε600	ε600		
Growth	%	ε15.0	ε15.0		
Inflation	%	ε1.4	ε5.0		
Debt	US$	2.0bn			
Def exp	US$	ε25m	ε25m		
Def bdgt	US$	13m	15m	15m	
FMA (US)	US$			0.1m	
US$1=L$ᵃ		1.0	1.0	1.0	

ᵃ Market rate **1999** US$1=L$41

Population	ε3,309,000 Americo-Liberians 5%		
Age	13–17	18–22	23–32
Men	177,000	147,000	204,000
Women	172,000	143,000	192,000

Total Armed Forces

ACTIVE ε11–15,000 mobilised

Total includes militias supporting govt forces. No further details. Plans for a new unified armed forces to be implemented at an unspecified date provide for: **Army** 4,000 • **Navy** 1,000 • **Air Force** 300

Madagascar Mdg

franc fr		1999	2000	2001	2002
GDP	fr	23.1tr	27tr		
	US$	5.2bn	5.6bn		
per capita	US$	700	700		
Growth	%	4.5	4.8		
Inflation	%	9.9	11.9		
Debt	US$	2.9bn			
Def exp	fr	ε273bn	ε295bn		
	US$	43m	42m		
Def bdgt	fr	ε273bn	ε295bn	ε310bn	
	US$	43m	42m	46m	
FMA (US)	US$	0.1m	0.1m	0.1m	
FMA (Fr)	US$	5m	5m		
US$1=fr		6,300	7,000	6,662	
Population					16,433,000
Age		13–17	18–22		23–32
Men		928,000	770,000		1,151,000
Women		905,000	751,000		1,140,000

Total Armed Forces

ACTIVE some 13,500

Terms of service conscription (incl for civil purposes), 18 months

Army some 12,500

2 bn gp • 1 engr regt
EQUIPMENT
  LT TK 12 PT-76
  RECCE 8 M-8, ε20 M-3A1, 10 *Ferret*, ε35 BRDM-2
  APC ε30 M-3A1 half-track
  TOWED ARTY 76mm: 12 ZIS-3; **105mm:** 5 M-101;
    122mm: 12 D-30
  MOR 82mm: M-37; **120mm:** 8 M-43
  RL 89mm: LRAC
  RCL 106mm: M-40A1
  AD GUNS 14.5mm: 50 ZPU-4; **37mm:** 20 Type-55

Navy† 500

(incl some 100 Marines)
BASES Diégo-Suarez, Tamatave, Fort Dauphin, Tuléar, Majunga
AMPHIBIOUS craft only
  1 LCT (Fr *Edic*)
SUPPORT AND MISCELLANEOUS 1
  1 tpt/trg

Air Force 500

12 cbt ac, no armed hel
FGA 1 sqn with 4 MiG-17F, 8 MiG-21FL
TPT 4 An-26, 1 BN-2, 2 C-212, 2 Yak-40 (VIP)
HEL 1 sqn with 6 Mi-8
LIAISON 1 Cessna 310, 2 Cessna 337, 1 PA-23
TRG 4 Cessna 172

Paramilitary 8,100

GENDARMERIE 8,100
incl maritime police with some 5 PCI<

Malawi Mlw					
kwacha K		1999	2000	2001	2002
GDP	K	64bn	73bn		
	US$	1.5bn	ε1.5bn		
per capita	US$	900	900		
Growth	%	4.2	2.5		
Inflation	%	44.9	30.0		
Debt	US$	2.6bn	2.8bn		

contd		1999	2000	2001	2002
Def exp	K	ε1,170m	ε1,300m		
	US$	27m	26m		
Def bdgt	K	ε1,170m	ε1,300m	ε1,500m	
	US$	27m	26m	19m	
FMA (US)	US$	0.3m	0.3m	0.4m	
US$1=K		44.1	48.7	77.6	
Population				11,164,000	
Age		13–17	18–22	23–32	
Men		679,000	538,000	801,000	
Women		673,000	530,000	828,000	

Total Armed Forces

ACTIVE 5,300 (all services form part of the Army)

Army 5,300

2 inf bde each with 3 inf bn • 1 indep para bn • 1 general spt bn (incl arty, engr) • 1 mne coy (+)
EQUIPMENT (less than 20% serviceability)
  RECCE 20 *Fox*, 8 *Ferret*, 12 *Eland*
  TOWED ARTY 105mm: 9 lt
  MOR 81mm: 8 L16
  AD GUNS 14.5mm: 40 ZPU-4
  SAM 15 *Blowpipe*

MARITIME WING (220)
BASE Monkey Bay (Lake Nyasa)
  PATROL, INSHORE 2
  1 *Kasungu* PCI<†, 1 *Namacurra* PCI<, some boats
AMPHIBIOUS craft only
  1 LCU

AIR WING (80)
no cbt ac, no armed hel
  TPT AC 1 sqn with 2 Basler T-67, 2 Do-228, 1 HS-125-800 (VIP)
  TPT HEL 1 SA-330F, 1 AS-350L, 1 *Super Puma* (VIP)

Forces Abroad

UN AND PEACEKEEPING
DROC (MONUC): 17 obs

Paramilitary 1,500

MOBILE POLICE FORCE (MPF) 1,500
8 Shorland armd car **ac** 3 BN-2T *Defender* (border patrol), 1 *Skyvan* 3M, 4 Cessna **hel** 2 AS-365

Ls Lb Mdg Mlw

Sub-Saharan Africa

Mali RMM

CFA fr		1999	2000	2001	2002
GDP	fr	1.7tr	1.8tr		
	US$	2.9bn	3.1bn		
per capita	US$	600	697		
Growth	%	6.4	4.8		
Inflation	%	-0.8	-0.7		
Debt	US$	3.2bn			
Def exp	fr	ε21bn	ε21bn		
	US$	34m	30m		
Def bdgt	fr	21bn	21bn	21bn	
	US$	34m	30m	28m	
FMA (US)	US$	0.3m	0.3m	0.3m	
FMA (Fr)	US$	5m	4m	4m	
US$1=fr		616	708	748	
Population			**11,514,000**	Tuareg 6–10%	
Age		13–17	18–22	23–32	
Men		663,000	534,000	792,000	
Women		688,000	557,000	835,000	

Total Armed Forces

ACTIVE about 7,350 (all services form part of the Army)
Terms of service conscription (incl for civil purposes), 2 years (selective)

Army about 7,350

2 tk • 4 inf • 1 AB, 2 arty, 1 engr, 1 SF bn • 2 AD, 1 SAM bty

EQUIPMENT†
MBT 21 T-34, 12 T-54/-55
LT TK 18 Type-62
RECCE 20 BRDM-2
APC 30 BTR-40, 10 BTR-60, 10 BTR-152
TOWED ARTY **85mm:** 6 D-44; **100mm:** 6 M-1944; **122mm:** 8 D-30; **130mm:** M-46 reported
MRL **122mm:** 2 BM-21
MOR **82mm:** M-43; **120mm:** 30 M-43
AD GUNS **37mm:** 6 M-1939; **57mm:** 6 S-60
SAM 12 SA-3

NAVY† (about 50)
BASES Bamako, Mopti, Segou, Timbuktu
PATROL, RIVERINE 3 PCR<

AIR FORCE (400)
16† cbt ac, no armed hel
FGA 5 MiG-17F
FTR 11 MiG-21
TPT 2 An-24, 1 An-26
HEL 1 Mi-8, 1 AS-350, 2 Z-9
TRG 6 L-29, 1 MiG-15UTI, 4 Yak-11, 2 Yak-18

Forces Abroad

UN AND PEACEKEEPING
DROC (MONUC): 1 obs SIERRA LEONE (UNAMSIL): 8 obs

Paramilitary 4,800 active

GENDARMERIE 1,800
8 coy
REPUBLICAN GUARD 2,000
NATIONAL POLICE 1,000
MILITIA 3,000

Mauritius Ms

rupee R		1999	2000	2001	2002
GDP	R	106bn	106bn		
	US$	4.6bn	5.1bn		
per capita	US$	17,200	19,000		
Growth	%	5.9	3.6		
Inflation	%	6.9	4.2		
Debt	US$	1.2bn	1.2bn		
Def exp	R	ε2.3bn	ε2.3bn		
	US$	91m	89m		
Def bdgt	R	218m	235m	256m	
	US$	8m	9m	9m	
FMA (US)	US$	0.1m	0.1m	0.1m	
US$1=R		25.2	25.9	28.5	
Population				**1,163,000**	
Age		13–17	18–22	23–32	
Men		51,000	55,000	100,000	
Women		50,000	54,000	100,000	

Total Armed Forces

ACTIVE Nil

Paramilitary 1,600

SPECIAL MOBILE FORCE ε1,100
6 rifle, 2 mob, 1 engr coy, spt tp
RECCE BRDM-2, *Ferret*
APC 11 VAB (2 with 20mm), 7 *Tactica*
MOR **81mm:** 2
RL **89mm:** 4 LRAC

COAST GUARD ε500
PATROL CRAFT 4
PATROL, OFFSHORE 1
1 *Vigilant* (Ca *Guardian* design) PCO, capability for 1 hel
PATROL, COASTAL 1
1 SDB-3 PCC

PATROL, INSHORE 2

2 Sov *Zhuk* PCI< (in refit), plus 26 boats

MR 1 Do-228-101, 1 BN-2T *Defender*, 3 SA-316B

POLICE AIR WING

2 *Alouette* III

Mozambique Moz

metical M		1999	2000	2001	2002
GDP	M	29tr	30.2tr		
	US$	2.3bn	2.4bn		
per capita	US$	1,400	1,500		
Growth	%	9.7	3.8		
Inflation	%	1.5	11.4		
Debt	US$	7.3bn	9bn		
Def exp	M	ε1,200bn	ε1,400bn		
	US$	94m	87m		
Def bdgt	M	ε1,200bn	ε1,400bn	ε1,600bn	
	US$	94m	87m	82m	
FMA (US)	US$	2.1m	2.7m	2.2m	
US$1=M		12,775	16,100	19,500	
Population					20,069,000
Age		13–17	18–22		23–32
Men		1,184,000	993,000		1,484,000
Women		1,193,000	1,008,000		1,521,000

Total Armed Forces

ACTIVE ε10,600–11,600

Terms of service conscription, 2–3 years

Army ε9–10,000

5 inf, 3 SF, 1 log bn • 1 engr coy

EQUIPMENT† (ε10% or less serviceability)

MBT some 80 T-54/-55 (300+ T-34, T-54/-55 non-op)

RECCE 30 BRDM-1/-2

AIFV 40 BMP-1

APC 150+ BTR-60, 80 BTR-152, 5 *Casspir*

TOWED ARTY 136+: **76mm**: 40 M-1942; **85mm**: 12 D-44, 6 D-48, 12 Type-56; **100mm**: 24 M-1944; **105mm**: 12 M-101; **122mm**: 12 D-30; **130mm**: 6 M-46; **152mm**: 12 D-1

MRL 122mm: 12 BM-21

MOR 82mm: M-43; **120mm**: 12 M-43

RCL 75mm; 82mm: B-10; **107mm**: B-11

AD GUNS 20mm: M-55; **23mm**: ZU-23-2; **37mm**: M-1939; **57mm**: S-60 towed, ZSU-57-2 SP

SAM SA-7

Navy† 600 (ε400 naval inf)

BASES Monkey Bay, Lake Malawi

PATROL AND COASTAL COMBATANTS 3†

PATROL, INSHORE 3 PCI< (non-op)

plus 2 LCU

Air Force 1,000

(incl AD units); no cbt ac, 4† armed hel

TPT 1 sqn with 5 An-26, 2 C-212, 4 PA-32 *Cherokee* (non-op)

TRG 1 Cessna 182, 7 ZLIN-326

HEL 4† Mi-24*, 5 Mi-8 (all non-op, with exception of 2 Mi-8)

AD SAM †SA-2, 10 SA-3 (all non-op)

Forces Abroad

UN AND PEACEKEEPING

DROC (MONUC): 2 obs **EAST TIMOR** (UNTAET): 12 incl 2 obs

Namibia Nba

dollar N$		1999	2000	2001	2002
GDP	N$	18bn	24bn		
	US$	2.7bn	2.9bn		
per capita	US$	5,200	5,537		
Growth	%	2.9	3.9		
Inflation	%	8.5	9.2		
Debt	US$	85m	161m		
Def exp	N$	732m	ε750m		
	US$	120m	105m		
Def bdgt	N$	559m	617m	ε700m	
	US$	92m	96m	87m	
FMA (US)	US$	1.2m	0.5m	0.3m	
US$1=N$		6.1	7.1	7.96	
Population					1,741,000
Age		13–17	18–22		23–32
Men		115,000	95,000		144,000
Women		114,000	94,000		143,000

Total Armed Forces

ACTIVE 9,000

Army 9,000

6 inf bn • 1 cbt spt bde with 1 arty, 1 AD, 1 ATK regt

EQUIPMENT

MBT some T-34, T-54/-55 (serviceability doubtful)

RECCE 12 BRDM-2

APC 20 *Casspir*, 30 *Wolf*, 10 BTR-60

TOWED ARTY 140mm: 24 G2

MRL 122mm: 5 BM-21

MOR 81mm; 82mm
RCL 82mm: B-10
ATK GUNS 57mm; 76mm: 12 M-1942 (ZIS-3)
AD GUNS 14.5mm: 50 ZPU-4; **23mm:** 15 *Zumlac*
  (ZU-23-2) SP
SAM ε50 SA-7

AIR WING

FGA 2 MiG-23
TPT 1 *Falcon* 900, 1 Learjet 36, 2 Y-12
SURVEILLANCE 5 Cessna 337/02-A
HEL 2 SA-319 *Chetak*, some Mi-8, Mi-24 reportedly
  delivered
TRG 4 K-8

Coast Guard ε200

(fishery protection, part of the Ministry of Fisheries)
BASE Walvis Bay
PATROL, OFFSHORE/COASTAL 2
  1 *Osprey* PCO, 1 *Oryx* PCC
AIRCRAFT
  1 F406 *Caravan* ac, 1 hel

Forces Abroad

DROC: 1,400 (to withdraw by 31/08/01)
UN AND PEACEKEEPING
ETHIOPIA/ERITREA (UNMEE): 5 incl 3 obs

Paramilitary

SPECIAL FIELD FORCE 6,000

Niger Ngr

CFA fr		1999	2000	2001	2002
GDP	fr	1,022bn	1,326bn		
	US$	1.7bn	1.8bn		
per capita	US$	826	844		
Growth	%	2.0	3.5		
Inflation	%	-0.6	2.9		
Debt	US$	1.6bn			
Def exp	fr	ε17bn	ε19bn		
	US$	28m	27m		
Def bdgt	fr	ε17bn	ε19bn	ε22bn	
	US$	28m	27m	29m	
FMA (US)	US$			0.1m	
FMA (Fr)	US$	7m	2m		
US$1=fr		616	708	748	
Population			11,068,000 Tuareg 8–10%		
Age		13–17	18–22	23–32	
Men		618,000	498,000	716,000	
Women		621,000	506,000	745,000	

Total Armed Forces

ACTIVE 5,300
Terms of service selective conscription (2 years)

Army 5,200

3 Mil Districts • 4 armd recce sqn • 7 inf, 2 AB, 1 engr coy
EQUIPMENT
  RECCE 90 AML-90, 35 AML-60/20, 7 VBL
  APC 22 M-3
  MOR 81mm: 19 Brandt; **82mm:** 17; **120mm:** 4 Brandt
  RL 89mm: 36 LRAC
  RCL 75mm: 6 M-20; **106mm:** 8 M-40
  ATK GUNS 85mm; 90mm
  AD GUNS 20mm: 39 incl 10 M-3 VDA SP

Air Force 100

no cbt ac or armed hel
TPT 1 C-130H, 1 Do-28, 1 Do-228, 1 Boeing 737-200
  (VIP), 1 An-26
LIAISON 2 Cessna 337D

Forces Abroad

UN AND PEACEKEEPING
DROC (MONUC): 13 incl 12 obs

Paramilitary 5,400

GENDARMERIE 1,400
REPUBLICAN GUARD 2,500
NATIONAL POLICE 1,500

Nigeria Nga

naira N		1999	2000	2001	2002
GDP	N	ε4.6tr	ε4.7tr		
	US$	ε50bn	ε53bn		
per capita	US$	1,300	1,359		
Growth	%	1.8	3.2		
Inflation	%	9.5	5.9		
Debt	US$	33bn	29bn		
Def exp	US$	ε2.2bn	ε2.4bn		
Def bdgt	N	26bn	34bn		
	US$	340m	340m		
FMA (US)	US$	0.1m	0.6m	0.7m	
US$1=N		92.3	102.4	113.9	

Population			ε113,007,000

North Hausa and Fulani South-west Yoruba South-east Ibo; these tribes make up ε65% of population

Age	13–17	18–22	23–32
Men	7,652,000	6,693,000	10,056,000
Women	7,631,000	6,735,000	10,450,000

Total Armed Forces

ACTIVE 78,500

RESERVES

planned, none org

Army 62,000

1 armd div (2 armd bde) • 1 composite div (1 mot inf, 1 amph bde, 1 AB bn) • 2 mech div (each 1 mech, 1 mot inf bde) • 1 Presidential Guard bde (2 bn) • 1 AD bde • each div 1 arty, 1 engr bde, 1 recce bn

EQUIPMENT
MBT 50 T-55†, 150 Vickers Mk 3
LT TK 100 *Scorpion*
RECCE ε120 AML-60, 60 AML-90, 55 *Fox*, 75 EE-9 *Cascavel*, 72 VBL (reported)
APC 10 *Saracen*, 250 Steyr 4K-7FA, 70 MOWAG *Piranha*, EE-11 *Urutu* (reported), *Saladin* Mk2
TOWED ARTY 105mm: 200 M-56; **122mm**: 200 D-30/ -74; **130mm**: 7 M-46; **155mm**: 24 FH-77B (in store)
SP ARTY 155mm: 27 *Palmaria*
MRL 122mm: 25 APR-21
MOR 81mm: 200; **82mm**: 100; **120mm**: 30+
ATGW *Swingfire*
RCL 84mm: *Carl Gustav*; **106mm**: M-40A1
AD GUNS 20mm: some 60; **23mm**: ZU-23, 30 ZSU-23-4 SP; **40mm**: L/60
SAM 48 *Blowpipe*, 16 *Roland*, ε100 SA-7
SURV RASIT (veh, arty)

Navy 7,000

(incl Coast Guard)
BASES Lagos **HQ Western Comd** Apapa **HQ Eastern Comd** Calabar
PRINCIPAL SURFACE COMBATANTS 1
FRIGATES 1†
FFG 1 *Aradu* (Ge MEKO 360)† with 8 *Otomat* SSM, *Albatros* SAM, 1 × 127mm gun, 2 × 3 ASTT, 1 *Lynx* hel
PATROL AND COASTAL COMBATANTS 8
CORVETTES 2† *Erinomi* (UK Vosper Mk 9) FS with 1 × 3 *Seacat* SAM, 1 × 76mm gun, 1 × 2 ASW mor
MISSILE CRAFT 3
3† *Ayam* (Fr *Combattante*) PFM with 2 × 2 MM-38 *Exocet* SSM, 1 × 76mm gun

PATROL, COASTAL 3
3 *Ekpe* (Ge *Lurssen* 57m) PCC with 1 × 76mm gun
MINE WARFARE 2
MINE COUNTERMEASURES 2†
2 *Ohue* (mod It *Lerici*) MCC (both non-op)
AMPHIBIOUS 1
1 *Ambe* (Ge) LST, capacity 220 tps, 5 tk
SUPPORT AND MISCELLANEOUS 5
3 AT, 1 nav trg, 1 AGHS

NAVAL AVIATION
EQUIPMENT
HELICOPTERS
MR/SAR 2† *Lynx* Mk 89

Air Force 9,500

86† cbt ac, 10† armed hel (only 50% serviceability)
FGA/FTR 3 sqn
1 with 19 *Alpha Jet* (FGA/trg)
1 with 5† MiG-21MF, 1† MiG-21U, 12† MiG-21B/FR
1 with 15† *Jaguar* (12 -SN, 3 -BN)
ARMED HEL 10† Bo-105D (being phased out), 6 Mi-35
TPT 2 sqn with 5 C-130H, 3 -H-30, 17 Do-128-6, 16 Do-228-200 (incl 2 VIP), 5 G-222 **hel** 4 AS-332, 2 SA-330, 3 Mi-34
PRESIDENTIAL FLT ac 1 Boeing 727, 2 *Gulfstream*, 2 *Falcon* 900, 1 BAe 125-1000
TRG ac† 22* L-39MS, 12* MB-339AN, 59 *Air Beetle* **hel** 13 Hughes 300
AAM AA-2 *Atoll*

Forces Abroad

UN AND PEACEKEEPING
CROATIA (UNMOP): 1 obs **DROC**(MONUC): 22 incl 21 obs **ERITREA/ETHIOPIA** (UNMEE): 10 incl 6 obs **IRAQ/KUWAIT** (UNIKOM): 5 obs **SIERRA LEONE** (UNAMSIL): 3,265 incl 4 obs **WESTERN SAHARA** (MINURSO): 5 obs

Paramilitary ε82,000

COAST GUARD
incl in Navy
PORT SECURITY POLICE ε2,000
about 60 boats and some 5 hovercraft
SECURITY AND CIVIL DEFENCE CORPS (Ministry of Internal Affairs)
POLICE 80,000: UR-416, 70 AT-105 *Saxon*† APC **ac** 1 Cessna 500, 3 Piper (2 *Navajo*, 1 *Chieftain*) **hel** 4 Bell (2 -212, 2 -222)

Rwanda Rwa

franc fr		1999	2000	2001	2002
GDP	fr	727bn	789bn		
	US$	2.2bn	2.4bn		
per capita	US$	500	627		
Growth	%	5.0	5.8		
Inflation	%	-2.4	3.9		
Debt	US$	1.2bn	1.3bn		
Def exp	fr	ε45bn	ε45bn		
	US$	135m	125m		
Def bdgt	fr	ε45bn	ε45bn	ε45bn	
	US$	135m	125m	104m	
FMA (US)	US$	1.1m	0.5m	0.5m	
US$1=fr		333	359	433	
Population		ε**8,823,000** **Hutu** 80% **Tutsi** 19%			
Age		*13–17*	*18–22*	*23–32*	
Men		581,000	469,000	671,000	
Women		597,000	486,000	703,000	

Total Armed Forces

ACTIVE ε56–71,000 (all services, incl *Gendarmerie*; up to 90,000 reported)

Army ε49–64,000

6 inf bde, 1 mech inf regt

EQUIPMENT
> **MBT** 12 T-54/-55
> **RECCE** ε90 AML-60/-90/-245, 16 VBL
> **AIFV** some BMP
> **APC** ε50: some BTR, Panhard, 16 RG-31 *Nyala*
> **TOWED ARTY** 35: **105mm**†; **122mm**: 6 D-30; **152mm**
> **MRL 122mm**: 5 RM-70
> **MOR** 250: **81mm**; **82mm**; **120mm**
> **AD GUNS** ε150: **14.5mm**; **23mm**; **37mm**
> **SAM** SA-7

Air Force ε1,000

At least 5 cbt ac, no armed hel
> **FGA** At least 5 MiG-21
> **TPT** Some An-2, 2–3 An-8, 1 B-707, 1 Bn-2A Islander
> **HEL** 8-12 Mi-17MD, 3 Mi-24
> **TRG** Some L-39

Forces Abroad

DROC: 15–20,000 reported

Paramilitary ε9,000

GENDARMERIE 6,000

COMMUNAL POLICE ε1,000

LOCAL DEFENCE FORCES ε2,000

Opposition

ε15,000 Hutu rebels in DROC (incl former govt tps, *Interahamwe* and other recruits) of which ε5,000 have been integrated into DROC armed forces

Senegal Sen

CFA fr		1999	2000	2001	2002
GDP	fr	3.2tr	3.3tr		
	US$	5.2bn	5.6bn		
per capita	US$	2,000	2,118		
Growth	%	5.1	5.5		
Inflation	%	0.9	0.7		
Debt	US$	3.2bn	3.4bn		
Def exp	fr	ε50bn	ε49bn		
	US$	81m	69m		
Def bdgt	fr	43bn	ε44bn	ε46bn	
	US$	70m	62m	61m	
FMA (US)	US$	0.8m	0.7m	0.8m	
FMA (Fr)	US$	7m	6m		
US$1=fr		616	708	748	
Population				**9,683,000**	
Wolof 36% **Fulani** 17% **Serer** 17% **Toucouleur** 9% **Mandingo** 9% **Diola** 9%, of which 30–60% in Casamance)					
Age		*13–17*	*18–22*	*23–32*	
Men		617,000	500,000	729,000	
Women		611,000	494,000	734,000	

Total Armed Forces

ACTIVE 9,400–10,000
Terms of service conscription, 2 years selective

RESERVES n.k.

Army 8,000 (3,500 conscripts)

7 Mil Zone HQ • 1 armd bn • 1 engr bn • 6 inf bn • 1 Presidential Guard (horsed) • 1 arty bn • 3 construction coy • 1 cdo bn • 1 AB bn • 1 engr bn

EQUIPMENT
> **RECCE** 10 M-8, 4 M-20, 30 AML-60, 27 AML-90
> **APC** some 16 Panhard M-3, 12 M-3 half-track
> **TOWED ARTY 75mm**: 6 M-116 pack; **105mm**: 6 M-101/HM-2; **155mm**: ε6 Fr Model-50
> **MOR 81mm**: 8 Brandt; **120mm**: 8 Brandt
> **ATGW** 4 *Milan*
> **RL 89mm**: 31 LRAC
> **AD GUNS 20mm**: 21 M-693; **40mm**: 12 L/60

Navy 600

BASES Dakar, Casamance
PATROL AND COASTAL COMBATANTS 10
PATROL, COASTAL 5
    1 *Fouta* (Dk *Osprey*) PCC
    1 *Njambuur* (Fr SFCN 59m) PCC
    3 *Saint Louis* (Fr 48m) PCC
PATROL, INSHORE 5
    3 *Senegal* II PFI<, 2 *Alioune Samb* PCI<
AMPHIBIOUS craft only
    2 *Edic* 700 LCT

Air Force 800

8 cbt ac, no armed hel
MR/SAR 1 EMB-111
TPT 1 sqn with 6 F-27-400M, 1 Boeing 727-200 (VIP), 1 DHC-6 *Twin Otter*
HEL 2 SA-318C, 2 SA-330, 1 SA-341H
TRG 4* CM-170, 4* R-235 *Guerrier*, 2 *Rallye* 160, 2 R-235A

Forces Abroad

UN AND PEACEKEEPING
DROC (MONUC): 555 **IRAQ/KUWAIT** (UNIKOM): 5 obs

Paramilitary ε5,800

GENDARMERIE ε5,800
12 VXB-170 APC
CUSTOMS
2 PCI<, boats

Opposition

MOUVEMENT DES FORCES DÉMOCRATIQUES DE CASAMANCE **(MFDC)** 2–3,000 eqpt with lt wpns

Foreign Forces

FRANCE 1,170: 1 mne inf bn (14 AML 60/90); **ac** 1 *Atlantic*, 1 C-160 **hel** 1 SA-319

Seychelles Sey

rupee SR		1999	2000	2001	2002
GDP	SR	3.3bn	3.3bn		
	US$	618m	570m		
per capita	US$	4,400	4,500		
Growth	%	1.4	1.4		
Inflation	%	2.7	6.7		
Debt	US$	163m	165m		

contd		1999	2000	2001	2002
Def exp	SR	61m	60m		
	US$	11m	10m		
Def bdgt	SR	56m	62m	62m	
	US$	11m	11m	11m	
FMA (US)	US$	0.1m	0.1m	0.1m	
US$1=SR		5.34	5.75	5.82	
Population					**78,000**
Age		13–17	18–22	23–32	
Men		4,000	4,000	6,000	
Women		4,000	4,000	6,000	

Total Armed Forces

ACTIVE 450 (all services, incl Coast Guard, form part of the Army)

Army 200

1 inf coy
1 sy unit
EQUIPMENT†
    RECCE 6 BRDM-2
    MOR 82mm: 6 M-43
    RL RPG-7
    AD GUNS 14.5mm: ZPU-2/-4; **37mm**: M-1939
    SAM 10 SA-7

Paramilitary 250 active

NATIONAL GUARD 250

COAST GUARD (200)
(incl 20 Air Wing and ε80 Marines)
BASE Port Victoria
PATROL, COASTAL/INSHORE 5
1 *Andromache* (It *Pichiotti* 42m) PCC, 1 *Zhuk* PCI<, 3 PCI<
plus 1 *Cinq Juin* LCT (govt owned but civilian op)

AIR WING (20)
No cbt ac, no armed hel
MR 1 BN-2 *Defender*
TPT 1 Reims-Cessna F-406/*Caravan* 11
TRG 1 Cessna 152

Sierra Leone SL

leone L		1999	2000	2001	2002
GDP	L	1,227bn	1,425bn		
	US$	724m	770m		
per capita	US$	676	712		
Growth	%	-8.1	3.8		
Inflation	%	34	10		
Debt	US$	1.2bn	1.3bn		
Def exp	US$	ε11m	ε9m		
Def bdgt	US$	11m	9m	10m	
FMA (US)	US$		0.1m	0.1m	
FMA (UK)	US$	7.3m			
US$1=L		1,804	2,232	1,894	
Population					ε4,883,000
Age		13–17	18–22		23–32
Men		297,000	247,000		383,000
Women		298,000	245,000		387,000

Total Armed Forces

ACTIVE ε6,000+

The Lome Peace Agreement between the govt and RUF rebels broke down in May 2000. A ceasefire agreement was signed on 10 Nov 2000, however, sporadic fighting continues with govt forces supported by UNAMSIL. An estimated 2,000 RUF rebels have been de-mobilised. A new, UK-trained, national army is forming and will have an initial strength of 8,000

EQUIPMENT (in store)

  MOR 81mm: ε27; **82mm**: 2; **120mm**: 2
  RCL 84mm: *Carl Gustav*
  AD GUNS 12.7mm: 4; **14.5mm**: 3
  SAM SA-7
  HEL 3 Mi-24 (only 2 operational), 3† Mi-8/17 (contract flown and maintained)

Navy† ε200

BASE Freetown

PATROL AND COASTAL COMBATANTS 3†

  1 PRC *Shanghai* II PFI<, 1 *Swiftship* 32m† PFI<, 1 *Fairy Marine Tracker* II (all non-op)<

Foreign Forces

UK 660: incl short term trg team **RUSSIA** 110: 4 Mi-24
UN (UNAMSIL): 274 obs and 11,841 tps from 31 countries

Opposition

REVOLUTIONARY UNITED FRONT (RUF) ε8,000

Somali Republic SR

shilling sh		1999	2000	2001	2002
GDP	US$	ε874m	ε900m		
per capita	US$	1,100	1,100		
Growth	%				
Inflation	%	ε16			
Debt	US$	3.2bn			
Def exp	US$	ε40m	ε40m		
Def bdgt	US$	ε13m	ε15m	ε15m	
FMA (US)	US$	1.1m	1.3m	1.6m	
US$1=sh		2,620	2,620	2,620	
Population			ε10,317,000 Somali 85%		
Age		13–17	18–22		23–32
Men		626,000	511,000		726,000
Women		625,000	508,000		727,000

Total Armed Forces

ACTIVE Nil

Following the 1991 revolution, no national armed forces have yet been formed. The Somali National Movement has declared northern Somalia the independent 'Republic of Somaliland', while insurgent groups compete for local supremacy in the south. Hy mil eqpt is in poor repair or inoperable.

Clan/Movement Groupings

'SOMALILAND' (northern Somalia) Total armed forces reported to be some 12,900

UNITED SOMALI FRONT str n.k. **clan** Issa **leader** Abdurahman Dualeh Ali

SOMALI DEMOCRATIC ALLIANCE str n.k. **clan** Gadabursi

SOMALI NATIONAL MOVEMENT 5–6,000 **clan** Issaq, 3 factions (Tur, Dhegaweyne, Kahin)

UNITED SOMALI PARTY str n.k. **clan** Midigan/ Tumaal **leader** Ahmed Guure Adan

SOMALIA

SOMALI SALVATION DEMOCRATIC FRONT 3,000 **clan** Darod **leader** Abdullah Yusuf Ahmed

UNITED SOMALI CONGRESS str n.k. **clan** Hawiye **sub-clan** Habr Gidir **leaders** Hussein Mohammed Aideed/Osman Atto

ALI MAHDI FACTION 10,000(-) **clan** Abgal **leader** Mohammed Ali Mahdi

SOMALI NATIONAL FRONT 2–3,000 **clan** Darod **sub-clan** Marehan **leader** General Omar Hagi Mohammed Hersi

SOMALI DEMOCRATIC MOVEMENT str n.k. **clan** Rahenwein/Dighil

SOMALI PATRIOTIC MOVEMENT 2–3,000 **clan** Darod **leader** Ahmed Omar Jess

'PUNTLAND' (northeastern Somalia)
MARITIME SECURITY FORCE (70 civilians, based at Bosaso under Puntland govt control)
1 PCO for fisheries protection

South Africa RSA

rand R		1999	2000	2001	2002
GDP	R	780bn	874bn		
	US$	128bn	122bn		
per capita	US$	6,000	6,281		
Growt	%	1.2	3.1		
Inflation	%	5.1	0		
Debt	US$	41bn	38bn		
Def exp	R	10.7bn	13.9bn		
	US$	1.8bn	1.9bn		
Def bdgt	R	10.7bn	13.8bn	15.8bn	
	US$	1.8bn	1.9bn	2.0bn	
FMA (US)	US$	1.0m	0.8m	0.8m	
US$1=R		6.1	7.14	7.9	
Population					40,792,000

Age	13–17	18–22	23–32
Men	2,570,000	2,327,000	3,855,000
Women	2,537,000	2,309,000	3,870,000

Total Armed Forces

ACTIVE 61,500

(incl 5,500 South African Military Health Service; 8,640 women; excluding 17,141 civilians)
Terms of service voluntary service in 4 categories (full career, up to 10 yrs, up to 6 yrs, 1 yr voluntary military service)
Racial breakdown 38,159 black, 16,153 white, 6,327 coloured, 855 Asian

RESERVES 89,189

Army 86,700 **Navy** 1,330 **Air Force** 434 **Military Health Service** (SAMHS) 725

Army 41,750

(incl women)
PERMANENT FORCE

8 'type' formations
Formations under direct comd and control of SANDF Chief of Joint Operations:
  5 regional joint task forces (each consists of HQ, tps are provided when necessary by permanent and reserve force units from all services)
  1 SF bde (2 bn)
  2 bde HQ
1 tk, 1 armd car bn
18 inf bn (incl 2 mech, 3 mot, 12 lt inf, 1 AB)

2 arty (incl 1 AD), 3 engr bn, 6 engr sqn
RESERVE FORCE

cadre units comprising 8 armd, 26 inf (incl 1 AB), 7 arty, 5 AD, 4 engr bn
some 183 'cdo' (bn) home defence units

EQUIPMENT

MBT some 168 *Olifant* 1A/-B (125 in store)
RECCE 242 *Rooikat-76* (94 in store)
AIFV 1,200 *Ratel* Mk III-20/-60/-90 (666 in store)
APC 429 *Casspir*, 538 *Mamba*
TOWED ARTY 140mm: 75 G-2 (in store); **155mm**: 72 G-5 (51 in store)
SP ARTY 155mm: 43 G-6 (31 in store)
MRL 127mm: 25 *Bataleur* (40 tube) (4 in store), 26 *Valkiri* (24 tube) (in store)
MOR 81mm: 1,190 (incl some SP); **120mm**: 36
ATGW 52 ZT-3 *Swift* (36 in store)
RL 92mm: FT-5
RCL 106mm: 100 M-40A1 (some SP)
AD GUNS 23mm: 36 *Zumlac* (ZU-23-2) SP; **35mm**: 40 GDF
SURV *Green Archer* (mor), *Cymbeline* (mor)
UAV some *Vulture*

Navy 5,000

(incl 560 women)
FLOTILLAS SS, strike, MCM
BASES Simon's Town (HQ), Durban (Salisbury Island)
SUBMARINES 2

SSK 2 *Spear* (Mod Fr *Daphné*) with 550mm TT
PATROL AND COASTAL COMBATANTS 11

MISSILE CRAFT 8 *Warrior* (Il *Reshef*) PFM with 6 *Skerpioen* (Il *Gabriel*) SSM (incl 2 in refit)
PATROL, INSHORE 3 T craft PCI<
MINE WARFARE 8

MINE COUNTERMEASURES 8

4 *Kimberley* (UK *Ton*) MSC (incl 2 in reserve)
4 *River* (Ge *Navors*) MHC (incl 2 in refit)
SUPPORT AND MISCELLANEOUS 36

1 *Drakensberg* AO with 2 hel and extempore amph capability (perhaps 60 tps and 2 small LCU)
1 *Outeniqua* AO with similar capability to *Drakensberg*
1 diving spt
3 AT
28 harbour patrol PCI<
1 AGHS (UK *Hecla*)
1 Antarctic tpt with 2 hel (operated by private co for Ministry of Environment)
plus craft: 8 LCU

Air Force 9,250

(incl 1,350 women); 86 cbt ac, ε7 attack and several extempore armed hel

Air Force office, Pretoria, and 5 type formations
FTR/FGA 2 sqn
  1 sqn with 28 *Cheetah* C, 10 *Cheetah* D
  1 sqn with 27 *Impala* Mk2, 21 *Impala* Mk1
TPT/TKR/EW 1 sqn with 5 Boeing 707-320 (EW/tkr)
TPT 5 sqn
  1 with 3 *King Air* 200, 1 *King Air* 300, 13 Cessna-208 *Caravan*, 1 PC-12
  1 (VIP) with 2 *Citation* II, 2 *Falcon* 50, 1 *Falcon* 900, 1 Boeing Business Jet
  1 with 11 C-47 TP (5 maritime, 4 tpt, 1 PR, 1 EW trg)
  1 with 12 C-130
  1 with 4 CASA-212, 1 CASA-235, 11 Cessna 185
HEL 1 cbt spt with 7* *Rooivalk*. 4 tpt, 1 flying school with 44 *Oryx*, 10 BK-117, 30 SA-316/319
TRG 1 flying school with 53 PC-7
UAV 3 *Seeker* with 1 control station
MISSILES
  ASM *Raptor*, ZT-3, *Mokopa* ZT-6, *Mupsow*
  AAM V-3C, V4
  SAM *Cactus* (*Crotale*), SAHV3 limited operational
GROUND DEFENCE
RADAR 2 Air Control Sectors (Hoedspruit and Bushveld), 3 fixed and 6 mob radars (2 long-range – Ellisras and Mariepskop – and 4 tactical)
SAAF Regt: 12 security sqn

South African Military Health Service (SAMHS) 5,500

(incl ε2,700 women); a separate service within the SANDF; 3 Type, 1 spt, 1 trg formation

Forces Abroad

UN AND PEACEKEEPING
DROC (MONUC): 107 incl 12 obs **ETHIOPIA/ ERITREA** (UNMEE): 7 incl 5 obs

Sudan Sdn

pound S£		1999	2000	2001	2002
GDP	US$	ε8.7bn	ε9.5bn		
per capita	US$	1,570	1,709		
Growth	%	5.5	7.2		
Inflation	%	14.0	8.0		
Debt	US$	18bn	16.4bn		
Def exp	US$	ε424m	ε580m		
Def bdgt	US$	ε424m	ε425m	581m	
US$1=S£		2,526	2,588	2,588	
Population				ε29,632,000	

Muslim 70% mainly in North Christian 10% mainly in South African 52% mainly in South Arab 39% mainly in North

Age	13–17	18–22	23–32
Men	1,990,000	1,693,000	2,542,000
Women	1,904,000	1,620,000	2,441,000

Total Armed Forces

ACTIVE ε117,000
(incl ε20,000 conscripts)
Terms of service conscription (males 18–30), 3 years

Army ε112,500

(incl ε20,000 conscripts)
1 armd div • 1 mech inf div • 6 inf div • 1 AB div • 1 engr div • 1 border gd bde • 8 indep inf bde (incl 1 mech) • 5 SF coy
EQUIPMENT
  MBT 200 T-54/-55
  LT TK 100 PRC Type-62
  RECCE 6 AML-90, 30 *Saladin*, 80 *Ferret*, 60 BRDM-1/ -2, 42 HMMWV
  AIFV 30 BMP-1/-2
  APC 90 BTR-50/-152, 42 OT-62/-64, 42 M-113, 19 V-100/-150, 120 *Walid*
  TOWED ARTY 450 incl: **85mm**: D-44; **105mm**: M-101; **122mm**: D-74, M-30, Type-54/D-30; **130mm**: M-46/PRC Type 59-1
  SP ARTY 155mm: ε10 M-114A1, F-3
  MRL 600: **107mm**: Type-63; **122mm**: BM-21, Type-81
  MOR 81mm; **82mm**; **120mm**: M-43, AM-49
  ATGW 4 *Swingfire*
  RL 73mm: RPG-7
  RCL 106mm: 40 M-40A1
  ATK GUNS 40 incl: **76mm**: M-1942; **100mm**: M-1944
  AD GUNS 1,000+ incl: **14.5mm**: ZPU-2/-4; **23mm**: ZU-23-2; **37mm**: M-1939/Type-63, Type-55; **57mm**: S-60, Type-59; **85mm**: M-1944
  SAM 54 SA-7
  SURV RASIT (veh, arty)

Navy ε1,500

BASES Port Sudan (HQ), Flamingo Bay (Red Sea), Khartoum (Nile)
PATROL AND COASTAL COMBATANTS 6
  PATROL, INSHORE 2 *Kadir* PCI<
  PATROL, RIVERINE 4 PCR<, about 12 armed boats
AMPHIBIOUS craft only
  some 2 *Sobat* (FRY DTK-221) LCT (used for trans-porting stores)

Air Force 3,000

(incl Air Defence); 35† cbt ac, 10 armed hel
FGA 9 F-5 (7 -E, 2 -F), 7 PRC J-6 (MiG-19) (GA/adv

trg), 12 F-7 (MiG-21), 4 MiG-23
BBR 3 An-24 modified as bombers
TPT 4 C-130H (of which 2 grounded), 4 DHC-5D, 2 F-27, 2 *Falcon* 20/50
HEL 8 AB-212, 8 IAR/SA-330, 11 (1 op) Mi-8, 10* Mi-24V
TRG 12 PT-6A
AD 5 bty SA-2 SAM (18 launchers)

Paramilitary 7,000

POPULAR DEFENCE FORCE 7,000 active

85,000 reserve; mil wg of National Islamic Front; org in bn of 1,000 (to be disbanded – loyalty in doubt)

Opposition

NATIONAL DEMOCRATIC ALLIANCE

coalition of many gp, of which the main forces are:

SUDANESE PEOPLE'S LIBERATION ARMY (SPLA) 20–30,000

four factions, each org in bn, operating mainly in southern Sdn; some captured T-54/-55 tks, BM-21 MRL and arty pieces, but mainly small arms plus **60mm** and **120mm** mor, **14.5mm** AA, SA-7 SAM

SUDAN ALLIANCE FORCES ε500

based in Er, operate in border area

BEJA CONGRESS FORCES ε500

operates on Er border (composed mainly of ε250–300 'White Lion Fighters')

NEW SUDAN BRIGADE ε2,000

operates on Er border only

Tanzania Tz

shilling sh		1999	2000	2001	2002
GDP	sh	6.3tr	6.4tr		
	US$	8.5bn	8.0bn		
per capita	US$	700	737		
Growth	%	3.9	5.2		
Inflation	%	8.2	5.9		
Debt	US$	7.8bn	6.9bn		
Def exp	sh	ε105bn	ε115bn		
	US$	141m	144m		
Def bdgt	sh	102bn	115bn	ε125bn	
	US$	137m	144m	140m	
FMA (US)a	US$	0.2m	0.2m	0.2m	
US$1=sh		745	799	890	

a Excl ACRI and East Africa Regional funding

Population				34,527,000
Age	13–17	18–22	23–32	
Men	1,989,000	1,600,000	2,380,000	
Women	2,034,000	1,696,000	2,520,000	

Total Armed Forces

ACTIVE ε27,000
Terms of service incl civil duties, 2 years

RESERVES 80,000

Army ε23,000

5 inf bde • 1 tk bde • 6 arty bn • 2 AD arty bn • 2 mor bn • 2 ATK bn • 1 engr regt (bn)
EQUIPMENT†
　MBT 15 PRC Type-59, 30 T-54/-55
　LT TK 25 PRC Type-62, 30 *Scorpion*
　RECCE 20 BRDM-2
　APC ε35 BTR-40/-152, ε25 PRC Type-56
　TOWED ARTY 76mm: ε60 ZIS-3; **85mm**: 75 PRC Type-56; **122mm**: 20 D-30, 80 PRC Type-54-1; **130mm**: 30 PRC Type-59-1
　MRL 122mm: 58 BM-21
　MOR 82mm: 100 M-43; **120mm**: 50 M-43
　RCL 75mm: PRC Type-52

Navy† ε1,000

BASES Dar es Salaam, Zanzibar, Mwanza (Lake Victoria)
PATROL AND COASTAL COMBATANTS 6
TORPEDO CRAFT 2 PRC *Huchuan* PHT< with 2 533mm TT
PATROL, COASTAL 4
　2 PRC *Shanghai* II PFC
　2 *Vosper Thornycroft* PCC
AMPHIBIOUS craft only
　2 *Yunnan* LCU

Air Defence Command 3,000

(incl ε2,000 AD tps); 19 cbt act†, no armed hel
Virtually no air defence assets serviceable
FTR 3 sqn with 3 PRC J-5 (MiG-17), 10 J-6 (MiG-19), 6 J-7 (MiG-21)
TPT 1 sqn with 3 DHC-5D, 1 PRC Y-5, 2 Y-12(II), 3 HS-748, 2 F-28, 1 HS-125-700
HEL 4 AB-205
LIAISON ac 5 Cessna 310, 2 Cessna 404, 1 Cessna 206 **hel** 6 Bell 206B
TRG 2 MiG-15UTI, 5 PA-28
AD GUNS 14.5mm: 40† ZPU-2/-4; **23mm**: 40 ZU-23; **37mm**: 120 PRC Type-55
SAM† 20 SA-3, 20 SA-6, 120 SA-7

Forces Abroad

UN AND PEACEKEEPING
DROC (MONUC): 5 obs **ETHIOPIA/ERITREA**

(UNMEE): 11 incl 8 obs **SIERRA LEONE** (UNAMSIL): 11 obs

Paramilitary 1,400 active

POLICE FIELD FORCE 1,400

18 sub-units incl Police Marine Unit
    MARINE UNIT (100)
      boats only
    AIR WING
      ac 1 Cessna U-206 **hel** 2 AB-206A, 2 Bell 206L, 2 Bell 47G

Togo Tg

CFA fr		1999	2000	2001	2002
GDP	fr	929bn	903bn		
	US$	1.5bn	1.6bn		
per capita	US$	1,426	1,481		
Growth	%	3.5	-0.5		
Inflation	%	-1.6	2.5		
Debt	US$	1.3bn			
Def exp	fr	ε21bn	ε22bn		
	US$	34m	31m		
Def bdgt	fr	ε21bn	ε22bn	ε23bn	
	US$	35m	31m	30m	
FMA (Fr)	US$	4m	4m		
FMA (US)	US$			0.1m	
US$1=fr		616	708	748	
Population					4,701,000
Age		13–17	18–22	23–32	
Men		316,000	239,000	347,000	
Women		314,000	249,000	374,000	

Total Armed Forces

ACTIVE some 9,450

Terms of service conscription, 2 years (selective)

Army some 9,000

2 inf regt
    1 with 1 mech bn, 1 mot bn
    1 with 2 armd sqn, 3 inf coy; spt units (trg)
1 Presidential Guard regt: 2 bn (1 cdo), 2 coy
1 para cdo regt: 3 coy
1 spt regt: 1 fd arty, 2 AD arty bty; 1 log/tpt/engr bn
EQUIPMENT
    MBT 2 T-54/-55
    LT TK 9 *Scorpion*
    RECCE 6 M-8, 3 M-20, 10 AML (3 -60, 7 -90), 36 EE-9 *Cascavel*, 2 VBL
    AIFV 20 BMP-2
    APC 4 M-3A1 half-track, 30 UR-416

TOWED ARTY 105mm: 4 HM-2
SP ARTY 122mm: 6
MOR 82mm: 20 M-43
RCL 57mm: 5 ZIS-2; **75mm**: 12 PRC Type-52/-56; **82mm**: 10 PRC Type-65
AD GUNS 14.5mm: 38 ZPU-4; **37mm**: 5 M-39

Navy ε200

(incl Marine Infantry unit)
BASE Lomé
PATROL AND COASTAL COMBATANTS 2
PATROL, COASTAL 2
    2 *Kara* (Fr *Esterel*) PFC

Air Force †250

16 cbt ac, no armed hel
FGA 5 *Alpha Jet*, 4 EMB-326G
TPT 2 *Baron*, 2 DHC-5D, 1 Do-27, 1 F-28-1000 (VIP), 1 Boeing 707 (VIP), 2 Reims-Cessna 337
HEL 1 AS-332, 2 SA-315, 1 SA-319, 1 SA-330
TRG 4* CM-170, 3* TB-30

Paramilitary 750

GENDARMERIE (Ministry of Interior) 750
1 trg school, 2 reg sections, 1 mob sqn

Uganda Uga

shilling Ush		1999	2000	2001	2002
GDP	Ush	9.0tr	9.5tr		
	US$	8.0bn	8.5bn		
per capita	US$	1,900	2,000		
Growth	%	7.0	3.5		
Inflation	%	3.4	4.2		
Debt	US$	3.8bn			
Def exp	Ush	290bn	400bn		
	US$	199m	251m		
Def bdgt	Ush	200bn	210bn	207bn	
	US$	138m	132m	115m	
FMA (US)a	US$	0.4m	0.4m	0.4m	
US$1=Ush		1,455	1,588	1,787	

a Excl ACRI and East Africa Regional funding

Population				22,302,000	
Age		13–17	18–22	23–32	
Men		1,244,000	1,110,000	1,587,000	
Women		1,274,000	1,083,000	1,698,000	

Total Armed Forces

ACTIVE ε50–60,000

Ugandan People's Defence Force

ε50–60,000

4 div (2 with 3, 2 with 4 bde)

EQUIPMENT†

MBT ε140 T-54/-55

LT TK ε20 PT-76

RECCE 40 *Eland*, 60 *Ferret* (reported)

APC 20 BTR-60, 4 OT-64 SKOT, 20 *Mamba*, 20 *Buffel*

TOWED ARTY 225 incl: **76mm**: M-1942; **122mm**: M-1938; **130mm**; **155mm**: 4 G5

MRL 122mm: BM-21

MOR 81mm: L 16; **82mm**: M-43; **120mm**: 60 Soltam

AD GUNS 14.5mm: ZPU-1/-2/-4; **37mm**: 20 M-1939

SAM 200 SA-7

AVN 10 cbt ac†, 2 armed hel

FGA some 6 MiG-19, 4 MiG-21. Total of 7 MiG-21 (5 - MF, 2 -UTI) reportedly on order

TRG 3†* L-39, 1 SF*-260 (non-op)

ARMED HEL 2 Mi-24

TPT HEL 3 Bell 206, 2 Bell 412, 4 Mi-17, 1 Mi-172 (VIP) (only 3 Mi-17, 1 Mi-24 op)

Forces Abroad

DROC: some 2,000

Paramilitary ε1,800 active

BORDER DEFENCE UNIT ε600

small arms

POLICE AIR WING ε800

hel 1 *JetRanger*

MARINES ε400

8 riverine patrol craft<, plus boats

LOCAL DEFENCE UNITS ε15,000

Opposition

LORD'S RESISTANCE ARMY ε1,500

(ε200 in Uga, remainder in Sdn)

ALLIED DEMOCRATIC FRONT ε500

Zambia Z

kwacha K		1999	2000	2001	2002
GDP	K	7.4tr	9.52tr		
	US$	3.5bn	3.7bn		
per capita	US$	900	1,000		
Growth	%	1.3	3.5		
Inflation	%	20.6	25.5		
Debt	US$	6.2bn	6.3bn		
Def exp	K	ε210bn	ε200bn		
	US$	88m	66m		
Def bdgt	K	186bn	ε196bn	ε211bn	
	US$	79m	65m	64m	
FMA (US)	US$	0.2m	0.5m	0.6m	
US$1=K		2,388	3,018	3,250	
Population					9,188,000
Age		13–17	18–22		23–32
Men		652,000	530,000		775,000
Women		641,000	520,000		795,000

Total Armed Forces

ACTIVE 21,600

Army 20,000

(incl 3,000 reserves)

3 bde HQ • 1 arty regt • 9 inf bn (3 reserve) • 1 engr regt • 1 armd regt (incl 1 armd recce bn)

EQUIPMENT†

MBT 10 T-55, 20 PRC Type-59

LT TK 30 PT-76

RECCE 90 BRDM-1/-2 (ε12 serviceable)

APC 13 BTR-60

TOWED ARTY 76mm: 35 M-1942; **105mm**: 18 Model 56 pack; **122mm**: 25 D-30; **130mm**: 18 M-46

MRL 122mm: 50 BM-21

MOR 81mm: 55; **82mm**: 24; **120mm**: 12

ATGW AT-3 *Sagger*

RCL 57mm: 12 M-18; **75mm**: M-20; **84mm**: *Carl Gustav*

AD GUNS 20mm: 50 M-55 triple; **37mm**: 40 M-1939; **57mm**: 55 S-60; **85mm**: 16 KS-12

SAM SA-7

Air Force 1,600

71† cbt ac, some armed hel. Very low serviceability.

FGA 1 sqn with 12 F-6 (MiG-19)†, 1 sqn with 12 MiG-21 MF† (8 undergoing refurbishment)

TPT 1 sqn with 4 An-26, 4 C-47, 4 DHC-5D, 4 Y-12(II)

VIP 1 fleet with 1 HS-748, 2 Yak-40

LIAISON 5 Do-28

TRG 2*F-5T, 2* MiG-21U†, 12* *Galeb* G-2, 15* MB-326GB, 8* SF-260MZ, 8 K-8

HEL 1 sqn with 4 AB-205A, 5 AB-212, 12 Mi-8

Tg Uga Z

Sub-Saharan Africa

LIAISON HEL 12 AB-47G
MISSILES
  ASM AT-3 *Sagger*
  SAM 1 bn; 3 bty: SA-3 *Goa*

Forces Abroad

UN AND PEACEKEEPING
DROC (MONUC): 5 obs **ETHIOPIA/ERITREA**
(UNMEE): 14 incl 10 obs **SIERRA LEONE**
(UNAMSIL): 840 incl 11 obs

Paramilitary 1,400

POLICE MOBILE UNIT (PMU) 700
1 bn of 4 coy
POLICE PARAMILITARY UNIT (PPMU) 700
1 bn of 3 coy

Zimbabwe Zw

dollar Z$		1999	2000	2001	2002
GDP	Z$	210bn	ε200bn		
	US$	6.8bn	6.6bn		
per capita	US$	2,300	2,300		
Growth	%	1.2	-5.0		
Inflation	%	58.5	60		
Debt	US$	5.4bn	4.8bn		
Def exp	Z$	ε16bn	ε15bn		
	US$	418m	401m		
Def bdgt	Z$	6.4bn	9.0bn	7.8bn	
	US$	168m	235m	142m	
FMA (US)	US$	1.0m	1.5m	1.3m	
US$1=Z$		38.3	38.2	55	
Population					11,781,000
Age		13–17	18–22		23–32
Men		837,000	675,000		1,023,000
Women		826,000	670,000		1,019,000

Total Armed Forces

ACTIVE ε39,000

Army ε35,000

5 bde HQ • 1 arty bde, 1 Presidential Guard gp • 1
armd sqn • 20 inf bn (incl 2 guard, 1 mech, 1 cdo, 1 para)
• 1 fd arty regt • 1 AD regt • 1 engr regt
EQUIPMENT
  MBT 30 PRC Type-59, 10 PRC Type-69
  RECCE 80 EE-9 *Cascavel* (**90mm** gun)
  APC 30 PRC Type-63 (YW-531), UR-416, 40 *Crocodile*,
    260 ACMAT
  TOWED ARTY 122mm: 18 PRC Type-60, 12 PRC
    Type-54
  MRL 107mm: 18 PRC Type-63; **122mm**: 52 RM-70
  MOR 81mm/82mm 502; **120mm**: 14 M-43
  AD GUNS 215 incl **14.5mm**: ZPU-1/-2/-4; **23mm**:
    ZU-23; **37mm**: M-1939
  SAM 17 SA-7

Air Force 4,000

52 cbt ac, 32 armed hel
Flying hours 100
FGA 2 sqn
  1 with 11 *Hunters* (9 FGA-90, 1 -F80, 1 T-81) (in store)
  1 with 5 *Hawk* Mk 60/60A (0 serviceable)
FTR 1 sqn with 9 PRC F-7 (MiG-21) (6 serviceable)
RECCE 1 sqn with 14* Reims-Cessna 337 *Lynx*
TRG/RECCE/LIAISON 1 sqn with 22 SF-260 *Genet* (9 -
  C, 6* -F, 5* -W, 2* TP)
TPT 1 sqn with 6 BN-2, 8 C-212-200 (1 VIP), some An-
  12
HEL 1 sqn with 24 SA-319, 6 Mi-35/2 Mi-35P (armed/
  liaison), 1 sqn with 8 AB-412, 2 AS-532UL (VIP)

Forces Abroad

DROC: 8,000

Paramilitary 21,800

ZIMBABWE REPUBLIC POLICE FORCE 19,500
(incl Air Wg)
POLICE SUPPORT UNIT 2,300

The 'European Rapid Reaction Force'

There are serious doubts about whether the European Union will meet its goal of achieving a fully operational European Rapid Reaction Force (ERRF), in accordance with its stated aspirations, by 2003. These doubts have been fuelled by the relatively low level of defence spending planned so far by the EU countries for the period up to 2003 and the allocation of this limited funding. Furthermore, the military restructuring required for prospective missions appears to be behind schedule. The following is an analysis of how short of its goals the ERRF is likely to fall and what needs to be done.

SETTING THE GOALS

At their December 1998 summit in St Mâlo, British Prime Minister Tony Blair and French President Jacques Chirac called for the 'full and rapid implementation of the provisions on Common Foreign and Security Policy (CFSP)', which had been introduced as part of the 1997 Amsterdam Treaty. Blair and Chirac envisaged the 'progressive framing of a common defence policy', with the EU developing a 'capacity for autonomous action, backed up by credible military forces'. The Cologne European Council in June 1999 agreed to absorb the Western European Union (WEU) by the end of 2000, and the nascent European Security and Defence Policy (ESDP) began to take shape six months later. A 'headline goal' was agreed at the December 1999 Helsinki European Council, whereby the EU 'must be able, by 2003, to deploy within 60 days and sustain for at least one year military forces of up to 50,000–60,000 persons'. Popularly described as the 'European Rapid Reaction Force' (ERRF) – a term, like 'European Army', guaranteed to irritate those governments that insist the Helsinki initiative is about identifying capabilities, rather than constructing a discrete force – the force would be roughly equivalent to an army corps, but organised at the level of independently deployable brigades. The force would be expected to carry out the full range of Petersberg tasks. Devised at a meeting of the Council of the WEU in June 1992 and incorporated into the Amsterdam Treaty, the Petersberg tasks include 'humanitarian and rescue tasks, peace-keeping tasks and tasks of combat forces in crisis management, including peacemaking'. The declaration on ESDP attached to the Nice Treaty (essentially a list of amendments to the Amsterdam Treaty), which was signed in February 2001, insisted that 'the objective for the European Union is for [the ESDP] to become operational quickly'.

The EU also agreed at Helsinki to establish various new committees and staff organisations (military and civilian) in Brussels. A standing Political and Security Committee (PSC) at the ambassadorial level now has competence in all aspects of the EU's foreign, security and defence policies. A Military Committee (MC), made up of the military representatives of the national chiefs of defence, provides advice to the PSC and direction to the European Union Military Staff (EUMS). The EUMS is designed to carry out early warning, situation assessment and strategic planning for Petersberg tasks, including identification of European national and multinational forces. In February 2001, PSC ambassadors held the first of a series of regular meetings with their counterparts from NATO's North Atlantic Council.

The next step was the November 2000 'Capabilities Commitment Conference' in Brussels, where EU governments made offers amounting to 100,000 troops, 400 aircraft and 100 ships. This 'reservoir' of manpower and equipment suggested to some that the headline goal could easily be achieved in time. It was noted, however, that for the EU's military capability to be anything like effective by 2003, particularly if the EU expected to undertake the most demanding of the Petersberg tasks without relying upon NATO assets, then it would also be necessary to meet certain 'collective capability goals', listed in a 'force catalogue' which had been drawn up with NATO help. Medical and other combat support services were still lacking. Even more debilitating were deficiencies in strategic air and sea transport, and in command, control, communications, computers, intelligence, surveillance and reconnaissance (C^{4}ISR), where 'serious efforts' would be needed. In many respects, these observations merely confirmed what had already been established by other reviews. NATO's Defence Capabilities Initiative (DCI) of April 1999 had listed as many as 58 deficiencies in European military capabilities, including suppression of enemy air defences (SEAD), airborne battlefield command, control and communications (C^3), interoperable and secure communications systems, defensive and offensive electronic-warfare capabilities, and combat search and rescue (CSAR). With the implementation of NATO's new strategic concept in mind, the DCI had also produced its own 'capability goals', including improvements in deployability, mobility and sustainability, an emphasis on SEAD and on the use of precision-guided munitions (PGM), and on interoperable command, control, communications and intelligence (C^{3}I). The WEU's November 1999 audit of the capabilities necessary to conduct the full range of Petersberg tasks made similar observations. Collective capabilities would need to be built up, particularly in strategic intelligence and strategic planning, and among the areas for improvement (including sustainability, survivability and interoperability), it was noted that WEU strategic lift would need to be 'considerably reinforced'.

As far as the EU's military ambitions are concerned, expressions of political intent have been in abundant supply. In terms of equipment, a host of capability analyses have made very clear what is required for the Helsinki initiative to become a military reality. In May 2001, Turkey withdrew its objections to negotiations between NATO and the EU regarding EU access to NATO assets under the 'Berlin plus' arrangement. It later reasserted its concerns and, despite inventive diplomatic intervention by the UK, persisted in blocking the needed access by the EU to NATO resources. Even with the access issue still under discussion, the EU has declared that it expects to achieve an initial operating capability (IOC) for the ERRF by 31 December 2001, and a full operating capability (FOC) by the end of 2003. The IOC would involve operations at the low end of the Petersberg range, such as humanitarian relief or national evacuation operations (NEO). Since operations on this scale could already be achieved by several national armed forces, the EU can be confident of achieving this goal. Full operating capability, however, would encompass the entire range of Petersberg tasks, even up to the level of the 1999 Kosovo operation. But can – or will – European governments deliver FOC by 2003, by some later date, or indeed, ever? An assessment of the prospects for the ESDP–ERRF must focus on four key issues: the availability of military personnel; the ability to deploy sufficient forces; the availability and capability of operational support for an expeditionary force; and the realities of defence spending in the EU.

MILITARY PERSONNEL

At the November 2000 Capabilities Commitments Conference, EU governments made pledges amounting to a notional personnel pool of about 100,000. Although significantly more than the 60,000 envisaged, a built-in surplus is essential in order to guarantee the full Helsinki commitment. However, 100,000 may still not be enough to sustain the force for a year as stated in the goals. Given that the EU has some 1.7 million men and women in its member states' active armed forces (that is, not including reserve units – see Table 27), the provision of a force of 60,000, or just 3.5% of the total, in theory should not be too demanding.

But how easy would it be for EU governments to provide a force of 60,000? EU active armed forces contain some 530,000 conscript troops, generally thought to be unsuitable for service away from home on Petersberg tasks. Additionally, roughly 110,000 EU troops are already deployed

Table 27 European Union Armed Forces: Active, Conscripts and Deployed[1]

	Active	Conscripts	Deployed
Austria	35,500	17,500	1,161
Belgium	39,250		3,450
Denmark	21,810	5,025	1,325
Finland	31,700	23,100	1,938
France	294,430	58,710	35,391
Germany	321,000	128,400	7,693
Greece	159,170	98,321	1,930
Ireland	11,460		885
Italy	250,600	111,800	8,344
Luxembourg	899		23
Netherlands	51,940		5,999
Portugal	44,650	5,860	1,447
Spain	166,050	51,700	2,500
Sweden	52,700	32,800	1,353
United Kingdom	212,450		36,459
Total	**1,693,609**	**533,216**	**109,898**

Note   [1] As at December 2000

outside their home country on peacekeeping and other deployments. Admittedly, some of these troops – such as British Army units based in Germany – would be available for Petersberg deployments. However, they are already committed in one way or another, and so changes to current commitments would have to be made. Many analysts argue that to guarantee the 60,000-strong force, a much greater pool would be necessary. Military planners often apply a rule of three to one: any long-term commitment of troops (and the Helsinki initiative envisages deployments lasting up to one year) requires three equivalent forces to be earmarked: one deployed, one in training and one post-deployment. Some analysts would argue that a multiple of three is inadequate, but when it is applied, the projected size of the ERRF increases to 180,000, representing 17% of the EU's available armed forces. When the rule of three is then applied, as it must be for consistency, to the 110,000 EU forces already on deployment, EU available forces reduce to around 840,000. If the Helsinki initiative could involve 180,000 active troops – and some would say a figure of 210,000–230,000 would be more reasonable – this could represent as much as 21% of the EU's active and available armed forces. This represents a very large-scale commitment and one which, realistically, could only be achieved by multiple-earmarking of troops rather than by dedicating specific units or formations.

Whatever the feasibility and likelihood of EU governments committing over one-fifth of their available armed forces to the Helsinki initiative, there would still be other personnel concerns to address. Small units of troops, or even a few individuals, would be appropriate for some Petersberg tasks, such as observer missions. However, when high-end missions are contemplated – those involving the possibility of combat – the level and standardisation of military training, interoperability and the integration of command-and-control systems will all be crucial considerations. NATO, with decades of experience in marshalling armed forces, accepted the impossibility of achieving alliance-wide standardisation in all functions throughout the command chain, but was of sufficient size to absorb the inevitable disconnects, inefficiencies and duplication of effort. How well the ERRF – a tiny force compared to the collection of armies and air forces that

NATO balked at homogenising – will manage the inevitable diversity in national operational and tactical practices, techniques and preferences, remains to be seen.

DEPLOYMENT

The ERRF will be expected to operate as an expeditionary force, although its precise radius of action is not yet clear. By some accounts, the force should be able to operate globally, although others have argued that the ERRF would be most suitable for crises on the borders of the EU or around the Mediterranean. Since the commitments conference, reference has frequently been made to an ERRF operational radius of 4,000km from Brussels. While not officially endorsed, the 4,000km radius has been adopted informally as a planning guideline, thus encompassing north-west Africa (including the western Sahara, North Africa and some of Sudan), the Middle East (including almost all of Iraq and some of Iran), the Caucasus region, central and eastern Europe (including the Balkans), and western Russia.

Whatever the wisdom of contemplating military operations in these areas, for most members of the European Union, an expeditionary capability clearly represents a marked break from a military tradition of home defence and static deployments dominated by armoured units. With this in mind, the credibility of the ERRF will – assuming the availability of armed forces – to a large degree be decided by European political will to acquire expeditionary capabilities.

The capacity for strategic deployment by sea and air is a theme common to all the capability audits. During the 1990 Gulf War, nearly 95% of the equipment deployed by the US-led coalition reached the theatre by sea. Certainly, a full-scale deployment of the ERRF, with 60,000 troops and all their equipment, would require a substantial sea-transport effort, making use of merchant shipping readily available for lease. Leasing can, however, be a lengthy and unreliable process. For a guaranteed, rapid-response capability, dedicated military sealift will be vital, and here the EU has very little to offer. EU military sealift and airlift capabilities are shown in Tables 31 and 32. Amphibious capabilities will also be important (Table 28). Even without the inevitable shortfalls for political, operational or maintenance reasons, the maximum capacity available to European Union members is around 10,000 troops. This compares uneasily with a maximum US amphibious lift of almost 37,000 troops, but could nevertheless offer some rapid-response capability. As a comparison, the US has 50 large ships dedicated to sealift, while the EU has two small ships.

Table 28 **European Union Amphibious Capabilities**	
	Amphibious Platforms and Craft
France	4 LPD (2×450 tps, 2×350 troops); 5 LSM (140 tps each); 26 craft
Greece	7 LST (5×300 tps, 2×400 troops); 57 craft
Italy	3 LPD (350 tps each); 33 craft
Netherlands	1 LPD (600 tps); 11 craft
Spain	2 LST (400 tps each); 2 LPD (620 tps each); 13 craft
United Kingdom	1 LPD (350 tps); 1 LPH (800 troops); 4 LSL (340 tps each); 2 LCL; 29 craft

The European (*not* EU) Amphibious Capability Initiative of October 2000 is worth noting; however, this minor innovation to operational planning was not designed to find ways of enhancing resources, but was merely an effort to coordinate existing resources and to increase interoperability.

For quicker reaction to a crisis closer to Europe, military sealift and amphibious capabilities alone will not suffice. The deployment to Kosovo of 40,000 troops took some five months:

certainly not 'rapid', and almost disqualifying itself as a 'reaction'. What is also required is light, tactical and strategic airlift capacity, together with in-flight refuelling to extend reach. The combined EU military airlift capability is considerable, but consists mainly of light and tactical transport aircraft.

The only strategic lift assets immediately available to EU troops are the four C-17 *Globemaster* aircraft currently leased for seven years by the UK Royal Air Force. This shortfall severely limits the capacity to deploy ERRF armoured and artillery units to combat situations. EU potential orders for the new Airbus A-400M amount to almost 200. This will greatly improve the European airlift capacity, enabling larger numbers of troops, together with vehicles and medium armour, to be moved greater distances. The A-400M fleet will not, however, be available until 2008 at the very earliest. Until then, the ERRF will be forced to rely mainly on tactical airlift (such as the C-130), calling on the small British C-17 fleet and on the United States when heavier strategic airlift is required. An alternative solution is to hire Russian An-124 aircraft or more C-17s. Another would be to buy or lease the An-70 from Russia or the Ukraine. However, the An-70 is not in full production yet. Completion of flight testing was delayed by the prototype's emergency gear-up landing, following a double engine failure after take-off from Omsk on 27 January 2001. Nevertheless, the first five An-70 are still scheduled for delivery in 2003, several years ahead of the first A-400M deliveries. The Westernised variant, the An-7X, is considered by some analysts to perform better than the A-400M. It is also believed to be cheaper. Both aircraft can meet the European Staff requirement for operations involving short take-offs and landings on temporary airstrips, whereas the C-17 cannot.

OPERATIONAL SUPPORT

Having arrived in theatre – most probably at the level of 2–4 brigades, rather than anything approaching the full corps strength of 50–60,000 – the ERRF will immediately require support in four key force-multiplying areas: headquarters and command; communications; intelligence collation and analysis; and air power.

• **Headquarters and command** Each force component (land, sea, air) of an ERRF deployment will require a Component Command Headquarters (CCHQ). At present, Europe lacks a dedicated naval CCHQ capability, although the British HMS *Ocean* is being fitted for this purpose and will be operational by 2003. There will also be a need for a Force Headquarters (FHQ), able to deploy rapidly to the operational theatre, taking under command the various multinational contributions. There are at present seven multinational FHQs within NATO: Eurocorps; Eurofor; Euromarfor; Multinational Division (Central) (MND (C)) of the Allied Rapid Reaction Corps (ARRC); the Spanish–Italian Amphibious Force; the UK–Netherlands Amphibious Force; and the German–Dutch Corps. Of these, only three (Eurocorps, Eurofor and MND (C)) could form an FHQ to command an ERRF operation. And it should be borne in mind that the most capable of these headquarters – Eurocorps – needed extensive support from ARRC and NATO Land Centre (LANDCENT) when it assumed command of KFOR.

• **Communications** While several European countries make use of civilian systems for their military satellite communications, a number of satellite projects dedicated to military communications should provide ERRF deployments with the necessary communications support: Italy's *Sicral*, Britain's *Skynet*-4 and France's *Syracuse* III. France is considering a wholly military replacement for the *Syracuse*, while Britain is examining a *Skynet*-5, an industry-provided replacement for *Skynet*-4. That said, interoperability among the different European systems – particularly in the ground sector – is limited, indicating a need not just to modernise existing national satellite assets, but also to rationalise technical specifications among European allies.

• **Surveillance and Target Acquisition** European battlefield-surveillance and target-acquisition capabilities are limited. Two main procurement initiatives are underway: the SOSTAR-X programme involving France, Germany, Italy, the Netherlands and Spain; and the UK ASTOR/RISTA project. Neither SOSTAR-X nor RISTA is likely to be available before 2003, and it could be as long as another decade before the ERRF could rely upon a European battlefield-surveillance capability.

The unmanned aerial vehicle (UAV) came into its own in the 1999 Kosovo campaign. Yet, there are few UAVs available in Europe, and those are older systems rather than High/Medium Altitude Long Endurance (HALE/MALE). In this critical area, therefore, dependence on the United States is likely to continue. Alternatively, the ERRF could, for the foreseeable future, be deployed only on low-end Petersberg task scenarios, where accurate, real-time tactical and operational intelligence would be less important.

Space-based surveillance assets are even scarcer. In imagery intelligence, the only dedicated European system is the tri-national *Helios* (France, Italy and Spain), with two operational satellites in orbit. France and Italy have plans to introduce about six low-orbit satellites to take over *Helios'* imagery-gathering role. Germany has similar plans, creating an obvious opportunity for coordination of the two European projects. It is very unlikely that any European capability could match that of the US, but there is plainly scope for a European satellite intelligence capacity commensurate with the objectives of the Helsinki project.

• **Air power** Air support for an ERRF expeditionary deployment will involve: airborne early warning (AEW), command and control; air superiority combat aircraft; suppression of enemy air defences; precision guided munitions; and – at least in the early stages of a deployment, which may be some distance away from operating bases, and may be opposed – maritime air power.

Airborne early warning, command and control During the Kosovo operation, the European airborne early-warning and command-and-control capabilities were limited, amounting to just five surveillance and command aircraft, as compared to the 41 provided by the United States. Between them, European countries could now field some 11 E-3 *Sentry* AEW aircraft (7 E3-D from the UK and 4 E3-F from France). If this force were pooled, a European expeditionary force could be guaranteed permanent airborne early-warning coverage, but only with one aircraft. To increase this cover, and to allow for maintenance and repair, reinforcements are needed. The most likely source would be the NATO airborne early-warning force of 17 E-3A *Sentry*, although there would be a risk of a national veto by Turkey on use of NATO assets.

Air superiority and SEAD Control of the air is vital to the success of any military operation. Any expeditionary deployment by the ERRF is likely to attract considerable political and media interest, and with it, the requirement to use air power to minimise the risk of casualties. European capabilities amount to some 500 aircraft equipped with modern radar systems and the Beyond Visual Range (BVR) missiles necessary to ensure the safety of the attacking aircraft. European air forces can also muster almost 400 all-weather air-defence aircraft. From 2002, with the EF-2000 *Typhoon*, the *Rafale* and a new range of BVR missiles, Europe should enjoy a decade or so of leading-edge air superiority, more than enough to support ERRF operations. The European suppression of enemy air defence (SEAD) capability is very limited, amounting to 50 *Tornado* electronic combat and reconnaissance (ECR) aircraft from Germany and Italy, together with a large fleet of ground-attack aircraft capable of launching anti-radiation missiles.

Precision Guided Munitions (PGMs) The use of PGMs will increasingly be seen as a political necessity in situations where there might otherwise be excessive collateral damage. Some European air forces – particularly those of Britain and France – are by now highly experienced in the use of laser guidance for bombs or missiles. Other European air forces, however, have less experience and capability. As far as cruise missiles are concerned, Britain has a limited Tomahawk Land-Attack Missile (TLAM) capability; there is little available elsewhere in Europe.

Maritime air power If the European Union seriously intends to acquire a long-range power-projection capability – even confined to the Petersberg tasks, and at no more than the corps-scale promised under the Helsinki initiative – aircraft-carrier groups will be at the centre of operations. At least in the early stages of an ERRF deployment, particularly when out of range of friendly air bases, aircraft carriers will be crucial for the provision of air cover and superiority. Carrier groups are, however, in very short supply in Europe. Only Britain (two) and France (one) operate carriers at present. The British government has announced its intention to build two new carriers by 2012–15 to replace its present ageing ships. Even if this project comes to fruition, there could at most be two out of the three European carriers operational at any one time. It is not only a question of providing the ships: a maritime aviation capability of some 150 combat aircraft would also be needed for the British carriers alone.

THE REALITIES OF EUROPEAN UNION DEFENCE SPENDING

The Helsinki headline and capability goals are being pursued in an unfavourable defence-economic climate, but just how unfavourable is a matter of contention. After the Cold War, defence expenditure fell dramatically across Europe, reflecting the global trend. The achievement

Table 29 **European Union Defence Expenditure**		constant 2000 local currency			
		1998	1999	2000	ε2001
Austria	schilling	23,409	23,363	23,000	22,061
Belgium	franc	138,382	139,009	140,256	141,814
Denmark	kroner	19,850	19,821	19,349	19,639
Finland	markka	10,520	9,794	10,159	9,655
France	franc	247,930	248,427	242,800	239,074
Germany	deutschmark	60,684	61,065	59,617	56,657
Greece	drachma	1,794,318	1,890,690	1,981,984	2,174,886
Ireland	pound	527	588	602	696
Italy	lira	42,410,344	43,933,406	43,002,000	43,893,117
Luxembourg	franc	5,407	5,438	5,468	5,500
Netherlands	guilder	14,109	14,828	14,192	13,766
Portugal	escudo	437,654	462,007	475,178	510,453
Spain	peseta	1,169,480	1,203,954	1,266,429	1,308,955
Sweden	kronor	46,715	47,302	47,268	49,923
United Kingdom	pound	23,385	23,004	22,823	22,740

Analyses and Tables

of the Helsinki initiative hinges upon whether the recession in European defence spending has bottomed out, and whether recovery is envisaged. Table 29 shows trends in EU defence spending over the past four years, measured in local currency.

By this account, spending in the EU's three largest economies (France, Germany and the United Kingdom) fell on average by 2% between 1998–2000. Estimates for 2001 indicate a continuing downward slide: 1.5% for France, 5% for Germany, and 0.4% for the United Kingdom. When measured in constant US dollars, the trends are even less auspicious, as Table 30 indicates.

In dollar terms, defence spending in the three largest economies fell by an average of 14.7% between 1998–2000, with estimates for 2001 showing a further fall of 8.6% for France, 11.8% for Germany and 6.1% for the United Kingdom.

Given that much of the debate about the Helsinki initiative concerns the improvement or acquisition of military capabilities, there is little, if any, room for optimism, no matter how defence spending is measured. Large-scale increases in European defence spending are not taking place and are politically inconceivable in the near-term. Thus, the achievement of full operating capability by 2003 seems unlikely. In the time available, the best that can be hoped for are improvements in the quality – rather than quantity – of European defence spending. Assuming the political will to consolidate or specialise, improvements and efficiencies could be achieved in a number of areas. Dedicated military sealift is lacking, but until capacity improves, arrangements for leasing merchant shipping could be expedited, even to the extent of pre-chartering transport ships, tankers and other vessels for use by the ERRF. Closer rationalisation might be suitable in airlift, perhaps with the creation of a European air-transport command, pooling the C-130, C-17 and eventually A-400M fleets. Something similar could be achieved with tanker aircraft, creating an EU on-call capability. With combat airpower, there is a pressing case for improvements in Europe's SEAD capabilities, perhaps even to the extent of inviting one or two EU air forces to specialise in this role. Given that the new *Eurofighter* will be procured by at least five EU members, there is also an argument for a shift to an EU, multinational equivalent of the large airbase concept, enabling significant savings in logistic, maintenance and repair facilities. The procurement of precision-guided munitions would be another obvious target for standardisation. At the tactical level, possibly the most pressing case for rationalisation – on both military and economic grounds – would be in the provision of secure communications networks down to the tactical level

CONCLUSION

The ERRF is likely to achieve initial operating capability by the December 2001 deadline. This will doubtless be seen as an encouraging first step; however, it represents little more than existing national capabilities. What really matters is the potential to move towards full operating capability. Analysis of available EU armed forces, strategic-lift capabilities, operational support (mainly combat air power) and trends in EU defence spending suggests that achievement of full operating capability by December 2003 is unlikely. EU member states currently lack the capabilities necessary to organise, deploy and sustain the ERRF on a long-term, high-level Petersberg task, and it is barely conceivable that these shortfalls could be met in a little over 24 months, even given the political determination to achieve this.

Optimists believe that, at the very least, the Helsinki initiative could reduce the rate of decline in post-Cold War European defence spending and, at best, that it might in future encourage Europeans to begin spending more. But there is a prospect of failure ahead, which can only be prevented by the acquisition of the appropriate capabilities. As a result of the various audits, there can be no doubt as to what is needed. Progress reports on the DCI clearly show that the rate of acquisition is painfully slow and inadequate. Since the early 1990s, the prospects for an EU military posture have often been summarised in the expression 'capabilities-expectations gap'. When the EU's military project was open-ended and the deadline 'eventual', the 'gap' was very much an abstract notion Since then, however, the deadline has become fixed – December 2003 – and talk of a 'capabilities-expectations gap' fails to grasp the severity of the looming crisis. In December 2003, when expectations of the EU as a military actor are found largely to lack substance, there will be a 'capabilities and expectations collapse'. To prevent such an outcome, two steps must be taken. First, EU governments should not overstate the 'achievement' of initial operating capability later this year, as this would only fuel expectations that cannot be met on schedule. Second, the EU must acknowledge openly that final operating capability can only be achieved by a much later date, say 2012. It could be approached incrementally, with 2003 then becoming the target date for the ability to deploy two or three brigade-level formations; something which might reasonably be achieved in the time available.

Table 30 European Union Defence Expenditure — constant 2000 US$bn

	1998	1999	2000	ε2001
UK UK	38,737	37,104	34,580	32,486
France Fr	42,026	38,576	34,986	31,962
Germany Ge	34,486	31,813	28,800	25,407
Italy It	24,427	23,123	20,977	19,861
Spain Sp	7,828	7,373	7,196	6,926
Netherlands Nl	7,112	6,853	6,170	5,484
Greece Gr	6,072	5,311	5,567	5,605
Sweden Swe	5,876	5,526	5,371	4,866
Belgium Be	3,812	3,511	3,403	3,080
Denmark Da	2,962	2,715	2,449	2,308
Portugal Por	2,430	2,348	2,241	2,239
Austria A	1,891	1,731	1,575	1,511
Finland SF	1,968	1,677	1,577	1,424
Ireland Irl	752	760	725	782
Luxembourg Lu	149	137	128	117

Analyses and Tables

MILITARY AIRLIFT

In 1991, *Operation Desert Storm*, the last major multinational military intervention, demonstrated the critical importance of airlift and also its limitations. The air and maritime bases available to the coalition forces in Saudi Arabia and the neighbouring Gulf States were crucial to their success in the conflict. These seaports and airfields, which rank among the best in the world, permitted the unhindered movement of thousands of troops and tons of equipment into the theatre, and the doubling of allied combat aircraft in theatre from roughly 900 in early September 1990 to approximately 1,800 in January 1991. During the build-up, Iraqi forces never attacked the coalition bases and the deployment of allied troops went ahead unimpeded.

It is unlikely that international intervention forces will be as fortunate in future, in terms of either facilities or the lack of opposition. Without these advantages, and the quantity of available airlift, the conduct of *Operation Desert Storm* would have been very different.

Military airlift is an inherently vulnerable asset, which depends on particular infrastructure and logistical resources. Nevertheless, it remains vital to modern warfare, enabling equipment and troops to be transported rapidly over long distances. There are obvious limits to its use: it takes around 500 sorties by C-141 *Starlifters*, one of the most capable aircraft in airlift terms, to move a light division with minimal supplies and no armoured vehicles. Airlift is best suited to moving relatively light forces and logistical support, leaving bulky and heavy materiel to go by sea.

Despite the limitations, demand for airlift is rising, with its use to deliver humanitarian resources and peacekeeping troops as rapidly as possible becoming as important as its role in transporting fighting forces. Paratroopers evacuating nationals from troublespots must now share airlift capacity with the need to, for example, assist flood-relief efforts in places such as Mozambique using heavy-lift helicopters. It is symptomatic of how the strategic environment has changed since the end of the Cold War that the specifications for the A-400M Military Airbus, the aircraft chosen by European nations as the solution to their airlift capability gap, did not include the ability to carry a main battle tank.

The aircraft listed in the following table are not usually dedicated to a particular type of mission or specific loads of troops or vehicles.

Table 31 **Military Air Transport** by country of origin

Definition Major fixed-wing military transport aircraft currently in service. Payload and range data should be treated with care; one can be reduced to increase the other.

	Maker	Designation	Name	Gross wt (lb)	Payload (lb)	Range (nm)
France/Germany						
	EADS	**C-160**	*Transall*	112,435	35,275	1,000
Italy						
	Alenia	**G-222/C-27A**	*Spartan*	61,730	19,840	680
	Alenia	**C-27J**	*Spartan*	66,138	22,046	540
Japan						
	Kawasaki	**C-1**		85,320	17,416	700

	Maker	Designation	Name	Gross wt (lb)	Payload (lb)	Range (nm)
Poland						
	PZL	An-28	*Cash*	14,350	3,858	560
Russia						
	Ilyushin	Il-76MD	*Candid*	418,870	105,820	2,160
	Ilyushin	Il-76MF		462,966	132,160	2,160
Spain						
	CASA	C-212	*Aviocar*	17,857	6,217	450
	CASA	C-295M		51,150	19,850	1,115
Spain/Indonesia						
	Airtech	CN-235	*Persuader*	36,376	13,227	800
Ukraine						
	Antonov	An-12	*Cub*	134,500	44,000	1,800
	Antonov	An-22	*Cock*	500,000	132,000	2,840
	Antonov	An-26	*Curl*	52,920	12,100	594
	Antonov	An-32	*Cline*	59,525	14,700	450
	Antonov	An-70		286,000	77,161	2,051
	Antonov	An-72/74	*Coaler B/C*	80,500	22,045	800
	Antonov	An-124	*Condor*	863,000	265,000	2,600
UK						
	Shorts	C-23	*Sherpa*	25,600	7,280	446
US						
	Boeing	C-17	*Globemaster*	585,000	169,000	3,000
	Boeing	C-40A		171,500	40,000	3,000
	Lockheed	C-5B	*Galaxy*	837,000	261,000	2,982
	Lockheed	C-130H	*Hercules*	155,000	42,673	2,046
	Lockheed	C-130J	*Hercules*	155,000	41,800	2,835
	Lockheed	C-141B	*Starlifter*	343,000	90,880	2,550

MILITARY SEALIFT

The only country with significant sealift (ships specifically designed to transport military resources) in its military inventory is the United States. The US Navy's Military Sealift Command (MSC) operates two major sealift programmes: 'Prepositioning' and 'Sealift'. The former consists of approximately 25 merchant ships, on full-time charter, permanently loaded with equipment for the army, air force and marine corps and based in Diego Garcia, Guam/Saipan or the western Mediterranean. The sealift programme's ships are sometimes used for prepositioning, but generally transport equipment for specific operations and are based in the US. Their number will increase to 28 in 2002 with the delivery of the final ships in the *Bob Hope* and *Watson* classes. Both classes were ordered in the aftermath of the Gulf War, when, mainly due to lack of dedicated military sealift, it had taken six months to transport all the equipment needed for the campaign. The US military has access to further sealift through the Department of Transport's Ready Reserve Force, which has over 70 sealift ships kept at a readiness notice of between four and 20 days; when activated they come under the operational control of the MSC. In addition, the 1997 Voluntary Intermodal Sealift Agreement (VISA) allows the Department of Defense (DoD) to use

Analyses and Tables

ships of ocean-shipping companies in times of national emergency, in return for which the companies receive governmental subsidies or peacetime defence-cargo movement contracts. The DoD can also charter transport ships for the short term on the commercial shipping market.

Chartering has been the preferred policy of all other countries needing sealift. However, some are considering ordering dedicated ships, due to the high cost of commercial chartering and the increased need to transport military equipment rapidly to theatres of operations anywhere in the world. The UK, whose sealift currently comprises two merchant transport ships on short-term charter, intends to order six sealift ships from a UK-registered company for a 20-year period. It is planned that the company will own, crew and operate the ships and will undertake to have three permanently available for the UK government; two of the remaining three will be available for commercial charter. France and the Netherlands have also announced plans to acquire sealift ships jointly. Other countries, such as New Zealand and Australia, have recently chartered merchant transport ships for short periods. One of these, the trimaran *Jervis Bey* proved particularly useful to Australia for transporting troops and equipment for the International Force in East Timor (INTERFET). Countries lacking either military sealift ships or merchant ships on long- or short-term contract, or which need to supplement their resources temporarily, generally hire merchant transport ships on the commercial market. Due to the global nature of the shipping industry, such ships are often registered in countries other than the hirer, and the owners and crew are often from elsewhere.

Table 32 **Military Sealift** by country of origin

Definition Covers all military ships above 1,000 tonnes (t) in active service designed to transport military resources. Does not include amphibious shipping. The figures given in parentheses are an illustration of the amount and type of military equipment that the ship's tonnage capacity allows it to transport.

MC Marine Corps **MSC** Military Sealift Command **prepo** prepositioned ship **MS** merchant ship **Mch** merchant charter.

Ship/class	No.	Estimated Capacity (t)	Speed (knots)	Age (yrs)	Remarks
Brazil					
Barroso Pereira	× 3	4,000 (1,970 tps)	15	36	
Chile					
Aquiles	× 1	1,800 (250 tps)	18	13	
China					
Qiongsha	× 4	350 (400 tps)	16	20	
India					
Nicobar	× 2	n.k. (1,200 tps)	16	3	MS owned by Andaman Administration
Indonesia					
Frosch II	× 2	650	18	22	
Tisza	× 4	875	12	40	
Italy					
Major	× 1	4,000	n.k.	17	MS; long-term charter to It Army
Malaysia					
Sri Indera Sakti	× 2	n.k. (17 tk; 600 tps)	16	21	

Ship class	No.	Capacity (t)	Speed (knots)	Age (yrs)	Remarks
Mexico					
Rio Lerma	× 1	**775**	14	39	
Morocco					
Dakhla	× 1	**800**	12	4	
Russia					
Antonov	× 8	**2,500**	17	26	Op by RF Border Guard
Spain					
El Camino Espanol	× 1	**3,500** (24 tk, 120 veh)	15	17	Op by Sp Army
Martin Posadillo	× 1	**n.k.** (70 veh)	10	28	Op by Sp Army
Taiwan					
Wan An	× 1	**1,700** (600 tps)	17	22	
Wu Kang	× 3	**2,000** (1,400 tps)	20	21	2 more to enter service 2002
UK					
Sea Centurion	× 1	**9,500** (350 veh)	19	5	Short-term charter to MOD until end 2002
Sea Crusader	× 1	**9,500** (350 veh)	19	5	Short-term charter to MOD until 2003
US					
Shughart	× 3	**22,000** (58 tk, 950 veh)	24	5	MSC ship
Gordon	× 2	**24,000** (58 tk, 950 veh)	24	29	MSC ship
Algol	× 8	**25,500** (183 tk)	30	28	MSC ship; 8 together carry 93% equip for full army mech div
Bob Hope	× 5	**13,000** (58 tk, 950 veh, 300 tps)	24	3	MSC ship; 2 more to enter service 2002
Watson	× 7	**13,260** (58 tk, 950 veh, 300 tps)	24	3	MSC ship; 1 more to enter service 2002
American Cormorant	× 1	**45,000** (cargo handling gear)	16	27	Mch to MSC; prepo at Diego Garcia with army cargo
Strong Virginian	× 1	**21,000** (cargo handling gear)	23	17	as above
Green Valley	× 1	**46,000**	16	27	as above
Green Ridge	× 1	**9,400**	17	22	as above
Green Harbour	× 1	**30,000**	27	29	as above
Jeb Stuart	× 1	**50,000** (LASH)	16	31	as above
Calvin P. Titus	× 3	**24,500** (sustainment cargo)	19	16	Mch to MSC; prepo at Guam with army cargo
Keystone	× 1	**10,400**	20	n.k.	as above
Buffalo Soldier	× 1	**20,000** (breakbulk)	16	23	Mch to MSC; prepo at Deigo Garcia with air force cargo
Steven L. Bennett	× 1	**41,000** (LASH)	16	17	Mch to MSC; prepo in W. Med with air force cargo
Louis J. Hauge Jr	× 5	**23,000** (20% of equip for MEB)	17	17	Mch to MSC; prepo at Diego Garcia/ Saipan/W. Med with MC cargo
Matej Kocak	× 3	**25,000** (25% of equip for MEB)	20	15	as above
John P. Bobo	× 5	**25,000** (1,400 veh)	18	15	as above

Analyses and Tables

The International Arms Trade

TRENDS

The international arms trade fell significantly in 2000, with the value of deliveries at $29.3bn compared with $37.2bn in 1999. Regional rankings were unchanged, with the Middle East continuing to spend more than any other region, and accounting for at least 40% of the world market. The largest Middle Eastern buyer, Saudi Arabia, took deliveries worth $7.3bn, an increase from $6.2bn in 1999. However, this figure is likely to fall in coming years as no significant new transfer agreements were signed with Saudi Arabia in 2000. A number of recent developments mean that the Middle East will probably remain the main destination for global arms exports for the foreseeable future. These include the signing of a $6.4bn licensed commercial agreement under which the United Arab Emirates will buy 80 F-16 aircraft from the US. Also, increased diplomatic and military contacts between Russia and Iran resulted in an agreement, signed by the two countries in March 2001, to resume trading in conventional weapons for the first time since 1979. It is thought that Iran would like to buy weapons worth up to $7bn, including fighter aircraft, helicopters and S-300 air-defence missiles. Other major weapons agreements that will have an impact on international arms deliveries in coming years include the extensive package offered by the US to Taiwan, including 4 *Kidd*-class destroyers, 8 diesel-electric submarines and 12 maritime reconnaissance aircraft, and the deal between Russia and India for up to 140 Su-30MKI aircraft and 310 T-90S main battle tanks (MBT). Russia is also seeking new markets in South Asia and may sell Su-30K fighter aircraft to Indonesia.

Table 33 **Arms deliveries: leading suppliers in 2000**		
current US$m		
1	US	14,187
2	UK	5,100
3	Russia	3,500
4	France	1,500
5	Germany	800
6	Sweden	600
7	China	500
8	Ukraine	400
9	Italy	300
10	Israel	300
11	Belarus	200

MARKET SHARE

The US is credited with nearly 50% of global arms deliveries. Among its major exports in 2000 were 53 F-16 aircraft to Bahrain, Egypt, Jordan and Singapore; over 350 armoured combat vehicles sold to 11 countries; two amphibious ships to Spain and one frigate to Turkey. The UK remained the second-largest exporter, with 17.4% of total arms deliveries. Among the recipients of UK transfers, Jordan took delivery of a further batch of 76 *Challenger* I MBTs, out of its original order of 288. Meanwhile, the lifting of an EU arms embargo imposed on Indonesia after the violence in East Timor allowed delivery of five *Hawk* aircraft, the last to fulfil a longstanding order. The UK also exported 10 *Super Lynx* attack helicopters, with South Korea receiving seven and Germany three, while Greece took delivery of its second *Hunt*-class mine countermeasure vessel.

Russia reported arms sales of $3.5–4bn in 2000. Its main customers remain China and India, which accounted for 50% and 22% of Russian exports respectively. Of particular note was China's acquisition of a second *Sovremenny*-class destroyer in 2000, as well as the transfer of a tenth *Kilo* submarine to India, making naval equipment Russia's main export.

Note

The methodology used in measuring the value of US arms exports has been revised. The US is the only major arms supplier that has two distinct systems for exporting weapons: the government-to-government (foreign military sales (FMS)) system, and the licensed commercial export system. Whereas data for the FMS programme, which accounts for the majority of conventional arms sales, is collected and revised on an ongoing basis, data maintained on commercial sales is less comprehensive.

Once an exporter receives from the State Department a commercial license authorization to sell – valid for four years – there is no current requirement for the exporter to provide to the State Department, on a systematic and on-going basis, comprehensive details of any final sales contract resulting from the original license approval.

Following research by the State Department's Office of Defense Trade Controls, it seems likely that the number of licenses resulting in a physical delivery of equipment is smaller than previously assessed.

Sources

The primary source for US government figures is *Conventional Arms Transfers to Developing Nations 1993–2000* (Richard F. Grimmett, Congressional Research Service, Washington DC, August 2001). Historical arms-trade data are also taken from *World Military Expenditures and Arms Transfers*, the *UN Register of Conventional Arms* and statistics obtained directly from governments.

Analyses and Tables

Table 34 Value of global arms deliveries and market share, 1993–2000

constant 2000 US$m, % in italics

	Total	Russia		US		UK		France		Germany		China		Others	
1993	37,287	3,941	10.6	17,584	47.2	5,331	14.3	1,739	4.7	1,970	5.3	1,391	3.7	5,331	14.3
1994	33,423	1,930	5.8	15,148	45.3	5,902	17.7	1,476	4.4	1,930	5.8	681	2.0	6,356	19.0
1995	39,844	3,875	9.7	17,703	44.4	5,867	14.7	3,100	7.8	2,214	5.6	775	1.9	6,310	15.8
1996	38,837	3,361	8.7	16,068	41.4	7,047	18.1	3,903	10.1	2,060	5.3	651	1.7	5,746	14.8
1997	44,127	2,760	6.3	17,273	39.1	7,218	16.4	6,687	15.2	1,274	2.9	1,061	2.4	7,854	17.8
1998	37,748	2,289	6.1	17,148	45.4	3,954	10.5	7,075	18.7	1,457	3.9	624	1.7	5,202	13.8
1999	37,274	3,163	8.5	18,298	49.1	5,203	14.0	3,163	8.5	1,938	5.2	306	0.8	5,203	14.0
2000	29,387	3,500	11.9	14,187	48.3	5,100	17.4	1,500	5.1	800	2.7	500	1.7	3,800	12.9

Table 35 Arms deliveries to the Middle East and North Africa, 1987, 1993–2000

constant 2000 US$m

	Saudi Arabia	Iran	Egypt	Israel	UAE	Kuwait	Algeria
1987	10,518	2,436	2,579	3,295	278	287	1,003
1993	9,853	1,277	2,214	1860	664	1,152	155
1994	8,978	443	1,329	1,362	587	917	159
1995	9,964	554	2,104	852	1,052	1,440	255
1996	10,185	443	1,771	1,007	830	1,826	278
1997	11,677	849	1,167	886	886	743	498
1998	11,048	664	1,079	1,107	997	554	554
1999	6,227	491	861	1,534	747	320	408
2000	7,300	300	1,300	1,000	500	1,000	300

Table 36 Arms deliveries to East Asia, 1987, 1993–2000

constant 2000 US$m

	Japan	Taiwan	ROK	Vietnam	China	Thailand	Malaysia	Singapore	Indonesia	Myanmar
1987	1,605	1,495	1,074	2,723	930	616	101	444	372	29
1993	2,981	1,160	1,981	22	667	162	313	151	104	151
1994	2,481	1,135	2,402	91	295	443	964	261	56	113
1995	2,547	1,329	1,894	221	803	1,217	830	221	188	155
1996	2,602	1,882	1,771	278	1,661	774	498	554	886	278
1997	2,379	7,197	1,440	165	443	525	333	498	443	333
1998	2,214	6,643	1,450	188	498	333	354	942	388	320
1999	1,904	2,657	1,884	178	510	418	1,224	632	783	332
2000	n.k.	1,200	700	n.k.	1,600	n.k.	400	n.k.	700	n.k.

Table 37 International comparisons of defence expenditure and military manpower, 1985, 1999 and 2000 — constant 1999 US$

Canada • US • NATO Europe • Non-NATO Europe

	Defence Expenditure US$m			Defence Expenditure US$ per capita			% of GDP			Numbers in Armed Forces (000)		Estimated Reservists (000)	Para-military (000)
	1985	1999	2000	1985	1999	2000	1985	1999	2000	1985	2000	2000	2000
Canada	11,597	8,395	7,456	457	275	239	2.2	1.3	1.2	83.0	59.1	43.3	9.4
US	382,548	292,147	294,695	1,599	1,061	1,059	6.5	3.2	3.0	2,151.6	1,365.8	1,211.5	89.0
NATO Europe													
Belgium	6,100	3,442	3,335	619	339	328	3.0	1.4	1.4	91.6	39.3	152.1	n.a.
Czech Republic	n.a.	1,155	1,133	n.a.	112	111	n.a.	2.2	2.2	n.a.	57.7	240.0	5.6
Denmark	3,098	2,661	2,401	606	504	454	2.2	1.6	1.5	29.6	21.8	64.9	n.a.
France	48,399	37,811	34,292	877	642	580	4.0	2.8	2.6	464.3	294.4	419.0	95.0
Germany	52,246	31,182	28,229	688	380	343	3.2	1.6	1.6	478.0	221.1	364.3	n.a.
Greece	3,451	5,206	5,457	347	491	513	7.0	4.8	4.9	201.5	159.2	291.0	4.0
Hungary	3,517	768	777	330	76	77	7.2	1.6	1.7	106.0	43.8	90.3	14.0
Iceland	n.a.	n.a.	n.a.	n.a.	n.a.	n.a.	n.a.	n.a.	n.a.	n.a.	n.a.	n.a.	0.1
Italy	25,459	22,664	20,561	446	395	359	2.3	2.0	1.9	385.1	250.6	65.2	252.5
Luxembourg	95	135	126	258	316	291	0.9	0.8	0.8	0.7	0.8	n.a.	0.6
Netherlands	8,812	6,193	6,392	608	394	405	3.1	1.6	1.9	105.5	51.9	32.2	5.2
Norway	3,067	3,241	2,856	738	730	640	3.1	2.2	1.8	37.0	26.7	222.0	0.3
Poland	8,533	3,222	3,191	229	83	82	8.1	2.0	2.0	319.0	217.3	406.0	21.5
Portugal	1,816	2,302	2,197	178	233	222	3.1	2.1	2.2	73.0	44.7	210.9	45.8
Spain	11,164	7,227	7,053	289	183	178	2.4	1.3	1.3	320.0	166.0	447.9	75.8
Turkey	3,401	9,717	10,609	68	148	159	4.5	5.2	5.2	630.0	609.7	378.7	218.0
United Kingdom	47,240	36,368	33,894	835	619	576	5.2	2.5	2.4	334.0	212.5	302.8	n.a.
Subtotal NATO Europe	226,397	173,291	162,503	475	353	332	4.0	2.2	2.2	3,575.3	2,417.5	3,687.3	738.4
Total NATO	620,542	473,834	464,654	540	388	368	4.0	2.2	2.2	5,809.9	3,842.4	4,942.1	836.8
Non-NATO Europe													
Albania	280	140	111	95	44	36	5.3	3.7	3.0	40.4	54.0	155.0	13.5
Armenia	n.a.	159	149	n.a.	44	42	n.a.	8.6	8.0	n.a.	41.3	210.0	1.0
Austria	1,913	1,696	1,609	253	208	196	1.2	0.9	0.8	54.7	40.5	75.0	n.a.
Azerbaijan	n.a.	203	213	n.a.	26	28	n.a.	4.4	4.5	n.a.	72.1	55.7	15.0
Belarus	n.a.	466	366	n.a.	45	36	n.a.	5.0	4.0	n.a.	83.1	289.5	8.0
Bosnia	n.a.	365	183	n.a.	90	46	n.a.	8.3	3.7	n.a.	30.0	150.0	46.0
Bulgaria	2,425	392	347	288	47	42	14.0	3.3	2.8	148.5	79.8	303.0	34.0
Croatia	n.a.	662	509	n.a.	146	114	n.a.	3.5	2.7	n.a.	61.0	220.0	40.0
Cyprus	129	353	453	194	406	577	3.6	4.1	4.8	10.0	10.0	60.0	0.8
Czechoslovakia	3,472	n.a.	n.a.	223	n.a.	n.a.	8.2	n.a.	n.a.	203.3	n.a.	n.a.	n.a.
Estonia	n.a.	71	79	n.a.	50	57	n.a.	1.4	1.4	n.a.	4.8	14.0	2.8
Finland	2,226	1,644	1,522	453	318	294	2.8	1.3	1.3	36.5	31.7	485.0	3.4
FYROM	n.a.	67	76	n.a.	32	37	n.a.	2.0	2.1	n.a.	16.0	60.0	7.5
Georgia	n.a.	111	116	n.a.	22	23	n.a.	2.8	2.5	n.a.	26.9	250.0	6.5
Ireland	474	745	684	133	201	183	1.8	0.9	0.7	13.7	11.5	14.8	n.a.
Latvia	n.a.	58	70	n.a.	24	30	n.a.	1.0	1.0	n.a.	5.0	14.5	3.5

Non-NATO Europe contd • Middle East and North Africa • Central and South Asia

	Defence Expenditure US$m			US$ per capita			% of GDP			Numbers in Armed Forces (000)		Estimated Reservists (000)	Para-military (000)
	1985	1999	2000	1985	1999	2000	1985	1999	2000	1985	2000	2000	2000
Lithuania	n.a.	107	195	n.a.	29	53	n.a.	1.0	1.8	n.a.	12.7	27.7	3.9
Malta	24	27	26	66	69	67	1.4	0.8	0.7	0.8	2.1	n.a.	n.a.
Moldova	n.a.	27	21	n.a.	6	5	n.a.	2.5	1.7	n.a.	9.5	66.0	3.4
Romania	2,067	607	809	91	27	36	4.5	1.8	2.2	189.5	207.0	470.0	75.9
Slovakia	n.a.	305	340	n.a.	57	63	n.a.	1.7	1.8	n.a.	38.6	20.0	2.6
Slovenia	n.a.	337	223	n.a.	169	112	n.a.	1.8	1.2	n.a.	9.0	61.0	4.5
Sweden	4,730	5,245	5,190	566	590	583	3.3	2.3	2.2	65.7	52.7	570.0	35.6
Switzerland	2,860	3,108	2,900	443	439	393	2.1	1.3	1.2	20.0	27.7	351.2	n.a.
Ukraine	n.a.	1,437	1,081	n.a.	28	21	n.a.	2.9	3.4	n.a.	303.8	1,000.0	116.6
FRY (Serbia/Montenegro)	4,951	1,654	1,790	212	155	168	3.8	12.4	10.0	241.0	97.7	400.0	38.0
Total	**25,550**	**19,984**	**19,062**	**251**	**131**	**130**	**4.3**	**3.2**	**2.8**	**1,024.1**	**1,328.5**	**5,322.4**	**462.5**
Russia	n.a.	56,800	58,810	n.a.	386	400	n.a.	5.1	5.0	n.a.	1,520.0	2,400.0	423.0
Soviet Union	364,715	n.a.	n.a.	1,308	n.a.	n.a.	16.1	n.a.	n.a.	5,300.0	n.a.	n.a.	n.a.
Middle East and North Africa													
Algeria	1,412	3,086	2,930	64	104	97	1.7	6.6	6.8	170.0	124.0	150.0	181.2
Bahrain	224	441	435	537	726	706	3.5	7.7	6.4	2.8	11.0	n.a.	10.2
Egypt	3,827	2,988	2,821	79	45	45	7.2	3.4	3.2	445.0	448.5	254.0	230.0
Gaza and Jericho	n.a.	n.a.	n.a.	n.a.	n.a.	n.a.	n.a.	n.a.	n.a.	n.a.	n.a.	n.a.	35.0
Iran	10,523	5,711	7,329	236	85	108	18.0	6.1	7.5	610.0	513.0	350.0	240.0
Iraq	13,752	1,500	1,470	897	66	64	37.9	7.6	9.7	1,000.0	429.0	650.0	50.0
Israel	7,486	8,846	9,373	1,768	1,465	1,512	21.2	8.9	8.9	142.0	172.5	400.0	8.0
Jordan	892	588	510	255	95	76	15.9	7.7	6.9	70.3	103.9	35.0	45.0
Kuwait	2,661	3,275	3,210	1,556	1,744	1,628	9.1	11.1	9.8	12.0	15.3	23.7	5.0
Lebanon	296	563	553	111	164	168	9.0	3.4	3.5	17.4	63.6	n.a.	13.0
Libya	2,000	1,311	1,176	531	236	210	6.2	5.1	3.2	73.0	76.0	40.0	0.5
Mauritania	77	24	23	46	9	9	6.5	2.0	2.8	8.5	15.7	n.a.	5.0
Morocco	950	1,761	1,680	43	62	59	5.4	5.1	5.1	149.0	198.5	150.0	42.0
Oman	3,196	1,631	1,733	1,998	677	682	20.8	10.9	10.0	29.2	43.5	n.a.	4.4
Qatar	445	1,468	1,427	1,411	2,156	2,065	6.0	13.7	11.7	6.0	12.3	n.a.	n.a.
Saudi Arabia	26,618	21,876	18,321	2,306	1,041	848	19.6	15.5	10.1	62.5	201.5	20.0	15.5
Syria	5,161	989	760	491	63	47	16.4	5.6	5.6	402.5	316.0	396.0	108.8
Tunisia	618	348	350	87	37	36	5.0	1.7	1.7	35.1	35.0	35.0	12.0
UAE	3,027	3,187	3,338	2,162	1,203	1,368	7.6	6.2	5.9	43.0	65.0	n.a.	1.0
Yemen	725	429	489	72	24	27	9.9	6.7	7.8	64.1	66.3	40.0	70.0
Total	**83,891**	**60,023**	**57,931**	**771**	**526**	**513**	**11.9**	**7.1**	**6.7**	**3,342.4**	**2,910.6**	**2,508.7**	**1,076.6**
Central and South Asia													
Afghanistan	425	250	245	24	11	10	8.7	14.1	13.0	47.0	400.0	n.a.	n.a.
Bangladesh	370	667	670	4	5	5	1.4	1.9	1.8	91.3	137.0	n.a.	n.a.
Bhutan	8	20	20	18	10	10	4.9	5.3	5.6	3.0	6.0	n.a.	n.a.

Central and South Asia contd • East Asia and Australasia • Caribbean

	Defence Expenditure US$m			US$ per capita			% of GDP			Numbers in Armed Forces (000)		Estimated Reservists (000)	Para-military (000)
	1985	1999	2000	1985	1999	2000	1985	1999	2000	1985	2000	2000	2000
India	9,281	13,895	14,472	12	14	14	3.0	3.2	3.1	1,260.0	1,303.0	528.4	1,069.0
Kazakstan	n.a.	291	357	n.a.	18	22	n.a.	2.0	2.0	n.a.	64.0	n.a.	34.5
Kyrgyzstan	n.a.	35	31	n.a.	8	7	n.a.	3.2	2.4	n.a.	9.0	57.0	5.0
Maldives	5	41	44	27	166	176	3.9	9.6	9.5	n.a.	n.a.	n.a.	5.0
Nepal	53	42	49	3	2	2	1.5	0.8	0.9	25.0	50.0	n.a.	40.0
Pakistan	3,076	3,523	3,579	32	23	23	6.9	5.7	5.8	482.8	612.0	513.0	288.0
Sri Lanka	338	807	862	21	43	46	3.8	5.1	5.3	21.6	115.0	4.2	88.6
Tajikistan	n.a.	92	80	n.a.	15	13	n.a.	7.6	6.5	n.a.	6.0	n.a.	1.2
Turkmenistan	n.a.	144	173	n.a.	29	35	n.a.	4.2	4.0	n.a.	14.5	n.a.	n.a.
Uzbekistan	n.a.	1,230	1,481	n.a.	52	61	n.a.	7.7	8.0	n.a.	59.1	n.a.	20.0
Total	**13,557**	**21,038**	**22,064**	**18**	**30**	**33**	**4.3**	**5.4**	**5.2**	**1,930.7**	**2,775.6**	**1,102.6**	**1,551.3**
East Asia and Australasia													
Australia	8,068	7,775	6,952	512	415	368	3.4	1.9	1.9	70.4	50.6	20.2	1.0
Brunei	304	402	348	1,356	1,252	1,060	6.0	6.7	5.8	4.1	5.0	0.7	3.8
Cambodia	n.a.	176	192	n.a.	16	17	n.a.	5.1	6.1	35.0	140.0	n.a.	220.0
China	29,414	39,889	41,167	28	32	32	7.9	5.4	5.3	3,900.0	2,810.0	600.0	1,100.0
Fiji	21	35	32	30	44	39	1.2	1.9	2.1	2.7	3.5	6.0	n.a.
Indonesia	3,469	1,502	1,493	21	7	7	2.8	1.1	1.0	278.1	297.0	400.0	195.0
Japan	31,847	40,383	44,417	264	319	351	1.0	0.9	1.0	243.0	236.7	49.2	12.0
Korea, North	6,158	2,100	2,049	302	87	95	23.0	14.3	13.9	838.0	1,055.0	4,700.0	189.0
Korea, South	9,323	12,088	12,496	227	257	263	5.1	3.0	2.8	598.0	683.0	4,500.0	4.5
Laos	81	22	19	23	4	4	7.8	2.3	1.1	53.7	29.1	n.a.	100.0
Malaysia	2,614	3,158	2,708	168	141	122	5.6	4.0	3.1	110.0	96.0	49.8	20.1
Mongolia	51	19	19	27	7	7	9.0	1.9	2.0	33.0	9.1	140.0	7.2
Myanmar	1,302	1,995	2,058	35	44	45	5.1	6.9	0.6	186.0	343.8	n.a.	85.3
New Zealand	957	824	788	294	217	204	2.9	1.6	1.5	12.4	9.2	5.5	n.a.
Papua New Guinea	53	46	55	15	10	11	1.5	1.4	1.2	3.2	4.4	n.a.	n.a.
Philippines	702	1,627	1,497	13	22	20	1.4	2.1	1.9	114.8	106.0	131.0	42.5
Singapore	1,760	4,696	4,707	688	1,364	1,320	6.7	5.6	4.9	55.0	60.5	213.8	108.0
Taiwan	9,541	14,964	17,248	492	687	785	7.0	5.2	5.6	444.0	370.0	1,657.5	26.7
Thailand	2,777	2,638	2,464	54	43	40	5.0	1.9	2.0	235.3	301.0	200.0	115.6
Vietnam	3,556	890	931	58	11	12	19.4	3.0	3.0	1,027.0	484.0	3,000.0	40.0
Total	**112,000**	**135,230**	**141,643**	**242**	**249**	**240**	**6.4**	**3.8**	**3.3**	**8,243.7**	**7,093.9**	**15,673.7**	**2,270.7**
Caribbean, Central and Latin America													
Caribbean													
Antigua and Barbuda	3	4	4	42	60	58.7	0.5	0.6	0.6	0.1	0.2	0.1	n.a.
Bahamas	14	26	25	61	97	94.4	0.5	0.7	0.6	0.5	0.9	n.a.	2.3
Barbados	17	12	13	77	44	47.9	0.9	0.5	0.5	1.0	0.6	0.4	n.a.
Cuba	2,366	750	735	235	67	65.6	9.6	4.8	4.5	161.5	58.0	39.0	26.5

Analyses and **Tables**

Caribbean contd • Central America • South America • Horn of Africa • Central Africa

| | Defence Expenditure | | | | | | | | | Numbers in Armed Forces (000) | | Estimated Reservists (000) | Para-military (000) |
| | US$m | | | US$ per capita | | | % of GDP | | | | | | |
	1985	1999	2000	1985	1999	2000	1985	1999	2000	1985	2000	2000	2000
Dominican Republic	76	114	112	12	14	13.2	1.1	0.9	0.8	22.2	24.5	n.a.	15.0
Haiti	46	50	48	8	6	5.9	1.5	1.6	1.5	6.9	n.a.	n.a.	5.3
Jamaica	30	51	49	13	20	19.1	0.9	0.8	0.7	2.1	2.8	1.0	0.2
Trinidad and Tobago	108	40	35	91	31	26.8	1.4	0.6	0.5	2.1	2.7	n.a.	4.8
Central America													
Belize	6	17	17	36	72	69.1	1.4	2.5	2.4	0.6	1.1	0.7	n.a.
Costa Rica	43	69	84	17	18	21.0	0.7	0.7	0.8	n.a.	n.a.	n.a.	8.4
El Salvador	373	171	168	78	28	26.8	4.4	1.7	1.6	41.7	16.8	15.0	12.0
Guatemala	174	149	115	22	13	10.1	1.8	1.1	0.8	31.7	31.4	35.0	21.5
Honduras	107	95	93	24	15	14.4	2.1	1.8	1.6	16.6	8.3	60.0	6.0
Mexico	1,839	4,289	5,229	23	44	52.9	0.7	0.9	1.0	129.1	192.8	300.0	15.0
Nicaragua	327	25	26	100	5	5.1	17.4	0.9	0.8	62.9	16.0	n.a.	n.a.
Panama	133	128	127	61	45	44.6	2.0	1.3	1.3	12.0	n.a.	n.a.	11.8
South America													
Argentina	5,366	5,418	4,658	176	149	125.8	3.8	1.9	1.7	108.0	71.1	375.0	31.2
Bolivia	188	149	128	29	18	15.7	2.0	1.7	1.4	27.6	32.5	n.a.	37.1
Brazil	5,738	15,978	17,545	42	95	103.1	1.8	2.6	2.8	276.0	287.6	1,115.0	385.6
Chile	2,380	2,586	2,891	197	172	190.0	10.6	3.2	3.4	101.0	87.0	50.0	29.5
Colombia	628	2,164	1,955	22	53	46.2	1.6	2.8	2.4	66.2	152.0	60.7	95.0
Ecuador	421	339	314	45	27	24.8	1.8	1.8	1.6	42.5	57.5	100.0	0.3
Guyana	47	7	7	59	8	7.6	6.8	0.9	0.8	6.6	1.6	1.6	1.5
Paraguay	89	128	121	24	24	21.9	1.3	1.4	1.3	14.4	20.2	164.5	14.8
Peru	950	888	861	51	35	33.5	4.5	1.4	1.3	128.0	115.0	188.0	78.0
Suriname	12	11	11	32	27	26.1	2.4	2.7	2.7	2.0	2.0	n.a.	n.a.
Uruguay	354	317	356	117	96	106.8	3.5	2.3	2.6	31.9	23.7	n.a.	0.9
Venezuela	1,221	1,328	1,377	71	56	57.0	2.1	1.6	1.5	49.0	56.0	8.0	23.0
Total	23,055	35,304	37,104	63	48	47.7	3.2	1.6	1.6	1,344.2	1,262.3	2,512.4	819.7
Sub-Saharan Africa													
Horn of Africa													
Djibouti	47	22	23	110	30	30.0	7.9	5.0	5.0	3.0	8.4	n.a.	4.2
Eritrea	n.a.	309	206	n.a.	81	53.6	n.a.	43.1	31.5	n.a.	200.0	120.0	n.a.
Ethiopia	662	444	448	16	8	7.6	17.9	7.1	6.8	217.0	352.5	n.a.	n.a.
Somali Republic	68	40	39	13	6	5.9	6.2	4.6	4.5	62.7	50.0	n.a.	n.a.
Sudan	158	424	568	7	14	19.3	3.2	4.9	6.1	56.6	104.5	n.a.	15.0
Central Africa													
Burundi	52	69	65	11	10	9.8	3.0	6.1	5.6	5.2	40.0	n.a.	5.5
Cameroon	236	154	154	23	10	10.2	1.4	1.5	1.4	7.3	13.1	n.a.	9.0
Cape Verde	5	7	7	17	16	17.4	0.9	2.7	2.7	7.7	1.1	n.a.	0.1
Central African Republic	26	45	43	10	13	11.9	1.4	4.0	3.7	2.3	3.1	n.a.	2.3

Central Africa contd • **East Africa** • **West Africa** • **Southern Africa**

	Defence Expenditure US$m			Defence Expenditure US$ per capita			% of GDP			Numbers in Armed Forces (000)		Estimated Reservists (000)	Para-military (000)
	1985	1999	2000	1985	1999	2000	1985	1999	2000	1985	2000	2000	2000
Chad	55	47	47	11	6	6.2	2.9	2.9	2.8	12.2	30.1	n.a.	4.5
Congo	83	73	72	44	25	24.5	1.9	2.7	2.5	8.7	10.0	n.a.	5.0
DROC	120	411	392	4	9	8.0	1.5	8.5	8.4	48.0	55.9	n.a.	37.0
Equatorial Guinea	4	10	12	12	19	23.8	2.0	1.9	1.7	2.2	1.3	n.a.	0.3
Gabon	117	135	123	117	92	81.3	1.8	2.4	2.2	2.4	4.7	n.a.	2.0
Rwanda	49	135	109	8	16	12.6	1.9	6.2	4.7	5.2	70.0	n.a.	6.0
East Africa													
Kenya	379	327	307	19	11	10.2	3.1	3.1	2.9	13.7	22.2	n.a.	5.0
Madagascar	80	43	41	8	3	2.6	2.0	0.8	0.8	21.1	21.0	n.a.	7.5
Mauritius	4	91	87	4	79	75.3	0.3	1.9	1.8	1.0	n.a.	n.a.	1.8
Seychelles	12	11	10	182	150	132.8	2.1	1.8	1.8	1.2	0.2	n.a.	0.3
Tanzania	207	141	141	9	4	4.2	4.4	1.7	1.8	40.4	34.0	80.0	1.4
Uganda	79	199	247	5	9	11.3	1.8	2.5	3.0	20.0	50.0	n.a.	0.6
West Africa													
Benin	31	34	36	8	6	5.9	1.1	1.4	1.4	4.5	4.8	n.a.	2.5
Burkina Faso	50	75	68	6	6	5.7	1.1	2.1	1.8	4.0	6.8	n.a.	4.5
Côte d'Ivoire	113	130	132	11	9	8.9	0.8	1.0	0.9	13.2	8.4	12.0	7.0
Gambia, The	3	16	15	4	13	11.3	1.5	3.5	3.2	0.5	0.8	n.a.	n.a.
Ghana	93	121	95	7	6	4.7	1.0	1.2	0.9	15.1	7.0	n.a.	1.0
Guinea	77	60	57	12	8	7.6	1.8	1.7	1.5	9.9	9.7	n.a.	9.6
Guinea Bissau	16	6	6	18	5	4.8	5.7	1.9	1.7	8.6	7.3	n.a.	2.0
Liberia	41	25	25	19	8	7.8	2.4	5.6	5.6	6.8	15.0	n.a.	n.a.
Mali	44	34	29	6	3	2.6	1.4	1.2	1.0	4.9	7.4	n.a.	7.8
Niger	18	28	26	3	3	2.5	0.5	1.7	1.5	2.2	5.3	n.a.	5.4
Nigeria	1,112	2,237	2,340	12	20	20.2	3.4	4.5	4.5	94.0	76.5	n.a.	30.0
Senegal	93	81	68	14	9	7.2	1.1	1.6	1.2	10.1	9.4	n.a.	6.0
Sierra Leone	7	11	9	2	2	1.8	1.0	1.5	1.2	3.1	3.0	n.a.	0.8
Togo	28	34	30	9	7	6.6	1.3	2.3	2.0	3.6	7.0	n.a.	0.8
Southern Africa													
Angola	959	1,005	1,250	109	81	97.1	15.1	16.5	19.2	49.5	107.5	n.a.	10.0
Botswana	55	259	245	51	163	150.8	1.1	5.2	5.5	4.0	9.0	n.a.	1.0
Lesotho	68	34	29	44	16	13.4	4.6	4.2	4.0	2.0	2.0	n.a.	n.a.
Malawi	31	27	26	4	2	2.3	1.0	1.8	1.8	5.3	5.0	n.a.	1.0
Mozambique	354	94	85	26	6	5.1	8.5	4.2	3.6	15.8	6.1	n.a.	n.a.
Namibia	n.a.	120	103	n.a.	70	59.6	n.a.	4.4	3.6	n.a.	9.0	n.a.	0.1
South Africa	4,256	1,755	1,912	127	44	47.4	2.7	1.3	1.6	106.4	63.4	87.4	8.2
Zambia	59	88	65	9	10	7.1	1.1	2.5	1.8	16.2	21.6	n.a.	1.4
Zimbabwe	252	418	394	30	36	33.7	5.6	6.1	6.1	41.0	40.0	n.a.	21.8
Total	10,206	9,830	10,184	28	26	24.4	3.1	4.4	4.0	958.5	1,504.1	299.4	228.4

Global Totals

	Defence Expenditure US$m			US$ per capita			% of GDP			Numbers in Armed Forces (000)		Estimated Reservists (000)	Para-military (000)
	1985	1999	2000	1985	1999	2000	1985	1999	2000	1985	2000	2000	2000
Global Totals													
NATO	620,542	473,834	464,654	540	388	368.2	4.0	2.2	2.2	5,809.9	3,842.4	4,942.1	836.8
				984	605	589.0	4.7	2.6	2.5				
Non-NATO Europe	25,550	19,984	19,062	251	131	129.7	4.3	3.2	2.8	1,024.1	1,328.5	5,322.4	462.5
				n.a.	108	102.8	n.a.	1.8	1.7				
Russia	n.a.	56,800	58,810	n.a.	386	400.2	n.a.	5.1	5.0	n.a.	1,520.0	2,400.0	423.0
Soviet Union	364,715	n.a.	n.a.	1,308	n.a.	n.a.	16.1	n.a.	n.a.	5,300.0	n.a.	n.a.	n.a.
Middle East and North Africa	83,891	60,023	57,931	771	526	513.5	11.9	7.1	6.7	3,342.4	2,910.6	2,508.7	1,076.6
				393	192	185.3	15.1	8.1	7.3				
Central and South Asia	13,557	21,038	22,064	18	30	32.6	4.3	5.4	5.2	1,930.7	2,775.6	1,102.6	1,551.3
				n.a.	15	15.5	n.a.	3.5	3.5				
East Asia and Australasia	112,000	135,230	141,643	242	249	240.1	6.4	3.8	3.3	8,243.7	7,093.9	15,673.7	2,270.7
				67	67	69.3	2.3	2.0	1.9				
Caribbean, Central and Latin America	23,055	35,304	37,104	63	48	47.7	3.2	1.6	1.6	1,344.2	1,262.3	2,512.4	819.7
				58	70	72.3	1.9	1.9	1.9				
Sub-Saharan Africa	10,206	9,830	10,184	28	26	24.4	3.1	4.4	4.0	958.5	1,504.1	299.4	228.4
				23	16	16.2	3.3	2.9	3.0				
Global Totals	1,253,517	812,043	811,452	399	223	219.3	6.7	4.1	3.8	27,953.5	22,237.4	34,761.3	7,669.0
				298	136	133.1	5.2	2.4	2.3				

Note Under Defence Expenditure per Capita and Defence Expenditure as a proportion of GDP, the top figure (123.4) is the arithmetic mean of individual country values, and the bottom number (123.4) is the arithmetic mean of the sum of regional and global totals.

Table 38 **Conventional Armed Forces in Europe** (CFE) **Treaty**

Manpower and Treaty Limited Equipment (TLE)
current holdings and CFE national ceilings on the forces of the Treaty members

Current holdings are derived from data declared as of 1 January 2001 and so may differ from *The Military Balance* listings

	Manpower Holding	Manpower Ceiling	Tanks[2] Holding	Tanks[2] Ceiling	ACV[2] Holding	ACV[2] Ceiling	Artillery[2] Holding	Artillery[2] Ceiling	Attack Helicopters Holding	Attack Helicopters Ceiling	Combat Aircraft[3] Holding	Combat Aircraft[3] Ceiling
Non-NATO												
Armenia	60,000	60,000	105	220	146	220	229	285	7	50	6	100
Azerbaijan	69,966	70,000	220	220	210	220	282	285	15	50	48	100
Belarus	83,083	100,000	1,683	1,800	2,496	2,600	1,473	1,615	58	80	218	294
Bulgaria	77,183	104,000	1,475	1,475	1,931	2,000	1,738	1,750	43	67	232	235
Georgia	24,529	40,000	90	220	114	220	109	285	3	50	7	100
Moldova	8,143	20,000	0	210	209	210	151	250	0	50	0	50
Romania	158,722	230,000	1,373	1,375	2,081	2,100	1,381	1,475	15	120	309	430
Russia [5]	653,299	1,450,000	5,330	6,350	9,542	11,280	6,171	6,315	587	855	2,636	3,416
Slovakia	38,929	46,667	272	478	622	683	383	383	19	40	82	100
Ukraine	310,000	450,000	3,928	4,080	4,670	5,050	3,726	4,040	240	330	874	1,090
NATO												
Belgium	38,785	70,000	140	300	565	989	282	288	46	46	135	209
Canada	0	10,660	0	77	0	263	0	32	0	13	0	90
Czech Republic [4]	53,636	93,333	652	957	1,211	1,367	648	767	34	50	97	230
Denmark	25,773	39,000	238	335	296	336	475	446	12	18	68	82
France	197,070	325,000	1,151	1,226	3,365	3,700	805	1,192	321	374	591	800
Germany	275,211	345,000	2,423	3,444	2,352	3,281	2,051	2,255	204	280	406	765
Greece	158,621	158,621	1,733	1,735	2,178	2,498	1,903	1,920	20	65	521	650
Hungary [4]	33,885	100,000	753	835	1,479	1,700	839	840	51	108	107	180
Italy	196,597	315,000	1,320	1,267	2,935	3,172	1,391	1,818	133	142	546	618
Netherlands	36,638	80,000	357	520	685	864	391	485	12	50	164	230
Norway	18,718	32,000	170	170	253	275	184	491	0	24	73	100
Poland [4]	194,190	234,000	1,668	1,730	1,438	2,150	1,554	1,610	108	130	234	460
Portugal	36,126	75,000	187	300	330	430	363	450	0	26	101	160
Spain	160,372	300,000	684	750	978	1,588	1,094	1,276	28	80	199	310
Turkey [5]	515,380	530,000	2,478	2,795	2,966	3,120	2,953	3,523	28	130	352	750
UK	188,328	260,000	612	843	2,355	3,017	418	583	228	350	504	855
US	99,382	250,000	657	1,812	1,706	3,037	326	1,553	134	396	237	784

Notes
[1] The adaptation of the CFE abandons the group structure (North Atlantic Group, Budapest/Tashkent Group) for a system of national and territorial ceilings. The amendment enters into force when CFE States Parties have ratified the change.
[2] Includes TLE with land-based maritime forces (Marines, Naval Infantry etc.)
[3] Does not include land-based maritime aircraft for which a separate limit has been set.
[4] Cz, Hu and Pl became NATO members on 12 March 1999.
[5] Manpower and TLE is for that in the Atlantic to the Urals (ATTU) zone only.

Definition In this table, a 'non-state armed group' is taken as being an organised and armed opposition force with a recognised political goal, which acts independently from state or government. Groups are only included if they have an effective command structure. The definition covers groups that might be variously described as guerrillas, militia forces, paramilitary or self-defence groups and also terrorist groups with political objectives that have caused significant damage and casualties over several years.

The table only includes non-state armed groups that are active or have recently been active and which represent, or have represented, a significant threat to states and governments. Groups operating in protracted conflicts where there is no internationally recognised government, such as in Afghanistan and Somalia, are excluded, as are armed groups with solely criminal objectives.

Notes

[1] Figures provided for strs are estimates

[2] **A** active, **C** cease-fire, **D** dormant (inactive for the past 12 months)

[3] Distinct Kurdish gps

Origin	Organisation • aka	Established	Strength[1]	Status[2]	Operates	Aims (Remarks)
Gr	**17th November Revolutionary Organisation**	1974	n.k.	A	Athens	Remove US bases from Gr; withdraw Tu tps from Cy; sever Gr ties to NATO and EU (Radical leftist)
	NATO AND NON-NATO EUROPE					
FYROM	**National Liberation Army** (NLA)	2001	500–1,000	A	north FYROM	Protect ethnic Albanian rights
Mol	**Dniestr**		5–10,000	D	Dniestr	Separate state of Trans-Dniestr
Sp	**Euskadi ta Askatasuna** (ETA)	1959	n.k.	A	Basque regions, Sp	Independent homeland on Marxist principles in Basque autonomous regions
Tu[3]	**Partiya Karkeren Kurdistan** (PKK)	1978	4–5,000	C	Tu, Europe, Asia, M. East	Independent Kurdish state in south-east Tu (Marxist–Leninist; in 1999 'peace initiative' claimed halt to use of force)
UK	**Continuity Irish Republican Army** (CIRA) • **Continuity Army Council**	1994	50+	A	UK, Irl	'Reunify Irl' (Armed wing of Republican Sinn Fein. Opposes Sinn Fein's adoption of Jul 1997 cease-fire)
UK	**Irish National Liberation Army** (INLA) • **People's Republican Army • Catholic Reaction Force**	1974	150	A	UK, Irl	Remove British forces from N. Ireland and unite it with Irl
UK	**Irish Republican Army** (IRA) • **Provisional Irish Republican Army** (PIRA/the Provos)	1969	n.k.	C	UK, Irl	Remove British forces from N. Ireland and unite it with Irl (Armed wing of Sinn Fein)
UK	**Loyalist Volunteer Force** (LVF)	1996	150+	C	UK, Irl	No political settlement with nationalists in N. Ireland (Faction of UVF)
UK	**Orange Volunteers**	1970s	20	C	UK, Irl	No political settlement with nationalists in N. Ireland
UK	**Real Irish Republican Army** (RIRA) • **True IRA**	1998	100+	A	UK, Irl	Oppose Sinn Fein's adoption of Jul 1997 cease-fire (Armed wing of 32 County Sovereignty Committee)
UK	**Red Hand Defenders** (RHD)	1998	20	A	UK, Irl	No political settlement with nationalists in N. Ireland (Hardliners split from loyalists observing cease-fire)

Origin	Organisation • aka	Established	Strength[1]	Status[2]	Operates	Aims (Remarks)
UK	Ulster Defence Association (UDA) • Ulster Freedom Fighters (UFF)	1971	200+	A	UK, Irl	Protect Loyalist community (Largest Loyalist paramilitary gp in N. Ireland. Backed 1998 Good Friday Agreement. Armed wing of Ulster Democratic Party)
UK	Ulster Volunteer Force (UVF) • Protestant Action Force • Protestant Action Group	1966	150+	A	UK, Irl	Safeguard N. Ireland's constitutional position within UK. Protect Loyalist community (Armed wing of Progressive Unionist Party)
FRY	Liberation Army of Presevo, Medvedja and Bujanovac (UCPMB)	2000	800	A	Presevo Valley	Annex Kosovo for ethnic-Albanians from south Serbia and west and north FYROM
RUSSIA						
RF	Chechen Rebels		2–3,000	A	Chechnya, Dagestan	Independent Islamic state (Many Muslim mercenaries)
MIDDLE EAST AND NORTH AFRICA						
Ag	Front Islamique du Salut (FIS) • Armée Islamique du Salut (AIS)	1989	n.k.	C	Ag	Socialist republic in Ag within framework of Islamic principles
Ag	Groupe Islamique Armée (GIA)	1992	1,500	A	Ag	Fundamentalist Islamic state in Ag (Refused Jan 2000 peace plan)
Ag	Groupe Salafiste pour la Prédication et le Combat (GSPC) • al-Safayya	1998	500	A	Ag	Fundamentalist Islamic state in Ag (Splinter faction of GIA)
Et	al-Jihad • Egyptian Islamic Jihad • Jihad Group • Islamic Jihad • Vanguards of Conquest	1973	1,000+	A	Cairo area	Islamic state in Et
Et	Islamic Group • al-Gama'at al-Islamiyya	1970s	1,000+	A	south Et	Islamic state in Et (Largest militant gp in Et)
Ir[3]	Kurdish Democratic Party of Iran (KDP)	1973	1,200–1,800	A	Ir	Kurdish autonomy in Ir
Ir[3]	Kurdistan Organisation of the Communist Party of Iran (KOMOLA)	1967	200	A	Ir	Communist govt in Ir (Formed Communist Party of Iran in 1983)
Ir	National Liberation Army (NLA) • People's Mujahideen of Iran (PMOI) • National Council of Resistance (NCR)	1965	6–8,000	A	Ir	'Democratic, socialist, Islamic republic in Ir' (Largest and most active armed Ir dissident gp. Armed wing of Mujahideen-e Khalq Organisation)
Irq[3]	Kurdish Democratic Party (KDP)	1946	15,000	A	Irq	Overthrow Irq govt (Ongoing conflict with PUK)
Irq[3]	Patriotic Union of Kurdistan (PUK)	1975	10,000	A	Irq	'Revitalise resistance and rebuild a democratic Kurdish society' (Evolved into a political movement, with political party structure. Ongoing conflict with KDP)

Origin	Organisation • aka	Established	Strength[1]	Status[2]	Operates	Aims (Remarks)
Irq	**Supreme Council for Islamic Revolution (SCIRI)**	1982	4–8,000	A	south Irq	'Oppose Irq aggression against Ir' (Shi'ite; mutual agreement signed with PUK against Irq)
RL	**Hizbollah (Party of God) • Islamic Jihad • Revolutionary Justice Organisation • Organisation of the Oppressed on Earth**	1982	2,000+	A	Bekaa Valley, Beirut, south RL	Iranian-style Islamic republic in RL; all non-Islamic influences removed from area (Shi'ite; formed to resist Il occupation of south RL with political representation in RL Assembly.)
Mor	**Frente Popular para la Liberación de Saguia el-Hamra y del Rio de Oro (Polisario Front)**	1973	3–6,000	A	Mor	Independent W. Sahara (Armed wing of Sahrawi People's Liberation Army)
GzJ	**Abu Nidal Organisation (ANO) • Fatah Revolutionary Council • Black September • Arab Revolutionary Brigades • Revolutionary Organisation of Socialist Muslims**	1974	300	A	international	Destroy Il (Ops in LAR and Et shut down by govts in 1999)
GzJ	**Al Saiqa**	1966	300	A	GzJ, Il	Mil wing of GzJ faction of Syr Ba'ath Party (Nominally part of PLO)
GzJ	**Arab Liberation Front**	1969	300	A	GzJ, Il	Achieve national goals of GzJ (Faction of PLO formed by leadership of Irq Al-Ba'ath party)
GzJ	**Democratic Front for the Liberation of Palestine (DFLP)**	1969	100+	A	GzJ, Il	Achieve GzJ national goals through revolution (Marxist–Leninist; splintered from PFLP)
GzJ	**Izz al-Din al-Qassem (IDQ)**	1987	500	A	GzJ, Il	Replace Il with Islamic state in GzJ (Armed wing of Harakat al-Muqawama al-Islamiyya (Hamas); separate from overt org)
GzJ	**Palestine Islamic Jihad (PIJ)**	1970s	ε500	A	GzJ, Il	Destroy Il with holy war and establish Islamic state in GzJ (One of the more extreme GzJ gps)
GzJ	**Palestine Liberation Front (PLF)**	1977	3–400	A	GzJ, Il	Armed struggle against Il (Splintered from PFLP)
GzJ	**Popular Front for the Liberation of Palestine (PFLP)**	1967	100+	A	GzJ, Il	Armed struggle against Il (Marxist–Leninist)
GzJ	**Popular Front for the Liberation of Palestine – General Command (PFLP–GC)**	1968	300–	A	GzJ, Il	Armed struggle against Il (Marxist–Leninist; Split from PFLP to focus on fighting rather than politics)

CENTRAL AND **SOUTH ASIA**

Origin	Organisation • aka	Established	Strength[1]	Status[2]	Operates	Aims (Remarks)
Afg	**al-Qaida**	1980s	1,000+	A	international	'Re-establish the Muslim state' worldwide (International network controlled from Afg by Osama Bin Laden)
Ind	**Harakat ul-Mujahideen (HUM)**	1993	450–500	A	Kashmir	Pro-Pak Islamic gp
Ind	**Hizb-ul-Mujahideen**	1989	1–1,200	A	Kashmir	Pro-Pak Islamic gp (Armed wing of Jamaat-e-Islami, Pak's largest Islamic party)

Origin	Organisation • aka	Established ⇩	Strength[1]	Status[2] ⇩	Operates	Aims (Remarks)
Ind	**Tehrik-e-Jihad**	1997	n.k.	A	Kashmir	Self-determination for Kashmir; Kashmir to join Pak
N	**Communist Party of Nepal (Maoist)**	1949	1–1,500	A	N	Overthrow N's constitutional monarchy; replace with Maoist republic (Declared 'People's War' in 1996)
Pak	**Al-Badr Mujahideen**	1998	n.k.	A	Kashmir	Liberate' Kashmir from Ind forces (Split from Hizb-ul Mujahideen)
Pak	**Lashkar-e-Tayyaba (LT)**	1992	300	A	Jammu, Kashmir	Create independent Islamic state in Kashmir (Armed wing of Markaz-ud-Dawa-wal-Irshad (MDI))
Ska	**Liberation Tigers of Tamil Eelam (LTTE) •** **World Tamil Association • World Tamil Movement**	1972	6,000	A	north and east Ska	Independent Tamil state (Began armed conflict in 1983. Now use mixture of terrorist and guerrilla tactics)
Tkm	**Islamic Movement of Turkestan (IMT)**	2001	n.k.	A	Uz, Tjk, Ir, Kgz, Afg	Fundamentalist Islamic states in all C. Asia (Coalition of Islamic militants from Tkm and other C. Asian states. Linked to IMU)
Uz	**Islamic Movement of Uzbekistan (IMU)**	1996	2,000+	A	Uz, Tjk, Ir, Kgz, Afg	Fundamentalist Islamic state in Uz (Coalition of Islamic militants from Uz and other C. Asian states. Linked to IMT)

EAST ASIA AND AUSTRALASIA

Origin	Organisation • aka	Established ⇩	Strength[1]	Status[2] ⇩	Operates	Aims (Remarks)
PRC	**Uighur Separatist Movement**	1990	n.k.	A	north-west PRC, C. Asia	Establish separate E. Turkestan state for Uighur population
Indo	**Gerakin Aceh Merdeka •** **Free Aceh Movement • Free Aceh •** **Aceh Security Disturbance Movement**	1976	2,000	A	Aceh	Independent Islamic state in Aceh (Underground since 1996)
Indo	**Laskar Jihad**	2000	2,000	A	Indo	Remove Christians from Maluku; Islamic state in Indo
Indo	**Organisasi Papua Merdeka (OPM)**	1962	150	A	Indo	Independence for W. Papua
J	**Aum Supreme Truth •** **Aum Shinrikyo**	1987	1,500–2,000	A	J	'Take over J and then the world' (Released Sarin on Tokyo subway in 1995 and other chemical attacks in J)
My	**All Burma Students Democratic Front**	1988	2,000	A	My	'Liberate My from dictatorship; establish democracy and transform into federal union'
My	**Democratic Karen Buddhist Army (DKBA)**	1994	1–500	C	My, Th	Independence for Karen minority (Splinter gp of Karen National Union (KNU). Armed wing of Democratic Karen Buddhist Organisation. Ongoing conflict with KNLA)
My	**Kachin Independence Army (KIA)**	1961	8,000	C	north My, Khmer range	Promote Buddhism (Armed wing of Kachin Independence Organisation)

Origin	Organisation • aka	Established ⇩	Strength[1] ⇩	Status[2] ⇩	Operates	Aims (Remarks)
My	**Karen National Liberation Army** (KNLA)	1947	4,000	A	Th border	Establish Karen State with right to self-determination (Armed wing of KNU. Ongoing conflict with DKBA)
My	**Mong Thai Army** (MTA)	1964	3,000	C	Th border	Protect Shan population
My	**Mon National Liberation Army** (MNLA)	1958	1,000	C	Th border	Represent Mon minority (Armed wing of New Mon State Party)
My	**National Democratic Alliance Army** (NDAA)	1989	1,000	C	east Shan State, PRC–Lao border	Oppose My mil rule (Formerly part of Communist Party of Burma (CPB))
My	**Palaung State Liberation Army** (PSLA)	1963	700	C	north of Hsipaw	Greater autonomy for Palaung population
My	**Shan State Army** (SSA) • **Shan State Progress Army** (SSPA)	1964	3,000	C	south Shan State	Freedom and democracy for Shan State
My	**United Wa State Army** (UWSA)	1989	12,000	C	Wa Hills	Splinter gp of CPB
Pi	**Abu Sayyaf Group** (ASG)	1991	1,500–	A	south Pi	Independent Islamic state in west Mindanao and Sulu (Split from Moro National Liberation Front (MNLF))
Pi	**Alex Boncayao Brigade** (ABB)	1980s	500	A	Manila, central Pi	Urban hit squad of Philippines Communist Party (Claimed alliance with the Revolutionary Proletarian Army in 1997)
Pi	**Bangsa Moro Army**	1970s	n.k.	C	south Pi	Muslim separatist movement (Armed wing of MNLF)
Pi	**Moro Islamic Liberation Front** (MILF)	1977	10,000–	C	south Pi	Independent Islamic state in Bangsa Moro and neighbouring islands (Split from MNLF. Signed cease-fire with Pi govt 7 Aug 2001)
Pi	**Moro Islamic Reformist Group**	1978	900–	A	south Pi	Independent Islamic state in south Pi (Split from MNLF)
Pi	**New People's Army** (NPA)	1969	9,500–	A	rural Luzon, Visayas and Mindanao	Overthrow Pi govt (Armed wing of Philippines Communist Party. Ended peace talks with govt after 1999 Pi–US agreement to resume joint mil exercises)
CARIBBEAN AND **LATIN AMERICA**						
Co	**Autodefensas Unidas de Colombia** (AUC)	1997	8,000	A	north and north-west Co	Coordinating gp for paramilitaries (Right-wing. Co govt refused to grant same 'political status' as guerrillas)
Co	**Ejercito de Liberación Nacional** (ELN)	1964	3,500–	A	north, north-east, south-west Co	Anti-US 'Maoist–Marxist–Leninist' gp (Peace talks with govt since 1999)
Co	**Ejercito Popular de Liberación** (EPL)	1967	500	A	Co	'Rid Co of US imperialism and Co oligarchies'

Origin	Organisation • aka	Established	Strength[1]	Status[2]	Operates	Aims (Remarks)
Co	**Fuerzas Armadas Revolucionarias de Colombia** (FARC)	1964	17,000–	A	Co	'Overthrow govt and ruling classes' (Armed wing of Colombian Communist Party)
Pe	**Movimiento Revolucionario Tupac Amaru** (MRTA)	1983	600	A	Pe	Establish Marxist regime and 'rid Pe of imperialist elements' (Less active since Pe govt's 1999 counter-terrorist op)
Pe	**Sendero Luminoso** (SL) • **Shining Path**	1960s	1,000+	A	Upper Huallaga river valley, Ene river valley	Establish peasant revolutionary regime in Pe (Less active since Pe govt's 2000 counter-terrorist op)
SUB-SAHARAN AFRICA						
Ang	**Frente de Libertação do Enclave de Cabinda** (FLEC)	1963	600	A	Ang	Independence of Cabinda region
Ang	**União Nacional para Independencia Total de Angola** (UNITA)	1966	20,000	A	Nba, Ang, DROC	Strive for govt proportionally representative of all ethnic gps, clans and classes' (Ang govt has recaptured much territory gained by UNITA during 1980s)
Bu	**Forces pour la Défense de la Démocratie** (FDD)	1994	10,000	A	DROC, west Tz, Bu	Restore constitution and institutions set by 1993 elections and form national army (To be disarmed under Lusaka Peace Accord but continues attacks against Bu govt and believed involved in DROC conflict. Armed wing of National Council for the Defence of Democracy)
Bu	**Parti pour la Libération du Peuple Hutu** (Palipehutu) • **Forces for National Liberation**	1980	2–3,000	A	Bu, Tz borders	Liberate Hutus and establish ethnic quotas based on 1930s Be census (Armed wing of Forces Nationales de Libération)
DROC	**Mouvement de Libération Congolais** (MLC)	n.k.	18,000	A	north DROC	'Fight dictatorship in DROC' (First faction to break from RCD)
DROC	**Rassemblement Congolais pour la Démocratie – Mouvement de Libération** (RCD–ML)	1999	2–3,000	A	DROC	Overthrow DROC govt
DROC	**Rassemblement Congolais pour la Démocratie – Goma** (RCD–GOMA)	1998	20,000	A	DROC	Establish democracy in DROC
Dj	**Front pour la Restauration de l'Unité et de la Démocratie** (FRUD)	1991	n.k.	C	Dj	Represent Afar population of Dj and establish multi-party elections (Following 1994 split, one faction signed agreement with govt to become legitimate political party, joined 1995 coalition govt)
Er	**Alliance of Eritrean Forces**	1999	3,000	A	Er	Overthrow Er govt (Coalition of Er armed gps)
Eth	**Ogaden National Liberation Front** (ONLF)	1984	n.k.	A	Eth	Restore rights of Ogaden population and obtain right to self-determination

Origin	Organisation • aka	Established	Strength[1]	Status[2]	Operates	Aims (Remarks)
Eth	Oromo Liberation Front (OLF)	1974	200+	A	Eth	Lead liberation struggle of Oromo population and overthrow Eth govt
Rwa	Interahamwe • Army for the Liberation of Rwanda (ALIR)	1994	2,000+	A	DROC, Rwa	Reinstate Hutu control of Rwa (Armed wg of Party for the Liberation of Rwanda. Consists of remnants of Hutu militias and former Rwa armed forces)
Sen	Mouvement des Forces Démocratiques de Casamance (MFDC)	1982	2–3,000	A	Sen	Independent Casamance (Involved in peace talks with govt since 2000)
SL	Revolutionary United Front (RUF)	1980s	8,000	A	Gui, SL	Overthrow SL govt (Disarmament began May 2001 following Nov 2000 Abuja cease-fire, but fighting continues)
RSA	People Against Gangsterism and Drugs (PAGAD)	1996	50	A	Cape Town area	Islamic state in RSA
Sdn	The Beja Congress	1993	500	A	east Sdn	Overthrow Sdn govt and establish autonomous Beja state (Controls area of eastern Sdn centred around Garoura and Hamshkoraib)
Sdn	New Sudan Brigade	n.k.	2,000	A	east Sdn	(Eastern branch of SPLA)
Sdn	Sudan Alliance Forces	1995	500	A	east Sdn	Overthrow Sdn govt and 'establish progressive and secular democracy' (Played major role in opening new war front in east since 1997)
Sdn	Sudan People's Liberation Army (SPLA)	1983	20–30,000	A	south Sdn	Secular and democratic Sdn (Armed wing of Sudan People's Liberation Movement (SPLM). Largely Christian and southern)
Uga	Allied Democratic Front • Uganda Allied Democratic Army	1996	500	A	west Uga	Replace Uga govt with regime based on Sharia law
Uga	Lord's Resistance Army (LRA)	1989	1,500	A	Gulu and Kitgum districts	'Rule Uga according to biblical ten commandments and create Great Nile Republic in northern Uga' (Christian fundamentalist)

Table 40 **Designations of aircraft**

Notes

1 [Square brackets] indicate the type from which a variant was derived: 'Q-5 … [MiG-19]' indicates that the design of the Q-5 was based on that of the MiG-19.
2 (Parentheses) indicate an alternative name by which an aircraft is known, sometimes in another version: 'L-188 … Electra (P-3 Orion)' shows that in another version the Lockheed Type 188 Electra is known as the P-3 Orion.

3 Names given in 'quotation marks' are NATO reporting names, e.g., 'Su-27… "Flanker"'.
4 When no information is listed under 'Country of origin' or 'Maker', the primary reference given under 'Name/designation' should be looked up under 'Type'.
5 For country abbreviations, see 'Index of Countries and Territories' (pp. 319–20).

Type	Name/designation	Country of origin / Maker

Fixed-wing

Type	Name/designation	Country of origin / Maker
A-1	AMX	**Br/It** AMX
A-1	Ching-Kuo	**ROC** AIDC
A-3	Skywarrior	**US** Douglas
A-4	Skyhawk	**US** MD
A-5	(Q-5)	
A-7	Corsair II	**US** LTV
A-10	Thunderbolt	**US** Fairchild
A-36	Halcón (C-101)	
A-37	Dragonfly	**US** Cessna
A-50	'Mainstay' (Il-76)	**RF** Beriev
A300		**UK/Fr/Ge/Sp** Airbus Int
A310		**UK/Fr/Ge/Sp** Airbus Int
A340		**UK/Fr/Ge/Sp** Airbus Int
AC-47	(C-47)	
AC-130	(C-130)	
Air Beetle		**Nga** AIEP
Airtourer		**NZ** Victa
AJ-37	(J-37)	
Alizé	(Br 1050)	**Fr** Breguet
Alpha Jet		**Fr/Ge** Dassault–Breguet/Dornier
AMX		**Br/It** Embraer/Alenia/Aermacchi
An-2	'Colt'	**Ukr** Antonov
An-12	'Cub'	**Ukr** Antonov
An-14	'Clod' (Pchyelka)	**Ukr** Antonov
An-22	'Cock' (Antei)	**Ukr** Antonov
An-24	'Coke'	**Ukr** Antonov
An-26	'Curl'	**Ukr** Antonov
An-28/M-28	'Cash'	**Ukr** Antonov/**Pl** PZL
An-30	'Clank'	**Ukr** Antonov
An-32	'Cline'	**Ukr** Antonov
An-72	'Coaler-C'	**Ukr** Antonov
An-74	'Coaler-B'	**Ukr** Antonov
An-124	'Condor' (Ruslan)	**Ukr** Antonov
Andover	[HS-748]	
Arava		**Il** IAI
AS-202	Bravo	**CH** FFA
AT-3	Tsu Chiang	**ROC** AIDC
AT-6	(T-6)	
AT-11		**US** Beech
AT-26	EMB-326	
AT-33	(T-33)	
Atlantic	(Atlantique)	**Fr** Dassault–Breguet
AU-23	Peacemaker [PC-6B]	**US** Fairchild
AV-8	Harrier II	**US/UK** MD/BAe
Aztec	PA-23	**US** Piper
B-1	Lancer	**US** Rockwell
B-2	Spirit	**US** Northrop Grumman
B-5	H-5	
B-6	H-6	
B-52	Stratofortress	**US** Boeing
B-65	Queen Air	**US** Beech
BAC-167	Strikemaster	**UK** BAe
BAe-125		**UK** BAe
BAe-146		**UK** BAe
BAe-748	(HS-748)	**UK** BAe
Baron	(T-42)	
Basler T-67	(C-47)	**US** Basler
Be-6	'Madge'	**RF** Beriev
Be-12	'Mail' (Tchaika)	**RF** Beriev
Beech 50	Twin Bonanza	**US** Beech
Beech 95	Travel Air	**US** Beech
BN-2	Islander, Defender, Trislander	**UK** Britten-Norman
Boeing 707		**US** Boeing
Boeing 727		**US** Boeing
Boeing 737		**US** Boeing
Boeing 747		**US** Boeing
Boeing 757		**US** Boeing
Boeing 767		**US** Boeing
Bonanza		**US** Beech
Bronco	(OV-10)	
BT-5	HJ-5	
Bulldog		**UK** BAe
C-1		**J** Kawasaki
C-2	Greyhound	**US** Grumman
C-5	Galaxy	**US** Lockheed
C-7	DHC-7	
C-9	Nightingale (DC-9)	
C-12	Super King Air (Huron)	**US** Beech
C-17	Globemaster III	**US** McDonnell Douglas
C-18	[Boeing 707]	
C-20	(Gulfstream III)	
C-21	(Learjet)	
C-22	(Boeing 727)	
C-23	(Sherpa)	**UK** Shorts
C-26	Expediter/Merlin	**US** Fairchild
C-27	Spartan	**It** Alenia
C-32	[Boeing 757]	**US** Boeing
C-37A	[Gulfstream V]	**US** Gulfstream
C-38A	(Astra)	**Il** IAI
C-42	(Neiva Regente)	**Br** Embraer
C-46	Commando	**US** Curtis
C-47	DC-3 (Dakota) (C-117 Skytrain)	**US** Douglas
C-54	Skymaster (DC-4)	**US** Douglas
C-91	HS-748	
C-93	HS-125	
C-95	EMB-110	
C-97	EMB-121	
C-101	Aviojet	**Sp** CASA
C-115	DHC-5	**Ca** De Havilland
C-117	(C-47)	
C-118	Liftmaster (DC-6)	
C-123	Provider	**US** Fairchild
C-127	(Do-27)	**Sp** CASA
C-130	Hercules (L-100)	**US** Lockheed
C-131	Convair 440	**US** Convair
C-135	[Boeing 707]	
C-137	[Boeing 707]	
C-140	(Jetstar)	**US** Lockheed
C-141	Starlifter	**US** Lockheed

Type	Name/designation	Country of origin Maker
C-160	*Transall*	**Fr/Ge** EADS
C-212	*Aviocar*	**Sp** CASA
C-235	*Persuader*	**Sp/Indo** CASA/Airtech
C-295M		**Sp** CASA
Canberra		**UK** BAe
CAP-10		**Fr** Mudry
CAP-20		**Fr** Mudry
CAP-230		**Fr** Mudry
Caravelle	SE-210	**Fr** Aérospatiale
CC-115	DHC-5	
CC-117	(*Falcon 20*)	
CC-132	(DHC-7)	
CC-137	(Boeing 707)	
CC-138	(DHC-6)	
CC-144	CL-600/-601	**Ca** Canadair
CF-5a		**Ca** Canadair
CF-18	F/A-18	
Cheetah	[*Mirage* III]	**RSA** Atlas
Cherokee	PA-28	**US** Piper
Cheyenne	PA-31T [*Navajo*]	**US** Piper
Chieftain	PA-31-350 [*Navajo*]	**US** Piper
Ching-Kuo	A-1	**ROC** AIDC
Citabria		**US** Champion
Citation	(T-47)	**US** Cessna
CJ-5	[Yak-18]	**PRC** NAMC (Hongdu)
CJ-6	[Yak-18]	**PRC** NAMC (Hongdu)
CL-215		**Ca** Canadair
CL-415		**Ca** Canadair
CL-600/604	*Challenger*	**Ca** Canadair
CM-170	*Magister* [*Tzukit*]	**Fr** Aérospatiale
CM-175	*Zéphyr*	**Fr** Aérospatiale
CN-212		**Sp/Indo** CASA/IPTN
CN-235		**Sp/Indo** CASA/IPTN
Cochise	T-42	
Comanche	PA-24	**US** Piper
Commander	Aero-/TurboCommander	**US** Rockwell
Commodore	MS-893	**Fr** Aérospatiale
CP-3	P-3 *Orion*	
CP-140	*Aurora* (P-3 *Orion*)	**US** Lockheed
	Acturas	
CT-4	*Airtrainer*	**NZ** Victa
CT-114	CL-41 *Tutor*	**Ca** Canadair
CT-133	*Silver Star* [T-33]	**Ca** Canadair
CT-134	*Musketeer*	
CT-156	*Harvard* II	**US** Beech
Dagger	(*Nesher*)	
Dakota		**US** Piper
Dakota	(C-47)	
DC-3	(C-47)	**US** Douglas
DC-4	(C-54)	**US** Douglas
DC-6	(C-118)	**US** Douglas
DC-7		**US** Douglas
DC-8		**US** Douglas
DC-9		**US** MD
Deepak	(HPT-32)	
Defender	BN-2	
DHC-3	*Otter*	**Ca** DHC
DHC-4	*Caribou*	**Ca** DHC
DHC-5	*Buffalo*	**Ca** DHC
DHC-6	*Twin Otter*, CC-138	**Ca** DHC
DHC-7	*Dash-7* (*Ranger*, CC-132)	**Ca** DHC
DHC-8		**Ca** DHC
Dimona	H-36	**Ge** Hoffman
Do-27	(C-127)	**Ge** Dornier
Do-28	*Skyservant*	**Ge** Dornier
Do-128		**Ge** Dornier
Do-228		**Ge** Dornier

Type	Name/designation	Country of origin Maker
E-2	*Hawkeye*	**US** Grumman
E-3	*Sentry*	**US** Boeing
E-4	[Boeing 747]	**US** Boeing
E-6	*Mercury* [Boeing 707]	**US** Boeing
E-26	T-35A (*Tamiz*)	**Chl** Enear
EA-3	[A-3]	
EA-6	*Prowler* [A-6]	
EC-130	[C-130]	
EC-135	[Boeing 707]	
EF-111	*Raven* (F-111)	**US** General Dynamic
Electra	(L-188)	
EMB-110	*Bandeirante*	
EMB-111	*Maritime Bandeirante*	**Br** Embraer
EMB-120	*Brasilia*	**Br** Embraer
EMB-121	*Xingu*	**Br** Embraer
EMB-145	(R-99A/-99B)	**Br** Embraer
EMB-201	*Ipanema*	**Br** Embraer
EMB-312	*Tucano*	**Br** Embraer
EMB-326	*Xavante* (MB-326)	**Br** Embraer
EMB-810	[*Seneca*]	**Br** Embraer
EP-3	(P-3 *Orion*)	
ERJ-145		**Br** Embraer
Etendard/Super Etendard		**Fr** Dassault
EV-1	(OV-1)	
F-1	[T-2]	**J** Mitsubishi
F-4	*Phantom*	**US** MD
F-5	-A/-B *Freedom Fighter*	
	-E/-F *Tiger* II	**US** Northrop
F-6	J-6	
F-7	J-7	
F-8	J-8	
F-10	J-10	
F-11	J-11	
F-14	*Tomcat*	**US** Grumman
F-15	*Eagle*	**US** MD
F-16	*Fighting Falcon*	**US** GD
F-18	[F/A-18], *Hornet*	
F-21	*Kfir*	**Il** IAI
F-22	*Raptor*	**US** Lockheed
F-27	*Friendship*	**Nl** Fokker
F-28	*Fellowship*	**Nl** Fokker
F-35	*Draken*	**Swe** SAAB
F-50/-60		**Nl** Fokker
F-104	*Starfighter*	**US** Lockheed
F-111	EF-111	**US** GD
F-117	*Nighthawk*	**US** Lockheed
F-172	(Cessna 172)	**Fr/US** Reims-Cessna
F-406	*Caravan*	**Fr** Reims
F/A-18	*Hornet*	**US** MD
Falcon	*Mystère-Falcon*	
FB-111	(F-111)	
FBC-1	*Feibao* [JH-7]	
FC-1	(*Sabre 2, Super-7*)	**PRC/RF/Pak** CAC/MAPO/Pak
FH-227	(F-27)	**US** Fairchild-Hiller
Firefly	(T-67M)	**UK** Slingsby
Flamingo	MBB-233	
FT-5	JJ-5	
FT-6	JJ-6	
FT-7	JJ-7	
FTB-337	[Cessna 337]	
G-91		**It** Aeritalia
G-115E	*Tutor*	**Ge** Grob
G-222		**It** Alenia
Galaxy	C-5	
Galeb		**FRY** SOKO
Genet	SF-260W	
GU-25	(*Falcon 20*)	

Type	Name/ designation	Country of origin Maker
Guerrier	R-235	
Gulfstream		**US** Gulfstream Aviation
Gumhuria	(*Bücker* 181)	**Et** Heliopolis
H-5	[Il-28]	**PRC** HAF
H-6	[Tu-16]	**PRC** XAC
H-36	*Dimona*	
Halcón	[C-101]	
Harrier	(AV-8)	**UK** BAe
Hawk		**UK** BAe
Hawker 800XP	(BAe-125)	**US** Raytheon
HC-130	(C-130)	
HF-24	*Marut*	**Ind** HAL
HFB-320	*Hansajet*	**Ge** Hamburger FB
HJ-5	(H-5)	
HJT-16	*Kiran*	**Ind** HAL
HPT-32	*Deepak*	**Ind** HAL
HS-125	(*Dominie*)	**UK** BAe
HS-748	[*Andover*]	**UK** BAe
HT-2		**Ind** HAL
HU-16	*Albatross*	**US** Grumman
HU-25	(*Falcon* 20)	
Hunter		**UK** BAe
HZ-5	(H-5)	
IA-50	*Guaraní*	**Arg** FMA
IA-58	*Pucará*	**Arg** FMA
IA-63	*Pampa*	**Arg** FMA
IAI-201/-202	*Arava*	**Il** IAI
IAI-1124	*Westwind, Seascan*	**Il** IAI
IAI-1125	*Astra*	**Il** IAI
Iak-52	(Yak-52)	**R** Aerostar
IAR-28		**R** IAR
IAR-93	*Orao*	**FRY/R** SOKO/IAR
IAR-99	*Soim*	**R** IAR
Il-14	'Crate'	**RF** Ilyushin
Il-18	'Coot'	**RF** Ilyushin
Il-20	'Coot-A' (Il-18)	**RF** Ilyushin
Il-22	'Coot-B' (Il-18)	**RF** Ilyushin
Il-28	'Beagle'	**RF** Ilyushin
Il-38	'May'	**RF** Ilyushin
Il-62	'Classic'	**RF** Ilyushin
Il-76	'Candid' (tpt), 'Mainstay' (AEW)	**RF** Ilyushin
Il-78	'Midas' (tkr)	**RF** Ilyushin
Il-82	'Candid'	**RF** Ilyushin
Il-87	'Maxdome'	**RF** Ilyushin
Impala	[MB-326]	**RSA** Atlas
Islander	BN-2	
J-5	[MiG-17F]	**PRC** SAF
J-6	[MiG-19]	**PRC** SAF
J-7	[MiG-21]	**PRC** CAC/GAIC
J-8	*Finback*	**PRC** SAC
J-10	[IAI *Lavi*]	**PRC** SAC
J-11	[Su-27]	**PRC** SAC
J-32	*Lansen*	**Swe** SAAB
J-35	*Draken*	**Swe** SAAB
J-37	*Viggen*	**Swe** SAAB
JA-37	(J-37)	
Jaguar		**Fr/UK** SEPECAT
JAS-39	*Gripen*	**Swe** SAAB
Jastreb		**FRY** SOKO
Jetstream		**UK** BAe
JH-7	[FBC-1]	**PRC** XAC
JJ-5	[J-5]	**PRC** CAF
JJ-6	[J-6]	**PRC** SAF
JJ-7	[J-7]	**PRC** GAIC
JZ-6	(J-6)	
K-8		**PRC/Pak/Et** Hongdu/E
KA-3	[A-3]	

Type	Name/ designation	Country of origin Maker
KA-6	[A-6]	
KC-10	*Extender* [DC-10]	**US** MD
KC-130	[C-130]	
KC-135	[Boeing 707]	
KE-3A	[Boeing 707]	
KF-16	(F-16)	
Kfir		**Il** IAI
King Air		**US** Beech
Kiran	HJT-16	
Kraguj		**FRY** SOKO
L-4	*Cub*	
L-18	*Super Cub*	**US** Piper
L-19	O-1	
L-21	*Super Cub*	**US** Piper
L-29	*Delfin*	**Cz** Aero
L-39	*Albatros*	**Cz** Aero
L-59	*Albatros*	**Cz** Aero
L-70	*Vinka*	**SF** Valmet
L-100	C-130 (civil version)	
L-188	*Electra* (P-3 *Orion*)	**US** Lockheed
L-410	*Turbolet*	**Cz** LET
L-1011	*Tristar*	**US** Lockheed
Learjet	(C-21)	**US** Gates
LR-1	(MU-2)	**J** Mitsubishi
M-28	*Skytruck*	**Pl** MIELEC
Magister	CM-170	
Marut	HF-24	
Mashshaq	MFI-17	**Pak/Swe** PAC/SAAB
Matador	(AV-8)	
Maule	M-7/MXT-7	**US** Maule
MB-326		**It** Aermacchi
MB-339	(*Veltro*)	**It** Aermacchi
MBB-233	*Flamingo*	**Ge** MBB
MC-130	(C-130)	
Mercurius	(HS-125)	
Merlin		**US** Fairchild
Mescalero	T-41	
Metro		**US** Fairchild
MFI-17	*Supporter* (T-17)	**Swe** SAAB
MiG-15	'Midget' trg	**RF** MiG
MiG-17	'Fresco'	**RF** MiG
MiG-19	'Farmer'	**RF** MiG
MiG-21	'Fishbed'	**RF** MiG
MiG-23	'Flogger'	**RF** MiG
MiG-25	'Foxbat'	**RF** MiG
MiG-27	'Flogger D'	**RF** MiG
MiG-29	'Fulcrum'	**RF** MiG
MiG-31	'Foxhound'	**RF** MiG
Mirage		**Fr** Dassault
Missionmaster	N-22	
Mohawk	OV-1	
MS-760	*Paris*	**Fr** Aérospatiale
MS-893	*Commodore*	
MU-2	LR-1	**J** Mitsubishi
Musketeer	Beech 24	**US** Beech
Mystère-Falcon		**Fr** Dassault
N-22	*Floatmaster, Missionmaster*	**Aus** GAF
N-24	*Searchmaster* B/L	**Aus** GAF
N-262	*Frégate*	**Fr** Aérospatiale
N-2501	*Noratlas*	**Fr** Aérospatiale
Navajo	PA-31	**US** Piper
NC-212	C-212	**Sp/Indo** CASA/Nurtanio
NC-235	C-235	**Sp/Indo** CASA/Nurtanio
Nesher	[*Mirage* III]	**Il** IAI
NF-5	(F-5)	
Nightingale	(C-9)	
Nimrod	[*Comet*]	**UK** BAe

Type	Name/designation	Country of origin / Maker
Nomad		**Aus** GAF
O-1	*Bird Dog*	**US** Cessna
O-2	(Cessna 337 *Skymaster*)	**US** Cessna
OA-4	(A-4)	
OA-37	*Dragonfly*	
Orao	IAR-93	
Ouragan		**Fr** Dassault
OV-1	*Mohawk*	**US** Rockwell
OV-10	*Bronco*	**US** Rockwell
P-3	*Orion* [L-188 *Electra*]	**US** Lockheed
P-92		**It** Teenam
P-95	EMB-110	
P-166		**It** Piaggio
P-180	*Avanti*	**It** Piaggio
PA-18	*Super Cub*	**US** Piper
PA-23	*Aztec*	**US** Piper
PA-28	*Cherokee*	**US** Piper
PA-31	*Navajo*	**US** Piper
PA-32	*Cherokee Six*	**US** Piper
PA-34	*Seneca*	**US** Piper
PA-36	*Pawnee Brave*	**US** Piper
PA-38	*Tomahawk*	**US** Piper
PA-42	*Cheyenne III*	**US** Piper
PBY-5	*Catalina*	**US** Consolidated
PC-6	*Porter*	**CH** Pilatus
PC-6A/B	*Turbo Porter*	**CH** Pilatus
PC-7	*Turbo Trainer*	**CH** Pilatus
PC-9		**CH** Pilatus
PC-12		**CH** Pilatus
PD-808		**It** Piaggio
Pillán	T-35	
PL-1	*Chien Shou*	**ROC** AIDC
PLZ M-28	[An-28]	**Pl** PZL
Porter	PC-6	
PS-5	[SH-5]	
PZL M-28	M-28 [An-28]	**Pl** PZL
PZL-104	*Wilga*	**Pl** PZL
PZL-130	*Orlik*	**Pl** PZL
Q-5	A-5 'Fantan' [MiG-19]	**PRC** NAMC (Hongdu)
Queen Air	(U-8)	
R-99A/B	EMB-145	**Br** Embraer
R-160		**Fr** Socata
R-235	*Guerrier*	**Fr** Socata
RC-21	(C-21, *Learjet*)	
RC-47	(C-47)	
RC-95	(EMB-110)	
RC-135	[Boeing 707]	
RF-4	(F-4)	
RF-5	(F-5)	
RF-35	(F-35)	
RF-104	(F-104)	
RG-8A		**US** Schweizer
RT-26	(EMB-326)	
RT-33	(T-33)	
RU-21	(*King Air*)	
RV-1	(OV-1)	
S-2	*Tracker*	**US** Grumman
S-208		**It** SIAI
S-211		**It** SIAI
SA 2-37A		**US** Schweizer
Sabreliner	(CT-39)	**US** Rockwell
Safari	MFI-15	
Safir	SAAB-91 (SK-50)	**Swe** SAAB
SC-7	*Skyvan*	**UK** Short
SE-210	*Caravelle*	
Sea Harrier	(*Harrier*)	
Seascan	IAI-1124	

Type	Name/designation	Country of origin / Maker
Searchmaster	N-24 B/L	
Seneca	PA-34 (EMB-810)	**US** Piper
Sentry	(O-2)	**US** Summit
SF-37	(J-37)	
SF-260	(SF-260W *Warrior*)	**It** SIAI
SH-5	PS-5	**PRC** HAMC
SH-37	(J-37)	
Sherpa	Short 330, C-23	**UK** Short
Short 330	(*Sherpa*)	**UK** Short
Sierra 200	(*Musketeer*)	
SK-35	(J-35)	**Swe** SAAB
SK-37	(J-37)	
SK-60	(SAAB-105)	**Swe** SAAB
SK-61	(*Bulldog*)	
Skyvan		**UK** Short
SM-90		**RF** Technoavia
SM-1019		**It** SIAI
SP-2H	*Neptune*	**US** Lockheed
SR-71	*Blackbird*	**US** Lockheed
Su-7	'Fitter-A'	**RF** Sukhoi
Su-15	'Flagon'	**RF** Sukhoi
Su-17/-20/-22	'Fitter-B' - '-K'	**RF** Sukhoi
Su-24	'Fencer'	**RF** Sukhoi
Su-25	'Frogfoot'	**RF** Sukhoi
Su-27	'Flanker'	**RF** Sukhoi
Su-29		**RF** Sukhoi
Su-30	'Flanker'	**RF** Sukhoi
Su-33	(Su-27K) 'Flanker-D'	**RF** Sukhoi
Su-34	(Su-27IB) 'Flanker-C2'	**RF** Sukhoi
Su-35	(Su-27) 'Flanker'	**RF** Sukhoi
Su-39	(Su-25T) 'Frogfoot'	**RF** Sukhoi
Super		**Fr** Dassault
Shrike Aerocommander		**US** Rockwell
Super Galeb		**FRY** SOKO
T-1		**J** Fuji
T-1A	*Jayhawk*	**US** Beech
T-2	*Buckeye*	**US** Rockwell
T-2		**J** Mitsubishi
T-3		**J** Fuji
T-6A	*Texan II*	**US** Beech
T-17	(*Supporter*, MFI-17)	**Swe** SAAB
T-23	*Uirapuru*	**Br** Aerotec
T-25	Neiva *Universal*	**Br** Embraer
T-26	EMB-326	
T-27	*Tucano*	**Br** Embraer
T-28	*Trojan*	**US** North American
T-33	*Shooting Star*	**US** Lockheed
T-34	*Mentor*	**US** Beech
T-35	*Pillán* [PA-28]	**Chl** Enaer
T-36	(C-101)	
T-37	(A-37)	
T-38	*Talon*	**US** Northrop
T-39	(*Sabreliner*)	**US** Rockwell
T-41	*Mescalero* (Cessna 172)	**US** Cessna
T-42	*Cochise* (*Baron*)	**US** Beech
T-43	(Boeing 737)	
T-44	(*King Air*)	
T-47	(*Citation*)	
T-67M	(*Firefly*)	**UK** Slingsby
T-400	(T-1A)	**US** Beech
TB-20	*Trinidad*	**Fr** Aérospatiale
TB-21	*Trinidad*	**Fr** Socata
TB-30	*Epsilon*	**Fr** Aérospatiale
TB-200	*Tobago*	**Fr** Socata
TBM-700		**Fr** Socata
TC-45	(C-45, trg)	
TCH-1	*Chung Hsing*	**ROC** AIDC

Type	Name/ designation	Country of origin Maker
TL-1	(KM-2)	**J** Fuji
Tornado		**UK/Ge/It** Panavia
TR-1	[U-2]	**US** Lockheed
Travel Air	Beech 95	
Trident		**UK** BAe
Trislander	BN-2	
Tristar	L-1011	
TS-8	*Bies*	**Pl** PZL
TS-11	*Iskra*	**Pl** PZL
Tu-16	*'Badger'*	**RF** Tupolev
Tu-22	*'Blinder'*	**RF** Tupolev
Tu-22M	*'Backfire'*	**RF** Tupolev
Tu-95	*'Bear'*	**RF** Tupolev
Tu-126	*'Moss'*	**RF** Tupolev
Tu-134	*'Crusty'*	**RF** Tupolev
Tu-142	*'Bear* F'	**RF** Tupolev
Tu-154	*'Careless'*	**RF** Tupolev
Tu-160	*'Blackjack'*	**RF** Tupolev
Turbo Porter	PC-6A/B	
Twin Bonanza	Beech 50	
Twin Otter	DHC-6	
Tzukit	[CM-170]	**Il** IAI
U-2		**US** Lockheed
U-3	(Cessna 310)	**US** Cessna
U-4	*Gulfstream* IV	**US** Gulfstream Aviation
U-7	(L-18)	
U-8	(*Twin Bonanza/Queen Air*)	**US** Beech
U-9	(EMB-121)	
U-10	*Super Courier*	**US** Helio
U-17	(Cessna 180, 185)	**US** Cessna
U-21	(*King Air*)	
U-36	(*Learjet*)	
U-42	(C-42)	
U-93	(HS-125)	
U-125	BAe 125-800	**UK** BAe
U-206G	*Stationair*	**US** Cessna
UC-12	(*King Air*)	
UP-2J	(P-2J)	
US-1		**J** Shin Meiwa
US-2A	(S-2A, tpt)	
US-3	(S-3, tpt)	
UTVA-66		**FRY** UTVA
UTVA-75		**FRY** UTVA
UV-18	(DHC-6)	
V-400	*Fantrainer* 400	**Ge** VFW
V-600	*Fantrainer* 600	**Ge** VFW
Vampire	DH-100	
VC-4	*Gulfstream* I	
VC-10		**UK** BAe
VC-11	*Gulfstream* II	
VC-25	[Boeing 747]	**US** Boeing
VC-91	(HS-748)	
VC-93	(HS-125)	
VC-97	(EMB-120)	
VC-130	(C-130)	
VFW-614		**Ge** VFW
Vinka	L-70	
VU-9	(EMB-121)	
VU-93	(HS-125)	
WC-130	[C-130]	
WC-135	[Boeing 707]	**US** Boeing
Westwind	IAI-1124	
Winjeel	CA-25	
Xavante	EMB-326	
Xingu	EMB-121	
Y-5	[An-2]	**PRC** Hua Bei
Y-7	[An-24/-26]	**PRC** XAC

Type	Name/ designation	Country of origin Maker
Y-8	[An-12]	**PRC** STAF
Y-12	*Turbo/Twin Panda*	**PRC** HAMC
Yak-11	*'Moose'*	**RF** Yakovlev
Yak-18	*'Max'*	**RF** Yakovlev
Yak-28	*'Firebar'* (*'Brewer'*)	**RF** Yakovlev
Yak-38	*'Forger'*	**RF** Yakovlev
Yak-40	*'Codling'*	**RF** Yakovlev
Yak-42	*'Clobber'*	**RF** Yakovlev
Yak-55		**RF** Yakovlev
YS-11		**J** Nihon
Z-143		**Cz** Zlin
Z-226		**Cz** Zlin
Z-326		**Cz** Zlin
Z-526		**Cz** Zlin
Zéphyr	CM-175	

Tilt-Rotor Wing

Type	Name/ designation	Country of origin Maker
V-22	*Osprey*	**US** Bell/Boeing

Helicopters

Type	Name/ designation	Country of origin Maker
A-109	*Hirundo*	**It** Agusta
A-129	*Mangusta*	**It** Agusta
AB-...	(Bell 204/205/206/ 212/214, etc.)	**It/US** Agusta/Bell
AH-1	*Cobra/Sea Cobra*	**US** Bell
AH-2	*Rooivalk*	**RSA** Denel
AH-6	(Hughes 500/530)	**US** MD
AH-64	*Apache*	**US** Hughes
Alouette II	SA-318, SE-3130	**Fr** Aérospatiale
Alouette III	SA-316, SA-319	**Fr** Aérospatiale
AS-61	(SH-3)	**US/It** Sikorsky/Agusta
AS-313 – AS-365/-366	(ex-SA-313 – SA-365/-366)	
AS-332	*Super Puma*	**Fr** Aérospatiale
AS-350	*Ecureuil*	**Fr** Aérospatiale
AS-355	*Ecureuil* II	**Fr** Aérospatiale
AS-365	*Dauphin*	**Fr** Aérospatiale
AS-532	*Cougar*	**Fr** Eurocopter
AS-550/555	*Fennec*	**Fr** Aérospatiale
AS-565	*Panthar*	**Fr** Eurocopter
ASH-3	(*Sea King*)	**It/US** Agusta/Sikorsky
AUH-76	(S-76)	
Bell 47	(*Sioux*)	**US** Bell
Bell 205		**US** Bell
Bell 206		**US** Bell
Bell 212		**US** Bell
Bell 214		**US** Bell
Bell 222		**US** Bell
Bell 406		**US** Bell
Bell 412		**US** Bell
Bo-105	(NBo-105)	**Ge** MBB
CH-3	(SH-3)	
CH-34	*Choctaw*	**US** Sikorsky
CH-46	*Sea Knight*	**US** Boeing-Vertol
CH-47	*Chinook*	**US** Boeing-Vertol
CH-53	*Stallion* (*Sea Stallion*)	**US** Sikorsky
CH-54	*Tarhe*	**US** Sikorsky
CH-113	(CH-46)	
CH-124	SH-3 (*Sea King*)	
CH-139	Bell 206	
CH-146	Bell 412	**Ca** Bell
CH-147	CH-47	
CH-149	*Cormorant* (*Merlin*)	
Cheetah	[SA-315]	**Ind** HAL

Type	Name/designation	Country of origin Maker
Chetak	[SA-319]	**Ind** HAL
Commando	(SH-3)	**UK/US** Westland/Sikorsky
EC-120B	*Colibri*	**Fr/Ge** Eurocopter
EH-60	(UH-60)	
EH-101	*Merlin*	**UK/It** Westland/Agusta
F-28F		**US** Enstrom
FH-1100	(OH-5)	**US** Fairchild-Hiller
Gazela	(SA-342)	**Fr/FRY** Aérospatiale/SOKO
Gazelle	SA-341/-342	
H-34	(S-58)	
H-76	S-76	
HA-15	Bo-105	
HB-315	*Gavião* (SA-315)	**Br/Fr** Helibras Aérospatiale
HB-350	*Esquilo* (AS-350)	**Br/Fr** Helibras Aérospatiale
HD-16	SA-319	
HH-3	(SH-3)	
HH-34	(CH-34)	
HH-53	(CH-53)	
HH-65	(AS-365)	**Fr** Eurocopter
Hkp-2	*Alouette* II/SE-3130	
Hkp-3	AB-204	
Hkp-4	KV-107	
Hkp-5	Hughes 300	
Hkp-6	AB-206	
Hkp-9	Bo-105	
Hkp-10	AS-332	
HR-12	OH-58	
HSS-1	(S-58)	
HSS-2	(SH-3)	
HT-17	CH-47	
HT-21	AS-332	
HU-1	(UH-1)	**J/US** Fuji/Bell
HU-8	UH-1B	
HU-10	UH-1H	
HU-18	AB-212	
Hughes 300		**US** MD
Hughes 500/520	*Defender*	**US** MD
IAR-316/-330	(SA-316/-330)	**R/Fr** IAR/Aérospatiale
Ka-25	'Hormone'	**RF** Kamov
Ka-27/-28	'Helix-A'	**RF** Kamov
Ka-29	'Helix-B'	**RF** Kamov
Ka-32	'Helix-C'	**RF** Kamov
Ka-50	*Hokum*	**RF** Kamov
KH-4	(Bell 47)	**J/US** Kawasaki/Bell
KH-300	(Hughes 269)	**J/US** Kawasaki/MD
KH-500	(Hughes 369)	**J/US** Kawasaki/MD
Kiowa	OH-58	
KV-107	[CH-46]	**J/US** Kawasaki/Vertol
Lynx		**UK** Westland
MD-500/530	*Defender*	**US** McDonnell Douglas
Merlin	EH-101	**UK/It** Westland/Augusta
MH-6	(AH-6)	
MH-53	(CH-53)	
Mi-2	'Hoplite'	**RF** Mil
Mi-4	'Hound'	**RF** Mil
Mi-6	'Hook'	**RF** Mil
Mi-8	'Hip'	**RF** Mil
Mi-14	'Haze'	**RF** Mil
Mi-17	'Hip-H'	**RF** Mil
Mi-24, -25, -35	'Hind'	**RF** Mil
Mi-26	'Halo'	**RF** Mil

Type	Name/designation	Country of origin Maker
Mi-28	'Havoc'	**RF** Mil
NAS-332	AS-332	**Indo/Fr** Nurtanio/Aérospatiale
NB-412	Bell 412	**Indo/US** Nurtanio/Bell
NBo-105	Bo-105	**Indo/Ge** Nurtanio/MBB
NH-300	(Hughes 300)	**It/US** Nardi/MD
NSA-330	(SA-330)	**Indo/Fr** Nurtanio/Aérospatiale
OH-6	*Cayuse* (Hughes 369)	**US** MD
OH-13	(Bell 47G)	
OH-23	*Raven*	**US** Hiller
OH-58	*Kiowa* (Bell 206)	
OH-58D	(Bell 406)	
Oryx	(SA-330)	
PAH-1	(Bo-105)	
Partizan	(*Gazela*, armed)	
RH-53	(CH-53)	
S-58	(*Wessex*)	**US** Sikorsky
S-61	SH-3	
S-65	CH-53	
S-70	UH-60	**US** Sikorsky
S-76		**US** Sikorsky
S-80	CH-53	
SA-313	*Alouette* II	**Fr** Aérospatiale
SA-315	*Lama* [*Alouette* II]	**Fr** Aérospatiale
SA-316	*Alouette* III (SA-319)	**Fr** Aérospatiale
SA-318	*Alouette* II (SE-3130)	**Fr** Aérospatiale
SA-319	*Alouette* III (SA-316)	**Fr** Aérospatiale
SA-321	*Super Frelon*	**Fr** Aérospatiale
SA-330	*Puma*	**Fr** Aérospatiale
SA-341/-342	*Gazelle*	**Fr** Aérospatiale
SA-360	*Dauphin*	**Fr** Aérospatiale
SA-365/-366	*Dauphin* II (SA-360)	
Scout	(*Wasp*)	**UK** Westland
SE-316	(SA-316)	
SE-3130	(SA-318)	
Sea King	[SH-3]	**UK** Westland
SH-2	*Sea Sprite*	**US** Kaman
SH-3	(*Sea King*)	**US** Sikorsky
SH-34	(S-58)	
SH-57	Bell 206	
SH-60	*Sea Hawk* (UH-60)	
Sokol	W3	
TH-50	*Esquilo* (AS-550)	
TH-55	Hughes 269	
TH-57	*Sea Ranger* (Bell 206)	
TH-67	*Creek* (Bell 206B-3)	**Ca** Bell
UH-1	*Iroquois* (Bell 204/205/212)	
UH-12	(OH-23)	**US** Hiller
UH-13	(Bell 47J)	
UH-19	(S-55)	
UH-34T	(S-58T)	
UH-46	(CH-46)	
UH-60	*Black Hawk* (SH-60)	**US** Sikorsky
VH-4	(Bell 206)	
VH-60	(S-70)	
W-3	*Sokol*	**Pl** PZL
Wasp	(*Scout*)	**UK** Westland
Wessex	(S-58)	**US/UK** Sikorsky/Westland
Z-5	[Mi-4]	**PRC** HAF
Z-6	[Z-5]	**PRC** CHAF
Z-8	[AS-321]	**PRC** CHAF
Z-9	[AS-365]	**PRC** HAMC
Z-11	[AS-352]	**PRC** CHAF

Index of **Countries and Territories**

Analyses and Tables

Index of Country Abbreviations

A	Austria
AB	Antigua and Barbuda
Afg	Afghanistan
Ag	Algeria
Alb	Albania
Ang	Angola
Arg	Argentina
Arm	Armenia
Aus	Australia
Az	Azerbaijan
Bds	Barbados
Be	Belgium
Bel	Belarus
BF	Burkina Faso
Bg	Bulgaria
BiH	Bosnia-Herzegovina
Bn	Benin
Bng	Bangladesh
Bol	Bolivia
Br	Brazil
Brn	Bahrain
Bru	Brunei
Bs	Bahamas
Btwa	Botswana
Bu	Burundi
Bze	Belize
C	Cuba
Ca	Canada
Cam	Cambodia
CAR	Central African Republic
CH	Switzerland
Cha	Chad
Chl	Chile
CI	Côte d'Ivoire
Co	Colombia
Cr	Croatia
CR	Costa Rica
Crn	Cameroon
CV	Cape Verde
Cy	Cyprus
Cz	Czech Republic
Da	Denmark
Dj	Djibouti
DPRK	Korea, Democratic People's Republic of (North)
DR	Dominican Republic
DROC	Democratic Republic of Congo
Ea	Estonia
Ec	Ecuador
EG	Equatorial Guinea
ElS	El Salvador
Er	Eritrea
Et	Egypt
Eth	Ethiopia
Fji	Fiji
Fr	France
FRY	Federal Republic of Yugoslavia (Serbia–Montenegro)

FYROM	Former Yugoslav Republic of Macedonia
Ga	Georgia
Gam	Gambia, The
Gbn	Gabon
Ge	Germany
Gha	Ghana
Gr	Greece
Gua	Guatemala
GuB	Guinea-Bissau
Gui	Guinea
Guy	Guyana
GzJ	Palestinian Autonomous Areas of Gaza and Jericho
HKJ	Jordan
Hr	Honduras
Hu	Hungary
Icl	Iceland
Il	Israel
Ind	India
Indo	Indonesia
Ir	Iran
Irl	Ireland
Irq	Iraq
It	Italy
J	Japan
Ja	Jamaica
Kaz	Kazakstan
Kgz	Kyrgyzstan
Kwt	Kuwait
Kya	Kenya
L	Lithuania
Lao	Laos
LAR	Libya
Lat	Latvia
Lb	Liberia
Ls	Lesotho
Lu	Luxembourg
M	Malta
Mal	Malaysia
Mdg	Madagascar
Mex	Mexico
Mgl	Mongolia
Mlw	Malawi
Mol	Moldova
Mor	Morocco
Moz	Mozambique
Ms	Mauritius
My	Myanmar (Burma)
N	Nepal
Nba	Namibia
Nga	Nigeria
Ngr	Niger
Nic	Nicaragua
Nl	Netherlands
No	Norway
NZ	New Zealand

O	Oman
Pak	Pakistan
Pan	Panama
Pe	Peru
Pi	Philippines
Pl	Poland
PNG	Papua New Guinea
Por	Portugal
PRC	China, People's Republic of
Py	Paraguay
Q	Qatar
R	Romania
RC	Congo
RF	Russia
RH	Haiti
RIM	Mauritania
RL	Lebanon
RMM	Mali
ROC	Taiwan
ROK	Korea, Republic of (South)
RSA	South Africa
Rwa	Rwanda
Sau	Saudi Arabia
Sdn	Sudan
Sen	Senegal
Sey	Seychelles
SF	Finland
Sgp	Singapore
Ska	Sri Lanka
SL	Sierra Leone
Slvk	Slovakia
Slvn	Slovenia
Sme	Suriname
Sp	Spain
SR	Somali Republic
Swe	Sweden
Syr	Syria
Tg	Togo
Th	Thailand
Tjk	Tajikistan
Tkm	Turkmenistan
Tn	Tunisia
TT	Trinidad and Tobago
Tu	Turkey
Tz	Tanzania
UAE	United Arab Emirates
Uga	Uganda
UK	United Kingdom
Ukr	Ukraine
Ury	Uruguay
US	United States
Uz	Uzbekistan
Ve	Venezuela
Vn	Vietnam
Ye	Yemen, Republic of
Z	Zambia
Zw	Zimbabwe

See *Index of Countries and Territories* (pp. 319–20) for country abbreviations

< under 100 tonnes
- part of unit is detached/less than
+ unit reinforced/more than
* training aircraft considered combat-capable
† serviceability in doubt
ε estimated
' ' unit with overstated title/ship class nickname

AAA anti-aircraft artillery
AAM/R air-to-air missile/refuelling
AAV assault amphibian vehicle
AAW anti-air warfare
AB(D) airborne (division)
ABM anti-ballistic missile
about the total could be higher
ac aircraft
ACM advanced cruise missile
ACP airborne command post
ACV air-cushion vehicle/vessel/armoured combat vehicle
AD air defence
adj adjusted
AE auxiliary, ammunition carrier
AEW airborne early warning
AF stores ship with RAS
AFB/S Air Force Base/Station
AG misc auxiliary
AGF command ship
AGHS hydrographic survey vessel
AGI intelligence collection vessel
AGM air-to-ground missile
AGOR oceanographic research vessel
AGOS ocean surveillance vessel
AH hospital ship/attack helicopter
AIFV armoured infantry fighting vehicle
AIP air-independent propulsion
AK cargo ship
aka also known as
AKR fast sealift ship
ALARM air-launched anti-radiation missile
ALCM air-launched cruise missile
amph amphibious/amphibian
AMRAAM advanced medium-range air-to-air missile
AO/T tanker(s) with/without RAS capability
AOE auxiliary, fuel and ammunition, RAS capability
AP armour-piercing/anti-personnel
APC armoured personnel carrier
APL anti-personnel land-mine
AR/C repair ship/cable
ARG amphibious ready group
ARM anti-radiation (radar) missile
armd armoured
ARS salvage ship
arty artillery
AR(R)V armoured recovery (and repair) vehicle
AS submarine depot ship
aslt assault
ASM air-to-surface missile
ASR submarine rescue craft

ASROC anti-submarine rocket
ASSM anti-surface-ship missile
AS/W/TT anti-submarine warfare/TT
ASUW anti-surface-unit warfare
AT/F tug/ocean-going
ATACMS army tactical missile system
ATBM anti-tactical ballistic missile
ATGW anti-tank guided weapon
ATK anti-tank
AVB aviation logistic ship
avn aviation
AWACS airborne warning and control system
AWT water tanker
BA budget authority (US)
bbr bomber
bde brigade
bdgt budget
BG battle group
BMD ballistic missile defence
bn battalion/billion
BOFI Bofors Optronic Fire control Instrument
bty battery
C³I command, control, communications and intelligence
cal calibration
CALCM conventional air-launched cruise missile
can cannon
CAS close air support
casevac casualty evacuation
CASM conventionally armed stand-off missiles
cat category
cav cavalry
cbt combat
CBU cluster bomb unit
CC/G/N cruiser/with GM/nuclear-fuelled
CCT combat-capable trainer
cdo commando
CEP circular error probable
CET combat engineer tractor
CFE Conventional Armed Forces in Europe
cgo freight aircraft
civ pol civilian police
CLOS command to line of sight
comb combined/combination
comd command
COMINT Communications Intelligence
comms communications
CONUS continental United States
coy company
CSAR combat search and rescue
CVBG carrier battle group
CV/N/S aircraft carrier/nuclear-fuelled/with VSTOL
CW chemical warfare/weapons
DD/E/G/H destroyer/escort/with GM/with hel
def defence
defn definition
det detachment
div division
ECM electronic countermeasures
econ aid economic aid with a military use
ECR electronic combat and reconnaissance

EDA Excess Defense Articles (US)
EEZ exclusive economic zone
ELINT electronic intelligence
elm element
EmDA Emergency Drawdown Authority (US)
engr engineer
EOD explosive ordnance disposal
eqpt equipment
ESM electronic support measures
est estimate(d)
EW electronic warfare
excl excludes/excluding
exp expenditure
FAC forward air control
fd field
FF/G/H frigate/with GM/with hel
FGA fighter, ground-attack
flo-flo float-on, float-off
flt flight
FMA/F/S Foreign Military Assistance/Financing/Sales
FROG Free Rocket Over Ground
FS/G corvette/with GM
ftr fighter (aircraft)
FW fixed-wing
FY fiscal year
g gramme
GA group army
gd guard
GDP gross domestic product
GM guided missile
GNP gross national product
gp group
GS General Service (UK)
GW guided weapon
HACV heavy armoured combat vehicle
HARM high-speed anti-radiation missile
hel helicopter
HMMWV high-mobility multi-purpose wheeled vehicle
HOT High-subsonic Optically Teleguided
how howitzer
HS Home Service (UK)
HWT heavy-weight torpedo
hy heavy
ICBM intercontinental ballistic missile
IMET International Military Education and Training
imp improved
incl includes/including
indep independent
inf infantry
IRBM intermediate-range ballistic missile
IRLS infra-red line scan
JDAM Joint Direct Attack Munition
JSF Joint Strike Fighter
JSTARS Joint Surveillance Target Attack Radar System
kg kilogramme
KT kiloton
LAM land-attack missile
LAMPS light airborne multi-purpose system
LANTIRN low-altitude navigation and targeting infra-red system night
LASH cargo ship barge

LAV light armoured vehicle
LAW light anti-tank weapon
LC/A/AC/H/M/T/U/VP landing craft/ assault/air-cushion/heavy/ mechanical/tank/utility/vehicles and personnel
LCC amphibious command ship
LGB laser-guided bomb
LHA landing ship, assault
LKA assault cargo ship
log logistic
LP/D/H landing platform, dock/helicopter
LS/D/H/M/T landing ship, dock/heavy/ medium/tank
lt light
LWT light-weight torpedo
maint maintenance
MBT main battle tank
MC/C/CS/D/I/MV/O mine countermeasures /coastal/command and support ship/diving spt/inshore/ vessel/ocean
MCLOS manual CLOS
MD Military District
mech mechanised
med medium
ME/F/B/U Marine Expeditionary/Force/ Brigade/Unit
MG machine gun
MH/C/D/I/O minehunter/coastal/drone/ inshore/ocean
mil military
MIRV multiple independently targetable re-entry vehicle
misc miscellaneous
MIUW mobile inshore undersea warfare
mk mark (model number)
ML minelayer
MLRS multiple-launch rocket system
mm millimetre
mne marine
mob mobilisation/mobile
mod modified/modification
mor mortar
mot motorised/motor
MP Military Police
MPA maritime patrol aircraft
MPS marine prepositioning squadron
MR maritime reconnaissance/motor rifle/ Military Region
MRAAM medium-range air-to-air missile
MRBM medium-range ballistic missile
MRD motor rifle division
MRL multiple rocket launcher
MRR motor rifle regiment
MRV multiple re-entry vehicle
MS/A/C/D/I/O/R minesweeper/auxiliary/ coastal/drone/inshore/ocean/riverine
msl missile
MT megaton
mtn mountain
n.a. not applicable
NASAMS Norwegian Advanced SAM System
NBC nuclear, biological and chemical

NCO non-commissioned officer
n.k. not known
nm nautical mile
NMD national missile defence
NMP net material product
nuc nuclear
obs observation
OCU operational conversion unit(s)
off official
O&M operations and maintenance
OOA out of area
OOV objects of verification
op/ops operational/operations
org organised/organisation
OTH/-B over-the-horizon/backscatter (radar)
OTHR/T over-the-horizon radar/targeting
PAAMS principal anti-air missile system
para paratroop/parachute
pax passenger/passenger transport aircraft
PC/C/I/M/O/R/T patrol craft/coastal/ inshore/with SSM/ocean/riverine/with torpedo
PDMS point defence missile system
pdr pounder
PF/C/I/M/O/T fast patrol craft, coastal/ inshore/with SSM/ocean/torpedo
PH/M/T patrol hydrofoil/with SSM/with torpedo
PKO peacekeeping operation
pl platoon
POMCUS prepositioning of materiel configured to unit sets
PPP purchasing-power parity
PR photo-reconnaissance
prepo pre-positioned
publ public
RAPID Reorganised Army Plains Infantry Division
RAM Rolling Airframe Missile
RAS replenishment at sea
RCL recoilless launcher
R&D research and development
recce reconnaissance
regt regiment
rkt rocket
RL rocket launcher
ro-ro roll-on, roll-off
RPV remotely piloted vehicle
RR/C/F rapid-reaction corps/force
RV re-entry vehicle
SACLOS semi-automatic CLOS
SAM surface-to-air missile
SAR search and rescue
sat satellite
SDV swimmer-delivery vehicles
SEAD suppression of enemy air defence
SEAL sea–air–land
SEWS satellite early-warning system
SF special forces
SHORAD Short Range Air Defence
SIGINT signals intelligence
sigs signals
SLAM stand-off land-attack missile

SLBM submarine-launched ballistic missile
SLCM sea-launched cruise missile
SLEP service life extension programme
SMAW shoulder-launched multi-purpose assault weapon
SOC special operations capable
some up to
Sov Soviet
SP self-propelled
spt support
sqn squadron
SRAM short-range attack missile
SRBM short-range ballistic missile
SS/B/C/I/K diesel submarine/with ballistic missile/coastal/inshore/ASW
SSBN ballistic-missile submarine nuclear-fuelled
SSGN SSN with dedicated non-ballistic- missile launchers
SSM surface-to-surface missile
SSN nuclear-fuelled submarine
START Strategic Arms Reduction Talks/ Treaty
STO(V)L short take-off and (vertical) landing
str strength
SUGW surface-to-underwater GW
SURV surveillance
svc service
sy security
t tonnes
TA Territorial Army (UK)
tac tactical
TASM tactical air-to-surface missile
TD tank division
tempy temporary
THAAD Theater High Altitude Area Defense (US)
tk tank
tkr tanker
TLE treaty-limited equipment (CFE)
TMD theatre missile defence
TOW tube-launched optically-tracked wire-guided missile
torp torpedo
tp troop
tpt transport
tr trillion
trg training
TRIAD Triple AD
TRV torpedo recovery vehicle
TT torpedo tube
UAV unmanned aerial vehicle
UN United Nations
URG under way replenishment group
USGW underwater-to-surface GW
utl utility
veh vehicle
VIP very important person
VLS vertical launch system
V(/S)TOL vertical(/short) take-off and landing
wg wing
WMD weapon(s) of mass destruction
wpn weapon